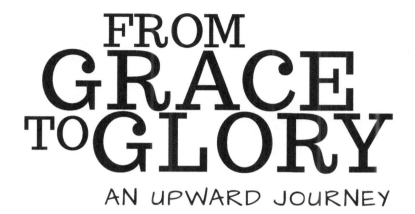

FROM GRACE TO GLORY

AN UPWARD JOURNEY

"Dear YHWH, grant me grace to run this race."

Marquis L. Harris

Published by
Olive Press Messianic and Christian Publisher
olivepresspublisher.com

Messianic & Christian Publisher

Printed in the USA.

Front cover design by Natasha Metzler.
Cover image copyright © 2014 by Shutterstock.
Author photo by Jennifer Reichert.

Scripture quotations marked:

ESV are taken from The Holy Bible, English Standard Version® (ESV®), copyright © 2001 by Crossway, a publishing ministry of Good News Publishers. Used by permission. All rights reserved.

NEB are taken grom the New English Bible © 1962 OXFORD UNIVERSITY PRESS || CAMBRIDGE UNIVERSITY PRESS. All rights reserved. NKJV are taken from New King James Version. Copyright © 1982 by Thomas Nelson, Inc. Used by permission. All rights reserved.

AKJV are taken from The Holy Bible, Authorized King James Version. 1611. The rights are vested in the Crown in the United Kingdom.

CEB are taken from the Common English Bible®, CEB® Copyright © 2010, 2011 by Common English Bible.™ Used by permission. All rights reserved worldwide.

ISV are taken from the Holy Bible: International Standard Version® Release 2.0. Copyright © 1996-2012 The ISV Foundation. ALL RIGHTS RESERVED INTERNATIONALLY.

WYC are taken from John Wycliffe Version. 1380. Public domain.

NIV are taken from Holy Bible, New International Version. Copyright © 1973, 1978, 1984 by International Bible Society. Used by permission. All rights reserved. The 1973 version is used in this book.

ASV are taken from The Holy Bible, American Standard Version.1901. Public domain.

TNIV are taken from the HOLY BIBLE, TODAY'S NEW INTERNATIONAL VERSION® TNIV® Copyright © 2001, 2005 by Biblica www.biblica.com. All rights reserved worldwide.

AMP are taken from e Ampli ed New Testament, Twenty-Second Edition, Zondervan Publishing, Grand Rapids, MI, 1958. All rights reserved.

Dedication

I dedicate this book to Olive Press Messianic and Christian Publisher, and to all the people who are traveling on the road to Glory with me. I also would like to thank those persons who have demonstrated kindness while I lived in Macon, GA, including: The Methodist Home for Children and Youth, Vineville United Methodist Church, Jeff Morris and First Assembly of God, Nachamu Ami, Thomas and Mamie Simmons, Matthew and Tammy Jerles, James Wren, and Don and Mary Evelyn Feibelman. Without these people and their contributions, this book would not be available. I also would like to thank those persons who made me apart of their family when I didn't have any in Macon, including: the Agus, the Olagunjus, the Parks, the Jarrells, the Hopsons, the Reicherts, the Greenes and the Fennells. Their love and kindness were invaluable.

A Note From The Author

Readers will notice throughout the book that the author has chosen to substitute the title "God" with the tetragrammato of his actual name—YHWH. In some instances I use the name YAH. I believe this is how our heavenly Father prefers to be called when speaking of or to him directly. Though I believe the latter should not be used in prayer. In the same way a man or woman would rather be called by their name, rather than by what they are—human. There are many members of Messiah's Body who have preferred to use the name Jehovah if they do refer to the Father by his name. I believe this pronunciation is non-preferable to the Father.

Moreover, rather than the English terms, "Old Testament" and "New Testament," I have chosen to use the Hebrew terms "Tanakh" and "B'rit Khadasha" as substitutes, respectively. It is my belief that in doing so, readers will better understand the Bible as a seamless book of instruction, and not as a book with two messages for two audiences—Jews and Christians. Readers will also notice that within the passages of Scripture used in this book, the name of the Father is always used when referring to him personally. The Hebrew name for Jesus, Yeshua, has also been substituted for the English. This was done to promote the truth of his heritage. However, there is nothing wrong with calling the Son by his English name.

"I and My Father are one." (John 10:30 NKJV)

" He who has seen Me has seen the Father." (John 1:9 NKJV),

"In the beginning was the Word, and the Word was with [YHWH], and the Word was [YHWH]. He was in the beginning with [YHWH]. All things were made through Him, and without Him nothing was made that was made" (John 1:1-3 NKJV),

These verses above show that Yeshua was with the Father throughout the Tanakh and the Father was with Yeshua throughout the B'rit Khadasha. The Father and Son are one. So what the Father did, the Son was doing. Yeshua was there in the Garden and on Mt. Sinai, etc. The converse is also true. What the Son did in the New Covenant, the Father was accomplishing.

Thus, the decision to use either name or title of the Father and Son in selected Bible verses and passages was not random, but prayerfully based on this Biblical understanding.

*   *   *

It is important for readers to ask the Father to be filled with the Holy Spirit and to be given wisdom, discernment, and understanding as they read this book, and to read it with their Bibles alongside. This book was written following the same advice.

Finally, it is necessary that readers read this book from beginning to end; in the order it was written, starting with the Preface. It would be unwise and confusing to the reader to skip around, or to dismiss a section entirely because you don't like the title. All sections are important, but only as they relate to the whole work. Readers, who choose to disregard this wisdom, will be frustrated and feel incomplete. It would be equally important to keep an open mind regarding the content in this book. Happy reading.

Preface

Suppose one of you has a servant plowing or minding sheep. When he comes back from the fields, will the master say, "Come along at once and sit down."? Will he not rather say, "Prepare my supper, fasten your belt, and then wait on me while I have my meal; you can have yours afterwards."? Is he grateful to the servant for carrying out his orders? So with you: when you have carried out all your orders, you should say, "We are servants and deserve no credit; we have only done our duty." (Luke 17:7-10 NEB)

All this happened in order to fulfill what [YHWH] declared through the prophet: "The virgin will conceive and bear a son, and he shall be called Emmanuel, a name which means, 'God is with us.'" (Matthew 1:22-23 NEB)

The following headings make up the acrostic REMEMBER ME that explains who YHWH is and what we can be when we know him.

Relational – The basis for our existence is to remain in an intimate relationship with the Father, through the Holy Spirit. Our secondary purpose, though no less important, is to build and sustain intimate relationships with one another in the Body of Messiah.

Our God is real and desires to have a relationship with those whom he created in his image and likeness. He doesn't demand to have a relationship with us, and he doesn't need to have one with us. But, to those who have accepted his Son as Savior, the Father does command their allegiance. It is a requirement for remaining on the road to Glory. To those whom he shamelessly calls brothers and sisters, as individuals, and his Bride as a Body, Messiah, the Head of the Church, demands faithfulness. His love is a jealous one—like that of a husband's—and he frowns severely upon his Bride's maidens who insist on fornicating with the world. Such behavior tarnishes the testimony of his death and resurrection. Messiah died so that his Bride might live…in union with him. In understanding that God is relational, he expects that his house will be a restored and united one. As such, his children must learn how to relate to one another. YHWH is real and expects his children to be real with one another. Where there is no authenticity, intimacy cannot exist. Where there is no intimacy, you are leaving enough space for the devil to come in and dwell. Wherever the devil dwells, deception and then destruction are sure to follow. The Bride of Messiah must divorce herself from the world—before the Bridegroom returns.

[Yeshua] then came with his disciples to a place called Gethsemane. He said to them, "Sit here while I go over there to pray." He took with him Peter and the two sons of Zebedee. Anguish and dismay came over him, and he said to them, "My heart is ready to break with grief. Stop here, and stay awake with me. " (Matthew 26:36-38 NEB)

Emotional - As a spiritual being who wants to relate to his creation, we serve a God with emotions. Yeshua does not remain tight-lipped about the behaviors of his creation. First and foremost, Yeshua is a loving being. The world, in its loveliness, was created by an act of love. Yeshua loved his creation even after they were disobedient, and continued to demonstrate his love from the moment Adam and Eve were expelled from the garden. YHWH's ultimate display of love was in sending his only Son to die a horrendous death on the cross for all of us who were lost. Yet, the Father has other emotions, too. Contrary to popular sentiment, he does indeed hate. He hates sin. He despises those who insist on tramping in the dark while professing to walk in the light. He hates posers because they give others a false impression of what the Son expects from his followers—absolute and total devotion; a monogamous relationship. Yeshua also expresses disappointment and sorrow. It saddens him when his creation demonstrates through their actions that they find death more attractive than Life. It saddens him to see his sheep suffer mercilessly, yet unnecessarily, at the hands of the enemy because they refuse to learn how to fight. And finally, like an earthly parent, our heavenly Father does not delight in watching the disciplining of his children or in watching their reaction. Yet, the Son rejoices when the flock, under his rod, run back to the road to Glory, which leads to life everlasting. Likewise, his children have emotions and the Father expects his children to learn to embrace them; though in moderation and with wisdom. Yeshua created man imago Dei (in the image of YHWH). It is man who creates mannequins. To the men in the Body, Messiah says that it is senseless to suffer in silence.

> At that very time there were some people present who told him about the Galileans whose blood Pilate had mixed with their sacrifices. He answered them: "Do you imagine that, because these Galileans suffered this fate, they must have been greater sinners than anyone else in Galilee? I tell you they were not; but unless you repent, you will all of you come to the same end. Or the eighteen people who were killed when the tower fell on them at Siloam—do you imagine they were more guilty than all the other people living in Jerusalem? I tell you they were not; but unless you repent, you will all of you come to the same end." (Luke 13:1-5 NEB)

Moral – We do not serve a God who sees the world in shades of gray. YHWH gave his children specific rules which he expects to be followed. It is indeed a matter of Life or death. The Ten Commandments were given to the Israelites in the Tanakh, and the ten were summed up with two in the B'rit Khadasha. YHWH's expectations did not change simply because a New Covenant was extended. Under the Old Covenant, obedience to the Law was a means to righteousness because the Israelites needed to see just how wrong their behavior was. Under the New Covenant obedience to the Law is the expected manifestation of our righteousness, given by grace, rather than earned by works. Nevertheless, consequences still abound for those who insist on living as if they are still dead. The wages of sinful living were never altered under the New Covenant, though many in the Body mistakenly believe that they were. Many shepherds in the Body teach that they have changed, when this is not truth. These shepherds must realize that in doing so, they are inadvertently promoting a "relativistic righteousness," and they are placing their stamp of approval on a cultural Christianity. YHWH/Yeshua's grace is a means of keeping us on the road to Glory. He bestows freely to those whose footsteps make valiant attempts at resembling righteousness. His grace is also extended to those who, while walking, occasionally stumble as a manifestation of their strengthening legs. His grace is not for cheapening by those who recklessly disregard their high standard for holy living in exchange for grotesquely feeding their lowest nature. YHWH is not fuzzy on what he requires of his children. However, to know it, requires reading the Bible. Messiah expects his shepherds to hold his sheep accountable. There is far too much leaven in the dough and it has infected the loaf. Those moldy pieces of bread need to be cleaned.

> And now, as he approached the descent from the Mount of Olives, the whole company of his disciples in their joy began to sing aloud the praises of [YHWH] for all the great things they had seen: "Blessings on him who comes as king in the name of the Lord! Peace in heaven, glory in highest heaven." Some Pharisees who were in the crowd said to him, "Master, reprimand your disciples." He answered, "I tell you, if my disciples keep silence the stones will shout aloud." (Luke 19:37-40 NEB)

Epochal – It is embarrassing to need to be reminded that YHWH is important, but our actions and apathetic attitudes reveal that we have forgotten. When our lives are structured so that we must fit YHWH into our schedules, rather than revolving our schedules around him, there is a problem. Without them we would cease to be. It is God's will that we remain dependent on him, and so suffering ensues. Man has shown that without suffering we would submit to self. But it is the Father's will that we submit to the Son until his work is done. Yeshua's epochal nature also speaks to his sovereignty. He is in ultimate control of the world he created. We do not serve a deistic god, one who crafted the universe, but then left man alone to worship his self and the rest of creation. We serve a God who is worthy of all our praise, glory, and honor. We serve a Shepherd who is the Head of his Body, the Church. It is imperative that after crafting a multitude of denominations, which has served to divide the Body, man understands there is only One Lord of all. As Messiah's disciples we need to ignore what the world says and focus only on the Holy Spirit, in striving to please the Son and the Father. Yeshua's approval is the only one that matters. Yeshua thought enough of us to make us in his image. It is time that our lives reflected our gratitude.

> [Yeshua] is good, a stronghold in the day of trouble; he knows those who take refuge in him. But with an overflowing flood he will make a complete end of the adversaries, and will pursue his enemies into darkness. What do you plot against the Lord? He will make a complete end; trouble will not rise up a second time. For they are like entangled thorns, like drunkards as they drink; they are consumed like stubble fully dried. From you came one who plotted evil against [YHWH], a worthless counselor. (Nahum 1:7-11 ESV)

Martial – YHWH is the Lord of Hosts. Yeshua and his angels are daily fighting on the side of his disciples. The Christian walk is also a Christian war. Christians must remember, in the same way that YHWH was with the Israelites during their mighty battles, he is there for them today. YHWH is emphatic in declaring that his children must learn how to duel with the devil. Shepherds must begin equipping

Messiah's sheep and desist from leaving them open to attacks by hungry wolves. The Holy Spirit is waiting and ready to empower. Though spiritual warfare remains largely an unpopular topic in most churches, ignorance can be blistering. Members must learn to guard their tongues, for there is where the potency lies. And the father of lies, along with the rest of the fallen angels, has been watching and listening to humanity with a keen interest. They know exactly how to make YHWH's people fall. Messiah is uninterested in keeping a wimpy staff on hand. It is time for his disciples to wise up and to pick up their swords and shields because this battle is for real.

The fear of [Yeshua] prolongs life, but the years of the wicked will be short. The hope of the righteous brings joy, but the expectation of the wicked will perish. The way of [Yeshua] is a stronghold to the blameless, but destruction to evildoers. The righteous will never be removed, but the wicked will not dwell in the land. (Proverbs 10:27-30 ESV)

Bi-conditional – It is true that YHWH is the same today as he was yesterday, and as he will be tomorrow. It is not him who has changed, only the perception of him. It is time that members begin seeing YHWH through both eyes, not just the one that posits him in their most favored light. He is loving and just. Our Lord and Savior is as meek and mild as a Lamb; and he was slaughtered in kind. However, Messiah is coming back to reign as the Lion of Judah. The Son of Man, who was fully human, was also the Son of YHWH—fully Divine. Our suffering would be more sufferable if we remembered that Messiah too suffered. It was his perfect, unblemished, human nature that allowed his own bodily sacrifice to be acceptable to the Father. We are expected to pattern our lives after his holy nature—not his Divine. Messiah is our Advocate. Yet he is also Lord of lords and King of kings. Christians also have dual natures. All have two seeds planted within. The seed of Messiah is holy. It is the seed of sin that must be crushed daily by the blood and grace of Yeshua Messiah, and by our will, divinely inspired by the Holy Spirit. Failure to daily crush this seed will lead the believer back to a life of weeds. The seed of Messiah must be daily watered so that fresh fruit can grow, and so that Messiah can see evidence of the fruit upon his return, when, alive or dead, believer or not, we will receive new bodies at the trumpet sound. The new temple for our spirits will remain with us for eternity, whether in heaven or in the lake of fire.

"I am the Alpha and the Omega, the Beginning and the End," says the Lord, "who is and who was and who is to come, the Almighty.". (Revelation 1:8 NKJV)

Eternal – Yeshua is the First and the Last, the Alpha and the Omega, the Beginning and the End. YHWH has always existed before time. He sees everything at once and is not bound by the same chronos that we are. Because of our myopic vision, at times it is difficult for believers to trust in him and his promises. Faith must step in when our reason insists on clouding our minds. YHWH always sees the big picture and so often his involvement in our lives will make little sense to the rest of us. Man is also eternal, but in a strict sense of the word. Man, of course, is a created being. However, Christians are promised an inheritance of eternal life upon accepting Yeshua Messiah as Lord and Savior. We must not forget that our actual home is in Heaven. The Body of Messiah must cease viewing the family of YHWH as some clever metaphor to help better explain the intentions of him whom the Father has made the Head of his house. Believers must start viewing the Body of Messiah as an actual family, rather than using the word "family" as an analogy to help explain the Body in a different light. We must begin to treat one another with all of the love of a true family and become intentional about expanding YHWH's kingdom family. Let none act so selfishly that we forget the millions still lost who need help finding their way home. We must ensure that the relationships we are building on earth are genuine and meaningful, for these are loved ones that we will see and worship with for eternity. Finally, each must remind one another that Satan's mirages are earth-bound; and though we are heaven-bound, we make our bodies rather weighty when we insist on eating from his fruit. Let none become so weighty that they are unable to take off when Messiah returns in midair.

> In the beginning, Elohim created the heavens and the earth. The earth was without form and void, and darkness was over the face of the deep. And the Holy Spirit was hovering over the face of the waters. And [Yeshua] said, "Let there be light," and there was light. And [Yeshua] saw that the light was good. And [Yeshua] separated the light from the darkness. [Yeshua] called the light day, and the darkness he called night. And there was evening and there was morning, the first day. (Genesis 1:1-5 ESV)

Rational – Creation itself was the first rational act of Elohim. He made a decision, spoke, and then judged his own actions. Whether or not it makes any sense to us, Yeshua had logic to the order of his creation. The Flood was a rational decision made by a rational God. YHWH saw the heightened level of sin—violence and corruption on earth—and so decided to destroy it. Perhaps he reasoned that such violence would have eventually led to the destruction of man anyway, and he was uninterested in seeing man to his final and perverse end. Or what if the Flood was simply an act of retribution? No one can say for sure because Scripture does not give us YHWH's rationale, other than that he didn't like what he saw. Members must believe that YHWH always has a reason for what he does and that his reasons are perfect and just and wise—even if we can't always understand them. Furthermore, Yeshua has an intellect that makes his creation intelligible. All of creation has order, just look at the field of mathematics. Our entire numbering system, no matter its variation, speaks of Yeshua. It is not true that YHWH purposely keeps us out of the loop of the rationale behind his decisions, or that believers are incapable of understanding his decisions—we who have the mind of Messiah. It is the case that believers seldom ask anything of the sort, and it is even more the case that believers barely, if ever, take time to sift through Scripture to find the answers. Man is also a rational creature; one of the main attributes separating us from the rest of Yeshua's creation, which is another tribute to our epochal nature. Man must be careful not to rely exclusively on his reasoning skills, however. Excessive reasoning can turn a relational-laden Christianity into a corpse-driven religion. Remember that Messiah needs for his disciples to move. Lastly, reason and emotion are not mutually exclusive; both have a place in the Body of Messiah.

> From east and west people will come, from north and south, for the feast in the kingdom of [YHWH]. Yes, and some who are now last will be first, and some are first who will be last. (Luke 13:29-30 NEB)

Multicultural – YHWH is spirit and therefore transcends all cultures and races. He is also intimately involved with all. That is, all that has as their foundation, Yeshua Messiah. It is foolish for individual members of the Body to pigeon hole YHWH as if he only exists through their monochromatic lenses. To say that he is multicultural does not suggest that he condones the secular multicultural philosophy, rooted in postmodernism; the philosophy which has as its foundation, moral relativism—absent of any truth. The synoptic Gospels can lay claim to promoting multiculturalism, as each book was written to a different cultural audience and in a slightly different format; with a slightly different tone and emphasis. Matthew was written to a Jewish audience, Mark to the Romans, and Luke to the Greeks. Yet all three have the same message and point to one truth—Yeshua Messiah. It does suggest that Yeshua is not housed on any one continent or country. His multicultural nature is indicative of his rational and creative self. That we have in the world a variety of ethnic groups, who have adopted unique worshiping styles and practices, does not imply that such is the result of original sinful living. Such diversity is only sinful when it becomes divisive. And the Body of Messiah is a divided Body today. There are those shepherds who insist on focusing on Messiah's color rather then teaching their sheep to focus on Messiah's character. Messiah is unimpressed. There are those members in the Body who refuse to worship together with someone of a different color, and yet claim that they still have love for their brothers. Messiah is disgusted. There are those whose focus is more on the music and less on the message, and so division occurs. Messiah is dismayed. There is only one Good Shepherd, who is Lord over all. To those who insist on remaining divided at the 11:00 hour, do you dare insist on remaining so until we approach our final minute? It is clear that man is multicultural. However, let no man ever place his temporal culture over the spiritual culture of Messiah.

> When day broke he went out and made his way to a lonely spot. But the people went in search of him, and they came to where he was they pressed him not leave them. But he said, "I must give the good news of the kingdom of [YHWH] to the other towns also, for that is what I was sent to do." So he proclaimed the Gospel in the synagogues of Judea. (Luke 4:42-43 NEB)

Ecumenical – YHWH is indeed the God of the universe. And he wants his people to know that, in carrying out the Great Commission of Messiah, he means for them to circle the globe. Christianity is not a country club religion, and therefore, other than sincere faith in the saving grace of YHWH through his Son, Yeshua Messiah, no one has any business declaring additional membership requirements. The apostle Paul was clear in his remarks to the church in Galatia. To the Romans, Paul reminded what the requirements are: acknowledgment of one's sinful nature and past sins, expression of remorse for past and current condition, a humble request that Yeshua Messiah become your personal Lord and Savior, and sincere renunciation of past sinful living. James also reminds readers that our newly found faith should be made manifest by our actions—a walking testimony of our Spirit-led tongues. In making all nations Messiah's disciples, it is going to require many to leave their boats. It is imperative that both short-term and long-term missionaries reflect the Messiah of the Bible, rather than the Messiah of their culture—the two are rarely the same. What people around the world need to see, including those in the United States, is a genuine reflection of the truth; perhaps less would reject Christianity if they actually saw Messiah. Nonetheless, as ecumenical creatures of our Creator, we must remember that while YHWH's house is big enough for all who desire, the Father nor the Son accepts all who desire to pollute. His love is universal, but so is his disdain for the dishonest, the deceptive, and the demoralizing. He does not tolerate those people who insist on spreading their immoral behavior while inside the Church. He does want the drunkards, adulterers, fornicators, homosexuals, gossips, liars, thieves, cheaters, murderers, sorcerers, witches, child-abusers, rapists, and racists. He wants them to live, and so the Church must open her doors to them and love them the way Messiah loved us, and so died on the cross. Such universalism must be accepted in order to change the universe. However, believers must remain leery of those within who insist on spreading sin throughout. If persisting in said practices, and if refusing to repent, then those unfaithful must be rooted out before their immoral behavior becomes amoralized. The amoralizing of immoral behavior is the pathway to apathy, which has its end—apostasy.

REMEMBER ME. While journeying and journaling, this mnemonic device should constantly remind as one continues to read and reflect. And now for a warning. What follows is not the Holy Bible. This book is not a paraphrasing or translation of the Holy Bible; neither is it a substitution. In fact, none reading this now should continue to the first entry without also having in their possession, an inspired translation of the word of YHWH. Nor should any make a decision of their translation without first prayerfully inquiring of our heavenly Father, in the name of his Son, our Lord and Savior, Yeshua Messiah, through the Holy Spirit—our Comforter, Intercessor, and Helper until the imminent return of our Redeemer. This is a compass to aid the believer (and prayerfully, the questioning unbeliever too), who, while traveling on the long, dusty, windy, and narrow road, is in need of redirection or assistance in making their way northbound. May all readers be encouraged, convicted, and empowered to continue walking until they see the gates of Glory. Walk with the provisions of the Father, the protection of the Son, and the power of the Holy Spirit. Amen.

Agape,

Marquis

The grace of [Yeshua] be with you. My love to you all in [Yeshua]. Amen. (1st Corinthians 16:23-24 ESV)

Table of Contents

Contents (cont.)

Contents (cont.)

Contents (cont.)

FROM GRACE TO GLORY
An Upward Journey

DEVOTIONALS

1. Miracular Degeneration I

First read: Isaiah 17:10

You are on the journey of life with both feet planted on the ground. You had no control over the path you were set on, and little control over where you find yourself today, but you are in complete control of determining where you go from here. So before you take another step, pause for a moment and look. Look long, but not for too long. Look back. Look back for two reasons, but not for too long. First, acknowledge that you may have had some obstacles in starting on your journey, and perhaps even a few hurdles along the way, but look how far you've come.

"For in baptism you were buried with him, in baptism also you were raised to life with him through your faith in the active power of [YHWH] who raised him from the dead." (Colossians 2:12 ESV)

How soon we forget the miracles of our Lord. How quickly we forget the bondage we were once in while living in sin, and how through the grace of YHWH we were delivered. For those believers under the New Covenant, who would rather discount the Tanakh as irrelevant to their lives today, I offer a word of caution. Yeshua Messiah, the Son of YHWH, relied upon Scripture verses from the Tanakh in converting the early Jewish sects to The Way. After his ascension into heaven, the apostles continued to use the messages of the Tanakh in converting both the Jews and Gentiles to Christianity. We find most of these occurrences taking place in the book of Acts, most notably with Peter, Stephen, and Paul. In addition, Paul's usage of the Tanakh can be found too in his instruction to the Romans. And again, we find the author of the book of Hebrews repeatedly referencing the Tanakh in delivering his message. It is clear, then, that Messiah through his Holy Spirit intended for believers everywhere, of all successive ages, to have within their reach the memorable accounts of both the Tanakh and B'rit Khadasha.

"I have told you all this while I am still here with you; but your Advocate [Helper], the Holy Spirit whom the Father will send in my name, will teach you everything, and will call to mind all that I have told you." (John 14:25-26 NEB)

"For all the ancient scriptures were written for our own instruction, in order that through the encouragement they give us we may maintain our hope with fortitude." (Romans 15:4 NEB)

Members of Messiah's Body should welcome learning about the events of our founding relatives. Not only was Yeshua Messiah himself a Hebrew by birth, but indeed Christianity could never have come into existence without the activities of those following the elder Jewish faith.

What follows? What Israel sought, Israel has not achieved, but the selected few have achieved it. The rest were made blind to the truth, exactly as it stands written, "[Yeshua] brought upon them a numbness of spirit; he gave them blind eyes and deaf ears, and so it is still." Similarly David says, "May their table be a snare and a trap, both stumbling-block and retribution! May their eyes become so dim that they lose their sight! Bow down their backs unceasingly." I now ask, did their failure mean complete downfall? Far from it. Because they offended, salvation has come to the Gentiles, to stir Israel to emulation. But if their offence means the enrichment of the world, and if their falling-off means the enrichment of the Gentiles, how much more their coming to full strength" (Romans 11:7-12 ESV).

Let us then neither bask in arrogance in discounting the significance of our Jewish siblings. For in the same way that many of their branches were chopped off for the benefit of our grafting, YHWH has made it clear that the day is near for the redemption of our elders. However, what's equally valuable in returning to the Tanakh are the lessons today's Christians can learn from reading of the Israelites' mistakes. What were those behaviors that induced their spiritual blindness? What miracles did they forget?

"You should understand, my brothers, that our ancestors were all under the pillar of cloud, and all of them passed through the Red Sea; and so they all received baptism into the fellowship of Moses in cloud and sea. They all ate the same supernatural food, and all drank the same supernatural drink; I mean, they all drank from the supernatural rock that accompanied their travels— and that rock was [Messiah]. And yet, most of them were not accepted by [YHWH], for the desert was strewn with the corpses. These events happened as symbols to warn us not to set our desires on evil things, as they did." (1st Corinthians 10:1-6 NEB)

Thus we are bound to pay all the more heed to what we have been told, for fear of drifting from our course. For if the word spoken through angels had such force that any transgression or disobedience met with due retribution, what escape can there be for us if we ignore a deliverance so great? For this deliverance was first announced through the lips of the Lord himself; those who heard him confirmed it to us, and [YHWH] added his testimony by signs, by miracles, by manifold works of power, and by distributing the gifts of the Holy Spirit at his own will. (Hebrews 2:1-4 NEB)

2. A Reflective Moment

Stuck in the Mud

First read: Philippians 3:12-14

Are you stuck in the past? Do you surround yourself with people who constantly remind you of the wretch you were prior to knowing Messiah? I believe some members have good intentions in attempting to keep their brothers and sisters humble. And in truth, it's necessary for all believers to remember the graciousness of YHWH in grafting us in:

> You will say, "Branches were lopped off so that I might be grafted in." Very well: They were lopped off for lack of faith, and by faith you hold your place. Put away your pride, and be on your guard; for if [YHWH] did not spare the native branches, no more will he spare you. Observe the kindness and severity of [YHWH] —severity to those who fell away, divine kindness to you, if only you remain within its scope; otherwise you too will be cut off, whereas they, if they do not continue faithless, will be grafted in; for it is in [YHWH]'s power to graft them in again. (Romans 11:19-23 ESV)

To this end Paul was speaking directly to the Gentiles, newly converted. He urged them not to think so highly of themselves as to forget what happened to the Israelites who were continuously disobedient, even after being delivered from the hands of Pharaoh. Again and again he spoke through judges, and then through prophets, to remind his children to return to him. He sent his own Son down to earth to plead and to save, and yet the Jews sent even Messiah to his grave.

> And he said, "The Son of Man has to undergo great sufferings, and to be rejected by the elders, chief priests, and doctors of the law, to be put to death and to be raised again on the third day." (Luke 9:22 NEB)

Though unfortunate, their rejection of the Master opened the door to allow the rest to serve—the wild olives, as Paul refers to members of the Body who aren't of Jewish descent. We would do well not to continue following in the same footsteps as our elder siblings. After grafting us in, Yeshua expects to see some growth.

> At last he sent to them his son. "They will respect my son," he said. But when they saw the son, the tenants said to another, "This is the heir; come on, let us kill him, and get his inheritance." And they took him, flung him out of the vineyard, and killed him. When the owner of the vineyard comes, how do you think he will deal with those tenants? "He will bring those bad men to a bad end," they answered, "and hand the vineyard over to the other tenants, who will let him have his share of the crop when the season comes." Then [Yeshua] said to them, "Have you never read in the scriptures: 'The stone which the builders rejected has become the main cornerstone. This is the Lord's doing, and it is wonderful in our eyes?' Therefore, I tell you, the kingdom of [YHWH] will be taken away from you, and given to a nation that yields the proper fruit. (Matthew 21:37-43 ESV)

Then Silas and Timothy came down from Macedonia, and Paul devoted himself entirely to preaching, affirming before the Jews that the Messiah was [Yeshua]. But when they opposed him and resorted to abuse, he shook out the skirts of his cloak and said to them, "Your blood be on your own heads. My conscience is clear; now I shall go to the Gentiles." (Acts 18:5-6 ESV)

Sin can have long-term repercussions even after we have put it aside. Our mind is like a camera in that through the passing of time some images remain sharp, even when we'd rather they fade. Nonetheless, past experiences are valuable because they often remind believers of their former state before being washed in Messiah's blood. Believers may feel a twinge of guilt when presented with the same temptations of their past. However, this time, rather than indulging, the decision is made to deny, and the believer can rejoice in their maturation. Another benefit of those irksome images is that they can serve as a reminder of YHWH's grace. We remember the words of Yeshua in speaking through the prophet Ezekiel:

…and say, "Thus says [Yeshua] to Jerusalem: Your origin and your birth are of the land of the Canaanites; your father was an Amorite and your mother a Hittite. And as for your birth, on the day you were born your cord was not cut, nor were you washed with water to cleanse you, nor rubbed with salt, nor wrapped in swaddling cloths. No eye pitied you, to do any of these things to you out of compassion for you, but you were cast out on the open field, for you were abhorred, on the day that you were born. And when I passed by you and saw you wallowing in your blood, I said to you in your blood, 'Live.' I said to you in your blood, 'Live.' I made you flourish like a plant of the field. And you grew up and became tall and arrived at full adornment. Your breasts were formed, and your hair had grown; yet you were naked and bare. When I passed by you again and saw you, behold, you were at the age for love, and I spread the corner of my garment over you and covered your nakedness; I made my vow to you and entered into a covenant with you, declares [Yeshua], and you became mine." (Ezekiel 16:3-8 ESV)

The imagery is a bit graphic, but I know of no better way to illustrate man's depravity. Indeed, other than Messiah's death on the cross, I see no better description of Yeshua's unfathomable love for his creation. If ever believers get on their spiritual high horse—if ever any begins thinking, after experiencing Yeshua and his goodness, that they can simply dismiss him and continue on their merry way—getting stuck in some mud for awhile can serve as a not-so-gentle reminder. Still, Messiah did not deliver us from the bondages of sin only to have believers continuously reading from the same old script—replaying the same old scene. What use is a servant who spends his time ruminating over regrettable decisions? How valuable is the servant who keeps her feet moving forward while always looking behind? Sooner or later an accident will ensue and new wounds will develop as a result. As a result, more time is spent on repairing self and less time on helping and encouraging others. YHWH, in his sovereignty, permits everything that happens in our lives. And if he permits, there must be a purpose, though there isn't a member alive or dead who hasn't had their share of circumstances they would rather forget.

Keeping our eyes on what's ahead doesn't necessitate members closing them completely on what happened five miles back. Oftentimes the heaviest loads we bear are the ones we refuse to share. In remaining concealed, members not only exacerbate their burden, they also thwart the healing purposes of Messiah. YHWH's call to the life above is a call for intimacy; foremost with the Godhead but also with one another. We reject his call when insisting that the road to Glory is based upon our own efforts or that we can reach our destination alone. How ironic that the members of the Body who attempt this route routinely find themselves stuck in the mud. At present there are those in the Church failing to win the prize because they are living in fear. They fear connecting with people and so not long after they begin walking, they stumble into the mud. Too afraid to ask for help, they are now stuck. For others, I believe the fear of rejection grips them mercilessly. In either situation wounds abounded somewhere in the believer's past, and they are now causing them to be rejected and displaced in the Church. When one body part rejects another body part, the Body can't function properly. While pressing for the goal, members must help one another, otherwise the whole Body remains stuck.

Little growth can take place, however, if we are constantly living in the past. Suffering is plenteous in the life of every believer. So allow them to rejoice in moments of maturity. Messiah does. Rather than crushing surrounding spirits by pushing them back into the mud, members of the Body should encourage one another. When a part of the body rejoices, the whole Body should rejoice. And when a part of the body stumbles back into the mud, rather than gloat over their mishap, the rest should help lift them up. For this is what family members do.

"Let hope keep you joyful; in trouble stand firm; persist in prayer. Contribute to the needs of [YHWH]'s people, and practice hospitality. Call down blessings on your persecutors—blessings, not curses. With the joyful be joyful, and mourn with the mourners. Care as much about each other as about yourselves. Do not be haughty, but go about with humble folk. Do not keep thinking how wise you are." (Romans 12:12-16 NEB)

3. Miracular Degeneration II

First read: Proverbs 4:26-27

Second, remember, as best you can and as far as your eyes will allow you, where all the ditches and twigs lay that you fell into or tripped over before. While not exact, there was a pattern. And as much as possible, you want to avoid stepping in those same spots.

Through revisiting the plight of the Israelites in the Tanakh, it is imperative that believers in the Church today remember the mistakes that were made. We are provided ample information of how the Hebrews sinned against YHWH once they were finally set free from Pharaoh's clutches. Prior to delivering a just judgment on his wayward people, YHWH would send a messenger to warn them of their impending punishment, should they persist in their sinful behavior and fail to repent. But the intent was never to scare them into submission by only informing them of what he would do to them. He would rather have his people focus on his goodness and remind them of the extent of their redemption out of Egypt—what he had done for them.

O my people, what have I done to you? How have I wearied you? Answer me. For I brought you up from the land of Egypt and redeemed you from the house of slavery, and I sent before you Moses, Aaron, and Miriam. O my people, remember what Balak king of Moab devised, and what Balaam the son of Beor answered him, and what happened from Shittim to Gilgal, that you may know the righteous acts of [YHWH]. (Micah 6:3-5 ESV)

Spiritual blindness begins to set in when believers start to forget the miracles of YHWH. For the Israelites, no sooner had they made it safely through the Red Sea into the wilderness of Shur, did they begin to grumble and complain. Apparently, all of the miracles that YHWH had delivered through Moses and Aaron while the Israelites still lived in Egypt were insufficient. It was clear that they lacked wisdom in understanding the purpose of YHWH through his choice of actions. Yeshua hardened Pharaoh's heart to obstinacy in order that the Israelites might see the extent of YHWH's power. What they saw should have been enlightening for their freedom. YHWH's acting in Egypt through Pharaoh was deliberate so that the Israelites might see, and once delivered, remain free.

What shall we say to that? Is [YHWH] to be charged with injustice? By no means. For he says to Moses, "Where I show mercy, I will show mercy, and where I pity, I will pity." Thus it does not depend on man's will or effort, but on [YHWH]'s mercy. For Scripture says to Pharaoh, "I have raised you up for this very purpose, to exhibit my power in my dealings with you, and to spread my fame over all the world." Thus he not only shows mercy as he chooses, but also makes men stubborn as he chooses.. (Romans 9:14-18 NEB)

It was the hope of YHWH that his miracles would sustain the Israelites as they traveled through the wilderness. However, it was their inability to see the future that clouded the memories of their recent past. When they failed to remember where they had been, they allowed their lapse to lead them to sin.

"In consequence, I say, [YHWH] has given them up to shameful passions. Their women have exchanged natural intercourse for unnatural, and their men in turn, giving up natural relations with women, burn with lust for one another; males behave indecently with males, and are paid in their own persons the fitting wage of such perversion." (Romans 1:26-27 NEB)

Do not be idolaters, like some of them; as Scripture has it, "the people sat down to feast and stood up to play." Let us not commit fornication, as some of them did—and twenty-three thousand died in one day. Let us not put the power of the Lord to the test, as some of them did—and were destroyed by serpents. Do not grumble against [YHWH], as some of them did—and were destroyed by the Destroyer. (1st Corinthians 10:7-10 NEB)

4. YHWH Is

Jeremiah 9:23-24

A is for accepting, abundant, and awesome
  for which no other god can compare

B is for breathtaking, a boundless blossom
  whose beauty no evil can bear

C is for caring, courageous, and candid
  a God who will capture your heart

D is for defender, designer, and devoted
  a God who shall never depart

E is for eager (an echo)...I said eager
  he is eager to end all of your pain

F is for faithful, flawless, and forbearing
  a Father, forgiving, a flame

G is glorious, gracious, and gentle
  guiltless, who speaks from within

H is for hallowed, heartfelt, a hero
  he gave of himself for our sin

I is for intimate, igniting, and inviting
  a God who invests in our growth

J is for joyous, jealous, a jurist
  there's justice and love in him both

K is for knowing, knightly, and kindly
  a King who shall never step down

L is for loving, living, a lantern
  a Lord whose might is renowned

M is for marvelous, majestic, a mover
  a God who moves with the wind

N is for necessary, nurturing, a noble
  whose narrow road to Glory won't bend

O is for omniscient, omnipotent, omnipresent
  a God who expects his own to obey

P is for parental, peaceful, and perceptive
  a paragon of Truth, Life, and the Way

Q is for quenching, qualified, and quieting
  the quintessence in all his has done

R is for radiant, righteous, a Redeemer
  who reconciled us all through his Son

S is for sacred, scorching, who sanctions
  who searches right down to the soul

T is for tenacious, thorough, and tender
  he takes what was torn and makes whole

U is for unusual, unbiased, and unseen
  the ultimate in all that is true

V is for valiant, vigilant, our Victor
  now from vices to virtues, we're new

W is for wonderful, whitening, a whisper
  whose wisdom is second to none

X is for exceptional, expressive, extending
  and so we extol the Father, Spirit, and Son

Y is for yearning, yes, YHWH, he is yearning
  to the Son we were yoked with a cost

Z is for zealous; YHWH's the zenith of zealous
  zero...the number of souls he wants lost

5. A Reflective Moment

Miracular Degeneration – III

Simply stated, miracular degeneration results in generations of sinfulness. When YHWH's people have forgotten his miracles of the past, when they fail to remember how YHWH delivered them from their bondage, immediately a false sense of security takes root until spiritual dependency no longer matters. In the United States, we easily forget YHWH's mercy in orchestrating our victory against Great Britain and the tyrant known as King George III; the man who first introduced the word "terrorist" to the American vocabulary. In schools, where the Declaration of Independence is examined, particular attention is often given to the opening lines of the second paragraph. In fact, most Americans are able to rattle off the thirty-five words reeking of hypocrisy. Words that did not fall upon blinded eyes and that YHWH would eventually allow to pierce the flesh and hearts of men during the American Civil War. However, it is the remaining portion of the document that offers rationale behind the colonists' desire for independence. It doesn't take much to convince a people that, among other acts of treachery, the burning down of villages and homes, obstructing and perverting justice for self-preservation while annihilating the people that such justice was instituted for, and finally, under the threat of death, forcing colonists to take part in the genocide of their own people, such a life is not genuine living.

> All these things that happened to them were symbolic, and were recorded for our benefit as a warning. For upon us the fulfillment of the ages has come. If you feel sure that you are standing firm, beware. You may fall. (1st Corinthians 10:11-12 NEB)

In comparing the forces of the ragtag Continental American Army with the incomparable Goliath known as Great Britain, only a fool in his arrogance would contend that American success was inevitable. Neither was securing our victory with the Battle of Yorktown, after first securing the support of the French, an obvious solution. George Washington was to receive assistance from the country he volunteered to attack just twenty-five years earlier in the French and Indian War. Many historians speculate over the motives of France in coming to the aid of a territory that had recently contributed to her gradual demise, both politically and economically. Some suggest that it was an opportunity for France to exact revenge behind the real culprit of the Seven Years War. Others have reasoned that it benefited France's own geo-political hegemonic attempts to cripple her nearest rival. Whatever the intention, America benefited and YHWH allowed, if not orchestrated, such an unlikely alliance to result in our achieving victory over King George III.

> In the sight of their fathers he performed wonders in the land of Egypt, in the fields of Zoan. He divided the sea and let them pass through it, and made the waters stand like a heap. In the daytime he led them with a cloud, and all the night with a fiery light. He split rocks in the wilderness and gave them drink abundantly as from the deep. He made streams come out of the rock and

caused waters to flow down like rivers. Yet they sinned still more against him, rebelling against the Most High in the desert. They tested [YHWH] in their heart by demanding the food they craved. (Psalms 78:12-18 ESV)

When YHWH delivers victory to his people, the expectation is that such deliverance will serve as a means for endless praise, devotion, and obedience. Instead, history has shown that YHWH's people repeatedly use his providence as a means for delving into prideful and disdainful disobedience. The Israelites seldom learned the lesson that when they were acting in submission to YHWH's will, then his hand was extended in protecting. And when through their actions the Israelites began to believe that they no longer needed him, or when they failed to take advantage of his offered respite as a means to repentance, the tides began to change.

6. Starting With Cymbals

First read: 1st Chronicles 15-16

Look around. Look around for two reasons, but not for too long. Recognize that the world is bigger than you are and that you're neither its center nor its sun. And then begin giving thanks to the one who created it all.

Each time we approach the Father in prayer, it should always begin with praise. So many in the Body struggle with prayer these days; it wasn't different yesterday either.

In the beginning, Elohim created the heavens and the earth. The earth was without form and void, and darkness was over the face of the deep. And the Holy Spirit was hovering over the face of the waters. And [Yeshua] said, "Let there be light," and there was light. And [Yeshua] saw that the light was good. And [Yeshua] separated the light from the darkness. [Yeshua] called the light day, and the darkness he called night. And there was evening and there was morning, the first day. (Genesis 1:1-5 ESV)

Before there is prayer, there is the Lord. Yeshua instructed well because he understood well. As the Son of YHWH, Yeshua Messiah was there in the beginning and everything created was created by him:

When all things began, the Word already was. The Word dwelt with [YHWH], and what [YHWH] was, the Word was. The Word, then, was with [YHWH] at the beginning, and by him all things came to be; no single thing was created without him. All that came to be was alive with his life, and that life was the light of men. The light shines on in the dark, and the darkness has never mastered it. (John 1:1-5 NEB)

So the Son understands fully the reverence and praise due to the Father, and the Father, the Son. It was the will of Messiah that his disciples also enter his Father's throne room with praise and then petition. The Father's name isn't hallowed when the prayers of his children are so hollow. When focused on our own needs, we instinctively hallow in haste and then race to ask for our needs to materialize, rather than taking time first to praise the Father for his goodness and then the Son for his place at the Head of the Body. In daily picking up our cross and following the Son we purposefully move that much closer to the Father.

[Yeshua] replied, "Anyone who loves me will heed what I say, then my Father will love him, and we will come to him and make our dwelling with him." (John 14:23 NEB)

Soon there will come an intimate moment with the Father where our newly molding spirits won't allow us to depart instantly. The Holy Spirit, now dwelling within, won't want to rush to the end. Instead the Spirit will want to begin with cymbals. Rather than pausing for praise out of obligation, it is Messiah's desire that his followers grow to develop a pattern of praise out of adoration. When believers believe that at the center of the universe sits both a Father and his Son, who as one, sustains all of life, only then will each in freedom and without shame, sound their cymbals in calling out his name.

Shout for joy in [Yeshua], O you righteous. Praise befits the upright. Give thanks to [Yeshua] with the lyre; make melody to him with the harp of ten strings. Sing to him a new song; play skillfully on the strings, with loud shouts. For the word of [Yeshua] is upright, and all his work is done in faithfulness. (Psalms 33:1-4 ESV)

Believe me when I say that I am in the Father and the Father in me; or else accept the evidence of the deeds themselves. (John 14:11 NEB)

7. The Call of the Wild The Cry of the Wise

First read: Habakkuk 1-3

There are some who are ahead of you. Accept it. There are some who are behind you. Expect it.

And respect both, because the decision to allow either comes from a sovereign God. Who dares to tell YHWH, what he wills is not fair? If he has placed you ahead in the race, it is not for the purposes of gloating, but for promoting the goodness and majesty of Messiah, and to encourage all of those behind you to continue in the race; at the pace Messiah has set for them.

> But you are a chosen race, a royal priesthood, a dedicated nation, and a people claimed by [YHWH] for his own, to proclaim the triumphs of him who has called you out of darkness into his marvelous light. You are now the people of [YHWH], who once were not his people; outside his mercy once, you have now received his mercy. (1st Peter 2:9-10 NEB)

> You did not choose me: I chose you. I appointed you to go on and bear fruit that shall last; so that the Father may give you all that you ask in my name. This is my commandment to you: love one another. (John 15:16-17 NEB)

To be elected through Messiah means being rejected by the common, but it also means remembering that Messiah died for the common too. Though, as ambassadors for the King, believers should expect that many commoners will refuse to accept their invitation to join them in the Kingdom. There are priestly responsibilities that commoners don't have to busy themselves with, and many will be uninterested in carrying out the required duties. The call of the wild is more appealing to the commoner than is the call of wisdom.

> Brother will betray brother to death, and the father of his child; children will turn against their parents and send them to their death. All will hate you for your allegiance to me; but the man who holds out to the end will be saved. When you are persecuted in one town, take refuge in another; I tell you this: before you have gone through all the towns of Israel the Son of Man will have come. (Matthew 10:21-23 NEB)

And yet there are those commoners who, while living in the wilderness, live like kings. Conversely, there are princes and priests who live like paupers. How baffling it all appears today, as it did to the prophet Habakkuk around 606 B. C. But, believers must not allow their bafflement to bamboozle. Such appearances might lead members of the Body to conclude that their Head is apathetic to the plight of his people. Don't be deceived—it's just the call of the wild. The prince of the wilderness wants Messiah's priests to become disgruntled with their work for the kingdom so that they will abdicate. It is best that the priests of the Lord not fall for the wiles of the wild, for a fire is already ensuing. Instead, members should keep their eyes on the prize and their hearts in the word, lest those wild be the victors in their attempts to woo.

He then dismissed the people, and went into the house, where his disciples came to him and said, "Explain to us the parable of the darnel [a Eurasian ryegrass weed] in the field." And this was his answer: "The sower of the good seed is the Son of Man. The field is the world; the good seed stands for children of the Kingdom, the darnel for the children of the evil one. The enemy who sowed the darnel is the devil. The harvest is the end of time. The reapers are angels. As the darnel, then, is gathered up and burnt, so at the end of time the Son of Man will send out his angels, who will gather out of his kingdom whatever makes men stumble, and all whose deeds are evil, and these will be thrown into the blazing furnace, the place of wailing and grinding of teeth. And then the righteous will shine brightly as the sun in the kingdom of their Father. If you have ears, then hear." (Matthew 13:36-43 NEB)

Like Job, Habakkuk struggled in understanding why it seemed the wicked should win in the midst of their sin. Yeshua's response to both was a reminder to all believers of our real struggle: myopia. It is tempting to displace our anger at our own deficiencies onto the Lord. It is also rather dimwitted, save for the merciful character of our Maker who, with perfect vision, knows the motivation despite our myopia. So he is gracious and tolerant while listening to our tirades.

[YHWH], how long shall I cry for help, and you will not hear? Or cry to you "Violence" and you will not save? Why do you make me see iniquity, and why do you idly look at wrong? Destruction and violence are before me; strife and contention arise. So the law is paralyzed, and justice never goes forth. For the wicked surround the righteous; so justice goes forth perverted. (Habakkuk 1:2-4 ESV)

Led by the Accuser, the call of the wild is filled with baseless accusations and believers should take care to see that their voices remain absent of venom. Our limited perspective changes not the plans of Messiah, but it may make our journey painful. The wicked are not on the same journey as the righteous, though Messiah wills that both paths cross. For how else will the Gospel be heard if the righteous never hear from the lost? So to compare the two roads does little but engender unnecessary aggravation. However, there is a place for the cry of the wise. To yearn for YHWH's intervention on behalf of his people and to cry out for help is wise. He takes no pleasure in the plight of his people who daily are bespattered with lies. And so a storm shall arise. Those wild will accuse and sully YHWH's name, defaming and defiling on a whim. While the wise will acknowledge the sovereignty of both and remain faithfully devoted to them.

After these words [Yeshua] looked up to heaven and said: "Father, the hour has come. Glorify thy Son, that the Son may glorify thee. For thou hast made him sovereign over all mankind, to give eternal life to all whom thou hast given him. This is eternal life: to know thee who alone art truly [YHWH], and [Yeshua Messiah], whom thou hast sent." (John 17:1-3 NEB)

8. Missing in The Midst

First read: Ruth 1:15-21

As you are looking around, if you find yourself comparing yourself, remind yourself to look first outside yourself and then beside yourself; look—you aren't by yourself. Second, the fruit bearing trees on high and the fruit bearing flowers below, attest to the fact that YHWH doesn't play favorites. The trees and the flowers are not equal, nor do they bear the same fruit. Yet, YHWH is equally concerned and involved with both, so both should produce. It wasn't an accident that you were born when or where you were. You don't have to walk another ten miles before you can start bearing fruit. YHWH is ready now. Are you?

After giving them a severe beating they flung them into prison and ordered the jailer to keep them under close guard. In view of these orders, he put them in the inner prison and secured their feet in the stocks. About midnight Paul and Silas, at their prayers, were singing praises to [YHWH], and the other prisoners were listening, when suddenly there was such a violent earthquake that the foundations of the jail were shaken; all the doors burst open and all the prisoners found their fetters unfastened. (Acts 16:23-26 NEB)

If walking for a distance, moments will arise when you begin to believe that Yeshua is no longer walking beside you. As members of the Body, we have a tendency to equate Yeshua's proximity in our lives with his blessings. But, what of those times when our bliss turns blistering? Are we still able to detect his blessings, or does spiritual immaturity leave us endorsing the belief of an absent Yeshua who is always missing in the midst of misery?

And Job again took up his discourse, and said: "Oh, that I were as in the months of old, as in the days when [YHWH] watched over me, when his lamp shone upon my head, and by his light I walked through darkness, as I was in my prime, when the friendship of [Yeshua] was upon my tent, when [the Spirit] was yet with me, when my children were all around me, when my steps were washed with butter and the rock poured out for me streams of oil. (Job 29:1-6 ESV)

Like the average American relating to poverty, most Christians in today's Body have yet to experience absolute suffering. Instead, our suffering is usually measured in relative terms. When, at present, we don't have in our possession those goods that others are enjoying, we are inclined to suggest that YHWH has turned his face. If one of our possessions is suddenly removed while our neighbor is still receiving, it *must* be because we are incurring YHWH's wrath, we think. But, YHWH doesn't live inside a box.

So, if there are members who have grown weary in fighting to make him fit, perhaps now is the time to quit.

There was a man named Lazarus who had fallen ill. His home was at Bethany, the village of Mary and her sister Martha (This Mary, whose brother,

Lazarus, had fallen ill, was the woman who anointed the Lord with ointment and wiped his feet with her hair) The sisters sent a message to him: "Sir, you should know that your friend lies ill." When [Yeshua] heard this he said, "This sickness will not end in death; it has come for the glory of [YHWH], to bring glory to the Son of [YHWH]." And therefore, though he loved Martha and her sister and Lazarus, after hearing of his illness [Yeshua] waited for two days in the place where he was. (John 11:1-6 NEB)

In the book of Ruth, Naomi is so overwrought with grief at the loss of her husband and two sons that she fails to see that YHWH is working for a greater good. Had the losses not occurred, Naomi would never have found reason to return to Judah. Ruth must have been grieving herself; after all, she was married to one of Naomi's sons. Still, she was able to look outside herself long enough to see the needs of another. Instead of nursing her own wounds, she found healing in helping Naomi to heal. Unfortunately, Naomi was so focused on her own disaster that for a while she was unable to see how YHWH was trying to deliver.

Then Job arose and tore his robe and shaved his head and fell on the ground and worshiped. And he said, "Naked I came from my mother's womb, and naked shall I return. [YHWH] gave, and [YHWH] has taken away; blessed be the name of [YHWH]." (Job 1:20-21 ESV)

Truthfully, in YHWH's omniscience and omnipresence he is constantly looking at the big puzzle; yet, all the while, never forgetting the broken pieces that need restoring. It is we, the short-sighted, who insist on viewing our Creator with myopic vision. If you don't have it now, YHWH may not see fit for you to have it now. That doesn't mean that it won't ever fit. Trying to force the pieces will only result in ruining the whole puzzle. If what you had was removed, YHWH may have allowed the connection for a season. The season is over now and YHWH has a different piece in store for you, perhaps one that is better fitting. While you wait, are you at peace and still working peacefully? Or in fearing the unknown, are you suddenly falling apart? Sitting in pieces will prolong what YHWH means for you to have sooner rather than later because you're no longer in the peace he left for you. He will patiently wait for you to pull yourself together. He will wait until your vision clears enough to see that He never left you in the first place. One question worth pondering: "Can I still produce when for the moment I'm not in use?" Such is a sign of spiritual maturity. To suggest that your fruit is only bearable when the sun is shining on you is an indication that some ripening is still needed. YHWH will continue to ripen.

Remember [Yeshua], risen from the dead, the offspring of David, as preached in my gospel, for which I am suffering, bound with chains as a criminal. But the word of [YHWH] is not bound. Therefore I endure everything for the sake of the elect, that they also may obtain the salvation that is in [Messiah Yeshua] with eternal glory. (2nd Timothy 2:8-10 NIV)

9. A Reflective Moment

The Significance of Suffering

First read: Genesis 37:1-24

Only now am I reaching the point in my walk with Messiah where I'm beginning to understand the significance of suffering. I haven't yet had a direct encounter where I suffer for my relationship with Christ; though while a student at Asbury College I recall hearing of such accounts. Now recently retired, Dr. Robert Neff, a God-fearing man and professor of history, had a heart for foreign missions. While teaching a course on communist Russia, he would tell stories of couples in China who were tortured for their mission work; tortured for their commitment to Messiah. There were also tales of Christians in Cuba who were dipped in feces for refusing to recant their faith. As I compare my own life in the United States, I can't help but wonder if I would have the strength to endure. There are moments when I thank YHWH for his graciousness.

These are times when I think back to the African Middle Passage, the Jewish Holocaust, the Russian Gulag, or the Japanese Internment, and I praise YHWH for his omniscience and goodness. Not that I haven't had my share of suffering. Sexually molested between the ages of three and ten by several men; physically and emotionally abused by a mother who herself was abused as a child; having gone from depression to suicidal ideations; from treatment facilities and foster homes to the Methodist Home for Children and Youth in Macon, Georgia, I've borne some burdens, and it's only by the grace of YHWH that I'm still living.

Only recently have I come to truly know Messiah, and, with my newly forged relationship, I've faced new hardships—rejection and alienation from long time acquaintances, gossip, and theft, to name a few. Nevertheless, I am reminded of five significant truths when I feel that my anguish has reached its pinnacle.

First, my suffering is inevitable. Messiah spoke of this while on earth. Second, my suffering is purposeful. And though I've yet to develop a perfect understanding, I'm better able to recognize and affirm that the purpose of suffering isn't entirely personal. Third, my suffering is relatable. The more I share, the more I see the journey I'm on doesn't require isolation. Pride is an aversion to peace. Each member of the body is a piece of the puzzle, and only when we begin connecting do we see the beauty in our brokenness. Fourth, my suffering is sufferable and YHWH has been with me every step of the way. I shall have no fear. Better still, the love of YHWH will not allow me to endure anything beyond my abilities, though I will continue to be stretched. Fifth, my suffering is temporary. Hallelujah. Messiah is on his way back. What is the significance of suffering? Through the wisdom of the Holy Spirit, the answers continue to reveal themselves through my everyday experiences. I am aware, however, that I shall never appreciate its significance until the appointed day of my glorification. I turn twenty-six tomorrow and whatever the day may bring I am already thankful for receiving the revelation that each bout of suffering brings with it a more complete understanding of YHWH's grace. I can't fathom a more perfect gift.

Take your share of hardship, like a good soldier of [Yeshua Messiah]. (2nd Timothy 2:3 NEB)

If you want a pattern of patience under ill-treatment, take the prophets who spoke in the name of the Lord. Remember: "We count those happy who stood firm." You have all heard how Job stood firm, and you have seen how [YHWH] treated him in the end. For [YHWH] is full of pity and compassion. (James 5:10-11 NEB)

10. Ploy of Perfection

First read: Ecclesiastes 7:20

Look down. Look down for two reasons, but not for too long. First, check to make sure that your shoelaces are tied. There will be plenty more ditches to fall into and plenty more branches to trip over along the way—yet, there are preventative steps you can take to ensure optimal protection. Wounds hurt, but the worst ones are those that could have been prevented. The wounds from another may hurt the most, but preventable wounds last the longest. For in the passing of time, others come and go and eventually your scars from the former will heal. But as for the latter, you will be perpetually plagued by guilt or shame, and so these scars will last. Tie your shoes.

> But when your Advocate [Helper] has come, whom I will send you from the Father—the Spirit of truth that issues from the Father—will bear witness to me. And you also are my witnesses, because you have been with me from the first." (John 15:26-27 NEB)

In understanding that there are bumps in the road as we travel the road to Glory, let none cavalierly invite unnecessary injuries. One injury often self-inflicted on a new believer, and even upon some seasoned, is unrealistic expectations of growth. To many, it may seem a tiny infraction on an otherwise well-armored warrior; a shoelace left untied. But, oh, the pains of the perfectionist. It is one thing in striving to reach for perfection, a task that, at present, so little of the Body seems interested in performing. And there is pain here as well. But the pain in perfecting isn't self-induced; rather it is a byproduct of the Holy Spirit's refining fire. The process is painful but it is also productive, manifested in a bountiful harvest.

> But the harvest of the Spirit is love, joy, peace, patience, kindness, goodness, fidelity, gentleness, and self-control. There is no law dealing with such things as these. And those who belong to [Messiah Yeshua] have crucified the lower nature with passions and desires. If the Spirit is the source of our life, let the Spirit also direct our course." (Galatians 5:22-25 ESV)

The Holy Spirit is the source of our life; self is always the source of our strife. The Spirit says, "I am perfecting." While self will reply, "I should be perfect." What a dangerous ploy from the great Deceiver. He who is perfect has no need for the Perfecter. This is not only a message for the unbeliever, but for the believer as well. For he who believes he no longer has to look down on the ground. The dirt isn't designed to perpetually guilt all into believing that our sins of old have to last forever. No, we have been redeemed and washed clean by the blood of the Lamb. However, though our ransom was paid, mistakes are still made because we're still growing. Thus says the Apostle Paul in speaking to the church in Philippi:

> It is not to be thought that I have already achieved this. I have not yet reached perfection, but I press on, hoping to take hold of that for which [Messiah] once took hold of me. My friends, I do not reckon myself to have got hold of

it yet. All I can say is this: forgetting what is behind me, and reaching out for that which lies ahead, I press towards the goal to win the prize which is [YH-WH]'s call to the life above, in [Yeshua]. (Philippians 3:12-14 ESV)

The question Messiah is currently asking his Body is not, "Why are you not yet perfect?" But rather, "Why are there so few of my members pressing toward perfection?" The perfectionist toils while in constant turmoil, out of grief that he can't measure up. He strains not to see that though completely free, he still has some cracks in his cup. In his quest for love he succumbs to loathing. What begins as resentment toward sin ends with resentment of self. The problem is that such unbridled idealism makes it difficult for any to distinguish between the old self and the new. The pain of the perfectionist will last until there is no more disdain for the cracks in his glass. But it's just one shoe lace—sigh. That can lead to the landing of some dirt in your eye—ouch.

I am the vine, and you the branches. He who dwells in me, as I dwell in him, bears much fruit; for apart from me you can do nothing. He who does not dwell in me is thrown away like a withered branch. The withered branches are heaped together, thrown on the fire, and burnt.. (John 15:5-6)

11. Down & Dirty

First read: 2nd Chronicles 5:2-7:22

Second, observe the dirty path. You have fallen before and you will fall again, but you have never really noticed the dirt until now. You will get dirty, but you don't have to stay on the ground. At the start of your journey, someone automatically picked you up when you fell, whether you wanted them to or not. You are now walking on your own two feet and the choice is yours to make. So when you fall, get back up. If you can't get back up by yourself and you find yourself comparing yourself, remind yourself to look, first outside yourself and then beside yourself. Grab the hand extended and help yourself up. Or when the situation arises, stick out your hands and help someone else up. As you are rising from the ground all excess dirt will fall away. Don't worry about trying to brush all the dirt off; it's impossible and you're just going to get dirty again on your next trip. As you continue on your journey, remember what it feels like to be dirty and don't hesitate to extend your hand.

My little children, these things I write to you, so that you may not sin. And if anyone sins, we have an Advocate with the Father, [Yeshua Messiah] the righteous. And He Himself is the propitiation for our sins, and not for our sins only but also for the whole world. (1st John 2:1-2 NKJV)

There is a difference between falling and jumping. Nowhere in the Bible does Messiah give his okay for his disciples to consciously and willfully engage in sinful behavior. Why anyone would make the decision to do wrong when presented with the same opportunity to do right is a question surrounding man's nature, still wrestling with sanctification. It is never YHWH's will that his people choose to do wrong. It is a just God who either punishes disobedience directly, or allows for the natural consequences of disobedience. On the other foot, falling results when the believer, still maturing, makes an unpremeditated decision that produces unforeseen negative circumstances. The road to Glory was designed to engender the occasional fall. The Father allows it or may even orchestrate it as a learning opportunity designed to strengthen, sharpen, and shape. But, whether from jumping or falling, the results are the same—now on the ground, you'll want to stay down.

To you, O [Yeshua], I call; my rock, be not deaf to me, lest, if you be silent to me, I become like those who go down to the pit. Hear the voice of my pleas for mercy, when I cry to you for help, when I lift up my hands toward your most holy sanctuary. (Psalms 28:1-2 ESV)

The original fall of man should really be called the original jump of man. Adam and Eve knew of the impending consequences when both made the decision to eat of the tree that YHWH had forbidden. After the jump, they landed on the ground and were dirty. With their fig-leaved loin cloths, they foolishly attempted to conceal what they believed were their dirty parts. At this point they would have done better to cover their entire body. When YHWH entered the garden, it was time for them to go. Though on the ground and deserving to die, Adam and Eve were given a glimpse of YHWH's dually just and merciful nature. Being permitted to live, although expelled from Eden, was the Father's way of saying, "Yes, you jumped and no, it was not okay. Here is your sentence, but no, you may not sulk." The believer has no right to sulk when they have consciously sinned. Yet, the same promise YHWH delivered to Solomon, upon the completion of his temple, is available to members in today's Body. YHWH has promised that the repentant sinner who turns his heart back (not just his lips through words) will once again enjoy his blessings. Yet, it must be emphasized that the conscious conscientious sinner will not escape Messiah's wrath.

Again the kingdom of Heaven is like a net let down into the sea, where fish of every kind were caught in it. When it was full, it was dragged ashore. Then the men sat down and collected the good fish into pails and threw the worthless away. That is how it will be at the end of time. The angels will go forth, and they will separate the wicked from the good, and throw them into the blazing furnace, the place of wailing and grinding of teeth." (Matthew 13:47-50 NEB)

For the fervent believer, it can seem depressing to consider that falls (and for some, the dreaded departure) will continue to occur while on the road to Glory.

After singing the Passover Hymn, they went out to the Mount of Olives. And [Yeshua] said, "You will all fall from your faith; for it stands written: 'I will strike the shepherd down and the sheep will be scattered.' Nevertheless, after I am raised again I will go on before you in Galilee." Peter answered, "Everyone else may fall away, but I will not.. (Mark 14:26-30 NEB)

But, Messiah wants to remind his faithful that falling does not always mean failure. Remember Peter's mishap? Not long after assuring his allegiance to Messiah, Peter was in the courtyard of the High Priest denying he ever knew him.

Again, a little later, the bystanders said to Peter, "Surely you are one of them. You must be; you are a Galilean." At this he broke out into curses, and with an oath he said, "I do not know this man you speak of." Then the cock crew a second time; and Peter remembered how [Yeshua] had said to him, "Before the cock crows twice you will disown me three times." And he burst into tears. (Mark 14:70b-72 NEB)

While the conscious sinner has no right to sulk, the consecrating sinner has no time. Peter had fallen, was on the ground, and was dirty. Make no mistake, Peter owed Messiah an apology for his actions and it is doubtless that he experienced severe emotional turmoil at the sound of the crows. Nevertheless, a Church still had to be built.

And I say this to you: "You are Peter, the Rock; and on this rock I will build my church, and the powers of death shall never conquer it. I will give you the keys of the kingdom of Heaven; what you forbid on earth shall be forbidden in heaven, and what you allow on earth shall be allowed in heaven.." (Matthew 16:18-19 NEB)

If Peter had wallowed in self-pity, allowed his decision to lead to depression, then the building of the Church might have been prolonged. It was vital that Peter get back up. Consecrating sinner? For the beginner, yes. A continuous consecrating sinner? No. As the believer strengthens, sharpens, and shapes, his proclivity to fall will fade; though never should his proclivity to fall remain attached to him who consecrates, nor should it hinder him from helping those who have fallen or jumped.

12. A Reason for Every Season I

First read: Leviticus 23:1-3

Look up. Look up for two reasons, but not for too long. First, survey the sky and then affirm that not even its expansiveness will limit you. You can go anywhere your feet will take you, if you have drive and perseverance. What are your limitations? Just name them. Second, watch how the clouds shift in shape, and then bear in mind that seasons will also change. There will be summers and winters. And through both of them you will have wind and rain, and even stormier weather. But none will last forever—eventually the sun will come out. And no, not always tomorrow; but there will be days when you'll be glad it didn't. For none of the conditions are good in excess, but all are good for a season.

Lift up your heads, O gates. And be lifted up, O ancient doors, that the King of glory may come in. Who is this King of glory? [Yeshua], strong and mighty, [Yeshua], mighty in battle. Lift up your heads, O gates. And lift them up, O ancient doors that the King of glory may come in. Who is this King of glory? [Yeshua], he is the King of glory.. (Psalms 24:7-10 ESV)

After this I looked and saw a vast throng, which no one could count, from every nation, of all tribes, peoples, and languages, standing in front of the throne and before the Lamb. They were robed in white and had palms in their hands, and they shouted together: "Victory to [YHWH] who sits on the throne, and to the Lamb." (Revelation 7:9-10 NEB)

Whether or not someone is a Christian has no bearing over YHWH's ruling status in the world. He doesn't cease being our God because one chooses not to recognize his sovereignty. For the Israelites, YHWH wanted them to fully understand that he truly was Lord of all. In as much, they would come to grasp his authority over time.

The Jews challenged [Yeshua]: "What sign," they asked "can you show as authority for your action?" "Destroy this temple," [Yeshua] replied, "and in three days I will raise it again." They said, "It has taken forty-six years to build this temple. Are you going to raise it again in three days?" But the temple he was speaking of was his body. After his resurrection his disciples recalled what he had said, and they believed the Scripture and the words that [Yeshua] had spoken." (John 2:18-22 NEB)

The Pharisees said to him, "You are witness in your own cause; your testimony is not valid." [Yeshua] replied, "My testimony is enough, even though I do bear witness about myself; because I know where I come from, and where I am going. You do not know where I come from or where I am going. You judge by worldly measurements. I pass judgment on no man, but if I do judge, my judgments are valid because it is not I alone who judge, but I and my Father who sent me. In the law it states that the testimony of two witnesses is sufficient. I am a witness in this cause, and my second witness is the Father who sent me." They asked, "Where is your second witness?" [Yeshua] replied, "You know neither me nor my Father; if you knew me you would know my Father as well.." (John 8:13-19 NEB)

In understanding who YHWH is, it is critical that Christians are able to identify with both his dual imminent and transcendent nature. Contrary to the belief of early Deists, those who aligned their faith with a belief in a God that was the creator of time, but decided to divorce himself from it not long after its creation. (In other words, Deists believe that a God made the clock, wound it up, and then decided to allow the hands to move on their own without any interference.) The more Biblical view to which Theists ascribe themselves, paints our God in a slightly different light. Yes, he made the clock, and of course wound it up. However, according to the theistic view, he is also intricately involved in the moving of its hands. In his sovereignty, he infringes upon man's free will as his perfect wisdom dictates.

Yet [Yeshua] my King is from of old, working salvation in the midst of the earth. You divided the sea by your might; you broke the heads of the sea monsters on the waters. You crushed the heads of Leviathan; you gave him as food for the creatures of the wilderness. You split open springs and brooks; you dried up ever-flowing streams. Yours is the day, yours also the night; you have established the heavenly lights and the sun. You have fixed all the boundaries of the earth; you have made summer and winter. (Psalms 74:12-17 ESV)

Leviticus describes the various festivals and seasons in which the Israelites were to celebrate, while at the same time carrying out assigned tasks. These were not seasons or festivals that the Israelites manufactured, in which they waited for YHWH to show his approval. Rather, each festival was created by YHWH and placed in its specific season for a specific reason. There was preparation involved leading to the days of celebration; work that wasn't always void of a struggle. But, all the toil made the Sabbath that much more gratifying. And while each offered a unique commemoration in the pilgrimage of the Israelites, like the Sabbath, all were designed to glorify the Father. Today, Yeshua is still the creator of all seasons. However, members of the Body will mature in their faith the moment they realize that both winter and summer are intended for their benefit. In any given season, obstacles will appear before the Christian. YHWH intends for the believer to view each obstacle as an opportunity. Each season has been appointed for specific reasons and the length of time each believer will spend in his or hers is also appointed. In authoring the Book of Ecclesiastes, wise Solomon attests to this truth:

For everything there is a season, and a time for every matter under heaven: a time to be born, and a time to die; a time to plant, and a time to pluck up what is planted; a time to kill, and a time to heal; a time to break down, and a time to build up; a time to weep, and a time to laugh; a time to mourn, and a time to dance; a time to cast away stones, and a time to gather stones together; a time to embrace, and a time to refrain from embracing; a time to seek, and a time to lose; a time to keep, and a time to cast away; a time to tear, and a time to sew; a time to keep silence, and a time to speak; a time to love, and a time to hate; a time for war, and a time for peace. (Ecclesiastes 3:1-8 ESV)

In truth, the believer will not pass to another season until he has grown and YHWH has been glorified.

13. Weathering the Weather

First read: 1st Kings 2:1-4

When balanced, the seasons operate in perfect recognition of the earth's potential, and when imbalanced they operate in perfect reflection of the earth's perversions. While on your journey, each season will aid and hinder; they have their role and so do you. Before taking another step, decide now which part you choose to play—is it the victim or the victor? Since you control no part of the weather, you have no control over its stability. You can only ensure that you don't lose sight of your destination. No matter the conditions, be prepared.

When they had gone for a long time without food, Paul stood up among them and said, "You should have taken my advice, gentlemen, not to sail from Crete; then you would have avoided this damage and loss. But now I urge you not to lose heart; not a single life will be lost, only the ship. For last night there stood by me a messenger of the God whose I am and whom I worship. 'Do not be afraid, Paul, he said, it is ordained that you shall appear before the Emperor; and, be assured, [YHWH] has granted you the lives of all who are sailing with you. So keep up your courage: I trust in [YHWH] that it will turn out as I have been told; though we have to be cast ashore on some island." (Acts 27:21-26 NEB)

The one constant in life is that everything is always changing. How true of the world the Father insists we remain in for just a little while longer. Sometimes life throws us a curve ball, which only compounds the difficulty of walking on a road that is less than straight. It is easy to get flustered and thrown into a tizzy over circumstances that don't announce themselves prior to crossing our path. "Why me?" the believer may ask when a sudden gust of wind blows and sends them reeling around, leaving them facing a direction that seems more foreign than the former. "Oh, no—not again," exclaims the member whose moment of bliss in the sun is interrupted by a blistering and biting chill. "What's the deal?" The deal is that while as Christians we would rather know the forecast of our future, we really can only prepare for today. Today is the day that my relationship with Messiah will strengthen because I acknowledge that I have no control over what tomorrow will bring, and so I find solace in his strength. In finding solace in his strength, my soul solidifies, and it becomes clearer that, whatever the weather, I will keep it together as a fortress who is fettered to faith.

Blessed be [Yeshua]. For he has heard the voice of my pleas for mercy. [Yeshua] is my strength and my shield; in him my heart trusts, and I am helped; my heart exalts, and with my song I give thanks to him. (Psalms 28:6-7 ESV)

How does the believer continue to believe when belief is believed to be baseless? When all those around count it folly to praise a God who allows such turbulence and chaos, what is your response? The mature member always has Messiah as their compass and the voice of a victor. We know that turbulence often precedes rest and returns the wayward back to the road. We know that chaos often has a way of sending the lost running back home, and of keeping those found from shutting the door. Indeed, Messiah has some strange ways of solidifying his Church. But it would behoove the whole Body if its members would quit acting like victims every time YHWH acts. What the lost need to see are those who never lose sight. Not believers who complain at every turn with every plight.

Be gracious to me, O [Yeshua], for I am in distress; my eye is wasted from grief; my soul and my body also. For my life is spent with sorrow, and my years with sighing; my strength fails because of my iniquity, and my bones waste away. Because of all my adversaries I have become a reproach, especially to my neighbors, and an object of dread to my acquaintances; those who see me in the street flee from me. I have been forgotten like one who is dead; I have become like a broken vessel. For I hear the whispering of many—terror on every side—as they scheme together against me, as they plot to take my life. But I trust in you, O [Yeshua]; I say, "You are my God." (Psalms 31:9-14 ESV)

Make no mistake in the fact that YHWH and Yeshua's ears are always open. He doesn't dissuade any of his people from approaching his throne and shedding a tear, no matter the day, month, or year. Messiah's death on the cross did grant us access to the Father, and he wants all to remember that he's always accessible. However, our tears in despair must never lead another to fear or despise. When the weather seems wrong prepare to do what is right.

In him we have access to [YHWH] with freedom, in the confidence born of trust in him. (Ephesians 3:12 NEB)

As the rain begins pouring and the wind starts to howl; when the clouds start to blacken and the weather seems afoul—be prepared. As the ground begins shaking and the trees start to fall; when the lighting starts answering to the sound of thunder's call—be prepared. And as souls begin to wail from their pits of despair; when sounds of anguish rise 'cause disasters in the air—be prepared. Members of the Body must first prepare to show the Gospel and then be prepared to share it.

No wonder we do not lose heart. Though our outward humanity is in decay, yet day by day we are inwardly renewed. Our troubles are slight and short-lived; and their outcome an eternal glory which outweighs them far. (2nd Corinthians 4:16-17 ESV)

14. Embracing in the Body

First read: Job 2:11-13

Whenever you find yourself frozen with fear, wet with worry, staggered with sickness, heated with hatred, or comparing yourself; remind yourself to first look outside yourself, and then beside yourself. There is someone there who can melt you with a smile, another to wipe your eyes with the extra tissue someone else gave them after first drying their own eyes, still another to heal you with words of affirmation, and yet one more still to help cool you off by simply loving you anyway.

Now that by obedience to the truth you have purified your souls until you feel sincere affection towards your brother Christians, love one another whole-heartedly with all of your strength. (1st Peter 1:22 NEB)

There are those in the Body who need to learn how to embrace without being embarrassed. Most men have difficulty embracing other men—no thanks to the highly sexualized overtones that Hollywood and society have imparted on the embrace. The type of sexuality embraced by the world has no room in the Body of Messiah and embarrassment should abound within for having tolerated such intrusiveness for so long. Likewise, even the embrace between an unmarried man and woman has of late become questionable. It is no question as to why such precautions have come into place; and it would seem an exercise of wisdom in avoiding awkwardness by avoiding intimacy. However, the believer must understand that such preventative behaviors only address the plausible effects and not the cause.

A man is commended according to his good sense, but one of twisted mind is despised. (Proverbs 12:8 ESV)

The Church needs healing. Members of the Body can't learn to embrace without first rejecting what the world has to offer. Messiah wants his Body to enjoy the intimacy he intended the Church to have, both spiritually and physically. It is the world and not the Word that confuses the intimacy of fraternity with the intimacy of matrimony. Yeshua did not fashion men or women to instantly think about sex the moment one came into contact with the other. It is not natural, though it has become normal. And the struggle occurs, nevertheless, because of sinful and demonic influences. Television shows, music, movies, and magazines bombard with messages of sensuality; educating YHWH's people on how each are suppose to act and react to given stimuli. The flesh devours every drop and soon lives begin to fashion themselves around the flesh. To those who presently reside outside of the Church, it is expected that many will readily embrace the opportunity to embrace. However, in responding, the Church should not now resist embracing; rather it should insist on embracing in the Spirit. Those who struggle with sensuous thoughts need to divorce themselves from sensuous material, not from sanctifying members. For the men who feel that embracing another man is a sign of effeminacy or that it will somehow lead to their emasculation, you are urged to look to the Son—not society. Messiah's was a ministry of reconciliation and it is impossible to reconcile without connecting. The disciple who is connected to Messiah needn't fear his image or identity, for misperceptions will remain until Messiah comes to claim. There is grave danger for the believer whose journey on the road is guided by judgments from the world. Do we desire the world's judgments now or Messiah's judgment soon?

A desire fulfilled is sweet to the soul, but to turn away from evil is an abomination to fools. (Proverbs 13:19 ESV)

The consequences for failing to embrace in the Body are too severe to dismiss as inconsequential. When disaster strikes the righteous, where will the righteous turn? When tempers start to flare up, who'll sit and watch them burn? Or will members in the Body learn to discern and see the effectiveness of embracing? If enough surround those suffering in flames, then eventually the fire will go out. Job's friends were not perfect, and much of the advice given by three of the four was flawed, based upon faulty assumptions about YHWH. However, their concern for Job was genuine. Though YHWH wants his people to turn first to him during moments of misery, he doesn't want any to underestimate or ignore the persons walking next to us who have been embattled, and so empowered to empathize and embrace.

And now, my friends, farewell. Mend your ways; take our appeal to heart; agree with one another; live in peace; and the God of love and peace will be with you. Greet one another with the kiss of peace. All [YHWH]'s people send you greetings. The grace of [Yeshua], and the love of [YHWH], and fellowship in the Holy Spirit, be with you all. (2nd Corinthians 13:11-14 NEB)

15. Perennial Pain

First read: Job 1-3

Look clearly ahead. Look ahead for two reasons, but not for too long. First, keep your destination in sight, but even more important, keep it in your head. Your eyes will perennially play tricks on you and the woods sometimes seem too thick for the sun to shine through. Inclement weather will be blinding or crippling in an attempt to throw you off course; but, keep a clear head and you will never lose sight.

> I have glorified thee on earth by completing the work which thou gavest me to do; and now, Father, glorify me in thy own presence with the glory which I had with thee before the world began. (John 17:4-5 NEB)

The Christian will face crises—that is plural and this is certain. And there is no believer in graver danger of departing from the road to Glory than the one ill-prepared to face gorier days. The most ill-prepared to handle such are the believers who simply disregard the crown of thorns he chose to wear, and who instead focus solely on his crown of glory. It is sometimes difficult to remember that Messiah suffered before he was raised. So too will the faithful follower rise from this earth when the final trumpet sounds. No more lies or moms who die, leaving child alone with tear-filled eyes. No more sorrow or food to "borrow"; no more wishing for no more tomorrows. No more aches or hearts that break, no more painful smiles to fake. One day soon we'll hear that tune and Messiah will take us home. But for now, every few miles will bring with them pain. How will you respond to rain? There are a couple of prayers that the Adversary would rather members avoid. From the Apostle Paul to the church in Ephesus:

> I pray that the God of [Yeshua], the all-glorious Father, may give you the spiritual powers of wisdom and vision, by which there comes the knowledge of him. I pray that your inward eyes may be illumined, so that you may know what is the hope to which he calls you, what the wealth and glory of the share he offers you among his people in their heritage, and how vast the resources of his power open to us who trust in him. They are measured by his strength and might." (Ephesians 1:17-19 NEB)

From the psalmist King David:

> Teach me your way, O [Yeshua], that I may walk in your truth; unite my heart to fear your name. I give thanks to you, O [YHWH] and [Yeshua], with my whole heart, and I will glorify your name forever. (Psalms 86:11-12 ESV)

Or the insight from King Solomon:

> So I turned to consider wisdom and madness and folly. For what can the man do who comes after the king? Only what has already been done. Then I saw that there is more gain in wisdom than in folly, as there is more gain in light than in darkness. The wise person has his eyes in his head, but the fool walks

in darkness. And yet I perceived that the same event happens to all of them. (Ecclesiastes 2:12-14 ESV)

The theme in these verses points to one truth: a focus on the Son and his light is a focus on internal convictions. However, the Adversary would like for believers to fixate on the external circumstances. He delights in the fickle believer whose faith is as whimsical as the weather appears to the world. Job's story is less an answer to the question, "Why do the righteous suffer?" The answer is two-fold, though not easily accepted. First, the righteous suffer because YHWH allows them to, or wills that they do. Why? In order that the righteous might display to him and to the world, YHWH's righteousness. Second, righteous suffering allows for the answer to a more important question: "As a believer, am I still right with the Father even when things are apparently going wrong?" Thus the story of Job aims not to address—"Why do the righteous suffer?"—but rather, "How should the righteous suffer?" The Apostle Paul proposes that Christians lead by example:

As [YHWH]'s people, we try to recommend ourselves in all circumstances by our steadfast endurance: in distress, hardships, and dire straights; flogged, imprisoned, mobbed; overworked, sleepless, starving. We recommend ourselves by the innocence of our behavior, our grasp of truth, our patience and kindliness; by gifts of the Holy Spirit, by sincere love, by declaring the truth, by the power of [YHWH]. (2nd Corinthians 6:4-6 NEB)

16. Success in Submitting

First read: 2nd Chronicles 20:31-37

Look clearly ahead and learn from those who have walked or are walking ahead of you, whether ten feet or ten miles. They have already walked where you are walking now and clearly they have done something right, or they wouldn't be where they are now. Learn from their mistakes. If you have been paying attention then you should have noticed where they tripped, when they slipped, and why they fell. Learn from their triumphs. How did they get back up? Who helped them to stand?

You heard me say, "I am going away, and coming back to you." If you loved me you would have been glad to hear that I was going to the Father; for the Father is greater than I. I have told you now, beforehand, so that when it happens you may have faith. I shall not talk much longer with you, for the Prince of this world approaches. He has no rights over me; but the world must be shown that I love the Father, and do exactly as he commands; so up, let us go forward. (John 14:28-31 NEB)

One notable trend with the kings of Judah who were declared to have done right in the eyes of the Lord was that each followed in the footsteps of a submissive sovereign. To many it might sound strange that a sovereign would need to submit, but even Yeshua, the Son of YHWH, and who by YHWH's decree is sovereign over all, acknowledged to the Pharisees that he acted not without the authority of his Father:

They did not understand that he was speaking to them about the Father. So [Yeshua] said to them, "When you have lifted up the Son of Man you will know that I am what I am. I do nothing on my own authority, but in all that I say, I have been taught by my Father. He who sent me is present with me, and has not left me alone; for I always do what is acceptable to him." (John 8:27-29 NEB)

What made only a few rulers of Judah acceptable to YHWH was that they were willing to submit to his rule. The wise successor followed upon the heels of a wise predecessor; both showing their wisdom in their willingness to bow to the Father's will. There is a distinction, however, between even the wisest earthly king and the King of kings. Messiah was perfect because of his ability and willingness to walk in intimacy with the Father, rather than behind him. Conversely, it is a dangerous position for the believer to believe that he or she can walk next to Messiah while here on earth. One day soon we shall, but for now it is imperative that the believer acknowledges, accepts, and acts upon the truth that Messiah is at the Head. For members of the Body, intimacy with the Father is granted only through intimacy with the Son. Some members may claim that Messiah is indeed in front of them, but the distance between the two is far too great. They have yet to grasp the meaning of reconciliation because they still know not the mission of the Reconciler:

He is, moreover, the head of the body, the church. He is its origin, the first to return from the dead, to be in all things alone supreme. For in him the complete being of [YHWH], by [YHWH]'s own choice, came to dwell. Through him [YHWH] chose to reconcile the whole universe to himself, making peace through the shedding of his blood on the cross—to reconcile all things, whether on earth or in heaven, through him alone. Formerly you were yourselves estranged from [YHWH]; you were his enemies in heart and mind, and your deeds were evil. But now by [Messiah's] death in his body of flesh and blood [YHWH] has reconciled you to himself, so that he may present you before himself as dedicated men, without blemish and innocent in his sight. (Colossians 1:18-22 NEB)

Sanctification then is the process of reconciling perfectly with the Father after justification by, and in continual submission to, the Son. Success starts with watching the wise walk, while taking notice of their occasional folly. Notice that their folly didn't end in failure because someone offered to help them regain their footing and they accepted. Perfect submission begins with admission but it also requires conditioning; the road to Glory is a training ground. The mind, heart, and soul are all continuously stretched to see if the body will continuously return to its source. Messiah's was and Messiah did. Not through his own folly, but man's. He who is sovereign did perfectly submit. His success was in the ability to offer salvation and reconciliation; now too should his subjects submit.

To this charge [Yeshua] replied, "In truth, in very truth I tell you, the Son can do nothing by himself; he does only what he sees the Father doing: what the Father does, the Son does. For the Father loves the Son and shows him all his works, and will show greater yet, to fill you with wonder. As the Father raises the dead and gives them life, so the Son gives life to men, as he determines." (John 5:19-21 NEB)

Be subject to one another out of reverence for [Messiah]. Wives, be subject to your husbands as to Christ; for the man is the head of the woman, just as [Messiah] also is the head of the church. [Messiah] is, indeed, the Savior of the body; but just as the church is subject to [Messiah], so must women be to their husbands in everything. (Ephesians 5:21-24 NEB)

17. Simple Supremacy

First read: Colossians 1:15-20

The image of the invisible YHWH
Firstborn over all creation
To those outside it seems rather odd
Why this man deserves such adoration

It's simple really...

By him all things on earth was created
As were all things above the earth, as well
And head of the Body, the Church, is he
Now in Messiah, we stand as one, related
In the Father's arms of mercy we dwell

It's simply really. . .

Un-condoned—yet, atoned
We adore this man who died to set us free

18. The Race of the Righteous

First read: Psalms 37:1-24

And now for some advice amid your journey: First, walk at your own pace. You are on a journey, not in a race - per se. Indeed, be mindful of the time. You do have a destination to reach and someone is expecting you to reach it in a timely manner. While you may be racing against a clock, you don't know when yours will stop ticking, so use your time wisely. Spend it and your energy mindful of those around you? Yes. Helping those in need? Yes. Learning from those on the same journey? Yes. But, waste neither time nor energy trying to out-walk someone else.

The pace for each believer while on their journey has already been set by YHWH. We each have the responsibility of ensuring that we keep up. The surest way to this end is by keeping your eyes focused on the prize and on all that is required to make certain of its attainment. In other words, a focus on faithful deeds, the fulfilling of another's needs, and keeping out of the devil's weeds. Should your attention avert from the road to Glory, reverting you back to days of old, know that all is not lost. Quickly find your way back to the road before once again your eyes grow accustomed to the dark and the light becomes an aversion. Remember your conversion.

Teach me your way, O [Yeshua], and lead me on a level path because of my enemies. Give me not up to the will of my adversaries; for false witnesses have risen against me, and they breathe out violence. (Psalms 27:11-12 ESV)

Come back to a sober and upright life and leave your sinful ways. There are some who know nothing of [YHWH]; to your shame I say it. (1st Corinthians 15:34 NEB)

It is tempting while walking, when the believer is intent on comparing themselves to everyone else, to look ahead at those whose bumpy road has finally evened out, and start rushing to catch up. What you don't notice are the bruises on their body that have only recently begun to heal. Your attempting to rush ahead of YHWH's schedule is only going to result in unintended scrapes. It is equally tempting in our weariness from walking on the occasionally painful road to Glory, to rush over to the side and partake in more leisurely activities. However, if our guard is down, we might find ourselves entering a different race. The prize for reaching the finish line of this other race? Whether slow or fast, first or last, the award will still be the same. An eternity of shame. Just remember that, while walking, your goal is to capture the attention of as many sideliners as possible. You first capture their hurts, then their hearing, and then move out of the way so that through the Holy Spirit, Messiah can capture their heart. However, in the event that Messiah's efforts are rebuffed, just remember that the clock is still ticking and keep moving.

Again I saw that under the sun the race is not to the swift, nor the battle to the strong, nor bread to the wise, nor riches to the intelligent, nor favor to those with knowledge, but time and chance happen to them all. For man does not know his time. Like fish that are taken in an evil net, and like birds that are caught in a snare, so the children of man are snared at an evil time, when it suddenly falls upon them. (Ecclesiastes 9:11-12 ESV)

The wisest man who ever lived appeared to ascribe to fatalist doctrine. Admittedly, from Solomon's limited perspective, Sheol was the end result for all. And so it was before Messiah. However, Solomon wasn't suggesting a world governed by a dead-beat father who left his children on their predestined road to hell. Rather, it is a world in which an active and involved Father chooses not to reveal to his people all the details of his make—for intimacy sake. From our finite and fleshly stance, events occur by chance. But for believers in the palm of his hand, our Father has a plan. It is not the Father's will that any of his people be caught unaware, unprepared, or left behind and not in the air. So yes, the race of the righteous is a daunting feat. Yet, the righteous will have won when their race is complete.

When evening fell, the owner of the vineyard said to his steward, "Call the laborers and give them their pay, beginning with those who came last and ending with the first." Those who had started work an hour before sunset came forward, and were paid the full day's wage. When it was the turn of the men who had come first, they expected something extra, but were paid the same amount as the others. As they took it, they grumbled at their employer: "These latecomers have done only one hour's work, yet you have put them on a level with us, who have sweated the whole day long in the blazing sun'. The owner turned to one of them and said, "My friend, I am not being unfair to you. You agreed on the usual wage for the day, did you not? Take your pay and go home. I choose to pay the last man the same as you. Surely I am free to do what I like with my own money. Why be jealous because I am kind? Thus will the last be first, and the first last." (Matthew 20:8-16 NEB)

You know (do you not?) that at the sports all the runners run the race, though only one wins the prize. Like them, run to win. But every athlete goes through strict training. They do it to win a fading wreath; we, a wreath that never fades. For my part, I run with a clear goal before me; I am like a boxer who does not beat the air; I bruise my own body and make it know its master; for fear that after preaching to others I should find myself rejected. (1st Corinthians 9:24-27 NEB)

19. Beatitude

First read: Matthew 5:1-21

More of him and less of me
is my faithful prayer each day;
to follow humbly in the footsteps
of my King

To deny myself in deeds and
words, it is the only way;
An adoring and accepted
offering

YHWH, he wipes away each tear
that falls upon my cheek;
He always comforts with the Spirit
as my guide

He strengthens me completely
when sorrows leave me weak;
As a faithful Groom who loves
and tends his Bride

I speak with words of affirmation
and walk with words of grace
I'm as gentle as my Lord,
who was a Lamb

I dare not speak in judgment,
for fear I shall disgrace
The Alpha and Omega,
the great I Am

It is holiness I crave each day
from the depths of my soul;
to walk thy path of righteousness
in love

To reach thy gates with gratitude
YAH, it is my only goal
Rain down your mercies please
from up above

I too shall show mercy, my God
to all who might offend;
I'll withhold revenge from cruel
and wicked man

May my mercies be the agent which
turns them from their sin,
and saves them from your just and
wrathful hand

My heart shall stay pure, YHWH
And lust not for the temporal;
No matter how charming some
fruits, at times, appear

My heart beats with my Savior's,
and my body, the Spirit's temple
So from all that may defile
I'll stay clear

Peace begins with prayer to you YHWH
then flows to those around;
I'll wear it on my feet for those
in need

If I help restore the shattered you'll
reward me with a crown
Help me plow those violent, bitter
and withered weeds

The pangs of arrows shot at me when
I know that I've done right;
sometimes it seems the pain will
never end

But the Lord redeems the righteous
and sharpens still their sight
Yes, Satan will attack, but
never win

20. Sensuous Nonsense

First read: Judges 16

If the image of running a race is helpful in keeping a clear head; a reminder to you that time will eventually lapse, then imagine that you are in a relay race and always remember two truths: One, rats never enter so rats never win. Two, you were strategically placed where your strengths could shine for the team, and yes, that does include you. Acknowledge your strengths and use them. Naturally, will your pace either increase or decrease. How will you know when? Adrenaline? No. If completely relied upon to complete a race, adrenaline can deceive, and depending on the situation, can kill. Listen to your heart, not your hormones. In the long run, you'll be glad you did.

But each of us has been given his gift, his due portion of [Messiah's] bounty. Therefore Scripture says: "He ascended into the heights with captives in his train; he gave gifts to men." (Ephesians 4:7-8 NEB)

And then there was a message to the men. It's amazing and yet at the same time sad, what many members of the Church will easily succumb to. Upon whom Messiah bestows gifts, he bestows for the betterment of the Body. When a believer forgets that his journey was never designed for walking solo, then there will exist the tendency to recklessly ill-consider one's function. Sensuous nonsense has traditionally been the Achilles heel for men in the Body. Does it seem possible that the physical strength, with which Yeshua has endowed his men, could easily falter over a lapse in his mental faculties? But from where does such folly derive?

One who is wise is cautious and turns away from evil, but a fool is reckless and careless. (Proverbs 14:16 ESV)

Samson's tragic tale should serve as a reminder that spiritual blindness is a possibility for all who lose sight of their appointed role. He failed to remember that his strength was not intended for his benefit exclusively, and as such he too forgot its source. Samson was holy, set apart as YHWH's vessel in delivering the Israelites from the Philistines. However, sensuality seemed to cloud his better sense. Alas, the wiles of an ungodly woman pose a threat to even the seasoned traveler whose head has parted from wisdom. For Samson, Delilah is likened to the woman Solomon speaks of in Proverbs:

The woman Folly is loud; she is seductive and knows nothing. She sits at the door of her house; she takes a seat on the highest places of the town, calling to those who pass by, who are going straight on their way, "Whoever is simple, let him turn in here." And to him who lacks sense she says, "Stolen water is sweet, and bread eaten in secret is pleasant." But he does not know that the dead are there, that her guests are in the depths of Sheol. (Proverbs 9:13-18 ESV)

Woe unto the woman who has made it a task to trip a man during his walk; her unrepentant strides will eventually provoke her own trip to the grave. Though,

Yeshua did not create man without the ability to make his own decisions. Adam's argument in Eden was as unacceptable to YHWH then as it is to Messiah now. If a woman is offering up illicit fruit, no matter how scintillating, no Christian, Spirit-sealed man is compelled to take a bite. It is the wisdom of the world which suggests that a man's masculinity is inextricably linked to his sexuality. The Church must divorce itself from the lie that Yeshua created men to be hormonally driven while giving only to women the desire for harmony; such were Yeshua's intentions for men and women. Upon carefully examining the manhood of Messiah, it is clear that while his mind was always on his Father, or rather because it was, he never ceased to speak from his heart.

The race to win is the race against sin. And through an act of the will, while Spirit-sealed, the Christian man must stop filling his head with sensuous nonsense. Apart from Messiah, his weaknesses will continue to abound. But Yeshua has assured that with his strength, man can indeed do all things. Rather than succumbing to their flesh in despair and defeat, men should begin fervently praying for one another in the words of the Apostle Paul:

> With this in mind, then, I kneel in prayer to the Father, from whom every family in heaven and on earth takes it name, that out of the treasures of his glory he may grant you strength and power through the Spirit in your inner being, that through faith [Messiah] may dwell in your hearts in love. With deep roots and firm foundations, may you be strong to grasp, of the love of [Messiah], and to know it, though it is beyond knowledge. So may you attain to fullness of being, the fullness of [YHWH] himself. (Ephesians 3:14-19 NEB)

21. A Reflective Moment

Boys Will Be Boys?

First read: Titus 1:15

Have you ever found yourself trying to reason with someone who holds a different set of values as you? One that I find common among men is the way in which many objectify women. We live in a culture that has ingrained into the minds of young boys that a woman's body is designed for lust; it's primal and instinctive and the way it's always been since the time of cave men. Hence, it is natural and healthy for a man to constantly have wayward eyes and to fantasize about women. We tell our boys that if they are not looking at girls in this fashion from the time of their youth, then there is something wrong with them and we begin to doubt their potential manhood. Sadly, we even have fathers who introduce their young sons to pornography as an instructional lesson on the female anatomy; the child's mind is warped from the gate. To suggest to such men that while this behavior is normal, it is nonetheless, unacceptable, is to challenge their preferred way of thinking. As long as these men are living for the world, one might as well speak Greek when attempting to prove their reasoning faulty.

Why do you not understand my language? It is because my revelation is beyond your grasp. (John 8:43 NEB)

Normal behavior is behavior that the majority of a particular sector of society, that is, the norm, currently engages in. In the stated scenario, it is indeed normal for young boys, young adults, and grown men to sexually objectify women. However, the relationship between the normalcy of the behavior and its goodness is mutually exclusive. In other words, just because most are engaging doesn't mean they necessarily ought to engage. As Christians we are called to a different standard of living—a higher one. When the rest of the world is answering for their unrighteousness, you won't want to be a part of the in-crowd then—so why now? While Yeshua designed man to become sexually drawn to the opposite sex, he never intended for women to become objects of unbridled lust. If he had, then there would have been no need to clarify the commandment concerning adultery:

You have learned that they were told, "Do not commit adultery." But what I tell you is this: If a man looks on a woman with a lustful eye, he has already committed adultery with her in his heart. (Matthew 5:27-28 NEB)

Neither is Messiah in the business of delivering a command that he knows man is incapable of adhering to. Fallen man? Indeed incapable. Justified and sanctifying man with the indwelling Holy Spirit? Quite. Admittedly, the problem with sexual lust is exacerbated by the media with all of its images and messages. However, fathers increase the likelihood that their sons will struggle with the same sin when they present the behavior as a natural right of passage or just a passing phase. Planting such seeds will produce weeds that threaten to entangle and eventually strangle. Don't turn to the world to rationalize immoral behavior, because the world, appealing to our lower nature, will only tell what we want to hear. Instead, in appealing to their spiritual nature, those members more mature should actively seek to capture the hearts and minds of our young boys, cultivate them into the men that Messiah has called them to, and then, bearing the responsibility, the Church must keep them captivated.

Make no mistake about this: [YHWH] is not to be fooled; a man reaps what he sows. If he sows seed in the field of his lower nature, he will reap from it a harvest of corruption, but if he sows in the field of the Spirit, the Spirit will bring him a harvest of eternal life. So let us never tire of doing good, for if we do not slacken our efforts we shall in due time reap our harvest. (Galatians 6:7-9 NEB)

What's the alternative? To continue perpetuating the myth that Yeshua understands the lustful nature of men because that's the way He designed them? Careful. While YHWH understands the struggle that most men will experience as it relates to sexual sin, he by no means excuses the sin. Instead, all should seek aid from the Holy Spirit to reduce the severity of the struggle. And though weariness may occur in the process, sanctification will take care of your rest.

22. Persistent Patterns

First read: Psalms 78:1-72

Second, stay alert. That is why you should look in all directions, at all times. This will also keep you from dealing with drowsiness or developing dry eyes. Again, look back, but not for too long. Neither ignoring nor bemoaning your past will get you any closer to your future. You can't learn from your past if you can't acknowledge that you have one—everyone does. If you spend your life hiding from it, you will remain hidden. If you are hidden, you are not moving. Moving is an essential element of your journey. You can't rejoice over success without recognizing times of failure; how will you know the difference? How will you learn from the failures and appreciate the successes if you can't tell them apart? Your past is behind you; it doesn't follow you, for that is impossible. And it is no more possible to take your whole past with you; it's too heavy, so why try?

It's a precarious task pondering your past. For some believers the past carries with it too many painful memories and so effort is made to walk without ever taking the opportunity to look back. This is understandable to a degree. But, remember that the Father nor the Son doesn't expect the road to Glory to be filled with grief from start to finish. Bemoaning the past can lead you off the road fast. With eyes perpetually filled with tears, there is no way anyone can see the direction they should always move in. For the Body to reach its destination in a timely manner, it mustn't spend excess time keeping all members walking in unison, so that little strength remains for enlarging its number. Again, walking on the road to Glory is a balancing act.

> Surely you know that the unjust will never come into possession of the kingdom of [YHWH]. Make no mistake: no fornicator or idolater, none who are guilty either of adultery or of homosexual perversion, no thieves or grabbers or drunkards or slanderers or swindlers, will possess the kingdom of [YHWH]. Such were some of you. But you have been through the purifying waters; you have been dedicated to [YHWH] and justified through the name of [Yeshua] and the Spirit of [YHWH]. (1st Corinthians 6:9-11 NEB)

However, ignoring one's past is a task appropriate only for the ignorant and not for believers who have already been informed. You ought to feel a twinge of discomfort when remembering what life was like before becoming a disciple of Messiah. A certain soreness should arise when thinking back to your persistent pattern of sinful living and how YHWH patiently awaited you to acknowledge him. You are where you are now on your journey because of YHWH's persistent patience. But consider that for the believer there does become a point, while walking, when present behaviors should no longer consist of the persistence of their past.

> You must therefore be mentally stripped for action, perfectly self-controlled. Fix your hopes on the gift of grace which is to be yours when [Yeshua] is revealed. As obedient children, do not let your characters be shaped any longer

by the desires you cherished in your days of ignorance. The One who called you is holy; like him, be holy in all your behavior, because Scripture says, "You shall be holy, for I am holy. " (1st Peter 1:13-16 NJKV)

The past is not intended to last forever, though, as long as you're walking, it should continue to serve with honorable intentions. What a privilege it is to walk on the road to Glory, while glancing back every now and again to commend Messiah on how far he has taken you on your journey. It can be discouraging when looking down at all the scrapes and bruises on our elbows and knees. Yet, it is near impossible to appreciate true liberty unless one has first suffered under the constraints of heavy chains. To the travelers who make a concerted effort to carry both their cross and chains, beware. Such blustering only screams at the Father that you obviously haven't had enough blisters.

When you were slaves to sin, you were free from the control of righteousness; and what was the gain? Nothing but what now makes you ashamed, for the end of that is death. But now, freed from the commands of sin, and bound to the service of [YHWH], your gains are such as make for holiness, and the end is eternal life. For sin pays a wage, and the wage is death, but [YHWH] gives freely, and his gift is eternal life, in union with [Yeshua]." (Romans 6:20-23 NEB)

23. A Reflective Moment

Eternal Sinner?

First read: 1st John:4-10

Have you ever met someone who attested to being a recovering alcoholic? I've met several, including my mother. There is something peculiar about how they discuss their recovery experience. First, it is the grace of YHWH that allows anyone suffering from an addiction to experience healing. Like the prodigal son, not only should these individuals be commended, but they also need encouragement and continual prayer. Now that their shackles have been unlocked and have fallen to the ground, they will begin to shimmer like freshly cut jewels. If those newly healed aren't Spirit-filled and daily reminded to keep their eyes on the road, tragedy may soon strike again.

The twelve step process that assists those in recovery has worked miracles in the lives of many. However, I cringe at a lie disguised as wisdom, to which most addicts insist on adhering –"Once an alcoholic, always an alcoholic." In other words, many believe that, even after seasons of sobriety, they will never be truly healed from their addiction. Harmfully enough, there are those in the Church living by this same faulty adage as it relates to sin, "Once a sinner, always a sinner." Throughout my life I can't count the number of Sunday school classes I've sat in on or services I've attended where I've heard variations of the following: "We're all sinners." Sadly, such humility can become crippling, as multitudes of sheep remain entrapped in the doorway to the slaughterhouse. Through the wisdom of the Holy Spirit, allow me to shed some light and prayerfully lift a burden that is heavy indeed. Sinners live a life consumed with sin in the same way that an alcoholic lives a life consumed with alcohol. Messiah came to earth while we were still sinners, slaves, and spiritually dead. Through Messiah we were justified, are at present being sanctified, and will one day experience glorification. Sanctification can't occur before justification, and justification is a one-time deal. Messiah was nailed once, bled once, and died once and for all. When believers invite Messiah into their life they are agreeing to give up their life of sin—once and for YAH.

To be sure, such a life of sinlessness is impossible by our own accord, and we will find miserably that all such human attempts are futile. However, the beauty of accepting Messiah is that along with his gift of salvation comes the gift of the Holy Spirit. It is our daily yielding to the Holy Spirit dwelling within us that makes it both possible and plausible to live a life free of sin. It is irreverent to suggest that YHWH really doesn't expect us not to sin. Such irreverence can soon lead to believing that his laws are irrelevant. YHWH would not deliver laws he knew we couldn't follow with aid from the Holy Spirit. The justification of Yeshua Messiah and sanctification through the Holy Spirit makes YHWH's goals reachable.

And if you and we belong to [Yeshua], guaranteed as his and anointed, it is all [YHWH]'s doing; it is [YHWH] also who has set his seal upon us, and as a pledge of what is to come has given the Spirit to dwell in our hearts. (2nd Corinthians 1:21-22 NEB)

Now to the One who can keep you from falling and set you in the presence of his glory, jubilant and above reproach, to the only God our Savior, be glory and majesty, might and authority, through [Yeshua], before all time, now, and for evermore. Amen. (Jude 1:24-25 NEB)

One common problem is that most novice Christians rarely see a model in which a veteran has led or is leading a life marked by an impenetrable devotion to Messiah. What they most often see are cultural Christians. Cultural Christians are compromising Christians striving to be accepted by their non-Christians peers who tell them to lighten up some. Usually their compromising takes the form of serving while sinning. As of late, committed Christians are in the minority while compromising Christians are in the majority, so they appear to be the rule of thumb. Careful, this is man's rule—not YHWH's. It's time for members to begin maturing and then becoming an exception to the rule.

As the Father has loved me, so I have loved you. Dwell in my love. If you heed my commands, you will dwell in my love, as I have heeded my Father's commands and dwell in his love. (John 15:9-10 NEB)

The part most believers have a hard time accepting is that the Christian walk is going to be a struggle. Like the alcoholic who comes to renounce her former ways (or any who has been healed from an addiction), believers will still be tempted with sin and will wrestle with the seed, still lodged within—but none have to give in. To deny your ability to live a sin free life is to deny the cleansing power of Yeshua. Blasphemy. In addition to the Holy Spirit, Messiah also gave us the Church. The Church should not be teaching, "Once a sinner always a sinner." Rather, it should teach, "Once a sinner, but now a beginner—a life no longer in sin. You once were lost, but with Messiah have been found, and will never turn back again."

What are we to say, then? Shall we persist in sin, so that there may be all the more grace? No, no. We died to sin: how can we live in it any longer? Have you forgotten that when we were baptized into union with [Yeshua] we were baptized into his death? By baptism we were buried with him, and lay dead, in order that, as [Yeshua] was raised from the dead in the splendor of the Father, so also we might set our feet upon the new path of life. (Romans 6:1-4 NEB)

24. Failure to Forgive

First read: Psalms 51:1-19

As previously acknowledged, you didn't pack your first bags, and in all likelihood you had help hauling. You never would have made it this far if you would've been forced to carry the whole load by yourself. Neither could you have made it this far without ever dropping off luggage that is no longer needed. Perhaps the image of the relay race will once again prove helpful. Just remember that rats never enter and you won't give in to the temptation to over pack, but tempted you will be. Keep a clear head: If you have luggage that is no longer needed, then you need to let the luggage go. Look back for too long and you will forget that which is equal in value—the people walking next to you.

Leave no claim outstanding against you, except that of mutual love. He who loves his neighbor has satisfied every claim of the law. For the commandments, "Thou shalt not commit adultery, thou shalt not kill, thou shalt not steal, thou shalt not covet," and any other commandment there may be, are all summed up in the one rule, "Love your neighbor as yourself." Love cannot wrong a neighbor; therefore, the whole law is summed up in love. (Romans 13:8-10 NEB)

It's bone chilling to consider the state of affairs our world would exist in had Messiah not died on the cross, forgiving the lost. That hell is not currently reining on earth is a testimony to the unfailing love of YHWH. That hell has nevertheless, been rather influential, is living proof that millions of souls still have yet to experience the sacrificial death that comes with accepting Messiah as Lord and Savior. There are millions claiming membership in the Body who haven't had much success in furthering their walk, due to excess luggage; excess baggage that if Messiah had chosen to continue carrying long after his resurrection, he never could have ascended into Heaven to sit at the right hand of his Father. Messiah spent hours in agony as the sins of the world rested heavily on his shoulders, yet he bore the weight:

Listen to me, O house of Jacob, all the remnant of the house of Israel, who have been borne by me from before your birth, carried from the womb, even to your old age I am he, and to gray hairs I will carry you. I have made, and I will bear; I will carry and will save. (Isaiah 46:3-4 ESV)

And when you stand praying, if you have a grievance against anyone, forgive him, so that your Father in heaven may forgive you the wrongs you have done. (Mark 11:25 NEB)

When Messiah was buried in the tomb, our sins were buried with him. It is man and not Yeshua who makes the choice to exert all of their energy digging up the past, hoisting it upon their shoulders and then complaining because of sin's impeding nature. So natural has sin become that man has hampered the Body's ability to live vivaciously and its members to walk victoriously. If Messiah had failed to excuse our transgressions then all would remain convicted and awaiting execution. The rest of the world savors tracking all wrongs, but not our Savior, and neither should any of his servants.

Then Peter came up and asked him, "Lord, how often am I to forgive my brother if he goes on wronging me? As many as seven times?" [Yeshua] replied, "I do not say seven times; I say seventy times seven." (Matthew 18:21-22 NEB)

Following his reply, Yeshua illustrated the seriousness of his command through a parable describing a debtor who, while he was exonerated by the King, went out and punished his own servant unable to repay his debts. Upon receiving the message of how the debtor mistreated his servant, the King's response was merciless:

And so angry was the master that he condemned the man to torture until he should pay the debt in full. And that is how my heavenly Father will deal with you, unless you each forgive your brother from your hearts. (Matthew 18:34-35 NEB)

Messiah never said it would be easy to forgive, but he does encourage his servants to remember why they have a chance to live.

25. A Reflective Moment

What Color Is Your Brother?

First read: 1st John 4:18-21

My dear friends, do not seek revenge, but leave a place for divine retribution; for there is a text which reads, "Justice is mine, says [Yeshua], I will repay." But there is another text: "If your enemy is hungry, feed him; if he is thirsty, give him a drink; by doing this you will heap live coals on his head." Do not let evil conquer you, but use good to defeat evil. (Romans 12:19-21 NEB)

I can recall a time during my stint at Asbury College when I was part of an effort to strengthen the racial diversity of the school. Every year, while a student, I attended the annual NCMSLC—that's National Christian Multicultural Student Leaders Conference. Each year college student leaders from around the country and from different ethnic groups, both domestic and foreign, would gather at a central location to discuss race relations. In particular, we met to seek out ways to promote unity among the various races and cultural groups attending Christian colleges throughout the United States. I can't recall a single year when I didn't leave the conference armed with a vision of how I would return to Asbury, ready to set it ablaze. The third year I attended, the conference was held in Grand Rapids, Michigan. I remember that year in particular because a statement was made in one of our ethnic caucuses that remains etched in my memory. The facilitator was describing how some of our racial difficulties are mirrored in the Church. She gave the sobering statistic of how 11:00am on Sunday mornings is still the most segregated hour in America. In asking those in attendance if any thought this presented a problem, another black woman raised her hand to enlighten the rest of us. She stated that she had no problem going to an all black church because for eight hours a day, five days a week, she was around all white people, and on Sunday's it felt good for her to finally be around her own. I can't remember how the facilitator responded because all I heard was a wave of "yep" and "that's right."

I may speak in tongues of men or of angels, but if I am without love, I am a sounding gong or a clanging cymbal. I may have the gift of prophecy, and know every hidden truth; I may have faith strong enough to move mountains; but if I have no love, I am nothing. I may dole out all I possess, or even give my body to be burnt, but if I have no love, I am none the better. (1st Corinthians 13:1-3 NEB)

Among blacks and whites I have heard the excuse of having different worshiping preferences to justify the de facto segregation of the Church. Without discounting the truth that there indeed are a variety of worshiping styles, I have been to a number of churches, of differing denominations, with equally all black and all white congregations and I see a multitude of similarities. Not only are worshiping styles similar in many of the churches, but all claim to believe in the same God. All claim to believe in the death and resurrection of Yeshua Messiah, that is, the Son of

YHWH. And all claim to believe that he will one day come back to redeem his own, that is, the whole Church. So what's the real problem? None seem too concerned with recognizing and admitting that the racial segregation of the Body is but one example of its damaging division.

Never cease to love your fellow-Christians. (Hebrews 13:1 NEB)

The Holy Spirit does indeed recognize that much healing needs to take place in the Church. However, the truth is that many in the Body insist on harboring and re-sowing seeds of hatred. At the root of this hatred are years of dejection giving rise to fears of continual or reversed rejection, and the gardener is Satan. There is no better way to hinder the Church's future then to have its members stuck in the past. In my short years of living I have learned some valuable lessons—here are three:

1) The road to revenge always leads to a dead end

2) Giving someone the silent treatment speaks volumes—about you

3) Forgiveness doesn't excuse, it accepts and amends what, in anger, will usually never end.

Then put on the garments that suit [YHWH]'s chosen people, his own, his beloved: compassion, kindness, humility, gentleness, patience. Be forbearing with one another, and forgiving, where any of you has cause for complaint: you must forgive as [Yeshua] forgave you. To crown all, there must be love, to bind all together and complete the whole. Let [Messiah's] peace be arbiter in your hearts; to this peace you were called as members of a single body. And be filled with gratitude. (Colossians 3:12-15 NEB)

Dear friends, let us love one another, because love is from [YHWH]. Everyone who loves is a child of [YHWH] and knows [YHWH], but the unloving know nothing of [YHWH]. For [YHWH] is love; and his love was disclosed to us in this that he sent his only Son into the world to bring us life. The love I speak of is not our love for [YHWH], but the love he showed us in sending his Son as the remedy for the defilement of our sins. If [YHWH] thus loved us, dear friends, we in turn are bound to love one another. Though [YHWH] has never been seen by any man, [YHWH] himself dwells in us if we love one another; his love is brought to perfection within us. (1st John 4:7-12 NEB)

26. Soiling the Sabbath

First read: Nehemiah 13:15-22

The longer you walk, the stronger your legs will become, and the muscles in your arms will also strengthen from the weight of the luggage carried while walking. And as time passes you will be able to carry more and for longer periods, but eventually every body needs respite from wear.

He also said, "The Son of Man is sovereign even over the Sabbath." (Luke 6:5 NEB)

Is there anyone in the Body who doesn't believe that each of the Ten Commandments still applies to each member today? There is a difference between obeying the Law in order to become justified and obeying the Law as a display of gratitude for your justification. The former is impossible while the latter is obligatory. However, it is the hope of the Father and the Son that all would comply with the commandments, though less out of compulsion and more out of conviction. When members begin to believe that YHWH's commandments are made for the good of the Body and that in all that the Father expects, he has in his heart and mind, the best interests of his people, then the Law will cease to look like a set of shackles and instead begin to look like the frame which keeps them free, through encouragement from the indwelling Holy Spirit. Contrary to popular belief, the Law did not die once Messiah was born:

> Do not suppose that I have come to abolish the Law and the prophets; I did not come to abolish, but to complete. I tell you this: so long as heaven and earth endure, not a letter, not a stroke, will disappear from the Law until all that must happen has happened. If any man therefore sets aside even the least of the Law's demands, and teaches others to do the same, he will have the lowest place in the kingdom of Heaven, whereas anyone who keeps the Law, and teaches others so, will stand high in the kingdom of Heaven. (Matthew 5:17-19 NEB)

Those who preach that the Law is the Old Testament and is therefore irrelevant are showing their ignorance and irreverence to Messiah. So then, what of the fourth commandment?

> Remember to keep the Sabbath day holy. You have six days to labor and do all of your work, for in six days the Lord made heaven and earth, the sea, and all that is in them, and on the seventh day he rested. Therefore the Lord blessed the Sabbath day and declared it holy. (Exodus 20:8-9, 11 ESV)

If there is recognition of its relevance, then why are so many soiling what YHWH has declared to be holy, or set apart for him? In truth, every day belongs to the Lord, but the Sabbath was especially set aside for abiding. If those who are weary and worn will give to YHWH what is due then he will gladly return to you. He yearns to give his people rest, but he won't while they insist on striving. Members were created to be holy and set apart from the world, but the Sabbath becomes soiled because of those who use it to continue toiling. You say you strive in order to stay alive, but in truth you amass because you think it will last. It won't.

And he told them this parable: "There was a rich man whose land yielded heavy crops. He debated with himself: 'What am I to do? I have not the space to store my produce. This is what I will do,' said he: 'I will pull down my storehouses and build them bigger. I will collect in them all my corn and other goods, and then say to myself, Man, you have plenty of good things laid by, enough for many years: take life easy, eat, drink, and enjoy yourself.' But [YHWH] said to him, 'You fool, this very night you must surrender your life; you have made your money—who will get it now?' That is how it is with the man who amasses wealth for himself and remains a pauper in the sight of [YHWH]." (Luke 12:16-21 NEB)

The Sabbath was created intentionally so that, in worshiping, believers could rest from their work while remembering Yeshua's commitment to his creation. Also on the seventh day, believers should remember and reassert their commitment to Messiah.

If you turn back your foot from the Sabbath from doing your pleasure on my holy day, and call the Sabbath a delight and the holy day of [Yeshua] honorable; if you honor it, not going your own ways, or seeking your own pleasure, or talking idly; then you shall take delight in [Yeshua], and I will make you ride on the heights of the earth; I will feed you with the heritage of Jacob your father, for the mouth of [Yeshua] has spoken. (Isaiah 58:13-14 ESV)

Such was the oath he swore to our father Abraham, to rescue us from enemy hands, and grant us, free from fear, to worship him with a holy worship, with uprightness of heart, in his presence, our whole life long. (Luke 1:73-75 NEB)

27. A Resting Request

First read: Leviticus 25:1-55

YHWH looks down upon the Earth
With eyes and a heart of grief
He sees past the outer-shell of flesh & bone,
At the souls that yearn for relief

He sees past the lies of busy lives,
At the souls who so yearn to breathe
He sees past the smiles which so often beguile,
At the minds that were once deceived

He sees past the lips with artful quips,
At the lives who refuse to believe

Yes, YHWH sees and he grieves

To his people he says through the Spirit,
"There is a plight that I need to address."

Remember your days? Your weary days?
When, by sin, you were foul and oppressed?
Remember how I called then patiently waited
For you to fall down on your knees and confess?

Remember how your senses would sour and sear
As the sun sat down in the west?
Remember all the nights you lay awake
With your mind so numb from distress?

Remember all the days you stayed in bed
With no strength to climb out and get dressed?

Remember? I do

So, into my house I invited you still
And to be so much more while my guest
And although I insist you press for holiness,
I still have yet, one request—

Learn to rest
With each breath—learn to rest

While on your quest for holiness
You must learn how to rest
For without rest you can't offer your best—
And in my house I expect nothing less

My Sabbaths are essential for all with potential
My commands I expect all to obey
To those who ignore, I have but one thing in store
Your blessings, I'll choose to delay.

28. Winning in Weakness

First read: 1st Chronicles 11-13

You were strategically placed where your weaknesses would be windows for the team, and yes, that does include you. Acknowledge your weaknesses and open up your window. Don't be ashamed of your foul odor. After all, you have been walking for some time now, what do you expect? Besides, if those around you would ever open their windows, you'd find that the odor hasn't omitted anyone, rather it is emitting from everyone. Either of you could be holding a piece of luggage that looks familiar to another—perhaps a piece carried before in the past. How was it hauled? When was it left? All of you could also have a free hand to offer. If helpful then think of it as a baton.

There will be times while on the road to Glory that walking will seem to believers an uphill battle. YHWH wills that his people develop stamina so that each can make it through this final stretch. However, it is ridiculous to think that YHWH wills for his people to complete their journey in isolation. While it is true that he will occasionally orchestrate solo encounters with a Goliath in order to stimulate faith within the timid, he will also allow some battles to ensue to ensure that his people learn how to depend on one another. Some of these battles will prove more strenuous than others, purposely. The believer will turn for help to a God who appears deaf. In fact, our God is not deaf, but definitive in his desire that the Body learn to act as One (like the Father and Son).

Consider my affliction and my trouble, and forgive all my sins. Consider how many are my foes, and with what violent hatred they hate me. Oh, guard my soul, and deliver me. Let me not be put to shame, for I take refuge in you. May integrity and uprightness preserve me, for I wait for you. Redeem Israel, O [Yeshua], out of all his troubles. (Psalms 25:18-22 ESV)

For many Christians the greatest battles are not fought on an open field, but rather in a closed space that most would prefer to keep on lock down. There are spiritual struggles that YHWH has allowed to seep into the most secret chamber of the human body—the heart. Unfortunately, so few members are willing to share theirs. It is not Messiah's intention that these struggles remain lodged; it is his desire that they linger. Why? Most importantly, it ensures that the committed Christian won't develop a sudden impulse to fly solo, apart from Messiah within.

We must not be conceited, challenging one another to rivalry, jealous of one another. If a man should do something wrong, my brothers, on a sudden impulse, you who are endowed with the Spirit must set him right again very gently. Look to yourself, each one of you; you may be tempted too. Help one another to carry these heavy loads, and in this way you will fulfill the law of [Messiah]. (Galatians 5:25-6:2 NEB)

Messiah died once so that we might take up our crosses daily. But even still, Messiah wills that Christians, in their weakness, help one another to carry their cross. Maybe you have asked YHWH to remove a thorn from your flesh and yet it still pierces. You will ache until you are ready to break. When you break then you will share until all is laid bare, but most members refuse to share because they're afraid they'll foul up the air. The Holy Spirit wants to remind believers that the air has been foul and it is now time to clear it; let those who have ears hear. It is true that YHWH granted David success in his fight against Goliath, and that it was done with a single shot. It wasn't that David needed to build up faith (his faith had brought him this far), but YHWH wanted others to see how faith could lead to victory. This victory, however, did not lead David into thinking that he was invincible or that he could achieve success while fighting the rest of his battles alone. In defeating the Philistines, David had no trouble acknowledging his weakness. He would need the support of other able-bodied men who had fought victoriously in previous battles, and so had proven themselves worthy. He shared his weakness and so he won. Members of the Body would do well to follow in the footsteps of a man after YHWH's own heart. Our God is more than capable of fighting every battle for each believer. Remember too that his heavenly host is doing precisely that behind the scenes. However, he has designed the road to Glory in such a manner that redemption would require the act of One, so that restoration could involve the actions of many.

We are free to do anything, you say. Yes, but is everything good for us? We are free to do anything, but does everything help the building of the community? Each of you must regard, not his own interests, but the other man's. (1st Corinthians 10:23-24 NEB)

74

29. **A Reflective Moment**

Self-Absorbed

First read: Philippians 2:1-4

Whether we wish to admit it or not, at some level we all desire acceptance. Actually, on a deeper level I believe we each have a desire to belong. Such is due to the relational make-up given to us by Yeshua. In the same way, from the beginning YHWH has desired to know us intimately, and he equally intended for his people to exist in relationships with one another. However, in order to commune with one another we need another to whom we can, in fact, relate. When those persons are not within our immediate reach, we begin to reach out to others. Yet, problems result when those persons are outside of the boundaries that YHWH has created for his people. Indeed, in sharing the Gospel with a dying world, it is necessary for Christians to step outside their yard frequently in order to cross the street. Of course to witness effectively, at times we must leave our own neighborhood to interact with the drug dealers and users, prostitutes, gang-bangers, pedophiles, rapists—in short, some of the lost. However, Messiah never advocated that his sheep become intimate with such sinners—not while they are actively sinning.

Walk with the wise and become wise, for a companion of fools suffers harm. (Proverbs 13:20 ESV)

Some might read this and think that such sentiments reek of snobbery. I would challenge readers to reconsider. The soul purpose of our becoming intimate with Messiah is so that we might learn how better to imitate Messiah. As the first born of the Father, he has given us a model to follow. If believers aren't careful, we can easily find ourselves imitating the behaviors of those we are seeking to save.

A friend loves at all times, and a brother is born for adversity. (Proverbs 17:17 ESV)

Again, Messiah has given members the Church where each might grow intimately with one another. The Church should be the natural place members turn to when experiencing loneliness, yet, often times, it is the place believers turn to the least. It is a sad commentary to hear stories in which individuals still feel isolated after going to the same church for years. When members feel as if they can't compete or compare with the lifestyle of others within, then those members begin looking outside to fulfill those same relational needs. How sad indeed. It is the responsibility of the Church to ensure that every member of the Body feels accepted. Many believers are delivered into the hands of the enemy when members more mature choose to turn a deaf ear. The old adage "negative attention is better than no attention at all" is often said of little children who grab at and gravitate toward anything or anyone that will respond. Messiah has not called us to attach our selves to just anything, and our Father is concerned with the intimate interactions of his children.

Currently, there is negative attention circulating throughout the Church where members are grasping at anything, whether dead or alive. The Church can only withstand so much deadness while still maintaining its spiritual vitality. Before too long the stench of death which has a grip on the world, will propagate a new breed of Christianity—the Christian corpse; leaving all others gasping for air. The response of the Church? Reach out to draw in, and then once drawn in, keep in. One marker of intimacy is self-disclosure. Members should know what's going on in the lives of other body parts. What will it take for members to begin laying down their own lives for the sake of each other? A sponge can only absorb so much before it is no longer usable. Then, how usable is a Christian that has become self-absorbed?

Pursue peace with everyone, and holiness, for without it no one will see [Yeshua]. See to it that no one comes short of the grace of [YHWH], that no one be like a bitter root springing up and causing trouble, and through him many become defiled. And see to it that no one becomes an immoral or godless person like Esau, who sold his own birthright for a single meal. For you know that later when he wanted to inherit his blessing, he was rejected, for he found no opportunity for repentance, although he sought the blessings with tears. (Hebrews 12:14-17 NEB)

30. Miracular Degeneration Part IV

First read: Exodus 20:18-21

You will always have memories to take with you—snapshots of your past—because every new step you take leaves another one behind. And if you are looking ahead as you walk then you are always taking pictures of the past. Like any snapshot, some images will remain sharper longer than others. Sometimes older pictures do retain the sharpness of their image longer than those more recently taken. Others don't. But, as the pictures are running their course, the images will start fading away on their own and in their own time—it's natural and inevitable—so let them fade. You may not clearly see the importance of letting go now, but that is okay, you're still developing. In the long run you'll be glad you did.

Believers must ensure they never suffer from selective memory. Another popular myth rampant within the Church today is that YHWH is not to be feared. There are shepherds who mistakenly believe they're helping their flock draw nearer to their God by offering them false comfort. There is danger in becoming too familiar with our Lord and Savior. Apparently, the encounter the Israelites had with YHWH wasn't as frightening as they led Moses to believe. So, too, for members of the Body of Messiah, there needs to remain etched in their minds a vision of a roaring, conquering lion that is as sharp as the image of a resting lamb. YHWH knew that the Israelites were struggling with displaying the appropriate amount of reverence, as evident by their persistent complaining at the onset of their exodus.

When Pharaoh drew near, the people of Israel lifted up their eyes, and behold, the Egyptians were marching after them, and they feared greatly. And the people of Israel cried out to [YHWH] and [Yeshua]. They said to Moses, "Is it because there are no graves in Egypt that you have taken us away to die in the wilderness? What have you done to us in bringing us out of Egypt? Is not this what we said to you in Egypt: 'Leave us alone that we may serve the Egyptians?' For it would have been better for us to serve the Egyptians than to die in the wilderness." (Exodus 14:10-12 ESV)

This was just the first of many panic-driven responses. YHWH understands his people and is equipped to handle our feelings and emotions. However, our response to him can become disrespectful and sinful. To suggest that living in bondage is preferable to dealing with the new storms that believers will encounter after redemption is a slap in the face to our Redeemer. It not only screams of disrespect to the one who rescued us from our deathbed, it is a clear indication that faith is lacking. In authoring the book of Proverbs, Solomon is unambiguous in stating that:

The fear of [Yeshua] is the beginning of knowledge; fools despise wisdom and instruction. (Proverbs 1:7 ESV)

And it is with knowledge and wisdom that all believers should courageously walk on the road to Glory. Perhaps there are those who have never had a fearful experience with Yeshua. The truth is that he has roared on multiple occasions and not too long ago. For several moments all shuddered in fear and responded favorably. How quickly time passes and memories fade. How much louder must the Lion roar before the sheep flee from the wolves and run to their Lamb permanently? Speaking through the Apostle Paul, the Holy Spirit reminded those members in the church at Philippi that fearing our God, both Father and Son, must remain an essential component of our journey—until our work is done.

> So you too, my friends, must be obedient, as always; even more, now that I am away, than when I was with you. You must work out your own salvation in fear and trembling; for it is [YHWH] who works in you, inspiring both the will and the deed, for his own chosen purpose. (Philippians 2:12-13 NEB)

31. Patching Up The Past

First read: 1st Chronicles 1-10

The further you walk away from your past the more difficult it will be to see the earlier stages of them—don't squint your eyes. The more you squint, the less you blink, which can lead to dry eye. There will be moments on your journey when your tears are going to come in handy, especially when a sudden and unexpected gust of wind blows dirt onto your face and into your eyes. The dirt itself will indeed hurt, but your inability to shed a tear and wash away the dirt will hurt the most because it was self-inflicted. And don't bother trying to walk back to see your past with greater clarity; you are simply wasting time already taken. If the thought of leaving your past behind is too burdensome to bear, then share those thoughts with those who are walking beside you and lessen your burden—they are probably thinking the same thing anyway. Think about your past, but not for too long. Don't allow burdensome thoughts to become excess baggage; you already have enough to carry while on your journey; more will only slow you down.

If any observation is worth making from the earlier chapters of 1st Chronicles, it's that Israel has an extensive past. As the genealogies from Adam to Saul are reviewed, the faithful reader should have little difficulty recalling the mishaps and misfortunes detailed in Genesis through 2nd Kings. Admittedly, it can become depressing rehashing the depravity of man. No person wants to be constantly reminded of their rather lousy lineage. Yet, the true believers must remember that regardless of denomination, race, nationality, gender, or age, all members share the same story. YHWH thought it necessary that his younger people know the experiences of their older siblings, and so they were recorded. It's difficult to become prideful in our present state when the past is branded or etched. Though, if stuck in the past too far or too long, in time you'll wind up a wretch. But, the only one you will have to blame is yourself.

Remember not the former things, nor consider the things of old. Behold, I am doing a new thing; now it springs forth, do you not perceive it? I will make a way in the wilderness and rivers in the desert. (Isaiah 43:18-19 ESV)

While we would rather old wounds and crusty scars completely disappear from sight, Messiah would rather they linger for a little while. He would actually prefer that we show and tell every now and again—and again and again until no one in the fold feels the need to feign. Yet, never confuse wounds for weights. There comes a point in everyone's journey where looking back no longer aids a fellow traveler. Through cathartic confession, revisiting the past has become an obsession. There's a real danger in obsessing over the past. With unnecessary weight added, the believer soon becomes stuck and unable to walk any further on the road to Glory.

You had time enough in the past to do all the things men want to do in the pagan world. Then you lived in license and debauchery, drunkenness, revelry, and tippling, and the forbidden worship of idols. Now, when you no longer plunge with them into all this reckless dissipation, they cannot understand it, and they vilify you accordingly; but they shall answer for it to him who stands ready to pass judgment on the living and the dead. Why was the Gospel preached to those who are dead? In order that, although in the body they received the sentence common to men, they might in the spirit be alive with the life of [YHWH]. (1st Peter 4:3-6 NEB)

Christians should rejoice that they always have access to their family tree. Never should any one find themselves wondering, "Where did I come from?" However, in reading and relating, neither should anyone lose sight of where they are going. Moreover, members of the Body should never cease giving the Father praise for allowing the story to continue past Chronicles. There is no need to patch up the past. Believers will simply look patchy and people are still going to ask. Instead, wear your wounds for the world. Yeshua did and he's been saving people ever since. But, there will come a time, while walking, when your wounds will start to heal. Let them and then rejoice over him who heals.

Then he raised his voice in a great cry: Lazarus, come forth. The dead man came out, his hands and feet swathed in linen bands, his face wrapped in a cloth. [Yeshua] said, "Loose him; let him go." Now many of the Jews who had come to visit Mary and had seen what [Yeshua] did, put their faith in him. (John 11:43-45 NEB)

32. Decimating Division - I

First read: Galatians 3:26-29

As you are looking around and taking in the scenery, perceiving its infinitude? Don't look for too long, for you will be deceived. The world is bigger than you are, but it is no more infinite. Refusing to look around for too long will help you to recognize that the world is, in fact, finite. It will also aid you in remembering that the world is fallible and, thus, everything in it is as well. As you are walking, you might find that trying to reconcile the world's duality—its immensity yet fallibility—proves puzzling. That's okay, for your journey in this world will be puzzling, and you will do well in remembering that you are just one of its many broken pieces. Behold and do not bemoan your brokenness because therein is where your beauty lies.

During this period, when disciples were growing in number, there was disagreement between those of them who spoke Greek and those who spoke the language of the Jews. The former party complained that their widows were being overlooked in the daily distribution. (Acts 6:1 NEB)

There is no question here of Greek and Jew, circumcised and uncircumcised, barbarian, Scythian, slave and freeman; but [Messiah] is all, and is in all. (Colossians 3:11 NEB)

Of late I've tried to reconcile a conundrum. How is it possible that on one hand each of us has an innate desire to belong, while on the other hand it seems that we are determined to segregate ourselves into different categories? The us and them phenomenon. This behavior pattern is not unique to American society, nor has it only been a recent trend. On the contrary, world history is full of examples in which people and cultures have chosen to separate for some of the most trivial reasons. How ironic that the most shallow of distinctions have produced the deepest wounds.

Do all you have to do without complaint or wrangling. Show yourselves guileless and above reproach, faultless children of [YHWH] in a warped and crooked generation, in which you shine like stars in a dark world and proffer the word of life. (Philippians 2:14-16 NEB)

The sociologist and historian alike have their own explanation, and at times even justification, as to why classism, racism, and sexism have abounded rampantly in the past, and why each continues to flourish today. As an avid reader of the social sciences, I respectfully attest to the merit of most arguments presented—with simple human nature most often topping the list. I have made it a personal goal of mine to no longer unnecessarily fret about the conditions of our fallen world. Not to suggest that I've simply quit caring about those around me, but I have come to the conclusion that the longer I look to the world, the more I expect the solutions to its problems to come from the world. Instead, I've decided to concentrate on the

Church, where many of the same problems abound. With the help of YHWH's Holy Spirit, I believe that if I can aid in curing her ills, then collectively we can have a greater impact on the world around. There is strength in numbers. Perhaps some in reading this entry will become instinctively defensive. "What? Classism, racism, and sexism in the Church? Not my church." Well, the beauty of the Church is that it involves all members universally. No single individual or single church need take blame for a virus that continues to plague the entire Body.

Conflict Resolution 101: Step 1) Admit there's a problem. Step 2) Accept personal responsibility for personal involvement. Step 3) Access the root of the problem. Step 4) Acknowledge present adverse circumstances. Step 5) Assess possible solutions. Step 6) Act, anticipating change.

It is with sadness that I believe the Church is today struggling with Step 1. Before addressing a problem, one must first acknowledge that the existing behavior is, at present, in conflict with a preexisting rule or law. As Christians we needn't look far to find our preexisting source. We are told that in the beginning was the Word, that the Word was with YHWH, and the Word was YHWH. Before all of creation existed, the Son of YHWH, that is, Yeshua Messiah, was. It was through Messiah that creation came into existence, for Yeshua spoke. As such, Messiah is both the source and the model for all Christian living.

This doctrine of the cross is sheer folly to those on their way to ruin, but to us who are on the way to salvation it is the power of [YHWH]. (1st Corinthians 1:18 ESV)

Messiah commanded that each love YHWH with all their hearts, minds, and souls, and simultaneously commanded all to love our neighbors like ourselves. If only we would follow these two simple commands. I say "would" rather than "could" because Messiah's death on the cross makes it possible for all to do so. Why won't we? Until members of the Body cease defining who their neighbor is and instead begin seeing all through the eyes of Messiah, who came to decimate division, then the Church will continue to struggle. The validity of the Church is inextricably bound to both the unity and vitality of its members.

And may [YHWH], the source of all fortitude and all encouragement, grant that you may agree with one another after the manner of [Yeshua], so that with one mind and one voice you may praise [YHWH], the Father of [Yeshua]. In a word, accept one another as [Messiah] accepted us, to the glory of [YHWH]. (Romans 15:5-7 NEB)

33. Decimating Division II

First read: Galatians 3:26-29

Sometimes it will be difficult for you to see the beauty in your brokenness. Though, if you drop some of the excess baggage, it might clear up your blur. And if at times your sight is still sore, it may merely serve as a reminder that you are still developing. Developing is good, though it is a process that requires movement. Movement is an essential element of your journey. Prepare to develop throughout your journey, and prepare to deal with the soreness. Need something soothing? Nothing is as natural or soothing to an eye as a tear that is shed or a drop from the sky. Thank Yeshua for tears and thank YHWH for rain.

As stated previously, the first step in resolving a conflict is admitting that there is a problem. Alas, the Church is struggling with this first step; the question is why? I'm sure you could come up with any number of truthful responses, but I'd like to offer up one of my own. I believe that most people lack the intrapersonal skills necessary to admit individual deficiencies. For some it's a matter a pride. These people love looking into the mirror—that is, until a blemish becomes noticeable. It's easier not to address what one chooses not to see. When others, in wisdom, attempt to point out the flaw—to correct, not to criticize—then these people rebuff such efforts with accusations of envy or trouble-stirring. In these situations, it is best not to respond in kind, but in love. Simply apologize for their perception and assure them that you have their best interest in mind and at heart. Then ask to end the meeting in prayer. No matter the fracture, Yeshua should always be the common denominator.

How blest are the peacemakers; [YHWH] shall call them his sons. (Matthew 5:9 NEB)

Of that you may be certain, my friends. But each of you must be quick to listen, slow to speak, and slow to be angry. For a man's anger cannot promote the justice of [YHWH]. Away then with all that is sordid, and the malice that hurries to excess, and quietly accept the message planted in your hearts, which can bring you salvation. (James 1:19-21 NEB)

Apart from prideful conflicts, many lack intrapersonal skills because they haven't taken the time to develop them. In my experiences I've found that some of the most successful relationally-driven people are also some of the most introspective. I'm not necessarily talking about the extrovert who has a natural knack for interacting with other people. Most of their relationships are superficial because they spend little time cultivating the necessary intimacy. Neither am I particularly addressing the introvert, who while possessing the natural ability to look within, may not always take the time to do so. The bottom line is that the longer we insist on remaining disconnected with who we are, the longer we will remain disconnected with those around us.

83

For no one of us lives, and equally no one of us dies, for himself alone. If we live, we live for [Yeshua]; and if we die, we die for [Yeshua]. Whether therefore we live or die, we belong to [Yeshua]. (Romans 14:7-8 NEB)

In connecting with who we are, our primary purpose is to ensure that we first know whose we are. The secondary purpose then becomes getting to know him. The more we know of Yeshua and his character then the more we realize where we fall short. However, YHWH did not send his Son to constantly remind his creation of their shortcomings—the Law already took care of that. No, Yeshua came to earth so that we who lived in sin could have the victory through him. The closer we draw ourselves to Yeshua the more we see his willingness and ability to make up for what we lack. When believers examine the life and teachings of Yeshua Messiah no ambiguity should exist concerning his expectations for us. And this is how introspection should take place: As we come to know more fully who Messiah is—the image of the invisible Father—we must ask ourselves continuously, "Where in my life am I missing the mark?" Why was Yeshua able to live a sinless life while on earth? Some might answer, "Because he was the Son of YHWH." This response is only partially true. Yeshua is the Son of YHWH. But, the success of Yeshua lay in the fact that he recognized both who he was and whose he was. In recognizing his identity, Yeshua equally recognized his responsibilities.

[Yeshua] said, "If [YHWH] were your father, you would love me, for [YHWH] is the source of my being, and from him I come. I have not come of my own accord; he sent me." (John 8:42 NEB)

First, he had the responsibility of obeying the will of his Father from birth to death. Second, Yeshua had the responsibility of maximizing intimacy with his Father while on this earth. Third, he had the responsibility of reflecting the character of his Father even in the midst of temptation, suffering, and death. What Yeshua exhibited perfectly while on this earth was faith, hope, and love—most of all, love. Through perfect faith, hope, and love—no sin exists. Our life journey is one in which we aim to perfect our faith, our hope, and our love.

Now we see only puzzling reflections in a mirror, but then we shall see face to face. My knowledge now is partial; then it will be whole, like [YHWH]'s knowledge of me. In a word, there are three things that last forever: faith, hope, and love; but the greatest of them all is love. (1st Corinthians 13:12-13 NEB)

34. A Reflective Moment

Pocketing Possessions

First read: Hebrews 13:5-6

Are we ready to admit another truth? There are some in the Church who find their sole existence in pocketing and polishing their possessions; in the process they are losing their souls. And while saving the soul is the most significant goal while walking the earth, it is by no means the only objective. If we are mindful in remembering that Messiah commands each member to look after one another, then we must continue to eradicate those areas which thwart such efforts and instead convince each to look after his or her own self. Focusing on possessions is one such area some members need to eradicate from their lives. What greater evil exists than that which redirects our affection toward our family members to adoration for material wealth?

> Each person should give as he has decided for himself; there should be no reluctance, no sense of compulsion; [YHWH] loves a cheerful giver. And it is in [YHWH]'s power to provide you richly with every good gift; thus you will have ample means in yourselves to meet each and every situation, with enough and to spare for every good cause. Scripture says of such a man: "He has lavished his gifts on the needy, his benevolence stands fast forever." (2nd Corinthians 9:7-9 NEB)

One of my favorite passages in Scripture comes from the book of Acts. Here is an illustration which best exemplifies the purpose of the possessions that YHWH has graciously loaned us:

> The whole body of believers was united in heart and soul. Not a man of them claimed any of his possessions as his own, but everything was held in common, while the apostles bore witness with great power to the resurrection of [Yeshua]. They were all held in high esteem; for they had never a needy person among them, because all who had property in land or houses sold it, brought the proceeds of the sale, and laid the money at the feet of the apostles; it was then distributed to any who stood in need. (Acts 4:32-35 NEB)

No, this is not a passage advocating a particular economic or political system such as socialism or communism, as many such egalitarian-driven humanitarians have suggested. What is illustrated in the above passage is an example of how the early Church promoted the general welfare—not from coercion by some outside source, but through conviction and compassion from the inside. Of particular significance is the magnitude of these charitable activities; due only to the transformative and unifying power of the indwelling Holy Spirit who surpasses human nature. Not too long before this verse, we find another in chapter two where the new converts have just celebrated Pentecost, been baptized by the Holy Spirit, and received instruction from Peter.

They met constantly to hear the apostles teach, and to share the common life, to break bread, and to pray. A sense of awe was everywhere, and many marvels and signs were brought about through the apostles. All whose faith had drawn them together held everything in common: they would sell their property and possessions and make a general distribution as the need of each required. With one mind they kept up their daily attendance at the temple, and, breaking bread in private houses, shared their meals with unaffected joy, as they praised [YHWH] and enjoyed the favor of the whole people. And day by day [Yeshua] added to their number those whom he was saving. (Acts 2:42-47 NEB)

Not everyone around agreed to these new arrangements. There were those who scoffed at the idea of sharing anything they had worked hard for or had inherited. But Luke informs readers that only those whose faith had drawn them together held everything in common. There are many in the churches who espouse their belief in the faith, but of what faith do they speak? For certain, all whose faith lay in their wealth are all serving the same master. We will continue to struggle with unity in the Body until we can corporately agree that nothing we individually possess belongs to us; everything belongs to YHWH. What do we gain through pocketing and polishing our temporal possessions while simultaneously becoming spiritually impoverished? Perhaps Ananias and Sapphira could've answered this question had they lived.

When the people saw that neither [Yeshua] nor his disciples were any longer there, they immediately went aboard these boats and made for Capernaum in search of [Yeshua]. They found him on the other side. "Rabbi, they said, when did you come here?" [Yeshua] replied, "In very truth I know that you have not come looking for me because you saw signs, but because you ate the bread and your hunger was satisfied. You must work, not for this perishable food, but for the food that lasts, the food of eternal life." (John 6:24-27 NEB)

Instruct those who are rich in this world's goods not to be proud, and not to fix their hopes on so uncertain a thing as money, but upon [YHWH], who endows us richly with all things to enjoy. Tell them to do good and to grow rich in noble actions, to be ready to give away and to share, and so acquire a treasure which will form a good foundation for the future. Thus they will grasp the life which is life indeed." (1st Timothy 6:17-19 NEB)

Perhaps all that is polished wouldn't perish so easily if people would begin opening up their purses and pockets and giving to YHWH what is due him first. Our first fruits are what we owe to YHWH, not the rest that has already been bitten into and chewed. Again, the firsts are due. There are the shepherds who preach that tithing ten-percent of our income is an Tanakh mandate; true, but not exclusively.

In the Tanakh:

I am [YHWH], unchanging; and you, too, have not ceased to be sons of Jacob. From the days of your forefathers you have been wayward and have not kept my laws. If you will return to me, I will return to you, says [YHWH].

You ask, 'How can we return?' May man defraud [YHWH] and [Yeshua] that you defraud me? You ask, 'How have we defrauded thee?' Why, in tithes and contributions. There is a curse, a curse on you all, the whole nation of you, because you defraud me. Bring the tithes into the treasury, all of them; let there be food in my house. Put me to the proof, says [YHWH], and see if I do not open windows in the sky and pour a blessing on you as long as there is need. I will forbid pests to destroy the produce of your soil or make your vines barren, says [YHWH]. All nations shall count you happy, for yours shall be a favored land, says [YHWH]. (Malachi 3:6-12 ESV)

In the B'rit Khadasha:

When he had finished speaking, a Pharisee invited him to dinner. He came in and sat down. The Pharisee noticed with surprise that he had not begun by washing before the meal. But [Yeshua] said to him, "You Pharisees. You clean the outside of cup and plate; but inside you there is nothing but greed and wickedness. You fools. Did not he who made the outside make the inside too? But let what is in the cup be given in charity, and all is clean. Alas for you Pharisees. You pay tithes of mint and rue and every garden-herb; but have no care for justice and the love of [YHWH]. It is these you should have practiced, without neglecting the others. (Luke 11:37-42 NEB)

A number of Pharisees and men of Herod's party were sent to trap him with a question. They came and said, "Master, you are an honest man, we know, and truckle [to be servile or submissive] to no one, whoever he may be; you teach in all honesty the way of life that [YHWH] requires. Are we or are we not permitted to pay taxes to the Roman Emperor? Shall we pay or not?" He saw how crafty their question was, and said, "Why are you trying to catch me out? Fetch me a silver piece, and let me look at it. "They brought one, and he said to them, "Whose head is this, and whose inscription?""Caesar's, "they replied. Then [Yeshua] said, "Pay Caesar what is due to Caesar, and pay [YHWH] what is due to [YHWH]. And they heard him with astonishment. (Mark 12:13-17 NEB)

Notice how Messiah's rebuke to the Pharisee was two-fold. First, he was selecting which portions of the Law he was going to carry out. Second, even in tithing, the Pharisee's motivation was misplaced. He was tithing purely for ritual purposes, rather than for righteous ones. Moreover, it appears that none of his actions followed the rule of Law that Moses gave under the Old Covenant and that Messiah reiterated under the new:

Hear, O Israel:[YHWH] and [Yeshua] are one. You shall love [YHWH] and [Yeshua] with all your heart and with all your soul and with all your might. (Deuteronomy 6:4-5 ESV)

Perhaps readers are already aware of these points and are in firm agreement; if so, then good. But readers should also observe the fact that in his rebuke to the

Pharisee, Yeshua never reprimanded him for tithing. He told him that he should not have neglected his love for YHWH or for justice, while continuing to tithe in obedience to the Law. In the passage from Mark, Yeshua makes it clear that in living within our secular system we are to give according to the secular laws – i.e. we must pay taxes. Those shepherds and sheep who mask behind Christianity to avoid their earthly duties are disobeying Messiah. In the same sentence, Messiah maintains that we are to simultaneously pay "YHWH what is due to YHWH." What is due to YHWH? Our first fruits. The word 'tithe' literally means a tenth. The commandment is that we give to YHWH our first fruits; not a portion of our fruits remaining after Caesar has taken his share, as that would be our second fruits. For those shepherds and sheep who still insist that this is a custom strictly tied to the Law, it must be pointed out that the act of tithing actually preceded the Law. Notice what the author of Hebrews says about the exchange between Abraham and Melchizedek:

This Melchizedek, king of Salem, priest of [YHWH], met Abraham returning from the route of the kings and blessed him; and Abraham gave him a tithe of everything as his portion. His name, in the first place means "king of righteousness"; next he is the king of Salem, that is, "king of peace." (Hebrews 7:1-2 NEB)

It is a matter of fact that Abraham's life preceded Moses, and thus, the Law. Therefore, none should use Old Testament "legalism" as an excuse for not carrying out Messiah's commandment. Tithing is not an option for those wanting to obey Messiah. However, offerings are. Offerings are what Paul is referring to in his letter to the churches in Corinth:

Remember: sparse sowing, sparse reaping; sow bountifully, and you will reap bountifully. Each person should give as he has decided for himself; there should be no reluctance, no sense of compulsion; [YHWH] loves a cheerful giver. And it is in [YHWH]'s power to provide you richly with every good gift; thus you will have ample means in yourselves to meet each and every situation, with enough and to spare for every good cause. Scripture says of such a man: "He has lavished his gifts on the needy, his benevolence stands for ever." Now he who provides seed for sowing and bread for food will provide the seed for you to sow; he will multiply it and swell the harvest of your benevolence, and you will always be rich enough to be generous. Through our action such generosity will issue in thanksgiving to [YHWH], for as a piece of willing service this is not only a contribution towards the needs of [YHWH]'s people; more than that, it overflows in a flood of thanksgiving to [YHWH]." (2nd Corinthians 9:6-12 NEB)

After giving YHWH what is due to him, Christians are now encouraged to show their love for him and for their neighbor, by providing extra for neighbors in need. Though, in truth, for the Christian disciple, offerings are not really optional, unless of course you are genuinely unable to give. There are those who, because of personal economic conditions, financial setbacks, or other unforeseen fiscal emergencies, are in no position to give extra. Messiah understands and therefore you are indeed under no compulsion to give; you need your resources to live. Perhaps it is you whom the Body of Messiah needs to come and relieve, so that you can continue to breathe. On the other hand, YHWH has monetarily blessed some. As such, he expects them to use their wealth to bless someone else. We tithe to please our God by respecting and obeying his command. We bless him when we take the remainder of what he has blessed us with, and use a portion of it to help those in need. Now listen as Messiah pleads:

In my Body there are masses
who ignore my Father's call.
To give to him, what is due to him-
tis but a tenth, it's not your all.

Continue disregarding
what my Father says to do,
and soon another crash shall come;
but no one shall there be to save you.

35. Am I There Yet?

First read: 2nd Kings:14-15

So why then should you look around? Because, failing to do so will also result in your forgetting the world's finitude and fallibility, as well as of all those who dwell in it. Amnesia, whether in great supply or not, is nevertheless too costly and you can't afford to have it, not while the clock is still ticking. There are a few exercises you can engage in, however, to help jog your memory in the likely event that amnesia kicks in while on your journey. First, look down just long enough to get an estimate of the number of dark, dead tree-limbs, and dark, desiccate ditches, one right after another. The tree limbs were once living and the ditches were once sodden. But, no drop from the sky and now they're all dry; alas, a sore sight indeed. Then, look around and begin counting the number of people you see stumbling, tripping, and falling. You could count without ceasing and they'd still keep increasing. Can you hear in your ear the echoes...echoes of finite earth? You should, but not for too long. Take comfort in counting those who fall for too long, and soon you too will be down for the count.

There was a troubling trend occurring in Israel while she was divided into the northern kingdom of Israel and the southern kingdom of Judah. The northern kingdom, inhabiting ten of the twelve tribes, could arguably have been considered the more sinful of the two. Remember that this was the kingdom given first to Jeroboam son of Nebat, one of Solomon's courtiers. Remember too how Jeroboam's insecurity led to his leading the rest of Israel astray by creating a pair of golden calves at Bethel and Dan, and requiring everyone to worship them, rather than traveling back to Jerusalem in Judah, home to the altar of the living God. It was also the northern kingdom of Israel that had Ahab as their king; the man described as having done "more that was wrong in the eyes of the Lord than all his predecessors." In comparing Israel to Judah, one could suggest that Judah stood shoulders above her sister in righteousness. This is, after all, the tribe from which the Son of YHWH derives his lineage. Jerusalem is also the city in which Messiah was crucified.

Even a child makes himself known by his act, by whether his conduct is pure and upright. (Proverbs 20:11 ESV)

Though rarely cast in the same light as her northern neighbor, Judah was far from perfect. In fact, king Amaziah, son of Joash, and his son and successor, king Azariah, both fell short of YHWH's standard. While each is credited for having done "what was right in the eyes of the Lord," neither destroyed the hill-shrines in the southern kingdom, where sacrifices continued to be slaughtered and burnt. Perhaps they reasoned that as long as they weren't engaging in the same types of sin as their northern neighbor then our God would be pleased in comparing. For their half-baked efforts, Amaziah was murdered in a conspiracy, and Azariah was struck with leprosy for the rest of his life.

Condemnation is ready for scoffers, and beating for the backs of fools. (Proverbs 19:29 ESV)

While traveling on the road to Glory, members will no doubt meet some former travelers who have decided to relax in the shade and enjoy their scintillating fruit. Others will have only recently joined them on the road. After sitting in the shade for so long, they are unable to walk for long periods of time without stumbling or falling. How tempting it is to shake our heads in disgust when no one on the road has reached their destination yet. Such an attitude does not come from a Messiah-centered heart. Messiah is unimpressed with those who have their feet on the road, but whose hearts are still rotten from their former fruit. When I see someone fall and all I do is stare, I am not yet there. With such an unhealthy heart, it won't be long before these members make their way back to the side of the road.

Let us therefore cease judging one another, but rather make this simple judgment: that no obstacle or stumbling-block be placed in a brother's way. (Romans 14:13 NEB)

For we all stumble in many ways. If someone does not stumble in what he says, he is a perfect individual, able to control the entire body as well. (James 3:2 NEB)

36. Fasting Forward

First read: Ezra 8:21-23

Movement is an essential element of your journey.

A simple statement, yes, but nonetheless, it is one that's worth repeating from time to time. For many on the road to Glory often find themselves stuck—not always in the mud, in a hole, or on the ground, but just stuck. While YHWH places people on the road and orchestrates situations that will occasionally propel us forward, he still ultimately desires that believers turn to him when moments arise where mobility seems like a dim possibility. Most of the time it's because members of the Body have become bloated from overindulgence. If there exists a daily spiritual struggle where the believer is having difficulty denying self, then fasting provides an opportunity to practice pruning.

It's embarrassing to admit that we find ourselves going to the Father with a wish list; filled with earthly wants, and with the expectation that he's to respond immediately. Our God is not a genie who, because we have found him, is now obligated to obey our every command. When our wishes are not granted, we often deduce that it's because he is either hard of hearing or that he isn't interested in our well-being. Such thinking will cause the committed Christian to begin stagnating in their spiritual walk. When the Body has become bloated it is necessary for members to hollow themselves in order that they might become hallowed. The process of becoming sanctified involves the believer coming to grips with the reality that our God is chiefly concerned with our spiritual well-being. He delights in his people who share his chief concern. There are situations that arise in the Church in which no earthly solution exists; a spiritual crisis requires Messiah. There is a spiritual crisis in the Church today, and of the multitudes who attest to believe, few are crying out to YHWH. Before Messiah began his journey, he spent forty days and nights in the wilderness, fasting and hollowing his body. It should not be forgotten that Moses did the same thing atop Mt. Sinai while recording YHWH Commandments, an act which should serve to remind all shepherds that a leader always leads by example.

And [YHWH] said to Moses, "Write these words, for in accordance with these words I have made a covenant with you and with Israel." So he was there with [YHWH] forty days and forty nights. He neither ate bread nor drank water. And he wrote on the tablets the words of the covenant, the Ten Commandments. (Exodus 34:27-28 NEB)

The similarity between Messiah and Moses is that both recognized the spiritual crisis that existed in their respective times, and through faith and obedience, both sacrificed in order to sanctify. The difference was that Moses initiated the process in pointing out sinful behavior. On the other hand, Yeshua was sent to fulfill the process through his death on the cross, and then, with the Father, sending the Holy Spirit. The hollowing of their bodies could lead to the hallowing of their people's.

For from his fullness we have all received, grace upon grace. For the law was given through Moses; grace and truth came through [Yeshua]. (John 1:16-17 NEB)

This Son of Man must be lifted up as the serpent was lifted up by Moses in the wilderness, so that everyone who has faith in him may in him possess eternal life. (John 3:15 NEB)

Fasting demonstrates to the Father, the believer's willingness to give up in order to gain more. Currently, there are those in the Body who have yet to understand what it means to go without; to them fasting is a foreign concept. However, all members should pay close attention to those who have fasted before them. Notice how the fasting never centered on getting YHWH to fulfill a selfish desire. Whether to remove an obstacle or to grant special favor, those who were successful in capturing YHWH's attention were those whose intentions were to see that everyone on the road moved ahead in their spiritual walk. Queen Esther acted upon this insight while concerned about the welfare of her own people living precariously in Persia.

Then Esther told them to reply to Mordecai, "Go, gather all the Jews to be found in Susa, and hold a fast on my behalf, and do not eat or drink for three days, night or day. I and my young women will also fast as you do. Then I will go to the king, though it is against the law, and if I perish, I perish." Mordecai then went away and did everything as Esther had ordered him. (Esther 4:15-17 NEB)

So to when you fast, do not look gloomy like the hypocrites: they make their faces unsightly so that other people may see that they are fasting. I tell you this: they have their reward already. But when you fast, anoint your head and wash your face, so that men may not see that you are fasting, but only your Father who is in the secret place; and your Father who sees what is secret will give you your reward. (Matthew 6:16-18 NEB)

37. Dismissed from Distrust

First read: 1st Kings 17:1-24

Can you hear in your ear the echoes...echoes of finite earth? You should, but not for too long. Focus on the deadness in life for too long and soon everything alive will look dead.

Our God did not give his people a pair of rose-colored glasses when he placed them on the road to Glory, and so none should walk baffled by the smell of rotting fruit; bewildered by the endless piles of broken tree limbs scattered throughout and on the sides of the dusty road; or befuddled over the darkness that daily engulfs the sun's rays and occasionally obstructs the traveler's vision. The glass is half full—true, but the other half is still rather empty. Believers need to acknowledge their perpetual thirst while focusing on filling the remainder of their glass with Living water, rather than feign contentment in settling for less than what the Father is yearning to give. Not only is the glass half empty, but the cracks are real—the ones you keep trying to conceal—and so what little water there is, is fast depleting. There is nothing wrong with Pollyanna, so long as Pollyanna can still see the pollution and is willing to help clean up.

But do not trust any and every spirit, my friends; test the spirits, to see whether they are from [YHWH], for among those who have gone out into the world there are many prophets falsely inspired. This is how we may recognize the spirit of [YHWH]: every spirit which acknowledges that [Yeshua] has come in the flesh is from [YHWH], and every spirit which does not thus acknowledge [Yeshua] is not from [YHWH]. This is what is meant by "Antichrist"; you have been told that he was to come, and here he is, in the world already. (1st John 4:1-3 NEB)

Nevertheless, Messiah doesn't demand that his sheep spend all their time and energy bemoaning their surroundings. There is danger in having our eyes focused on the failures and the fallen. With so much attention given to the degenerate, you will miss opportunities when our God wants to rejuvenate you. In truth, there are times when members will be renewed through their renewing of others. All should make efforts to ensure that such opportunities are never missed. Indeed the only reason a member could fail to see is if his vision was obstructed by wearing rose-colored glasses. But, what of those who are traveling with you? Our God is equally interested in your restoration while traveling and will use other believers to aid. So, then members must desist with distrusting those whom YHWH has sent to disentangle.

The incredulous widow of Zarephath struggled with believing that YHWH had sent Elijah because she found his instructions outlandish and his promises unlikely. She was not unlike many members of today's Body who would rather hold to their "reverential" beliefs of a God who is removed and solely transcendent, than to accept an immanent and hence, intimate Father who is daily concerned with the well-being of his people. It is clear that while the widow did comply, she wasn't convinced that Elijah wasn't a lie. YHWH blessed and yet she still needed another test. "Why are you really here?" These words never left her lips, yet they were etched on her heart. God listened and then he responded. It wasn't until Elijah revived her dead son to life that readers find these words upon her lips:

> And the woman said to Elijah, "Now I know that you are a man of [YHWH], and that the word of [YHWH] in your mouth is truth." (1st Kings 17:24 ESV)

Yeshua was dismissed because the Pharisees and Sadducees did not trust him. Some were not convinced until he showed them signs and wonders. And still others upon seeing such miracles claimed it was the work of the devil. Today, even those who profess to believe only believe in a Messiah from yesteryear, but they refuse to believe that the same Messiah, through the Holy Spirit, is still working and renewing today. What then is Yeshua to do with such a doubting generation? Are there those who have forgotten that the Son of YHWH was crucified, yes; died and was buried, yes; was resurrected from the grave, yes; and ascended into Heaven to sit at the right hand of his Father? Messiah is not dead, but alive. Hence, those who serve the Son, and are sent by the Son, are driven by the same living Spirit. Learn to discern so that those who doubt don't wind up without. Speaking to his disciples before sending them out, Yeshua says:

> To receive you is to receive me, and to receive me is to receive the One who sent me. Whoever receives a prophet as a prophet will be given a prophet's reward, and whoever receives a good man because he is a good man will be given a good man's reward. (Matthew 10:40-41 NEB)

38. Broken but Beautiful

First read: Isaiah 52-54

In looking around learn to see the beauty in your brokenness. The beauty from your brokenness will not be perfectly seen until you reach your destination. However, the beauty in your brokenness can be clearly seen while on your journey, but only through bringing the broken pieces together. Look around you and you can't help to see the broken. Don't look around too long or you'll become fixated on the brokenness. Remember too that you are not the only one on this journey. There are others around you whose strengths or weaknesses will be better suited for one "particular worn." You must also remember that while you were already in pieces when you started on your journey, you have contributed to the wears and tears. Nonetheless, never fixate on fixing. If you insist on waiting until you are fixed before deciding to help someone else, your contributions will be invisible to everyone else on the journey.

Isn't it breathtaking how Yeshua sees his tattered creation? We are torn and yet Messiah still claims us as his adoring Bride—broken, but beautiful:

Fear not, for you will not be ashamed; be not confounded, for you will not be disgraced; for you will forget the shame of your youth, and the reproach of your widowhood you will remember no more. For your Maker is your husband, [YHWH] is his name; and [Yeshua] of Israel is your Redeemer, the God of the whole earth he is called. For [YHWH] has called you like a wife deserted and grieved in spirit, like a wife of youth when she is cast off, says your God. (Isaiah 54:4-6 ESV)

In former generations this was not disclosed to the human race; but now it has been revealed by inspiration to his dedicated apostles and prophets, that through the Gospel the Gentiles are joint heirs with the Jews, part of the same body, sharers together in the promise made in [Yeshua]. (Ephesians 3:5-6 NEB)

The time is drawing near when the Jews will once again be grafted back into their native stock. Until then the Bride of Messiah is not fully dressed, though he loves us nonetheless. While our God works to mend their wounds, those wild olives that Messiah saved still have some growing to do. Yeshua the Son forsook his beauty to restore the broken, but only through breaking, himself. Hence, we are beautiful by virtue of his breaking, his blood, and his body. Those who are not yet members of the Church and therefore cannot see, remain unsightly looking in the eyes of Messiah (as once did we). Though even their features are less repulsive than are the redeemed who won't repent; who no longer give a second thought as to why the Son was sent. To them, a reminder from Messiah to the church at Ephesus:

Fortitude you have; you have borne up in my cause and never flagged. But I have this against you: you have lost your early love. Think from what a height you have fallen; repent, and do as you once did. Otherwise, if you do not repent, I shall come to you and remove your lamp from its place. (Revelation 2:3-4 NEB)

It is impossible to see the beauty in your brokenness when you are trying in vain to fix what YHWH has the power to do. Our human efforts look pretty hideous, and they only hinder our God's grace. Moreover, while it is important to acknowledge our role in the spreading of sin, Messiah does not want his Bride's maidens replaying or reprising the same old song time and time again.

I have blotted out your transgressions like a cloud and your sins like mist; return to me, for I have redeemed you. (Isaiah 44:22 ESV)

There are multitudes that need to receive wedding invitations. Focusing on our failures where Messiah has forgiven won't get the invitations out any faster. In fact, there are too many believers waiting for personal instructions to go out and invite. Messiah already commanded it before he ascended into Heaven, and the clock is still ticking.

During supper [Yeshua] took bread, and having said the blessing he broke it and gave it to the disciples with the words: "Take this and eat; this is my body." Then he took a cup, and having offered thanks to [YHWH] he gave it to them with the words: "Drink from it, all of you. For this is my blood, the blood of the covenant, shed for the forgiveness of sins." (Matthew 26:26-28 NEB)

In the same way that Messiah extended his broken body to his disciples in the Upper Room, we are to extend ours to the world, and shamelessly too. Messiah has equipped the broken pieces of his Body to share themselves with the world, so that in sharing those lost may be drawn to the Head, and receive the living bread; and drink of the beauty in the blood that was shed.

When after some days he returned to Capernaum, the news went round that he was at home; and such a crowd collected that the space in front of the door was not big enough to hold them. And while he was proclaiming the message to them, a man was brought who was paralyzed. Four men were carrying him, but because of the crowd they could not get him near. So they opened up the roof over the place where [Yeshua] was, and when they had broken through they lowered the stretcher on which the paralyzed man was lying. When [Yeshua] saw their faith, he said to the paralyzed man, "My son, your sins are forgiven." (Mark 2:1-5 NEB)

39. A Reflective Moment

Can I Serve?

First read: 2nd Timothy 2:20-21

Therefore, friends, look out seven men of good reputation from your number, men full of the Spirit and of wisdom, and we will appoint them to deal with these matters, while we devote ourselves to prayer and to the ministry of the Word. This proposal proved acceptable to the whole body. They elected Stephen, a man full of faith and of the Holy Spirit, Philip, Prochorus, Nicanor, Timon, Parmenas, and Nicolas of Antioch, a former convert to Judaism. These they presented to the apostles, who prayed and laid their hands on them. (Acts 6:3-6 NEB)

What does it take to be a servant of Christ? There are many who err in their understanding of the requirements for Christian servant-hood. At one extreme is the view that Messiah demands a perfected rather than a perfecting soul. These are members of the Body who believe that their inadequacy lies in their brokenness, instead of realizing that it is their brokenness which makes them equipped to aid in the repairing of others broken. For the call of the Christian is to spend all allotted earthly time helping others to restore themselves unto our God. While each is at work helping others to restore, YHWH is restoring them. Messiah made this a possible goal and members of the Body have the responsibility of making it a plausible one.

The other extreme suggests that Yeshua, in recognizing that all of his creation is sinful by default (or more precisely—by the fall), understands our disobedient nature, and is willing to allow us to serve him while we are still actively engaging in sinful behavior. In other words, YHWH endorses the serving sinner. The problems with this view are manifold. First, as previously mentioned, while our God understands our struggle with sin due to man's original act of disobedience in the Garden of Eden, he does not accept continual and consistent defiance of his commandments. Messiah was sent to earth to deliver man not only from the clutches of death (for death is merely the end result), he was also sent to deliver man from the source of death, which is sin. Second, while it is possible to serve while sinning, Christians need to realize that while doing so, the god they are serving is not the God of creation. So what does it take to be a servant of Christ? It takes a believer who is willing to submit their entire being—mind, body, and soul. Trying to serve Messiah without complete submission to him is like trying to take an unfamiliar long distance road trip with no map, no money, and half a tank of gas. You won't get very far and the distance you are able to travel will bring with it trepidation and uncertainty. So what does submission look like? Submission may take on various forms depending on the situation and the players involved. However, ultimately one must surrender self; less emphasis on "I" and more on him; less focusing on "me" and more on them.

And again, the Father does not judge anyone, but has given full jurisdiction to the Son; it is his will that all should pay the same honor to the Son as to the Father. To deny honor to the Son is to deny it to the Father who sent him. (John 5:22-23 NEB)

Each of us must consider his neighbor and think of what is for his good and will build up the common life. For [Messiah] too did not consider himself, but might have said, in the words of Scripture, "The reproaches of those who reproached thee fell upon me." (Romans 15:2-3 NEB)

Finally, a servant of Messiah must always be observant of his commandments; but not just observant, obedient. No matter how many hours a Christian is sacrificing to support a worthy cause, all service is considered worthless if when off the clock, the servant is sinning. And perhaps that's just it. Whether awake or asleep, in the presence of many or none, we're always in the presence of One. As such, the Christian servant is never off the clock. While serving Messiah will bring with it moments of pure joy, members of the Body should not count it accidental when brief bouts of suffering ensue. Instead, those members more mature should embrace and encourage the fainthearted and remind one another that we serve a benevolent Master who promises that our labor is never in vain. Can you serve? Messiah says you can. Will you?

He who thus shows himself a servant of [Messiah] is acceptable to [YHWH] and approved by men. (Romans 14:18 NEB)

The language of ecstasy is good for the speaker himself, but it is prophecy that builds up a Christian community. I should be pleased for you all to use the tongues of ecstasy, but better pleased for you to prophesy. The prophet is worth more than the man of ecstatic speech—unless indeed he can explain its meaning, and so help to build up the community. (1st Corinthians 14:4-5 NEB)

My brothers, whenever you have to face trials of many kinds, count yourselves supremely happy, in the knowledge that such testing of your faith breeds fortitude, and if you give fortitude full play you will go on to complete a balanced character that will fall short in nothing. (James 1:2-4 ESV)

40. Fixing Friends

First read: Job 3-8

If in vain you aim to fix what, in fact, you didn't break, you have no one but yourself to blame for the bigger mess you'll make.

As he went on his way [Yeshua] saw a man blind from birth. His disciples put the question, "Rabbi, who sinned, this man or his parents? Why was he born blind?" "It is not that this man or his parents sinned," [Yeshua] answered; "he was born blind so that [YHWH]'s power might be displayed in curing him. While daylight lasts we must carry on the work of him who sent me; night comes, when no one can work. While I am in the world I am the light of the world." With these words he spat on the ground and made a paste with the spittle; he spread it on the man's eyes, and said to him, "Go and wash in the pool of Siloam." (The name means "sent.") The man went away and washed, and when he returned he could see. (John 9:1-7 NEB)

How noble is the friend who wants to end the plight of his brother or sister. It is the Messiah-centered heart filled with compassion, which cringes at the sight of another's suffering. Messiah is pleased, as is the Father, when the Body seeks to ensure that her fellow members remain secure. Only, each should exercise caution when delivering words of wisdom. Even the well-meaning Christian can err when approaching a suffering soul with the intention of fixing what is obviously a broken vessel. First, always remember that there is nothing we can do to fix anybody else because we aren't the manufacturers. Only our God can fix his people, and the Father made such possible by sending his Son, Yeshua Messiah, to bleed on the cross. Messiah's blood is the only paste capable of permanently binding the broken, no matter the size or condition. And it's the Holy Spirit who seals what Messiah has healed. All other attempts at fixing merely resemble a broken piece of pottery whose pieces are held loosely together with scotch tape; one small misstep and…. Messiah's paste was freely given, but it is up to members of his Body to help one another come together and to stay together. Speaking to the church in Ephesus, the Apostle Paul reminds its members:

You are built upon the foundation laid by the apostles and prophets, and [Yeshua] himself is the foundation-stone. In him the whole building is bonded together and grows into a holy temple in [Yeshua]. In him you too are being built with all the rest into a spiritual dwelling for [YHWH]. (Ephesians 2:20-22 NEB)

Second, although the robe of righteousness, saturated with the blood of the Son, is capable of fitting all sanctifying members no matter their size, not all can put it on the same way. Each vessel is broken differently, intentionally. Therefore, when attempting to aid another in their plight, make sure to recognize the uniqueness of their fractures. Yeshua did not have a batch of cookies in mind when he decided to make man in his own image, so no cookie cutter should be used when attempting to repair the broken. Thus Eliphaz and Bildad only frustrated Job more when both insisted that YHWH would restore Job only after he repented of his unrighteousness.

> Behold, blessed is the one whom [YHWH] reproves; therefore despise not the discipline of the Spirit. Although wounding, there is binding; while shattering, there are healing hands. (Job 5:17-18 ESV)

> While yet in flower and not cut down, they wither before any other plant. Such are the paths of all who forget [YHWH]; the hope of the godless shall perish. (Job 8:12-13 ESV)

It isn't that Eliphaz or Bildad gave Job bad advice or misinformation. Eliphaz provided Job with information that believers can find in Hebrews 12:5. None should reject YHWH's discipline. And YHWH would eventually heal Job's wounds. However, Job, at this point, was not being rebuked by YHWH. Bildad's metaphor of the godless and the withering flower is accurate. During his earthly ministry, Messiah would use similar metaphors in describing the fate of the unfaithful. Yet, Job's withering condition resulted not from his forgetting his God. While quite appropriate for the wayward walker, their cookie-cutter comments did not fit the specific circumstances of Job. Carefully examine the believer's walk before predicating on their predicament, and don't rule out the possibility that YHWH may desire that you do nothing more than console the suffering while they suffer. It is dangerous to assume and then to act on the assumption that only the sinful suffer at the hands of our God. Doubting begins when knowing ends. He who walks with YHWH should never base his place on the suspicions of another. The suffering saint is only a conundrum to those who have yet to identify fully with the process of sanctification.

> We are [YHWH]'s heirs and [Messiah's] fellow-heirs, if we share his sufferings now in order to share his splendor hereafter. For I reckon that the sufferings we now endure bear no comparison with the splendor, as yet revealed, which is in store for us. (Romans 8:17-18 NEB)

> If you suffer, it must not be for murder, theft, or sorcery, nor for infringing the rights of others. But if anyone suffers as a Christian, he should feel it no disgrace, but confess that name to the honor of [Yeshua]. (1st Peter 4:15-16 NEB)

41. Whistle While You Work

First read: 2nd Thessalonians 2:6-12

Somewhere earlier on your journey you were told by someone wise that you couldn't help repair somebody else while you were still broken. A fool lied to you somewhere earlier on your journey. Don't go back to the same fool asking why. You will get a foolish response. Keep walking and learn how to spot a fool before they open their mouth. It may be difficult for you now, but keep walking and you'll pass by several fools, and hopefully, you'll keep walking. Otherwise, look around for too long and you'll try to take it all in. Look around for too long and you'll start listening to everyone you're looking at. Look around for too long and you'll start believing everything you hear. Look around for too long and you'll start believing foolish talk. Look around for too long and you will start imitating foolish behavior. Look around for too long and before too long you will find yourself on the ground—looking up, down, and all-around—looking like a fool.

[Yeshua] replied, "My kingdom does not belong to this world. If it did, my followers would be fighting to save me from arrest by the Jews. My kingly authority comes from elsewhere." (John 18:36 NEB)

An idle brain is the devil's playground. And idle hands are tools used for destroying, rather than rebuilding the Church, which is what the Holy Spirit is reminding members of the Body to partake in. As stated before, Messiah does not expect his servants to be inactive. One of the many problems facing the Body is the inability of its members to grasp what it is that Messiah expects for them to do while on this earth. One thing is for certain—sleeping while on the job is a sure way to get the Enemy's attention:

Wherever the corpse is, there the vultures will gather. (Matthew 24:28 NEB)

Answering the call of Messiah and returning to his fold is perhaps our most important job on this earth, but it is not the only task given to the Church. While there does exist a multitude of tasks in which the Christian servant is to engage, they all can be divided into three primary categories: Serving Messiah, reflecting Messiah, and sharing Messiah. Serving Messiah first requires our acknowledging his sovereignty over the Church.

He put everything in subjection beneath his feet, and appointed him as supreme head to the Church, which is his body and as such holds within it the fullness of him who himself receives the entire fullness of [YHWH]. (Ephesians 1:22-23 NEB)

The Father has bestowed onto Messiah the honor of being the Head of his household. As such, he has equally employed him with the task of getting his house back in order. We know that Messiah's first mission in completing his task was to die on the cross; laying the foundation on which the rest of his house might stand firm. However, it should be remembered that Messiah wasn't just born to die. No, Messiah walked the earth for a little over three years in order to instruct and to train in the truth those who would replace him—not as Savior, but as carpenters. After salvation, servants should begin maturing, that is, through sanctification with the Holy Spirit's aid. In the course of our service to Messiah, we are steadily growing into members fit for service; in hopes that through restoring we are more clearly reflecting his image.

> From first to last this has been the work of [YHWH]. He has reconciled us men to himself through [Messiah], and he has enlisted us in his service of reconciliation. What I mean is, that [YHWH] was in [Messiah] reconciling the world to himself, no longer holding men's misdeeds against them, and that he has entrusted us with the message of reconciliation to [YHWH]. [Messiah] was innocent of sin, and yet for our sake [YHWH] made him one with the sinfulness of men, so that in him we might be made one with the goodness of [YHWH] himself. (2nd Corinthians 5:18-21 NEB)

It is also true that we are each called to the position of ambassador. The primary function of an ambassador is to represent the position of his or her homeland while an envoy in another country. It's really rather simple. As Christians, this world is not our home—we are citizens of Heaven. It is imperative that while on earth we not misrepresent the interests of Messiah, whom the Father has made ruler of both Heaven and earth. Our words, our actions, our thoughts—all must align with the desires of Yeshua. Currently, this is the task the Church is struggling with the most, which, in turn, inhibits members from carrying out their other functions.

> So [Yeshua] continued, "You belong to this world below, I to the world above. Your home is in this world, mine is not. That is why I told you that you would die in your sins. If you do not believe that I am what I am, you will die in your sins." (John 8:23-24 NEB)

> In very truth I tell you, if anyone obeys my teaching he shall never know what it is to die. (John 8:51 NEB)

And this our most joyous charge: to share Messiah and the message of his Gospel. But, how enthusiastically can one share whom they barely know themselves?

> I have spoken thus to you, so that my joy may be in you, and your joy complete. This is my commandment: love one another, as I have loved you. There is no greater love than this, that a man should lay down his life for his friends. You are my friends, if you do what I command you. (John 15:11-15 NEB)

If we love our neighbors as Messiah commands us, flocks of his sheep should seek to bring others into the fold so that they too may experience eternal life. The house we are to rebuild is made up of both wood and glass. Messiah already took care of laying and sealing the foundation with nails and blood. With every ounce of energy remaining we are to continue building where the early disciples stopped. When Messiah returns he expects to see his servants still working and for considerable progress to have been made. Only when we reach the gates of Glory will we see the finished product. What a glorious day we shall see when finally we are able to see ourselves—perfectly reflected through the casting of the Son's light.

I saw no temple in the city; for its temple was the sovereign God and the Lamb. And the city had no need of sun or moon to shine upon it; for the glory of [YHWH] gave it light, and its lamp was the Lamb. By its light shall the nation walk, and the kings of the earth shall bring into it all their splendor. (Revelation 21:22-24 NEB)

42. Purposefully In Pieces

First read: 2nd Chronicles 3-5:1

Are you puzzled? Good. In the long run you'll be glad that you were. Because, in pieces is the only way you can help someone else who is broken. And in pieces is the only way a puzzle can come together. Don't fear not fitting in. What is even more puzzling is how puzzle pieces fit, not in spite of, but because of their similarities and differences. What is similar about a puzzle is that every single piece is broken. Puzzle pieces fit because they come already broken. You'll fit right in. What is different in a puzzle is every single broken piece. No two pieces are exactly the same, no matter how similar any of them may look. Each piece, in their brokenness, was beautifully crafted to one day reflect the beauty of the whole craft. Each piece was crafted differently, intentionally. In your brokenness you too were crafted to one day reflect the beauty of the whole craft, and in doing so, perfectly reflect the beauty of the Crafter.

Yeshua's temple began in pieces but ended whole so that he who is holy could dwell therein. YHWH had a plan but trusted David to handle the details of its execution. From the porches and doorways to the vessels and lamp-stands, our God had a plan. From the tables and tossing-bowls to the cherubim and the altar, our God had a purpose. Though varied in make-up, all the pieces used in creating the temple had at least one thing in common; they each were designed specifically and purposefully for YHWH. Not one was an afterthought, mistake, or left over from some other project. It is impossible to rebuild YHWH's temple without first ensuring that certain conditions have been met. To begin building they need builders. Make no mistake—he only needs builders by choice. Father, in his sovereignty and omnipotence, could have crafted a temple capable of constructing itself or could have simply spoken and extended the work week by creating his temple so he could have a place to rest on the Sabbath, which would then have been the eighth day. But, it was his will to use his creation in creating. Second, for our God's purpose he needs not the perfected pawn, but the disciplined disciple. What need would a "perfect" builder have in relying on his co-workers for help, or still yet, what need would he have in seeking wisdom from the Crafter if he could do it by himself? It is our God's purpose that we pray so that none will stray.

The end of all things is upon us, so you must lead an ordered and sober life, given to prayer. Above all, keep your love for one another at full strength, because love cancels innumerable sins. Be hospitable to one another without complaining. Whatever gift each of you may have received, use it in service to one another, like good stewards dispensing the grace of [YHWH] in its varied forms. Are you a speaker? Speak as if you uttered oracles of [YHWH]. Do you give service? Give it as in the strength which [YHWH] supplies. In all things so act that the glory may be [YHWH]'s through [Yeshua]; to him belong glory and power for ever and ever. Amen. (1st Peter 4:7-11 NEB)

Third, YHWH needs every piece of his temple to come together in order to reflect the whole. He already has some committed builders whom he continues to take delight in, yet he desires that others begin stepping up to the plate before it is too late. However, there is concern over the number of vessels who refuse to acknowledge their brokenness.

Then he said to them, "Suppose one of you has a friend who comes to him in the middle of the night and says, 'My friend, lend me three loaves, for a friend of mine on a journey has turned up at my house, and I have nothing to offer him'; and he replies from inside, 'Do not bother me. The door is shut for the night; my children and I have gone to bed; and I cannot get up and give you what you want.' I tell you that even if he will not provide for him out of friendship, the very shamelessness of the request will make him get up and give him all he needs." (Luke 11:5-8 NEB)

As long as persons are already "whole" they shall never see holiness. YHWH cannot dwell among the unholy because he is wholly unacceptable to them. His people are in pieces purposely designed to connect with one another intimately. No piece already whole is capable of fitting in with the rest because every single piece is in pieces. Believers need to pray for peace and ask YHWH to grant them the courage to connect, which is impossible to do while their brokenness is concealed.

For a man's ways are before the eyes of [Yeshua], and he ponders all his paths. (Proverbs 5:21 ESV)

Here and now, dear friends, we are [YHWH]'s children; what we shall be has not yet been disclosed, but we know that when it is disclosed we shall be like him, because we shall see him as he is. Everyone who has this hope before him purifies himself, as [Yeshua] is pure. (1st John 3:2-3 NEB)

Members of the Body would do well to remember that nothing is hidden from YHWH, including what many would rather not reveal. It is not his desire to stay removed, but he can't reside in what so many choose to hide—themselves. The temple of YHWH is both an individual as well as a corporate dwelling place. The Holy Spirit desires to abide in each believer, while simultaneously abiding in the Body. The re-building of both requires the assistance of all. Every believer should assist one another by being real with each other, in realizing that the Holy Spirit can't dwell where deceit lives—it's too dark.

When [Yeshua] came to the place, he looked up and said, "Zacchaeus, be quick and come down; I must come and stay with you today. He climbed down as fast as he could and welcomed him gladly. At this there was a general murmur of disapproval. "He has gone in, they said, "to be the guest of a sinner." But Zacchaeus stood there and said to [Yeshua], "Here and now, sir, I give half my possessions to charity; and if I have cheated anyone, I am ready to repay him four times over." [Yeshua] said to him, "Salvation has come to this house today.—for this man, too, is a son of Abraham, and the Son of Man has come to seek and save what is lost." (Luke 19:5-10 NEB)

Finally, all must commit to reject none that they see. Instead, focus on the fact that what will be, will be beautiful. Nevertheless, in focusing on the future, don't neglect what's in front. While none will look pleasant, none should forget the condition they were in when YHWH first invited them into his presence. Yeshua wants holy servants who will follow him wholly, but the only ones who are invited to serve are the ones with the nerve to come to him in pieces.

> Later, when he went out, he saw a tax-gatherer, Levi by name, at his seat in the custom-house, and said to him, "Follow me." And he rose to his feet, left everything behind, and followed him. Afterwards Levi held a big reception in his house for [Yeshua]; among the guests was a large party of tax-gatherers and others. The Pharisees and the lawyers of their sect complained to his disciples: "Why do you eat and drink," they said, "with tax-gatherers and sinners?" [[Yeshua]] answered them: "It is not the healthy that need a doctor, but the sick; I have not come to invite virtuous people, but to call sinners to repentance." (Luke 5:27-32 NEB)

43. The Road of Restoring

First read: Nehemiah 1-3

In your brokenness don't look to fix or to get fixed because both are impossible pursuits while on this earth. Instead, prepare to repair and in repairing you too shall be repaired. Moreover, through reparations you are making preparations for the end of this journey and for the beginning of the next. But, be cognizant of the time. The only step necessary to take before you can aid in the repairing of another is to acknowledge that you too need repairing. In doing as much you are recognizing that you need restoring, not fixing. A call for restoration acknowledges the role you played in the deterioration process—yours and others—and requires you to engage in the discomforting refining process that is necessary before completion. In traveling, you are both on the road of restoring, as well as on the road to restoration. This road may require some refining, but it will not require any redesigning. While on your journey expect to be refined and to aid in the refining of others; but, leave the redesigning to the Designer.

You will discover another striking similarity between Yeshua and his followers while traveling the road to Glory. Like Messiah's, our journey has as its aim, to restore; Messiah walked to restore his younger siblings to the Father. It is vital that as members are traveling, they do not have as their goal to fix anyone—themselves or others. The problem is sin, and no human being alive can fix sin. Messiah died so that soon sin would one day die too. But until then, his death means that we can die daily to the sin still lodged within:

> Wherever we go we carry death with us in our body, the death that [Yeshua] died, that in this body also life may reveal itself, the life that [Yeshua] lives. For continually, while still alive, we are being surrendered into the hands of death, for [Yeshua] sake, so that the life of [Yeshua] also may be revealed in this mortal body of ours. Thus death is at work in us, and life in you. (2nd Corinthians 4:10-12 NEB)

Death is not pleasant but none should hesitate to crucify "self" because "self" isn't invited into the Kingdom. There are too many hesitant because there are too many hypocrites. How unfair that the Pharisees should continue parading inside the Church. It seems that many have been indulging in their leaven. Perfection is not a necessity to reach the gates of Heaven. It is foolery for anyone to think that Messiah will not use anyone unless they glisten; though by the end of this journey you shall. Still, Messiah does expect each believer to partake in the perfecting process and to accept both the painful, as well as the pleasurable experiences that accompany. Expect them and then accept them.

> So he came and proclaimed the good news: peace to you who were far off, and peace to those who were near by; for through him we both alike have access to the Father in the one Spirit. Thus you are no longer aliens in a foreign land,

but fellow-citizens with [YHWH]'s people, members of [YHWH]'s household. (Ephesians 2:17-19 NEB)

Around 445 B. C. Nehemiah was given the task of leading the Israelites in rebuilding decimated Jerusalem. In the opening chapters it is clear that this was no one-man job. Nehemiah relied upon the talents from all those present to work faithfully. Though no one working was directly responsible for the destruction of Jerusalem, all recognized that it was their sinful behavior that initiated the process. However, only after repenting did YHWH allow them to revive.

44. A Woman of Worth: Abigail

First read: 1st Samuel 25:1-40

Beauty is in the eye and ear of the beholder. When looking at the darkness in others, make sure you can still see and hear. It's difficult to see or hear anything in a crowded space. When your head gets too crowded with hate, it will close, but lose the crowd and you'll once again be open for business.

Isn't it funny how we find ourselves placing ridiculous stereotypes on members of both sexes? We say that men are thinking creatures. Women, on the other hand, are feeling creatures. Men are more rational, while woman are more emotional. The truthfulness of such observations depends upon geographic location as well as the environmental conditions in which said men and women have been raised. But, comments that resemble those stated above not only stifle individuality for those in the world, they also limit the roles that each could perform for the greater good of Messiah's Body. Yeshua did create men and women distinctly with unique attributes that serve to complement one another in the areas of marriage and parenting, as well as in the ministry. However, too often will man pen to one what Yeshua created in both. He gifted both sexes with the ability to reason, as well as to experience and convey emotion. Equally true is that given free-will, coupled with the capacity to yield to lesser natures, both sexes can display either ability in its perfecting or per-verted states. It's a choice between daily reflecting the fresh fruits of the Holy Spirit, or by default, the fleshly fruits.

Live as people who are free, not using your freedom as a cover-up for evil, but living as servant's of [YHWH]. (1st Peter 2:16 ESV)

We find in 1st Samuel a woman of worth, gifted with good sense and sent by YHWH to temper David who, in rashness, would have murdered her husband, Nabal. Abigail doesn't often stand out as a figure that Christians have come to em-brace as a symbol of righteousness. If given the chance to rank the most influential Biblical characters, Abigail probably would not make anyone's top ten. Yet, her actions—bowing in boldness—strike at the heart of the Christian servant. Finding strength in submission is a challenge for many in the Body and Abigail's efforts were not unrewarded.

How blest are those of a gentle spirit; they shall have the earth for their pos-session. (Matthew 5:5 NEB)

There is no quicker route to hell than by fanning its flames in fury while in the midst of anger. When emotions run high it is time to lay low. Even the seasoned believer should get into the habit of daily asking to be filled with the Holy Spirit. In this account, David demonstrates how easily a godly man can quickly go from righ-teous to outrageous if left malnourished. Yeshua understood that harboring such ha-tred and anger toward any other could lead to spiritual blindness. When filled with such perversion it is difficult for the servant to see the possibilities in their offender. It isn't that our God is blind, and so doesn't see the ills of his people; it is that our job is to kindle a fire; admittedly, not always a simple task when we have been burned. Where the fire lands is the prerogative of the Father. In the Gospels, Yeshua reminds his followers what the penalty is for aiming at any place other than the heart.

> You have learned that our forefathers were told, "Do not commit murder; anyone who commits murder must be brought to judgment." But what I tell you is this: Anyone who nurses anger against his brother must be brought to judgment. If he abuses his brother he must answer for it to the court; if he sneers at him, he will have to answer for it in the fires of hell." (Matthew 5:21-22 NEB)

Fortunately for David, Abigail's reasoning skills proved life-saving. There is little doubt that David's hastiness would have been viewed unfavorably by our God, and might have cost him the crown. Instead, in his goodness, YHWH stirred a woman to win the heart of his servant by humbling him through the power of humility.

> For whoever exalts himself will be humbled; and he who humbles himself will be exalted. (Luke 14:11 NEB)

45. Beauty and the Beast

First read: 2nd Samuel 13:1-39

Yes, behold the beauty of those around you, but not for too long. For if you behold the beauty of another for too long, you will soon go blind. Blindness may hinder your movement. Movement is an essential element of your journey. Your eyesight is already less than perfect and you want to make sure that you can see clearly, the fruits in the trees and the fruits on the flowers.

There is quite a bit to take in while walking on the road to Glory. It's impossible to walk a short distance without coming across something or someone pleasing to the eye. And there is nothing wrong with looking at the beauty that is in Yeshua's creation. It is not necessary to close your eyes as if what you are looking at is a figment of your imagination. Moreover, all that which is poisonous is off to the side of the road, rather than on it. You will have people walking next to, in front of, or behind you, on the same journey, whose beauty you'll find breathtaking. Relax. Breathe. Messiah is not going to condemn those who admire his creation. There are those in the Body who think it essential to separate themselves from all who "might tempt." No, believers need to learn to discern. Stop fearing the flesh and start focusing on their fruit. If what they are producing is fit for the Father and acceptable to the Son then it will benefit the entire Body, that is, everyone. However, if your eyes remain closed out of fear of falling then you will never receive what Messiah would have for you.

> In the same way, a good tree always yields good fruit, and a poor tree bad fruit. A good tree cannot bear bad fruit, or a poor tree good fruit. (Matthew 7:17-18 NEB)

Nevertheless, a word to the wise: Breathtaking beauty may take your last breath. It was Amnon's desires which led to his death. After beholding the beauty of his half-sister, Tamar, Amnon made the decision to pervert what our God intended pure. His sinful actions, like many within the Body, had long-term consequences that were not immediately apparent. At her father's request Tamar obediently went to Amnon's chambers where she faithfully served, despite his maleficent intent. It is possible that YHWH could have used Tamar's servant heart to altar her brother's purpose and maybe he would have repented of his lust. But, in choosing to stare at the flesh, Amnon could no longer see her fruit, and in his blindness he resorted to beast. There are many in the Body who, in forgetting that they were made in the image of Yeshua, regularly resort to beast. "But I can't help myself and I know the limits of my flesh. So to keep from resorting to beast it is best that I keep away." Sounds noble doesn't it? The problem is that the problem hasn't left—just you. Remember the words of the Apostle Paul:

> Stand up to the devil and he will turn and run. Come close to [YHWH], and he will come close to you. (James 4:7 NEB)

If temptation is the issue, consider the source. Indeed, there will appear those fruits on the side of the road that tantalize, scintillate, and are from Satan. Speak out in faith, rather than in fear, while reminding Satan that you serve only one master and are not interested in his illusions. Watch how the fruits wither and fade while there in the shade and then keep walking. A fellow traveler may catch your eye, only they are not the ones enticing. In those moments when you would rather flee, ask YHWH instead to help you see. The fellow traveler may bear fruit that will aid in your journey. Cease with foolish thinking, for the beauty of one does not guarantee that a beast will come out of another. Those who walk in the flesh focus on the flesh and will find themselves floundering in their faith. Yet, the mature member understands that even while still in the flesh, we walk in the Spirit, who is forever taming our hearts and our minds.

It follows, my friends, that our lower nature has no claim upon us; we are not obliged to live on that level. If you do so, you must die. But if by the Spirit you put to death all the base pursuits of the body, then you will live. (Romans 8:12-13 NEB)

46. Where Did I Go Wrong?

First read: 1st Kings-2nd Kings

In looking at the trees and then at the flowers, perhaps you think it strange how the former are taller and the latter are shorter, though both still get sun and rain. But don't look for too long at the differences in height, for growth can only be measured by the fruit that each produce. However, don't think it strange or slightly unfair when you see that few will bear fruit while most will stay bare. Both were planted in the same ground. Both were given rain and sun. Yet, some grew to bear delicious fruit; others grew to bear none. In recognizing the fruits in both the trees and flowers you will come to realize that the Gardner doesn't play favorites after all.

Imagine a parent who raises an entire household of children; treats each fairly, though not equally; and showers them all with love. Yet, despite all efforts, many choose a life of destruction, while only a few continue to walk the path set rightly before them. There are parents in the Body who can attest to having had such experiences. Grief often accompanies, as they struggle to look in the mirror and not see the reflection of a failure. "Where did I go wrong?" or, "What could I have done differently?" they ask. While there are individual circumstances that warrant recognition of admitted mistakes, parents mustn't always assume that they're the ones who took a wrong turn.

A foolish son is a grief to his father and bitterness to her who bore him. (Proverbs 17:25 ESV)

As a parent who chose to endow his children with choice, our heavenly Father understands disappointment. Even before the creation of man, YHWH first had to watch as a third of his elder creation, the angels, choose to give up their home in heaven. They were the first to exchange an eternity of righteousness for an eternity of rebellion. At the prompting of those already fallen, man chose to follow suit. What more could a son or daughter have asked for than what their Father had blessed them with in the Garden of Eden? Yes, they had the animals and the leaves; the fruit off the trees. But nothing could have been more delightful than their dwelling with the living God. Nothing should have been, but there was. And when man made his choice, YHWH responded in kind. What believers must remember is that our God's response was indeed kind, because rather than permanent banishment from his presence (like the fallen angels who tempted), man was offered redemption.

Remember too the angels, how some of them were not content to keep the dominion given to them but abandoned their proper home; and [YHWH] has reserved them for judgment on the great Day, bound beneath the darkness in everlasting chains. (Jude 1:6 NEB)

Though expelled from the Garden of Eden, man was placed on the road to Glory in hopes that the prodigal son might one day soon become reunited with his Father. The story of the Tanakh is one illustrating man's failed attempts at staying on the road and the bruises incurred, resulting from their wayward walking. As an extension of his patience and kindness, the Father sent his only Son—not to make the path smoother, but to make it visible. There is a catch, however: The Father's children still have a choice. The kings of Israel were all placed on the same path and albeit imperfect, each had a model in King David that could have been emulated. Yet, the books of Kings indicate that out of twenty rulers from the southern kingdom of Judah, only eight did what was right in the eyes of Yeshua, and two of them, Joash and Josiah were just seven and eight-years-old, respectively, when they ascended to the throne. What of the other twelve? Did their later rebellion against YHWH indicate that somewhere earlier our God had gone wrong? Of course not. YHWH is a perfect parent who allows his children to make less than perfect choices. Their choices are a reflection of their own character, not his. The Father's desire is that his children develop the character of Messiah, who is, himself, a perfect reflection of the Father. Parents obedient to Scripture will raise their children in the way of Yeshua. However, the child who has grown, although he has known, must choose to continue knowing, and he must choose to keep going.

Fathers, do not exasperate your children, for fear they grow disheartened. (Colossians 3:21 NEB)

Therefore, since we are surrounded by such a great cloud of witnesses, we must get rid of every weight and the sin that clings so closely, and run with endurance the race set out for us, keeping our eyes fixed on [Yeshua], the pioneer and perfecter of our faith. For the joy set out for him he endured the cross, disregarding its shame, and has taken his seat at the right hand of the throne of [YHWH]. Think of him who endured such opposition against himself by sinners, so that you may not grow weary in your souls and give up. (Hebrews 12:1-3 NEB)

47. Why the Wicked Win

First read: Job 21

As you hear in your ear the echoes...echoes of finite earth, remember not to focus on its deadness for too long, or soon you too will find yourself deaf.

Honor and dishonor, praise and blame, are alike our lot: we are the imposters who speak the truth, the unknown men whom all men know; dying we still live on; disciplined by suffering, we are not done to death; in our sorrows we have always cause for joy; poor ourselves, we bring wealth to many; penniless, we own the world. (2nd Corinthians 6:8-10 NEB)

Why do the wicked win? They don't. At times it only seems that they do to the suffering saint—at least here in this world. But, then therein lies the problem. To the suffering saint what do the wicked seem to win? The book of Job focuses on what the rest of us who are sanctifying tend to focus on in determining the winners and losers; the posh versus the impoverished. However, it is not the case that the wealthy are all winners in YHWH's eyes. Believers must remember that for the present, wickedness rules this world and therefore the wicked will continue to win; though not always and not forever. It is vital that the suffering saint not fixate on the diamonds of the dead, lest he begin cursing the Author of life. Remember too, that Satan tempted Yeshua with wealth while he walked in the wilderness:

Once again, the devil took him to a very high mountain, and showed him all the kingdoms of the world in their glory. "All these," he said, "I will give you, if you will only fall down and do me homage." (Matthew 4:8 NEB)

So, for the time being the devil has the power to enhance all who will give him the chance. There is no better way for the devil to keep the dead in their grave then by convincing them that all of their diamonds are a reward for their goodness. The "good" will stay in the grave only to rise shortly to an eternity of suffering. On the other hand, the righteous, made right by the blood of Messiah, will suffer toward sanctification, but shortly will ascend to an eternity of splendor. When saints suffer it is not a sign that they have lost, but a reminder that Messiah has won.

To those who pursue glory, honor, and immortality by steady persistence in well-doing, he will give eternal life; but for those who are governed by self-ish-ambition, who refuse obedience to the truth and take the wrong for their guide, there will be the fury of retribution. There will be trouble and distress for every human being who is an evil-doer, for the Jew first and for the Greek also; and for every well-doer there will be glory, honor, and peace, for the Jew first and also for the Greek. (Romans 2:7-10 NEB)

How quickly we compare when "life isn't fair." But, believers must remember that our God has a method, and getting mad over what is difficult or presently impossible to understand won't for a second change his plans, nor will it alter his disposition. YHWH tolerated the sinner who became a saint and for the present he shall continue in his tolerance. So it is less that the wicked are winning and more that the Father continues to patiently wait. It is not for the believer to contemplate over whom the Father shall condemn, nor should any decide on whom he should. Messiah would condemn none if he could. Unfortunately, there exists those whose souls won't break; whose hearts are in love with the money they make; whose lips are as toxic as the smiles they fake; whose hands are like daggers with the lives they take; whose minds are depraved whether sleep or awake. In the very end, the wicked who sin won't win. But the saint who suffers must refrain from asserting as much, before he can no longer discern our God's hand and the devil's touch.

48. Living Out Loud: The Spirit Filled Church I

First read: Acts 13:8-12

As you are walking on your journey and looking around, you may miss a fruit here or there that is falling from a live tree. But, in deafness, you won't hear it hit the ground and you just may go hungry. The fruits up high and the fruits down low are not the same, but still—both will soon fall to earth, and both can hurt or heal. You want to make sure you can tell the difference. Somewhere earlier on your journey someone wise told you that what was on the outside didn't matter. A fool lied to you somewhere on your journey and you passed him about ten miles ago. He was by the side of the road, passed out with some half-eaten piece of fruit rotting by his side. In finding good fruit, turn to their hearts—for here is where the rotting starts. But, it ends on the outside. Don't be foolish. What's rotten on the outside was rotting on the inside. You don't need to look too long. Look too long at the rotten and soon what's fresh will be forgotten. Look too long at the rotten and soon you'll be tempted when you see it. Look too long at the rotten, you'll soon grow hungry and soon you'll eat it. Eat too long what's rotten and soon you too will be left out to rot. Self-inflicted rotting? Two words. Hot. Rancid.

However, when the Spirit of truth comes, you will be guided into all the truth; for the Spirit will not speak by self authority, but will tell only what is heard; and the Spirit will make known to you the things that are coming. The Spirit will glorify me, for everything that the Spirit makes known to you will be drawn from what is mine. (John 16:13-14 NEB)

Throughout the B'rit Khadasha believers are cautioned by the Son of YHWH and his apostles to stay clear of false prophets and wolves. Those members who are walking in their wake are clearly unable to distinguish a genuine prophet from a false one. Neither can they spot a wolf in a flock of sheep, let alone a wolf masquerading in sheep skin. As such, it has become easy for these false prophets and wolves to lead those who are blind further away from the truth. Unknown to themselves, many who had been set apart before they were born for discipleship unto Messiah—members of his herd—are instead adding to the pack. When Messiah returns to judge the earth it will be a sad day for the sheep that he finds among the wolves. Moreover:

For this we tell you as [Yeshua]'s word: we who are left alive until [Yeshua] comes shall not forestall those who have died; because at the word of command, at the sound of the messenger's voice and [YHWH]'s trumpet call, [Yeshua] himself will descend from heaven; first the Christian dead will rise, then we who are left alive shall join them, caught up in the clouds to meet [Yeshua] in the air. Thus we shall always be with [Yeshua]. Console one another, then, with these words. (Thessalonians 4:15-18 NEB)

In reclaiming his own to join him in the air, Yeshua's head will face only the direction of his flock. Therefore it is crucial that members of the Body learn to discern now so that they are not found among the pack later. A Spirit-filled body is a discerning body. A Spirit-filled body doesn't merely dismiss a new teaching because it is different from what they are accustomed to hearing, unless what they are already accustomed to hearing is legitimate. The most assured way of spotting a lie is by cross-checking all that is heard with the Spirit of truth. Little difficulty is had here because a Spirit-filled body is filled with the word.

It is imperative that the welfare of one remains the concern of all. The Spirit-filled body recognizes that strength lies in numbers and that in order to effectively combat the enemy, they mustn't allow theirs to dwindle. The quickest way to reduce the Christian ranks is not by instantly killing one off. Others, in seeing, will know not to follow in the same footsteps, and the enemy's attempt will have been in vain. Instead, by adding a little leaven to the dough the Body will have successfully ingested his poison. His success lies less in the one who ate and more in the one who shares. Remember Adam and Eve? What's dangerous is that there are many passionate members in the Church who are concerned for the welfare of all. However, without the Holy Spirit's filling, these well-meaning believers are simply passing the poison. But, whether listening to the latest craze or the oldest gem, the Spirit-filled Body learns to look for the leaven. An emboldened and discerning Christian poses a threat to the false prophet and wolf. The discerning Christian may sniff them out, but it is with boldness that they are snuffed out.

> Beware of false prophets, who come to you in sheep's clothing but inwardly are ravenous wolves. You will recognize them by their fruits. Are grapes gathered from thornbushes, or figs from thistles? (Matthew 7:15-16 ESV)

> You therefore, beloved, knowing this beforehand, take care that you are not carried away with the error of lawless people and lose your own stability. But grow in the grace and knowledge of our Lord and Savior [Yeshua Messiah]. To him be the glory both now and to the day of eternity. Amen. (2nd Peter 3:17-18 ESV)

49. The Warrior's Creed

First read: 2nd Timothy 2:1-5

I will raise my banner to the sky
While in the army of the Lord
And march close behind him 'til I die
When I shall receive my just reward

Why should I ever feel discouraged
When in my hand I wield a sword?

The Holy Spirit gives me courage
As I walk on open battlefield
I have but one single message
As I carry faith as my open shield

'Yeshua Messiah is the Son of YAH'
The Father's love for us revealed

In Messiah's hand are both staff and rod
They're used to keep me on the path
No time for play, no time to plod
Lest my enemies see and laugh

No time for tears to cloud my sight
Lest I fall amidst their violent wrath

I have strength within to stand and fight
While covered in my Savior's blood
Whether arrows fly by day or night
I'll rise above the deadly flood

As I sail on to my victory
I won't be mired in deadly mud

As I stand equipped with a Holy three
I battle with those who fight unseen;
Who practice their craft with jubilee
I fight against all who come between

My mission to reclaim the lost
On behalf of he who once redeemed

By shedding blood upon the cross
With shoes of peace upon my feet
I gladly bear the dangerous cost
I march assured, but with no vain conceit

To release the souls who sit enchained
No time to moan or fear defeat

If they do not hear, I am to blame
My helmet atop must remain intact
For this is why my Lord was slain
My daily bread I shall not lack;

My every need shall be supplied
The truth I speak will thus attract

All hungry souls who've fed on lies
While fighting for the Prince of Peace
Who showed no sins, but still he died
I'll pine for sinners' prompt release

Then teach them how to run this race;
To always pray and without cease

Keep their eyes upon their Captain's face
I'll intercede for those still weak
And keep them at a steady pace
When at times it seems a just critique

Will keep the weak on steady course
I am sure I'll hone a fair technique

To keep them sound, though without force
Thy coat of mail I shall maintain;
From what is right I shall not divorce
Until all thy enemies are slain,

Until my battles have been won
You held your captives in your train;

Their deadly hold did come undone
And though, with stealth, they seek to kill
I shall stand and fight, I will not run
For that, my Lord, is thy perfect will

And you've trained me well enough to win
I'll fight by faith on both toe and heel

And stay a thousand miles away from sin
Until that day when the trumpet sounds;
When all the saints shall enter in
Thy rest, far from earth's temporal ground

We shall rejoice with thy holy host
And watch the righteous as they're crowned
But, for now I shall keep to my post
And follow you without grave despair

While deep in battle from coast to coast
All thine enemies, my God, beware

50. Wounded but Wiser

First read: 1st Samuel 15:1-23

Sometimes the fruit will be in its earliest stage of rotting. The core is degenerating and the shell still scintillating, and so you may not capture a scent. You must learn to discern. Discerning is a skill that will take time to learn and time to develop. But remember that your time is limited, so embrace all efforts to learn efficiently. How do you learn how to discern efficiently? Sometimes by eating the fruit with the scintillating shell in its earliest stage of rotting. Because it is in its earliest stage, it will not prove terminal if you eat; it should, however, prove memorable. A picture is worth a thousand words. A putrid picture is priceless. So, the one taken of this experience should speak volumes. Keep the volume up, but don't blow your eardrums blasting and blaring. You can't discern if you can't hear.

No one likes to experience pain. It's painful. Parents don't like for their children to experience pain either because watching their writhing is heart-wrenching. It is no different with our heavenly Father. How foolish it is to suggest that YHWH enjoys the suffering of his children. So then why ask the question, "If YAH is good and if he is loves then why does he allow his children to suffer?" Here, instead, is a better question worth pondering: "If we are good and if we love our Father, then why do we wander?" Why do we allow ourselves to sin? Thankfully, our Father's goodness is not contingent upon the wickedness of his Son's creation. YHWH doesn't cease in his goodness simply because some choose to sin. YHWH is neither the author of sin nor of suffering.

The author of sin is Satan and with the birth of man's lower nature resulting from original sin, came the unnatural extension of suffering into the world. YHWH is the author of salvation through his Son, Yeshua. From the moment man sinned, he, in his goodness, put forth his plan to restore the shattered. However, restoration never precluded affliction; indeed suffering is included.

To the woman he said, "I will surely multiply your pain in childbearing; in pain you shall bring forth children. Your desire shall be for your husband, and he shall rule over you. " And to Adam he said, "Because you have listened to the voice of your wife and have eaten of the tree of which I commanded you, 'You shall not eat of it,' cursed is the ground because of you; in pain you shall eat of it all the days of your life; thorns and thistles it shall bring forth for you; and you shall eat the plants of the field. By the sweat of your face you shall eat bread, till you return to the ground, for out of it you were taken; for you are dust, and to dust you shall return." (Genesis 3:16-19 ESV)

Believers would do well to remember that repairing is always at the forefront of YHWH's mind. If it were possible to repair without using despair then surely he would oblige. But, our God is a God of love and not of impression. His imposing would guarantee the opposition of his children, and those who did comply would do so begrudgingly—not exactly an act of love.

The history of the Israelites, and of modern day Christians, is a picture of peculiarity. When YHWH has blessed, his people have wandered off. When he has wounded, the people come running back; only to wander off once again the moment their wounds have healed. Perhaps the road to Glory is marked by suffering because in suffering one stays on the road. Though suffering will still occur among the faithful, it is the foolish that will have the hardest time healing. YHWH would have it no other way. At times the faithful suffer because of the faithless' actions, not our God's. Yet, the hope of the faithful rests in their Redeemer who, while having perfect faith, suffered nonetheless. They resonate well with Paul:

Yet indeed I also count all things loss for the excellence of the knowledge of [Yeshua], for whom I have suffered the loss of all things, and count them as rubbish, that I may gain [Yeshua] and be found in him, not having my own righteousness, which is from the law, but that which is through faith in [Yeshua], the righteousness which is from [YHWH] by faith; that I may know [Yeshua] and the power of his resurrection, and the fellowship of his sufferings, being conformed to his death, if, by any means, I may attain to the resurrection from the dead. (Philippians 3:8-11 NEB)

The foolish suffer because of their folly. Though having received instructions from Yeshua on how to prevent unnecessary and unintended painful encounters, they still choose to ignore. Rather than blaming the Father or Son for their wounds, as they lay there on the ground, they should, through the Holy Spirit, begin asking for wisdom. Our Father's desire is not that his children writhe in their wounds, but that they learn how to discern. If it is found that the experience is not worth having again, then it was worth having once.

Whoever heeds instruction is on the path to life, but he who rejects reproof leads others astray. (Proverbs 10:17 ESV)

51. The Counterfeit Counselor

First read: 1st Kings 22:1-53

While looking around on your journey, perhaps the most difficult task you will encounter will be in distinguishing between that fruit which is too rotten and that which is too ripe. Both grow and fall from flowers and trees, and both have similar hearts. Stare at either fruit from near or afar and soon you won't tell them apart. While on this journey aim for irregularity, in the long run you'll be glad you did.

To whom do you run when seeking wise counsel? It is tempting for members in Messiah's Body to seek out only those members who will tell us precisely what we want to hear. If what we seek is only that which sounds pleasant to our ears, what we have ultimately decided is to receive counsel from a counterfeit. A true member of the Body will always speak what is truthful even if what is spoken brings tears to him who hears. Sometimes tears are the only available instrument capable of clearing the vision of those momentarily mesmerized by the wiles of the world.

Do not stifle inspiration, and do not despise prophetic utterances, but bring them all to the test and then keep what is good in them and avoid the bad of whatever kind. (1st Thessalonians 5:19-22 NEB)

There are members of the Body whom Yeshua has designated as eyes and ears for the Church. Because of his providence they have been given a direct line to the Father, and are especially attuned to the sound of his voice. It is unfortunate that these members are ignored in some circles and despised in others because they have information that would benefit the entire Body. In our own wisdom we turn to fools to provide us foolish counsel, though not always intentionally.

The tongue of the wise uses knowledge rightly, but the mouths of fools pours forth foolishness. The eyes of [Yeshua] are in every place, keeping watch on the evil and the good. (Proverbs 15:2-3 NKJV)

Admittedly it can be difficult at times to distinguish between the heathen and the hypocrite. But in truth, it is because they really aren't dissimilar. Both are lost and blind, though the heathen doesn't claim to have sight. The hypocrite, on the other hand, often appears the most pious and is always willing to offer his two cents. If the believer has any sense, then he won't turn to either the heathen or the hypocrite for advice, but will, instead, search out those members whom the Father has connected to the Head.

But if you are harbouring bitter jealousy and self ambition in your hearts, consider whether your claims are not false, and a defiance of the truth. This is not the wisdom that comes from above; it is earth-bound, sensual, demonic. For with jealousy and ambition come disorder and evil of every kind. (James 3:14-16 NEB)

Jehoshaphat and Ahab serve as symbols as to what befalls the member who chooses to either accept or reject wise counsel. Jehoshaphat, the fourth king of the southern kingdom of Judah, sought direction from YHWH before engaging in battle with the Aramaeans. He enlisted the help of Micaiah, recognized as a legitimate prophet from the northern kingdom of Israel. However, Ahab, Israel's reigning sovereign, reviled the prophet because Micaiah insisted on speaking only what was truthful. Ahab was only interested in hearing from his own false prophets who, out of fear, regularly flattered the king.

Caution: flattery will leave you flattened.

A lying tongue hates its victims, and a flattering mouth works ruin. (Proverbs 26:28 ESV)

All is not well in the Church, though there are a multitude of counterfeiters who continue to suggest otherwise. "Yeshua is pleased with his Body, and so will grant victory to members from all of their enemies," they say. Continue listening to such counsel without regard for needed change, and find out how much protection will be afforded on the battlefield.

The righteous is delivered from trouble, and the wicked walks into it instead. (Proverbs 11:8 ESV)

52. A Reflective Moment

Lover of Truth

First read: 2nd Thessalonians 2:8-12

As a member of the Body of Messiah are you a lover of truth? Are you at a place in your walk with Messiah that you can readily distinguish truth from falsehood? Are you seeking to know the truth? I would encourage those members who are to continue seeking, and, little by little in YHWH's perfect timing, you shall continue to find. It's amazing how YHWH knows exactly what to reveal to us at the moment it needs revealing. I believe that he wants to reveal more to his children than what at present has already been revealed. Because the closer we come to spiritual truth, the greater protection we have against Satan who is the father of lies. Speaking to those who refuse to accept his teachings as truth, Yeshua said:

> Your father is the devil and you choose to carry out your father's desires. He was a murderer from the beginning, and is not rooted in the truth; there is no truth in him. When he tells a lie he is speaking his own language, for he is a liar and the father of lies. But I speak the truth and therefore you do not believe me. Which of you can prove me wrong? If what I say is true, why do you not believe me? He who has [YHWH] for his father listens to the words of [YHWH]. You are not [YHWH]'s children; that is why you do not listen. (John 8:44-47 NEB)

Yeshua was speaking to a people who refused to accept his identity. Without accepting who he was, the Son of YHWH, it was in vain that they acknowledged ties to the Father, since according to Yeshua,

> … they may all be one, just as you, Father, are in me, and I in you, that they also may be in us, so that the world may believe that you have sent me. The glory that you have given me I have given to them, that they may be one even as we are one. (John 17:21-22 ESV)

The growing concern in this age is the venomous idea that all truth is relative. How appealing is such an assertion to a people who denounce accountability as meddlesome and restrictive.

> Justice is turned back, and righteousness stands far away; for truth has stumbled in the public squares, and uprightness cannot enter. Truth is lacking, and he who departs from evil makes himself a prey. [Yeshua] saw it, and it displeased him that there was no justice. (Isaiah 59:14-15 ESV)

On the contrary, truth, as a rule, is the means to freedom. Truth alone holds the key to unlocking the chains that have kept millions deprived of their opportunity to live a life of holiness. A life filled with love and marked by perpetual faith, hope, wisdom, and integrity. If, then, you are a lover of truth what evidence exists that you are seeking it, speaking it, living it, and are also a defender of it? As we are preparing for the return of Messiah, it is imperative that members of the Body boldly resist all attempts to subjectify the road to Glory—for there is indeed only one.

Buy truth, and do not sell it; buy wisdom, instruction, and understanding. (Proverbs 23:23 ESV)

Prove me, O [YHWH], and try me; test my heart and my mind. For your steadfast love is before my eyes, and I walk in your faithfulness. (Psalms 26:2-3 ESV)

53. A Hindrance to Deliverance I

First read: Deuteronomy 30:11-20

While walking awhile in the blaze of heat, some glitter will shimmer below. A reason, un-rare, is rampant to share: "Look down to capture its glow." You could pause to gaze at your gold. You should peek and then keep going. A pondering mind will wander when parched—keep yours saturated with wisdom. Look down for too long and you'll take notice to neat-looking seeds. But if veiled are your eyes and scorched are your veins, no way shall you tell of their weeds. You would leave but you don't; your curiosity has peaked with a purr. "I could meet all of my needs with such neat-looking seeds," so with those same seeds you'll sow. So then before too long, the seeds have been planted and sooner or later they grow.

There are a multitude of hindrances to YHWH's deliverance, but perhaps none stand to delay things the most than the believer's impatience. It is a fact worth remembering that our God is omniscient and we are not. At times it may appear that he has inadvertently left us in a season that should have passed years ago. But, if after walking for a season you find that the temperature hasn't changed, keep moving; you're still walking for a reason. Like Yeshua's experience in the desert, the mirages will usually begin to appear in the dead of heat. If we allow the natural to overshadow the spiritual, then disaster is soon to follow. Road-signs with promises of short cuts are always enticing, as are attractive anesthetics offering false security from the blaze. Just a sip of some worldly water? In attempting to hasten your day in the desert, there is no quicker way to induce the wrath of YHWH than for one of his children to turn to another "father" for aid or relief.

One who is righteous is a guide to his neighbor, but the way of the wicked leads them astray. (Proverbs 12:26 ESV)

But our forefathers would not accept his leadership. They thrust him aside. They wished themselves back in Egypt, and said to Aaron, "Make us gods to go before us. As for Moses, who brought us out of Egypt, we do not know what has become of him." That was when they made the bull-calf, and offered sacrifice to the idol, and held a feast in honor of the thing their hands had made. But [YHWH] turned away from them and gave them over to the worship of the host of heaven, as it stands written in the book of the prophets: "Did you bring me victims and offerings those forty years in the desert, you house of Israel? No, you carried aloft the shrine of Moloch and the star of the god of Rephan, the images which you had made for your adoration. I will banish you beyond Babylon." (Acts 7:39-43 NEB)

And it's tempting. Above all the commandments given to the Israelites, the one repeated most often was the prohibition against the worshiping of other gods. Had it not been for the intervention of Moses in Horeb, the Israelites (including Aaron) in their impatience and impudence would have roasted alongside their golden bull-calf. The opening words of Moses to the Israelites while delivering the Ten Commandments were:

> I am the [YHWH] who brought you out of the land of Egypt, out of the house of bondage. "You shall have no other gods before Me." (Deuteronomy 5:6-7 NKJV)

It was a reminder to all that no other god should have been desired, when it was YHWH that had set them free from captivity. And yet due to discontentment with their present circumstances, the Israelites turned from YHWH and turned to gold. Sound familiar? How easy it is for Christians in today's Body to sneer at the foolishness of our elders. "What were they thinking?" we ask. The Holy Spirit is presently asking the same question. We think it odd that anyone would worship a golden-calf as if it was a god. However, there are believers who will faithfully enter a season of summer until it seems to them that YHWH is no longer accompanying them on their journey. Dehydration sets in because no water did they drink prior to summer; choosing instead to fill their bodies with worldly water. So to end their misery they turn to money. Others trade in their sorrows for sex, or their angst for alcohol; compromising their eternity with momentary ecstasy. No different from the exercises of the earlier Israelites in worshiping their false gods. Rather than allowing dehydration to delay our deliverance, Messiah offers an alternative solution to drawing and drinking worldly water:

> [Yeshua] said, "Everyone who drinks this water will be thirsty again, but whoever drinks the water that I shall give him will never suffer thirst any more. The water that I shall give him will be an inner spring always welling up for eternal life." (John 4:13-14 NEB)

The water Messiah has to offer is more than sufficient to sustain all believers who find themselves waiting for their deliverance while walking in the desert. A body dehydrated will turn to any source to quench their thirst. But the waters of this world, while quenching the body, will squelch the soul. When the sun is beaming down, what are you seeking to fill your cup? To whom do you turn to fill you up?

54. Wealthy With Wisdom I

First read: Proverbs 10:16

Monetarily mesmerized (only for a moment) by the mirage below, your senses become marred. And in time others, still on their own journey, are passing you by; determined not to waste what little they have on curing your ills. Consequently, you are now clutched—trapped, though not in time. For time continues to travel without telling you where it has been or where it is going. It is demanding. However impossible it may be to outrun, time, nevertheless, expects you to keep up and to stay on track. Whether on your heels or flying by, time savors while nipping, and, in essence, gains value by averting you from getting lost.

Therein lies the richness of [YHWH]'s free grace lavished upon us, imparting full wisdom and insight. He has made known to us his hidden purpose—such was his will and pleasure determined beforehand in [Yeshua]—to be put into effect when the time was ripe: namely, that the universe, all in heaven and on earth, might be brought into a unity with [Messiah]. (Ephesians 1:8-10 NEB)

There isn't a trace of evidence in any of the Gospels to convince us that Messiah's primary purpose in coming to earth was to monetarily enrich the lives of his followers. The Great Commission calls on Christians to go out and make disciples for Messiah. So there is no reason why any shepherd should be adding his two cents to a message that already speaks of a great cost.

A doctor of the law came up, and said, "Master, I will follow you wherever you go. [Yeshua] replied, "Foxes have their holes, the birds their roosts; but the Son of Man has nowhere to lay his head." (Matthew 8:19-20 NEB)

But the problem is not prosperity. There is nothing inherently wrong with wealth. Money is not in of itself maleficent, and the King of kings finds no fault with those who have used their material blessings to bless others. The fault is with those who have become imprisoned by their prosperity, or their quest for it.

He who earnestly seeks good finds favor, but trouble will come to him who seeks evil. He who trusts in his riches will fall, but the righteous will flourish like foliage. (Proverbs 11:27-28 ESV)

What I mean, my friends, is this. The time we live in will not last long. While it lasts, married men should be as if they had no wives; mourners should be as if they had nothing to grieve them, the joyful as if they did not rejoice; buyers must not count on keeping what they buy, nor those who use the world's wealth on using it to the full. For the whole frame of this world is passing away. (1st Corinthians 7:29-31 NEB)

Moreover, Messiah is concerned with those shepherds who, out of dimness or deceit, would mislead his sheep into believing that their relationship with him is defined by the amount of their riches. I hope that his concern now does not turn into condemnation later.

Alas, alas for you, lawyers and Pharisees, hypocrites that you are. You shut the door of the kingdom of Heaven in men's faces; you do not enter yourselves, and when others are entering, you stop them. (Matthew 23:13 NEB)

For no sooner has the sun risen with a burning heat than it withers the grass; its flower falls and its beautiful appearance perishes. So the rich man also will fade away in his pursuits. (James 1:11 NEB)

Bear in mind that there are those in the Body whose wealth has not come from their Savior; for at the present moment he is not the sole distributor of gifts. YHWH is not in the business of setting his people up for failure, so there is no reason to believe that he is going to bestow gifts so that a believer can break. Remember that Messiah was a carpenter by trade and as such, is interested in rebuilding. Through the Holy Spirit, he will only dispense those heavier tools to those whom he knows can carry the weight. Members need discerning eyes in order to see that most, with their money, are in bondage and have yet to experience true freedom. Unfortunately, most are also heavily deluded into believing that they've found their deliverance, though Messiah is still waiting patiently to deliver.

While each believer shares the individual responsibility of discovering the truth, Messiah counts on his shepherds to aid in the findings. Therefore, shepherds will answer for the weeds that have grown through the seeds *they* have sown:

For I know the plans I have for you, declares [Yeshua], plans for welfare and not for evil, to give you a future and a hope. (Jeremiah 29:11 ESV)

Yeshua's message did not end there. If YHWH's children are ever going to find rest then many need to learn to read the rest of the Scripture passages that speaks on the same topic.

Time is running out and it will mean tragedy for all those whom Messiah finds, upon returning, still sitting in prison, though his blood was shed to set them free. Penalties await believers who hide the key.

Well you know that it was no perishable stuff, like gold or silver, that bought your freedom from the empty folly of your traditional ways. The price was paid in precious blood, as it were of a lamb without mark or blemish—the blood of [Yeshua]. (1st Peter 1:18-19 NEB)

With such a focus on prosperity, shepherds are missing the point. YHWH's ultimate purpose for his lost children is salvation through repentance. This is the prosperity Gospel: that upon adoption, YHWH's children may dwell in the richness of his presence in following whole-heartedly after his Son.

Or again, if a woman has ten silver pieces and loses one of them, does she not light the lamp, sweep out the house, and look in every corner till she has found it? And when she has, she calls her friends and neighbors together, and says, "Rejoice with me. I have found the piece that I have lost." In the same way, I tell you, there is joy among the angels of [YHWH] over one sinner who repents. (Luke 15:8-10 NEB)

All material gain is immaterial to our Messiah. To seek after anything else is to show our ungratefulness for the Father's gift. If any worth comes from time, it's in reminding us how quickly things depreciate—except for the Father's love. Some years have gone by since Messiah's death, resurrection, and ascent into the sky. Time has been running since the Holy Spirit's coming. How have you shown your appreciation?

> Crowds of people came out to be baptized by him, and he said to them: "You vipers brood. Who warned you to escape from the coming retribution? Then prove your repentance by the fruit it bears; and do not begin saying to yourselves, "We have Abraham for our father." I tell you that [YHWH] can make children for Abraham out of these stones here. Already the axe is laid to the roots of the trees; and every tree that fails to produce good fruit is cut down and thrown on the fire. The people asked him, "Then what are we to do?" He replied, "The man with two shirts must share with him who has none, and anyone who has food must do the same." (Luke 3:7-11 NEB)

55. The Hindrance to Deliverance II

First read: Numbers 33:51-56

Don't covet and you won't get clutched. What is the name of the garden you've grown? Your garden that grew from the seeds that were sown? Your garden from glitter that grips with its weeds? The garden you grew to meet all your needs? Before breaking free from its clutches, you will have to break free from your own. In order to break free, you must first be willing to break. Breaking is painful. Breaking requires movement. Movement is an essential element of your journey.

Are you far enough along in your journey that you have begun to resent sin? A clear indication of your spiritual growth is not just your resistance to sinful acts, but your resentment of sin itself. YHWH frowns upon his children engaging in sinful behavior, but he loathes sin. It is sin that engenders the sinful behavior. I'm sure it must have seemed to the Israelites that YHWH placed some fine print in the advertisement they had been given; telling of the land "flowing with milk and honey." Our God promised them that he'd deliver them from their enemies; first Pharaoh, and then:

> When [YHWH] brings you into the land that you are entering to take possession of it, and clears away many nations before you, the Hittites, the Girgashites, the Amorites, the Canaanites, the Perizzites, the Hivites, and the Jebusites, seven nations more numerous and mightier than you, and when [YHWH] gives them over to you, and you defeat them, then you must devote them to complete destruction. You shall make no covenant with them and show no mercy to them. You shall not intermarry with them, giving your daughters to their sons or taking their daughters for your sons, for they would turn away your sons from following me, to serve other gods. Then the anger of [YHWH] would be kindled against you, and they would destroy you quickly. But thus shall you deal with them: you shall break down their altars and dash in pieces their pillars and chop down their Asherim and burn their carved images with fire. For you are a people holy to [YHWH]. [YHWH] has chosen you to be a people for his treasured possession, out of all the peoples who are on the face of the earth. (Deuteronomy 7:1-6 ESV)

But, the Israelites still had to resist. Deliverance by the Master is not without some assistance by his servants. Our God chose this pattern by design. Again, he does not need our assistance, but he desires it. Our willingness to assist through resistance is actually a symbol of submission, an act of obedience. The irony of it all, however, is that it's our submission which activates YHWH's assistance; and his assistance always brings deliverance.

But the Day of [YHWH] will come; it will come, unexpected as a thief. On that day the heavens will disappear with a great rushing sound, the elements will disintegrate into flames, and the earth with all that is in it will be laid bare. Since the whole universe is to break up in this way, think what sort of people you ought to be, what devout and dedicated lives you should live. Look eagerly for the coming of the Day of [YHWH] and work to hasten it on; that day will set the heavens ablaze until they fall apart, and will melt the elements in flames. But we have his promise, and look forward to new heavens and a new earth, the home of justice. With this to look forward to, do your utmost to be found at peace with him, unblemished and above reproach in his sight. (2nd Peter 3:10-14 NEB)

The nations surrounding the Israelites represented sin, all of whom insisted on engaging in behavior that blatantly violated YHWH's commandments. As previously stated, our God so ordered their destruction to both instruct and protect their people. In the same manner done when the Hebrews began to sin in the desert, YHWH wanted to remind them of the consequences of disobedience. Nevertheless, Yeshua, as creator of humanity, also understands their nature and with it two fundamental truths. First, sin appeals to the lowest nature. And second, all lowest natures appeal to one another. Because the lowest nature won't die fully until the end of our journey, it is best to isolate our lowest nature from sinful behavior. Hence, our God's decree to the Israelites not to intermarry wasn't racist, but righteous; as was his command to destroy the roots of their weed. Unfortunately, the enticement of the nations led to the entanglement of YHWH's people; and for years afterward their actions demonstrated their disinterest in freedom. The season of deliverance was prolonged until the Israelites came to resent sin. Before Yeshua will rescue us from sin we have to first resent it, then repent of it, and finally resist it. But it is the resentment of sin that ensures our repentance will prove meaningful and our resistance victorious.

Dear friends, I beg you, as aliens in a foreign land, to abstain from the lusts of the flesh which are at war with the soul. Let all your behavior be such as even pagans can recognize as good, and then, whereas they malign you as criminals now, they will come to see for themselves that you live good lives, and will give glory to [YHWH] on the day when he comes to hold assize (court). (1st Peter 2:11-12 NEB)

56. Submitting to Self

First read: 2nd Chronicles 28:1-27

In carefully examining all that you seek, you may find the questions quieting and the answers alarming. Both questions and answers should serve as a daily wake-up call. The truth, however unsightly, will, in time, draw back both of your eyes. Waste your time sleeping in banking for beauty and you'll find that you've soon overspent. Truthfully, you will have everything you need while on your journey. This truth will continue to serve sufficiently until you start looking around for too long and then back at yourself—comparing yourself to everyone else. Look around for too long and you'll soon find yourself looking down. And down is where you found your glittering seeds, a shimmering sight for the hunt. But alas, it is you who is trapped in the game; caught by the Weeds of the Want.

The current zeitgeist (spirit of the age) embodies a principle of old: *Carpe Diem* (seize the day). Messiah would have no trouble advocating such an axiom if the seized days were spent seizing souls. The key to seizing souls is submitting to the Son. The trouble is that there are many within the Body who, at present, are consumed with submitting to themselves. Submission to self is the pathway to sin.

The iniquities of the wicked ensnare him, and he is held fast in the cords of his sin. He dies for lack of discipline, and because of his great folly he is led astray. (Proverbs 5:22-23 ESV)

Christians must understand that "self," while once the ruler of their souls, should no longer be the captain of their ship, who wills that they remain anchored in sin. When Messiah died on the cross, man inherited the ability to live in complete freedom from the clutches of self, but only by walking faithfully in the Spirit, through the grace of our Father and Lord Yeshua Messiah. That is, those who are sealed with the Spirit (every genuine believer), must also be daily filled with and daily yielded to the Holy Spirit. Those who walk in the Spirit need never to look to the world for fullness, because the Spirit will never deprive a genuine follower of Messiah from his or her nourishment. The Holy Spirit also acts as a faithful check to self and its wants. Until the believer reaches the gates of Glory, self will whisper worrisome words in an attempt to convince the convert that their wants are actually needs. The Holy Spirit was not given so that the believer, once deaf to the voice of YHWH, would now become deaf to the world. For where does an act of love come from if the heart is unable to choose? Walking in the Spirit not only provides the opportunity for Christian submission, it allows the faithful follower to express love for the Father and Son. The danger in submitting to self is that it is never satisfied. Monetary greed is a common weed in the world and believers must desist in believing that this god will make their journey smoother.

He who loves money will not be satisfied with money, nor he who loves wealth with his income; this also is vanity. When goods increase, they increase who eat them, and what advantage has their owner but to see them with his eyes?

Sweet is the sleep of a laborer, whether he eats little or much, but the full stomach of the rich will not let him sleep. (Ecclesiastes 5:10-12 ESV)

Moreover, it is not wealth that is necessary to seize souls, rather it is will. If believers would spend more time cultivating will, in ensuring that theirs is continuously aligned with our God's, then less time would exist for cultivating captivating gardens. It is the will of the Father that his children invest in the expansion and growth of his family. It is the will of Messiah that his disciples practice denying self in order to strengthen their spiritual health. And the Holy Spirit wills that members of the Body become sensitive to instruction, chiefly through self-discipline and always through fasting and praying, while ingesting Scripture.

Or do you think the Scripture means nothing when it says that the Spirit that [YHWH] caused to live in us jealously yearns for us? But he gives all the more grace. And so he says, "[YHWH] opposes the arrogant but gives grace to the humble." Therefore, submit yourselves to [YHWH]. (James 4:5-7 ISV)

57. Re-sanctifying the Sanctuary - I

First read: 2nd Chronicles 29:1-11

Congratulations. While on your journey, naming the source of your struggle is moving one step in the right direction. Look around, but not for too long. You have named the garden and so now you can go. You have taken a good step— make that a great step—because sadly, you will find that many on your journey won't ever get their feet back on track, and therefore, never will they reach their destination. In the clutches of despair, they insist and deny while first hiding how they feel and then waving hi. Tick. Tick. Tick. In the clutches of despair, they resist and deny while cursing as the time and the people pass them by bye."
Tick. Tick. In the clutches of despair they persist and deny, so in the clutches of despair there they sit, and there they die. Tick. But wait, don't despair. They will die in denial.

The Body should count it a blessing that there are members who have had their painful encounter with repentance, and as a result are seeing the fruits of YHWH's goodness and grace. The goodness may or may not, at present, be manifested monetarily, but then material wealth should never be the marker used to determine whether our God is delighted in a member's maturity. Indeed, the truest indicator of YHWH's delight is in the believer's spiritual journey. How much and how well is our God allowing you to see or hear? The keener your hearing and sight then the closer you are in becoming fully reconciled to the Father. Once a member has matured enough in his sanctifying process, YHWH will allow him to begin aiding in the sanctification of Messiah's sanctuary.

Hezekiah began to reign when he was twenty-five years old, and he reigned twenty-nine years in Jerusalem. His mother's name was Abijah the daughter of Zechariah. And he did what was right in the eyes of [YHWH], according to all that David his father had done. (2nd Chronicles 29:1-2 ESV)

Hezekiah did right at the age of twenty-five and so our God was able to use him at the age of twenty-five. There are those in the Body younger still whom the Father is allowing to see and hear, and what is before them isn't very appealing. The obstinate elders and the unyielding youth refuse to acknowledge that the Church needs re-sanctifying. Hezekiah saw the pollution that had entered in the sanctuary. In his maturity, he recognized that YHWH's anger was real, righteous, and would be relentless if his people refused to repent. Moreover, Hezekiah understood that hollow words and deeds would never please; unless the repentance was real, Judah would never experience healing.

As for me, I said, "O [YHWH], be gracious to me; heal me, for I have sinned against you." (Psalms 41:4 ESV)

Denial is a spiritually dangerous place to sit. It's a place which suggests that what is, is okay, when Messiah is saying that what is, is unacceptable. The Holy Spirit, on occasions, will lead the believer through the desert where it may seem that our God is momentarily distant. However, a spirit of denial is never from the Father. Denial sits on the opposite end of admittance, next to death, whereas admittance rests in the company of repentance.

[Yeshua] said, "It is for judgment that I have come into this world—to give sight to the sightless and to make blind those who see." Some Pharisees in his company asked, "Do you mean that we are blind?" "If you were blind," said [Yeshua], "you would not be guilty, but because you say, 'We see,' your guilt remains." (John 9:39-41 NEB)

Where the believer chooses to sit will determine his eternal destination. Messiah is not pleased with the status quo and so neither should be any of his disciples. At present there is much pollution in the Body because its members have been complacent with regards to what has entered. Members have also allowed the pollutants to remain for too long, contributing to their blindness and deafness. If the children of YHWH are determined to hear and to see, all must work diligently to remove those which detract and distract from his word.

58. Re-Sanctifying the Sanctuary II

First read: 2nd Chronicles 31:1

Fortunately, you've learned how to cite your source and so you won't drown in denial. But, before you can enjoy complete freedom from your weeds there is still an axe that needs grinding. And if you know what's good for you, you'd do well to grind it good. If you want to keep it real, you will keep it real by getting dirty; but, that's what usually happens when you start pulling up weeds. Why? Because, that's the only way you're going to get to their roots. Yet, this time you know exactly where you are falling, and why, because you have already been looking down. Unfortunately, in getting down you will need to fall down. In citing the source you have only scratched the surface. No, it wasn't easy, but it was essential in moving to the next step. Sometimes stepping down will be an essential element of your journey.

Hopefully there aren't any believers within the Body who believe that re-sanctifying the Church is easy or that Christian passivity passes off as effective. Contrary to some popular sentiments there are many in the world that have come to view Christianity as a feeble religion; filled with feeble-minded followers who will accept whatever is thrown their way if it means keeping the peace. It isn't hard to view what sits in plain sight. Submitting to Messiah doesn't mean sacrificing your sanctification for reconciliation with the world. In instructing his disciples before sending them out to proclaim, Yeshua solemnly warned:

Whoever then will acknowledge me before men, I will acknowledge him before my Father in heaven; and whoever disowns me before men, I will disown him before my Father in heaven. You must not think that I have come to bring peace to the earth; I have not come to bring peace, but a sword. I have come to set a man against his father, a daughter against her mother, a son's wife against her mother-in-law; and a man will find his enemies under his own roof. (Matthew 10:32-35 NEB)

But wait. Isn't Yeshua referred to as the Prince of Peace? Yes. And, didn't he say while delivering the Sermon on the Mount, "How blest are the peacemakers; YHWH shall call them his sons?" Yes. Messiah is the Prince of Peace, not of appeasement. And blest are the peacemakers; not the pleasers or appeasers.

Prompted by her mother, she said, "Give me here on a dish the head of John the Baptist." The king was distressed when he heard it; but out of regard for his oath and for his guests, he ordered the request to be granted, and had John beheaded in prison. The head was brought in on a dish and given to the girl; and she carried it to her mother. Then John's disciples came and took away the body, and buried it; and they went and told [Yeshua]. (Matthew 14:8-12 NEB)

Messiah is concerned with the soul and not with the roles that his sheep enjoy playing. He is aware that millions of souls are in turmoil, while the flesh is feigning contentment. Most make their feigning a family affair. But, for the sake of our souls, Messiah will slice through whichever layers are producing more liars. How blessed are those who are willing to slice in order to save, and how blessed still are those who are willing to slice in order to sanctify. Messiah has provided us with a tool whose blade is as sharp as his sword of truth.

For the word of [YHWH] is alive and active. It cuts more keenly than any two-edged sword, piercing as far as the place where life and spirit, joints and marrow, divide. It sifts the purposes and thoughts of the heart. There is nothing in creation that can hide from him; everything lies naked and exposed to the eyes of the One with whom we have to reckon. (Hebrews 4:12-13 NEB)

In re-sanctifying his Body, Messiah's blade will require that some members forsake their lofty temporal posts for the sake of gaining a higher eternal position in the Kingdom. Every member of the Body is expected to get their hands dirty at one time or another in rooting out the weeds. If there are any too pristine to pull from the ground then it is worth remembering that this is where you were found.

59. Weed Whacking

First read: Isaiah 1-5

While perhaps a dirtier task, you will experience less pain and greater success pulling from the ground, on the ground, than you would in trying to pull up the weeds while you're still standing. It is cooler on the ground and the roots are easier to root out. Remember, however, to concentrate on the task at hand rather than on the dirt in your hands. You still have work to do. Do it. But don't stay on the ground for too long; the clock is still ticking. Besides, you won't be effective in whacking the weeds if you're whacking the weeds with an axe. You will use your weed whacker to whack your weeds; the axe is for using when you stand back up.

It is the Father's preference that his children engage in their own garden tending. It is the Son's desire that his disciples acknowledge his status as the one and only true Vine from which real fruit is ripened.

I am the real vine, and my Father is the gardener. Every barren branch of mine he cuts away; and every fruiting branch he cleans, to make it more fruitful still. You have already been cleansed by the word that I spoke to you. Dwell in me, as I in you. No branch can bear fruit by itself, but only if it remains united with the vine; no more can you bear fruit, unless you remain united with me. (John 15:1-4 NEB)

It is the Father's preference, but it his prerogative to intervene whenever he feels the need. The Book of Isaiah is considered, by most, the greatest of all the prophetic books in the Tanakh, as evidenced by its constant citing in the B'rit Khadasha—even from the Lord Yeshua Messiah. In Isaiah there is telling of past, present, and future events all in one volume, and Messiah's quoting only illuminates its validity. What believers can glean from their reading is the necessity of cleaning. There are members in the Body who are content in deceiving themselves with the lie that the God of the Tanakh and B'rit Khadasha are two different beings. It is this lie that leaves so many content with clinging to their weeds, thus accounting for their barren branches. The truth is that while we live under a New Covenant, the conditions of its execution haven't altered. Under the old contract, YHWH had conditions that he expected the Israelites to meet, and consequences were doled out accordingly, deliberately. While the New Covenant provides a permanent expiation for sins through Messiah, it doesn't change our God's expectation for obedience, for holiness.

You love evil more than good, and lying more than speaking what is right. You love all words that devour, O deceitful tongue. But [YHWH] will break you down forever; he will snatch and tear you from your tent; he will uproot you from the land of the living. The righteous shall see and fear, and shall laugh at him, saying, "See the man who would not make [YHWH] his refuge, but trusted in the abundance of his riches and sought refuge in his own destruction. (Psalms 52:3-7 ESV)

Admittedly, this is the typical characterization of one who opposes the Father. However, believers mustn't forget the times in Israel's history when she too epitomized such opposition; equally must they receive the Gardner's pruning. Being our heavenly Father, and through Messiah and the Holy Spirit, YHWH will prune, no matter how painful, if it means preventing our prideful demise. To those who find solace in, "Nope, not my God—he wouldn't do that; he is a God of love." Please be advised and then be wise: our God is a lover of righteousness and a hater of wickedness.

Whoever loves discipline loves knowledge, but he who hates reproof is stupid. A good man obtains favor from [Yeshua], but a man of evil devices he condemns. No one is established by wickedness, but the root of the righteous will never be moved. (Proverbs 12:1-3 ESV)

His discipline is aimed at correcting for the long-run. For some this will require short-term crippling. But, don't despair; know that YHWH is still there. And there are no short-cuts; you will fine-tune as you prune.

60. Universal Umbrage - I

First read: Isaiah 23-26

And standing back up is a must if you are to continue moving ahead. However, not before the head of your axe also makes contact with the Garden of Wanting Weeds. As has been stated already, naming the source of your struggle is only half the battle won. Before your dance with victory, first, another dance is done. Beware, for before this dance is over you will find yourself by yourself dancing solo. The name of this number? "Waste Not, Want Not." Keep up. An axe, in its acuity, may keep you on your toes. But, if not alert you soon shall dance to sounds of wailing woes. Don't look around for too long. You do not want to lose any toes; you need toes to dance and you need toes to walk. Walking is an essential element of your journey. Yet, there is another reason for using an axe rather than a hoe. The weeds were pulled while on the ground, and no hoe had you in hand. The strength of your axe, as soon you shall see, is found in shaking land—before the curtain closes.

It is not the case that Messiah wants his disciples to remain uninformed about the events around them. There are many members of the Body who have opted to avoid any involvement in the political institutions of their land or abroad; choosing instead to bask in their ignorance. Intimately knowing the nature of man, it was YHWH's preference that such entanglements should never have transpired to begin with. But, for the Israelites, their obduracy towards faith and obedience continued to reveal an already scarred Achilles' heel. Thus the Israelites to the judge and prophet Samuel:

> Then all the elders of Israel gathered together and came to Samuel at Ramah and said to him, "Behold, you are old and your sons do not walk in your ways. Now appoint for us a king to judge us like all the nations." (1st Samuel 8:4-5 ESV)

Their concerns regarding Samuel's sons were well-founded, who, according to previous verses in the same chapter, "did not follow in their father's footsteps" but were intent on their own profit, taking bribes and perverting the course of justice. Warranted were the Israelites complaints, yet unwise was their conceived cure. They should have asked YHWH to reproach Joel and Abiah for their unrighteousness, and then to remove them if necessary. Such actions would have demonstrated their faithfulness to a concerned Father. Samuel, sensitive to and sharing in our God's sentiments, received this response after approaching him in prayer:

> And [YHWH] said to Samuel, " Heed the voice of the people in all that they say to you; for they have not rejected you, but they have rejected me, that I should not reign over them. According to all the works which they have done since the day that I brought them up out of Egypt, even to this day—with which they have forsaken me and served other gods—so they are doing to you also. (1st Samuel 8:7-8 NEB)

YHWH then tells Samuel to warn the Israelites what their request will mean: And he said, "This will be the behavior of the king who will reign over you: He will take your sons and appoint them for his own chariots and to be his horsemen, and some will run before his chariots. He will appoint captains over his thousands and captains over his fifties, will set some to plow his ground and reap his harvest, and some to make his weapons of war and equipment for his chariots. He will take your daughters to be perfumers, cooks, and bakers. And he will take the best of your fields, your vineyards, and your olive groves, and give them to his servants. He will take a tenth of your grain and your vintage, and give it to his officers and servants. And he will take your male servants, your female servants, your finest young men, and your donkeys, and put them to his work. He will take a tenth of your sheep. And you will be his servants. And you will cry out in that day because of your king whom you have chosen for yourselves, and the Lord will not hear you in that day." (1st Samuel 8:11-18 NEB)

YHWH tried to reason by providing concrete examples of what their "king" would do, but to no avail. An insatiable soul devoid of the Spirit, will never be able to see the Truth, no matter how clear or unmasked, so in truth they shall never be free.

61. A Reflective Moment

Universal Umbrage - II

First read: Isaiah 23-26

As it stands now it is the man-made political institution which shapes the direction of our country. As members of the Body of Messiah, we have a spiritual obligation to acknowledge those decisions which have driven this nation into the tentacles of iniquity and to correct them. While delivering YHWH's laws to the Israelites, Moses gave the following instructions:

> When you come to the land that [YHWH] is giving you, and you possess it and dwell in it and then say, "I will set a king over me, like all the nations that are around me, " you may indeed set a king over you whom [YHWH] will choose. One from among your brothers you shall set as king over you. You may not put a foreigner over you, who is not your brother. Only he must not acquire many horses for himself or cause the people to return to Egypt in order to acquire many horses, since [YHWH] has said to you, "You shall never return that way again." And he shall not acquire many wives for himself, lest his heart turn away, nor shall he acquire for himself excessive silver and gold. (Deuteronomy 17:14-17 NEB)

There is wisdom to be gleaned from these historic words as it applies to present day America. Believers must remember that when Messiah died, the wild olives (that is, the Gentiles) were grafted into the same tree as the cultivated olive (that is, the Jews or Israel); thereby creating a new stock, attached to the same Vine. The United States has a history of detaching herself from the Vine. Her kings and princes of late have not come from Israel's stock, but have been foreigners of another Rock; intent on leading the nation back into Egypt. Her wants and desires have engendered from Spiritless souls; culminating in the most unholy of polygamous marriages, where economic prosperity has ensued at the expense of spiritual poverty. What started off as a blessing from YHWH, quickly gave license to licentiousness. Not because of our God's gifts, but because of man's grandiosity. It is Messiah's desire that members of his Body begin mourning for the moral decay that has come to exemplify the United States. Silver and gold? Riches untold?

It is by the faithfulness of a few gems that YHWH's grace has continued to abound in this nation, but not for long. The Father is pleased with those who, in earnestness, persist in their prayers for the lost. Their prayers have not gone unheard nor will they go unanswered. On the contrary, our God will wield his axe for the precise purpose of responding to prayer. At times the only way to get the sleep to wake, the blind to see, or the deaf to hear is by sounding several trumpets—loud and clear.

> And in that day a great trumpet will be blown, and those who were lost in the land of Assyria and those who were driven out to the land of Egypt will come and worship [Yeshua] on the holy mountain at Jerusalem. (Isaiah 27:13 ESV)

62. Wealthy With Wisdom II

First read: Proverbs 5:15-21

When you stand back up, (hurry up) you have little time to waste. Take your axe and with its head start chopping ground in haste. You may find yourself asking, "Why use an axe when chopping earth?" The head of an axe is sharp. The head of a hoe is dull in comparison. Do not use a hoe for chopping and digging in a drained effort to regain your footing. In use, its predictable motions, while rhythmic, provoke habits that will hinder. You have little time to waste.

In the same way you women must accept the authority of your husbands, so that if there are any of them who disbelieve the Gospel they may be won over, without a word being said, by observing the chaste and reverent behavior of their wives. Your beauty should reside, not in outward adornment—the braiding of the hair, or jewelry, or dress—but in the inmost centre of your being, with its imperishable ornament, a gentle, quiet spirit, which is of high value in the sight of [YHWH]. (1st Peter 3:1-4 ESV)

Any married couple in the Body of Messiah can contend that what YHWH intends for a blessing isn't always so blissful. In fact, there are those whose marriages have been outright plagued with blisters. Marriages will, on occasions, appear as rocky as the road to Glory itself because both partners are imperfect. A marriage sanctioned by the Father should ideally involve two members who have both received the gift of salvation, and who are both working out their salvation. But, at times, even the ideal can seem like a raw deal if either member becomes too distracted.

When they were indoors again the disciples questioned him about this matter; he said to them, "Whoever divorces his wife and marries another commits adultery against her: so too, if she divorces her husband and marries another, she commits adultery." (Mark 10:10-12 NEB)

When our God is no longer the center of attention because something else has captured your view; when working for wealth keeps you busy, so you're only at home for a few—danger lurks. Time commitment is a major factor in determining the duration of a successful marriage. How much time does the head of the house commit to the Head of the Body? What about his spouse? How much time do the two spend in prayer? Does either even care?

"How much are you really into me?" is a question of intimacy, and it arises when either spouse feels neglected because of time ill-spent. It is also a question that YHWH regularly asks of children who claim him as Father, but whose actions often tell a different story. So what happens when blisters begin appearing after one has been burned? You hurt so badly that your journey holds no joy and so all you can do is sit. To whom do you turn? Sadly, within the Body, there are members who have turned to bodies outside of their own, and against the commands of their Creator:

145

He answered, "Have you not read that he who created them from the beginning made them male and female, and said, 'Therefore, a man shall leave his father and his mother and hold fast to his wife, and the two shall become one flesh?' So they are no longer two but one flesh. What therefore [YHWH] has joined together, let not man separate." (Matthew 19:4-6 NEB)

Copulating is no way to cope. Fornicating with foreign flesh only fans the flames of hell. In their selfishness, fornicators don't realize how much damage is done while they're out having "fun" and some won't know 'til they're dead. The Father is unwilling to accept the excuse from his people, "but everyone else is doing it." Indeed everyone is not a child of YHWH. You are and therefore such actions are deplorable.

Do you not know that he who unites himself with a prostitute is one with her in body? For it is said, "The two will become one flesh." But whoever is united with the Lord is one with him in spirit. Flee from sexual immorality. All other sins a person commits are outside the body, but whoever sins sexually, sins against their own body. Do you not know that your bodies are temples of the Holy Spirit, who is in you, whom you have received from God? You are not your own; you were bought at a price. Therefore honor God with your bodies. (1st Corinthians 6:16-20 NIV)

And yet such actions are forgivable while time still permits, if only the offenders will relinquish and repent. For those marriages that have allowed the mirages of this world to distract to the point of destruction, it is time to rewind. Remember the moment that you walked down the aisle after saying, "I do." The same love that flowed through your veins then can begin re-circulating now, if you will only return to your first Love.

63. A Reflective Moment

Selective Seething

First read: 1st Corinthians 6:12-20

[Yeshua] answered, "A man was giving a big dinner party and had sent out many invitations. At dinnertime he sent his servant with a message for his guests, 'Please come, everything is now ready.' They began one and all to excuse themselves. The first said, 'I have bought a piece of land, and I must go and look over it; please accept my apologies.' The second said, 'I have bought five yoke of oxen, and I am on my way to try them out; please accept my apologies.' The next said, 'I have just got married and for that reason I cannot come.' When the servant came back he reported this to his master. The master of the house was angry and said to him, 'Go out quickly into the streets and alleys of the town, and bring me in the poor, the crippled, the blind, and the lame.' The servant said, 'Sir, your orders have been carried out and there is still room.' The master replied, 'Go out on to the highways and along the hedge-rows and make them come in; I want my house to be full. I tell you that not one of those who were invited shall taste my banquet.' (Luke 14:16-24 NEB)

Tick. Tick. Tick. Do you hear that sound? It is the sound of temporal time slowly coming to the end of an era. Thump. Tick. Thump. Do you hear this sound of time? It is the sound of the human heart synchronized with temporal time. If you find that your heart is beating with the rhythms of the world then perhaps it is time to reset. The Church is in daily spiritual warfare, and its members are finding themselves losing a battle in which they have already been guaranteed the victory. The question is why. I believe it has everything to do with members of the Body having an adulterous affair with the world. And what's not to love? You want it? Just name it and you don't have to look far to find it. Sex? The world tells you that it's the most satisfying activity (and it is quite accessible). Some of the most moral people admit to accepting illicit sexual activity as a natural way of life, so long as it's not homosexual sex. For many in the Church it may come as a surprise to know that homosexual sex is not the only activity currently threatening the sanctity of marriage. The number of members engaging in premarital or adulterous heterosexual activity is just as rampant and is also offensive to YHWH.

Food is for the belly and the belly for food, you say. True; and one day [YHWH] will put and end to both. But it is not true that the body is for lust; it is for [Yeshua]—and [Yeshua] for the body. [YHWH] not only raised our Lord from the dead; he will also raise us by his power. Do you not know that your bodies are limbs and organs of [Messiah]? Shall I then take from [Messiah] his bodily parts and make them over to a harlot? Never. (1st Corinthians 6:13-15 NEB)

What is unfortunate is that, within the Body, sex remains a topic of taboo. Many parents find themselves too embarrassed to discuss the issue of sex and sexuality with their children and likewise, save for a few here and there, the Church chooses to remain silent on the issue. Unless there is controversy in the air; only then do members become outspoken critics of what society insists is natural. The Church's refusal to comply is commendable, but there is still work to do nevertheless. Rather then taking a defensive stance that is often hateful in delivery, the Holy Spirit is urging members of the Body to take a more "offensive" approach that is firm, yet compassionate—such was the way of Messiah. Remember that we too were once lost. However, equally remember that compassion must never equate with compromise. What's disturbing is that while the Church largely denounces homosexuality (and appropriately so), the same ecumenical disdain isn't shown for those engaging in heterosexual premarital or adulterous affairs. Presently, is the heart of the Church beating rhythmically in time with American culture? While American acceptance of homosexuality is on the rise, it is, thankfully, still largely viewed as immoral. On the other hand, premarital and adulterous sex is largely viewed as non-preferable, yet tolerable.

> Now they had forgotten to bring bread, and they had only one loaf with them in the boat. And he cautioned them, saying, "Watch out; beware of the leaven of the Pharisees and the leaven of Herod." (Mark 8:14-15 NEB)

Regardless of the behavior our surrounding culture is condoning, the Church must cease engaging in selective seething. More importantly, the Church must discontinue its passive and then reactive rants. Such sentiments are generally emotion driven and engender resentment rather than results. Instead, members of the Body should take an assertive, preventative, and proactive position that is prayerfully driven. The results? Not a resentful and divided Body, but a repentant and united one. The bottom line? YHWH intended for his gift of sex to occur between a man and a woman within the confines of marriage. The Church's selective seething has created an atmosphere that suggests the Father, rather than man, is tolerant of all types of sexual deviance except one. As such, sexually illicit behavior is on the rampage, and ravaging members of the Church—among all age groups; both single and married; male and female.

> Keep turning blind to such a plight and soon it will be hard to see.
> If left alone this tainted seed may choke all those now free.

64. Foolish Friends I

First read: 1st Kings 12:1-17

From the gazing at the glitter to the sowing of the seeds; from the citing of the source to the whacking of the weeds; it was you who chose to engage. Remember that while on your journey, what surrounds you is your stage. Each act is different but the choice of roles will remain the same. Once again, it is advantageous to decide before the act begins whether you will play the victim or victor. Conversely, you may have some help in choosing your role because your stage around isn't yours alone. You share the stage with members of your company. Know the members of your company and know which members to keep. However, if too many members are adversely affecting your performance, know when to part with the company.

When [Yeshua] saw the crowd around him, he gave orders to cross to the other side of the lake. Then a teacher of the law came to him and said, "Teacher, I will follow you wherever you go." [Yeshua] replied, "Foxes have holes and birds of the air have nests, but the Son of Man has no place to lay his head." Another disciple said to him, "Lord first let me go and bury my father." But [Yeshua] said to him, "Follow me, and let the dead bury their own dead." (Matthew 8:18-22 TNIV)

Every Christian has a past life that includes past relationships, many of which were bad ones. Part of the struggle in becoming a new creature is in understanding the necessity of letting go the loved ones who aren't in love with the idea of joining you on your new journey. To some this screams of insensitivity, "I can't just up and leave the people who I care about so much, and who have been with me through thick and thin—that doesn't sound very Christ-like." Actually it's quite Christ-like and we only need look to the Gospels for conformation. Prior to the Twelve's quest to begin capturing souls, Yeshua delivered a heart-piercing revelation:

No man is worthy of me who cares more for father or mother than for me; no man is worthy of me who cares more for son or daughter; no man is worthy of me who does not take up his cross and walk in my footsteps. (Matthew 10:37-38 NEB)

And while on the road to Jerusalem, Yeshua was stopped by a few men appearing eager to follow:

To another he said, "Follow me." But he said, "Lord, let me first go and bury my father." And [Yeshua] said to him, "Leave the dead to bury their own dead. But as for you, go and proclaim the kingdom of [YHWH]." Yet another said, "I will follow you, Lord, but let me first say farewell to those at my home." [Yeshua] said to him, "No one who puts his hand to the plow and looks back is fit for the kingdom of [YHWH]." (Luke 9:59-62 NEB)

Messiah is not suggesting that believers ignore the concerns of their loved ones. In truth, however, if, while on the road to Glory, those whom you love won't follow suit, then you must, out of love, give them the boot; out of love for Messiah. From time to time members should ask themselves, 'Whom do I love the most?' If any names other than YHWH fall on your tongue then stop and ask yourself, "To whom do I belong?" Your response should remind you of where your heart is. No one likes the thought of leaving anyone behind, but you must if they are keeping you from moving ahead. They are dead and in their present state have nothing more to offer you, other than their excess weight. Your cross is heavy enough, so there's no need to add lead to your luggage. Nevertheless, it doesn't mean you have to stop caring. You care enough for the lost to show them the cross. But then it's up to them to decide. When they've made their decision, it is time to make yours. Choosing to remain with the same old crowd is sending a message to Messiah: "I'm not ready to follow you now." Messiah will continue respecting your disrespectful decision for the time being. However, members should consider the fact that the Master's patience is wearing thin.

65. Foolish Friends II

First read: 1st Kings 12:1-17

You should have parted earlier with the fools you were partying with. Many of them were just as eager in enticing your sow, as they were eager to leave when your garden did grow. Their comedy was your tragedy and at your expense. And though costly it was, it has brought good since. Chopping with the axe will strengthen you. As your company returns regaling, prepare to part ways. To all do the foolish regale of their folly, to remove all doubt that they're fools.

Rehoboam had an opportunity that YHWH offers to all of his children in every generation. The opportunity to regain the footing lost by foolish family members of the past, and to continue on the path set before us by our heavenly Father; to once again walk the road still less traveled by most, but has nevertheless been required of us by the Son. Unfortunately, members don't always pay attention to those who have walked ahead of them and stumbled. Because of road-side distractions or lack of development, the continued falls of their predecessors fall on blind eyes and deaf ears. Sometimes we are so enraptured by those around us—our peers—that we fail to focus on the prize. As a prince there is no explanation as to why Rehoboam would not have been aware of Solomon's declining popularity with the people of Israel. It is worth noting that the moment Solomon turned to sin, he focused on sin; turning within while his people went without. There is no explanation except for that which plagues so many youth. Rehoboam was infatuated with his friends, and as such, paid little attention to the concerns of his father's kingdom. The Father understands childhood and the innocence which accompanies. Indeed, there is something special about a child's place and there is no expectation from the Father for his children to focus all of their attention on the affairs of adults. Like the Apostle Paul, however, there is a moment when all children are to grow up:

> When I was a child, my speech, my outlook, and my thoughts were all childish. When I grew up, I had finished with childish things. (1st Corinthians 13:10-11 NEB)

Growing up will necessitate leaving behind all childish principles. Childish ideas are no longer childish when children have become adults—they're foolish. Rehoboam failed when he insisted on accepting advice from his childhood friends who had grown into fools. Foolish friends are also fair-weather friends, and when menacing clouds begin to commence, oh how quick will the foolish flee. And there you are left bereaved and bereft while wondering how it all came to be. Learn to discern and learn when to cut the ties.

Rehobaom didn't come from a family of fools. His father Solomon had been granted unprecedented wisdom. What he lacked, at times, was willpower. When members persist in sin, they lose their power to do the Father's will. They soon forget that it is the Holy Spirit within that empowers them to obey, but the choice is always theirs. Even still, his grandfather David, himself anointed by our God, understood a thing or two about staying in good company:

Praise [YHWH]. I will give thanks to [YHWH] with my whole heart, in the company of the upright, in the congregation. (Psalms 111:1 ESV)

I am a companion of all who fear you, of those who keep your precepts. (Psalms 119:63 ESV)

Members of Messiah's Body who fear losing their friends should remember that neither the Father nor the Son is interested in isolating you from people. YHWH values relationships, and did not place before you a road designed for traveling in seclusion. Your loving Father is interested in insulating you from people who will prove more harmful than helpful to you while traveling. Leave the foolish behind, and prayerfully, in time, they will choose to catch up. Instead, ask the Father to send you fellow believers whose sights are equally set on reaching the finish line; peers who too have their eyes on the prize.

66. A Reason for Every Season: III

A Season for Rejection

First read: Numbers 16:1-35

Yes, you are the odd one out, and now the rest want to get even. They stand united as they find strength in their numbers. Moreover, no drop from the sky, so the soil is dry. In perceiving that you are now powerless, you, perhaps, find yourself paralyzed with fear. The sense of fear compounds as you struggle with standing on your own two feet; forgetting that it was on your own two feet that you wrenched free from the weeds. Seize your present fear before it becomes excess baggage.

Keep your conscience clear, so that when you are abused, those who malign your Christian conduct may be put to shame. It is better to suffer for well-doing, if such should be the will of [YHWH], than for doing wrong. For [Messiah] also died for our sins once and for all. He, the just, suffered for the unjust, to bring us to [YHWH]. (1st Peter 3:16-18 NEB)

In the Gospels, Messiah reminds his disciples that in following him, each would have his own cross to bear. In spreading the Gospel, it is imperative that seasoned believers don't forget to share. To bear the cross of Messiah is to share in his rejection. While journeying, believers will experience rejection, and each would do well to remember in experiencing that they have already been accepted by the One who matters.

For [YHWH] will not forsake his people; he will not abandon his heritage; for justice will return to the righteous, and all the upright in heart will follow it. (Psalms 94:14-15 ESV)

While walking the earth, Messiah was always cognizant of whom it was he had already been accepted by; the same One who sent him to be rejected. Nevertheless, Yeshua, being fully human, still felt the twinge of pain that comes with such encounters; first by word and tales, then through wood and nails. It is necessary that believers become rejected by the world so that we too remember why Messiah sends us out. But another painful truth also bears sharing; Yeshua was rejected by his own.

He was despised and rejected by men; a man of sorrows, and acquainted with grief; and as one from whom men hide their faces he was despised, and we esteemed him not. (Isaiah 53:3 ESV)

And a man will find his enemies under his own roof. (Matthew 10:36 NEB)

Just as he was speaking, Judas, one of the Twelve, appeared. With him was a crowd armed with swords and clubs, sent from the chief priests, the teachers of the law, and the elders. Now the betrayer had arranged a signal with them: "The one I kiss is the man; arrest him and lead him away under guard." Going at once to [Yeshua], Judas said, "Rabbi!" and kissed him. The men seized [Yeshua] and arrested him. (Mark 14:43-46 NIV)

When reading the tales of Moses and Aaron in the book of Exodus, it resonates well to know that YHWH delivered them from the blatant malevolence of Pharaoh. The Egyptians embodied everything that the Israelites were not, and Pharaoh, as king, was the epitome of the enemy. However, fast forward to the Book of Numbers and we see enemies of a different color; ones who are actually closer in complexion to Moses. Some of the same people that the Father had earlier delivered, and that been assigned special duties among their God's people, were now conspiring evil against the man YHWH had chosen as their instrument for deliverance. Moses was to be rejected by Korah, Dathan, and Abiram—not Egyptians, but fellow Israelites.

Now you are Messiah's body, and each of you a limb or organ of it. Within our community [YHWH] has appointed, in the first place apostles, in the second place prophets, thirdly teachers; then miracle-workers, then those who have gifts of healing, or ability to help others or power to guide them, or the gift of ecstatic utterance of various kinds. Are all apostles? All prophets? All teachers? Do all work miracles? Have all gifts of healing? Do all speak in tongues of ecstasy? Can all interpret them? The higher gifts are those you should aim at. (1st Corinthians 12:27-31 NEB)

Yeshua was rejected due to the jealousy of religious leaders, and so were Moses and Aaron. That YHWH always chooses some for the sake of all should elicit rejoicing, not rejection. But alas, selfishness and pride are present. Rather than asking for and cultivating the gifts the Father has preordained especially for us in helping to rebuild the Body, we would rather turn to various parts in doubtful condemnation. While Moses and Aaron did occasionally struggle, in this particular instance, they, like Messiah, did not allow the fear of rejection to deter them from the path their God had already set before.

Neither did Moses turn to himself for redemption, because his trust was in YHWH. Whether from outside the family or from within, the Father will allow his people to go through seasons of rejection, as a reminder from where their help comes. He will allow until the younger bear a resemblance to their Elder. Ultimately, the Shepherd wants his flock to know that rejection is for their own protection. Yes, it hurts the heart. Yes, it stings the soul. But, those who find anybody more worthy of adoration than the Father and Yeshua Messiah will find themselves losing out on eternal life.

As you come to him, a living stone rejected by men but in the sight of [YHWH] chosen and precious, you yourselves like living stones are being built up as a spiritual house, to be a holy priesthood, to offer spiritual sacrifices acceptable to [YHWH] through [Yeshua]. (1st Peter 2:4-5 NEB)

67. Dealing with Divorce

First read: Psalms 139:24

Adding in feelings of betrayal and seclusion, you begin looking around dazed; and before long you're gazing in peril. Caution. If you continue to gaze, in your head will it haze. Hazed with delusions of desire to connect with everyone within reach, you'll follow without first looking to see in which direction they're heading. Or, hazed with delusions of defeat, you'll decide that everyone within reach will remain at a distance. Undoubtedly, this will include those who want the best for you; those around you with integrity and wisdom. Learn to discern. Decide before you're in a daze for too long, for your dazing could lead to your death. Learn to discern before deciding. You can't discern if you're trapped in a daze.

Immediately upon receiving the gift of salvation and upon entering into a marriage-like relationship with Messiah, the believer will find many of their former friends "filing for divorce." Even with the new imparted Holy Spirit, believers will find themselves, nevertheless, seeking human companionship. Not only are such feelings expected and natural, they're okay. Yeshua created his people for relational purposes.

> If then our common life in [Messiah] yields anything to stir the heart, any loving consolation, any sharing of the Spirit, any warmth of affection or compassion, fill up my cup of happiness by thinking and feeling alike, with the same love for one another, the same turn of mind, and a common care for unity. (Philippians 2:1-2 NEB)

So it seems only natural that hurt should ensue when loved ones are no longer interested in loving you. It is during these moments of misery that believers must guard their hearts, for concern that the seed set in should sour. Embrace your emotions without allowing them to embarrass you or any member of the Body, especially its Head. Recognize that after entering into a covenant with Messiah, he will want to introduce you to his family members and that they will help to ensure you arrive at the gates of Glory still intact.

Peter said, "We here have left our belongings to become your followers." [Yeshua] said, "I tell you this: there is no one who has given up home, or wife, brothers, parents, or children, for the sake of the kingdom of [YHWH], who will not be repaid many times over in this age, and in the age to come have eternal life." (Luke 18:28-30 NEB)

This will require the believer to part ways with previous company. For some, this departure will last for a season or two, or until Messiah feels you are mature enough to rejoin in helping to repair. Others, Messiah will insist that you maintain adequate distance from until they are no longer hazardous to your spiritual health. Still, whether they "file" or you, there are things you mustn't do. First, you mustn't rush to replace what Messiah has removed in an attempt to eradicate your feelings of loneliness.

[Yeshua] settles the solitary in a home; he leads out the prisoners to prosperity, but the rebellious dwell in a parched land. (Psalms 68:6 ESV)

A departure from sin shouldn't creep up again in the image of another conscientious sinner. Yet, this is precisely what happens to many recent "divorcees." Ironically, codependency keeps many believers from ever experiencing the intimacy that the Father desires to have with his children, and that the Son seeks to have with his Body. Members must trust in Yeshua to lead them on this journey, and know that seasonal solitude isn't intended for their suffering, it's to encourage surrendering. Second, your "divorce" mustn't leave you distrustful of everybody else. Just because you mustn't trust everybody, it doesn't mean that you cannot trust anybody. Your solitude will exist in seasons, not indefinitely. If you should happen upon a fellow traveler whom YHWH has gifted with an ear to hear both you and them, then take advantage of the opportunity. They will have words of wisdom from which you can glean. Of course, their credentials lie not in a robe or a suit, but in the freshness of their fruit.

"For a good tree does not bear bad fruit, nor does a bad tree bear good fruit. For every tree is known by its own fruit. For men do not gather figs from thorns, nor do they gather grapes from a bramble bush. A good man out of the good treasure of his heart brings forth good; and an evil man out of the evil treasure of his heart brings forth evil. For out of the abundance of the heart his mouth speaks.. (Luke 6:43-45 NKJV)

Dealing with friendship divorce is difficult. After deciding to die for the sake of living, it is difficult to consider and accept that some of our closest friends will decide, for a time, to remain some of the Father's staunchest enemies. But the pathway to Heaven is not convergent and so the believer should pray ceaselessly that former friends will appear again with a passion for perfecting their soul—as they join you on the road.

Thorns and snares are in the way of the crooked; whoever guards his soul will keep far from them. (Proverbs 22:5 ESV)

68. A Reflective Moment

The Potency of Repentance: I

First read: Luke 23:39-43

Members of the Body must remember that when Messiah died to set us free, those who received his gift of salvation were no longer convicts, they became converts. Convicts have the heavy burden of carrying with them the guilt and shame which brought them to their present circumstances. If one can imagine the two criminals hanging on both sides of Messiah while on the cross, perhaps a clearer picture will emerge. The criminal on the cross who chose to taunt Messiah represents the unrepentant man who will assuredly carry with him the dead weight of sin to his grave and beyond.

But as for the cowardly, the faithless, and the vile, murderers, fornicators, sorcerers, idolaters, and liars of every kind, their lot will be the second death, in the lake of fire that burns with sulphurous flames. (Revelation 21:8 NEB)

It is possible that up until the moment his legs were broken, this man endured emotional turmoil, as well as physical pain; a regrettable choice that secured the inevitability of his death, coupled with the uncertainty of what would follow. Perhaps he thought, "What was I thinking when I. . ." and, "If I had only reconsidered that decision, I wouldn't have gotten caught." On the other hand, I do believe that for the other criminal—the one who appealed rather than antagonized—his remaining moments were different. It is important for believers to understand the following truth: There are temporal consequences for sinful behavior; consequences that don't always appear temporary, though they are. As Messiah lay dying he could have arranged it so that the criminal's confession resulted in his temporal release from physical torture. But, he didn't. Though he was assured a place in Paradise, while the criminal lived, suffering would continue until he died. In the same way, when believers repent of their past sinful behavior, they are set free from a life of sin, but not necessarily from its effects.

The conclusion of the matter is this: there is no condemnation for those who are united with [Yeshua], because in [Yeshua] the life-giving law of the Spirit has set you free from the law of sin and death. What the law could never do, because our lower nature robbed it of all potency, [YHWH] has done: by sending his own Son in a form like that of our own sinful nature, and as a sacrifice for sin, he has passed judgment against sin within that very nature, so that the commandment of the law may find fulfillment in us, whose conduct, no longer under the control of our lower nature, is directed by the Spirit. (Romans 8:1-4 NEB)

What Paul is saying is that believers are no longer compelled to sin now that they have a new nature. Because the seed of sin remains, a struggle remains. The struggle doesn't always seem easy to face. Compared to those who have yet to repent, the convert has a tougher road to travel. It is tempting to believe that the convict's

157

relative ease is a sure sign of YHWH's approval. The Father does allow for all things, but he doesn't allocate every thing. The wicked may enjoy a temporal life of bliss, but it is indeed only temporary.

> Fret not yourself because of evildoers, and be not envious of the wicked, for the evil man has no future; the lamp of the wicked will be put out. (Proverbs 24:19-20 ESV)

If left unrepentant, their eternal condition will leave them blistered. For the newly converted, however, there is absolute (though not unconditional) freedom from eternal condemnation for past sinful leaving, but not from its temporal consequences. What is offered to every believer is the Father's grace to persevere amidst those consequences, while clinging to the hope of what lies in store for all who faithfully endure. For the repentant criminal on the cross, I believe that while his physical suffering continued, the moment he confessed, Messiah graciously afforded him a peace not extended to the other. While heaving his last breaths he could also see Paradise on the horizon; thereby, making his suffering bearable.

69. Reflection or Rejection?

First read: Psalms 69:1-36

In feeling betrayed one seeks to betray, while bemoaning bouts of betrayal. The oddity of such behavior soon becomes obvious. You may reason that in leaving the crowd, the crowd, in turn, would leave. Alas, remember that after walking with the same crowd for a time they grow to love you. And in their love they cannot bear you parting company; but you did and now they are miserable.

And being no longer a con, how should you now respond? Many new converts often find themselves wrestling with old convicts, members of their former circle. For some the struggle with their past is an issue of temptation. Long after a believer's conversion experience, the flesh will continue to crave poisonous fruit. Because of her newly Spirit-filled diet, the further along the believer is in her walk, then the less inclined she is to give in to those yearnings. It will benefit the believer to realize that the goal while walking on the road to Glory is to starve the old flesh to death. It is impossible to enter into the gates of Heaven without first receiving a new body from Messiah. But what motive does Messiah have in giving you a new body if, upon reaching Heaven's gates, your old one still looks satiated.

What I mean, my brothers, is this: flesh and blood can never possess the kingdom of [YHWH], and the perishable cannot possess immortality. (1st Corinthians 15:50 NEB)

But now you must yourselves lay aside all anger, passion, malice, cursing, filthy talk—have done with them. Stop lying to one another, now that you have discarded the old nature with its deeds and have put on the new nature, which is being constantly renewed in the image of its Creator and brought to know [YHWH]. (Colossians 3:8-10 NEB)

Other converts struggle less with leaving their past behind and more with their past leaving them alone. How ideal, if every time a convict converted to Messiah, his entourage, sharing in his former misery, converted with equal zeal. This is a fleshly ideal which would prefer the path of least resistance so that the believer never shares in the sufferings of Messiah.

Then they led him away to be crucified. On their way out they met a man from Cyrene, Simon by name, and pressed him into service to carry his cross. So they came to a place called Golgotha (which means "Place of a skull") and there he was offered a draught of wine mixed with gall; but when he had tasted it he would not drink. (Matthew 27:32-34 NEB)

Neither does it strengthen the disciple who must continuously overcome rejection while wearing the robe of righteousness. The Father's ideal is to win convicts over—not through a shared emotional experience, being both temporal and temporary—but by seeing a reflection of Messiah in the convert. The believer does not reflect Messiah immediately upon conversion; this is the continuing work of sanctification, requiring daily submission to the Holy Spirit. However, it is the gift of salvation which grants former convicts access to the Holy Spirit, and allows them to suffer toward reflection. Suffering for Messiah should engender compassion for the convict. All convicts need compassion; all convicts need Messiah. That it is difficult for the convict to part ways with the newly converted, and that misery is their mode of flattery isn't comforting; but, neither should it confound. The convict spreads misery so that others will know he's still confined, and as such, miserable. What is painful for the convert is equally painful for the convict, whose soul seeks conversion. Perhaps he doesn't yet realize that your rejection is a reflection of Messiah. The believer though, needs to remember that Messiah's death on the cross was a rejection of sin and not the sinner. Separation from sinners is necessary for the beginner who needs to digest some wisdom before walking. However, when journeying and reproached by your past, remember that your approach in the present will influence their future. As a convert to Messiah are you a walking reflection or rejection?

70. A Reason for Every Season: III

A Season for Persecution

First read: Numbers 21:21-25

As they stand seething and scheming, their senses will sere, adding to the deadness they seek. Watch as the weight of the withered in their wake to get even will worsen the soil still weak. While still undecided they'll fall still united. If reason calls forth through their winds of despair, hopefully they'll break and divide rather than sit like flocking dodos. Even so, don't bother going over to see if you can carry the remainder. Take any number, even or odd, then divide that number by One. The fool entertains to find what remains; the wise move on when they're done.

When day broke, the Jews banded together and took an oath not to eat or drink until they had killed Paul. There were more than forty in this conspiracy. They came to the chief priests and elders and said, "We have bound ourselves by a solemn oath not to taste food until we have killed Paul. It is now for you, acting with the Council, to apply to the commandant to bring him down to you, on the pretext of a closer investigation of his case; and we have arranged to do away with him before he arrives." (Acts 23:12-15 NEB)

Admit it. Persecution is one of the last things any Christian wants to consider as a component of their journey. Yet, YHWH has never withheld from his children the opportunity to endure. Both the Tanakh and B'rit Khadasha are filled with accounts of how the Israelites, and then the Christians, were subjected to mistreatment or attempts at mistreatment. Still, this is another part of the Gospel that's seldom shared when carrying out the Great Commission. It is no wonder then that the Christian faith doesn't feel so appealing to many converts the moment persecution stares them in the face. They haven't been told the Good News. What is so good about persecution? To begin with, all believers have the assurance that the Father will never lay upon their shoulders more than each is able to bear. If you are bearing it as a believer, it's because Messiah says you can. And while you are bearing it, Messiah is holding your hand.

So far you have faced no trial beyond what man can bear. [YHWH] keeps faith, and he will not allow you to be tested above your powers, but when the test comes he will at the same time provide a way out, by enabling you to sustain it. (1st Corinthians 10:13 NEB)

Hard pressed on every side, we are never hemmed in; bewildered, we are never at our wits' end; hunted, we are never abandoned to our fate; struck down, we are not left to die. (2nd Corinthians 4:8-9 NEB)

Second, our God is constantly about the business of strengthening his children. For a weak limb is no help to the Body, who depends upon the strength of every member, no matter its size. Often times the only way to strengthen muscles is through work, stretching just beyond their accustomed capacity. Painful? Yes. But necessary. And he will continue to strengthen until we no longer choose to wallow in the pits of the despair—Satan's lair. Third, believers need to remember that, "all eyes are on me." The novice believers as well as the unbelievers whom YHWH seeks to make his own; all are watching your responses to rejection and persecution. Some are listening, but all are watching. Messiah is using your obstacles as opportunities to increase his family size. What's his is yours. When we remember that within the Body of Messiah none is an only child, our framework when doing anything will cease to center around self.

> Remember [Yeshua], risen from the dead, born of David's line. This is the theme of my gospel, in whose service I am exposed to hardship, even to the point of being shut up like a common criminal; but the word of [YHWH] is not shut up. And I endure it all for the sake of [YHWH]'s chosen ones, with this end in view, that they too may attain the glorious and eternal salvation which is in [Yeshua]. (2nd Timothy 2:8-10 NEB)

Finally, like the Israelites in dealing with the Amorite king Sihon, the Father will allow his people to go through seasons of persecution so that in engendering perseverance they too might experience seasons of deliverance. It is a not so gentle reminder as to why YHWH sent his Son to earth and why Messiah commands the Great Commission. The good news is that for the unbeliever, Messiah continues to stand ready to deliver from death. But, in exercising wisdom, even the seasoned traveler acknowledges their need for daily deliverance. Not from death, but from the dirt deposits which had accumulated while the body was lying beneath the ground.

71. Weight of The Cross

First read: Luke 14:25-35

Shame, glares,
hateful stares;
this is the weight I choose to bear

To live a life that is filled
with bouts of grief
and brief dismay

Condemnation, scorn,
painful thorns;
ever since I've been reborn

My cross is rather heavy
from wicked men
whose sins betray

Gossip, dejection,
induced reflection;
while on the path toward perfection

It is the cost of my devotion
to Messiah the King
who brings true peace

Isolation, lies,
at times despised;
by those who hope for my demise

This is the price I must pay
to walk the road;
my load, my fleece

Persecution, tears,
weathered years;
but, staying clear of misplaced fears

While walking behind the Lord
with faithful speech
and with each breath

Abused, maligned
ill-defined
It is the lot I've been assigned

It is the weight of the cross I bear
so I will comply

72. Surrendering To Suffering

First read: Job 32-37

You will not always find yourself in the midst of unpleasant company. But if, in fact, you do, remember that it is your choice to do so. It is fear that confines those in denial to mere existence, and often a short one; too afraid of stumbling, tripping, or falling—too afraid of walking. First, they will fear falling, and so falling first they will. And, when in fervid angst to break the fall they'll fall harder still; their piercing pain is self-inflicted. Having fallen, they now fear people rushing to condemn; condescending, castigating, and judging on a whim. In the likely event they're seen, they change their grimace into a grin and exchange a wince for a wave. With eager hands hiding ebbing hearts, they will wave to you as you're passing. Beggars can indeed be choosers and those begging often choose suffering over surrendering.

Upon realizing that Eliphad, Bildad, and Zophar were not providing adequate counsel, Job should have dismissed them (if only for the season). Instead, he allowed their comments to frustrate him to the point of spiritual exasperation. YHWH does not expect his people to accept the advice of every sojourner, especially if the origin of their message is either unclear or unknown.

Then Job answered and said: "How you have helped him who has no power. How you have saved the arm that has no strength. How you have counseled him who has no wisdom, and plentifully declared sound knowledge. With whose help have you uttered words, and whose breath has come out from you?" (Job 26:1-4 ESV)

Who among the Body has not experienced such anguish at one juncture or another while journeying? We must never allow our mental anguish to further degenerate into spiritual arrogance. The first sign of arrogance is when our assumptions about the Father turn into accusations; as if any of us actually have the capacity to put our Creator on trial. Perhaps our God will redirect here, or perhaps he will just continue to hear patiently. The next sign of conceit is when the believer begins to believe that he is so righteous that YHWH has no right to approve of his suffering. It is here that the believer must remember that the only person who was ever so righteous was Yeshua Messiah, and his Father did approve.

For he grew up before him like a young plant, and like a root out of dry ground; he had no form or majesty that we should look at him, and no beauty that we should desire him. (Isaiah 53:2 ESV)

Job's friends had such twisted explanations that it wasn't too long before his defense began to sound offensive to YHWH. Pain is the prerequisite for genuine progress because only pain promises the avoidance of any future repeats, and thus any future regrets. The road to Glory is painful at times because the Father is interested in your progress. You must suffer as you repair, but despairing is never a demand. Our God does not demand that his people despair. Though, such sentiments are a sign that submission to Messiah's will is still lacking. Failure to surrender our entire beings when suffering ensues will engender spiritual failure. It isn't that the failure will necessarily prove irredeemable or that YHWH will inevitably view us as such. Believers often beat themselves when they fail to trust in the Father. He has a purpose that's beyond our conception; but, when we insist on despair then it alters our perception. All of a sudden friends become foes, and those once trustworthy are now seen as traitors. When our perceptions of our God change, so too will our impressions of life. To avoid gratuitous anguish, it is best that believers learn how to surrender when they suffer. The choice to surrender when suffering is tough. But, it doesn't require the believer to wink when they'd rather weep. Neither does it demand that he feign contentment when he'd rather cry out to YHWH. Yeshua both wept and cried out to his Father while dying on the cross to save the lost. Surrendering requires that the believer remember who's in control, so that when it's time to get out he won't stay in the hole.

> Darkness fell over the whole land from midday until three in the afternoon; and about three [Yeshua] cried aloud, "Eli, Eli, lema sabachthani?" which means, "My God, my God, why hast thou forsaken me?" (Matthew 27:45-46 NEB)

73. Fishing for the Floundering

First read: 2nd Kings 4:8-37

In continuing on your journey you will continue to see the fallen; be sure to take time out to help up those who need help. You are not being foolish in spending your time trying to help others get back on track. You are being foolish if you don't. However, in pursuing, you will find that some people are resistant to receiving. Be not be deceived, for it is not pride, but fear, that cripples those who die in denial.

No one lights a lamp and puts it in a cellar, but rather on the lamp-stand so that those who enter may see the light. The lamp of your body is the eye. When your eyes are sound, you have light for your whole body; but when the eyes are bad, you are in darkness. See to it then that the light you have is not darkness. If you have light for your whole body with no trace of darkness, it will all be as bright as when a lamp flashes its rays upon you. (Luke 11:33-36 NEB)

Are you aware of the fact that there is a multitude on the side of the road who are looking for an excuse to get on board? There is no biblical indication that Messiah expects his followers to walk with such tunnel-vision that we forget to occasionally glance at the side of the road while walking. Members must not forget that the road to Glory is positioned so that all lost sheep are in plain view, no matter how much the shade may attempt to shield. Members mustn't become so enraptured in their own walk that it causes them to ignore the longing of the lame. Those with eyes to see must begin looking. Sometimes our minds are so fixated on our own spiritual growth, or we're so caught up in the service that Messiah has called us to inside the Church, that we unintentionally neglect our Commission. It's alright; it happens to even the veteran of the veterans. It is good to know that believers serve a Master who knows the depths of their hearts and who is aware of the tiniest intention. Therefore, no defense is necessary for believers who: "Never [are] lacking in zeal, but keep your spiritual fervor, serving [Yeshua]" (Romans 12:11 NEB).

However, with equal energy and in the same ardor of spirit when serving Yeshua, believers must too remember to seek the lost.

It is Messiah who ultimately saves and yet he expects his disciples to bring him those who are floundering. This in no way implies that those on the side are an easy catch. Indeed, there exists a greater struggle now than there has ever been in the past, due to the present conditions of the sea. Not only are there sharks, but many of Messiah's fish have become content swimming in sewage. Others are discontent in their murky depths, but would rather stay than swim over and join those at the shallower end; not that they've received an invitation.

One day as he stood by the Lake of Genneesaret, and the people crowded upon him to listen to the word of [YHWH], he noticed two boats lying at the water's edge; the fishermen had come ashore and were washing their nets. He

166

got into one of the boats, which belonged to Simon, and asked him to put out a little way from the shore; then he went on teaching the crowds from his seat on the boat. When he had finished speaking, he said to Simon, "Put out into deep water and let down your nets for a catch." Simon answered, "Master, we were hard at work all night and caught nothing at all; but if you say so, I will let down the nets." They did so and made a big haul of fish; and their nets began to split. So they signaled to their partners in the other boat to come and help them. This they did, and loaded both boats to the point of sinking. When Simon saw what had happened he fell at [Yeshua]'s knees and said, "[Yeshua], leave me, sinner that I am." For he and all his companions were amazed at the catch they had made; so too were his partners James and John, Zebedee's sons. "Do not be afraid, said [Yeshua] to Simon; "from now on you will be catching men." As soon as they had brought the boats to land they left everything and followed him. (Luke 5:1-11 NEB)

Consequently, it is up to those who have already tasted the living Water to reel in the rest of the fish. It is time for the floundering to have rest. Though Elisha was a mighty man of YHWH, in following on the heels of Elijah, he wasn't so mighty as to turn down an opportunity to raise somebody else up. While seated on the judgment throne, Messiah will turn toward his servants and inquire of their catch. What will you have in your net? Anything that you are bound to regret?

Rescue those who are being taken away to death; hold back those who are stumbling to the slaughter. If you say, "Behold, we did not know this," does not he who weighs the heart perceive it? Does not he who keeps watch over your soul know it, and will he not repay man according to his work? (Proverbs 24:11-12 ESV)

74. Light of the World

First read: Matthew 5:14-16

While graced to walk the earth each day
I see darkness all around,
and hear the muffled sounds of souls
who cry aloud

I wonder if the light I bear
is easily on display
and if it's bright enough
to illuminate those bound

Does my light shine on the hurting soul
whose nourishment is crack?
Who would steal his mother's soul
for one more high?

Whose body craves the substance
as its only goal,
convinced he has to have it
or he will die.

Does my light shine on the husband
who yearns for one more drink?
Who drinks for peace to please
just one more glass

He drinks to ease the pain he feels
when his mouth is dry again,
then he pours another and
hopes the pain won't last

Does my light shine on the crafty thief
Who robs both day and night?
Who steals for no good reason
but some cheap thrill?

She cons them with her clever curves
His trade is through his might
If either meet the less than meek
they will kill

Does my light shine on the lonely wife
who misses the caress
of the one who once adored
her very soul?

She gives her self to other men—
a most deceitful life
She sleeps to seek a man
who will make her whole

Does my light shine on the dark morose
Who sees no other way?
Who feels that only death will solve
the troubles they ensue?

A knife wound here or there or
with some pills to overdose
Do the sullen cry out in vain
to me and you?

Does my light shine on the battered son
whose father loves to touch?
and whose mother tells him that
he's full of lies?

He can't stay home another day,
so now's he's on the run
He finds comfort on the street
and there he hides

Does my light shine on those with vain conceit
who love money more than men?
Whose thirst for greed keeps them
reaching for the sky?

Whose quest for power pushes them
towards goals they cannot meet,
without pushing others down
to claim their prize?

Does my light shine on the little girl
whose mother loves to hit?
And whose father left the home
when she was two?

She's never heard the words before
"You're more precious than a pearl. "
She limps because both legs
are black and blue

Does my light shine on the angry teen
who's found safety in a gang?
Yes, a family who supplies
his wants and needs?

Though leery in his daily walk,
he desires to be seen
as someone with more gifts
than smoking weed

Does my light shine on the pregnant youth
who thought that it was love?
Who thought that he would
never leave her side?

She thought that sex would fix it
but now she knows the truth
The love she had is gone,
a lustful lie.

Does my light shine on the base and cruel
whose eyes are filled with lust?
Whose venom spews on those with
skin of different shades?

They are deadly with their poison
'cause their blood is filled with bile
Thus, they fill their hearts with hate
and there it stays

Messiah says, "To the world you are light,"
a reflection of the King
of the one who came to heal
the deaf and blind

By my words and through my deeds,
does my light give others sight?
Or do my actions toward the lost
leave the King maligned?

75. Acting on Assumptions

First read: 2nd Samuel 19:15-30

As you are walking do not make assumptions about those who are sitting on the side of the road. The fool assumes those waving, wave in haughtiness and pride. The wise still know those waving wave because they're hurt inside. The fool, with pride, keeps walking. The wise, with wounds, starts talking. Learn to discern. If those on the roadside were full of pride, they would not be waving with masks of silent contentment. Those on the side of the road do not think of themselves as too good to ask for help. They don't think much of themselves at all.

How easy it is to make assumptions about those people who, for whatever reason, have not made the decision to join the rest of us on the road to Glory. The only conjecture we have any business conceiving concerning those on the side is that they are lost. No matter their actions, it should never fail to fill us with compassion. There was never a more perfect demonstration of this truth then when the Son of YHWH, bludgeoned, bloody, and before his last breath spoke aloud:

[Yeshua] said, "Father, forgive them; they do not know what they are doing." (Luke 23:34 NEB)

How many believers are beside themselves, bewildered at the response of the King of kings? Perhaps no less than those who are equally puzzled at the plight of King David in the middle of 2nd Samuel who we find is on the run again—not from Saul—but rather his own son, Absalom:

When King David came to Bahurim, there came out a man of the family of the house of Saul, whose name was Shimei, the son of Gera, and as he came he cursed continually. And he threw stones at David and at all the servants of King David, and all the people and all the mighty men were on his right hand and on his left. And Shimei said as he cursed, "Get out, get out, you man of blood, you worthless man. [YHWH] has avenged on you all the blood of the house of Saul, in whose place you have reigned, and [YHWH] has given the kingdom into the hand of your son Absalom. See, your evil is on you, for you are a man of blood." (2nd Samuel 16:5-8 ESV)

It appears that a member of David's entourage, Abishai son of Zeruiah, sought revenge. In fact, what he was seeking was relief. So too was Shimei. But, to get the message they seek to convey, we must look past what they do and beyond what they say. For out of a broken heart comes the desire to break hearts. The mature member must keep in mind that Messiah, the carpenter, was in the business of repairing. While walking on the road to Glory, believers must perceive the possibilities of those on the side, as they remember that someone once saw the possibility in them, and so they didn't condemn.

When the days drew near for him to be taken up, he set his face to go to Jerusalem. And he sent messengers ahead of him, who went and entered a village of the Samaritans, to make preparations for him. But the people did not receive him, because his face was set toward Jerusalem. And when his disciples James and John saw it, they said, "Lord, do you want us to tell fire to come down from heaven and consume them?" But he turned and rebuked them. And they went on to another village. (Luke 9:51-56 NEB)

We too were once of their number: we all lived our lives in sensuality, and obeyed the promptings of our own instincts and notions. In our natural condition we, like the rest, lay under dreadful judgment of [YHWH]. But [YHWH], rich in mercy, for the great love he bore us, brought us to life with [Messiah] even when we were dead in our sins; it is by his grace you are saved. (Ephesians 2:3-5 NEB)

In the verses that followed, David's response to Abishai reminds all why YHWH chose to establish the throne of Yeshua through the son of Jesse. David understood that his plight, while painful, was the will of the Father's, so he chose to endure. Moreover, it is possible that David identified with Shimei's pain. Though not quite the same, remember that the King not only grieved over the death of Saul and Jonathan; it wasn't too long ago that he experienced the lost of his newborn son, and more recently, the lost of his eldest, Amnon. Like Shimei, David was acquainted with heartache. Still, what can top the response of our Redeemer? To whom was he responding? It was to a disappointed people who, while seeking a deliverer, put their Deliverer to death. Yeshua asked his Father to look past what they were doing to see what they wanted. Messiah got the message. And yet, it was not their actions he sought to excuse. But, he appealed to his Father: Their hearts have been bruised; forgive them. "By pride comes nothing but strife, but with the well-advised is wisdom" (Proverbs 13:10 NEB).

For in the tender compassion of our God the morning sun from heaven will rise upon us, to shine on those who live in darkness, under the cloud of death, and to guide our feet into the way of peace. (Luke 1:78-79 NEB)

76. Narrow Gate Narrow Mind

First read: Proverbs 22:6

Use your time wisely in walking over and talking to Those-Needy. Don't forget that you still have a journey to complete and that you are already behind due to your recent garden tending. Remember, too, that though you cannot make up time lost, if you stay focused, it is possible to catch up to time passed. Don't waste time scrubbing your hands. You will never get them clean enough and in vain you will do little but add to the stench of seasoned sweat. Not only is it unnecessary, you will also find it to be counterproductive. It is unfamiliarity that breeds contempt. Those-Needy need to hear of all the seeds you use to sow. They need to hear the painful echoes of your past. They need to see that you aren't spotless—there's still dust—yet even so, they can see how filthy sand can turn to glass. Let Those-Needy see your dust. Showing your dust to Those-Needy will keep dirt from flying into faces; thereby, eliminating any unnecessary vision problems. During the exchange you both will need a clear head.

I became a lover of language at an early age. Yet, I didn't say much at all. Thanks to my shameful stutter; I was shamed into silence. Between the ages of seven and ten I had to stomp either foot to utter even a few words. If the stomping failed me then I past the test with the twisting of my head and neck; every so often I would have to employ both. But most of the time it was too emotionally painful, so I figured why bother trying to employ both when I knew neither would lend me what I wanted. The stomping and twisting juxtaposing sounds of sorrow slipping from lips were my introduction to music. Since I was too ashamed to show my face, my interactions with those black or white were primarily confined to the words written within the pages of my books. Words became my life and through words I also learned how to live. Though, at the time I wasn't fully living because I had been silenced. I needed healing, but I also needed help to heal. How do you heal from that which you feel, when that which you feel is deep inside?

As I sat listening to the sermon being delivered one Sunday at a church in Macon, Georgia, I was saddened to hear that only a meager percentage of my generation, that is, generation Y, profess to have a relationship with Jesus Christ. Of greater interest is finding out the number walking the talk. Again, I was saddened, but I wasn't surprised. Though I can recall professing on multiple occasions, even as young as eleven, my own lips and legs didn't begin moving simultaneously until roughly six years ago.

It's difficult not to feel frustrated with the parents of today's teens. As a former foster care youth, I can grasp what it feels like to not have any parental figures in which to relate. Up until the age of fourteen, when I still lived with my mother, I never felt comfortable telling her anything. I know this had everything to do with how she responded to me when I first told her that I was being sexually molested by her second husband. She called me a liar and accused me of trying to ruin her marriage. She also sent me away several times to get help with some of my issues. I spent months at various short-term and long-term treatment facilities. At the age of seven when I saw that I wasn't getting any positive attention from my mother, I began to act out negatively. I became angry, vengeful, and began lying about everything. I also began sexually acting out, stealing, breaking into houses, and setting fires; all while still being sexually molested, and all before I turned eight years old. When my mother was stationed at Ft. Leonard Wood, Missouri, on two separate occasions, I was sent to a hospital in nearby Nevada, Missouri. Once while she was still stationed in Missouri, I was sent to a long-term facility in Tulsa, Oklahoma.

When I entered the fifth grade, after having been in and out of residential treatment centers for the last two years, I discovered the art of running away. My mother had recently divorced her second husband and her new boyfriend arrived on the scene, while husband number three waited in the wings. She and her new boyfriend had appetites for alcohol, though both were well-masked; his as a Marine, and hers as a drill sergeant in the Army. I hated my life, though the sexual molestation had stopped by now. I hated how everything always looked so disciplined and orderly on the outside, while on the inside hellish chaos reigned supreme. Constantly running away did little but fester the brewing hatred I believed my mother had toward me while I still lived with her; a feeling that was mutual. When it was time to move, I believed my mother thought that a change in the outside would mean a change for the better. After all, who wouldn't love living in Hawaii? Exit boyfriend and enter husband number three. He was a former career military official whom my mother had met while we were living in Germany, and while she was married to her first husband. I don't know when it happened, but I believe after having served almost twenty years he fell from grace, due to his own greed. He began to steal from the military and then went AWOL to avert authorities. It didn't take long for the military to find him, fine him, and put him in jail. Facing the inevitably of a major reduction in rank, he opted, instead, for a dishonorable discharge. He arrived on our doorsteps about a month before we left for Hawaii. In addition to his own drinking demons, he would also introduce my mother to drugs.

My point in relating much is to establish credibility in understanding what it feels like not to have a set of ears or a heart to share with. A majority of the youth that I come in contact with today have two parents at home. But sometimes a warm body, even if it's two, isn't enough. There are three incidents that come to mind when I think of the challenge facing our youth today, and why I believe parents need to stand up and start engaging in the task given to them by YHWH. One has to do with sex, another, drugs, and the last, alcohol.

Several years ago I was asked to participate in a commercial for a local restaurant. With me in the scene were a couple of girls from a local private high school. In between takes of the commercial, a scene from the movie *Mean Girls* began to take form. The two girls were incredulous as they berated some of their female friends for their "stupidity." Apparently, the other girl's boyfriends were regularly traveling to a nearby city for weekly massages. At least that's what they had been telling the girls. In truth, the gentlemen were also paying for sexual favors at the parlor. I tried to conceal the shocked look on my face, though I don't believe I was very successful. I chimed in, "Are you serious?" They looked at me as if I was from another planet. I then made the mistake of asking, "And are they still coming back and having sex with their girlfriends?" One of the girls turned to me and replied almost impatiently, "Um, yeah." She wasn't being rude, but it was another way of saying, "Duh." Duh? As if I'm supposed to already know how common this behavior is? I was stunned and then frustrated. "Where are the parents in all of this?" I thought. Then I realized, they are the ones giving away the keys, car, and money, which enable their "trustworthy" youth to engage in such reckless behavior.

On another occasion while mentoring some youth from the school where I taught, we left a local theater and headed to a nearby fast-food spot for a quick bite to eat. As is my custom when hanging out with youth, I was dressed casually that evening—black athletic running pants, shirt, and a baseball cap turned to the back. The scene was typical of that area with dozens of youth from public and private schools, mixed races, many in cars, all congregating together. Not long after ordering our food, one of my youth was invited to a nearby table where he was asked to follow the perpetrator to his car to examine his "special." There was a sign separating the culprits from our table. Yet, this particular youth was in plain sight. He did walk over, but showed his uneasiness about going over to the car. I listened to their goading for a little while longer before standing up to make my presence known. I was black, as were the dealers, but not the youth. When they saw me, I was called over to try and convince the youth that he was safe and that they were not going to hurt him. I knew otherwise. They also wanted me to come and view their "special." It was obvious from their bloodshot eyes, giddy behavior, and stammering speech that they were high. I politely but sternly told them that I was not interested and neither was the youth. They stared at me in disbelief, and with the youth at my side I left them there staring. A few days later I relayed the events with some other youth and wasn't shocked to learn that this particular establishment, in the "good" part of town, is a well known spot for drug dealers and users. This is the side of town that parents drop their kids off at all hours of the night, with plenty of money and no supervision.

And finally, one evening I spoke to a former student of mine who was struggling with getting others to like him for who he really is, rather than for whom they had grown comfortable getting to know. "Jake" is intelligent, compassionate, and an obvious leader. He possesses qualities that, when Messiah gets a hold of him, will prove invaluable for the Kingdom. In the meantime, however, Jake is seen as a suave, narcissistic, lady's man who's never short of a crass joke. He is at the age where he believes experimenting with everything is a sure way of finding that one thing he's searching for. In listening to Jake describe his parents, it is clear that he has a father who gives him wise counsel. Unfortunately, he views his father as meddlesome and any advice given as a way of ruling or ruining his life. One summer, Jake explained to me how, shortly after the graduation ceremony of a local private school, he was invited to a celebration where he drank alcohol and tried marijuana for the first time. He said there was plenty of alcohol, plenty of weed, plenty of teenage boys and girls, and no parents.

America, we have a problem. The Body in America has a problem and so the Church has a problem. When are parents going to recognize that they are spoiling the gifts that YHWH has given them? When are parents going to understand that their children really don't belong to them after all? As I heard one believer put it, "God doesn't have any grandchildren." The expectation is for every earthly parent to introduce their son or daughter to their Heavenly Father through their eldest brother, Yeshua Messiah. Some parents are giving their children too much rope and others are actually placing the noose around their neck. In the name of independence, children are becoming dependent on the world and all of its evils. In refusing to properly raise their sons and daughters in the way of YHWH, generations X, Y, and the one coming after are assuring that the youth of today and tomorrow continue to have Satan for their father. Now more than ever parents mustn't rely on their own strength and wisdom in child-rearing, but on their heavenly Father, Messiah, and the mighty power of the Holy Spirit. It is unwise for parents to trust today's youth to make the right decisions, no matter how mature they appear. The Holy Spirit is the only one capable of ensuring that our youth will make the right decisions when parents are out of sight. Parents first have the responsibility of getting their child sealed with the Holy Spirit, in receiving the gift of salvation from Messiah. And then parents must teach their children to daily ask the Father for the Holy Spirit's filling. As a rule of thumb, believers must make it a habit of trusting no one who is not sealed by, and daily yielding to, the Holy Spirit.

To some this may scream of narrow-mindedness. I make no apologies. It is only with narrow minds that believers will travel safely while on the narrow road leading to the narrow-gates of Glory. It is my prayer that parents will take time to reexamine the unique role given to them by our heavenly Father. The greater the God-driven discipline instilled within youth while they are still young, the less discipline Yeshua will need to exert on them when they enter adulthood.

Enter by the narrow gate. The gate is wide that leads to perdition, there is plenty of room on the road, and many go that way; but the gate that leads to life is small and the road is narrow, and those who find it are few. (Matthew 7:13-14 NEB)

Children, obey your parents, for it is right that you should. "Honor your father and mother" is the first commandment with a promise attached, in the words: "that it may be well with you and that you may live long in the land." You fathers, again, must not goad your children to resentment, but give them the instruction, and the correction, which belong to a Christian upbringing. (Ephesians 6:1-4 NEB)

77. On Behalf of Those Silenced

First read: Psalms 139:13-16

On behalf of those silenced who shall never be seen
Because they were never a part of the deal
Though the passion was real
But, mommy and daddy were just barely sixteen
And were drinking while seeking a thrill

No, Rachel or Derrick won't ever know joy
That comes from walking the earth
Or its intrinsic worth
What started as life has now been destroyed
No sunlight, no laughter, no birth

To those who conceived through carousing
And feel burdened by what shall ensue
Because of the things you do
Do not bring death because of your fling
'Cause there are others who won't ever be due

Is there anyone in Israel who'll give them a voice?
Who will stand up and loudly proclaim,
While having no shame,
That YAH is aware of those making the choice
To end life in ending their pain

Oh, the womb of Eve and the daughters of seeds
What a blessing to carry and bear
Though some do not share
Yes, our God sees all the red blood and grieves
Over lives that could have been spared

Yes, there are those who carry from affliction
They are victims of violence and more
Our God will settle that score
But give not the child a lasting conviction
For that violence our God too abhors

To those wounded by the lust and anger of men
Oh, how YAH wants to step in to heal
Yes, your scars are real
But the seed within need not offend
And your anger need not kill to reveal

On behalf of those silenced who will never be seen
And whose voices will never be heard
Our God has just one word:
"Enough of the slaughter of souls left demeaned
Lest the earth feel my ire now deferred."

175

78. Hands from Hell

First read: Psalm 30:2

I was touched by hands from hell
But, so as not to seem weak
I refused to speak
so the hands that were touching
still touched me

I was touched by hands from hell
But, so as not to seem gay
I had nothing to say
So he continued to caress
and to clutch me

I was touched by hands from hell
But, so as not to show fear
whenever he was near
I stood still while he kneeled
to invade me

I was touched by hands from hell
But when I decided to tell,
my mother just yelled
While the man sat still
and forgave me

I was touched by hands from hell
But, so as not to cause static
with my mother, the addict,
I kept silent
and suffered for years

I was touched by hands from hell
But, so as not to seem timid
I pushed all limits
And proudly kept back
all my tears

As time started passing,
my spirit started asking
"When is my time up
from this jail?"

"How much longer
must I keep acting stronger
while doused in the
flames of hell?"

And then I could hear it—
my God's own Spirit
A voice that rattled
my soul

"On behalf of those weak
It is time to speak;
there are pieces that now
must be whole."

To those sons who've been touched
by hands from hell,
To those who've been tortured
while sitting in jail,

To those who've been silent
while wanting to yell
I have a message of mending
for you:

"You have a Father in Heaven
with hands to heal
with a Brother who is sorrowed
by the pain that you feel

And they both are real
So, let them heal,
let them heal,
Let them heal.

And when our Father is finally done
You'll be one step closer
To reflecting his Son

A Savior who defeated the
powers of hell—
Nail after nail,
after nail, after nail."

79. A Reflective Moment

Carrying My Torch

Child abuse. Not exactly a topic of choice among most circles. There was a time when I dwelt among those circles. For me it wasn't an issue of indifference relating to a topic that was unfamiliar to me and therefore irrelevant to my daily living. Instead, it was an issue of having grown weary of its familiarity. For awhile, after graduating from high school, I refused to acknowledge any meaningful aspect of my past, because I no longer cared to wear it as an appendage to my identity. Most people don't realize that I married at the age of sixteen. Yes. It happened in December of 1997 when I first arrived at the Methodist Home for Children & Youth in Macon, Georgia. I didn't even realize that I was getting married but someone else decided that I was. And so my surname was exchanged for a new one. For roughly the next fifteen months I was no longer Marquis L. Harris. My new last name became "From the Methodist Home." Whenever I was introduced by others it was rarely as Marquis Harris, but rather Marquis from the Methodist Home. It didn't take long for the annoyance to set in. At the time I wasn't ashamed of where I lived. In truth I had more of my needs met there than any foster home had ever provided for me. I've heard horror stories, and had experienced some of my own before moving to the Methodist Home. I didn't mind that everyone knew where I lived. I did mind that in the eyes of those around, I wasn't a person, but an object—who I was became affixed to where I lived. In May of 1999, upon graduating from Central High School, I decided that prior to leaving for Asbury College, I was getting a divorce. I was taking back my own name.

Only in the past three years, as of this writing, have I come to understand the necessity of remembering who I am; a child of YHWH who had an abused start. But because of Yeshua's goodness and grace, I am experiencing a healing that only he can offer and render. Though never delightful to our heavenly Father, my bruising then was allowed for my using now. Even as I type these words, a peace flows through my body and it is breathtaking. When I first invited Messiah into my life nearly fifteen years ago, my identity was still found in the world. In the summer of 2006 I experienced the pain of repentance and agreed—not to a quasi, co-relational partnership with Yeshua—but to an unconditional surrendering of my entire being in acknowledging him as Lord of my life. In receiving the Father's gift of the Holy Spirit, I am now content in revisiting my past as I realize that my identity is firmly secured in Heaven. Who I was isn't all, but it is a part, of who I am. I no longer dread sharing who I am with others out of fear of rejection because I have already been accepted by the One who redeems.

A dispute arose among them: which of them was the greatest? [Yeshua] knew what was passing in their minds, so he took a child by the hand and stood him at his side, and said, "Whoever receives this child in my name receives me; and whoever receives me receives the One who sent me. For the least among you all—he is the greatest." (Luke 9:46-48 NEB)

The despised in this world hold a special place in the heart of our God. Children are abused, abandoned, and neglected every waking moment under the sun. For many travelers on their road to Glory, the orphaned are afforded no more attention than a passing pit stop; a pause, some pity, and then continued passing. Others are treated no better than the dirt trampled under the soles of dirty feet. However, YHWH is clear in his directives toward the treatment of the youngest persons and the Church's role in caring for the orphans. It is with newly found freedom that I count myself among the rejected, who was accepted by Messiah to shine a light on those whom the world would just as soon leave in the dark. I pray that the Holy Spirit will continue pressing upon others to join me in walking with my candle in carrying my torch.

Never despise one of these little ones; I tell you, they have their guardian angels in heaven, who look continually on the face of my heavenly Father. (Matthew 18:10-11 NEB)

So put away all filth and evil excess and humbly welcome the message implanted within you, which is able to save your souls. But be sure you live out the message and do not merely listen to it and so deceive yourselves. For if someone merely listens to the message and does not live it out, he is like someone who gazes at his own face in a mirror. For he gazes at himself and then goes out and immediately forgets what sort of person he was. But the one who peers into the perfect law of liberty and fixes his attention there, and does not become a forgetful listener but one who lives it out—he will be blessed in what he does. If someone thinks he is religious yet does not bridle his tongue, and so deceives his heart, his religion is futile. Pure and undefiled religion before the Father is this: to care for orphans and widows in their misfortune and to keep oneself unstained by the world. (James 1:21-27 NEB)

80. Benevolence

First read: Psalm 127:3-4

They promised to hold you,
Give and adore you
They wanted to show you
Off to the world

What joy they would bring you
Songs they would sing you
A family to help you
Hide from the world

The time has now come to
Meet those who will love you
Two people who picked you
Out of the world

But not too long with you
They happen to see you
There's baggage now with you
Brought from the world

Daddy doesn't want you
Mama can't stand you
They both want to send you
Back to the world

The clothes that came with you
The scars you take with you
Don't let the door hit you
As you enter the world

81. Enabling the Unable

First read: Psalms 102:19-20

As you are walking over to help, be mindful of the situation and tell yourself that as you empathize, you will not enable. Listen? Yes. Cry? If you need to. Wearing your feelings is only a weakness if your wearing them weakens them still. Be mindful of your task in going over to the side of the road. To look down on Those-Needy? Well, yes, actually, and no. Don't be foolish. You, of course, need to look down so they can see you.

> For we are not as many, which corrupt the word of [YHWH]: but as of sincerity, but as of [YHWH], in the sight of [YHWH] speak we in [Yeshua]. (2nd Corinthians 2:17 AKJV)

Yes, Messiah did cry while upon the cross dying to save the lost. But, it was blood, not tears that set free those who had been held in captivity. There is nothing wrong with weeping for those needy, for they are indeed in a sad state of affairs. However, what those on the side of the road need is not someone to rock and lull them into a deeper slumber. They need a sharpened and jagged rock to hold on to so they don't lose their footing when rising up. At this juncture they don't need coddling, they need converting. In the book of Acts, we find that, while on their way to pray at three in the afternoon, Peter and John are stopped by a crippled man begging for pity. Yes, the apostles listened to his plea, but they could also see:

> But Peter fixed his eyes on him as John did also, and said, "Look at us." Expecting a gift from them, the man was all attention. And Peter said, "I have no silver or gold; but what I have I give you: in the name of [Yeshua] of Nazareth, walk." Then he grasped him by the right hand and pulled him up; and at once his feet and ankles grew strong; he sprang up, stood on his feet, and started to walk. He entered the temple with them, leaping and praising [YHWH] as he went. (Acts 3:4-8 NEB)

Apparently the beggar had been getting by on sympathy, which, while helpful, continued to render him helpless. Though it is true that the Gospel doesn't need conveying in the same fashion to every cripple, the presentation must never lose its potency. It is one thing to empathize with the broken in acknowledging that we too were once members of the waking wake. Empathy is vital when in pursuit of revival. Your ability to relate is what's going to make you reliable; those needy have no other proof of your passion. Moreover, there is no empathy where there is no intimacy. A disciple of Messiah mustn't avoid intimacy. No heart to heart? No eye to eye? Then no surprises should exist when they don't buy into your "lie." Paul understood this and in writing a letter of encouragement to the church in Thessalonica, he begins by reminding the Macedonians of their own wakening experience:

> For neither at any time used we flattering words, as ye know, nor a cloke of covetousness; God is witness: nor of men sought we glory, neither of you, nor yet of others, when we might have been burdensome, as the apostles of

[Messiah]. But we were gentle among you, even as a nurse cherisheth her children: so being affectionately desirous of you, we were willing to have imparted unto you, not the gospel of God only, but also our own souls, because ye were dear unto us. (1st Thessalonians 2:5-8 AKJV)

However, we are never to sympathize with the plight of the spiritually pitiful. The Savior didn't sympathize with the perpetually sinful anymore than he sympathized with sin. Start sympathizing with the person sitting in a leaky boat and you shall soon find yourself in the same boat, equally unholy and drowning. Instead, think back to the days when you were drowning and then extend your hand.

Righteous lips are the delight of a king, and he loves him who speaks what is right. (Proverbs 16:13 ESV)

A man who flatters his neighbor spreads a net for his feet. (Proverbs 29:5 ESV)

When they heard this they were cut to the heart, and said to Peter and the apostles, "Friends, what are we to do?" "Repent," said Peter, "repent and be baptized, every one of you, in the name of [Yeshua] the Messiah for the forgiveness of your sins; and you will receive the gift of the Holy Spirit. For the promise is to you, and to your children, and to all who are far away, everyone whom [YHWH] may call." (Acts 2:37-39 NEB)

82. Trail of Tears

First read: Job 9-14

Walk down the trail of tears for too long and soon you'll find that you're walking in circles. If ever you find yourself walking in circles, somewhere you took a bad step. You need to stop and ask for some directions; preferably not from the person walking next to you.

He also offered them a parable: "Can one blind man be guide to another? Will they not both fall into the ditch?" (Luke 6:39 NEB)

The trail of tears is a dangerous path to walk down. It appears at the moment when both doubt and frustration decide to make a fashionably late appearance at the pity party a believer will occasionally throw for himself while in the midst of suffering. Job began walking down the trail of tears after years of walking on the road to Glory. Why the sudden departure? After entertaining the wisdom of Eliphaz, Bildad, and Zophar, Job's confidence in his relationship with YHWH began to erode. In the beginning it was easy for Job to dismiss Eliphaz's conjecture that his suffering was punitive rather than purposeful. Though, in speaking to YHWH, it is clear that the seed of uncertainty had been planted nonetheless.

If I sin, what do I do to you, you watcher of mankind? Why have you made me your mark? Why have I become a burden to you? Why do you not pardon my transgression and take away my iniquity? For now I shall lie in the earth; you will seek me, but I shall not be. (Job 7:20-21 ESV)

There are days when tears can clear up the haze, and then there are times when tears can blur the vision. What once was seen clearly now becomes questionable. It is wrong and unfair to the Father to assume that the relationship with child and sheep shifts simply because their circumstance has changed. But how easily and definitively we make the assumption. YHWH expects that tears will fall when the winds appear harsh; winds tend to have that effect. However, when our tears begin to water the seed of uncertainty, then it isn't long before the believer finds herself entangled in the weeds of indictment. Clutched by the weeds, she begins walking in circles while asking the question, "Why?" Not long after circling, her assumptions will quickly turn into accusations. Bildad accurately points out that Job sounds foolish in his diatribe, yet he fails to provide adequate counsel. Rather than encouraging Job to remember the road he's been traveling on and then wisely guiding him back, Bildad instead reinforces Eliphaz's supposition that Job must have sinned, because in his experiences only the sinful have suffered. Bildad's response only ensures that Job's stint along the trail of tears will remain secure.

You have granted me life and steadfast love, and your visitation has preserved my spirit. And these things you hid in your heart; I know that this was your purpose. If I sin, you watch and do not forgive me of my iniquity. (Job 10:12-14 ESV)

Job's response to YHWH illustrates how his decision to remain on this trail has only exacerbated his anguish. On the one hand, Job concedes that his heavenly Father has always protected him, and in the same breath he proclaims to know the heart of YHWH and accuses him of being malicious. What psychologists regularly refer to as displacement, Messiah asserts is disrespectful. The Father's heart is without malice and it is foolish for the suffering to suggest otherwise. The trail of tears can lead to a distorted, if not a sordid, view of our God. The protector is now seen as the predator and so there is no motivation to pray. It is imperative that in the midst of suffering, the tearful kind don't suddenly go blind.

83. A Reflective Moment

The Potency of Repentance: Part III

The Pain of Resistance

First read: Luke 23:26

While not knowing for sure, I am fairly certain that Simon from Cyrene found the cross of Yeshua Messiah weighty. The rod that Yeshua bore was for our sins, not his own. And again, the repentant criminal lying next to him, he too suffered before entering into the promised Paradise. Readers will recognize that the common experience shared by all three was their acquaintance with pain. As repentant believers, it is wise to understand that the road to Glory will have with it painful experiences, but they won't all come from external situations. In truth, most aching will come from internal changes, as the Holy Spirit presses all toward glorification:

I mean this: if you are guided by the Spirit you will not fulfill the desires of your lower nature. That nature sets its desires against the Spirit, while the Spirit fights against it. They are in conflict with one another so that what you will to do you cannot do. But if you are led by the Spirit you are not under the law. (Galatians 5:16-18 NEB)

This is the discipline that the author of Hebrews describes as never pleasant and that at times seems painful. Simon of Cyrene was illustrating the conditioning that members of the Body would continuously emulate if they were interested in following Messiah. Upon conversion there will exist moments of euphoria, as believers embrace their newly given freedom. Most importantly, their souls will shout praises to Yeshua Messiah for setting them free from captivity.

Praise [Yeshua]. Praise [Yeshua], O my soul. I will praise [YHWH] as long as I live; I will sing praises to [Yeshua] while I have my being. Put not your trust in princes, in a son of man, in whom there is no salvation. When his breath departs, he returns to the earth; on that very day his plans perish. Blessed is he whose help is the God of Jacob, whose hope is in [Yeshua], who made heaven and earth, the sea, and all that is in them, who keeps faith forever; who executes justice for the oppressed, who gives food to the hungry. [Yeshua] sets the prisoners free; [Yeshua] opens the eyes of the blind. [Yeshua] lifts up those who are bowed down; [Yeshua] loves the righteous. (Psalms 146:1-8 ESV)

Believers will thank Messiah for giving their aching wrists and ankles respite after having been in shackles for so long; and YHWH and his angels will share in their delight. The celebration is short lived, however. The lower nature, still influenced by Satan, sits pouting while the believer enjoys his mountain top experience. Soon it's time for members to begin walking on the road, and so now the struggle begins. Prior to accepting Messiah, there did exist a slight struggle as the soul acknowledged that it really belonged to a higher power. But being powerless to act against his then current master, the seed of sin, the soul sat sulking while the body continued to self-destruct.

184

In my inmost self I delight in the law of [YHWH], but I perceive that there is in my bodily members a different law, fighting against the law that my reason approves and making me a prisoner under the law that is in my members, the law of sin. Miserable creature that I am, who is able to rescue me out of this body doomed to death? (Romans 7:22-24 NEB)

Still, the believer who has been sealed and then filled by the Holy Spirit needn't feel defeated any longer.

[YHWH] alone, through [Yeshua]. Thanks be to [YHWH]. In a word then, I myself, subject to [YHWH]'s law as a rational being, am yet, in my unspiritual nature, a slave to the law of sin. The conclusion of the matter is this: there is no condemnation for those who are united with [Yeshua], because in [Yeshua] the life-giving law of the Spirit has set you free from the law of sin and death. (Romans 7:25-8:2 NEB)

It doesn't mean that we won't have occasional feelings of heightened frustration. The truth is that the lower nature will continue to fight in vain to have its way, and it will annoy most after the new journey has lasted but for a short time. Satan and his fallen kingdom, including demons, will use all former experiences of the believer in an effort to trip. While the Holy Spirit and Satan are not evenly matched, without the intervention of the Holy Spirit, the convert doesn't stand a chance. There is good news, however. The author of Hebrews makes it clear that a disciplined life will eventually lead to an honest life. Though pains will exist in the beginning—saying no to old lifestyles, choices, and probably old friends—the committed believer will begin to appreciate the Father's gift. It is with necessity that those shackles stay visible. In maturing, the soul will look with disdain at its former prison, and, in union with the Spirit, will be encouraged to continue resisting. What's more is that with each disciplined step, the Holy Spirit is also strengthening the believer. It is with the Spirit's imparting wisdom that the believer views such strength as a means of remaining connected to the Vine, and not as an instrument for flying solo. Greater pain will ensue in crashing.

He will keep you firm to the end, without reproach on the Day of [Yeshua]. It is [YHWH] himself who called you to share in the life of his Son [Yeshua Messiah] our Lord; and [YHWH] keeps faith. (1st Corinthians 1:8-9 NEB)

[Messiah] bought us freedom from the curse of the law by becoming for our sake an accursed thing; for Scripture says, " Cursed is everyone who is hanged on a tree." And the purpose of it all was that the blessing of Abraham should in [Yeshua] be extended to the Gentiles, so that we might receive the promised Spirit through faith. (Galatians 3:13-14 NEB)

84. Shaming the Sham

First read: Psalms 94:1-23

Those-Needy, while not inferior, need to see clearly that, presently, they are in an inferior position. In truth, they can see others walking by, and a distinction in position is apparent. That is until their daze induces haze and all becomes blurred. Then they really can't see a distinction anymore. Because they have resolved to giving in to rejection and thus to giving up on life, their senses, much like their emotions, become deadened. What you see as you are walking by are the waking waves of Those-Needy, signaling what will soon transpire as they grow weaker in their wake. At this point Those-Needy need to be awoken. Standing over and looking down should first clear up the haze, allowing them once again to clearly see their inferior position. You also want them to see that they don't have to stay there.

Yea, so have I strived to preach the gospel, not where [Messiah] was named, lest I should build upon another man's foundation: but as it is written, To whom he was not spoken of, they shall see: and they that have not heard shall understand. (Romans 15:20-21 AKJV)

Whether they care to admit it, those who have yet to make it onto the road of Glory are needy and in need of your help. If attuned to the Holy Spirit, then you will have no trouble detecting those who are crying out; though no tears will you see falling from their eyes. Many of these have entered a church or two in search of some truth, but were offered little incentive to stay. Others never received an invitation. It is a costly endeavor to ignore the waves of the wake. It is no different then a jewelry store placing a fine diamond in their display window, upon seeing the display, in walks a man wearing tattered clothing and a wearied look. The shop owner has left the jewelry store into the care of several employees. As the wearied man enters the door he notices how busy the store is and so decides to wait patiently near the back. There are dozens of other customers scurrying around who appear to have the attention of every sales clerk. For a few moments the scene looks odd because there are more clerks in the store then there are customers, and yet none of the clerks are available. Some customers have two or even three clerks swarming around them like bees attracted to a honey comb. One has the manager's undivided attention. To the wearied man, the scene no longer looks odd, it looks old. While continuing to wait patiently he mutters to himself, "Oh, um, yeah. It isn't honey, it's their money." Dressed to the nines are all the customers in the store, except for the man who looks ragged and poor. After waiting for almost thirty minutes without so much as a hello, he turns to go. With the same reoccurring reaction, the man's interest in quality diamonds has waned and he turns instead to the seedy pawn shop up the road.

Treat others as you would like them to treat you. (Luke 6:31 NEB)

There was once a rich man, who dressed in purple and the finest linen, and feasted in great magnificence every day. At his gate, covered with sores, lay a poor man named Lazarus, who would have been glad to satisfy his hunger with the scraps from the rich man's table. Even the dogs used to come and lick his sores. One day the poor man died and was carried away by the angels to be with Abraham. The rich man also died and was buried, and in Hades, where he was in torment, he looked up; and there, far away, was Abraham with Lazarus close beside him. "Abraham, my father," he called out, "take pity on me. Send Lazarus to dip the tip of his finger in water, to cool my tongue, for I am in agony in this fire." But Abraham said, "Remember, my child, that all the good things fell to you while you were alive, and all the bad to Lazarus; now he has his consolation here and it is you who are in agony. But that is not all: there is a great chasm fixed between us; no one from our side who wants to reach you can cross it, and none may pass from our side to us." (Luke 16:19-26 NEB)

It is the Church's responsibility to ensure that no one is walking around wearing a cubic zirconium thinking to themselves, "I don't know if it's real, but it's cheap, barely cost a dime, and it's mine." Before too long they'll forget that what they are wearing is phony. While on the side of the road those in their wake will begin flashing what's fake and the Holy Spirit will usher you over to inform. How will you convince those needy to replace their gem with something genuine? Simply walking over to them and shoving your diamond in their face will prove insufficient. At this point, telling them where you bought the diamond from will prove disastrous. While admittedly difficult, this is the unfortunate position the Church often finds herself in today; attempting to rectify the mishaps of other members. Messiah takes issue with shepherds and sheep with sham testimonies. The authenticity of the faith is found in the actions of his followers, but a problem arises when those seeking Truth are repelled by the "truth" that they see. Yes, it is a choice to buy into a lie, and those who choose to remain attached to such will soon find themselves without much. However, the Church must begin taking steps to show those needy that the Truth is not only viable, it is of greater value.

Whoever despises his neighbor is a sinner, but blessed is he who is generous to the poor. (Proverbs 14:21 ESV)

'Therefore, you shepherds, hear the word of [YHWH]: "As I live," says [Yeshua], "surely because my flock became a prey, and my flock became food for every beast of the field, because there was no shepherd, nor did my shepherds search for my flock, but the shepherds fed themselves and did not feed my flock"—therefore, O shepherds, hear the word of [YHWH]! Thus says [Yeshua]: "Behold, I am against the shepherds, and I will require my flock at their hand; I will cause them to cease feeding the sheep, and the shepherds shall feed themselves no more; for I will deliver my flock from their mouths, that they may no longer be food for them."(Ezekiel 34:7-10 NKJV)

Here is another picture of the kingdom of Heaven. A merchant looking out for fine pearls found one of very special value; so he went and sold everything he had, and bought it. (Matthew 13:45-46 NEB)

My brothers, believing as you do in [Yeshua], who reigns in glory, you must never show snobbery. For instance, two visitors may enter your place of worship, one a well-dressed man with gold rings, and the other a poor man in shabby clothes. Suppose you pay special attention to the well-dressed man and say to him, "Please take this seat." while to the poor man you say, "You can stand; or you may sit here on the floor by my footstool." do you not see that you are inconsistent and judge by false standards? (James 2:1-4 NEB)

85. Through Heaven's Eyes

First read: James 2:1-13

I am driving down a busy street-
rushing home from work again
when my car is forced to stop
and spend,at the changing of
the light
I am thinking of the days affairs;
one more day of some more hot air
when something from the side of me
begins obstructing
my sight
A man who is roughly six feet tall,
with an unclean face and crooked teeth—
he has the nerve to place his hands
on the corner of
my pane
Thank YAH the light just changed
I certainly don't need another bum
playing dumb, coming up to me
begging, pleading, like he hasn't already
been stealing
I keep driving until once again I am
stopped by yet another red
It's 6pm and already dim
and he's wearing a hood
I understood
It is perfectly plain to see
My doors lock as I stare at my clock
and I'm hoping his eyes
won't turn
to me
Thank YAH the light just changed
I certainly don't need a blood
or crip trying to pistol whip
coming up to me thuggin', bangin'
while high
My foot hits the gas once more
and I cruise with the pedal to the floor
"No more red, no more red."
I just want to make it home to bed;
my heart throbs
I was almost robbed
while leaving downtown behind
and now my head, it aches
Yet, there's still one more sign,
it's red
She walks out of the shadows
it's dim just after 6pm,
but I can see her legs, her supplies -
flesh stockings thigh high,
and her red dress
Now my head is a mess
"Oh no, not tonight;
not with this scarlet harlot."
Thank YAH I can pass the sign
just now
I certainly don't need a two-bit tramp
wearing her hooker stamp
coming up to me with a price
being nice as she tries
to entice
I skid off into the night
now to my home where I'll be safe
and content
Until a sign is sent
from above—

"Pop" goes my tire and then
a bag is whacked in my face
Now I find myself
in a new place with
white space
I'm in a momentary daze
Now I see a throne, am I home?
A man in white with an unclean face,
and a hooded cloak appears to me;
His flesh with scarlet stains
"You are to blame," he says
"Your judgments have become your judge
and now you won't ever know what was
until you see
my face again."
"For your tire was going flat around 6pm,
while it was dim;
so three persons I sent to warn,
and you sat content with your contempt,
in judgment, with scorn, while you claimed
to have been re-born."
"You claimed to have Heaven's eyes
but it was only a disguise;
You claimed to have Heaven's eyes,
but that was
a lie.
You claimed to have Heaven's eyes,
but you used them to despise;
You claimed to have Heaven's eyes,
but tonight all you saw were
size, highs, and thighs.
You claimed to have Heaven's eyes
after you were baptized in my name.
But tonight, three times,
I was defamed and you are
to blame."
I meekly reply to him who spoke to me;
though my voice is weak,
"Lord, I am to blame
for defaming
your name.
I ask for your pardon, please.
Forgive me
for my judging eyes;
I have not one
alibi."
His reply was quick and to the point,
"You are forgiven my sheep,
but when you wake,
and have been healed,
speak, my friend.
Tell my sheep that I despise
those whose hearts speak utter lies;
that if a moment should arise
I expect them to see through
Heaven's eyes.
Heaven's eyes, Heaven's eyes.
I expect them to see
through Heaven's eyes,
lest they meet their
own demise."
Now I lie here in bed
still
with EXIT signs overhead;
and their lights are red,
red.

86. A Reflective Moment

The Worth of the Worthless

First read: Philemon 1:1-25

Give, and gifts will be given to you. Good measure, pressed down, shaken together, and running over, will be poured into your lap; for whatever measure you deal out to others will be dealt to you in return. (Luke 6:38 NEB)

A slave—historically considered valuable as property, but worthless as a human being. Today, there are the professions in our society that we have collectively come to revere deeply: Doctors, lawyers, and certain political figures; in essence, those positions that bring with them prestige, prominence, and power. We have also come to expect that these figures will continue to enjoy their status for as long as time allows. On the other end of the spectrum are the widows, children, orphans, abused, and persons in the world that are continuously derided at best, and ignored, at worst; in essence, those positions that bring with them castigation, condemnation, and contempt. And some are treated no better than a slave.

Whoever oppresses a poor man insults his Maker, but he who is generous to the needy honors him. (Proverbs 14:31ESV)

And yet, somewhere within each of our psyche lies indivisible rulers and scales used to measure and determine the general worth of the individuals we come in contact with. Most of the time it's easy for us to size another up before even getting to know them. We usually only have to ask ourselves one question: "How valuable are they to me?" If the answer is, "Not at all" or, "Very little" then we guiltlessly dismiss them.

Then he said to his host, "When you are having a party for lunch or supper, do not invite your friends, your brothers or other relations, or your rich neighbors; they will only ask you back again and so you will be repaid. But when you give a party, ask the poor, the crippled, the lame, and the blind; and so find happiness. For they have no means of repaying you; but you will be repaid on the day when good men rise from the dead." (Luke 14:12-14 NEB)

Actually, the real question is, "What can he or she do for me, for my career, or for my status in society?" It's amazing how quickly we're able to determine the worth of another individual. Before we meet them we have already prepared a mental check-list; all we have to do is watch. Typically, we have six scales used to weigh another's worth: physical attractiveness, skin color, gender, socio-economic status, popularity, and influence. Now some might say, "Hey, what's wrong with that? Everybody does it, it's just the way of the world." And they're right. However, it becomes problematic when members of the Church begin emulating the same behavior and applying the same standards to other members of the Body.

But if a man has enough to live on, and yet when he sees his brother in need shuts up his heart against him, how can it be said that the divine love dwells in him? (1st John 3:17 NEB)

190

Scripture isn't silent on showing favoritism in the Church. James, an earthly brother of Yeshua Messiah and leader of the early church, wrote ecumenically. He admonished the practice of Christian snobbery, that is, blatantly lavishing some while dismissing others on the basis of outward appearance. While such behavior is obviously disdainful for any church to engage in officially, it is sadly too common among individual members of the Body.

But if you fulfill the royal law as expressed in this scripture, "You shall love your neighbor as yourself" you are doing well. But if you show prejudice, you are committing sin and are convicted by the law as violators. (James 2:8-9 NEB)

Whether preached or taught, Philemon is one of those books in the Bible rarely discussed in most churches. It's the one-chapter, Paulian epistle appearing just before the book of Hebrews. To make a short story even shorter, Paul makes an appeal to Philemon, the owner of a runaway slave. Paul wasn't an abolitionist, worried exclusively about the external well-being of Onesimus. Rather he was a Christian, concerned with Philemon's internal well-being; imploring that he no longer treat Onesimus as a slave, but instead as a brother in Messiah. In the eyes of YHWH, every one of his children is of equal value. Perhaps as Christians we would do better to cease viewing each other as a possible commodity and instead look upon each member as they truly are—an extension of Messiah whose worth isn't based on worldly standards. When it's time to kneel before the judgment throne, how many times will Messiah accuse you of dismissing him?

87. Consoling the Suffering

First read: Job 15-17

Don't allow what you see sitting before you to become so overwhelming that fear sets in. "What if I get pulled down?" As an emotion, fear, if uncontrolled, can also cloud your ability to reason and to remember. What if you get pulled down? You get back up. You've been in stickier places before and yet somehow here you are. What once you could remember is suddenly unfamiliar. Unfamiliarity breeds contempt. It won't be long now before you do begin to think of Those-Needy as inferior by design. "How can they allow themselves to sit in such filth?" You are no longer looking outside yourself and so you can no longer see the dirt on yourself. In looking to yourself, you forget to hold out your dirty hands.

He was once in a certain town where there happened to be a man covered with leprosy; seeing [Yeshua], he bowed to the ground and begged his help. "Sir, he said, "if only you will, you can cleanse me." [Yeshua] stretched out his hand, touched him, and said, "Indeed I will; be clean again." The leprosy left him immediately. [Yeshua] then ordered him not to tell anybody. "But go," he said, "show yourself to the priest, and make the offering laid down by Moses for your cleansing; that will certify the cure." But the talk about him spread all the more; great crowds gathered to hear him and to be cured of their ailments. (Luke 5:12-15 NEB)

One of the best methods for consoling the suffering is to freely attest to your own suffering; and when the opportunity presents itself, reveal your battle scars to show them how Messiah healed. Unfortunately, many believers forget that there was a purpose for their own brokenness and so fail to consider how their consoling might appear condescending to those needing to ascend. Like it or not, the children of YHWH are all related to one another, and in reaching the suffering, it is best to show how the two of you relate. The righteous have quite a bit in common, most importantly, that all started off as unrighteous. Second, all were made right by the Son of YHWH. It is imperative that believers remember the moments when they too have sat on the ground sulking while they suffered. What was the response of Messiah?

For he has not despised or abhorred the affliction of the afflicted, and he has not hidden his face from him, but has heard, when he cried to him. (Psalm 22:24 ESV)

And the name of [Yeshua], by awakening faith, has strengthened this man, whom you see and know, and this faith has made him completely well, as you can all see for yourselves. (Acts 3:16 NEB)

It is equally imperative that those consoling remember that they are to act as compasses for Messiah. Our experiences are a vital part of the journey, and yet they are valuable only as they are shared with those whose footsteps may cross our path.

However, our experiences are *not* the Gospel. Fear can only set in when the focus is within. Our spiritual death and resurrection is not what brings repentance or renewal to those who are lost or lamenting. Rather, the Gospel of Yeshua Messiah should forever sound inside the ear of those who suffer, and it should continue sounding until it has reached their souls.

> You yourselves can testify that I said, "I am not the Messiah; I have been sent as his forerunner. It is the bridegroom to whom the bride belongs. The bridegroom's friend, who stands by and listens to him, is overjoyed at hearing the bridegroom's voice. This joy, this perfect joy, is now mine. As he grows greater, I must grow less." (John 3:28-30 NEB)

As a compass for Messiah, we know that we're functional when our consoling prompts the suffering to rise once more and begin walking in the right direction. The Gospel doesn't include personal experiences, though our experiences should include the Gospel if we are presently on the road to Glory. This is what the suffering need to hear: that Messiah came to save the lost, so that each who now lives must carry their cross. The suffering saint isn't lost so why lambaste them with the message of salvation? No, this message is more fitting for the suffering sinner. Thus the response of Job to Eliphaz the Temanite who maintains that Job suffers for his wickedness:

> I have heard many such things; miserable comforters are you all. Shall windy words have an end? Or what provokes you that you answer? I also could speak as you do, if you were in my place; I could join words together against you and shake my head at you. I could strengthen you with my mouth, and the solace of my lips would assuage your pain. (Job 16:2-5 ESV)

It isn't hard to figure out what the suffering saint needs to hear because Job tells us. They need words of encouragement, a reminder that their cross to bear is bearable. Words of affirmation—you suffer because your heavenly Father loves his younger children in the same way he loves his Eldest child. Messiah went to the cross because "YHWH so loved the world." He suffered for salvation, we suffer for sanctification. His was for the world and ours is for the Body.

> And the God of all grace, who called you into his eternal glory in [Messiah], will himself, after your brief suffering, restore, establish, and strengthen you on a firm foundation. He holds dominion for ever and ever. Amen. (1st Peter 5:10-11 NEB)

88. Wealthy With Wisdom III

First read: Proverbs 17:5

Those-Needy are not concerned with reason. If they didn't ask you to come over in the first place, they assuredly are not going to ask why you aren't holding out your hands. No dirt? Suddenly nothing about you looks familiar to them. Unfamiliarity breeds contempt. Oh, except for your disgusted facial expressions— they have seen those before from those who pass them by. Those-Needy begin raising their hands, ready to return to their waking waves once more. But, in your present state of unfamiliarity, you don't recall the wave that won you over. You are startled by their foreign gesture, and in an attempt to avert their filth from touching you, you trip and fall. Look down, but not for too long. When walking over to help Those-Needy make sure your arms are already extended. You will be recognizable and less likely to lose your footing.

"Go and learn what this means: 'I want mercy and not sacrifice,' because I did not come to call righteous people, but sinners." (Matthew 9:13a ISV)

Do not think you've made it home free simply because you decide to deliver the Gospel. For the efficacy of the Gospel is determined by its delivery. The attitude of Messiah's servants must always stand above reproach, though especially when approaching the suspicious soul who is already seething and seeing through slits. Some in the Body seem to believe that only the most holy are worthy of witnessing, and so in their most broken state, they sit and they wait. For what? Until restoration is complete? What dangerous strategizing for delivering the Gospel. Complete restoration doesn't occur until the end of the road. In the meantime those on the side need lifting up. There are others in the Body who, even while recovering from their wreck, will indeed go out to witness. Nevertheless, they rush to hide their scars for fear that they'll poorly reflect the healing power of Messiah. "I want them to see what Messiah can do." If you want those needy to see, then let them see all of you. The real you; the you that is wrecked, but still walking.

At that time [Yeshua] spoke these words: "I thank thee, Father, Lord of heaven and earth, for hiding these things from the learned and wise, and revealing them to the simple. Yes, Father, such was thy choice." (Matthew 11:25-26 NEB)

While our masquerading may seem benign, there will come a time when it comes back to bite. Whether we care to admit it, our scars are a part of our identity while here on earth. What we choose to hide soon begins to appear ugly on the outside. Why? Because our visible scars remind us of the victory afforded to us by Messiah alone; and he alone is the focus of the Gospel. With our scars out of sight, we forget our mission, and soon we no longer remember the moment when we lived spiritually impoverished. Moreover, the Father is interested in the broken pieces of his Son's Body becoming whole. A piece isn't complete until all connections are made and a piece can't connect to a whole. That's why the Father sent his Holy Son to be bruised, so that he could be used to save the broken world.

It was clearly fitting that [YHWH] for whom and through whom all things exist should, in bringing many sons to glory, make the leader who delivers them perfect through sufferings. (Hebrews 2:10 NEB)

But it is a Holy Head who makes the rest of his Body holy. Messiah wants his servants to remember that the holy will still have holes while walking on the road and that those on the side need to see them. Like Thomas was with Yeshua, there will come times when only your scars will substantiate the Gospel.

One of the Twelve, Thomas, that is "the Twin," was not with the rest when [Yeshua] came. So the disciples told him, "We have seen the Lord." He said, "Unless I see the mark of the nails in his hands, unless I put my finger into the places where the nails were, and my hands into his side, I will not believe it." A week later his disciples were again in the room, and Thomas was with them. Although the doors were locked, [Yeshua] came and stood among them, saying, "Peace be with you." Then he said to Thomas, "Reach your finger here; see my hands. Reach your hand here and put it into my side. Be unbelieving no longer, but believe." Thomas said, "My Lord and my God." (John 20:24-28 NEB)

While not ideal, no harm is done if your story centers on the Father's only begotten Son. Remember that there are those whose slumber is deep.

It is not ourselves that we proclaim; we proclaim [Yeshua] as Lord, and ourselves as your servants, for [Yeshua]'s sake. For the same God who said, "Out of darkness let light shine." has caused his light to shine within us, to give the light of revelation—the revelation of the glory of [YHWH] in the face of [Yeshua]. (2nd Corinthians 4:5-6 NEB)

What those on the side of the road are craving is authenticity. From his disciples, Messiah demands absolute devotion, because the legitimacy of the Gospel will lie in the credibility of the deliverer, and your only bait is to show that you can relate. Though Messiah wills that his sheep do rejoice in the richness that comes with knowing him, while walking on the road to Glory, believers must never forget the time when they too were paupers. The stakes are too high and those on the side are already acquainted with the pretense of the pretentious. What they need is the Father's present, and they need to see his presence in you.

89. A Reflective Moment

The Potency and Pain of Repentance: Part IV

First read: Luke 23:39-43

Another point worth considering when viewing the repentant criminal on the cross: the repenting itself was painful. One can imagine that by this time all three on Calvary were in the midst of some terrible discomfort. After having already been whipped and beaten, nails driven into hands and feet, it is probable that every muscle in their bodies ached. And yet, the repentant criminal mustard up enough energy to face Yeshua, in admitting that his own sentence was indeed just; in acknowledging Messiah's identity, and then in asking him for access to his kingdom. Yeshua's reaction?

He answered, "I tell you this: today you shall be with me in Paradise." (Luke 23:43 NEB)

How soothing a promise while in the midst of pain. For believers a genuine repentant experience shouldn't fall far from this mark. Yeshua is less interested in hearing the words that are coming from our lips and more so in the words that are coming from our heart and the faith exclaimed by our feet.

But what do you think about this? A man had two sons. He went to the first, and said, "My boy, go and work today in the vineyard." "I will, sir", the boy replied; but he never went. The father came to the second and said the same. "I will not", he replied, but afterwards he changed his mind and went. Which of these two did as his father wished? "The second." they said. Then [Yeshua] answered, "I tell you this: tax-gatherers and prostitutes are entering the kingdom of [YHWH] ahead of you. For when John came to show you the right way to live, you did not believe him, but the tax gatherers and prostitutes did; and even when you had seen that, you did not change your minds and believe him." (Matthew 21:28-32 NEB)

But what does it say? "The word is near you: it is upon your lips and in your heart." This means the word of faith which we proclaim. If on your lips is the confession, "[Yeshua] is Lord." and in your heart the faith that [YHWH] raised him from the dead, then you will find salvation. For the faith that leads to righteousness is in the heart, and the confession that leads to salvation is upon the lips. (Romans 10:8-10 NEB)

In truth, it is difficult to conceal on the face what is brewing in the heart; difficult, but not impossible. The world has masquerading down to an art because it has had plenty of time to practice. But, it takes more effort to conceal than it does to be real; only instead, members of the Body have preferred to take painstaking efforts to hide the pain inside of their hearts. What might fool members of the Body only frustrates her Head.

Not everyone who calls me "Lord, Lord" will enter the kingdom of Heaven, but only those who do the will of my heavenly Father. When that day comes, many will say to me, "Lord, Lord, did we not prophesy in your name, cast out devils in your name, and in your name perform many miracles?" Then I will tell them to their face, "I never knew you; out of my sight, you and your wicked ways." (Matthew 7:21-23 NEB)

Part of the healing process associated with forgiveness comes in realizing the ugliness of who we really are. The Father will not allow us to come before him asking for forgiveness unless we are willing to look into the mirror extended to us while on our knees. Looking into the mirror can be a painful experience; for some it is gut-wrenching. However, it is truth we seek while staring at our reflection because only the truth will set us free. The truth is rarely pretty. Unfortunately, many who go seeking forgiveness merely glance into the mirror and tell themselves, "Oh, I'm not that bad after all." This follows with a quick, "Yeshua-I-know-that-I'm-a-sinner-save-me-from-my-sins-Amen." and then a sigh of relief. "Whew, I'm glad that's through; that was easier than I thought." Easy? Repentance? Not much longer after standing back up do they find themselves on the ground again, having fallen into a hole. A member more mature ought not simply stare at them in haughty self-righteousness, but explain to them where they erred. And then after helping them out of their hole, take out a mirror and ask them if they are really ready to look.

Repentance requires more than just a casual glance into the mirror. If members of the Body expect forgiveness from YHWH then they must forfeit that which keeps them from staring. For some it is fear; for other's it is pride; though pride is really nothing more than a coping mechanism for masquerading fears. In staring, one finds themselves comparing. Good. Only make sure that the comparison is to Messiah and not to others who we might think are less attractive. Falling on our knees and comparing ourselves to Messiah should induce tears from the hardest of hearts. When once we have persevered through the pain of repentance, the Holy Spirit is now made available for respite. Members should delight in receiving the Father's gift, for he means for you to benefit. However, in enjoying your new found freedom, remember that respite from repentance is breaking ground in preparing for your resistance.

90. Conciliation through Confession

First read: Ezra 10:1-44

If for no other reason then to be reminded of its vastness, whenever you trip and fall be sure to look up immediately at the sky above. In remembering that in its vastness, not even the sky will limit you, it becomes clear that neither shall the ground; get up. When you do get up, continue to look up. How far away you seem from the heights of the clouds; so there is no reason why your head should ever get stuck.

Moreover many of those who had become believers came and openly confessed that they had been using magical spells. And a good many of those who formerly practiced magic collected their books and burnt them publicly. The total value was reckoned up and it came to fifty thousand pieces of silver. In such ways the word of [Yeshua] showed its power, spreading more and more widely and effectively. (Acts 19:18-20 NEB)

There is only one way to conciliate with the Father and it isn't through concealing. It makes little sense to try and conceal anything from the One who knows every detail of the heart, mind, and soul. But, still there are those who seek to conceal. Many believers rush through their prayers as if YHWH really isn't there. As if he doesn't even care. As if he is unaware of the fact that there isn't an ounce of sincerity in the words that are passing from libelous lips. Those who are under such an impression have been walking on a path with their head stuck in the clouds, unaware that they left the road to Glory several miles back.

Ah, you hide deep from [Yeshua] your counsel, whose deeds are in the dark, and who say, "Who sees us? Who knows us?" You turn things upside down. Shall the potter be regarded as the clay, that the thing made should say of its maker, "He did not make me"; or the thing formed say of him who formed it, "He has no understanding?" (Isaiah 29:15-16 ESV)

When Ezra was informed by some of the leaders of Israel that many in the family, including priests and Levites, were intermarrying with members of the foreign population, his reaction was not to conceal, but to confess:

And at the evening sacrifice I rose from my fasting, with my garment and my cloak torn, and fell upon my knees and spread out my hands to [YHWH], saying: "O [YHWH], I am ashamed and blush to lift my face to you, [YHWH], for our iniquities have risen higher than our heads, and our guilt has mounted up to the heavens." (Ezra 9:5-6 ESV)

Ezra then proceeded to cry out to YHWH in acknowledging Israel's specific iniquities. Remember that repentance is painful because it requires the believer to stare at his ugly reflection, not just glance. Where there is no pain there is no incentive to change, and so the believer remains the same; still only half-believing, and still with only one foot in the door to the Kingdom. "But I'm too ashamed to utter out loud." Get your head out of the clouds and recognize that you haven't done anything so shameful that the Father won't forgive; remember that he wants you to live shame-free. If you insist on walking around filled with shame then you only have yourself to blame. "But, how can I possibly lift up my head and recap to my Lord everything I have said? Oh, how I wish I were dead." That's what Satan wants you to wish, so that you will stay on the ground clutched by his weeds. It is Messiah's intention that you do die to your "self" and your pride. However, confession should never lead the believer into a state of depression. The servant who sits and ruminates over past mistakes after purging is of little use to the Master who needs his repentant servant to rise and aid others in their restoration. There are those in the Church who are waiting for the Father to respond to their prayer; to show that he's there and is aware of their plight. Alright.

Again I tell you this: if two of you agree on earth about any request you have to make, that request will be granted by my heavenly Father. For where two or three have met together in my name, I am there among them. (Matthew 18:19-20 NEB)

The Holy Spirit is urging all members to first confess. There are sins that still have yet to be spoken; hearts that have hardened that need to be broken. Messiah does not enjoy the sight of his sheep running to and fro aimless and without a shepherd. Messiah is not content with any of his sheep receiving an inadequate diet or with any suffering from dehydration.

When he came ashore, he saw a great crowd; and his heart went out to them, because they were like sheep without a shepherd; and he had much to teach them. (Mark 6:9 NEB)

He recognizes that the wilderness has been hot, dry, and at times debilitating. He knows that the road to Glory is filled with moments of uncertainty and frustration. Messiah has been both in the wilderness and on the road before—he knows. There is an oasis of water he longs to give, and a fresh fire so that all may live. There are those who are weary and yearning for rest; so, confess.

91. Wealthy With Wisdom - IV

First read: Proverbs 1:20-33

You don't want your head in the clouds for obvious reasons. If clarity is what you aim for, there is no faster road to haze then by walking through fog. The farther you walk through fog the fogger it gets, until eventually you freeze. Frozen from fear of the fog. How will you get through this maze? How will you clear up the haze? You certainly won't get through by continuing to walk, though you could try. You are better off waiting on the wind. Can you hear? Is it clear? As the wind blows, quietly listen as reason whispers in your ear. Stay away from the fog; you are limiting yourself. Look up, but not for too long.

Hopefully none has read through the Book of Proverbs thinking that Solomon's wisdom was a one time deal, and that all Christians living today have not a prayer when it comes to having the ability to perpetually exercise Godly wisdom. If so, then you need reminding that Solomon's wisdom came not from him, but from YHWH. Go figure, then reconsider. What set Solomon apart in delighting the Father's heart was that he asked for wisdom above all else. The wisdom of our God is indeed priceless, and oh, how Messiah wishes that his disciples would spend more time amassing it instead of wealth. Most of the binds that believers find themselves in come from having cloudy minds. When the head is cloudy, it becomes impossible to think clearly. Cautiousness is replaced with callousness, prudence is replaced with pride, and reason is replaced with rebellion. In short, what was once sensible is now sinful. While a prisoner in Rome, what was it that led the Apostle Paul to have to send the following admonition to the church in Ephesus?

> This then is my word to you, and I urge it upon you in [Yeshua]'s name. Give up living like pagans with their good-for-nothing notions. Their wits are beclouded, they are strangers to the life that is in [YHWH], because ignorance prevails among them and their minds have grown hard as stone. Dead to all feeling, they have abandoned themselves to vice, and stop at nothing to satisfy their foul desires. (Ephesians 4:17-20 NEB)

> This I say, therefore, and testify in the Lord, that you should no longer walk as the rest of the Gentiles walk, in the futility of their mind, having their understanding darkened, being alienated from the life of God, because of the ignorance that is in them, because of the blindness of their heart; who, being past feeling, have given themselves over to lewdness, to work all uncleanness with greediness. (Ephesians 4:17-19 NKJV)

Since specific infractions had not yet been reported to Paul concerning the church in Ephesus, it is possible that his previous travels and interactions with recent converts had convinced him that some general guidelines were needed for any follower of the true faith. Most notable, that all behaviors generally associated with the world cease being defensible for a disciple of Messiah. What had at one time been chalked up to ignorance is now plain stupidity, should a disciple continue to delve.

For it is impossible, in the case of those who have once been enlightened, who have tasted the heavenly gift, and have shared in the Holy Spirit, and have tasted the goodness of the word of [YHWH] and the powers of the age to come, and then have fallen away, to restore them again to repentance, since they are crucifying once again the Son of [YHWH] to their own harm and holding him up to contempt. (Hebrews 6:4-6 ESV)

Believers have at their disposal a treasure chest filled with insight on how to stay out of the darkness and keep to the daylight. There's a depth of perception that if readers would read more, then less they would weep—a wealth of wisdom that is free for the taking, learning, and shaping. For anyone who appreciates their freedom and can daily relate to its cost; Proverbs was left for all who once were lost. For many in the Body, their heads are not as clear as they were on the day they accepted Messiah into their life. Don't be surprised. When you were adopted into the Father's family you sparked a family feud. Confusion is the cousin of doubt and doubt is the brother of fear. And Satan is the father of them all. As the father of confusion, it is in his nature to cloud up the minds of any "willing" mark. You are a mark if you've made Yeshua Messiah your Savior, and by adoption, your Eldest brother. However, you are "willing" if you choose to walk on the road to Glory wisdom-free. Instead, hear the words of Wisdom:

And now, o sons, listen to me: blessed are those who keep my ways. Hear instruction and be wise, and do not neglect it. Blessed is the one who listens to me, watching daily at my gates, waiting beside my doors. For whoever finds me finds life and obtains favor from [Yeshua], but he who fails to find me injures himself; all who hate me love death. (Proverbs 8:32-36 ESV)

[Yeshua] answered them, "Have faith in [YHWH]. I tell you this: if anyone says to this mountain, 'Be lifted from your place and hurled into the sea,' and has no inward doubts, and believes that what he says is happening, it will be done for him. I tell you, then, whatever you ask for in prayer, believe that you have received it and it will." (Mark 11:22-24 NEB)

92. Wasteful Worrying

First read: Isaiah 44:1-23

As you are walking, worry will occasionally drop by for a visit. It is aware that every so often you entertain foolish company and worry will stay in the midst, clouding up of the conversation. "Where are you going?" "Who do you think you are?" "What makes you so special?" "Why are you here?" Soon you stagnate and then soon you become stuck. If you are stuck, then you are not moving. Moving is an essential element of your journey. Eventually worry will be relieved by misery. Misery will enjoy your company, but only until you've finished stewing. You won't be much fun when you decide you're ready to move on. In time, you will feel a cool breeze brush by. Be quiet and listen to the beckoning voice of reason. Shhh...though faint you will hear its gentle whisper...2, 3, 4.... whisper......2, 3, 4. . . .in rhythm, in time. Can you hear? Is it clear? As the wind blows, the fog begins to lift, carrying away worry and giving you respite. Move.

We learned how to worry when we were living for the world. Worrying is the result of wanting, but fearing that we won't have. It is born out of the worshiping of our wants. When Messiah is invited into our lives as personal Lord and Savior, the expectation is that we cease worrying because we cease wanting the world:

> Have no fear, little flock; for your Father has chosen to give you the Kingdom. Sell your possessions and give in charity. Provide for yourselves purses that do not wear out, and never-failing treasure in heaven, where no thief can get near it, no moth can destroy it. (Luke 12:32-33 NEB)

It takes a few miles of walking before we begin to realize that our former desires didn't really fulfill our deepest longings, and yet those longings linger. As believers continue to mature in their faith, Satan will continue in his mission: to knock us out of commission. Worrying never comes from YHWH who, in his perfect wisdom, knows that this wind will only blow his people off course. Satan wants the Father's people to rely on their feelings rather than their faith. If he can get members to second guess their decision to die, then he is succeeding in his job, which is to rob you of your joy. He hopes that you will return to those idols so idle and mute, which offered you plenty, but gave you no fruit. There is room for growth while on the road to Glory, but no room for graves; all of which remain off to the side of the road. When Satan begins to whisper in your ear, know that a different death is near and refuse to accept its invitation. There is not much space between musing and misery, and so members must learn to discern. Musing as encouraged by the Holy Spirit may on occasion spring misery, but only momentarily. The Spirit's misery is always a means to a righteous end. However, Satan means for your musing to be the end of you. What may begin as amusing will always end in misery. Many members of the Body have found themselves here, and admittedly it is alarming. But, for all those whom Messiah has ransomed know this:

What the wicked dreads will come upon him, but the desire of the righteous will be granted. When the tempest passes, the wicked is no more, but the righteous is established forever. (Proverbs 10:24-25 ESV)

Believers can't keep Satan from whispering, but we don't have to whimper when he does. Unlike the wicked, whose worrying is only exacerbated by the width of their woes, the believer must know that our God won't sit idle if you ask for his intervention, though you must pay attention. Remember the exasperated prophet Elijah in the cave of Horeb, who, in fear, sought out YHWH?

And he said, "Go out and stand on the mount before [YHWH]." And behold, [YHWH] passed by, and a great and strong wind tore the mountains and broke in pieces the rocks before [YHWH], but [YHWH] was not in the wind. And after the wind an earthquake, but [YHWH] was not in the earthquake. And after the earthquake a fire, but [YHWH] was not in the fire. And after the fire the sound of a low whisper. And when Elijah heard it, he wrapped his face in his cloak and went out and stood at the entrance of the cave. And behold, there came a voice to him and said, "What are you doing here Elijah?" He said, "I have been very jealous for [YHWH]. For the people of Israel have forsaken your covenant, thrown down your altars, and killed your prophets with the sword, and I, even I only, am left, and they seek my life, to take it away." (1st Kings 19:11-14 ESV)

When Yeshua finally speaks, members have a choice to either listen and obey, or continue to worry and go on wasting each day while others are quickly wasting away. Messiah's words? "All who are mine I hold in my hand. Now heed my command: Time is of the essence: don't worry, work."

He said, "The kingdom of [YHWH] is like this. A man scatters seed on the land; he goes to bed at night and gets up in the morning, and seed sprouts and grows—how, he does not know. The ground produces a crop by itself, first the blade, then the ear, then full-grown corn in the ear; but as soon as the crop is ripe, he plies the sickle, because harvest-time has come." (Mark 4:26-29 NEB)

Therefore, a Sabbath rest still awaits the people of [YHWH]; for anyone who enters [YHWH]'s rest, rests from his own work as [YHWH] did from his. Let us then make every effort to enter that rest, so that no one may fall by following this evil example of unbelief. (Hebrews 4:9-11NEB)

93. Destination or Denomination

First read: Colossians 2:6-8

Confusion gets the invite and now your company really begins to party. And you will start crying if this party lasts for too long. Oh, and confusion brings a ravishing guest. Meet doubt, what a knock out. But doubt isn't a foreign guest; the two of you have already been acquainted. It's getting a little crowded and confusion is the life of the party; entertaining all through, mixing and mingling. While the music is blaring, worry will sit staring, waiting; Tick. Tick. Tick. If you insist on listening, you soon will fail to feel. You will no longer sense time nipping at your heel. But, listen you do, and soon worry walks up and starts whispering, telling you to enjoy your party for as long as you want. You aren't enjoying the party at all; but, since listening to the voices surrounding, you didn't notice that fear slipped in late; unexpected, unannounced, uninvited.

And now I appeal to the elders of your community, as a fellow-elder and a witness of [Yeshua]'s sufferings, and also a partaker in the splendor that is to be revealed. Tend that flock of [Yeshua] whose shepherds you are, and do it, not under compulsion, but of your own free will, as [YHWH] would have it; not for gain but out of sheer devotion; not tyrannizing over those who are allotted to your care, but setting an example to the flock. And then, when the Head Shepherd appears, you will receive for your own the unfading garland of glory. (1st Peter 5:1-4 NEB)

There's a pink elephant sitting in the middle of the Church, obstructing the view of the cross, and thus the road to Glory. This, at present, is presenting a problem for those believers who once knew what the cross looked like, but have been staring at the elephant for so long that the cross is no longer visible, much less the road. For others, the elephant, in all its pinkness, has captivated the believer so much that although he may see the cross, it pales in comparison with its wooden insipidity. And so for both types, when sharing the Gospel, the focus is on the elephant while Messiah becomes irrelevant. Does the elephant have a name? Yes, in fact it shares a multitude. Anglican, Armenian, Baptist, Christian & Missionary Alliance, Church of God, Episcopalian, Evangelical Free, First Assembly, Free Methodist, Holiness, Lutheran, Nazarene, Orthodox, Pentecostal, Presbyterian, Salvation Army, Seven-Day, Southern-Baptist, United Methodist, and Wesleyan—just to name a few. Is the suggestion that Messiah is nowhere among any of the mentioned denominations? Of course not. Observation, however, has shown that Messiah is often forgotten in the believer's attempt to fervently prove his or her allegiance to a part of the body rather than to its Head. Unless members reexamine their motives, denominational division will be the Achilles' heel of the Body of Messiah. Paul prefaces his first letter to the church in Corinth with this same word of caution:

I appeal to you, my brothers, in the name of our Lord [Yeshua Messiah]; agree among yourselves, and avoid divisions; be firmly joined in unity of mind and thought. I have been told, my brothers, by Chloe's people that there are quarrels among you. What I mean is this: each of you is saying, "I am Paul's man," or I am for Apollos; "I follow Cephas." Or "I am [Messiah's]." Surely [Messiah] has not been divided among you. Was it Paul who was crucified for you? Was it in the name of Paul that you were baptized? Thank [YHWH], I never baptized one of you—except Crispus and Gaius. So no one can say you were baptized in my name. Yes, I did baptize the household of Stephanas; I cannot think of anyone else. [Messiah] did not send me to baptize, but to proclaim the Gospel; and to do it without relying on the language of worldly wisdom, so that the fact of [Messiah] on his cross might have its full weight. (1st Corinthians 1:10-17 NEB)

No doubt that there have been men of past who've left a commendable mark on the Christian faith. And in truth, if they were doing the will of YHWH then their efforts will not go unrewarded when standing before the judgment throne of Messiah. But even Paul, an apostle and early architect of the Church, encouraged his followers to keep their eyes on Messiah. When believers take their eyes off Messiah to concentrate on creeds or on those who crafted them, it becomes easier to leave the road leading to their promised destination. In the process we are inviting doubt and confusion to join our company, while leaving the ranks that Messiah intended to remain united. Where doubt and confusion tie, rest assured the Enemy isn't far behind.

So never make mere men a cause for pride. For though everything belongs to you—Paul, Apollos, and Cephas, the world, life, and death, the present and the future, all of them belong to you—yet you belong to [Messiah], and [Messiah] to [YHWH]. (1st Corinthians 3:21-23 NEB)

It took some time to push the pink elephant in front of the cross. How much longer is it going to take before the pink loses its luster and members grow tired of its obstruction? Tick. Tick. Tick. Members need to act now and remove the elephant from blocking their destination. The Holy Spirit is urging the Body to remember the red that once appeared on the cross. And, unlike the pink elephant sitting in the middle of the Church, the cross wasn't always red. Someone's blood was shed.

Be on your guard; do not let your minds be captured by hollow and delusive speculations, based on traditions of man-made teaching and centered on the elemental spirits of the universe and not on [Messiah]. (Colossians 2:8 NEB)

For in [Messiah] our release is secured and our sins are forgiven through the shedding of his blood. (Ephesians 1:7 NEB)

94. A Hindrance to Deliverance III

First read: Deuteronomy 20:1-4

On your journey you will do well to remember that fear never shows up at the beginning of a party, because fear is never invited. No one with a clear mind would invite fear because it always leaves a mess behind and expects the host to clean it up. However, whenever worry wanders in, with confusion close behind; dressed and through the door will doubt appear. After sitting for a second, soon unraveling will commence; and what you thought was doubt is actually fear. You were flirting with doubt earlier and now fear, flattered by your gestures, has grabbed a hold of you, hungry. And now a word of caution: If you insist on staying for the show, don't resist it when you get caught. You need to let go of fear; because long after it has fled will you still be left in a haze. Frozen from fear of the fog. Left alone to clean a mess that keeps you in a blaze.

Before the Israelites could settle in the promise land they would first encounter a little resistance. But, through Moses, YHWH also gave these instructions:

See, [YHWH] your God has set the land before you. Go up, take possession, as [YHWH] the God of your fathers, has told you. Do not fear or be dismayed. (Deuteronomy 1:21 ESV)

One night in a vision [Yeshua] said to Paul, "Have no fear: go on with your preaching and do not be silenced, for I am with you and no one shall attempt to do you harm; and there are many in this city who are my people." So he settled down for eighteen months, teaching the word of [YHWH] among them. (Acts 18:9-11 NEB)

Believers should know that the Father commands his children not to fear man. The fear of man will always prove a hindrance to Yeshua's deliverance. Fear and faith are inseparable. As irony would have it, whomever we fear is who we will find our faith draws us near. Faith in man's power will gradually render one powerless to resist it because, whether fearfully or in awe, he will begin to perceive his enemy's as insurmountable while his own as insufficient. It is through paralysis (manifested as passivity or inactivity) that the enemy is able to gain victory. Therefore, Messiah has zero tolerance for those who would render his flock fearful of anyone other than him or the Father. While journeying, times will abound when circumstances—strange places or unfamiliar faces—threaten to cloud the believer's mind with dismay over their demise. Like the Israelites in the wilderness of Paran, oftentimes fellow travelers will offer up words of wisdom.

Where are we going up? Our brothers have made our hearts melt, saying, "The people are greater and taller than we. The cities are great and fortified up to heaven. And besides, we have seen the sons of Anakim there." (Deuteronomy 1:28 ESV)

In other words, "If you are smart, you won't go." The decedents of the Anakim were considered giants of men. Our God doesn't scoff at common sense. Any Israelite would naturally fear one man who could easily snap them into two. And yet their brethren were telling of a whole community. Hence, the response of Moses:

> Then I said to you, "Do not be in dread or afraid of them. [YHWH] your God who goes before you will himself fight for you, just as he did in Egypt before your eyes, and in the wilderness, where you have seen how [YHWH] your God carried you, as a man carries his son, all the way that you went until you came to this place. (Deuteronomy 1:29-31 ESV)

Here the Israelites had the choice to either remain wrapped in their fear or to begin walking in their faith. But it wasn't even blind faith; the Israelites had already seen with their own eyes, the mighty hand of YHWH. Moreover, YHWH's spokesperson told them not to fear because the Creator of the universe was walking, not next to them, but in front. There is no better armor. Nevertheless,

> Yet in spite of this word you did not believe [YHWH] your God, who went before you in the way to seek you out a place to pitch your tents, in fire by night and in the cloud by day, to show you by what way you should go. (Deuteronomy 1:32-33 ESV)

Then, for the believer, what are the possible consequences for choosing to live in fear of man? Perhaps a delay in their deliverance; possibly death. For the fearful Israelites, their journey through the wilderness was extended for another forty years, with a whole generation dying along the way. Those who engendered the fear among the family were put to death immediately. Messiah is neither unaware of, nor insensitive to, the natural feelings of his flock. However, as Christians we are commanded to walk in the spiritual, guided by the Spirit. Wrapping ourselves in fear doesn't just hinder our deliverance. With arms and legs transfixed, it becomes impossible to carry the candle needed in lighting the road to Glory. With no light in sight, those on the road can't see—all those sitting on the side of the road waiting to be set free.

95. A Reflective Moment

The Road to Glory

First read: Philippians 2:5-11

When serving Messiah, where should the Christian center his focus? Does this sound like a trick question? Perhaps for some the answer is rather easy; the order goes a bit like this: First Messiah, then myself, and finally my brothers and sisters. After all, how can I help build others if I don't have my own house in order first, right? As tempting as this pearl appears, it's really a set-up for ineffectiveness. Without question, our attention should always center on the Master first. The moment we take our eyes off him then we are asking for trouble. If we examine the life of Yeshua Messiah, we see that every ounce of his being was devoted to the service of humanity, even unto his death on the cross. There has never been and will never be another alive more deserving of the title: Son of Man. From the moment he succeeded in the desert, Yeshua began focusing on the redemption of his siblings.

From that day [Yeshua] began to proclaim the message: "Repent; for the kingdom of Heaven is upon you." (Matthew 4:17 NEB)

Notice that his message was not "Repent; for the King of Heaven is among you." Though he would have been speaking truth, such was not his purpose while walking the earth. Instead, he urged everyone to correct their behavior so as to please their Father.

But what I tell you is this: Love your enemies and pray for your persecutors; only so can you be children of your heavenly Father, who makes his sun rise on good and bad alike, and sends rain on the honest and the dishonest. (Matthew 5:44-45 NEB)

Be careful not to make a show of your religion before men; if you do, no reward awaits you in your Father's house in heaven. (Matthew 6:1 NEB)

But when you pray, go into a room by yourself, shut the door, and pray to your Father who is there in the secret place; and your Father who sees what is secret will reward you. (Matthew 6:5-6 NEB)

For if you forgive others the wrongs they have done, your heavenly Father will also forgive you; but if you do not forgive others, then the wrongs you have done will not be forgiven by your Father. (Matthew 6:14-15 NEB)

Yeshua, in obedient service to his Father, came to serve man, not himself. It is equally important to note that Messiah did not come only to preach. After instructing others on how to serve their Father, he too begins to serve.

After he had come down from the hill he was followed by a great crowd. And now a leper approached him, bowed low, and said, "Sir, if only you will, you can cleanse me." [Yeshua] stretched out his hand, touched him, and said, "Indeed I will; be clean again." And his leprosy was cured immediately. Then [Yeshua] said to him, "Be sure you tell nobody; but go and show yourself to the priest, and make the offering laid down by Moses for your cleaning; that will certify the cure." (Matthew 8:1-4 NEB)

The Gospels are filled with examples of Messiah's service to mankind. Led by the Holy Spirit, Yeshua never seemed to tire from doing the will of his Father (though being fully human, Messiah did need, and partook in, physical rest). From the above account we also know that neither was Messiah interested in making a spectacle of himself or his works. His purpose was to reflect the character of his Father, and in doing so, demonstrate to the world the purpose of his Father in restoring both body and soul. Even while in the Garden, hours before his crucifixion, Yeshua, in the midst of emotional anguish, directed his attention to mankind and continued to serve in prayer:

Father, I want those you have given me to be with me where I am, and to see my glory, the glory you have given me because you loved me before the creation of the world. Righteous Father, though the world does not know you, I know you, and they know that you have sent me. I have made you known to them, and will continue to make you known in order that the love you have for me may be in them and that I myself may be in them. (John 17:24-26 ISV)

We know the rest of the story. Messiah, in leaving his throne, came to this world to redeem his siblings for his Father. In Messiah we have the perfect pattern of how to serve so that in serving, we are also restoring. Messiah's road to Glory began with his giving up himself, that is, his glorious splendor as a member of the Godhead, was marked by a life of continual giving, and ended with him being given up in death. So then how are we to live? We who identify ourselves as consecrated servants of Yeshua? Like Messiah, our road to Glory has to begin with our deciding to give up ourselves. That is, we must first leave our past behind, but then quickly we must learn to look outside ourselves. We must give up self for the sake of others. I can't recall a Scriptural reference in which Yeshua spent time reminding his Father of his own needs. This is because YHWH already knew what Yeshua needed and provided for him in the right season for the right reason. Yeshua too reminded us that we have the same certainty.

In your prayers do not go babbling on like the heathen, who imagine that the more they say the more likely they are to be heard. Do not imitate them. Your Father knows what your needs are before you ask him. (Matthew 6:7-8 NEB)

No, do not ask anxiously, "What are we to eat? What are we to drink? What shall we wear?" All these are things for the heathen to run after, not for you, because your heavenly Father knows that you need them all. Set your mind on [YHWH]'s kingdom and his justice before everything else, and all the rest will come to you as well. So do not be anxious about tomorrow; tomorrow will look after itself. Each day has troubles enough of its own. (Matthew 6:31-34 NEB)

When we remove "self," our heavenly Father is allowed to move. The Holy Spirit is urging members to revamp their prayer life. The material possessions that we often find ourselves petitioning for mean little to our God when our spiritual lives are still in disarray. Rather than seeking to self-indulge, members should begin asking the Father for tools to aid in rebuilding the Church; the Holy Spirit has an abundant supply waiting to give believers who are willing to give of themselves. Nothing should gratify a servant of Messiah more than to spend his or her life serving; not just for the kingdom in the future, but while in the kingdom even now.

> The Pharisees asked him, "When will the kingdom of [YHWH] come?" He said, "You cannot tell by observation when the kingdom of [YHWH] comes. There will be no saying, 'Look, here it is. ' or 'There it is.' for in fact the kingdom of [YHWH] is among you." (Luke 17:20-21 NEB)

Christian service is most gratifying when believers are serving in the area that YHWH ordained for them. Many spend more time building up resentment than they do the Church, when choosing to compare themselves with everyone else in the Body. Rather than complaining about not having an office that the Father hasn't equipped you for, members should instead spend time in prayer asking our God to reveal to them what he intended for them. When YHWH feels that you are ready he will begin to open doors; and then it is up to the believer to faithfully walk through. Members need not wait until they have mastered the skill before executing their service, for the Father delights in working through a willing heart. Mastering will come with cultivating and cultivating only through practice. As long as all eyes remain on Messiah, then service in the Church should itself be redeeming. In truth, mistakes will occur while working in the Church, but as long as believers are open to correction and have a repentant heart then, YAH will always forgive the sorrowful servant. However, Messiah is disinterested in the servant whose primary interest is in serving self. We see strong admonishment given by Peter in the Book of Acts to Simon, the converted sorcerer from Samaria who wanted to use the power of the Holy Spirit's baptism for selfish gain.

> Your money go with you to damnation, because you thought [YHWH]'s gift was for sale. You have no part nor lot in this, for you are dishonest with [YHWH]. Repent of this wickedness and pray to [YHWH] to forgive you for imagining such a thing. I can see that you are doomed to taste the bitter fruit and wear the fetters of sin. (Acts 8:20-23 NEB)

It is foolish to assert that Christians will not grow weary in working for Messiah, and there is indeed a time for rest, which our God acknowledges in providing for us a Sabbath. It is equally foolish for the worker not to obey YHWH in taking a Sabbath. Remember, however, that time off from work does not grant us time apart from the Father. When Yeshua rested from the masses, he spent his time in prayer maximizing the degree of intimacy with his Father still afforded to him, though limited while on earth.

Messiah's final act of service was in dying, so that all others might live. Martyrs have played a vital role in the history of the Church, and indeed there is a special place reserved for each in Heaven. The road to Glory is shorter for some than for others. Our God has purposefully allowed for the physical death of some in the hopes of saving the masses. But one truth continues to sound clearly, if only ears will open: Messiah expects each member to die daily to themselves.

[Yeshua] then said to his disciples, "If anyone wishes to be a follower of mine, he must leave self behind; he must take up his cross and come with me. Whoever cares for his own safety is lost; but if a man will let himself be lost for my sake, he will find his true self. What will a man gain by winning the whole world, at the cost of his true self? Or what can he give that will buy that self back? For the Son of Man is to come in the glory of his Father with his angels, and then he will give each man the due reward for what he has done." (Matthew 16:24-27 NEB)

The focus of the Christian should remain on the road to Glory. But, herein is the conundrum: staying on the road to Glory requires a daily death, while the road to self-glory ends in death. Which road are you on?

96. Illusionary Luster

First read: Jeremiah 44:1-30

With the haze clearing, it will be necessary for you to step outside yourself long enough to look up. Remind yourself that like you, the sky is confined to the chains of time, limited by the same striking hands. On occasion you will be blinded by its thickness in haze—its massive maze. The skies are indeed vast, but remember that no matter the clouds, they too shall pass. Look up, but not for too long. It's hard to see clearly when your head is stuck in the clouds.

There has to come a point, while walking, when you have had enough of all your stuff. While living in sin, it was impossible to see the light, due to the haziness of our sight. The accepting of Yeshua Messiah as Lord and Savior meant clarity. Unfortunately, there remains a large number of Israelites still living in Egypt and who still have their heads stuck in the clouds. These are the believers who have the illusion that all of their riches and stored wealth is a sure sign that YHWH is content with their performance. The Israelites of Jeremiah's day suffered from the same illusion. When attempts were made to clear up the haze, the Hebrews were content in keeping their gaze, gripped by their delusions of grandeur.

As for the word that you have spoken to us in the name of [YHWH], we will not listen to you. But we will do everything that we have vowed, make offerings to the queen of heaven and pour out drink offerings to her, as we did, both we and our fathers, our kings and our officials, in the cities of Judah and in the streets of Jerusalem. For then we had plenty of food, and prospered, and saw no disaster. But since we left off making offerings to the queen of heaven and pouring out drink offerings to her, we have lacked everything and have been consumed by the sword and by famine. (Jeremiah 44:16-18 ESV)

Their analysis was faulty; sin will do that. Because all went well with them in the midst of their sinning, but then things went wrong the moment they ceased, they reasoned that their rebellion was more profitable. What they failed to understand was that their respite from ruin was a sign of the Father's tolerance, not to be mistaken for acquiescence. It is no different from the modern day member who believes in the gratuitousness of our God's grace (while shamelessly sponging off its effects) and therefore sees no reason to press for perfection. They are content in settling for spiritual mediocrity at best and flirting with apostasy at worst. But Paul's message to the converts in Rome varied little from Jeremiah's response to the Israelites, concerning the wicked:

Thus, because they have not seen fit to acknowledge [YHWH], he has given them up to their own depraved reason. This leads them to break all rules of conduct. (Romans 1:28 NEB)

It is admitted that [YHWH]'s judgment is rightly passed upon all who commit such crimes as these; and do you imagine, you who pass judgment on the guilty while committing the same crimes yourself; do you imagine that you, any more than they, will escape the judgment of [YHWH]? Or do you think lightly of his wealth of kindness, of tolerance, and of patience, without recognizing that [YHWH]'s kindness is meant to lead you to a change of heart? In the rigid obstinacy of your heart you are laying up for yourself a store of retribution for the day of retribution, when [YHWH]'s just judgment will be revealed, and he will pay every man for what he has done. (Romans 2:2-6 NEB)

Herein lies the difference between what became of the Israelites under King Nebuchadrezzar of Babylon, and the opportunity that Christians of today have in avoiding their mistake through repentance. Although the Hebrews ceased momentarily from their sinful behavior, there is no indication that genuine repentance transpired. In fact Jeremiah, speaking on behalf of Yeshua, says this:

To this day you have shown no remorse, no reverence; you have not conformed to the law and the statues which I set before you and your forefathers. These, therefore, are the words of [Yeshua]: I have made up my mind to bring calamity upon you and exterminate the people of Judah. (Jeremiah 44:10-11 ESV)

To the members who allege belief in the Father, yet persist in their wickedness: The hands that first struck twelve will soon strike one. You persisted in plenty. Will you still insist with none?

When he broke the third seal, I heard the third creature say, "Come." And there, as I looked, was a black horse; and its rider held in his hand a pair of scales. And I heard what sounded like a voice from the midst of the living creatures, which said, "A whole day's wage for a quart of flour, a whole day's wage for three quarts of barley-meal. But spare the olive and the vine." (Revelation 6:5-6 NEB)

97. A Reflective Moment

Walking the Talk

First read: Titus 1:16

Whatever you are doing, whether you speak or act, do everything in the name of the [Yeshua], giving thanks to [YHWH] the Father through him. (Colossians 3:17 ESV)

So, you're a Christian. Can anyone attest besides you? "You can't judge me. I may curse sporadically, cheat occasionally, and connive when it suits me, but my God knows my heart." So, you have the eyes and mind of Christ? Can anyone else see him working in you besides you? "You can't judge me. My music may be racy, movies raunchy, and marriage rocky, but my God knows my heart." Indeed, Yeshua does know the heart of all because he created all. Somehow members have become convinced that their attitudes and actions matter little so long as their "heart is in the right place." There's a little problem here. The heart can become deceptively rotten—to the core.

The heart is deceitful above all things, and desperately sick; who can understand it? "I [YHWH] search the heart and test the mind, to give every man according to his ways, according to the fruit of his deeds." (Jeremiah 17:9-10 ESV)

And once rotting has begun it becomes almost impossible to produce good fruit. In dealing with the hypocritical Pharisees of his day, Yeshua was unmistakable in his message.

Either make the tree good and its fruit good, or make the tree bad and its fruit bad; you can tell a tree by its fruit. You viper brood. How can your words be good when you yourselves are evil? For the words that the mouth utters come from the overflowing of the heart. A good man produces good from the store of good within himself; and an evil man from evil within produces evil. (Matthew 12:33-35 NEB)

Whether we care to admit it, what sinfully transpires on the outside has been steadily conspiring on the inside. Its manifestation is merely a reflection of lowered spiritual inhibitions. In other words, we have let our guard down, removed our spiritual armor, and turned deaf ears to the convicting voice of the Holy Spirit. When this happens we have allowed our lower nature to get the better of us. With our lower nature in control, Messiah won't work because it is the domain of the devil. It is the arrogant believer who expects the Son of YHWH to compete with Satan for their attention and affection when he already demonstrated his commitment to us by dying on the cross. Without Messiah in control of your life, Messiah isn't seen in your life. Hence, every heart that he hasn't captured is a heart still up for grabs. And grabbed it will be by this world and by the prince of this world.

He went on, "It is what comes out of a man that defiles him. For from inside, out of a man's heart, come evil thoughts, acts of fornication, of theft, murder, adultery, ruthless greed, and malice; fraud, indecency, envy, slander, arrogance, and folly; these evil things all from inside, and they defile a man." (Mark 7:20-23 NEB)

Members of the Body whose hearts haven't permanently been claimed by Messiah will find themselves becoming first inattentive, then inactive, and finally, indifferent. However, once Messiah has captured the heart, then we must take care to ensure that every sound uttered and step taken is a reflection of his character. Members also bear another responsibility. Messiah can capture our hearts, but we have to keep them captivated, shielded from possible contamination. On one hand, a captured heart should remain a humbled heart. Pride is poisonous and poison will damage good fruit. On the other hand, a captive heart must also remain an active heart. Activity is the hallmark of the Christian. Every member of the Body should ensure that theirs is never questionable, but always above reproach. So you're a Christian. Can anyone attest besides you? More importantly, on the Day of Judgment, will Messiah?

98. Where YAH Says Go

First read: Jonah 1:1- 4:11

Collectively, use the clouds as your compass while journeying. While occasionally observing, it will occur to you that their shapes are often shifting. Rather than a source of confusion, their shifting should instead aide as a resource for recognition. Recognize that change is inevitable, unavoidable, and usual. You will get no further on your journey by attempting to control what you cannot. In trying, you will find yourself stuck while the world continues to change around you and without you. Ironically, in insisting on resisting its inevitability, change will nevertheless occur, as you deteriorate in obscurity. Little repairing and restoring is possible if change isn't a part of the process. Accepting change as certain will better prepare you for its arrival.

[Yeshua] said to him, "Go at once to Straight Street, to the house of Judas, and ask for a man from Tarsus named Saul. You will find him at prayer; he has had a vision of a man named Ananias coming in and laying his hands on him to restore his sight." Ananias answered, "Lord, I have often heard about this man and all the harm he has done to thy people in Jerusalem. And he is here with authority from the chief priests to arrest all who invoke thy name." But [Yeshua] said to him, "Go, for he is a chosen instrument of mine to carry my name before the Gentiles and kings and the children of Israel. For I will show him how much he must suffer for the sake of my name." (Acts 9:11-16 NEB)

Where YHWH say go, will we say no? How futile is it to try and resist his will. It is like the image of a cloud going opposite from the direction of the earth rotating on its axis. The image is practically impossible to imagine no matter how hard one may try. If any attempts were made on the part of the cloud, it is difficult not to see how the wind would not tear it apart from the start. So, not only would it be futile, it would be equally foolish. Some may read the story of Jonah and gawk in disbelief at his brazen stubbornness. "How dare he say no to where YAH says to go." Perhaps some are tempted to sympathize with Jonah's rationalization. After all, the Father was instructing him to go to a ruthless nation; to a wicked people infamous for their barbarous warfare tactics, such as live human flaying and pyramid building with freshly severed heads. The Assyrians were unmerciful, relentless in their sins, and overflowing with pride. Yet, our God was willing to set all aside as he questioned an indignant Jonah.

And should I not pity Nineveh, that great city, in which are more than one hundred and twenty thousand persons who cannot discern between their right hand and their left—and much livestock?" (Jonah 4:11 NKJV)

In other words, why should YHWH not have compassion for the spiritually insolent whose roots lie in their ignorance? The Book of Jonah does not describe a God who has gone soft and no longer takes exception to sin. Rather it depicts a God who is sovereign and willing to accept all men who turn from their sin. Jonah should have felt honored to have been called by the Father to go. But he said no. Why? It is clear that Jonah didn't think it right that such a sin-filled people should receive clemency.

> But it displeased Jonah exceedingly, and he became angry. So he prayed to [YHWH], and said, "Ah, [YHWH], was not this what I said when I was still in my country? Therefore I fled previously to Tarshish; for I know that you are a gracious and merciful God, slow to anger and abundant in lovingkindness, One who relents from doing harm. (Jonah 4:1-2 NKJV)

> For these are our instructions from [Yeshua]: "I have appointed you to be a light for the Gentiles, and a means of salvation to earth's farthest bounds." (Acts 13:47 NEB)

While not explicitly cited, the self-righteous Jonah perhaps could have even reasoned that such a people were incapable of repentance, being the sinners that they were. What a dangerous thought, to believe that a sovereign God is incapable of changing the hardest of hearts. In speaking of the Great Commission: "Why go if it isn't so?" But Messiah has commanded that we go to Nineveh and it is not for any of us to say that we will not. Messiah is only commanding that we go back into the country from which we came and to share his name. But you say, "I was never a Ninevite." How quickly we forget our former foreign status. "But, I never killed anyone; let alone partook in the stripping of skin." But you still lived in sin.

Therefore you were a citizen of Nineveh. And just as Moses left the place he was born when Yeshua commanded him to return for the rest of his family, Messiah has given the same instructions to the Church. We are to go and retrieve the rest of his flock and lead them to our Rock. Believers must know, however, that Messiah doesn't need us to go. On the contrary, we need him to go with us. And he will if we will. But, he will if we won't, though questions will arise later. Change is upon the Church and the wind is about to blow. Which direction will you go?

> So Ananias went. He entered the house, laid his hands on him and said, "Saul, my brother, [Yeshua], who appeared to you on your way here, has sent me to you so that you may recover your sight, and be filled with the Holy Spirit." And immediately it seemed that scales fell from his eyes, and he regained his sight. Thereupon he was baptized, and afterwards he took food and his strength returned. (Acts 9:17-19 NEB)

99. Breaking Bad Habits

First read: 2nd Kings 9:1-37

How do you prepare for change? First, by refusing to carry on as a creature of habit. Refuse to excuse bad habits and engage in refining good ones. You pick up bad habits by habiting with bad company. Break your bad habits before you are broken—beyond repair.

Who does your circle of friends consist of? Are you one of those believers who insist that opposites attract and then wonder why you're constantly floundering in your faith? One habit worth breaking is the act of selecting friends based upon outside appearances and worldly aspirations. So you may walk in the way of goodness, and keep to the paths of righteousness. For the upright will dwell in the land, and the blameless will remain in it; but the wicked will be cut off from the earth, and the unfaithful will be uprooted from it. (Proverbs 2:20-22 NEB)

It's tempting to have by our side those people who make us look better than the person we have come to accept as real. Yeshua counts such a decision as folly because these relationships typically result in his servants choosing to separate themselves from him. Jezebel is an attractive friend. As a Phoenician princess who later married Ahab, king of Israel, it is clear that this queen had wealth. Many members in the Church too, find it necessary to surround themselves with the wealthy. This isn't always healthy. Most of the wealthy are impressed with their wealth, and most leave a lingering impression on those surrounding. Before too long, the member will have made a new master. When Jehu son of Jehoshaphat entered the city of Jezreel to carry out YHWH's vengeance, Queen Jezebel was found in her usual insouciant state. With face painted, hair pinned, and dressed up to the nines, Jezebel openly displayed her contempt for Jehu; unaware that she was approaching her final hour. In all her pomposity, perhaps Jezebel failed to recall her own murderous activity. But, the Father had neither forgotten about Naboth nor his promise to return the queen's sentiment. Members, who find that they often associate with those whose favorite pastime is primping in order to look the part, will soon find themselves playing the same roles. Their new-found attraction will begin to corrode their appearance until eventually the Shepherd can no longer recognize what once was his sheep.

It is not a coincidence that the believer will find not a single verse recorded in the Gospels making mention of the Messiah's financial assets or his physical appearance. One fact is clear, however. To the world, the Son of YHWH didn't look attractive. It is equally clear that Messiah often surrounded himself with people deemed worthless to the naked eye. Why? In order to show the world what he really considers valuable. It isn't beauty, fortune, or fame, but the hearts made pure after pouring out their shame.

The disciples had gone away to the town to buy food. Meanwhile a Samaritan woman came to draw water. [Yeshua] said to her, "Give me a drink." The Samaritan woman said, "What? You, a Jew, ask a drink of me, a Samaritan woman?" (Jews and Samaritans, it should be noted, do not use vessels in common.) [Yeshua] answered her, "If only you knew what [YHWH] gives, and who it is that is asking you for a drink, you would have asked him and he would have given you living water." (John 4:8-10 NEB)

There is nothing inherently evil about money or beauty, for both are gifts from YHWH. But, the lower nature is full of evil, and those living outside of the Shepherd's fold daily operate in their lowest. It is a bad habit to seek the company of those whose actions continually threaten to divorce the believer from her new nature. While on the road to Glory, the Father will provide his children with playmates who are accustomed to and intent on playing by the same rules of repairing. Those who are seeking must now begin speaking and asking their heavenly Father for friends who will help them go far on the road to Glory. When searching for intimacy away from the flock and friendships outside of the fold, believers will only break the heart that Messiah is trying to mold.

100. Accepting Accountability

First read: 1st Thessalonians 5:14

As you are walking if you see that someone is habitually tripping over their shoestrings, falling down, getting back up, and tripping once again, begin to discern. Don't follow in dimness' step, believing that the foolish traveler has secretly discovered a new source of pleasure. You won't step too far and the only experience you will have is with pain. Instead, walk over and ask if the traveler needs assistance in tying their shoes. If the reply is, "I can't help it, I'm just a creature of habit." Take a look at their bleeding nose, elbows, knees, and chin. Look at their chipped tooth and blackened eye, and then ask again, pointing out to them their aesthetic peculiarity. If the reply is, "Oh, it's bound to happen sooner or later, so why prolong the inevitable?" Throw the fool a band-aid and keep walking—after first making sure your shoes are tied. Listening to dimness' "wisdom" will lead to your folly. Prevention isn't focused on preventing what's for sure. For what is sure will occur when it's time. Prevention is for curbing what is tragic, but not rare: senseless falling to your death, in your prime.

But when Cephas came to Antioch, I opposed him to his face, because he was clearly in the wrong. For until certain persons came from James he was taking his meals with Gentile Christians; but when they came he drew back and began to hold aloof, because he was afraid of the advocates of circumcision. The other Jewish Christians showed the same lack of principle; even Barnabas was carried away and played false like the rest. But when I saw that their conduct did not square with the truth of the Gospel, I said to Cephas, before the whole congregation, "If you, a Jew born and bred, live like a Gentile, and not like a Jew, how can you insist that Gentiles must live like Jews?" (Galatians 2:11-14 NEB)

Most people dislike being corrected by another. And Christians are often the worst when it comes to reproach—both the messenger and receiver. While at times the methods employed seem faulty, Yeshua, nevertheless, still expects members of his Body to hold each other accountable for sinful behavior. There is a lie circulating throughout the Church, which would have members to believe that holding one another accountable is equivalent to judging; and because Messiah warned against judging each other, then no accountability should occur. Does the following exchange sound familiar?

Member A to B: "You really shouldn't be having sex outside of marriage."

Member B to A: "Who are you to judge me? The Bible says not to judge."

Member A to B: "Oh, I'm sorry I was just saying that…"

Member B to A: "Why don't you just mind your own business and let my God be my God?"

Unfortunately, this scenario is all too common among Christian believers. Members who are attempting to redirect a wayward believer are chastised and made to feel as if they are committing a sin. What then is Messiah speaking of when he says,

> Judge not, that you be not judged. For with the judgment you pronounce you will be judged, and with the measure you use it will be measured to you. (Matthew 7:1-2 NEB)

First, he speaks to the arrogance of some individuals who believe that some people are just broken beyond repair. The type of condemnation which ties a believer's present circumstance (or an unbeliever as well) to their eternal destination; dismissing some as bad seeds, incapable of ever producing fresh fruit. Bad root, bad fruit? Not necessarily. Take the roots and place them in different soil and watch what happens. Yeshua warns us that it is not our job to pronounce ultimate judgment on anyone. Second, unlike the Father, members of the Body are not omniscient. We can no more see into the future than we can into someone else's past. And the admonition is to resist judging someone's future based upon what is only seen at present. Often we are looking at a glass that has several cracks in it; a glass that looks as if it will completely shatter at any moment.

> Therefore do not pronounce judgment before the time, before [Yeshua] comes, who will bring to light the things now hidden in darkness and will disclose the purposes of the heart. Then each one will receive his commendation from [YHWH]. (1st Corinthians 4:5 ESV)

> You have heard what my manner of life was when I was still a practicing Jew: how savagely I persecuted the church of [Yeshua], and tried to destroy it; and how in the practice of our national religion I was outstripping many of my ancestors. But then in his good pleasure [YHWH], who had set me apart from birth and called me through his grace, chose to reveal his Son to me and through men, in order that I might proclaim him among the Gentiles. (Galatians 1:13-16a NEB)

Fortunately, our God is simultaneously looking at the present cracked glass, as well as the sparkling diamond, buffed and brilliant, that will be presented to him in the near future.

> And immediately he proclaimed [Yeshua] in the synagogues, saying, "He is the Son of [YHWH]." And all who heard him were amazed and said, "Is not this the man who made havoc in Jerusalem of those who called upon this name? And has he not come here for this purpose, to bring them bound before the chief priests?" But Saul increased all the more in strength, and confounded the Jews who lived in Damascus by proving that [Yeshua] was the [Messiah]. (Acts 9:20-22 NEB)

Rather than judging based upon what we can and can't see, we should instead spend our time aiding in the buffing. However, there are occasions where admonition of an individual member's immoral behavior is necessary because such behavior is an ill-reflection of the Body of Messiah. It is crucial that each member is consistently conscious of his or her actions, not only as a display of spiritual maturity, but also as a beacon of light for those still lost. The reality is that there are multitudes needing to enter the fold, but who, at present, are still outside. With each passing act of Christian hypocrisy, the light grows dimmer. Parents often tell their children to display their best behavior when they go out in public because their behavior is a reflection of them. Yeshua has the same expectations. We are his people—his sheep, a part of his flock. And just how is the rest of the flock supposed to hear Yeshua's voice to enter into the fold?

> And [Yeshua] came and said to them, "All authority in heaven and on earth has been given to me. Go therefore and make disciples of all nations, baptizing them in the name of the Father and of the Son and of the Holy Spirit, teaching them to observe all that I have commanded you. And behold, I am with you always, to the end of the age." (Matthew 28:18-20 ESV)

The answer is found by looking into the mirror. Some have been adopted into the fold and our God expects us to find the rest of our brothers and sisters who are still lost. The Father has placed his firstborn Son in charge of the family. Yeshua is not only our Lord and Savior, the Head of the household who is himself a reflection of the Father, he is also our eldest brother.

> For [YHWH] never said to any angel, "Thou art my Son; today I have begotten thee." or again, "I will be Father to him, and he shall be my Son." Again, when he presents the first-born to the world, he says, "Let all the angels of [YHWH] pay him homage." (Hebrews 1:5-6 NEB)

> For a consecrating priest and those whom he consecrates are all of one stock; and that is why the Son does not shrink from calling men his brothers, when he says, "I will proclaim thy name to my brothers; in full assembly I will sing thy praise." and again, "I will keep my trust fixed on him. " and again, "Here I am, and the children whom [YHWH] has given me." The children of a family share the same flesh and blood; and so he too shared ours, so that through death he might break the power of him who had death at his command that is, the devil; and might liberate those who, through fear of death, had all their lifetime been in servitude. (Hebrews 2:11-15 NEB)

It is clear then that our God's intention was for each member to become and remain a part of one family. So then, in public we are representing not only ourselves, but also our brothers and sisters in the Body of Messiah. We have a tremendous responsibility in ensuring that we are not embarrassing Messiah or the Father, in embarrassing our family. Unfortunately, unchecked immoral behavior continues to abound within the Church, stifling its growth. YHWH is not pleased. It's a daunting task for members to hold one another accountable. For some, the fear of alienation or rejection often impedes their attempts. Others have allowed weeds of timidity to grip them. In either circumstance, believers must turn to the Father for strength, while heeding the words of the apostle:

Let the word of [Yeshua] dwell in you richly, teaching and admonishing one another in all wisdom, singing psalms and hymns and spiritual songs, with thankfulness in your hearts to [YHWH]. (Colossians 3:16 ESV)

Why would the Holy Spirit, speaking through Paul, instruct us to do so? Because as a Body, we are to care enough about each other to let one another know when something is awry.

Do not judge superficially, but be just in your judgments. (John 7:24 NEB)

Better to have correction now by members within the Body than to face condemnation later by the Head of the Body. We are to do so with the utmost of wisdom and never out of selfish motives or foolish ambition. In truth, correction will continue to meet resistance.

So with many other exhortations he preached good news to the people. But Herod the tetrarch, who had been reproved by him for Herodias, his brother's wife, and for all the evil things that Herod had done, added this to them all, that he locked up John in prison. (Luke 3:18-20 ESV)

Some will respond with blazing hostility. Others won't respond at all. These are typically the ones who are content in misbehaving and living double lives. No amount of warning will convince them to change their behavior. They are only able to learn through self-discovery. So, leave them alone to discover.

101. A Hindrance to Deliverance - IV

First read: Deuteronomy 6:1-3

How do you prepare for change? If you are a creature of habit, you are also a creature of comfort. But, if comfort is your measure of success while walking, at the end of your journey you will come up short. Behaviors become habitual when they become comfortable. On the road to Glory remember that you will refine as you repair. Perhaps it needs reinforcing that both steps are perpetual and concurrent, and you will not complete either step until your last. Change is not always comfortable. Sometimes it's painful. But, prolonged comfort will eventually lead to eternal misery. Because you are continuing to grow while on your journey, good habits are great for a season, but eventually even those grow stale. Nothing smells quite as fetid as a habit no longer fitting. Know when to stop before the stench makes you drop.

It's amazing the similarities between adults and children. Children typically have no problem expressing to one another, and occasionally even to their authority figures, how much they despise authority. Whether from a parent that's laying down the law, or a teacher who's carefully explaining classroom rules, most children, whether younger or older, will routinely articulate their feelings to such with sighs and groans. When asked about their sentiments, the general consensus is that youth don't mind having the authority as long as those figures aren't going to keep them from doing what they want. In their immaturity, children often view rules as punitive rather than as protective. They believe that regulations are made to add to their misery, rather than to save them from it. It is time for the adults in the Church to grow up.

Discretion will watch over you, understanding will guard you, delivering you from the way of evil, from men of perverted speech, who forsake the paths of uprightness, to walk in the ways of darkness, who rejoice in doing evil and delight in the perverseness of evil, men whose paths are crooked, and who are devious in their way. (Proverbs 2:11-15 ESV)

Deuteronomy is just as unpopular now among most Christian circles as it was then among most Israeli. While the Israelites obviously didn't have the book, they still knew the rules. Before Moses' death in the land of Moab, YHWH instructed him to deliver a message that would forever remain etched onto the minds of those whom he had rescued from slavery. The sermon contained a detailed list of commandments that the Father expected his people to follow daily. In addition, like the loving Shepherd he is, Messiah had no problem giving an explanation for his expectations. In the words of Moses:

And now, O Israel, listen to the statutes and the rules that I am teaching you, and do them, that you may live, and go in and take possession of the land that [Yeshua] is giving you. You shall not add to the word that I command you, nor take from it, that you may keep the commandments of [YHWH] that I command you. (Deuteronomy 4:1-2 ESV)

The idea was simple really. Actually, it was lovely. The love of Messiah compels him to tell of those behaviors which threaten to destroy the intimacy he desires to share with his sheep. His love moves him to warn of those decisions that spell death. And in the same breath, he continuously speaks of the bountiful blessings that come only with obedience. It is indeed a loving God that would fathom offering to a stubborn people:

. . . houses full of all good things that you did not fill, and cisterns that you did not dig, and vineyards and olive trees that you did not plant. . . (Deuteronomy 6:11a ESV)

The Father would have been justified in destroying all Israelites for their activities in the wilderness; and yet for the growth of all, he destroyed only a few. Contrary to popular sentiment, and while admittedly uneasy, today's Church has not been relieved of her duty to obey the Father's and Messiah's commandments. No, adhering to all of them won't extend to any, the gift of eternal life. Such a gift was offered freely to us while we were still yet stubborn. However, our God's provisions are for our own protection. Only with the indwelling Holy Spirit and YHWH's grace, do believers have the ability to comply; and in doing so, we ensure that our gift remains secure. YHWH's rules are not meant as a hindrance, but are the means to deliverance—from messing up our lives. .

102. The Holy Spirit: Dead or Alive I

First read: Acts 8:14-17

You will not always wear the same shoes while traveling. The pair you're wearing today should not be the same ones you are wearing fifty miles down the road. Shoes wear out and what may be ideal and therefore comfortable for your feet now, will be harmful and discomforting later. Learn to discern and know when to change shoes. Some fools will insist on keeping the same pair because they've had them for miles and are now used to the comfort. Those fools will find themselves walking the next few miles alone. Their comfort is not very comfortable for anyone else within—make that near—their radius. Which is a bit problematic for all whom rely and are reliant upon anyone else for their restoration, and that should be everyone. If a habit seems to place you in the perils of seclusion and it seems that no one else worth having hangs around. Then consider (make that question) your dilemma in reflection. If your habit reeks from aging, put it down. Your journey will get lonely sometimes (another inevitability and equally discomforting truth); no need to induce isolation by self-indulging.

Other fools will insist on keeping the same pair to prove that they've still got it. Really, they don't have it at all and most never had it, and are therefore looking to get it from others. These fools have an even more precarious plight than the former fools. Isolation will not work as admonition because they will always have people around them. Above—using; in back—mocking; in front— pitying; beside—copying; below—fearing. Yet, all the while, all are smiling at them. Their habits will be the toughest to break because no one will break it to them. Stop. Do not be deceived. These fools don't really believe that all around them condone their habits. They hear the laughing and the sighing; the "friend" who is lying, and still they will walk on to obtain. But in trying to prove they still have what they want, they'll walk while they still hide their pain.

While on your journey, don't emulate either of these fools. Both are walking with limps that can be seen from a mile ahead. Yet, both are limping with airs of comfort. The former feigning contentment in walking the next fifteen or twenty miles alone, and the latter pretending that pain is pleasurable. While perhaps comfortable, both are also concealing their latest fashion—foot fungus. You would do well in not attempting to put them on for size. In the long run you'll be glad you didn't. The clouds are shifting once more; signaling a change in color and with it, a novelty you will come to embrace. Drip.

Therefore, brothers, be all the more diligent to confirm your calling and election, for if you practice these qualities you will never fall. For in this way there will be richly provided for you an entrance into the eternal kingdom of [Yeshua]. (2nd Peter 1:10-11 ESV)

There's a foulness that is rank circulating throughout the Body, and it will continue to debilitate the entire Church unless its members quickly come to grips with the sober truth. The odor has been lingering for so long that members have simply become accustomed to smelling its stillness, which has inevitably rendered most of them paralyzed. Any outsider walking in will immediately detect this strangely familiar ambiance if they have ever attended a funeral. It is the stench of staleness—stifled souls, whose condition would fare far better if they realized they were asphyxiating. As it stands, however, the oxygen has been gone for so long that members of the Body have grown to believe that heaving and gasping is assuredly how Messiah intended for his Bride to survive while waiting for his return. This is a lie. Members must know that even while still on this earth, Messiah doesn't want the Church to merely survive. He wants his Bride to thrive. Members must believe that Messiah wants his Body to actually breathe.

Praise [YHWH]. Praise, O servants of [Yeshua], praise the name of [YHWH]. Blessed be the name of [YHWH] from this time forth and forevermore. From the rising of the sun to its setting, the name of [YHWH] is to be praised. (Psalms 113:1-3 ESV)

There's a tiny problem, though. With our own spirit we may indeed survive, but just barely, and it will be a sight for sore eyes. But the vitality needed to walk on the road to Glory (for weary days will abound), the vigor needed to resist the devil while walking, the vivacity necessary for encouraging fellow believers to continue walking, and the verve required to lead the blind unto the road—so they too can walk—comes only from the Holy Spirit. There are many currently on the road attempting to travel without the Spirit's baptism. They've been sealed with the Holy Spirit, but they have yet to be filled. While they aren't convicts, they do bare an uncanny resemblance to a mummified corpse; bandages everywhere from unnecessary tripping and falling, and stiff as a "bored" in their spiritual walk. Though blind, convicts can still hear; otherwise they couldn't respond and through repentance, receive sight. A walking corpse, however, (or zombie, more precisely), parades among the living, masquerading as if it's lively. And herein lies the danger.

The Spirit alone gives life; the flesh is of no avail; the words which I have spoken to you are both spirit and life. (John 6:63 NEB)

Once again, these believers do have life if they have been sealed with the Holy Spirit; only they don't know it yet and so, they still haven't begun to really live. Where is the joy that Messiah promised? The Holy Spirit has it. However, believers must daily ask the Father to be filled with the Holy Spirit. Only then will the mummy be able to mirror his Master who doesn't expect his disciples' walk to Glory to depict the perpetual dirge, as if they had never left the ranks of the dead.

103. Embracing Emotions

First read: Psalms 1-10

It may not occur to you during your journey that you will, on occasion, seasonally perhaps, need to remind yourself of your humanness. Not only as an acknowledgment of your finitude and fallibility, but also as a recognition of your easily forgotten, though equally significant, plural nature. On the road to Glory you are engaging in restoring all of you. All of you can't be refined or restored with only a part of you, or even parts of you, in use. Thus, restoring all of you is going to require finding all of you. You are one person who has more than one dimension. You are plural, personal, and three dimensional, made up of heart, soul, and mind. Your walk is a balancing act and the road leading to your destination, pretty narrow. However, you will experience greater freedom, if you can learn to walk in harmony.

When Yeshua speaks of the rigidness of the road to Glory, what comes to your mind? If you are honest with yourself and with Messiah then you wouldn't mind readily acknowledging that the rigidness of the road is, at times, frustrating. It isn't our spirit that is exasperated with Messiah's expectations, rather it's the flesh. Prior to accepting Messiah as our personal Lord and Savior, our flesh was allowed to reign freely; leading us to the deadest of paths and darkest of woods. However, if the Holy Spirit has taken captive your heart, soul, and mind, then the flesh should no longer reign. Consequently, it is the flesh that is frustrated. And until our last step carries us to the gates of Glory, there will continue to be a struggle between spirit and flesh.

Stay awake, all of you; and pray that you may be spared the test. The spirit is willing, but the flesh is weak. (Mark 14:38 NEB)

For those who are resistant to the idea of a spiritual struggle—those who believe that they have been cheated out of a glamorous walk—it is time to grow up. Nowhere in any of the Gospels does Messiah make mention of glamour. What Messiah said was that his disciples were guaranteed victory. King David was well acquainted with the battlefield. When reading the Psalms, believers might do well to associate some of David's physical struggles with their spiritual ones. Though Yeshua expected his servant to stand strong while in the midst of his battles, he didn't expect him to be expressionless. The strong need not be the stoic. For many members in the Body, primarily men, it is difficult to resonate with the idea that Yeshua too created them with emotions. There are too many men walking on the road to Glory refusing to resonate with their humanity; resisting their responsibilities to the Body. The Body cannot harmonize as long as its members refuse to open their mouths. No sound, no solution. There is something melodic about the expression of misery. Actually, in the Body it isn't the expression, but the effects of the expression that one might hear in melody. It's antiphonic, or rather, it should be.

The "call and response" technique used widely in both Renaissance and Baroque music might find, once more, meaning within the walls of the Church if the broken would dare to sing. If the broken would call, then the broken would respond, that's antiphony. Perhaps if there was more antiphony within the Body then less antipathy would exist throughout. Sadly, the claustrophobia felt by many while walking on the narrow road to Glory is self-induced. Such closed spaces are necessary if the Father is going to mold and shape according to his purposes. However, the frustrating feelings of being closed-in would lessen, if members would learn how to open up. And if walking, sealed and daily filled with the Holy Spirit, then you should have nothing to hide.

...and I shall walk in a wide place, for I have sought your precepts. (Psalms 119:45 ESV)

But, frustration isn't the only feeling one encounters while walking. Joy, sadness, excitement, confusion, desperation, alarmed, anger betrayal, and contentment are all common emotions that accompany the Christian experience, and the Son is equipped to handle them all. And if the Son, then too his Body.

I waited patiently for [YHWH]; and he inclined to me, and heard my cry. He also brought me up out of a horrible pit, out of the miry clay, and set my feet upon a rock, and established my steps. He has put a new song in my mouth—praise to [Yeshua]; many will see it and fear, and will trust in [YHWH]. (Psalms 40:1-3 NEB)

104. Protocol for the Prodigal

First read: Isaiah 55-59

The earth, with its multiple dimensions, has more than one season. And while you must learn to see the virtue in each, collectively their natural changes implore the steadiness of your walk. There's no better time to ponder over this puzzle then in the pouring rain. Majestic earth's way of reminding you that it's okay. Do you think you're too old—is that why? Is that why you won't cry? Majestic earth, quite your elder, cries in laughter over such foolish thinking. Do you think it'll make you look less masculine—is that why? Is that why you won't cry? Majestic earth, with its cliffs and mountains, cries in laughter over such foolish thinking. Do you think it'll make you look weak—is that why? Is that why you won't cry? Majestic earth, full of cracks and valleys, cries in laughter over such foolish thinking. The earth—ancient, almighty, and admittedly broken—cries and is fine. You are not crying? Why?

Why won't all who are needy address it? Why won't all who are hungry air it? Why won't all who are weary confess it? And, why won't all who are thirsty declare it? The sad reality is that there are a slew of people sitting on the side of the road ragged and worn, who at one time knew what it was like to walk with vitality. Unfortunately, the weather got the best of them because no one taught them how to weather. When they were offered the option to rest for a few, they had no clue that such an opportunity would prove costly. They've been sitting out for some time now, content under the shady tree that Satan has provided for comfort. In truth, their souls are more discontented now than they ever have been before because they were once connected to their Source. What's worse is that they won't admit to anyone (though they've been asked) that while hiding out of the sun and eating their succulent fruit, they are starving, dehydrated, and more enervated than ever before. They are hungry for more. And it is their foolish pride which keeps them from yelling: "Satan, you lied. "

Up to the present, we know, the whole created universe groans in all its parts as if in pangs of childbirth. Not only so, but even we, of whom the Spirit is given as first-fruits of the harvest to come, are groaning inwardly while we wait for [YHWH] to make us his sons and set our whole body free. For we have been saved, though only in hope. Now to see is no longer to hope: why should a man endure and wait for what he already sees? But if we hope for something we do not yet see, then, in waiting for it, we show our endurance." (Romans 8:22-25 NEB)

There is nothing wrong with crying out in admitting that we made a mistake. All have moments on the road when they'd rather run off. It is the pesky conflict between the new and the old. During these times, believers must remember they've already been sold, and then they must keep walking. But, many of the faithful have not remained faithful; many have given in to the frustration of their flesh. The good news is that Messiah is just to pardon if they would just part with their sin. It is with joy that the Father will embrace a wayward son or daughter, but it starts with a tear:

> So he set out for his father's house. But while he was still a long way off his father saw him, and his heart went out to him. He ran to meet him, flung his arms round him, and kissed him. The son said, "Father, I have sinned, against [YHWH] and against you; I am no longer fit to be called your son." But the father said to his servants, "Quick. Fetch a robe, my best one, and put it on him; put a ring on his finger and shoes on his feet. Bring the fatted calf and kill it, and let us have a feast to celebrate this day. For this son of mine was dead and has come back to life; he was lost and is found. " And the festivities began. (Luke 15:20-24 NEB)

Tears of remorse will put you on course to return to the road left behind. Cry out to our Lord who is just to forgive, and once again you will hear, "You are mine." But, those who insist on the shade of the tree, who forget their souls have been bought, in danger they stand of hearing these words: "Depart, because thee I know not."

> It may be that the house of Judah will hear all the disaster that I intend to do to them, so that every one may turn from his evil way, and that I may forgive their iniquity and their sin. (Jeremiah 36:3 ESV)

> Here lies the test: the light has come into the world, but men preferred darkness to the light because their deeds were evil. Bad men hate the light and avoid it, for fear their practices should be shown up. The honest man comes to the light so that it may be clearly seen that [YHWH] is in all he does. (John 3:19-21 ESV)

105. A Reflective Moment

The Potency of Repentance: Part III

First read: Luke 23:39-43

In your struggle against sin, you have not yet resisted to the point of shedding your blood. You have forgotten the text of Scripture which addresses you as sons and appeals to you in the these words: "My son, do not think lightly of [Yeshua]'s discipline, nor lose heart when he corrects you; for [Yeshua] disciplines those whom he loves; he lays the rod on every son whom he acknowledges." You must endure it as discipline: [YHWH] is treating you as sons. Can anyone be a son, who is not disciplined by his father? If you escape the discipline in which all sons share, you must be bastards and no true sons. Again, we paid due respect to the earthly fathers who disciplined us; should we not submit even more readily to our spiritual Father, and so attain life? They disciplined us for this short life according to their lights; but he does so for our true welfare, so that we may share his holiness. Discipline, no doubt, is never pleasant; at the time it seems painful, but in the end it yields for those who have been trained by it the peaceful harvest of an honest life. Come, then, stiffen your drooping arms and shaking knees, and keep your steps from wavering. Then the disabled limb will not be put out of joint, but regain its former powers. (Hebrews 12:4-13 NEB)

Only one resisted sin from birth until the shedding of his blood, and that was Yeshua Messiah. For the remainder of us, repentance should lead to a lifetime of resistance (and continual repentance as the Holy Spirit convicts). The author of Hebrews is clear that, in convicting, the Father is disciplining his people. It is common for the average person to associate discipline with punishment only. If a child disobeys her parent or a student his teacher, then it is common practice and wise to correct their behavior. Often, the only way to correct deviant behavior is through punishment; typically intended for retribution and prevention. When looking at the criminals on the cross, it is clear that the intentions of the Romans were to seek vengeance. Through their public humiliation, it was also hopeful that onlookers would seriously consider the actions of their own behavior, lest they receive the same punishment for similar crimes. As illustrated throughout the Tanakh, our heavenly Father is not above using similar tactics in order to preserve the sanctity of his law, as well as the intended holiness of his people. Furthermore, our Father has given to Messiah the task of carrying out his just judgments on all who insist on adulterating righteousness.

When, however, we do fall under [Yeshua]'s judgment, he is disciplining us, to save us from being condemned with the rest of the world. (1st Corinthians 11:32 NEB)

But, there is another side of discipline that the author of Hebrews is addressing in this passage. Discipline can also mean self-control. When once we have repented, sin doesn't cease to exist. Because, while we are now free, the seed of sin is still embedded within our lower nature. On the contrary, the real fight begins in an effort to keep the freedom that Messiah afforded us through his death on the cross.

> For I am ready to fall, and my pain is ever before me. I confess my iniquity; I am sorry for my sin. (Psalms 38:17-18 ESV)

Herein lies the truth. If self is the instrument used to control self, you will continue to yield a net weight of zero and achieve nothing. No, there must be a more powerful force exerted on sin (coming from within) in order to keep it from resurfacing, re-captivating, and recapturing. Christians need look no further than to the Holy Spirit for the potency of repentance. It takes discipline and the grace of our God to walk that narrow road which leads to Glory. In looking at the writhing of the repentant criminal, believers are reminded that struggles will ensue along the way. Though, to help on those days it seems impossible, the Father has afforded his children a Helper who is willing to hold our hand; ever whispering in our hearts, telling us we can. Sadly, for many in the Body, freedom may have, in fact, been granted at one time. However, the chains which they once wore have consistently been re-shackled, because they choose to rely on their own strength. Effective resistance can only begin when I no longer insist on resisting through my own efforts.

> In the same way the Spirit comes to the aid of our weakness. We do not even know how we ought to pray, but through our inarticulate groans the Spirit is pleading for us, and [YHWH] who searches our inmost being knows what the Spirit means, because the Spirit pleads for [YHWH]'s people in [YHWH]'s own way; and in everything, as we know, the Spirit co-operates for good with those who love [YHWH] and are called according to his purpose. (Romans 8:26-28 NEB)

> Beloved, if our heart does not condemn us, we have confidence before [YHWH] and whatever we ask we receive from him, because we keep his commandments and do what pleases him. And this is his commandment, that we believe in the name of his Son [Yeshua] and love one another, just as he has commanded us. Whoever keeps his commandments abides in [YHWH], and [YHWH] in him. And by this we know that he abides in us, by the Spirit whom he has given us. (1st John 3:21-24 NEB)

106. Yoking the Youth

First read: Ecclesiastes 12:1-7

Clouds. Yes, looking up at the shifting of their shapes reminds you of the seasons change. And once again this should be a welcomed change, for each offers you an opportunity to reflect, refocus, and rejoice. Though, perhaps the most valuable assistance afforded by changing seasons is their aiding in your renewal. Refining will first require surrendering—not only to its necessity—but surrendering to its complexity as well. There is nothing simple about anything three-dimensional, and in attempting to simplify you will find yourself complicating and looking like a simpleton. To avoid complication, you must engage in contemplation. Clouds condense and then commence to release. Cathartic and cleansing for body and soul, soothing for swelter in kind. In clearing your pathway, curbing your pain, in pouring, it cleanses your mind.

Face it. It is hard being young. There are troubles that the youth of today face that, while not completely foreign to most adults, are nevertheless fiercer, and, at times, outright ferocious when compared to yesterdays. Adolescence brings with it enough anxiety on its own without having to add to the mix an enemy who is set on mayhem intermingling with the minds of our youth. The young must first understand that they have a heavenly Father who adores them. A Father who does not desire that the youngest of his people forfeit their youthfulness in exchange for the tribulations that will accompany adulthood. King Solomon offers the following words of encouragement:

Rejoice, young man, in your youth, and let your heart cheer you in the days of your youth. Walk in the ways of your heart and the sight of your eyes. But know that for all these things [YHWH] will bring you into judgment. (Ecclesiastes 11:9 ESV)

In adding the stipulation, Solomon is not trying to rain on anyone's parade. Though, it requires a paradigm shift in postmodern thinking to reign in and teach today's youth about absolute truth. But before remembering what, they must first be taught Who. Parents think their children know, when, in fact, most haven't a clue. But then neither do most parents. The youth must also be taught why. Tell them why a loving Father would send his only Son to die. And why the Father still expect even his youngest to conduct themselves like precious sons and daughters of a King.

Be most careful then how you conduct yourselves: like sensible men, not like simpletons. Use the present opportunity to the full, for these are evil days. (Ephesians 5:15-16 NEB)

But [YHWH] has laid a foundation, and it stands firm, with this inscription: "[YHWH] knows his own." and "Everyone who takes [YHWH]'s name upon his lips must forsake wickedness." Now in any great house there are not only utensils of gold and silver, but also others of wood or earthenware;

the former are valued, the latter held cheap. To be among those which are valued and dedicated, a thing of use to the Master of the house, a man must cleanse himself from all those evil things; then he will be fit for any honorable purpose. Turn away from the wayward impulses of youth, and pursue justice, integrity, love, and peace with all who invoke [Yeshua] in singleness of mind. (2nd Timothy 2:19-22 NEB)

Messiah does not feel that the youth of today are, "too young to get it now." Even for youth, the Master's yoke is good to bear. But, he does insist that those in charge begin training them in how.

The chief priests and doctors of the law saw the wonderful things he did, and heard the boys in the temple shouting, "Hosanna to the Son of David." and they asked him indignantly, "Do you hear what they are saying?" [Yeshua] answered, "I do; have you never read the text, 'Thou hast made children and babes at the breast sound aloud thy praise?'" (Matthew 21:15-16 NEB)

Training them requires discipline. Parents must remember that Messiah wants disciples—not delinquents. Developing a disciple with a devoted heart, mind, and soul is a parent's primary goal; and while not simple, it may save from an early grave. "But, but, but..." some parents will cry, "Shouldn't the youth enjoy their leisure?" Messiah is not against leisure. His antipathy is for the spiritually lazy. For those parents who pander to, Messiah has some candor to offer you:

But if a man is a cause of stumbling to one of these little ones who have faith in me, it would be better for him to have a millstone hung round his neck and be drowned in the depths of the sea. Alas for the world that such causes of stumbling arise. Come they must, but woe betide the man through whom they come. (Matthew 18:6-7 NEB)

Messiah is serious about the sanctity of his Father's youth. Encouraging reflection, so that they know who to reflect, is not an unreasonable task. Yes, allow the youth to bask, but in YHWH's glory.

107. Walking With Wisdom - I

First read: 2nd Chronicles 12:1-16

You should seek to saunter while pondering in the pouring rain. Don't fear reflection, for it is the only pathway to refocusing. Embrace the rain, and as it surges to clear your mind, spend some time soaking in solitude. Make reflecting an exclusive exercise before including the entourage. Remember that the refining process is an interpersonal experience, but it is also an intrapersonal experience as well. Both you and your fellow travelers should have your own reflection time. Insist on yours and theirs. In keeping your head soaked with insight that others will soon impart, ensure that the wisdom is gleaned from those who've given from their heart.

It would appear that Solomon's apple didn't fall far from his tree. Rehoboam, son of Solomon and heir to the throne of Israel, didn't make a habit of exercising good judgment. His first opportunity was botched when he failed to heed the advice of the older and wiser elders who cautioned him against ignoring the concerns of the Israelites. Truthfully, Rehoboam can't take complete responsibility here because Scripture indicates that YHWH orchestrated the turn of events in order to fulfill an earlier prophecy. It was because of Rehoboam's obstinacy that the kingdom of Israel was divided into the northern kingdom of Israel and the southern kingdom of Judah; ironically, the result of an unwise decision made by wise Solomon years before:

And [YHWH] was angry with Solomon, because his heart had turned away from [YHWH] the God of Israel,, who had appeared to him twice and had commanded him concerning this thing, that he should not go after other gods. But he did not keep what [YHWH] commanded. Therefore [Yeshua] said to Solomon, "Since this has been your practice and you have not kept my covenant and my statutes that I have commanded you, I will surely tear the kingdom from you and will give it to your servant. Yet for the sake of David your father I will not do it in your days, but I will tear it out of the hand of your son. However, I will not tear away all the kingdom, but I will give one tribe to your son, for the sake of David my servant and for the sake of Jerusalem that I have chosen." (1st Kings 11:9-13 ESV)

What is the similarity between Solomon's mishap and Rehoboam's? Solomon's sin came after he had finished building YHWH's temple. There came a time when Solomon grew complacent with his own wisdom after no longer acknowledging its source. This time came after the Father had established him on the throne. And his son?

When the rule of Rehoboam was established and he was strong, he abandoned the law of [YHWH], and all Israel with him. (2nd Chronicles 12:1 ESV)

During his reign, Rehoboam was said to have done what was wrong because he, "did not make a habit of seeking guidance of YHWH." Like father like son. It wasn't that they hadn't ever walked in wisdom, but neither made it a life long habit.

In their eminent positions it must have been a challenge to find alone time. But, even the Son of YHWH, while serving on earth, made it his business to spend time alone with his Father. Even the best servant can wind up sinning if she isn't taking time out to commune with the source of her service.

> That evening after sunset they brought to him all who were ill or possessed by devils; and the whole town was there, gathered at the door. He healed many who suffered from various diseases, and drove out many devils. He would not let the devils speak, because they knew who he was. Very early next morning he got up and went out. He went away to a lonely spot and remained there in prayer. (Mark 1:32-35 NEB)

There are some in the Body who fear solitude, so they serve instead; thinking that the Father will accept their service as a substitute. There are others who, at the beginning of their journey, regularly sought guidance of YHWH, as they weren't always sure of the next step to take. As they continued to walk, however, they grew less intimate with the Father and less dependent on the Holy Spirit. Our Father expects his children to seek after him regularly and to understand that there are times when he isn't interested in sharing you with others. It doesn't mean that he loves them less; his ecumenical nature is sufficient for all, but it should never be diluted for any.

> Immediately [Yeshua] made His disciples get into the boat and go before him to the other side, while he sent the multitudes away. And when he had sent the multitudes away, he went up on the mountain by himself to pray. Now when evening came, he was alone there. (Matthew 14:22-23 NKJV)

108. Indigestion

First read: 2nd Peter 2:21-22

While walking you will find yourself occasionally wandering off track. Whether from looking back, down, or around for too long, or from habiting with bad company, it is bound to happen. When you finally realize that you've ventured into vomit, you'll rush to wash. Unfortunately, the further you venture, the further you must venture back. Time will have lapsed and you will be fatigued in lapping. The longer you wonder, the longer you'll wander and soon you will find yourself lost. A drop on the head will keep you ahead and keep you from death by exhaust. Your journey is already a lengthy one and weariness promises to pay you several visits; so, no need to send out an invitation or reminder.

Vomit. Throw-up. Puke. Not exactly the most pleasant thought is it? What about the idea of vomiting and then going back later and ingesting it when, for a moment or two, you find yourself missing your old diet? Does this sound appetizing to you? No more so, I hope, than does accepting Messiah into your life, repenting of all your sins, getting all of the trash out of your life, and then once you find yourself hungry, going back to the trash-can to retrieve your former filth. Make no mistake, as Christians we will have days of nostalgia. If we are honest with ourselves, it wasn't the idea of sinning that intrigued us so much, as did the act itself. While walking and maturing in our faith, days of old will occasionally creep back into our minds. The life we used to lead was filled with activities that were pleasurable. Our walk with YHWH will sometimes feel painful, and at other times, seem insufferable. It is during these moments that we must not forget that before we accepted Messiah, some of those same memorable activities were equally, sinful.

> But he rescued Lot, who was a good man, shocked by the dissolute habits of the lawless society in which he lived; day after day every sight, every sound, of their evil courses tortured the good man's heart. Thus [Yeshua] is well able to rescue the godly out of trials, and to reserve the wicked under punishment until the day of judgment. (2nd Peter 2:7-9 NEB)

Peter reminds us of how foolish it is for the believer who has come to receive and experience the grace of the Father, through salvation in Yeshua Messiah, to whimsically decide in times of turmoil to turn to their former life-styles for refuge. In alluding to a proverb, he compares it to a dog returning to its own vomit. While we may find it disgusting, dogs see nothing wrong with it. That's because dogs are acting as they often do—instinctively. Careful, Yeshua did not create us to act instinctively. Rather he has called all to act spiritually and with discernment; to walk righteously and in holiness. Our instincts and our nature are inextricably bound. However, we must remember that our fallen nature is in constant battle with our newly kindled spirit. When in the midst of a hardship our nature alerts us of its discomforts. We then become fixated on our discomforts until the hardship, although temporary, at present seems eternal. It is this eternal perception which induces us to give in. While the Spirit is saying, "fight and endure," our nature is simultaneously screaming, "flee and surrender." Unless we learn to act from internal convictions and not external conditions, then we will continue to flounder in frustration. And if we are not careful, our floundering can lead us back to the life we originally fled.

And now what do you gain by going to Egypt to drink the waters of the Nile? Or what do you gain by going to Assyria to drink the waters of the Euphrates? Your evil will chastise you, and your apostasy will reprove you. Know and see that it is evil and bitter for you to forsake [YHWH]; the fear of me is not in you, declares [Yeshua]. (Jeremiah 2:18-19 ESV)

In truth, we will always have hunger pangs. The longer we walk with Messiah, the stronger they become, but the less apt we are to feel them. Not because they aren't there, but because after a time we learn to consistently feast on the word of YHWH. Moreover, the Church must always be in a position to feed. Perhaps the best opportunity for feeding is through fellowship. Fellowshipping in the Body can increase the likelihood that a believer will always have a choice other than vomit to eat when hungry. Witnessing to others and carrying out the Great Commission can also significantly reduce a relapse. For it is through perpetually witnessing to others that we stay reminded as to how our own lives were before accepting Messiah. In viewing others vomit we are less inclined to seek our own.

A child of [YHWH] does not commit sin, because the divine seed remains in him; he cannot be a sinner, because he is [YHWH]'s child. That is the distinction between the children of [YHWH] and the children of the devil: no one who does not do right is [YHWH]'s child, nor is anyone who does not love his brother. (1st John 3:9-10 NEB)

Once again, there will be days when it seems easiest to return to our former lives. Satan loves to tempt us into believing that the grass is always greener on the other side. But let none show daftness. We have already been on the other side, and it was with much of what that side had to offer that we found ourselves turning green to begin with. On those days you regale over what was fun, remember those nights when it all was done. How did you feel? Better yet, how do you think YHWH feels when any of his adopted children decide, through their actions, that they no longer are interested in him being their Father?

Who will have pity on you, O Jerusalem, or who will grieve for you? Who will turn aside to ask about your welfare? You have rejected me, declares [Yeshua]; you keep going backward, so I have stretched out my hand against you and destroyed you—I am weary of relenting. I have winnowed them with a winnowing fork in the gates of the land; I have bereaved them; I have destroyed my people; they did not turn from their ways. (Jeremiah 15:5-7 ESV)

In walking with Messiah, times of hardship will arise, but none will be insufferable. Rather than returning to your vomit, keep your sights on the Heavenly banquet. Vomit. Throw-up. Puke. Sound repulsive? What about sin?

The fear of [Yeshua] is hatred of evil. Pride and arrogance and the way of evil and perverted speech I hate. (Proverbs 8:13 ESV)

109. Cohabitation

First read: Colossians 3:1-11

The head and heart cohabitate, and if anything of worth is to enter or leave, the two must also collaborate. Wisdom from a head with no feelings attached is a head detached from the heart. Hence, the words delivered are dead and worthless. Wisdom from a heart with no meaning attached is a heart detached from the head. The words delivered are dead and worthless still. If what you glean comes from either source solely, slowly let it enter one ear, process it—not digest—and then let it quickly exit through the other. Because you are not one-dimensional, trying to digest the information that came from one part of one body intended for the whole will leave you sick to your stomach. However, all wisdom, departing, imparting, should have the same end and start. Sounds in your head may soon fade away, but they'll always remain in your heart. Don't allow dead words to settle in your heart.

Do you ever feel that there's a spiritual disconnect between you and YHWH? If you do, it isn't because Messiah didn't do his job. There did exist a spiritual disconnect between YHWH and his children after the original fall of man. See, in the Garden of Eden when YHWH warned Adam:

And [YHWH] commanded the man, saying, "You may surely eat of every tree of the garden, but of the tree of the knowledge of good and evil you shall not eat, for in the day that you eat of it you shall surely die." (Genesis 2:16-17 ESV)

What he was in fact saying was that "On the day that you choose to disobey me, Adam, you and I will become disconnected." Death is also separation from the Father. Though, for the believer, this separation is only temporary. It was only by his grace that YHWH decided to put into place his plan for man's redemption. Through sending his Son to die on the cross for our sins, YHWH granted us access to him once again. As a newly grafted member of the Body, once we accept Messiah as head of our lives, there's no reason we should still feel detached. Unless, of course, there's a disconnect between the Head and our hearts.

And in union with [Yeshua] he raised us up and enthroned us with him in the heavenly realms, so that he might display in the ages to come how immense are the resources of his grace, and how great his kindness to us in [Yeshua]. (Ephesians 2:6-7 NEB)

In order to maximize the relationship that the Father wants believers to have with his Son, cohabitation must exist between the two in the same way it exists between the two of them. Such was the prayer of Yeshua while in the garden:

And the glory which You gave Me I have given them, that they may be one just as We are one: I in them, and You in Me; that they may be made perfect in one, and that the world may know that You have sent Me, and have loved them as You have loved Me. (John 17:22-23 NKJV)

The way to determine if Messiah is the one heading your life is by monitoring your own behavior. What words are coming out of your mouth? If Messiah is your Head, then would these same words leave his mouth? What thoughts are you entertaining in your mind? If Messiah is your Head, then would he allow these thoughts to remain in his? What feelings are you allowing to manifest in your heart? If Messiah is your Head then that means you should also have his heart. And the heart of Messiah is what each member of the Body should constantly seek.

The thoughts of the wicked are an abomination to [Yeshua], but gracious words are pure. (Proverbs 15:26 ESV)

No bad language must pass your lips, but only what is good and helpful to the occasion, so that it brings a blessing to those who hear it. And do not grieve the Holy Spirit of [YHWH], for that Spirit is the seal with which you were marked for the day of our final liberation. Have done with spite and passion, all angry shouting and cursing, and bad feeling of every kind. (Ephesians 4:29-31 NEB)

The problem is, however, that while many Christians proclaim Messiah as their Head, they insist on keeping their own hearts. Problem? Yes. First, our own hearts are sin-filled from birth. When we accept Messiah into our lives, we are also offered a heart transplant. Sadly, there are those who turn it down, so they never experience the fullness that comes with having a relationship with Messiah; only the angst that comes with his absence. Second, Messiah isn't interested in having partners; he is our Lord and Master—we are not his equals. In the same way that there can exist only one Head, in order for the Body of Messiah to operate as one, only one Heart must beat and each member must ensure that all are connected to both.

[YHWH] is at hand; do not be anxious about anything, but in everything by prayer and supplication with thanksgiving let your requests be made known to [YHWH]; And the peace of [YHWH], which surpasses all understanding, will guard your hearts and your minds in [Yeshua]. Finally, brothers, whatever is true, whatever is honorable, whatever is just, whatever is pure, whatever is lovely, whatever is commendable, if there is any excellence, if there is anything worthy of praise, think about these things. (Philippians 4:5b-8 ESV)

110. Dueling With the Devil In Peace - I

First read: Ephesians 6:14-18

Neither you nor they can give from the heart without listening to its beat. You can't listen if you can't hear, and you can't hear if there's noise. Seek solace in silence. Perhaps you may think it dissonant, the tempo of the drizzling rain, juxtaposing that of your beating heart; especially when the drizzling turns into a downpour and eventually a thunderstorm. How can thoughtful reflection take place? Concentrate on the consonance found in the chords of contentment. These harmonic chords can be found in your soul. Find them and play them continuously. If and when you do, you will rejoice without ceasing, no matter how much dissonance is around you.

Peace to the brotherhood and love, with faith, from [YHWH] the Father and the Lord [Yeshua]. [YHWH]'s grace be with you all who love [Yeshua], grace and immortality. (Ephesians 6:23-24 NEB)

All members of the Body should understand that the Gospel of peace in no way promotes Christian passivism or even pacifism. On the contrary, the nature of spiritual warfare implies an ongoing battle that requires believers to remain active and aggressive. That is, actively serving Messiah while restoring others and self from our current broken state. That is, also, aggressively sifting out leaven within the parts of the Church that are threatening to destroy the whole. What Paul is encouraging believers to reflect and then remember is that Satan seeks to debilitate. If he can't destroy, spiritual debilitation is the next best option. YHWH tests those who profess to believe in him. He also tests those who say they believe him. In the same way that the Holy Spirit led Messiah into the wilderness before starting his ministry, at specific junctures while journeying, the Father will allow for each believer some time in the desert. This is no time for hesitation, but for dedication, education, investigation, and preparation. Once again, Satan is aware of human frailties, and he will occasionally drop by in an effort to castigate, debilitate, or humiliate. Whatever he can do to induce the believer to give up, or worse yet, reject YHWH. While walking through the desert on the hot sand, it is imperative that Christians have the shoes of peace on the soles of their feet.

At other times the Father will lead us to a storm. The believer must remember, if he is leading you to, then he will also lead you through. These chords of contentment are none other than the indwelling Holy Spirit. When facing tests or trials, the difficulty for most believers lies in remembering that YHWH is still present. This brings to mind the parable of the seeds—remember the ones sown among rocky soil? Members of the Body must share with those lost and with those newly converted, the message of the whole Gospel. While the truths of justification by grace through faith, and salvation from eternal separation from the Father, need to sound clearly, it isn't the beginning or end that most Christians struggle with. At present there are many who, while in the middle of their journey, leave the Body, or are, at best, hanging on by a severed tendon, because they were never fully prepared to serve Messiah because they were never told about the Gospel of peace. How then can they wear that which never was shown? Why must they wait until their seeds have been sown? As previously stated, the Church must begin taking preventive steps rather than tripping in reaction.

[YHWH] sits enthroned over the flood; [Yeshua] sits enthroned as king forever. May [YHWH] give strength to his people. May [Yeshua] bless his people with peace. (Psalms 29:10-11 ESV)

But the wisdom from above is in the first place pure; and then peace-loving, considerate; and open to reason; it is straightforward and sincere, rich in mercy and in the kindly deeds that are its fruit. True justice is the harvest reaped by peace-makers from seeds sown in a spirit of peace. (James 3:17-18 NEB)

When YHWH delivers a promise, we are eager to reap the harvest but don't always feel conditioned to sow the seeds. The Gospel of peace is not just a message of perpetual conciliatory efforts in a Body filled with resistant lower natures. It is a reminder to the believer that each will have their cross to bear. But in the midst of bearing their cross, the Father affords his peace that surpasses all understanding. This doesn't mean, however, that the cross won't feel heavier at times than at others. And Satan loves to add his own weight.

You trampled the sea with your horses, the surging of mighty waters. I hear, and my body trembles; my lips quiver at the sound; rottenness enters into my bones; my legs tremble beneath me. Yet I will quietly wait for the day of trouble to come upon people who invade us. Though the fig tree should not blossom, nor fruit be on the vines, the produce of the olive fail and the fields yield no food, the flock be cut off from the fold and there be no herd in the stalls, yet I will rejoice in [YHWH]; I will take joy in the God of my salvation. [Yeshua], the Lord, is my strength; he makes my feet like the deer's; he makes me tread on my high places. (Habakkuk 3:15-19 ESV)

111. Soul Searching

First read: Isaiah 38:9-20

Your soul is the most essential element of your 3-D nature in the same way that moving is the most essential element of your journey. While walking in the pouring rain, remind yourself that in listening to your heart and reflecting with your mind, you're refining and repairing your soul. For it is here that your journey prepares for reunion; where your half will one day be whole. There are other essential elements that rain induces and refines besides reflection. Delight in the dew. And with the drop from the skies, start dropping from your eyes. No tears will fall, however, if your heart has hardened.

Why does the rain fall on the just as well as the unjust? Because even the saint still has some stains. The stain of sin is so deep within that sometimes YHWH will press and press until he sees that our responses are nothing less than holy. It is not possible to eek out such holiness when we are consistently only basking in the Son's rays, because most of the time the light only highlights those areas that are most attractive. Make no mistake, such highlighting is also intentional because Messiah expects his disciples to shine. As we are preparing for his triumphant return, it is imperative that members of the Body intensify their brilliance, so that those who are blind might see.

O house of Jacob, come, let us walk in the light of [Yeshua]. (Isaiah 2:5 ESV)

We should remember, however, that such luminescence is all but impossible without having been tested. And while Messiah is elated when his hands and feet are able to draw others out of the pit; the midst of commotion is a test of devotion: "Will you stay when it's you who is hit?" Can believers of today pray the prayer of King David?

Why are you cast down, O my soul, and why are you in turmoil within me? Hope in [YHWH]; for I shall again praise him, my salvation and my God. (Psalms 43:5 ESV)

The purification of the soul doesn't come without suffering because without anguish we never learn how to relinquish. There is nothing a believer can do to purify his soul because the Father has given this job to the Son. But to purify the soul, the Holy Spirit must have control. Experience has shown that even the most seasoned believer is, at his base, reluctant to relinquish all. This is because, even while walking with Messiah, we are haunted by temporal experiences of the past. We haven't yet mastered how to let our luggage go, and so we ruminate. Our ruminations can lead us down a dangerous path spiritually if ever we forget our Savior's divinity. While we are to continuously connect with Messiah's human condition (as he selflessly connected to ours), unlike our countless broken human relationships, believers must never forget that Messiah will never fail us.

Lift up your eyes to the heavens, and look on the earth beneath; for the heavens will vanish like smoke, the earth will grow old like a garment, and those who dwell in it will die in like manner; but my salvation will be forever, and my righteousness will not be abolished. (Isaiah 51:6 NKJV)

Thusly, the Son has observed that it is often affliction which renders his disciples desperate. Messiah's call to salvation is a call to sacrifice "self." But, the end of self is not the end itself; it only secures our beginning. It is in our desperation for sanctification that we surrender our souls, and now the Holy Spirit is able to begin working. The Spirit was sent to search. Believers mistakenly believe that it is their job to search, but this is impossible. We have been given dominion over the outside, and Messiah expects his disciples to exhibit control over our new self, exemplified by Christian behavior. However, our inside is the domain of another. Once relinquished, only the Spirit may control our "selves." And yet, the goal is not to control, but to clean. Without question, there will be moments when members of the Body won't delight in what the Spirit is doing. Nevertheless, hearts must remain guarded against griping. Satan would like nothing more than for a believer to lose his grip. And when you slip be assured that he will rush in to "save." Certainly, be assured and beware.

112. Dueling With The Devil In Peace - II

First read: Ephesians 6:14-18

As you walk, there will be days, even weeks, with no drop from the sky. The sun will scorch mercilessly, sopping up moisture like a fuming sponge. With its rays on a rampage, the sun will desiccate and decimate, discriminating against nothing and no one. During these times of misery the earth will harden—guard your heart. Be sure to stay attuned to your chords of contentment and tune out all those jarring sounds. Deaf ears will lead to dead hearts. Fainter still will the beating sound, as your ears are congested with crank. Complaining and cursing all those around, but no one will they thank. You could offer them a cup of water and those with hardened hearts will throw it back in your face, demanding a gallon. Unfortunately, these are the same travelers whom you offered a towel to dry with during the rains, and yet, they threw it on the ground, demanding a larger one to cover their whole body. These fools aren't even fair-weather friends. Whether the sky is blue or whether the sky is gray, they always will sigh—with no tears in their eyes—whatever the sky is that day. You will profit by not playing with fire. Raising your temperature won't lower the sun's, and the fools around you, playing chicken with the sun, will soon find themselves roasting. And it won't stop there. Inflamed, the foolish feel that fury will somehow cool them off; while inflamed, a thousand enemies they earn. Inflamed, the fool in fury flounders, getting still no cooler; now in flames, a thousand watch the foolish burn. If raising your temperature when already heated will cause you to combust, then consider lowering your temperature when hot.

Only let your conduct be worthy of the gospel of [Messiah], so that whether I come and see you for myself or hear about you from a distance, I may know that you are standing firm, one in spirit, one in mind, contending as one man for the gospel faith, meeting your opponents without so much as a tremor. This is a sure sign to them that their doom is sealed, but a sign of your salvation, and one afforded by [YHWH] himself; for you have been granted the privilege not only of believing in [Messiah] but also of suffering for him. You and I are engaged in the same contest; you saw me in it once, and, as you hear, I am in it still. (Philippians 1:27-30 NEB)

The devil loves division. He also loves conflict, confusion, and chaos. In recognizing as much, it is in Satan's best interest for YHWH's children to remain divided. While traveling on the road to Glory, believers must quit reacting to the thorns and glass which will continue to appear in various shapes, sizes, and colors, and instead ensure that their feet remain protected by wearing the shoes of peace. How then is the Christian to defend himself when in the midst of cantankerous circumstances? Not by returning the sentiments. For many members, Messiah offers a seemly implausible solution.

You have learned that they were told, "Love your neighbor, hate your enemy." But what I tell you is this: Love your enemies and pray for your persecutors; only so can you be children of your heavenly Father, who makes his sun rise on good and bad alike, and sends rain on the honest and the dishonest. If you love only those who love you, what reward can you expect? Surely the tax-gatherers do as much as that. And if you greet only your brothers; what is there extraordinary about that? Even the heathen do as much. There must be no limit to your goodness, as your heavenly Father's goodness knows no bounds. (Matthew 5:43-48 NEB)

Truly, his commandments in no way resemble what society would have members believe is the way to respond. However, this should come as no surprise since Messiah's teachings continue to stand in contrast to the wisdom of the world. Many men in the Body may find that they struggle with conflict resolution, as most insist on secularizing the Father's intended depiction of masculinity.

The mouth of the righteous is a well of life, But violence covers the mouth of the wicked. (Proverbs 10:11 NKJV)

Whoever is slow to anger has great understanding, but he who has a hasty temper exalts folly. (Proverbs 14:29 ESV)

A soft answer turns away wrath, but a harsh word stirs up anger. (Proverbs 15:1 ESV)

113. Real Men Weep

First read: 2nd Samuel 1:1-27

Remember that your body comes complete with an automatic sprinkler. When you get heated, listen to your body and allow the water to start flying. The clouds have no shame in showing their tears and neither should you. On days when it's clear that little comforting is near, close your eyes then open them once more. If by chance you blur, then embrace what will occur; your tears are there, don't fight them; let them pour. There is nothing wimpy about weeping. If you find yourself feeling angry, anxious, or joyous while walking—good. It means you have no problem in recognizing your plurality. If, however, you find yourself shielding your tears—horrid. It means you have a hitch in embracing your humanity. Caution. You are carrying dead weight. Drop it. You should ask yourself why you won't cry.

For what is the measure of a man? That depends upon to whom you're directing the question. Turning to the world, one hears the suggestion that a man should be measured by his strength. And so the adage goes, "real men don't cry." Such a shame it is to allow the soul to suffer in an effort to mimic the masses. What the world expects of our young boys is that they learn how to mask all sentiment that doesn't mirror aggression. They are taught that to display any emotion with lesser intensity is a sign of effeminacy. As such, our young boys grow into young men whose expressions remain dormant. What the world is interested in producing then, aren't men, but mannequins.

Blessed are you who are hungry now, for you shall be satisfied. Blessed are you who weep now, for you shall laugh. (Luke 6:21 ESV)

Mannequins are made in the image of the world. Men are made in the image of Yeshua. How silly to believe that in crafting man, Yeshua would withhold from him the ability to reveal when and what the soul really feels. To reserve such a gift for women only would speak to cruelty; a suggestion that Yeshua created man for the sole purpose of carrying dead weight. And yet how common it is for society to place this boulder upon the shoulders of men who, while stumbling in agony, will, in turn, place a block of equal weight onto the backs of their sons. Then the world expects them all to walk. There is much relief to be found in reading the Bible. In looking through Scripture, men will find not a verse supporting a notion that the Father or Son winces at weeping.

So Mary came to the place where [Yeshua] was. As soon as she caught sight of him she fell at his feet and said, "O sir, if you had only been here my brother would not have died." When [Yeshua] saw her weeping and the Jews her companions weeping, he sighed heavily and was deeply moved. "Where have you laid him?" he asked. They replied, "Come and see, sir." [Yeshua] wept. The Jews said, "How dearly he must have loved him." (John 11:32-36 NEB)

Because members know that Yeshua is the perfect image of the invisible YHWH, it is safe to assume that all of his actions were met with approval by his Father. Yeshua displayed emotions that would fail to measure up to what the world deems manly. Compassionate, thoughtful, sensitive, and empathetic are just a few of the adjectives which appropriately describe Messiah. And yet today, what man dares to show that he cares? What's more, Yeshua did the unthinkable, and on more than one occasion.

> He himself withdrew from them about a stone's throw, knelt down, and began to pray: "Father, if it be thy will, take this cup away from me. Yet not my will but thine be done." And now there appeared to him a messenger from heaven bringing him strength, and in anguish of spirit he prayed the more urgently; and his sweat was like clots of blood falling from the ground. (Luke 22:41-44 NEB)

Sweat, blood, and anguish? In identifying with humanity while walking the earth, Yeshua never failed to show that he was human. Yes, we serve a warrior who weeps, but he is no wimp.

> Then I saw heaven wide open, and there before me was a white horse; and its rider's name was Faithful and True, for he is just in judgment and just in war. His eyes flamed like fire, and on his head were many diadems. Written upon him was a name known to none but himself, and he was robed in a garment drenched in blood. He was called the Word of [YHWH], and the armies of heaven followed him on white horses, clothed fine linen, clean and shining. From his mouth there went a sharp sword with which to smite the nations; for he it is who shall rule them with an iron rod, and tread the winepress of the wrath and retribution of [YHWH] the sovereign Lord. And on his robe and on his thigh there was written the name: King of kings and Lord of lords. (Revelation 19:11-16 NEB)

If the Son of Man, who is also the King of kings and Lord of lords, wept, then surely his younger brothers should have no shame in shedding. Once again, we find in David, "a man after YHWH's own heart," practically living on the battle field, his strength in open display. This is the same man who authored more than half of the poetry found in the Bible; shamelessly danced before YHWH; and cried bitterly over the death of Jonathan and Saul. Like Yeshua, David had no trouble embracing his humanity; they were both real men. For what is the measure of a man? In turning to the Father, man finds that he too measures by strength. The strength to walk with his heart on display; no matter what those in the world have to say.

114. Licking the Liar

First read: Nehemiah 6:1-19

In truth, you will struggle with tears, to keep from showing you're torn. As you're walking, a fool will tell you that what you are feeling is natural. It is not natural, it is unwise. Alas, the fool is speaking from their head and from their head alone; dead words—let them pass. Then, let the fool pass and keep walking. It only feels natural if you have become accustomed to not admitting your brokenness. It feels natural because it has become a habit. All habits feel natural, including bad habits. As you continue to walk, you'll continue to struggle and another fool will tell you that what you're feeling is normal. This fool is right. However, after slapping your back in pardoning your normality, the fool will continue walking and talking and aiding others in their demise. What you're feeling is normal because everyone else around you is feeling the same way. Everyone around you is exercising bad habits; senselessly tripping over the same shoes and hiding their foot fungus. None are repairing and none are refining. Congratulations, you're normal. How do you feel with fungus on your heel?

On the following Sabbath almost the whole city gathered to hear the word of [YHWH]. When the Jews saw the crowds, they were filled with jealous resentment, and contradicted what Paul said, with violent abuse. (Acts 13:44-45 NEB)

When it is time for the believer to begin rebuilding his or her temple after repenting of its deterioration, not only will he encounter those on the sidelines who aim to enervate through discouraging words and deeds, there will also exist those whom Satan has inspired to lie. If the believer isn't careful and discerning then there will be unnecessarily hard lessons learned. There is only one way to lick the liar and that is to stay immersed in the truth.

Lead me in Your truth and teach me, For You are the God of my salvation; On You I wait all the day. (Psalms 25:5 NKJV)

At Iconium similarly they went into the Jewish synagogue and spoke to such purpose that a large body both of Jews and Gentiles became believers. But the unconverted Jews stirred up the Gentiles and poisoned their minds against the Christians. (Acts 14:1-3 NEB)

My children, this is the last hour. You were told that Anti-[Messiah] was to come, and now many anti-[Messiahs] have appeared; which proves to us that this is indeed the last hour. They went out from our company, but never really belonged to us; if they had, they would have stayed with us. They went out, so that it might be clear that not all our company truly belong to it. You, no less than they, are among the initiated; this is the gift of the Holy One, and by it you all have knowledge. It is not because you are ignorant of the truth that I have written to you, but because you know it, and because lies, one and all, are alien to the truth. (1st John 2:18-21 NEB)

But even before repentance, there must be a willingness to acknowledge one's need. There are plenty of non-believers in the world who see nothing wrong with the current state of affairs; they are themselves in a sad state. While walking around in blindness, they see the world in shades of gray , and criticize all others who dare adhere to a binding standard of truth. In their eyes, those who bear and share the Truth are unenlightened simpletons who have yet to arrive. It is easy to fall into the trap of believing this lie because the accusers often have letters, both in front of, and behind their names, to illuminate their worldly insight. The Apostle Paul cautions against gawking at such genius.

Let no one deceive himself. If anyone among you seems to be wise in this age, let him become a fool that he may become wise. For the wisdom of this world is foolishness with [YHWH]. For it is written, "He catches the wise in their own craftiness"; and again, "[Yeshua] knows the thoughts of the wise, that they are futile." (1st Corinthians 3:18-20 NKJV)

But "he who glories, let him glory in [Yeshua]." For not he who commends himself is approved, but whom [Yeshua] commends. (2nd Corinthians 10:17-18 NKJV)

Nehemiah was able to avoid unnecessary hardship by relying upon Godly wisdom to rescue him from worldly ruses. If the worldly are able to confuse, then the world will be able to use. The truth is that only the broken are eligible for repairs and qualify for use by Messiah. When Yeshua created man, debilitating fear was not a part of his make-up because it is not a part of Yeshua's. Man was created in the image of Yeshua. Yeshua created the natural and all remained such until sin entered the picture. Sin was not natural, but a deviation from creation. When man fell, his nature became deviant. As a result of our sinful lineage, what was deviant eventually became the norm. However, when the sinner is saved, his deviant nature becomes outflanked by Messiah's who, while sharing man's nature while walking the earth, never allowed his behavior to deviate from his Father's. The believer, then, can lick the liar by proclaiming that what is normal in the eyes of the world is unnatural in the eyes of the Father. While on the road to Glory, the believer should aim for abnormality. In the long run, he'll be glad he did.

The wise lay up knowledge, but the mouth of a fool brings ruin near. (Proverbs 10:14 ESV)

Who is the liar? Who but he that denies that [Yeshua] is the [Messiah]? He is Anti-[Messiah], for he denies both the Father and the Son: to deny the Son is to be without the Father; to acknowledge the Son is to have the Father too. (1st John 2:22-23 NEB)

115. Seeing the Soul, Healing the Whole

First read: Psalms 19:7-14

When journeying, if you notice that many around will not look you in the eye, most likely it's because they have something to hide. If you feign comfort in concealing, you soon become resistant to revealing. All have come to accept that the eyes are the windows to their soul, and most would rather you not peek into theirs. For in peeking you will find that their soul sits in discomfort, and sits in chains. Peek long enough and you will soon hear their soul wailing for freedom. How sorrowful for those who walk with shackled souls. After a while their souls won't wail anymore, they'll just sulk.

Should any find it discomforting that the Father can see into the depths of our spirit? It's the only way he can determine the true essence of those who lay claim to his lineage. It's also how he knew to send his Son. If the Father would have made a decision based solely on what men showed outwardly, then every soul would have continued on their journey to hell without any Divine intervention. Speaking through David, the Holy Spirit made the following observation:

The fool says in his heart, "There is no God." They are corrupt, they do abominable deeds, there is none who does good. [YHWH] looks down from heaven on the children of man, to see if there are any who understand, who seek after Elohim. They have all turned aside; together they have become corrupt; there is none who does good, not even one. (Psalms 14:1-3 ESV)

How bleak. How true. The heart is as deceptive as the deeds it engenders, but how fortunate we are that the Father looked past our hearts in order to see our hurts. It is an affront to YHWH to have those in the Body of Messiah purporting to walk in freedom when so many are, in fact, sitting enslaved, as if Messiah never turned the key. It was Zechariah who made the glorious proclamation upon the birth of his son, John the Baptist:

And Zechariah his father was filled with the Holy Spirit and uttered this prophecy: "Praise to [YHWH]. For he has turned to his people, saved them and set them free, and has raised up a deliverer of victorious power from the house of his servant David. So he promised: age after age he proclaimed by the lips of his holy prophets, that he would deliver us from our enemies, out of the hands of all who hate us." (Luke 1:68-71 NEB)

Satan was the enemy and, with permission, continues to oppose every believer. And yet Messiah suffered for our sake, for the sake of our souls. There are those who are presently walking in body, but are sulking in spirit. The chains that bind are invisible to the blind, but all who are free can see. Those who can see have learned to look beyond, and are able to tell what is real. The Holy Spirit is urging all in the Body to reveal what they'd rather conceal.

Among them was a woman who had suffered from hemorrhages for twelve years; and nobody had been able to cure her. She came up from behind and touched the edge of his cloak, and at once her hemorrhage stopped. [Yeshua] said, "Who was it that touched me?" All disclaimed it, and Peter and his companions said, "Master, the crowds are hemming you in and pressing upon you." But [Yeshua] said, "Someone did touch me, for I felt that power had gone out from me." Then the woman, seeing that she was detected, came trembling and fell at his feet. Before all the people she explained why she had touched him and how she had been instantly cured. He said to her, "My daughter, your faith has cured you. Go in peace." (Luke 8:43-48 NEB)

Only those willing to put aside their foolish pride may have access to the Son. Only those who shamelessly acknowledge their need for him will ever experience genuine freedom. However, it isn't possible to face the Head without also looking at the rest of his Body.

Then turning to his disciples he began to speak: "How blest are you who are in need; the kingdom of [YHWH] is yours." (Luke 6:20 NEB)

116. Outrunning the Son

First read: Isaiah 18:4-6

It is natural for the rain to pour from the skies, and as natural for tears to pour from your eyes. Learn to reveal what you want to conceal so others will know what is there. If nothing is shown, then nothing is known; so, no one will know to repair. In refusing to reveal your brokenness, you're actually revealing just how much repairing you need. When you forget, from time to time, majestic earth will soon remind, shamelessly. Delight in the dew and don't run from the rays.

What a foolish thought, trying to outrun the sun. Can you imagine being stuck in the desert with no hint of shade in sight, and with no indication of the sun's relenting of its lingering light? So in order to find relief you "outwit" the sun by running here and there; delirious with vain conceit in attempting to dodge its rays. In the end, it's you who looks rather dim. An unpopular book among most Christian circles, the Book of Revelation, provides a not-so-chilling preview of what is to come when Messiah comes back to usher in his final judgments on the world; what the Tanakh prophets commonly referred to as the Day of the Lord. While exiled for his faith on the island of Patmos, the apostle John was shown multiple visions chronicling eschatological events. In one of the visions, a trumpet blowing messenger (the sixth) unleashes the four angels currently held bound at the great river Euphrates, along with their cavalry, to carry out one of YHWH's judgments:

> By these three plagues, that is, by the fire, the smoke, and the sulfur that came from their mouths, a third of mankind was killed. The power of the horses lay in their mouths, and in their tails also; for their tails were like snakes, with heads, and with them too they dealt injuries. The rest of mankind who survived these plagues still did not abjure the gods their hands had fashioned, nor cease their worship of devils and of idols made from gold, silver, bronze, stone, and wood, which cannot see or hear or walk. Nor did they repent of their murders, their sorcery, their fornication, or their robberies. (Revelation 9:18-21 NEB)

This isn't even a final judgment, as the seven angels with the seven bowels of plagues are to come still later. Yet, sadness should abound, not because of YHWH's just judgment, but because even after the death of a third, mankind is still obstinate in his disobedience. These are people who, saturated with pride, will try foolishly to outrun the rays of the Son, instead of succumbing to them in repentance.

When reading the prophetic books, including Revelation, believers ought not to read with horrific disbelief at the idea of a Father who judges righteously. In truth, YHWH's series of judgments speak to his patience as a parent, as each one is designed to reign in his wayward children. As in the former days of the Israelites, the Father never punishes beyond repair. Indeed, his goal is to draw attention to those areas of our life that remain lifeless and to put some strength into them. Messiah's preferred method is through the Holy Spirit:

> Nevertheless I tell you the truth: it is for your good that I am leaving you. If I do not go, your Helper will not come, whereas if I go, I will send your Helper to you. Upon arriving, the Helper will confute the world, and show where wrong and right and judgment lie. The Helper will convict them of wrong, by their refusal to believe in me: the Helper will convince them that right is on my side, by showing that I go to the Father when I pass from your sight; and the Helper will convince them of divine judgment, by showing that the Prince of this world stands condemned. (John 16:7-11 NEB)

However, when it becomes apparent that the Holy Spirit's heeding convinces little to none, then the Father has given authority to the Son to ensure that the job gets done. Once the rays of the Son embark on their rampage, it would be unwise to run and hide. Instead, those who have failed to heed his warnings should hurry to kill their pride. And yet there is still mercy even now. The sun is only beginning to rise. Better now to endure the correcting rod, when the sun is not yet overhead. For those who wait until the clock strikes twelve, will no doubt wish they were still dead.

> I call heaven and earth to witness against you today, that I have set before you life and death, blessing and curse. Therefore choose life, that you and your offspring may live, loving [YHWH] your God, obeying his voice and holding fast to him, for he is your life and length of days, that you may dwell in the land that [Yeshua] swore to your fathers, to Abraham, to Isaac, and to Jacob, to give them. (Deuteronomy 30:19-20 ESV)

> For the wound which is borne in [YHWH]'s way brings a change of heart too salutary to regret; but the hurt which is borne in the world's way brings death. (2nd Corinthians 7:10 NEB)

117. Rays of Son

First read: Isaiah 9-11

Delight in the dew, but don't drown in it. Remember that balance is the key and crying without ceasing will knock you off. No matter how hard or how long it may pour, eventually the rain does let up. And when it does, the clouds will continue shifting. No longer condensed, they now drift in divergence. Use the diverging of the clouds as a signal to pull your self together. In the same manner that crying shows, not a sign of weakness, but of strength, knowing when to stop also validates strength to grow. Nothing is as illustrative of vigor as the illuminating rays of the sun. Yes, at times its rays will be on a rampage, however, most of the time they will affectionately radiate warmth.

Making unjust laws; taking advantage of the poor, the elderly, the widow, and the orphan. These are a just a few of the behaviors commonly condemned by YHWH. Upon reading the short, though sinful, list, wisdom would dictate writing them off as conduct unbecoming of a Christian. Moreover, a glint of acuity might even compel one to believe that these actions would only occur in a nation devoid of God Almighty. Regrettably, the one hundred dollar question is not, "Does this describe a nation near you?" But rather, "In a nation such as this, what is Messiah going to do?" There is little that can be done among such deadness and so the Son must first revive. While unpopular, the history of the Israelites has shown that Yeshua's most effective tool in reviving the fool is to wound with his rod. Why must the rod induce repentance? The reality is that Messiah would rather use his light to lead. But for many, his light is only appreciated after they have first lost sight. For most it is the only means of authenticating the gravity of their blindness. Before his conversion on the road to Damascus, Saul was already walking blindly as a persecutor of the Christians. What he failed to realize was that his actions not only affected the Body, but the Head as well. Hence Messiah's question to Saul:

> While he was still on the road and nearing Damascus, suddenly a light flashed from the sky all around him. He fell to the ground and heard a voice saying, "Saul, Saul, why do you persecute me?" (Acts 9:3-4 NEB)

Readers are not given specific information regarding Saul's emotional condition following his encounter with Messiah, though we know some of his physical.

> Saul got up from the ground, but when he opened his eyes he could not see; so they led him by the hand and brought him into Damascus. He was blind for three days, and took no food or drink. (Acts 9:8-9 NEB)

One could reasonably infer that this three day period was not only one of fasting, but of seeking forgiveness from the Father. In fact, we read the instructions given to the disciple Ananias of Damascus:

> [Yeshua] said to him, "Go at once to Straight Street, to the house of Judas, and ask for a man from Tarsus named Saul. You will find him at prayer; he has had

a vision of a man named Ananias coming in and laying his hands on him to restore his sight." (Acts 9:11-12 NEB)

We know that upon the restoration of his sight, Saul spent the remainder of his years walking faithfully, (though not struggle-free), in the light of Yeshua. The contrasting personhoods of Saul the Benjaminite and Saul the Apostle reflect the contrast between one who claims heredity to the kingdom, and one who lives out his calling to the King. The Israelites enjoyed their status, but their country was plagued with sin. The Son is unequivocal in his message that his servants cannot have both. The message has not changed, though the ears of his servants have deafened. Genuine repentance seems rather unlikely without the Father's rod, which he has given to the Son. When the Son's rays are no longer on the rampage, then once again we shall find them useful as a rampart; first a pruning, and then protection for the fruitful flowers.

I cannot act by myself; I judge as I am bidden, and my sentence is just, because my aim is not my own will, but the will of him who sent me. (John 5:30 NEB)

118. Messengers of the Moment

First read: Ezekiel 1-3

After a downpour, when you have finishing soaking in silence, you will want to bask while bathing. Soaking implies passivity, and when reflecting, you really shouldn't be doing anything else. Bathing, however, requires activity. Much like any other activity, you will, of course, grow weary occasionally. Take a break and bask, but not for too long. When it seems like the rains had fallen forever, then soon you shall likely forget. In the strength of the sun for several short hours, sit around and soon you'll regret. Bask in the rays of the sun for too long and soon you will find yourself baked.

Then he said to them: "Go forth to every part of the world, and proclaim the Good News to the whole creation. Those who believe it and receive baptism will find salvation; those who do not believe will be condemned. Faith will bring it these miracles: believers will cast out devils in my name and speak in strange tongues; if they handle snakes or drink any deadly poison, they will come to no harm; and the sick on whom they lay their hands will recover." (Mark 16:15-18 NEB)

At the moment there are two messages that Messiah has for his Body. Both are words of wisdom and are full of grace. However, the first is given with a degree of frustration because he ought not to have to give it. The Word has been at the disposal of every believer for the past several centuries, and yet so few within the Body have believed. He should not have to rehash to the believers of today the same messages he gave to the churches of Ephesus, Smyrna, Pergamum, Thyatira, Sardis, Philadelphia, and Laodicea. He should not have to remind his disciples that while he is the Lamb who was slain, he is also the Lion who will slay.

But one of the elders said to me: "Do not weep; for the Lion from the tribe of Judah, the Root of David, has won the right to open the scroll and break its seven seals." (Revelation 5:5 NEB)

He ought not to have to remind us of any of his transcendent attributes; that while he is our Elder brother in whom we can confide every sorrowful situation—from the attacks of men to struggles with sin—he is also the King of kings and Lords of lords who commands faithful allegiance. Messiah does not mince words in declaring that, at present, he is displeased with the Body. Unequivocally, Messiah, whom the Father has ordained Master of his household, is declaring that now is the time for his house to get its act together, for it is in danger of being demolished.

For every house has its founder; and the founder of all is [YHWH]. Moses, then, was faithful as a servitor in [YHWH]'s whole household; his task was to bear witness to the words that [YHWH] would speak; but [Messiah] is faithful as a son, set over his household. And we are that household of his, if only we are fearless and keep our hope high. (Hebrews 3:4-6 NEB)

He ought not to have to say anything more because everything that is being said now has been said many times before. He should not have to, but he is; that's why it's grace. This is the message of the moment: That those with a message need to mature, so that out they may go unto souls uninsured. For there are multitudes on the outside and dozens within who still haven't grasped the gravity of sin.

For the Scripture says, "Whoever believes on him will not be put to shame." For there is no distinction between Jew and Greek, for the same Lord over all is rich to all who call upon him. For "Whoever calls on the name of [Yeshua] shall be saved." How then shall they call on him in whom they have not believed? And how shall they believe in him of whom they have not heard? And how shall they hear without a preacher? And how shall they preach unless they are sent? As it is written: "How beautiful are the feet of those who preach the gospel of peace, Who bring glad tidings of good things." But they have not all obeyed the gospel. For Isaiah says, "[YHWH], who has believed our report?" So then faith comes by hearing, and hearing by the word of [YHWH]. (Romans 10:11-17 ESV)

We are no better than pots of earthenware to contain this treasure, and this proves that such transcendent power does not come from us, but is [YHWH]'s alone. (2nd Corinthians 4:7 NEB)

Let all be clear, lest pride draws near. Messiah doesn't need us. God Almighty could have crafted the message for delivery in any number of ways, and at any moment he could still develop a new blue-print. Make no mistake: if ever we fail, Messiah shall still prevail. No, Messiah doesn't need us, but his desire is to use his disciples to deliver the message that only he is the deliverer from death.

So we sailed from Troas and made a straight run to Samothrace, the next day to Neapolis, and from there to Philippi, a city of the first rank in that district of Macedonia, and a Roman colony. Here we stayed for some days, and on the Sabbath day we went outside the city gate by the riverside, where we thought there would be a place of prayer, and sat down and talked to the women who had gathered there. One of them named Lydia, a dealer in purple fabric from the city of Thyatira, who was a worshipper of [YHWH], was listening, and [Yeshua] opened her heart to respond to what Paul said. She was baptized, and her household with her, and then she said to us, "If you have judged me to be a believer in [Yeshua], I beg you to come and stay in my house." And she insisted on our going. (Acts 16:11-15 NEB)

Thus to the members of the Body, the message of the moment is a reminder that we are the messengers of the moment. Messiah is still willing to extend grace to those who have gone astray so that they can aid in spreading the message of grace so desperately needed. However, to all who choose to ignore or rebuff, who hate the truth, but love the fluff; who never can seem to get enough of feasting on the lies. To them there soon shall come a day, while all is calm and all at play, while all are drunk as Satan's prey; you'll hear nothing less than cries.

Alas for you who laugh now; you shall mourn and weep. (Luke 6:25b NEB)

Accepting and proclaiming the messages of liability and redemption are just as relevant to the Church today as it was for Israel yesterday. Just as Messiah strengthened Ezekiel, so to will he empower all who are willing to obey. For all who are redeemed will be held liable if they fail to show others the way.

We must be regarded as [Messiah's] subordinates and as stewards of the secrets of [YHWH]. Well then, stewards are expected to show themselves trustworthy. (1st Corinthians 4:1-2 NEB)

119. A Reflective Moment

Fact or Fiction

First read: 2nd Peter 3:3-13

... knowing this first of all, that scoffers will come in the last days with scoffing, following their own sinful desires. They will say, "Where is the promise of his coming? For ever since the fathers fell asleep, all things are continuing as they were from the beginning of creation." For they deliberately overlook this fact, that the heavens existed long ago, and the earth was formed out of water and through water by the Word of [YHWH], and that by means of these the world that then existed was deluged with water and perished. But by the same Word the heavens and earth that now exist are stored up for fire, being kept until the day of judgment and destruction of the ungodly. (2nd Peter 3:3-7 NEB)

How many of you really believe that the Church is in its final stage before the return of Messiah? Or, are you one of those skeptics who claim that every generation believed that they were the ones who were going to see the return of Messiah. And that because they were obviously wrong—here we still sit—then, of course, all those who are currently on the street corners proclaiming "Get ready" are over-emotional Pentecostal zealots? The thing about personal beliefs is that we like to guise them in truth. Once this has occurred then it is easy for us to say that those who do not accept our truth, or those who are teaching anything contrary to what we claim is true, are, in fact, spreading lies. This is problematic.

Again the Word of [YHWH] came to me, saying, "Son of man, speak to the children of your people, and say to them: 'When I bring the sword upon a land, and the people of the land take a man from their territory and make him their watchman, when he sees the sword coming upon the land, if he blows the trumpet and warns the people, then whoever hears the sound of the trumpet and does not take warning, if the sword comes and takes him away, his blood shall be on his own head. He heard the sound of the trumpet, but did not take warning; his blood shall be upon himself. But he who takes warning will save his life. But if the watchman sees the sword coming and does not blow the trumpet, and the people are not warned, and the sword comes and takes any person from among them, he is taken away in his iniquity; but his blood I will require at the watchman's hand.'" (Ezekiel 33:1-6 ESV)

He also said to the people, "When you see clouds banking up in the west, you say at once, 'It is going to rain.' and rain it does. And when the wind is from the south, you say, 'There will be a heat-wave.' and there is. What hypocrites you are. You know how to interpret the appearance of earth and sky; how is it you cannot interpret this fateful hour?" (Luke 12:54-56 NEB)

Messiah is only an enemy to those who reject his intimacy. First, let me remind all that, in fact, no man, angel, or even the Son himself knows the hour of his return.

However, the Father knows and the date has already been set. It is also true that all attempts, past and present, to pin point an exact date of his return has been met with deserved ridicule. Nonetheless, a series of erroneous predictions in no way implies that Messiah's return must therefore lie in the far distant future. Sadly though, in response to the faulty hype, many in the Church have migrated "safely" toward the other end of the pendulum. The Holy Spirit is urging members of the Body to get their act together. Remember the parable of the bridesmaids, in which only half of them wisely prepared for their meeting with the bridegroom?

While they were away the bridegroom arrived; those who were ready went in with him to the wedding; and the door was shut. And then the other five came back. "Sir, sir," they cried, "open the door for us." But he answered, "I declare, I do not know you." Keep awake then; for you never know the day or the hour. (Matthew 25:10-13 NEB)

Assuredly, Messiah's return is very imminent. The Gospel of Matthew is clear in stating that the return of Messiah will be, for most, an unwelcomed surprise. Rather than wise preparation, many members of the Body are, at present, taking a sabbatical—enjoying an ill-deserved siesta. "As things were in Noah's days, so will they mirror when the Son of Man comes." Here is a snap shot at what was going on then:

Then [Yeshua] saw that the wickedness of man was great in the earth, and that every intent of the thoughts of his heart was only evil continually. And [Yeshua] was sorry that he had made man on the earth, and he was grieved in his heart. So [Yeshua] said, "I will destroy man whom I have created from the earth, both man and beast, creeping thing and birds of the air, for I am sorry that I have made them." But Noah found grace in the eyes of [YHWH]. This is the genealogy of Noah. Noah was a just man, righteous in his generations. Noah walked with [YHWH]. And Noah begot three sons: Japheth, Ham, and Shem. The earth also was corrupt before [YHWH], and the earth was filled with violence. So [YHWH] looked upon the earth, and indeed it was corrupt; for all flesh had corrupted their way on the earth. And [YHWH] said to Noah, "The end of all creation has come before Me, for the earth is filled with violence through them; and behold, I will destroy them with the earth." (Genesis 6:5-13 NKJV)

What's interesting is that nowhere in the account does it mention that anyone besides Noah was preparing for the flood. YHWH had already made his decision to save Noah and his family while destroying the rest of the earth, prior to delivering his instructions:

By faith Noah, being warned by [YHWH] concerning events as yet unseen, in reverent fear constructed an ark for the saving of his household. By this he condemned the world and became an heir of the righteousness that comes by faith. (Hebrews 11:7 NKJV)

It's now 2014 and the Father has made his plan known to the entire universe; there is no secret. If only members of the Body would arise from their slumber and ask the Father to remove the scales from their eyes and the plugs from their ears, all might see and hear. Messiah is on his way back and those on the street corners aren't crazy, they're concerned—as should be every member of the Body.

Likewise as it was also in the days of Lot—They ate, they drank, they bought, they sold, they planted, they built; but on the day that Lot went out of Sodom it rained fire and brimstone from heaven and destroyed them all—so will it be in the day when the Son of Man is revealed. (Luke 17:28-30 NKJV)

In very truth I tell you, he who receives any messenger of mine receives me; receiving me, he receives the One who sent me. (John 13:20 NEB)

Some days later Felix came with his wife Drusilla, who was a Jewess, and sending for Paul he let him talk to him about faith in [Yeshua]. But when the discourse turned to questions of morals, self-control, and the coming judgment, Felix became alarmed and exclaimed, "That will do for the present; when I find it convenient I will send for you again." At the same time he had hopes of a bribe from Paul; and for this reason he sent for him very often and talked with him. (Acts 24:24-26 NEB)

If proof is what you seek, then all you have to do is look. The problem is that most don't really want proof, they want permission. Permission to carry on as usual; believing that the return of Messiah is going to put a dent in their earthly plans. For those persons, here is proof—proof that the world is of greater interest to them than the Kingdom of Heaven. Careful, your thoughts of temporal finitude, if left unchecked, will lead to your spiritual solitude—eternally. It is time for all members to start asking the question: "Do I want to be left behind suffering from the severity of the Anti-Messiah, or would I rather join my family in Heaven while enjoying the security of Messiah?" Finally, what is everybody doing to ensure that nobody is left?

My brothers, if one of your number should stray from the truth and another succeed in bringing him back, be sure of this: any man who brings a sinner back from his crooked ways will be rescuing his soul from death and cancelling innumerable sins. (James 5:19-20 NEB)

120. Born to Bathe

First read: 2nd Kings 5:1-14

Nothing is as revealing as bathing in the nude. Be prepared to sunbathe. This is the time to look at your self and surrender yourself with everyone else. In nakedness you are natural and noticeable, having nothing to conceal. While sun bathing you are exposing yourself; leaving you in great discomfort. After being drenched in rain for a while, the warmth of the rays all over you is comforting. It is the vulnerability that comes with your public display that you find to be distressing. Ironically, the others bathing are either too busy ruminating over their own maladies to notice yours, or vice versa. Reflect, but don't ruminate. Notice your nakedness and theirs and then begin bathing. Ruminate for too long and your "note" shall shift to your stare. Ruminate for too long and you'll forget that you need to repair.

Why is it that the simplest commandments given to us by Messiah are often the most difficult to follow? Messiah summed up all of the Hebraic laws delivered by Moses in just two, and yet the pains still endured by earth stem from her human inhabitants' constant failure to abide. Messiah tells us to pick up our mat from which we laid limp and to carry it home. Yet, many within the Body are content walking while masking their mats, as if they were never lame. In the Gospel of John we read of Yeshua healing a man who had been blind from birth. Does anyone count it as strange or unfair that Messiah would have the blind man wash before he received sight? Is there a suggestion that Messiah's gift of freedom isn't so free after all? That somehow the lost must earn Yeshua's favor? Of course not. The Son died so that all might have the ability to walk in freedom through access to the Father and the Holy Spirit. Making freedom accessible was the role of Messiah. Seizing the opportunity is the responsibility of the convict and then the convert. Messiah's commandment to wash, though he has touched, is an indication that the believer's responsibility to repair doesn't end at the point of justification. Justification is a symbol that the clay is now salvageable. And while ready to return to the Potter upon receiving the gift, further washing is still in order.

Wash me thoroughly from my iniquity, and cleanse me from my sin. For I know my transgressions, and my sin is ever before me. Against you, you only, have I sinned and done what is evil in your sight, so that you may be justified in your words and blameless in your judgment. (Psalms 51:2-4 ESV)

Messiah commands us to bathe, but most members won't. Why? Because bathing first requires removing all that which conceals the Body. Some members struggle with rarely, if ever, feeling the rays of the sun, because while journeying they have bought into the latest fashion of layering. In refusing to share, we'll never be bare. It's difficult to bathe the Body when so many of her members are resistant to the nude.

And here is another parable that he told. It was aimed at those who were sure of their own goodness and looked down on everyone else. "Two men went up to the temple to pray, one a Pharisee and the other a tax-gatherer. The Pharisee stood up and prayed thus: 'I thank thee, O [YHWH], that I am not like the rest of men, greedy, dishonest, adulterous; or, for that matter, like this tax-gatherer. I fast twice a week; I pay tithes on all that I get.' But the other kept his distance and would not even raise his eyes to heaven, but beat upon his breast, saying, 'O [YHWH], have mercy on me, sinner that I am.' It was this man, I tell you, and not the other, who went home acquitted of his sins. For everyone who exalts himself will be humbled; and whoever humbles himself will be exalted." (Luke 18:9-14 NEB)

Unlike the unbeliever who mistakenly believes that his works will earn him favor with the Father, the sinner who has been saved still has work left undone. Truthfully, then, there are members in the Body who, while having been touched, still cannot see clearly. How sad. The Father has adopted children who won't wash. The sinner who has been saved, but still will not bathe doesn't realize that their seasoned sweat doesn't smell very sweet to YHWH. Even the most loving parent can only withstand so much stench.

121. A Reflective Moment

Living Out Loud: The Spirit Filled Church – II

First read: Acts 4:31

And when Elizabeth heard Mary's greeting, the baby stirred in her womb. Then Elizabeth was filled with the Holy Spirit and cried aloud, "[YHWH]'s blessing is on you above all women, and his blessing is on the fruit of your womb." (Luke 1:41-42 NEB)

It is no coincidence that the book of Acts speaks of the Holy Spirit more times than any other book in the B'rit Khadasha—including Revelation. Forty-five times, to be precise. The book of Acts tells the story of how the Christian Church was founded; when its members first discovered the art of breathing—of living. Because a significant number of bodies have yet to discover this art, and therefore are still walking in their wake, it is vital that believers spend time exploring how the early Church benefited from this gift.

It is my prayer that readers will prayerfully seek guidance from God Almighty in kindling, or re-kindling the flame in their own bodies. Still others should inquire as to how their fires can be made to burn even brighter. When a body of believers has received the Father's gift of the Holy Spirit's baptism—when the members who're already sealed, have now been filled—where is the evidence? While it is dangerous to associate the filling with the experience itself, this should not undermine the joy and other emotions that do accompany the baptism. In the same way, YHWH revealed himself in various forms to the Israelites upon their exodus from Egypt and while in the wilderness.

Throughout all their journeys, whenever the cloud was taken up from over the tabernacle, the people of Israel would set out. But if the cloud was not taken up, then they did not set out till the day that it was taken up. For the cloud of [YHWH] was on the tabernacle by day, and fire was in it by night, in the sight of all the house of Israel throughout all their journeys. (Exodus 40:36-38 ESV)

And the Son after his resurrection:

When he had risen from the dead early on Sunday morning he appeared first to Mary of Magdala, from whom he had formerly cast out seven demons. She went and carried the news to his mourning and sorrowful followers, but when they were told that he was alive and that she had seen him they did not believe it. Later he appeared in a different guise to two of them as they were walking, on their way into the country. These also went and took the news to the others, but again no one believed them. (Mark 16:9-13 NEB)

It is the prerogative of the Holy Spirit to become revealed through either a private or corporate encounter. Private repentance can result in a private experience, as it did with Saul.

So Ananias went. He entered the house, laid his hands on him and said, "Saul, my brother, [Yeshua], who appeared to you on your way here, has sent me to you so that you may recover your sight, and be filled with the Holy Spirit." And immediately it seemed that scales fell from his eyes, and he regained his sight. Thereupon he was baptized, and afterwards he took food and his strength returned. (Acts 9:26-28 NEB)

While collective repentance might yield a collective encounter:

Peter was still speaking when the Holy Spirit came upon all who were listening to the message. The believers who had come with Peter, men of Jewish birth, were astonished that the gift of the Holy Spirit should have been poured out even on Gentiles. For they could hear them speaking in tongues of ecstasy and acclaiming the greatness of God Almighty. Then Peter spoke: "Is anyone prepared to withhold the water for baptism from these persons, who have received the Holy Spirit just as we did ourselves?" Then he ordered them to be baptized in the name of [Yeshua]. After that they asked him to stay on with them for a time. (Acts 10:44-48 NEB)

But, whether public or private, the experience is always personal.

122. Living Out Loud: The Spirit Filled Church Part III

First read: Acts 4:31

This game of exhibition is not without heckling spectators from the sidelines. Tune out the cacophony and continue to strike your chords of contentment. The hecklers have chosen to remain veiled for the time being, sitting comfortably in the shade. Ignore them, for their shade is fading even as you walk. In the event that any of them come off the sidelines to interfere, don't allow them to convince you to join the crowd. There are more of them than there are you. They are in the majority and you in the minority. So? Keep bathing. Invite them to join you while informing everyone that there is enough sun to go around. Some will—most won't. By habit, most will prefer to heckle and criticize. While in the nude nothing is covered, all is laid bare. Easy to show and easy to tell all that needs repaired.

But Scripture says, "I believed, and therefore I spoke out." and we too, in the same spirit of faith, believe and therefore speak out; for we know that he who raised [Yeshua] to life will with [Yeshua] raise us too, and bring us to his presence, and you with us. (2nd Corinthians 4:13-14 NEB)

There is something to be said about the experience of being filled with the Holy Spirit, but then words should continue long after. Remember that emotions are only a partial piece of what the Father has given us in living out our faith. All must exercise caution, lest an overemphasis on emotional experience leaves one fluttering in a wind designed to blow them off course. What then is another characteristic of a Spirit-filled body? Boldness.

On the day I called, you answered me; my strength of soul you increased. All the kings of the earth shall give you thanks, O [YHWH], for they have heard the words of your mouth, and they shall sing of the ways of the [Yeshua], for great is the glory of the [YHWH]. (Psalms 138:3-5 ESV)

Because a Spirit-filled body has the Word of YHWH forever burning in their hearts, their entire being radiates with such a fire that the Gospel within is seen and heard from a million miles away. The Spirit-filled church, also yielding to the Spirit, dies daily to self and so cares little about how the world around them perceives their outspoken condemnation of unholy living. However, the Spirit-filled body doesn't merely ignore. Because a body without the Spirit's filling is lifeless and limp, they are inclined to turn a deaf ear, and most do. It takes a Spirit-filled body to condemn the behavior, while inviting the lost to become a believer.

Herod and Pontius Pilate conspired with the Gentiles and peoples of Israel to do all the things which, under thy hand and by thy decree, were foreordained. And now, [YHWH], mark their threats, and enable thy servants to speak thy word with all boldness. Stretch out thy hand to heal and cause signs and wonders to be done through the name of thy holy servant [Yeshua]. (Acts 4:27-30 NEB)

The jailer woke up to see the prison doors wide open, and assuming that the prisoners had escaped, drew his sword intending to kill himself. But Paul shouted, "Do yourself no harm; we are all here." The jailer called for lights, rushed in and threw himself down before Paul and Silas, trembling with fear. He then escorted them out and said, "Masters, what must I do to be saved?" They said, "Put your trust in [Yeshua], and you will be saved, you and your household." Then they spoke the word of [Yeshua] to him and to everyone in his house. At that late hour of the night he took them and washed their wounds; and immediately afterwards he and his whole family were baptized. He brought them into his house, set out a meal, and rejoiced with his whole household in his new-found faith in [YHWH]. (Acts 16:27-34 NEB)

Members of an emboldened body don't search for the path of least resistance. Rather, even while recognizing winning lost souls will indeed be an uphill battle, they stay the course and walk the distance. And with each step, members are calling out to those on the side of the road, inviting them to partake in their journey.

Whoever listens to you listens to me; whoever rejects you rejects me. And whoever rejects me rejects the One who sent me. (Luke 10:16 NEB)

What's more is that the emboldened body doesn't wait for situations but instead are constantly looking for opportunities that call for them to visit the side of the road when a simple invitation won't sway. With boldness the Spirit-filled believer will proclaim the truth about what lies in store for them at the end of their journey for those whom agree to join. With that same Spirit the believer doesn't shy away from sharing what awaits them, should they insist on lounging in the shade. So let all who are bold speak too with Wisdom:

Hear, for I will speak noble things, and from my lips will come what is right, for my mouth will utter truth; wickedness is an abomination to my lips. (Proverbs 8:6-7 ESV)

Prior to the baptism of the Holy Spirit, most bodies are marked by having a spirit of timidity. It is this timidity that has allowed many churches to fall into the trap of keeping to themselves. In doing so, not only has there been a failure by many to carry out the Great Commission, there has equally been a failure to carry out the second part of the greatest commandment. Many are finding it difficult to love their neighbor as themselves because many are too afraid to find out who their neighbors are. How can you love whom you don't even know?

When they had ended their prayer, the building where they were assembled rocked, and all were filled with the Holy Spirit and spoke the word of [YHWH] with boldness. (Acts 4:31 NEB)

123. Walking In Wisdom II

First read: 1st Kings 3:4-15

As you are bathing in the sun, a fool from the sidelines walks around address-ing the perversion in exposing to everyone; eventually it is your turn. During a diatribe the fool will demand that, in the name of decency, you cover up. The fool is trying to shame you and everyone else for bathing. In pointing to everyone else on the sidelines, the fool tries to make you look foolish in saying that exposing yourself is unnatural and abnormal. Unless your head is saturated with Wisdom from soaking in silence, you will quickly clothe with everyone else, and head to the sidelines. It won't be long before you grow comfortable in your new habitat and soon you too will heckle in the shade.

That course was urged only as a concession to certain sham-Christians, inter-lopers who had stolen in to spy upon the liberty we enjoy in the fellowship of [Yeshua]. These men wanted to bring us into bondage, but not for one mo-ment did I yield to their dictation; I was determined that the full truth of the Gospel should be maintained for you. (Galatians 2:4-5 NEB)

Exposing yourself? To be sure, it's not an activity on the top of anyone's agenda. Understandably so. Christians live in a society that encourages secrecy, indepen-dence, and individuality. That is unless you turn on the television and catch the lat-est craze of filming—so called "reality t.v." Here, it appears that everyone is seeking attention, and so they want cameras displaying their views. Everyone looks, talks, and acts the same, while playing the same game. Soon the viewer will understand that nothing or no one on the screen is real after all. Nevertheless, what the media has been able to capture is a truth worth considering. Despite the attempts of soci-ety and the god of this world to convince members to hide their hearts and to shield their souls—not to arm, but to keep everyone at arm's length—there's a natural inclination toward laying bare; people do want to share. What then is the battle?

Does not wisdom call? Does not understanding raise her voice? On the heights beside the way, at the crossroads she takes her stand; beside the gates in front of the town, at the entrance of the portals she cries aloud: "To you, O men, I call, and my cry is to the children of man. O simple ones, learn prudence; O fools, learn sense." (Proverbs 8:1-5 ESV)

The battle is between the wisdom of the world and the wisdom of the Word; and deciding, as Christians, which wisdom you are willing to walk with. For King Solomon it was a question worth considering. He understood the magnitude of God Almighty's calling on his life and wanted to ensure that every decision made was one pleasing to him. As members of the Body, we ought to consider that Mes-siah is concerned with repairing the broken. While it is folly to the world, Messiah's wisdom dictates that believers share their brokenness with others, so that in sharing, members are repairing. Does it take the broken to break the news to others that what the world teaches is nonsense? The Apostle Paul thought so.

Divine folly is wiser than the wisdom of man, and divine weakness stronger than man's strength. My brothers, think what sort of people you are, whom [YHWH] has called a few. Few of you are men of wisdom, by any human standard; few are powerful or highly born. Yet, to shame the wise, [YHWH] has chosen what the world counts folly, and to shame what is strong, [YHWH] has chosen what the world counts weakness. He has chosen things low and contemptible, mere nothings, to overthrow the existing order. And so there is no place for human pride in the presence of [YHWH]. You are in [Yeshua] by [YHWH]'s act, for [YHWH] has made him our wisdom; he is our righteousness; in him we are consecrated and set free. (1st Corinthians 1:25-30 NEB)

Presently, there are millions of broken spirits who, while desiring to share, don't dare. They have been instructed in and have mastered the art of deception. The Holy Spirit is calling for members to first seek inwardly and then to speak out. Divorce yourself from the wisdom of this world and invite the Holy Spirit in for a time of intimacy, where you can begin gleaning precious pearls. After soaking and saturating your head with wisdom, it is time for the Holy Spirit to lead you to that person, in that place, who needs to see your face. Never fear the reaction of those who will heckle; for those who heckle and jeer do so out of fear. Their end is near.

The teaching of the wise is a fountain of life, that one may turn away from the snares of death. (Proverbs 13:14 ESV)

How blest you are when men hate you, when they outlaw you and insult you, and ban your very name as infamous, because of the Son of Man. On that day be glad and dance for joy; for assuredly you have a rich reward in heaven; in just the same way did their fathers treat the prophets. (Luke 6:22-23 NEB)

124. A Woman of Worth: Esther

First read: Esther 4:1-16

It is not natural to keep yourself covered in the light, while exposing yourself in the dark. It is comfortable to keep covered in the light and so it becomes habitual. Remember that just because it's habitual, it doesn't mean it's natural. And yes, once again the fool is truthful in telling you that exposing yourself is abnormal, because no one on the sidelines—the norm—is doing it. Rather than entertaining foolish notions, embrace the rays and look to the sun for strength; strength to invite, then strength to resist; and when all else fails, the strength to insist.

Is there anyone struggling to reveal what for so long has been concealed? If so, then join the ranks of the many who have traveled before you and have somehow managed to reach their destination, free from the weightiness of guilty garments. Actually, there is only one way they have managed to reach their destination and that was through cloaking themselves in the righteousness and confidence of Messiah Yeshua. However, never forget that the cloak of righteousness, like the helmet of salvation, does not fit snuggly on the body of the believer who insists on layering. Bare exposure to the Son is a must before his clothing can be worn and a work can be done. Hear then the words of a sincere Shepherd:

Man, say to the Israelites, "You complain, 'We are burdened by our sins and offences; we are pining away because of them; we despair of life.' So tell them: 'As I live,' says [Yeshua], 'I have no desire for the death of the wicked. I would rather that a wicked man should mend his ways and live. Give up your evil ways, give them up; O Israelites, why should you die?'" (Ezekiel 33:10-11 ESV)

Is the problem in the Church that so few of its members are willing to boldly state how weary they are from wearing heavy clothing, or are there none articulating their burdens because so little are actually burdened? Must YHWH add to the burden of his children before they decide to cry out? The rod of correction isn't ideal, but it is real and helpful in inducing the Body to reveal all of its many fractures. Sparing the rod is still only an option for those members whose hearts are becoming fleshly and so can be persuaded to bathe with just a little more tugging. For the rest, the Son will do what's in the best interest of his flock.

Folly is bound up in the heart of a child, but the rod of discipline drives it far from him. (Proverbs 22:15 ESV)

Many theologians have questioned the legitimacy of the Book of Esther, while others have questioned its relevance. These scholars point out that the name "YHWH" is nowhere found in the Book. Therefore, most shepherds dismiss its contents as peripheral at best and with skepticism at worst. Besides, the book is about a woman who, because of her valor (and God Almighty's providence), was able to save an entire people from the clutches of death. It would behoove many in the Body to recognize their sexist sentiments as sinful and leave them at the foot of the cross. Esther contains some powerful truths that the entire Body would benefit from acknowledging. Most notably, that it is the Father's preference, for the time being, to work behind the scenes, though he is still at work nonetheless. Moreover, it is not YHWH's desire that his people live in fear of revealing whom they really are. Concealing for comfort? An indication of just how unsettled the soul really is. Mordecai reminded Esther of her responsibility, and it is the same one that Messiah has placed upon his disciples: to walk with a spirit of humility, yes, but also with confidence in understanding their royal role. Each has been placed intentionally for such a time as this. The time to unveil is now.

If anyone is ashamed of me and mine in this wicked and godless age, the Son of Man will be ashamed of him, when he comes in the glory of his Father and of the holy angels. (Mark 8:38 NEB)

125. Justified By Yeshua

First read: 2nd Samuel 11:1-12:14

Most normal habits are bad habits. While on your journey, you need to learn to discern and learn to deviate from the norm. Moreover, remember that just because it's normal, it doesn't mean it's natural. It is natural for the sun to light what dimness tries to hide; to expose the dirt that earth veils in the dark. Soon luminously shining down, all doubt is set aside; shortly, all of earth is stripped and left in stark—including those on the sidelines.

But we know that no man is ever justified by doing what the law demands, but only through faith in [Yeshua]; so we too have put our faith in [Yeshua], in order that we might be justified through this faith, and not through deeds dictated by law; for by such deeds, Scripture says, no mortal man shall be justified. (Galatians 2:16 NEB)

While relying upon the grace of Messiah, daily does every single member of the Body have to consciously make the decision not to engage in sin. In the process of restoring, all will wrestle while on the road to Glory. Sanctification will be a grueling experience at times (what Scripture refers to as, "working out your salvation"), but eventually those committed will learn the art of alleviation. Truthfully, members should take a holistic approach so that the whole Body benefits. However, at present there is an even thornier issue at hand which threatens to separate from YHWH, those whom Messiah has separated from the world. The issue is justification. The problem is that there are those among the Body who, while having already been justified, are still trying to justify their sinful behavior.

I have been crucified with [Messiah]: the life I now live is not my life, but the life which [Messiah] lives in me; and my present bodily life is lived by faith in the Son of [YHWH], who loved me and sacrificed himself for me. (Galatians 2:20 NEB)

Do not then throw away your confidence, for it carries a great reward. You need endurance, if you are to do [YHWH]'s will and win what he has promised. For "soon, very soon (in the words of Scripture), he who is to come will come; he will not delay; and by faith my righteous servant shall find life; but if he shrinks back, I take no pleasure in him." (Hebrews 10:35-38 NEB)

"No one is perfect," says the keen observer.

"True," replies the Holy Spirit.

"Everyone makes mistakes," adds the astute onlooker.

"Another truth," replies the Holy Spirit.

"Look around and you'll see just how much sin is in the world and in the Church," chimes the perceptive spectator.

"Still true," sighs the Holy Spirit.

"So, then," says the believer, "YHWH can't possibly expect anyone living on this earth to live a life free of sin; clearly it's impossible."

"No," replies the Holy Spirit, "that's a lie."

It is because of the justification through Messiah that members indeed have the opportunity to leave sin behind, and the penalty that comes with it. No one serving Messiah ever has any business engaging in behavior that allows them to blend in. Each should consistently ask themselves: "As a disciple of Messiah, am I being distinctive, or am I acting deceptive?" Make no mistake, what may pass in the Body now will not get past the Head soon; when the books are opened and all that has been concealed is finally revealed.

We know that the man we once were has been crucified with [Messiah], for the destruction of the sinful self, so that we may no longer be slaves of sin, since a dead man is no longer answerable for his sin. But if we thus died with [Messiah], we believe that we shall also come to life with him. We know that [Messiah], once raised from the dead, is never to die again: he is no longer under the dominion of death. For in dying as he died, he died to sin, once for all, and in living as he lives, he lives to [YHWH]. In the same way you must regard yourselves as dead to sin and alive to [YHWH], in union with [Yeshua]. (Romans 6:6-11 NEB)

Then he will do justice upon those who refuse to acknowledge [YHWH] and upon those who will not obey the gospel of [Yeshua]. They will suffer the punishment of eternal ruin, cut off from the presence of [Yeshua] and the splendor of his might, when on that great Day he comes to be glorified among his own and adored among all believers; for you did indeed believe the testimony we brought you. (2nd Thessalonians 1:8-10 NEB)

It is a dangerous phenomenon, what the Church is experiencing. A slew of believers regularly grieving God Almighty by dismissing his grace as gratuitous and the Spirit's sanctifying power as nonsense; they'd rather navigate to the norm and take others along with them. Once Messiah has saved and the Holy Spirit begins convicting, sin should begin to feel less and less natural. Soon, what once was natural should now seem strange. Eventually, the believer should find himself estranged from sinful living, as the new nature takes hold and they're changed from within.

The goal then, for members, is to divorce themselves from the norm, not in body, but in behavior. Daily must those in the norm see the distinctive nature of the Christian disciple, so that in watching they might one day gain sight. David, in all of is strength, was enervated by a common virus of his day and one that continues to plague both men and women still—lust. In his rapturous state, David failed to remember the Father's call to holiness; he would soon receive a painful reminder. That the world habitually feeds her lustful cravings, grants YHWH's children no permission to follow in step. He sent a cure for his children. In one Word: Messiah. Who, in dying, extended the gift to all. Perhaps those who accepted got more than expected, because Messiah has conditions with his cure.

I am the real Vine, and my Father is the gardener. Every barren branch of mine he cuts away; and every fruiting branch he cleans, to make it more fruitful still. You have already been cleansed by the word that I spoke to you. Dwell in me, as I in you. No branch can bear fruit by itself, but only if it remains united with the vine; no more can you bear fruit, unless you remain united with me. (John 15:1-4 NEB)

We have already been cleansed by the blood of Messiah. Hence, there is no sense in trying to justify today what had already been justified by Yeshua nearly 2,000 years ago. Instead, members should focus on their fruit. For there will exist no justification for those whose branches remain barren when the Vine returns. When Messiah comes to claim, will you still be the same?

126. Wealthy With Wisdom V

First read: Proverbs 13:5-6

While walking, if those on the sidelines won't stop heckling it could eventual-ly weigh you down. Insist that they leave immediately before you're lying on the ground—on the sidelines. Unfortunately, some around you will cave into canker and delusions, believing that they are disturbing those around them by insisting too forcibly. They also believe that by insisting, they are discouraging any other sideliners who may one day want to join in the wash. If you ever find yourself straying to the sidelines, you should stop immediately, look to the sun, and ask yourself why. Why would you rather lie? Do you think you're too young—is that why? Is that why you would rather lie? Mighty sun, forever young, in heralding the birth of a new day—each day—blazes in brilliance over such foolish think-ing.

And mark this: I am sending upon you my Father's promised gift; so stay here in this city until you are armed with the power from above. (Luke 24:49 NEB)

Salvation is no small matter. Neither is sanctification. Messiah's death on the cross did not come cheaply; neither did the Holy Spirit or the building of the Church. If all believers understood the value of these gifts then perhaps all would do better in guarding against encroachment. In both the spiritual and physical realms, there exists an army fighting against Yeshua and his disciples. Not only must Christians learn how to effectively battle in spiritual warfare, they too must defend themselves against its physical manifestations. Simply put, Messiah has empowered his disciples to deal with any who would attempt to dissuade them from staying on the road to Glory. Not only must members of the Body firmly guard themselves against the atheist and the agnostic, so too must they exercise discernment and wisdom when faced with self-proclaimed believers who are actually walking on a different path, though it bear semblances of the truth.

Weak men we may be, but it is not as such that we fight our battles. The weapons we wield are not merely human, but divinely potent to demolish strongholds; we demolish sophistries and all that rears its proud head against the knowledge of [YHWH]; we compel every human thought to surrender in obedience to Christ; and we are prepared to punish all rebellion when once you have put yourselves in our hands. (2nd Corinthians 10:3-6 NEB)

But you, my friends, must never tire of doing right. If anyone disobeys our instructions given by letter, mark him well, and have no dealings with him until he is ashamed of himself. I do not mean treat him as an enemy, but give him friendly advice, as one of the family. (2nd Thessalonians 3:13-14 NEB)

The young must remain leery and not allow worldly wisdom to lead them astray. There are many who say to them that only the weak-minded adhere to a faith that teaches one truth. The young must respond by acknowledging that their faith is rooted in weakness, but grounded in strength. The young Cretan pastor Titus was given some valuable advice by the Apostle Paul on dealing with these matters.

There are all too many, especially among Jewish converts, who are out of control; they talk wildly and lead men's minds astray. Such men must be curbed, because they are ruining whole families by teaching things they should not, and all for sordid gain. (Titus 1:10-11 NEB)

It is folly for any to believe that the young are ill-equipped by design to fend off a fool. It is treacherous for any shepherd to teach such foolishness. It is because of their design that Satan is after their mind; knowing that their vigor and vitality can infringe on his reality. Rather than enervating this generation by inducing their ignorance through ignoring or indifference, the Church must proactively empower by teaching and reinforcing how Messiah has equipped through the Holy Spirit.

Let no one slight you because you are young, but make yourself an example to believers in speech and behavior, in love, fidelity, and purity. (1st Timothy 4:12 NEB)

For the grace of [YHWH] that brings salvation has appeared to all men, teaching us that, denying ungodliness and worldly lusts, we should live soberly, righteously, and godly in the present age, looking for the blessed hope and glorious appearing of [Yeshua], who gave himself for us, that he might redeem us from every lawless deed and purify for himself his own special people, zealous for good works. Speak these things, exhort, and rebuke with all authority. Let no one despise you. (Titus 2:11-15 NEB)

All Christians everywhere, in remembering what Messiah did on Calvary, must guard against cowardly conceding when accused of baseless conceit. Messiah does not command his disciples to have a defeatist disposition; neither does he condone. For integrity's sake it is the duty of every disciple to defend the faith (though with dignity), and to demonstrate their knowledge of the truth, the whole truth, and nothing but the truth—so help us YAH.

127. Woman of Worth: Deborah

First read: Judges 5:1-11

Still others don't believe they have enough strength to stand and insist. If they believe such lies for too long they soon shall find themselves lying. They are mistaken, and in believing, are not very useful to those still on the road. Rather than insist, they would rather lie. If ever you find yourself straying to the sidelines, you should stop immediately, look to the sun, and ask yourself, why? Why would you rather lie? Do you think it will make you look less feminine—is that why? Is that why you would rather lie? Mighty sun, nurturing and sustaining all that is living through the warmth of its rays, blazes in brilliance over such foolish thinking.

And yet, in [Messiah's] fellowship woman is as essential to man as man to woman. If woman was made out of man, it is through woman that man now comes to be; and [YHWH] is the source of all. (1st Corinthians 11:11-12 NEB)

Othniel, Ehud, Shamgar, Deborah, Gideon, Abimelech, Tola…wait—Deborah? A woman? Yes, YHWH does use women. Women, of course, are a vital part of the Son's creation. Despite the modern advances of science, women are still needed in carrying out the reproductive process. Moreover, man can't accurately reflect what God Almighty's intentions were for marriage without the help of the other sex. Sadly, however, we still live in a society where the roles of women are continuously marginalized. While reproducing, parenting, and lending husbands a helping hand are far from insignificant functions, women have been made to feel as if these duties are the sole reasons for their existence.

Next day we left and came to Caesarea. We went to the home of Philip the evangelist, who was one of the seven, and stayed with him. He had four unmarried daughters who possessed the gift of prophecy. (Acts 21:8-9 NEB)

In the last several decades the Church has experienced the secularized reaction of the browbeaten woman. The Biblical woman has been waning for some time now, no thanks to the contributions of the waxing unbiblical man. History has never been shy of reminding all that a radical reaction always has, as its place of origin, a radical repression.

Husbands, love your wives, just as [Messiah] also loved the church and gave himself for her, that he might sanctify and cleanse her with the washing of water by the word, that he might present her to himself a glorious church, not having spot or wrinkle or any such thing, but that she should be holy and without blemish. So husbands ought to love their own wives as their own bodies; he who loves his wife loves himself. (Ephesians 5:25-28 NKJV)

The machismo woman of the new millennium would feel less inclined to compromise her role given by YHWH if the rest of the Church would begin to legitimize. However, this is impossible to do without both sexes agreeing to return to Scripture in seeing how the Father has truthfully related to women. It is becoming apparent that in today's Body, women are struggling to understand their femininity in the same way that men struggle to understand their masculinity. In adopting the wisdom of the world, both have substituted their spiritual identity for a secular one. When the wisdom of the world begins to infiltrate the ranks of God Almighty's army, the enemy simultaneously strengthens his stronghold. The results? Rejection leading to defection.

A golden ring in the nostrils of a sow, (is like) a woman fair and fool. (A gold ring in the nostrils of a pig, is like a woman who is comely, but foolish.) (Proverbs 11:22 WYC)

Through the eyes of many modern conservatives, Deborah should not have been a judge. Judges were military and spiritual leaders chosen by YHWH to lead the wayward nation of Israel. Deborah was a woman.

And the people of Israel again did what was evil in the sight of [Yeshua] after Ehud died. And [Yeshua] sold them into the hand of Jabin king of Canaan, who reigned in Hazor. The commander of his army was Sisera, who lived in Harosheth-hagoyim. Then the people of Israel cried out to [YHWH] for help, for he had 900 chariots of iron and he oppressed the people of Israel cruelly for twenty years. Now Deborah, a prophetess, the wife of Lappidoth, was judging Israel at that time. She used to sit under the palm of Deborah between Ramah and Bethel in the hill country of Ephraim, and the people of Israel came up to her for judgment. (Judges 4:1-5 ESV)

Is the Church then to conclude that the Father is a liberal? No. "Conservative" and "liberal" are man-made constructs used to further pit man against man. God Almighty is a liberator who chooses whomever he likes to unfetter the subjugated. Deborah was deemed worthy enough by YHWH to deliver a whole people—his people—from oppressive hands. Caution. A society that insists on defining a woman's worth by her sex is a society that will continue to see women finding their worth through sex; never the Father's intentions.

Many women have done excellently, but you surpass them all. Charm is deceitful, and beauty is vain, but a woman who fears [Yeshua] is to be praised. Give her of the fruit of her hands, and let her works praise her in the gates. (Proverbs 31:29-31 ESV)

In Joppa there was a disciple named Tabitha (in Greek, Dorcas, meaning a gazelle), who filled her days with acts of kindness and charity. (Acts 9:36 NEB)

Treat the younger men as brothers, the older women as mothers, and the younger as your sisters, in all purity. (1st Timothy 5:2 NEB)

128. Priceless

First read: Matthew 6:26

From time to time
it will cross my mind,
and a question do I pose;
the answer is well within my reach
for my Father in heaven knows

And though I may,
seek all day
from those upon the earth,
in vain I find, to my own demise,
the measure of my worth

"Oh how nice you look,
How well you cook,
Wow, your house is grand,
Your voice divine,
your manners fine;
the fairest in all the land."

Yet, all the praise I daily crave,
from the moment of my birth,
still leaves me rather empty
as I wonder what I'm worth
to YAH

And he says,
You're more precious than gold;
more valuable and worthy than
all the treasures of the world

You were worthy enough to die for,
while you lay dead in sin
You were worthy enough to rise for,
that you might live again

The price Messiah paid,
to secure your release,
proves your worth to him.
The cost of salvation –
your Savior's blood.

No ruby, no sapphire, no gem
The world may think you worthless
because you've no letters with your name
But to your Father in heaven
you're a precious jewel
so I love you just the same.

Though stock and bonds
may rise and fall
your worth to me remains
Though jobs will come
and jobs will go
My love will never wane

The Spirit will search
And the Spirit will press
and press, and press

Repeat

No perfect pearl
without some pain,
No diamond
without some heat

The world sees dirt,
worthless dirt,
without shape or name

Yes, today you are clay,
inside a jar
with ugly scars
and black as tar

But when I am through-
pressing and holding,
shaping and molding-

When I'm done with
the dirt that I bought;
the world will see then,
that coal is much more
than it seems,

A stone whose worth isn't
measured in dollars or cents
but by faith in your Rock
who redeems

First read: Proverbs 18:9-21

Do you think it will make you look haughty—is that why? Is that why you would rather lie? Mighty sun, humiliated by night, yet rising daily to herald, nurture, and sustain—blazes in brilliance over such foolish thinking. The sun— youthful, fruitful, and daily disgraced—blazes in might. You choosing to lie? That isn't right. Sometimes you need to stand up and fight. Remember, you are also fighting for the team. In not insisting you are risking, though uncommon, yet so tragic, that those standing by will try to swoon away. As you are walking don't fear talking; use the sun's light as your anchor, or as you walk, you'll see them fall out and they'll lay.

> They have eyes for nothing but women, eyes never at rest from sin. They lure the unstable to their ruin; past master in mercenary greed, [YHWH]'s curse is on them. They have abandoned the straight road and lost their way. They have followed in the steps of Balaam son of Beor, who consented to take pay for doing wrong, but had his offense brought home to him when the dumb beast spoke with a human voice and put a stop to the prophet's madness. (2nd Peter 2:14-16 NEB)

There is another group of members within Messiah's flock who choose not to ward off the attacks of those who would do harm to the Body, for belief that those on the side of the road will misperceive. These are the one's who have been convinced that they have no right to judge anybody because they have listened to shepherds or other sheep mischaracterize the Word:

> Pass no judgment, and you will not be judged. For as you judge others, so you will yourselves be judged, and whatever measure you deal out to others will be dealt back to you. Why do you look at the speck of sawdust in your brother's eye, with never a thought for the great plank in your own? Or how can you say to your brother, "Let me take the speck out of your eye," when all the time there is that plank in your own? You hypocrite. First take the plank out of your own eye, and then you will see clearly to take the speck out of your brother's." (Matthew 7:1-5 NEB)

There is no judgment in truth or justice, only in selfish aggrandizement. And now for some candor: There remains a multitude of members who can judge, but who won't. It isn't belief that grips, but lazy lips. Those sheep who sit idly by while wolves and lions run rampant will never see clearly, so long as the plank of complacence remains lodged in their eye. At the moment they are ready to listen to the Holy Spirit's conviction, it is time to put away foolish sophistry.

> Do not entertain a charge against an elder unless it is supported by two or three witnesses. Those who commit sins you must expose publicly, to put fear into the others. Before [YHWH] and the angels who are his chosen, I solemnly charge you, maintain these rules, and never pre-judge the issue, but act with

strict impartiality. Do not be over-hasty in laying on hands in ordination, or you may find yourself responsible for other people's misdeeds; keep your own hands clean. (1st Timothy 5:19-22 NEB)

Messiah was not discouraging his workers from speaking truth to those who are dying to hear. His disdain is for those who would attempt to utter truth while they are themselves living a lie. The shepherd's solution should not therefore consist of preaching a false and debilitating humility: "You are a sinner just like everyone else and therefore you have no right to speak." How defeatist. That's not preaching humility—it is teaching stupidity. Instead, shepherds need to encourage their flock to live a life of holiness through the indwelling Holy Spirit (and the grace of the Father) so that then each can speak out, and then weed out when necessary. More candor? Messiah did it, and thus, so can his sheep.

John was dressed in a rough coat of camel's hair, with a leather belt round his waist, and he fed on locusts and wild honey. His proclamation ran: "After me comes one who is mightier than I. I am not fit to unfasten his shoes. I have baptized you with water, he will baptize you with the Holy Spirit." (Mark 1:6-8 NEB)

In truth, in very truth I tell you, he who has faith in me will do what I am doing; and he will do greater things still because I am going to the Father. (John 14:12 NEB)

For others, there is a lack of fortitude. These members need to hear a message of strength; a reminder that Messiah commands because he is the Commander-in-Chief. What then accompanies dejection is a struggle with belief:

Once again [Yeshua] addressed the people: "I am the light of the world. No follower of mine shall wander in the dark; he shall have the light of life." (John 8:12 NEB)

He rescued us from the domain of darkness and brought us away into the kingdom of his dear Son, in whom our release is secured and our sins forgiven. (Colossians 1:13-14 NEB)

Messiah is depending on those disciples more mature to protect the newly converted—the infants who are still in need of milk. They are the most vulnerable. No, Satan cannot snatch the helmet of salvation off of the head of any sheep. His strategy is stealth; to convince the novice (often through wealth), to remove their own helmet, and to exchange it for something a little bit more hellacious. Just a little leaven to deaden the bread. Enough said.

Then I saw a great white throne, and the One who sat upon it; from his presence earth and heaven vanished away, and no place was left for them. I could see the dead, great and small, standing before the throne; and books were opened. Then another book was opened, the roll of the living. From what was written in these books the dead were judged upon the record of their deeds. The sea gave up its dead, and Death and Hades gave up the dead in their keeping; they were judged, each man on the record of his deeds. Then Death and Hades were flung into the lake of fire. This lake of fire is the second death; and into it were flung any whose names were not to be found in the roll of the living. (Revelation 20:11-15 NEB)

130. A Reflective Moment

Flattering or Furthering

First read: 1st Thessalonians 2:4-8

For all that, even among those in authority a number believed in him, but would not acknowledge him on account of the Pharisees, for fear of being banned from the synagogue. For they valued their reputation with men rather than the honor which comes from [YHWH]. (John 12:42-43 NEB)

When walking out your faith whose approval do you seek? If serving Messiah, then the only approval necessary is his. Mixed messages can be sent, even unintentional ones, when the servant is appealing to the masses rather than to YHWH. With chaos and confusion all around, one message should ring true above all else. If the Master is pursuing, then this message is capable of penetrating through even the hardest of hearts. It is the message of redemption through repentance. Unfortunately, members of the Body often find themselves in churches where the intention is to ignite but the delivery becomes diluted. The Holy Spirit is interested in igniting a fire within the Church that will remain ablaze until the return of Messiah; and even then the fires will continue to flash. However, the flames of the Holy Spirit are the flames of truth. Any message delivered where truth is ill-considered will result in squelching rather than reviving.

First of all, then, I urge that petitions, prayers, intercessions, and thanksgiving be offered for all men; for sovereigns and all in high office, that we may lead a tranquil and quiet life in full observance of religion and high standards of morality. Such prayer is right, and approved by [YHWH] our Savior, whose will it is that all men should find salvation and come to know the truth. For there is one God, and also one mediator between [YHWH] and men, [Yeshua], himself man, who sacrificed himself to win freedom for all mankind, so providing, at the fitting time, proof of the divine purpose. (1st Timothy 2:1-6 NEB)

It has been suggested by some that the goal of the Church is to bring in as many lost to the fold as time affords. Agreed. Furthermore, it is indeed wise to know the crowd that one is attempting to reach. In speaking to the church in Corinth Paul writes:

I am a free man and own no master; but I have made myself every man's servant, to win over as many as possible. To Jews I became like a Jew, to win Jews; as they are subject to the Law of Moses, I put myself under that law to win them, although I am not myself subject to it. To win Gentiles, who are outside [YHWH]'s law, I made myself like one of them, although I am not in truth outside [YHWH]'s law, being under the law of [Messiah]. To the weak I became weak, to win the weak. Indeed, I have become everything in turn to men of every sort, so that in one way or another I may save some. All this I do for the sake of the Gospel, to bear my part in proclaiming it. (1st Corinthians 9:19-23 NEB)

So, then, the Church bears the collective responsibility of being all things to all people, such is the role of each member. Nevertheless, however varied the approach might be, dependent upon demographics, the substance need not diverge from the Truth. There's little flattering about the message of the Gospel, lest we forget the cross to which Messiah was led, the thorns on his head, the words that he said, the tears that he shed, and the blood that he bled.

> But now [Messiah] has come, high priest of good things already in being. The tent of his priesthood is a greater and more perfect one, not made by men's hands, that is, not belonging to this created world; the blood of his sacrifice is his own blood, not the blood of goats and calves; and thus he has entered the sanctuary once and for all and secured an eternal deliverance. (Hebrews 9:11-12 NEB)

Understanding the sacrifice that was made by the Son of YHWH should serve to further our understanding of Messiah's expectation for each of us. Repentance is not merely regret over sin. It is refusing to give in to the temptations that will continue to resurface even as our relationship with Messiah strengthens. When Messiah feels that you're ready, this will become an almost daily exercise.

> Have nothing to do with those godless myths, fit only for old women. Keep yourself in training for the practice of religion. The training of the body does bring limited benefit, but the benefits of religion are without limit, since it holds promise not only for this life but for the life to come. Here are words you may trust, words that merit full acceptance: "With this before us we labor and struggle, because we have set our hopes on the living God, who is the Savior of all men."—the Savior, above all, of believers. (1st Timothy 4:7-10 NEB)

A trend within the Body is the growth of the so called mega church; named because of its incredible size and vast array of services provided. The mega church does, in fact, play a vital role in evangelizing. Because of their larger nets, these churches generally are able to catch more fish. As we are approaching the return of Messiah, these churches will continue to thrive. And now for a word of caution: In as much as Messiah is interested in the quantity of his flock, he is equally concerned with their quality. Mountain top experiences are valuable, but what is of greater value is teaching others how to cope when they are in the valley. The recovery of every one of Messiah's lost sheep is vital. It's also imperative that they remain covered. Flattering to find favor with the flock is a sure way to fall out of favor with the Father—just ask King Saul.

> After bringing the good news to that town, where they gained many converts, they returned to Lystra, then to Iconium, and then to Antioch, heartening the converts and encouraging them to be true to their religion. They warned them that to enter the kingdom of [YHWH] we must pass through many hardships. They also appointed elders for them in each congregation, and with prayer and fasting committed them to [Yeshua] in whom they had put their faith. (Acts 14:21-23 NEB)

131. Surviving Rivalry

First read: Jeremiah 51:1-64

You should find solace in seeing that with seasons' various changes there are at least two constants—the sun and rain. There is, in fact, stability to be found in the face of earth's fickleness.

There is no sword mightier than the one wielded by our Master.

I turned to see whose voice it was that spoke to me; and when I turned I saw seven standing lamps of gold, and among the lamps one like a son of man, robed down to his feet, with a golden girdle round his breast. The hair of his head was white as snow as snow-white wool, and his eyes flamed like fire; his feet gleamed like burnished brass refined in a furnace, and his voice was like the sound of rushing waters. In his right hand he held seven stars, and out of his mouth came a sharp two-edged sword; and his face shone like the sun in full strength. (Revelation 1:12-16 NEB)

Admittedly, it is not a comforting thought to know that if ever we wander without a thought of remorse and repentance, we are just as subject to Yeshua's just judgment as is the Accuser who daily attacks his subjects. We don't like to picture the Son's slaying, but, in truth, it should produce such sweet serenity in the soul of every believer.

The one who seeks to rob his will;
whose purpose is to pounce and kill;
who's hungry still after every meal –
his time is almost up.

The one who from the first did fall;
who searches for the soul to maul;
who tries to block the Savior's call –
his time is almost up.

The one who's always on the prowl;
who is as wise as is the wisest owl;
who was as evil then as he is now –
his time is almost up.

The one who plants the deadly seeds;
the ones that grow into deadly weeds;
who's always there to meet our needs –
his time is almost up.

The one who sought to overthrow;
who's the Father's, Son's, and Spirit's foe;
who once was high but now is low –
his time is almost up.

The one whose aim is never good;
who lies at length, as liars should;
who'd slay us all, if he only could –
his time is almost up.

The one who blinds the eyes from birth;
who seeks to keep us on his turf;
who tells us that our home is Earth –
his time is almost up.

The one who binds the soul to sin;
though Messiah did die and Messiah did win;
the one who seeks to bind again –
his time is almost up.

The one who always picks the fights;
who does his darkest deeds at night,
but who'll shriek in fear when he's sees the Light –
his time is almost up.

When the thousand years are over, Satan will be let loose from his dungeon; and he will come out to seduce the nations in the four quarters of the earth and to muster them for battle, yes, the hosts of Gog and Magog, countless as the sands of the sea. So they marched over the breadth of the land and laid siege to the camp of [YHWH]'s people and the city that he loves. But fire came down on them from heaven and consumed them; and the Devil, their seducer, was flung into the lake of fire and sulfur, where the beast and the false prophet had been flung, there to be tormented day and night forever. (Revelation 20:7-10 NEB)

It is important for believers to remember that while wearisome and at present, relentless, the enemy will not reign for eternity. Any illusions he had to the contrary were shattered while Yeshua was shedding his blood on the cross. Several times Satan sought to prevent the Father's Present from prevailing. First, while Yeshua walked wearily in the wilderness, and on another occasion in trying to get him to succumb to an impassioned Peter.

From that time [Yeshua] began to make it clear to his disciples that he had to go to Jerusalem, and there to suffer much from the elders, chief priests, and doctors of the law; to be put to death and to be raised again on the third day. At this Peter took him by the arm and began to rebuke him: "Heaven forbid." he said. "No, Lord, this shall never happen to you." Then [Yeshua] turned and said to Peter, "Away with you, Satan; you are a stumbling block to me. You think as men think, not as [YHWH] thinks." (Matthew 16:21-23 NEB)

And though he succeeded with neither strategy, Satan persisted in his mission until his mission became moot. The dragon is now waging war on the rest of spiritual-Israel's children and will continue to do so until his appointed time—now in the spirit, but soon through the flesh. However, let all members of the Body understand that the Son holds the victory sword and that our faithfulness in the midst of frustration will yield an eternity of reining with the King.

For already the secret power of wickedness is at work, secret only for the present until the restrainer disappears from the scene. And then he will be revealed, that wicked man whom [Yeshua] will destroy with the breath of his mouth, and end by the radiance of his coming. But the coming of that wicked man is the work of Satan. It will be attended by all the powerful signs and miracles of the Lie, and all the deception that sinfulness can impose on those doomed to destruction. Destroyed they shall be, because they did not open their minds to love of the truth, so as to find salvation. Therefore [YHWH] puts them under a delusion, which works upon them to believe the lie, so that they may all be brought to judgment, all who do not believe the truth but make sinfulness their deliberate choice. (2nd Thessalonians 2:8-12 NEB)

> When it seems that time and time again,
> Satan is about to win;
> when all seems lost and doubt sets in
> remember that his time is almost up.

And then pray to him who lights the way
 to usher in that final day
when Satan, at last, will have to pay.
But until then, my friends, look up.

And the God of peace will soon crush Satan beneath your feet. The grace of [Yeshua] be with you. (Romans 16:20 NEB)

132. Feeling Forsaken

First read: 1st King 19:1-21

During the changing of seasons you will sometimes look up at the shifting clouds and notice that there is no sky to be seen. The clouds, in their bleakness, will leave you blank and often speechless. No sun will you see; no rain will you feel; no time will you sense nipping at your heel. These are the moments of greatest despair, but you must still believe that all are still there. It will be difficult to accept; but, in accepting you must continue to step. Winters, springs, summers, and falls; they each bring gifts to share and burdens to bear. Take both their gifts and burdens, and share them with those traveling with you.

Think you've been forsaken? You are mistaken. To all whom are faithful, YHWH will never depart. This doesn't mean, however, that believers aren't going to feel, on occasion, like they have been neglected. It is an issue of the flesh and believers must learn not to judge the proximity of God Almighty by the conditions which surround them. Make no mistake, Messiah can relate to our feelings of abandonment. Remember the anguish of Messiah as he laid suffering for the sake of humanity?

From midday a darkness fell over the whole land, which lasted until three in the afternoon; and about three [Yeshua] cried aloud, "Eli, Eli, lema sabachthani?" which means, "My God, my God, why hast thou left me?"

(Matthew 27:45-46 NEB)

It was as if the whole earth entered into a time of depression, juxtaposing the emotions of her Creator. If members of the Body fail to remember that while he walked the earth, Yeshua Messiah was fully human, then it will make no sense why any should have their faith in someone merely transcendent. Our faith, hope, and love are in the One who once breathed the same air we do today. Our allegiance is to the Messiah who is able to connect with his creation in every human way. It is therefore acceptable to cry out to our heavenly Father whenever we feel forsaken.

Out of my distress I called on [YHWH]; [Yeshua] answered me and set me free. (Psalms 118:5 ESV)

Run the great race of faith and take hold of eternal life. For to this you were called; and you confessed your faith nobly before many witnesses. (1st Timothy 6:12 NEB)

What is unacceptable, however, is to allow our fleshly feelings to overshadow what our spirits know to be true. As we walk, our spirits should continuously align with the Holy Spirit. The indwelling Holy Spirit is the believer's linkage to eternal truth. As long as the internal is fixed on the eternal, then the plights of the external shall never leave an eternal bruise on the spirit. A spirit that has been eternally bruised can never enter the Kingdom of Heaven where there is only room for the spiritually healed. Even though in distress, while dying on the cross, Yeshua still understood that each nail pierced only his flesh. Perhaps it is easiest to feel forsaken when frightened. Elijah's life was sought when he delivered the message to Jezebel that her prophets were unacceptable. In fearing for his life, Elijah rightfully turned to the Father for refuge. However, forty days passed before God Almighty responded, and even then Elijah had to ensure that his spiritual ears remained opened to hear. When he didn't hear YHWH in the wind, through the earthquake, or from the fire, Elijah could have assumed he'd been abandoned and could have given up. But, it was because of his faith that he eventually heard the voice of YHWH-Shammah, which means, YHWH-is-There.

For the spirit that [YHWH] gave us is no fearful spirit, but one to inspire strength, love, and self-discipline. (2nd Timothy 1:7 NEB)

The Apostle Paul also knew what earthly abandonment felt like. In sensing the imminence of his death, he writes to his protégé:

Do your best to join me soon; for Demas has deserted me because his heart was set on this world; he has gone to Thessalonica, Crescens to Galatia, Titus to Dalmatia; I have no one with me but Luke. (2nd Timothy 4:9-10 NEB)

At the first hearing of my case no one came into court to support me; they all left me in the lurch; I pray that it may not be held against them. But [Yeshua] stood by me and lent me strength, so that I might be his instrument in making the full proclamation of the Gospel for the whole pagan world to hear; and thus I was rescued out of the lion's jaws. And [YHWH] will rescue me from every attempt to do me harm, and keep me safe until [Yeshua]'s heavenly reign begins. Glory to him for ever and ever. Amen. (2nd Timothy 4:16-18 NEB)

During heightened distress, members of the Body must make a choice. If walking in the flesh, then each will always feel a void, which will be filled by the wiles of the world. Yet, if walking in the spirit and yielding to the Spirit, then each will hear the Spirit's voice. And though it may not always ring out as clear, believers must know that the Spirit is near.

For he will hide me in his shelter in the day of trouble; he will conceal me under the cover of his tent; he will lift me high upon a rock. And now my head shall be lifted up above my enemies all around me, and I will offer in his tent sacrifices with shouts of joy; I will sing and make melody to [Yeshua]. Hear, O [Yeshua], when I cry aloud; be gracious to me and answer me. You have said, "Seek my face." My heart says to you, "Your face, [YHWH], do I seek." Hide not your face from me. Turn not your servant away in anger, O you who have been my help. Cast me not off; forsake me not, O [YHWH] of my salvation. For my father and my mother have forsaken me, but [Yeshua] will take me in. (Psalms 27:5-10 ESV)

133. Rock Solid

First read: Psalms 81-90

Perhaps, winter offers the heaviest burden to give you. However, if you can bear its burden then you should have no problem bearing anything. Will you? Will you handle its chill? Some days will prove so cold that each step threatens to freeze you solid. Bear the freeze and warmly embrace its solidifying role. Though stony you may feel, remember that rocks, with their rough and chipped edges, are far from whole; most are also far from hollow.

For many travelers winter can appear the most perplexing season of the four, with the most memorable of holidays sandwiched between the most miserable of weather. A celebration of the birth of Messiah juxtaposed with the constant chipping of ice; winter can often be anything but nice. The believer should relish the opportunity to solidify amidst such harsh conditions, because in solidifying you know that you are also sanctifying. The goal of the Father in sending a sudden chill is to support your efforts in becoming a reflection of Messiah the King. It may not be what you want, but then never is our heavenly Father so attuned to our wants that he forgets to provide for our needs. It is often when times get the roughest that our exterior becomes the toughest. The roughest of times can also produce the softest of hearts, which is what Messiah needs melted if we are going to follow in his hallowed footsteps.

Today, therefore, as the Holy Spirit says—Today if you hear his voice, do not grow stubborn as in those days of rebellion, at that time of testing in the desert, where your forefathers tried me and tested me, and saw the things I did for forty years. And so, I was indignant with that generation and I said, "Their hearts are for ever astray; they would not discern my ways; as I vowed in my anger, they shall never enter my rest." (Hebrews 3:7-11 NEB)

Why must the Christian be rock solid? There are a plethora of useful purposes for the jagged rock. For starters, most are pretty dense; making it difficult to blow them off the right road. With so many religious fads fading in and out of existence, it is imperative that believers stay the course by staying in the word.

You know how, in the days when you were still pagan, you were swept off to those dumb heathen gods, however you happened to be led. (1st Corinthians 1:2 NEB)

Timothy, keep safe that which has been entrusted to you. Turn a deaf ear to empty and worldly chatter, and the contradictions of so-called "knowledge." For many who lay claim to it have shot far wide of the faith. Grace be with you all. (1st Timothy 6:20-21 NEB)

If the Father finds that there are too many distractions which prevent his children from focusing on their journey, then he may find it necessary to freeze them in place for a little while. Although sad, there is proof that many only turn to the Truth when they have virtually nothing else to do. Such intervention is far from ideal, as the Father would rather his children choose him while they still freely have the option to pick a "better deal."

Now therefore fear [Yeshua] and serve him in sincerity and in faithfulness. Put away the gods that your fathers served beyond the River and in Egypt, and serve [Yeshua]. And if it is evil in your eyes to serve [YHWH], choose this day whom you will serve, whether the gods your fathers served in the region beyond the River, or the gods of the Amorites in whose land you dwell. But as for me and my house, we will serve [YHWH]. (Joshua 24:14-15 ESV)

Next, most solid rocks have jagged edges, which are ideal for sharpening the edges of another. At times it may be necessary to remind a fellow believer that no matter how far along on his journey, until he sees the gates of Glory, he must continue to go because he must continue to grow. To the world, the jagged look the most ragged and are therefore tossed to the side as unsightly, and thus inconsequential. To the world, the jagged are also painful. However, strategically placed on the road to Glory, the jagged can remind the proud and prominent that it is YHWH who is dominant, and that at any given moment, he can cut them down if the ground is the only place from which they can see clearly, their crown.

Iron sharpens iron, and one man sharpens another. (Proverbs 27:17 ESV)

Therefore it is also contained in the Scripture, "Behold, I lay in Zion a chief cornerstone, elect, precious; and he who believes on him will by no means be put to shame." Therefore, to you who believe, he is precious; but to those who are disobedient, "The stone which the builders rejected has become the chief cornerstone," and "A stone of stumbling and a rock of offense." They stumble, being disobedient to the word, to which they also were appointed. (1st Peter 2:6-8 NKJV)

Finally, in becoming rock solid it is vital that members not forget that a reflection does not replace the image. While walking the earth, Yeshua Messiah, the Son of YHWH, was the perfect image of the Father. And while our God, Yeshua Messiah is not the Father.

If you knew me you would know my Father too. From now on you do know him; you have seen him. Philip said to him, "Lord, show us the Father and we ask no more." [Yeshua] answered, "Have I been all this time with you, Philip, and you still do not know me? Anyone who has seen me has seen the Father." Then how can you say, "Show us the Father?" Do you not believe that I am in the Father, and the Father in me? I am not myself the source of the words I speak to you: it is the Father who dwells in me doing his own work." (John 14:7-10 NEB)

The Son is the radiance of [YHWH]'s glory and the exact representation of his being sustaining all things by his powerful word. After he had provided purification for sins, he sat down at the right hand of the Majesty in heaven. (Hebrews 1:3 NEB)

In the same way, there is only one whom the Father has crowned King of kings and Lord of lords. There is only one Rock. Messiah does not command copies of himself, for there are none. As rocks, we are to reflect the attitude and actions of Messiah, while respecting his essence. If winter provides the best means to this end, then let the chilling begin.

Then comes the end, when he delivers up the kingdom to God the Father, after abolishing every kind of domination, authority, and power. For he is destined to reign until [YHWH] has put all enemies under his feet; and the last enemy to be abolished is death. Scripture says, "He has put all things in subjection under his feet." But in saying "all things," it clearly means to exclude [YHWH] who subordinates them; and when all things are thus subject to him, then the Son himself will also be made subordinate to [YHWH] who made all things subject to him, and thus [YHWH] will be all in all. (1st Corinthians 15:24-28 NEB)

Let all Israel then accept as certain that [YHWH] has made this [Yeshua], whom you crucified, both Lord and Messiah. (Acts 2:36 NEB)

134. Fit From Fear

First read: 1st Samuel 15:24

The greater your hollowness, the greater ease harsh winds will have in blowing you off track. Density is not your enemy unless it is preventing you from penetrating pearls of wisdom. While walking, if you happen to pass those dense with ditz, then keep walking. Those who are dense with ditz will deliberate on glitz; and with their glitz they'll seek to feel secure. Deceptively at ease, they will flutter in the breeze; and if their glitz were gone, they'd soon detour. If you are going to be dense, be acutely dense. Astute enough to flee from fools who have discovered a different route and who will want you to tour with them. You have zero time for detours and zero time to waste, no matter how alluring they appear. In denseness you will struggle, because in denseness you won't budge, but in denseness you won't follow out of fear.

> Moreover, brethren, I declare to you the gospel which I preached to you, which also you received and in which you stand, by which also you are saved, if you hold fast that word which I preached to you—unless you believed in vain. (1st Corinthians 15:1-2 NKJV)

Do you realize that YHWH never fitted his children for fear? It is no wonder that much backsliding in the Body occurs, when its members insist on acting, or resist acting, out of fear. The Holy Spirit is the only person powerful enough to keep believers from blowing in the wind. The problem is that there are many in the Church who, in refusing to daily walk in, become filled with, and yield to the Holy Spirit, sway easily from the Truth. And who, without much effort, are persuaded to engage in acts of disobedience. What is it that affects them so? They talk and they walk and yet they don't grow. It's because they have an unhealthy desire to be accepted; hence, they fear rejection. On the surface the problem seems harmless. After all, what human alive doesn't want to be accepted? Certainly Messiah understands that his sheep need to be connected, right? Of course. Only, Messiah never intended his sheep to connect to the world.

> Do not love the world or the things in the world. If anyone loves the world, the love of the Father is not in him. For all that is in the world—the lust of the flesh, the lust of the eyes, and the pride of life—is not of the Father but is of the world. And the world is passing away, and the lust of it; but he who does the will of [YHWH] abides forever. (1st John 2:15-17 NKJV)

Without denying the genius of Shakespeare, he fell short when passing over the opportunity to tell of one of the greatest tragedies ever—the fall of Saul. It's difficult to read the accounts of Israel's first king without weeping. Here is a guy who, at the age of fifty, had the opportunity to deliver Israel from oppression and to steer them back unto the road to Glory. In truth, Saul should never have been king in the first place. It was YHWH's intentions that his people remain content with his rule. But, in wanting to imitate everyone else, the Israelites insisted on having an earthly king, even after the Father warned of the impending disaster. Nevertheless, a man was appointed who stood above the rest.

Then Samuel brought all the tribes of Israel near, and the tribe of Benjamin was taken by lot. He brought the tribe of Benjamin near by its clans, and the clan of the Matrites was taken by lot; and Saul, the son of Kish was taken by lot. But, when they sought him, he could hardly be found. So they inquired again of [YHWH], "Is there a man still to come?" and [YHWH] said, "Behold, he has hidden himself among the baggage." Then they ran and took him from there. And when he stood among the people, he was taller than any of the people from his shoulders upward. And Samuel said to all the people, "Do you see him whom [YHWH] has chosen? There is none like him among all the people. " And all the people shouted, "Long live the king." (1st Samuel 10:20-24 ESV)

But his reign would not last long. In hiding among the baggage, it was clear that from the beginning Saul struggled with fear. Fear delivered him into the arms of a wrathful God who would have delivered Saul from his fear, had he asked. Saul found solace in pleasing the crowd. Caution. Those who are eager to please the crowd will soon find themselves appeasing the crowd. The cause for unity is a noble one indeed; so long as all stand united with Truth. Unfortunately, the world has remained divided ever since man fell. The call of Christians is not to unite with the world, but to unite the world with Messiah. But, before they are fit for service, believers must first be fit from fear. By whom are you looking to be received? There are two choices. Only one counts.

Here are words you may trust: "If we died with him, we shall live with him; if we endure, we shall reign with him. If we deny him, he will deny us. If we are faithless, he keeps faith, for he cannot deny himself." (2nd Timothy 2:11-13 NEB)

135. Stepping With Steadfastness

First read: Psalms 108:1-2

With its freezing temperatures, winter will keep you focused. In solidifying, you will become steadfast and set on staying the course. Even with its biting winds in the severest weather, winter still lends support in keeping you alert. Alert enough to keep walking, while generating enough body heat to keep you from freezing to death.

It is decidedly more difficult to doze off when the windchill is below freezing. As Messiah was approaching his hour of power, with urgency he spoke of the final days before his return and encouraged all to remain alert—lest they be found sleeping on the job.

But about that day or that hour no one knows, not even the angels in heaven, not even the Son; only the Father. Be alert, be wakeful. You do not know when the moment comes. It is like a man away from his home: he has left his house and put his servants in charge, each with his own work to do, and he has ordered the door-keeper to stay awake. Keep awake, then, for you do not know when the master of the house is coming. Evening or midnight, cock-crow or early dawn—if he comes suddenly, he must not find you asleep. And what I am saying to you, I say to everyone: Keep awake. (Mark 13:32-37 NEB)

Messiah did not speak these words in order that his servants should pause indefinitely to ponder the hour of his return. In the winter such idleness could prove deadly. To prevent lethargy, believers need to remain active if the heat from the Holy Spirit is going to circulate throughout the Body. If it encourages others to wake from their slumber, there is nothing wrong with the eschatological enthusiast who wants to perpetually sound the alarm. Indeed, every true member of the Body has been assigned their task. It is not for a doubter to tell a believer that his assignment is bogus because of his own spiritual insecurities. However, it is imperative that the enthusiast inspire the slumbering to awaken, and then to begin walking out of adoration for YHWH. In their passion, well-intentioned watchmen speak of Messiah's imminent return so effectively that some of the dead do arise from their bed. But then there they stand—frozen and unsure of when or how to take the next step. The winter should leave none frozen. Those members more mature have the responsibility of teaching the novice or the ignorant how to kindle a holy fire.

You keep him in perfect peace whose mind is stayed on you, because he trusts in you. Trust in [Yeshua] forever, for [Yeshua] is an everlasting rock. (Isaiah 26:3-4 ESV)

Before [YHWH] and before [Yeshua], who is to judge men living and dead, I charge you solemnly by his coming appearance and his reign, proclaim the message, press it home on all occasions, convenient or in-convenient, use argument, reproof, and appeal, with all the patience that the work of teaching requires. (2nd Timothy 4:1-2 NEB)

It is the Holy Spirit who empowers believers to step with steadfastness, and keeps them from turning into icicles. Solid? Yes. Usable? No. The point in solidifying is to become confident in Messiah so that we remain useful. While awaiting the return of Messiah, the focus of the Christian should center on fulfilling the Great Commission. With each chilling wind all must press forward faithfully, while heeding the words of Moses to the Israelites:

You shall be careful therefore to do as [YHWH] has commanded you. You shall not turn aside to the right hand or to the left. You shall walk in all the way that [YHWH] has commanded you, that you may live, and that it may go well with you, and that you may live long in the land that you shall possess. (Deuteronomy 5:32-33 ESV)

Accept that our hope is now set on that which is eternal. The final hour is approaching; the destination has changed, but his declaration has not.

136. Intimacy with Emmanuel I

First read: Song of Songs: 1:1-17

You can only accumulate so much body heat in walking alone. Louder than any other season, winter will remind that you can't reach your destination walking alone. On one hand, body heat increases in proportion to the number of people amassed. Though, body heat accumulated depends less on percentage and more on proximity. Don't be foolish in deafness. This is not the season to fixate on your fear of intimacy. It is perhaps the season to address it. Intimacy is: Drawing in so that they can see. If you find that you are struggling, ask yourself why. Why do you fear drawing near?

It is the failure of members in two essential areas that prohibits the Church from functioning the way Messiah would see fit. First, there is the disconnect that members have with the Father, Son, and Holy Spirit. It is a fear of intimacy. Unfortunately, this is not the type of fear that YHWH had in mind when first he spoke through David and then Solomon. The Father encourages fear so that his people remain spiritually stable, not so that any should become disabled.

Serve [Yeshua] with fear, and rejoice with trembling. Kiss the Son, lest he be angry, and you perish in the way, for his wrath is quickly kindled. Blessed are all who take refuge in him. (Psalms 2:11-12 ESV)

Think it not a coincidence that those whose marriages are absent of any real intimacy are also marred by the same spiritual deficiency. Second, as a natural consequence of the first quandary, members equally struggle with becoming intimate with other members of their own body. Some believers who are members of smaller churches sneer at those incorporated into larger bodies, claiming that it is impossible for any of them to develop real relationships. The reality is that Messiah is unimpressed with the majority of present day congregations, of either size. Intimacy has nothing to do with numbers, but everything to do with nuptials. Says the Apostle Paul while addressing the church in Ephesus:

For no one ever hated his own body: on the contrary, he provides and cares for it; and that is how [Messiah] treats the church, because it is his body, of which we are living parts. Thus it is that (in the words of Scripture) "A man shall leave his father and mother and shall be joined to his wife, and the two shall become one flesh." It is a great truth that is hidden here. I for my part refer it to [Messiah] and to the church, but it applies also individually: each of you must love his wife as his very self; and the woman must see to it that she pays her husband all respect. (Ephesians 5:29-33 NEB)

Song of Songs offers compelling insight into examining three significant truths, the first being the most important. First, God Almighty is a jealous God and he adores his people. He equally deplores the depthless relationship that most of his people have come to seek with him.

Then Paul stood up before the Court of Areopagus and said: "Men of Athens,

I see that in everything that concerns religion you are uncommonly scrupulous. For as I was going round looking at the objects of your worship, I noticed among other things an altar bearing the inscription 'To an Unknown God.' What you worship but do not know—this is what I now proclaim." (Acts 17:22-23 NEB)

He desires devotion, and yet the Father's house is filled with deception. Next, marriage is a gift from YHWH, as is sex. However, couples miss the boat when they believe that sex is an even exchange for intimacy. It is but one expression, and while intended for enjoyment (within the Father's ordained confines), sex, like marriage, is also earth-bound.

[Yeshua] said to them, "The men and women of this world marry; but those who have been judged worthy of a place in the other world and of the resurrection from the dead, do not marry; for they are not subject to death any longer. They are like angels; they are sons of [YHWH], because they share in the resurrection." (Luke 20:34-36 NEB)

Therefore, to ensure monogamy in thwarting monotony, husbands and wives must search for even deeper ways of relating. The Holy Spirit is only too willing to offer guidance—who dares to ask? Finally, the Church is the Body of Messiah and the Holy Spirit's primary mode of operating. Messiah wills that members of his Body learn to relate. The potency of the Church lies in the potency of her members. An isolated fire here and there does virtually nothing in a world so full of darkness. However, if members would cease having fear in drawing near to one another, they would have greater ease in attracting the moths on the roadside, whose fluttering is fleeting. So bright and so high could the flames rise that Messiah only knows how many blind would see. But, intimacy starts with the Father; then and only then will any work get done.

I give you a new commandment: love one another; as I have loved you, so you are to love another. If there is love among you, then all will know that you are my disciples. (John 13:34-35 NEB)

Love in all sincerity, loathing evil and clinging to the good. Let love for our brotherhood breed warmth of mutual affection. Give pride of place to one another in esteem. (Romans 12:9-10 NEB)

137. Intimacy with Emmanuel II

First read: Song of Songs 4:1-16

Do you think that others won't like what they see inside—is that why? Is that why you fear drawing near? Don't be foolish. Inside is where your warmth resides. Failure to let others in will leave those around you cold. You too will stay cold, as body heat increases in proportion to the number of people amassed. Have you been burned in the past—is that why? Is that why you fear drawing near? Don't be foolish, it's winter. Hopefully you still retained some of that heat to keep warm and to keep you from freezing. If you feel that you were burned badly, even better, you have more heat to share with others.

In keeping with the Apostle Paul's analogy of the marriage-like relationship between Messiah and the Church, the bridegroom knows his bride like the back of his own hand, because indeed the two are one flesh. Concerning her members, he therefore knows the most intimate of details; he can relate to every experience and all emotions. There are moments when we as believers think back to the most hurtful of times and we think that there's no way YHWH could ever make use of them, or that some of our most disgraceful experiences are too shameful for Messiah. It is here that we must remember Messiah's love for us and how he can take the most shameful of stenches and turn it into the sweetest smell; an inviting and invigorating aroma.

But thanks be to [YHWH], who continually leads us about, captives in [Messiah's] triumphal procession, and everywhere uses us to reveal and spread abroad the fragrance of the knowledge of himself. We are indeed the incense offered by [Messiah] to [YHWH], both for those who are on the way to salvation, and for those who are on the way to perdition: to the latter it is a deadly fume that kills, to the former a vital fragrance that brings life. (2nd Corinthians 2:14-16 NEB)

A hallmark of intimacy is self-disclosure, and a hallmark of a destructive marriage is secrecy. God Almighty wants his people to recognize his dual transcendent and imminent nature. On the one hand, we serve an omniscient and omnipresent God who knows all because he sees all. However, we also serve a God who desires to have an intimate rapport with his people. Therefore, the purpose in disclosing is relational and not revelatory. Secrets can be destructive within human relationships,and YHWH, an emotional being, is hurt by his people's lack of trust. The other obvious reason for keeping secrets from the Father is sin—remember Adam & Eve?

And they heard the sound of [YHWH] walking in the garden in the cool of the day, and the man and his wife hid themselves from the presence of [Yeshua] among the trees of the garden. But [YHWH] called to the man and said to him, "Where are you?" And he said, "I heard the sound of you in the garden, and I was afraid, because I was naked, and I hid myself." (Genesis 3:8-10 ESV)

301

Only in the encounter, YHWH wasn't the only one hurt by the secret. Indeed, YHWH had already pronounced judgment prior to the act, and yet one wonders what possibly could have happened had both just confessed and repented. There too have been many earthly marriages destroyed by the keeping of secrets. It bears repeating that there isn't a single marriage that doesn't resemble the relationship that both partners have with the Father. If one is shallow, chances are the other isn't much deeper.

The husband must give the wife what is due to her, and the wife equally must give the husband his due. The wife cannot claim her body as her own; it is her husband's. Equally, the husband cannot claim his body as his own; it is his wife's. Do not deny yourselves to one another, except when you agree upon a temporary abstinence in order to devote yourselves to prayer; afterwards you may come together again; otherwise, for lack of self-control, you may be tempted by Satan. (1st Corinthians 7:3-5 NEB)

Messiah is equally concerned that members of his Body fail to relate intimately with one another because of prior bad experiences. To keep others out, these members enter with a cold shoulder and so have no fire to offer the rest. And because most churches have temperatures inside that are just as frigid, there's no opportunity for any thawing. Messiah places equal responsibility on the individual shoulders, as well as the Church's. Members entering need to remember that the fire of the Holy Spirit can only burn as bright as individual contributions allow. When feeling the most incensed, members need to think of incense. God Almighty can turn your burns into a blessing. He can use your story for his glory, while adding to the blaze of the Church—a blessing still.

The Church needs to remember that collectively it is a reflection of Messiah. When new members enter, or seasoned members transfer, they should already feel inclined to share. So hot should the temperature feel in that body, that any frozen shoulder is left bare.

138. Intimacy with Emmanuel - III

First read: Song of Songs 8:5-14

Do you think that you have nothing of value to offer—is that why? Is that why you fear drawing near? Don't be foolish, you are a body—your body emits heat—you are valuable. Of course you want to learn how to let people in where it is warmer. However, in the dead of winter, simply having a body to stand next to can make a difference between feeling cold and freezing to death.

Do not buy into the lie that you are worthless. The enemy would like nothing more than for YHWH's children to feel so distressed and useless that they become useless to the Body. Again, the power of the Church lies in her cohesiveness, and those who are lost need to hear from members who are coherent. It is possible to be so drunk with despair at our depravity, that we forget the place from which Messiah redeemed us. Our Light and shining armor loved us while we still slept in the dark, and from the dark is where we were rescued:

Then Peter, filled with the Holy Spirit, said to them, "Rulers of the people and elders of Israel: If we this day are judged for a good deed done to a helpless man, by what means he has been made well, let it be known to you all, and to all the people of Israel, that by the name of [Yeshua] of Nazareth, whom you crucified, whom [YHWH] raised from the dead, by him this man stands here before you whole." (Acts 4:8-10 NKJV)

Such vessels are we, whom he has called from among Gentiles as well as Jews, as it says in the Book of Hosea: "And I will say to Not My People, 'You are my people; and he shall say you are my God. For in the very place where they were told 'You are no people of mine,' they shall be called sons of the Living God." (Romans 9:24-26 NEB)

By the Head we were resuscitated for a reason—to take up residence in his Father's house and to become representatives of his Body—each of us. In recognizing our depravity, let us not forget to be disciples. (Perhaps Judas would have remained had he remembered his depravity, and in remembering, withstood the temptation to reflect it.) How much instruction could any of the twelve have received if all would have decided that because of their condition, they were incorrigible and therefore invalids, indefinitely? If Yeshua had believed so then he never would have invited them. Yes, he invites invalids to intimacy with him, so that he may heal; but only those who are real. In turn, the former invalid is able to proclaim his new perfectible nature and to share with all who are still invalid. From the eyes of the Father, in one word: priceless. Lest anyone misunderstand, the believer's ultimate value to God Almighty is that he believes. We are not priceless because of our performance. But, as extensions of the Body who faithfully act in love, we are continuously validating our value.

Therefore, my brothers, I implore you by [YHWH]'s mercy to offer your very selves to him: a living sacrifice, dedicated and fit for his acceptance, the worship offered by mind and heart. (Romans 12:1 NEB)

Throughout the Gospels we find Yeshua addressing fear, primarily in the context of witnessing and carrying out the Great Commission. He wills that none of his remain hindered by misplaced fear. Before sending them out he offers the following words of encouragement:

> Do not fear those who kill the body, but cannot kill the soul. Fear him rather who is able to destroy both soul and body in hell. Are not sparrows two a penny? Yet without your Father's leave not one of them can fall to the ground. As for you, even the hairs on your head have all been counted. So have no fear; you are worth more than any number of sparrows. (Matthew 10:28-31 NEB)

> After my return to Jerusalem, I was praying in the temple when I fell into a trance and saw him there, speaking to me. "Make haste," he said, "and leave Jerusalem without delay, for they will not accept your testimony about me." "Lord," I said, "they know that I imprisoned those who believe in thee, and flogged them in every synagogue; and when the blood of Stephen thy witness was shed I stood by, approving, and I looked after the clothes of those who killed him." But he said to me, "Go, for I am sending you far away to the Gentiles." (Acts 22:17-21 NEB)

Fear of self is still misplaced fear, and equally dangerous. Yes, you are depraved and the thought indeed is depressing at times. But during these times remember why Yeshua died—to make you his Bride. You are depraved and he is Divine. Put the two together and you have a new flesh; a disciple, no longer dead, with Messiah as the Head.

> In truth, in very truth I tell you, a time is coming, indeed it is already here, when the dead shall hear the voice of the Son of [YHWH], and all who hear shall come to life. For as the Father has life-giving power in himself, so has the Son, by the Father's gift. (John 5:25-26 NEB)

Don't allow your feelings of irrelevance to keep you distant from Messiah's Body. It is not the walls of the Church that emit heat, but the bodies within the walls. It can get cold standing outside in solitude. You're also more accessible to the hungry Accuser. There are those members of the Body who need to quickly make their way inside, where the heat resides. You are an invaluable member of the Body. Messiah desires your heat to help fan the fiery flames of Heaven, and to quickly carry them out to a world on its way to Hell.

> However, the Most High does not live in houses made by men: as the prophet says...." (Acts 7:48 NEB)

> The God who created the world and everything in it, and who is Lord of heaven and earth, does not live in shrines made my men. (Acts 17:24 NEB)

> I send you to open their eyes and turn them from darkness to light, from the dominion of Satan to [YHWH], so that, by trust in me, they may obtain forgiveness of sins, and a place with those whom [YHWH] has made his own. (Acts 26:18 NEB)

139. Withdrawing From The World

First read: Isaiah 17-20

Neither is winter the season to fixate on your fear of independence. Yet again, however, it is the ideal season for dealing with this dread. Do you fear that you will you get lost—is that why? Is that why you bemoan being alone? Don't be foolish—get up.

It is dangerous for any disciple of Messiah to dread independency. While there ought to always exist intimacy with Emmanuel and among members of his Body, members must equally resist whoring with the wiles of this world. There are, at present, entirely too many "saints" dependent on the world for survival, and it may wind up costing them their souls, if left uncorrected. Undeniably, some of the most frustrating times will come when believers are speaking out against the ills of a sin-filled society. For the earlier prophets such as Jeremiah, Ezekiel, and Amos, times were exceedingly difficult because YHWH had indeed raised them up for their solo acts. Hear the jeers:

> Then they said, "Come, let us make plots against Jeremiah, for the law shall not perish from the priest, nor counsel from the wise, nor the word from the prophet. Come, let us strike him with the tongue, and let us not pay attention to any of his words." Hear me, O [YHWH], and listen to the voice of my adversaries. Should good be repaid with evil? Yet they have dug a pit for my life. Remember how I stood before you to speak good for them, to turn away your wrath from them. (Jeremiah 18:18-20 ESV)

> Yes, persecution will come to all who want to live a godly life as Christians, whereas wicked men and charlatans will make progress from bad to worse, deceiving and deceived. (2nd Timothy 3:12-13 NEB)

The answer to Jeremiah's question is yes. In this world, those who are righteous will continuously be wronged; but, Yeshua will vindicate his virtuous. And, yet, believers would dislike less the thought of being shunned if all within the Body were speaking out as one. The reality is, however, that with so much relativity rampant within, those who would dare declare objective truth are indeed objects of ridicule.

> To the pure all things are pure; but nothing is pure to the tainted minds of disbelievers, tainted alike in reason and conscience. They profess to acknowledge [YHWH], but deny him by their actions. Their detestable obstinacy disqualifies them from any good work. (Titus 1:15-16 NEB)

Messiah compels his disciples to accept this truth as well: Those who diligently seek after him will find him, but know the cost of this find—all who are his will be lost. Those in the world who reject the truth of the Gospel because of their blinded minds will perhaps proclaim that you have lost yours. This is a trick of Satan's to convince Messiah's flock that his message is flawed; to re-harden the hearts of all that had thawed. Says the Apostle Paul to members of the church in Galatia:

I marvel that you are turning away so soon from him who called you in the grace of [Messiah], to a different gospel, which is not another; but there are some who trouble you and want to pervert the gospel of [Messiah]. But even if we, or an angel from heaven, preach any other gospel to you than what we have preached to you, let him be accursed. As we have said before, so now I say again, if anyone preaches any other gospel to you than what you have received, let him be accursed. (Galatians 1:6-9 NKJV)

When believers finally withdraw from the world, they must prepare for war. Without question, it is the responsibility of the Church to arm and equip the members of her Body with the weapons of warfare, and to teach them how to successfully duel in the spiritual realm, while dealing with the physical. To date, save for the pockets of parishes which are instructing, the Church has collectively ignored the topic of spiritual warfare and so her members remain ignorant and unarmed. The results? Attacks from the enemy lead millions running to his ranks. The Holy Spirit is urging all members to remember that when you accept and proclaim the Gospel, expect nothing less than a world that is hostile (both physical and spiritual).

The persons I have referred to are envious of you, but not with an honest envy: what they really want is to bar the door to you so that you may come to envy them. (Galatians 4:17 NEB)

Days will ensue when the enemy's ire will prove irksome, leaving you teary and worn But, know that it's simply some weight from your cross; the price that you pay for leaving the lost. It is not the Father who's rushing to condemn, but rather confirmation that you do belong to him. As the Potter continues to mold and shape, the prince will interfere. The vessel that he tries to crush, the Potter still holds dear. The vessel may cry, though he mustn't crack. The Potter hasn't left the wheel. There is nothing the prince can fracture that the Potter cannot heal. Our response to the world and its prince is every bit as telling of our testimony as is the Truth we proclaim with our tongues. Let our lips forever proclaim this truth: As a citizen of Heaven, this world has nothing for me.

140. Lonely? If Only

First read: Ezra 9:1-15

Caution. In the dead of winter you will be tempted to warm up with the nearest body, but if you aren't careful, you'll wind up burning at a temperature that not even a glacier of ice could lower. Know when to break from the crowd to take in some cool air. Fixate for too long on your fear of independence and you will soon find yourself suffocating. If you find yourself struggling with breaking free to breathe, ask yourself why. Why do you bemoan being alone? Do you feel like you're nobody unless you're with some body—is that why? Don't be foolish. No "body" can breathe if nobodies exist. You are breathing, so clearly you are somebody; capable of breathing by yourself. Learn to discern. In the event you do need assistance in breathing, you don't want simply some "body," sickly or dead. You want a living body, and preferably one that isn't reliant upon you to also breathe.

Fear of loneliness. Admittedly, we have all at one time or another cringed at the idea of being alone.

Turn to me and be gracious to me, for I am lonely and afflicted. The troubles of my heart are enlarged; bring me out of my distresses. (Psalms 25:16-17 ESV)

To the unmarried and to widows I say this: it is a good thing if they stay as I am myself; but if they cannot control themselves, they should marry. Better be married than burn with vain desire. (1st Corinthians 7:8-9 NEB)

Sound familiar? Some, in desperation, have taken steps in the past that have led them off the road to Glory. Hopefully, there were mature members within the Body who were able to lead the reverted back unto the road, and hopefully he or she learned a valuable lesson. Earthly marriage is not the cure for loneliness, though YHWH did ordain and sanctify this institution so that neither man nor woman would have to live alone. The truth is that there is no body on earth capable of satisfying the loneliness that entered man's soul the moment Adam and Eve were expelled from Eden. Messiah died on the cross so that the soul could reconnect with its Maker. All who attempt to kindle an earthly fire in hopes of fulfilling a spiritual desire will soon find that they are fanning such flames in vain.

Let him kiss me with the kisses of his mouth. For your love is better than wine; your anointing oils are fragrant; your name is oil poured out; therefore virgins love you. Draw me after you; let us run. The king has brought me into his chambers. (Song of Songs 1:2-4 ESV)

There are travelers who must learn to ignore what those on the sidelines suggest is the only way to live. There are even fellow travelers who have the mistaken view that the Father wills everybody to marry.

It is a good thing for a man to have nothing to do with women; but because there is so much immorality, let each man have his own wife and each woman her own husband. (1st Corinthians 7:1-2 NEB)

As such, there have been shepherds who have unintentionally led sheep to the slaughter house, in giving the impression that singleness is nonsense; even those whom the Father created for such purposes. During a conversation with the Pharisees, Yeshua stated that divorce was never a part of God Almighty's original plan and that Moses' allowance was a result of man-made sinful behavior. Upon hearing God Almighty's guidelines for marriage and divorce, the disciples responded to Yeshua:

"...if that is the position with husband and wife, it is better not to marry." To this he replied, "That is something which not everyone can accept, but only those for whom [YHWH] has appointed it. For while some are incapable of marriage because they were born so, or were made so by men, there are others who have themselves renounced marriage for the sake of the kingdom of Heaven. Let those accept it who can." (Matthew 19:10-12 NEB)

Worried about being an outcast, many members have rushed into a marriage that was never designed by YHWH, resulting in the destruction of two souls, if not more. Others have allowed lust, rather than love, to lead them down the aisle. "But we love each other," is the proclamation of the believer who is attempting to justify his decision to bed an unbeliever; and soon the believer will completely forget his first Love. When it happens, hopefully someone near will help jog his memory, and hopefully it will happen before his first Love returns to claim his Bride. A marriage is only successful when it has been sanctioned by YHWH, when husband and wife have been saved by Messiah, and when the Holy Spirit is actively working to guide. Finally, neither man nor woman should solely depend on the other for spiritual survival. Rather, each should check that both are staying connected to the cross, so that neither one gets lost.

Since therefore we have a great high priest who has passed through the heavens, [Yeshua] the Son of [YHWH], let us hold fast to the religion we profess. For ours is not a high priest unable to sympathize with our weaknesses, but one who, because of his likeness to us, has been tested every way, only without sin. Let us therefore boldly approach the throne of our gracious God, where we may receive mercy and in his grace find timely help. (Hebrews 4:14-16 NEB)

141. From Insolence to Intimacy

First read: Hosea 9-14

Do you fear you will be forgotten—is that why? Is that why you bemoan being alone? Don't be foolish. Everyone around you will not vanish into thin air the instant you decide to take in some. In your fear of being forgotten, don't forget to turn back around and rejoin the group. You have no cause to bemoan if while walking, you choose to remain alone.

There is no room for insolence while being intimate with YHWH. When he deems it necessary that you give up anything in your life in order to return to your first Love, will you comply? How will you reply? We mistakenly believe that the Father is trying to punish us by insisting that we have no other gods before him. When Messiah insists on an annulment between you and the world, will you wonder why? Will you begin to cry? It is the ultimate test of fidelity when the Bridegroom asks his Bride to set aside her sin and to return to him. It is a forgiving husband who is willing to take back an unfaithful spouse, and it is a foolish wife who willingly rebuffs. To his Bride; to all who have an ear to hear the Spirit deep inside, the question is indeed: "Why am I not enough?" Before the Father would secure Abraham's blessing, Abraham would first have to faithfully prove through active obedience that he was enough.

And the messenger of [YHWH] called to Abraham a second time from heaven and said, "By myself I have sworn, declares [Yeshua], because you have done this and have not withheld your son, your only son, I will surely bless you, and I will surely multiply your offspring as the stars of heaven and as the sand that is on the seashore. And your offspring shall possess the gate of his enemies, and in your offspring shall all the nations of the earth be blessed, because you have obeyed my voice." (Genesis 22:15-18 ESV)

God Almighty will continue to ask his people to give up whatever is standing between them, until the believer finally gives in. Sometimes solitude is the only way we can hear the Holy Spirit without the interference of our idols. Find our idols and we find our identity. Lose our idols and then we are able to identify with Messiah completely. It is wise for the believer not to resist giving up their idols, in thinking that Messiah wills for the solo soul. Messiah only wills for the solely soul; the soul whom depends solely on YHWH-Jireh (YHWH-Who-Provides) to meet all of their needs. The believer must stand with Messiah in his prayer:

"I do not pray for these alone, but also for those who will believe in Me through their word; that they all may be one, as You, Father, are in Me, and I in You; that they also may be one in Us, that the world may believe that You sent Me. And the glory which You gave Me I have given them, that they may be one just as We are one: I in them, and You in Me; that they may be made perfect in one, and that the world may know that You have sent Me, and have loved them as You have loved Me. (John 17:20-23 NKJV)

When the believer sees that unity in the Body isn't achievable without each member's union with the Head, only then is he ready to return to his siblings in helping to prepare for the Son's triumphant arrival. And return to the Body he must; for an isolated walk, left unchecked and discouraged, may engender an insolent one.

Behold, how good and pleasant it is when brothers dwell in unity. It is like the precious oil on the head, running down on the beard, on the beard of Aaron, running down on the collar of his robes. It is like the dew of Hermon, which falls on the mountains of Jerusalem. For there [YHWH] has commanded the blessing, life forevermore. (Psalms 133:1-3 ESV)

It is no easy task to trade in our insolence for intimacy with YHWH, but it is an essential one. The Holy Spirit is a gift to all believers, who is, being from the Father, the only one capable of capturing the essence of Messiah. Let all members thus seek the Spirit out, in order that all may be drawn in.

During this time he went out one day into the hills to pray, and spent the night in prayer to [YHWH]. (Luke 6:12 NEB)

142. Benefits of Belonging

First read: James 5:16

This is not your first winter. You will do well in remembering that this will not be your last. During an unexpected blizzard, not addressing either your fear of intimacy or independence where appropriate, could engender a snowball effect. You will find yourself quickly buried under, while bringing others to their death along the way. Winter comes and winter goes, shorting day for night. Through even the darkest hour, it sharpens still your sight. A sharpened sight will allow you to appreciate all the beauty that abounds in spring.

We can only begin to take advantage of the benefits of belonging when we realize to whom and what we belong. The first part requires acknowledging that we, in fact, belong to someone else; never have we belonged to ourselves. Prior to accepting Messiah as our Lord and Savior, we belonged to this world and to the temporary ruler of this world, that is, Satan.

Formerly, when you did not acknowledge [YHWH], you were slaves of beings which in their nature are no gods. (Galatians 4:8 NEB)

When we accepted Messiah, we also accepted a new Master, for we were purchased with his blood on the cross. But we have a benevolent Master who desires for us to accept him as much more. While we were still sinners, we were slaves to sin. Yet, the chains that once bound us are still visible and within our reach. To live for Messiah is to daily make the decision to leave the chains on the ground. The longer they stay, the more likely they are to disintegrate. But the chains will remain there for the longest time; not always to tempt, but to remind. The chains remind us of how powerless we were while in bondage. The chains remind us of how pointless our life was; for while in chains we weren't living, but merely existing.

And you, my brothers, like Isaac, are children of [YHWH]'s promise. But just as in those days the natural-born son persecuted the spiritual son, so it is today. But what does Scripture say? "Cast out this slave woman with her son, for the son of this slave woman shall not be heir with my son Isaac." You see, then, my brothers, we are no slave-woman's children; our mother is the free woman. [Messiah] set us free, to be free men. Stand firm, then, and refuse to be tied to the yoke of slavery again. (Galatians 4:28-5:1 NEB)

Now that we have a new Master in Messiah Yeshua, we are to remember how powerful we are against the enemy. It is important for us to learn how to use the weapons given to us in dueling with the devil. More imperatively, we are also to remember how purposeful our life is in Messiah.

Once we accept Messiah, the journey isn't over, it's actually just beginning—only on a new path; narrower, hillier, and rockier. Herein are the benefits of belonging. As adopted sons and daughters of the Father, we now have a new family, one that will last for eternity. Pause to think about this significant truth. The body of believers we are building on earth will be the same Body we will fellowship with in

Heaven, forever. It is up to us to take advantage of the benefits of belonging. What meaningful group have you ever been a member of where a degree of transparency wasn't in order? All of the major support groups have several common themes. First, in the beginning, every new member is a little apprehensive about attending, and it takes a couple of meetings before the ice begins to melt. It's natural because it is a new environment and a new experience. Second, every new member is hesitant about sharing experiences, believing at first that no one can possibly relate to their story. In addition, there is concern of judgment in sharing one's hurts and hurdles. Third, after all initial fear has waned, healing is allowed to begin as masks come off. Authenticity is encouraged among members because all recognize that none have any place to go but up. Finally, encouragement and accountability are hallmarks which help make the recovery not just a possibility, but a reality. The road to recovery is certainly not an easy one; but knowing that the bumpy road doesn't have to be a lonely one makes the trip not only bearable, but worth it.

And because you are sons, [YHWH] has sent forth the Spirit into your hearts, crying out, "Abba, Father." Therefore you are no longer a slave but a son, and if a son, then an heir of [YHWH] through [Messiah]. (Galatians 4:6-7 NEB)

As Christians, we are all former addicts to sin. The church should be the place and the Church should be the Body we run to for support. Sadly, most Christians feel the most discomfort on Sunday mornings. Christians regularly discuss their disgust with church, out of concern of being judged. For many, if they do decide to go, every Sunday for them feels like the first time and so the ice never melts. And because the ice hasn't melted, there's no desire to share anything with anyone. Moreover, rarely do these members see the practice modeled in front of them; no one else is sharing so why should they, and how do they? Until a significant number of members in the Body begin to acknowledge how broken we are, and all come to recognize that none have any place to go but up, the Church will never be the vessel that Messiah intended it to be. The road we travel is the road less traveled, but traveled down before it has been. If while walking down the road, we would simply share our load; then others won't be apt to leave again. The Holy Spirit is waiting to heal. Is the Church ready?

Therefore, as opportunity offers, let us work for the good of all, especially members of the household of faith. (Galatians 6:10 ESV)

143. From Old to New: Only a Few

First read: Ezekiel 40-48

It is springtime. The clouds are beginning to separate once more and you can actually see the color blue. It occurs to you only briefly that you never appreciate the beauty in contrasting colors until you have spent a significant portion of your winters staring at clouds of monochrome. You will soon reflect over this revelation in greater detail. In the meantime you are thankful for the signs of life. Birds sing, heralding the arrival of their newborns. Flowers open tauntingly to reveal their first rounds of ripening fruit. And, the people around you are hastening their steps after miles of trek. Congratulations, you have survived another winter without freezing to death. Be thankful for the thaw. But you mustn't forget the duality of each season. In exchange for revamping, renewing your path, through the thawing and blooming of flowers, spring must insist that you partake amidst its purging and plentiful showers.

For the covenant I will make with the house of Israel after those days, says [YHWH], is this: I will set my laws in their understanding and write them on their hearts; and I will be their God, and they shall be my people. And they shall not teach one another, saying to brother and fellow-citizen, "Know the Lord!" For all of them shall know me, from small to great; I will be merciful to their wicked deeds, and their sins I will remember no more at all. By speaking of a new covenant, he has pronounced the first one old; and anything that is growing old and ageing will shortly disappear. (Hebrews 8:10-13 NEB)

Submission is the standard for acceptance onto the road to Glory. If we are to enjoy the new life which Messiah wills for his sheep to have, then we must accept that the old is no longer an option. It will always be in sight—in the open. But it must never be an option. The moment it becomes an option, we grant Satan free access to cloud our minds and our memories. After he clouds, he is then able to present a convincing argument of why the old (when our hearts were still cold) is, in fact, better than the new. Hence it is imperative for believers to realize that nothing Satan suggests is fact; it is all fictitious.

He told them this parable also: "No one tears a piece from a new cloth, to patch an old one; if he does, he will have made a hole in the new cloak, and the patch from the new will not match the old. Nor does anyone put new wine into old wine-skins; if he does, the new wine will burst the skins, the wine will be wasted, and the skins ruined. Fresh skins for new wine. And no one after drinking old wine wants new; for he says, 'The old wine is good.'" (Luke 5:36-39 NEB)

The necessity then, for the believer, is to submit his will entirely to the Father's gift of the Holy Spirit because the only thing acceptable is the new. It is the seed of sin still embedded within that desires to cling to the old. Thank YHWH for the boldness of the Spirit; the only one capable of squelching the seed still tied to the

313

Law. Once the Holy Spirit has captured the heart, our new options are now: Living life more abundantly or merely living, rejoicing while conforming or reluctantly complying. It marks a distinction between the Christian who thrives while being daily filled with the Holy Spirit and yielding to the Spirit's guidance, and the one content with surviving in being solely sealed with the Holy Spirit. Though it is Messiah's desire that we not settle for the latter, only a few choose the former.

> The thief does not come except to steal, and to kill, and to destroy. I have come that they may have life, and that they may have it more abundantly. (John 10:10 NKJV)

Precision is the prerequisite for walking the narrow road which leads to the gates of Glory.

> In visions of [YHWH] he brought me to the land of Israel, and set me down on a very high mountain, on which was a structure like a city to the south. When he brought me there, behold, there was a man whose appearance was like bronze, with a linen cord and a measuring reed in his hand. And he was standing in the gateway. And the man said to me, "Son of man, look with your eyes, and hear with your ears, and set your heart upon all that I shall show you, for you were brought here in order that I might show it to you. Declare all that you see to the house of Israel." (Ezekiel 40:2-4 ESV)

Apart from the construction of a building, Ezekiel was also afforded an opportunity to see the exactitude in building Yeshua's temple. The measurements were as specific then as the measurements for the rebuilding of our temple are now—Yeshua's temple still. Such conscientiousness in our rebuilding is necessary because the parameters Messiah has given must remain consistently in our conscious. Yes, we have room for error because of the Father's grace, but consistent carelessness can prove costly when our rebuilding time is finite. While admittedly uneasy, it is nevertheless demanded. But, it's also doable. Yet, only a few are doing, so only a few are actively renewing.

> But the priesthood which [Yeshua] holds is perpetual, because he remains for ever. That is why he is also able to save absolutely those who approach [YHWH] through him; he is always living to plead on their behalf. Such a high priest does indeed fit our condition—devout, guileless, undefiled, separated from sinners, raised high above the heavens. He has no need to offer sacrifices daily, as the high priests do, first for his own sins and then for those of the people; for this he did once and for all when he offered up himself. (Hebrews 7:24-27 NEB)

Perfection is the condition by which we are granted access to the gates of Glory to dwell for eternity with our High Priest. Many members, thankfully, are now no longer defeated. And the same are eager to behold the beauty of the completed, but are wholly disinterested with partaking in the pains of perfecting. From this they must purge. Messiah already partook in the pains; now, so must we. No rain? No gain because there's no growth. Rebuilding our temple will not always be fun, but the mundane will one day radiate magnificence; when our work is finally done. But only a few shall behold its splendor.

A pupil is not superior to his teacher; but everyone, when his training is complete, will reach his teacher's level. (Luke 6:40 NEB)

We are oppressed because we do not want to have the old body stripped off. Rather our desire is to have the new body put on over it, so that our mortal part may be absorbed into life immortal. [YHWH] himself has shaped us for this very end; and as a pledge of it he has given us the Spirit. (2nd Corinthians 5:4-5 NEB)

144. A Reflective Moment

His Best, Our Rest

First read: Leviticus 1-10

So Aaron drew near to the altar and killed the calf of the sin offering, which was for himself. And the sons of Aaron presented the blood to him, and he dipped his finger in the blood and put it on the horns of the altar and poured out the blood at the base of the altar. But the fat and the kidneys and the long lobe of the liver from the sin offering he burned on the altar, as [YHWH] commanded Moses. The flesh and the skin he burned up with fire outside the camp. Then he killed the burnt offering, and Aaron's sons handed him the blood, and he threw it against the sides of the altar. And they handed the burnt offering to him, piece by piece, and the head, and he burned them on the altar. And he washed the entrails and the legs and burned them with the burnt offering on the altar. (Leviticus 9:8-14 ESV)

Whole offering, shared offering, sin offering, guilt offering, etc, etc... Right? No doubt that it is once again tempting to dismiss these rituals as antiquated and irrelevant practices by a group of has-beens. Is this not what many in the Body find themselves suggesting when attempting to plow through the book of Leviticus? What on earth could the Holy Spirit want the believers of today's Church to glean from reading this third book of the Pentateuch? Well, for starters I think it best to admit that there are many who have come to believe that YHWH will accept anything less than our best. It is true that in coming to Messiah, nothing more than our worst is expected. In fact, when the decision is made to repent of our former selves, it is necessary that we bring before the feet of Messiah, the dirtiest of our dirt. However, afterwards, when he has made us a new creation and the Father has imparted within us the Holy Spirit, expectations change. No longer are we to simply come as we are, as if who we are hasn't changed from who we were. And when it is time to kneel before the throne of Messiah, our hands-on activities won't be an effective guise for an unchanged heart.

In sacrifice and offering you have not delighted, but you have given me an open ear. Burnt offering and sin offering you have not required. Then I said, "Behold, I have come; in the scroll of the book it is written of me: I delight to do your will, O [YHWH]; your law is within my heart. (Psalms 40:6-8 ESV)

After the building of the Tabernacle, YHWH instructed Moses and the Israelites on how to bring forth an offering to him. With the exception of a few, YHWH most often required the sacrificing of an unblemished animal for an offering to be rendered acceptable. Unblemished. The premise was that untainted blood was required for the expiation of a tainted or sinful act. However, not all offerings were propitiatory in nature. The burnt offering for example, a type of whole-offering, was dedicatory. Again, in most instances the offerings required the priests to not only use unblemished animals, they also were instructed to burn the best parts on the altar—most notably, the fat—while either eating or destroying the rest.

Thus we find that the former covenant itself was not inaugurated without blood. For when, as the Law directed, Moses had recited all the command-ments to the people, he took the blood of the calves, with water, scarlet wool, and marjoram, and sprinkled the law-book itself and all the people, saying, "This is the blood of the covenant which [YHWH] has [made with] you." In the same way he also sprinkled the tent and all the vessels of divine ser-vice with blood. Indeed, according to the Law, it might be said, everything is cleansed by blood and without the shedding of blood there is no forgiveness. (Hebrews 9:18-22 NEB)

We should offer endless praise to the Father for sending his best to die for the expiation of our sins. The Father's love for us, in spite of our sinful nature, was best illustrated by sending us the One who is of him. Messiah's redemption also guar-antees our rest. Because Yeshua died once and for all, thankfully the gory sacrificial rituals are not necessary for the present. We have been granted permission to simply come and kneel at his feet.

For you will not delight in sacrifice, or I would give it; you will not be pleased with a burnt offering. The sacrifices of [YHWH] are a broken spirit; a broken and contrite heart, [Yeshua], you will not despise. (Psalms 51:16-17 ESV)

Nonetheless, there is still work to be done. It is wise for believers to restrain from viewing their assigned tasks as mandatory labor, as if they were carrying out a sentence. Remember, you are a convert on patrol, not a convict on parole. Instead, each should view their missionary acts as dedicatory or thanksgiving offerings; an opportunity to return the Father's sentiment in sending us his best. Let us then, not seek to tire ourselves out during the day by engaging in mindless activities, so that by night we only have for an offering, the rest of us. Rather, in all that we do, we ought to give the Father, our best. And, in daily giving our best while on the road to Glory, there's the assurance of an eternal rest that awaits us at the end of our journey.

Offer to [YHWH] a sacrifice of thanksgiving, and perform your vows to [Yeshua]. (Psalms 50:14 ESV)

145. Pebble Patterns

First read: Ezekiel 9-16

In solidifying during the winter you want to make sure that you haven't hard-ened your heart. The temptation will be there, especially if you're still struggling with your fear of intimacy or independence. You will fear to frustration and bemoan to bitterness. Deal with it so you can embrace the freedom that comes in rejuvenating spring.

Do not love the world or the things in the world. If anyone loves the world, the love of the Father is not in him. For all that is in the world, the lust of the flesh, the lust of the eyes, and the pride of life—is not of the Father but is of the world. And the world is passing away, and the lust of it; but he who does the will of [YHWH] abides forever. (1st John 2:15-17 NKJV)

From time to time the temptation will arise to allow our lives to become patterned after pebbles. Even after a solidifying season when the Holy Spirit has been at work in strengthening those areas still weak, we still might not fully believe that YHWH isn't interested in having anything less than all of us. It is like the struggling married couple who, in the dead of winter, goes off to a cabin in the woods to repair what's broken. In the midst of their marriage the bridegroom discovered that though he had been faithful, his wife had become wayward. Yet, despite her adulterous affairs he was still committed to affirming his adoration. Unfortunately, not long into the weekend the bride begins to feel the pangs of resentment slowly swelling within her soul, as her husband's cry for greater intimacy is perceived as intrusive. Still, she says nothing of this to him, preferring instead to keep it inside. The weekend ends with the couple returning home. The bridegroom believes that progress was made and wishes they could've stayed longer. But the bride's heart has developed some bile, and if it stays for a while it'll grow stronger. Boulders are unbearable, but everyone else can see them and some may try to ease your burden. And yet the pebble is more painful. While tiny, it's still a stone; and when lodged in the center of the soul—where the heart lies—the effects are piercing.

But [Messiah] offered for all time one sacrifice for sins, and took his seat at the right hand of [YHWH], where he waits henceforth until his enemies are made his footstool. For by one offering he has perfected for all time those who are thus consecrated. (Hebrews 10:13-14 NEB)

If, as the Body of Messiah, we belong to the Bridegroom, we have no right to resent. At the very least we should express gratitude for his advances, despite the fact that, as a Body, we have a sad history of adultery.

Therefore, O prostitute, hear the word of [YHWH]: Thus says [Yeshua], "Because your lust was poured out and your nakedness uncovered in your whorings with your lovers, and with all your abominable idols, and because of the blood of your children that you gave to them, therefore, behold, 'I will gather all your lovers with whom you took pleasure, all those you loved and all those you hated. I will gather them against you from every side and will uncover your nakedness to them, that they may see all your nakedness. And I will judge you as women who commit adultery and shed blood are judged, and bring upon you the blood of wrath and jealousy. And I will give you into their hands, and they shall throw down your vaulted chamber and break down your lofty places. They shall strip you of your clothes and take your beautiful jewels and leave you naked and bare. They shall bring up a crowd against you, and they shall stone you and cut you to pieces with their swords. And they shall burn your houses and execute judgments upon you in the sight of many women. I will make you stop playing the whore, and you shall also give payment no more.' So will I satisfy my wrath on you, and my jealousy shall depart from you. I will be calm and will no more be angry. Because you have not remembered the days of your youth, but have enraged me with all these things, therefore, behold, I have returned your deeds upon your head, declares [Yeshua]. Have you not committed lewdness in addition to all your abominations?" (Ezekiel 16:35-43 ESV)

Messiah is indeed a jealous husband. Even a pebble takes up too much space for the place that Messiah wants to have in our hearts and in our lives. What we resent is that a relationship with Messiah means no secrets. We resent that we no longer belong to ourselves, but that we are now under the authority of a righteous Head. We resent that our new life with the Bridegroom means that many old relationships must die. Such resentment springs not from the Spirit, whom we received when we said, "I do," but from a flesh that is still fighting to win, and from the one who's still trying to woo. As our relationship with Messiah rebounds off the shaky ground we've stood, still a voice so small will speak of better routes. But any stone that separates the Bridegroom from his Bride, must quickly be a stone that we cut out.

Set me as a seal upon your heart, as a seal upon your arm; For love is as strong as death, Jealousy as cruel as the grave; Its flames are flames of fire, a most vehement flame. (Song of Songs 8:6 ESV)

You cannot be unaware, my friends—I am speaking to those who have some knowledge of law—that a person is subject to the law so long as he is alive, and no longer. For example, a married woman is by law bound to her husband while he lives; but if her husband dies, she is discharged from the obligations of the marriage-law. If, therefore, in her husband's lifetime she consorts with another man, she will incur the charge of adultery; but if her husband dies she is free of the law, and she does not commit adultery by consorting with another man. (Romans 7:1-3 NEB)

146. The Mysteries of Our Maker

First read: Jeremiah 33:1-26

Already you have come to recognize the reflective inducing power of rain through listening to its tranquil pour. Remember that inner tranquility can be achieved by concentrating on striking your chords of contentment, regardless of the rain's intensity.

But as it is written: "Eye has not seen, nor ear heard, Nor have entered into the heart of man The things which [YHWH] has prepared for those who love Him." 10 But [YHWH] has revealed them to us through His Spirit. For the Spirit searches all things, yes, the deep things of [YHWH]. For what man knows the things of a man except the spirit of the man which is in him? Even so no one knows the things of [YHWH] except the Spirit of [YHWH]. Now we have received, not the spirit of the world, but the Spirit who is from [YHWH], that we might know the things that have been freely given to us by [YHWH]. (1st Corinthians 2:9-12 NKJV)

It is time to debunk one of the worst myths that has ever been conjured up and allowed to infect the Body of Messiah. It is a myth that has infiltrated the ranks of Messiah's warriors for so long that members have become resolute in believing that anything contrary to their beliefs must be bogus. Unfortunately, its acceptance has created such a schism between YHWH and his children that Christians continue to struggle with identifying with their Father. What is the myth creating such rifts? That it is YHWH's desire that he remain a mystery to members of his household. While this perception of him clothes itself in reverence, it's ridiculous.

"You are my witnesses," says [YHWH], "and my servant whom I have chosen, that you may know and believe me, and understand that I am he. Before me there was no god formed, nor shall there be after me. I, even I, am [Yeshua], and besides me there is no savior. I have declared and saved, I have proclaimed, and there was no foreign god among you; therefore you are my witnesses," says [YHWH], "that I am [YHWH]. Indeed before the day was, I am he; and there is no one who can deliver out of my hand; I work, and who will reverse it?" (Isaiah 43:10-13 ESV)

No one has ever seen [YHWH]; but [YHWH]'s only Son, he who is nearest to the Father's heart, he has made him known. (John 1:18 NEB)

Why would YHWH keep himself hidden from his children? We acknowledge the Scripture which points to Messiah as the image of the invisible YHWH, which suggests accepting that the Father did mean for family members to know him. Nevertheless, we have well-meaning shepherds who teach their flock that YHWH's ways are unknowable. It is not that they are unknowable, but that they are on a need-to-know basis. There is some information that YHWH has decreed should only get disseminated according to his perfect timetable; we won't know beforehand, because we don't need to know. YHWH knows that sharing such ahead of time will only disrupt the plans he's already fashioned. Yet, there is knowledge about the Father and his purposes that he wants to share, if any of his children would care to inquire. And those who belong to Messiah have been given his mind, and hence, the capacity to understand.

And because we are interpreting spiritual truths to those who have the Spirit, we speak of these gifts of [YHWH] in words found for us not by our human wisdom but by the Spirit. A man who is unspiritual refuses what belongs to the Spirit of [YHWH]; it is folly to him; he cannot grasp it, because it needs to be judged in the light of the Spirit. A man gifted with the Spirit can judge the worth of everything, but is not himself subject to judgment by his fellow-men. For (in the words of Scripture) "Who knows the mind of [Yeshua]? Who can advise him?" We, however, posses the mind of [Yeshua]. (1st Corinthians 2:13-16 NEB)

It is only to those who persist in sin that access to the Father has been denied, and thus his ways will remain a mystery. But to all others:

Adapt yourselves no longer to the pattern of this present world, but let your minds be remade and your whole nature thus transformed. Then you will be able to discern the will of [YHWH], and to know what is good, acceptable, and perfect. (Romans 12:2 NEB)

There is a rare peace which is only experienced in knowing YHWH fully in all of his knowable ways. However, it is impossible to embrace such peace, and thus unfeasible to intimately connect with the Father, without Messiah and the Holy Spirit. The Father wants his children to know more of him, not less. Scripture provides the basis for understanding his character. Members of the Body would feel far less disconnected from the Father if they would connect more with the Bible. There are some hidden truths in Scripture, but only for those who insist on hiding. For all the rest who have turned to him who is real, it takes but a request of the Father to unlock what only the Spirit can reveal. Only the Holy Spirit has the ability to make the mysteries of our Maker make sense. It was Messiah's prayer that his disciples share the same union that he has with the Father; his death on the cross made it possible. Now it is up to the members of his Body to make the next move.

Grace and peace be yours in fullest measure, through the knowledge of [YHWH] and [Yeshua]. His divine power has bestowed on us everything that makes for life and true religion, enabling us to know the One who called us by his own splendor and might. Through this might and splendor he has given us his promises, great beyond all price, and through them you may escape the corruption with which lust has infected the world, and come to share in the very being of [YHWH]. (2nd Peter 1:2-4 NEB)

147. Sin: Walking With vs. Walking In

First read: Ezekiel 33-34

You will have numerous encounters with nature's roguery, so be prepared. Prepare yourself for those days during the spring when the sky will be blue, yet the drops will accrue. Those days during the spring when the sun is close up, but the rain won't let up. Spring offers the distinct gift, in greater vividness than the other three seasons, of teaching you how to deal with the greatest puzzle and struggle on your journey—your desire to remain standing and to continue traveling on the road to Glory, conflicted with your propensity to fall down or wander off while walking. For you will have days where the sun shines down, lighting your path that darkness tries to hide. Concurring, the rain will fall, dousing and drenching in washing your dirt aside. The sun will shine in radiance to warm you and to warn you. Warning you not to venture off in a direction where its rays are not illuminating, as well as signaling where to step in specific areas where its rays are illuminating. It makes sense to you. You know that you haven't been afforded infinite time to reach your destination. You know that you haven't time to waste on detours or unnecessary pitfalls. You know that you aren't someone who desires or enjoys hardship. Nevertheless, in wondering you will find yourself wandering. With the luggage you'll haul, there will be days you do fall.

When first we begin our journey on the road to Glory, we are excited.

For the created universe waits with eager expectation for [YHWH]'s sons to be revealed. It was made the victim of frustration, not by its own choice, but because of him who made it so; yet always there was hope, because the universe itself is to be freed from the shackles of mortality and enter upon the liberty and splendor of the children of [YHWH]. (Romans 8:19-21 NEB)

But then we begin to walk. It isn't until we have gone a few miles that we begin to feel slightly fatigued. While tolerable, it is nonetheless irritating. "Could it possibly be the seed of sin wedged between my soul and me?" How can something so tiny be so weighty? For the believer, perhaps one of the more difficult truths to grip is the reality of the sin still lodged within.

I confess my iniquity; I am sorry for my sin. (Psalms 38:18 ESV)

Many members within the Body have come to grasp this truth. However, most don't like to grip it. Good. We would exist not in our present condition if only Adam and Eve had refused to grip in the Garden. But they did. Christians of today have no power to change the cause of our condition, and only Messiah has the power to change the effects. What choice, then, is left for the believer? To remain grounded, rooted, and attached to the Vine. And yet even with our attachment to the Son, the rains will still fall and the winds will still blow. "Does that mean that the seed to which I was bound will still grow?" No. At least it is not compelled to.

If we claim to be sinless, we are self-deceived and strangers to the truth. (1st John 1:8 NEB)

There is a difference between walking with sin and walking in it. Before knowing Messiah, sin saturates man. But after accepting Messiah as Lord and Savior, man is saturated in the blood of the Lamb which covers sin's multiple faces. It is Messiah's blood that keeps the seed from germinating. His robe of righteousness keeps the blood from drying out. What's more, members must remember that with the gift of the Holy Spirit come new seeds, each capable of bearing sustaining good fruit. It is the blood of Messiah which activates these seeds as well. What determines which seeds the believer will walk in is whether or not he or she keeps wearing Messiah's robe. It takes time and instruction to learn how to endure the heat and weight of his robe. It also takes time to grow into it. Until endurance has developed, the propensity will remain for believers to take it off regularly. Immediately his blood begins to dry and the seed of sin takes root again, and it will begin to pull you down. And before too long the seeds of sin will have you on the ground, on the side of the road.

I will greatly rejoice in [YHWH]; my soul shall exult in [Yeshua], for he has clothed me with the garments of salvation; he has covered me with the robe of righteousness, as a bridegroom decks himself like a priest with a beautiful headdress, and as a bride adorns herself with her jewels. (Isaiah 61:10 ESV)

What will make you distinguishable as one of Messiah's sheep, when he returns, is not what once you were doing when you actually wore his robe, but, rather, will you still have it on when he returns? Have no fear; you are secure from Satan's thievery. He can't yank off what was given to you. But he laughs every time you do. It is the shepherd's responsibility to care for Messiah's sheep and to make sure that each are growing into his or her robe. He will hold each accountable for their reckless disregard. Though, admittedly, it's difficult to discern whether the sheep haven't grown, if the shepherd is still too small for his own.

148. ThanksLiving

First read: Psalms 42-50

With prudence you won't plan for your occasional departure or trip; but when it happens you will find yourself in anguish. Some of the anguish will actually benefit, as it forces you to reflect over and perhaps acknowledge any contributions you may have made in making the trip a success. You won't like how you feel—dirty, inside and out. Thus you will aim to sharpen your acuity, tighten your shoestrings, and part existing company to prevent senseless, though costly, trips. However, in the midst of your anguish, you will begin to feel a fine mist that will develop into a drizzle and eventually progress into a pour. Remember that as you get back up, or back on track, any loose dirt will fall away on its own. Allow the rain to wash aside the dirt that is more resistant. It should comfort you to know that on the day you are dirtiest from falling into a mud hole, you have a cleansing opportunity anyway.

Through [Yeshua], then, let us continually offer up to [YHWH] the sacrifice of praise, that is, the tribute of lips which acknowledge his name, and never forget to show kindness and to share what you have with others; for such are the sacrifices which [YHWH] approves. (Hebrews 13:15-16 NEB)

At least once a year believers gather around the family table with thankful ardor to tell of their blessings. It is a sure time of ceremony, celebration, and for many, sincerity. Sadly, for most, it is also short-lived. YHWH takes no exception to the sincere heart which pauses briefly to acknowledge his role as provider, though he delights in the heart which daily recognizes this same truth. During Thanksgiving do we also give thanks to him who, in his providence, decides that in order to propel us farther along on the road to Glory, the occasional setback is necessary?

Oh come, let us sing to [YHWH]; let us make a joyful noise to the rock of our salvation. Let us come into his presence with thanksgiving; let us make a joyful noise to him with songs of praise. (Psalms 95:1-2 ESV)

Are we grateful that, for the moment, we are not yet spotless and are therefore recognizable to all those who still need help getting up out of the mud or off the sidelines? Are we appreciative of the times that we ask our Father for such and such, or so and so, and he says no because he understands that it won't help us to grow? How indebted are we to our Father for sending his only Son to die so that while still dying in filth, we might live through faith? We are thankful for our materials, but what about Messiah's misery?

Make a joyful noise to [YHWH], all the earth. Serve [Yeshua] with gladness. Come into his presence with singing. Know that [Yeshua], he is God. It is he who made us, and we are his; we are his people, and the sheep of his pasture. Enter his gates with thanksgiving, and his courts with praise. Give thanks to him; bless his name. For [Yeshua] is good; his steadfast love endures forever, and his faithfulness to all generations. (Psalms 100:1-5 ESV)

It is difficult for some in the Body to consider thanking YHWH at any juncture on their journey other than on a festive holiday, because they have never been taught to do otherwise. Others have little trouble considering, but great difficulty with consistency. These members affirm the importance and can appreciate the habit of regularly giving YHWH what is due; yet, they struggle with following through. Why? Because a genuine relationship with God Almighty and Messiah has to go beyond affirming and appreciating, it has to be adoring. When giving thanks, believers affirm and appreciate internally, and their righteous speech is the external manifestation. However, the true believer shows evidence of living thankfully by living righteously. Our adoration of the Father allows for no division between the internal or external, because it has less to do with behavior and everything to do with identity. Christians were created to adore and to do no more. We are worshipful beings. Prior to Messiah's death on the cross we worshiped self, the world, and the present ruler of this world. Every action, word, and thought was an illustration of our idolatry. Thankfully, the Father sent his Son, Yeshua Messiah, to justify our sinful selves so that we could continue what Adam and Eve could not.

But the time approaches, indeed it is already here, when those who are real worshipers will worship the Father in spirit and in truth. Such are the worshipers whom the Father wants. [YHWH] is spirit, and those who worship him must worship in spirit and in truth. (John 4:23-24 NEB)

As a believer, how thankful are you to YHWH for such an opportunity? How often do you tell him? How often do you show him? On Thanksgiving, then, let us give thought to distinguishing between manifested mouthfuls and reflected righteousness.

Oh come, let us worship and bow down; let us kneel before [YHWH] our Maker. For he is [YHWH], and we are the people of his pasture, and the sheep of his hand. (Psalms 95:6-7a ESV)

149. An Interlude for Thanksgiving

First read: 1st Thessalonians 5:16-18 / Psalms 50:23

From the moment you arise in the morning,
you're greeted by the sun so bright—
Take some time out to thank Yeshua,
who gave you the gift of sight

As you rise from the ground to reach for the sky,
look first to your hands and then feet—
Take some time to thank the Maker,
who made your body complete

As you're walking along and gazing above,
admiring birds, the clouds, and sun—
Take some time to thank the Creator,
whose work is second to none

Some days will prove more perilous;
you will see nothing but rain and wind—
Still take some time to thank the Sustainer,
Who took the time to send

If ever you fail to receive what you want
never should you fall prey to greed
Instead, take some time to thank YHWH-jireh,
who'll forever supply what you need

Never should you feel need to walk in despair,
although at night the lights will fade
From dawn until dusk you should thank Yeshua,
who in dimness so dark still made

While on the road to Glory,
there will be times of tears and strife
Still give some time to the generous Savior,
the One who gave you life

I thank you, Father, for who you are
I thank you for your only Son
I thank you for the Holy Spirit
You're our God who is second to none

150. A Reflective Moment

Cha-Ching $$

First read: 1st Peter 2:16

And now, as you see, I am on my way to Jerusalem, under the constraint of the Spirit. Of what will befall me there I know nothing, except that in city after city the Holy Spirit assures me that imprisonment and hardships await me. For myself, I set no store by life; I only want to finish the race, and complete the task which [Yeshua] assigned to me, of bearing my testimony to the gospel of [YHWH]'s grace. (Acts 20:22-24 NEB)

Do you believe that you've hit the jackpot now that Messiah has entered your life? Did part of your conversion conversation sound a little like this? "Christ-died-to-save-you-from-the-clutches-of death-and-his-grace-is-more-than-sufficient-to-forgive-you-of-all-your-sins." Again, I think that for many newly converts, grace is an alluring word. And for veterans it is a word often abused. For both categories and for many in between, it remains misunderstood. The grace of YHWH most visibly became manifested through his Son, by his death on the cross. I believe this was the most gracious act in recorded history. For YHWH's grace is always undeserved. Until we become humble enough to accept this fact, we will continuously abuse it. It is painful to hear stories of past where new members of the Body share how they came from some unforgiving circumstances.

Personally, grace was never a word that entered my vocabulary until my relationship with Messiah solidified. My mother was a career military official for roughly the first thirteen years of my life. Perhaps the worst times came while she served as a drill sergeant in the U. S. Army. As a drill sergeant it was not my mother's job to distribute grace, it was to get basic training cadets into shape via discipline. Sadly, my mother brought her work home with her. Hence, discipline was a regular member of our household. I didn't revere my mother; I was afraid of her. I not only feared being disobedient, the thought of making a mistake petrified me. Yet, I made many, nonetheless. Undoubtedly, there are members of the Body who can relate to my own experiences. In some ways it's unfortunate that we take our unpleasant experiences with us when we first meet Messiah. Yes, Messiah welcomes all that we bring him, and he wants to assure all that there is nothing we can bring him that he hasn't taken before, and that he isn't willing to accept now. What's unfortunate is that many attempt to displace their distorted reflections of the past unto the perfect image of Messiah. I tried and sometimes still do. A small but significant truth: Messiah can never be any more or any less than he is. If we are to make any substantial gains in our relationship with him, we have to believe that he is a gracious Master.

For all alike have sinned, and are deprived of the divine splendor, and all are justified by [YHWH]'s free grace alone, through his act of liberation in the person of [Yeshua]. For [YHWH] designed him to be the means of expiating sins by his sacrificial death, effective through faith. [YHWH] meant by this to demonstrate his justice, because in his forbearance he had overlooked the sins of the past—to demonstrate his justice now in the present, showing that he is himself just and also justifies any man who puts his faith in [Yeshua]. (Romans 3:23-26 NEB)

When we invite him into our lives it should be a time of joy, not trepidation. For we have entered into an eternal covenant; been adopted into an eternal family, and have escaped an eternal judgment, that is the Great White Throne. Moreover, we can begin our new journey with confidence, knowing with certainty that if we should happen to stumble and fall into a hole, our Father will graciously greet us at the door of repentance. There is another side to the coin, though. There is a distinction between stumbling into a hole and jumping feet first. There are many Christians who mistakenly believe that each time they jump in, the Father is required to hold out his hand to lift them out; that the New Covenant conveys such a message. "After all," they say, "he is gracious and his grace is sufficient." Sounds Christian right? Well, God Almighty's grace is sufficient, but it is not infinite, there will, in fact, come a time when it is no longer available. Unless members of the Body come to understand this truth then true repentance will continue to be met with resistance. Without genuine repentance the soul is still in bondage, no matter how loose the chains appear. Until the chains have been completely removed, it is impossible to walk fully in the Spirit. Accepting Messiah into your life doesn't mean you've hit the jackpot. Start off viewing him in this light and the odds will continue to stack up against you. Continue to view Messiah in the same light and you will soon find yourself spiritually bankrupt.

151. Inconsistently Intimate

First read: Nahum 1-3

Even the rain won't wash aside the dirt's residue, especially if the sun, with its own prerogative, decided that today was the day to radiate its warmth.

For the Ninevites that warmth radiated in 612 B.C. though Jonah had warned them of their sin over a hundred years prior. At that point, they repented and turned from their sins:

So the people of Nineveh believed [YHWH], proclaimed a fast, and put on sackcloth, from the greatest to the least of them. Then word came to the king of Nineveh; and he arose from his throne and laid aside his robe, covered himself with sackcloth and sat in ashes. And he caused it to be proclaimed and published throughout Nineveh by the decree of the king and his nobles, saying, "Let neither man nor beast, herd nor flock, taste anything; do not let them eat, or drink water. But let man and beast be covered with sackcloth, and cry mightily to [YHWH]; yes, let every one turn from his evil way and from the violence that is in his hands. Who can tell if [YHWH] will turn and relent, and turn away from his fierce anger, so that we may not perish?" Then [YHWH] saw their works, that they turned from their evil way; and [YHWH] relented from the disaster that he had said he would bring upon them, and he did not do it. (Jonah 3:5-10 ESV)

The Assyrians repented and YHWH relented, but then they returned to their sins again. They went back on their word and so YHWH went back to his. There are multitudes within the Body who mistakenly believe that the lip service they paid to Messiah when they first believed will keep them from receiving his rod. As such, they are content in being inconsistently intimate with the Father. Much of their contentment stems from the false security many shepherds adorn them with: "As long as you confess and profess then you will forever be blessed, and protected by the Prince of Peace." It does have a ring of rightness doesn't it? Except that it's wrong. Messiah's protection isn't contingent upon a single profession, but upon our continual professing. As the Father's gift to Messiah's disciples, the Holy Spirit is an enabler and an encourager, but is not an enforcer. Thus, while sovereign and capable of intervening at will, the Spirit nevertheless refrains from imposing until invited, and even then the main objective is to disclose the will of the Son, and then to equip and enable us to get the job done. However, the decision to comply remains our own.

When the Son of Man comes in his glory (his majesty and splendor), and all the holy angels with him, then he will sit on the throne of his glory. All nations will be gathered before him, and he will separate them [the people] from one another as a shepherd separates his sheep from the goats; And he will cause the sheep to stand at his right hand, but the goats at his left. Then the King will say to those at his right hand, Come, you blessed of my Father [you favored of {YHWH} and appointed to eternal salvation], inherit (receive as your own) the kingdom prepared for you from the foundation of the world. For I was hungry and you gave me food, I was thirsty and you gave me something to drink, I was a stranger and you brought me together with yourselves and welcomed and entertained and lodged me, I was naked and you clothed me, I was sick and you visited me with help and ministering care, I was in prison and you came to see me. (Matthew 25:31-36 AMP)

What motivation does Messiah have to reward, if his disciples choose not to feed, quench, house, clothe, aide, or visit, but instead are coerced into doing so? No, we can choose or refuse to do those good deeds. Likewise, we can refuse to comply with Messiah's rules for righteousness, loudly declaring our disinterest in remaining intimate with him. When we do—when our disobedience clogs our ears and so all that we hear from the Holy Spirit begins to sound like dissonance—then disaster is close at hand. It is arrogant for any disciple to believe that Messiah is obligated to protect the prodigal—the faithless. Scripture promises the prodigal neither provisions nor protection. There is, however, a perpetual plea for the prodigal to fall prostrate, and then a promise of a pardon. It is an act of grace that YHWH should induce prostration among his prodigal people. For better now to be drenched in dew—to be made new—than to wait for the Son's return and hear him say to you: "We're through."

If his children forsake my law and do not walk according to my rules, if they violate my statutes and do not keep my commandments, then I will punish their transgression with the rod and their iniquity with stripes, but I will not remove from him my steadfast love or be false to my faithfulness. I will not violate my covenant or alter the word that went forth from my lips. (Psalms 89:30-34 ESV)

He who believes in him is not condemned; but he who does not believe is condemned already, because he has not believed in the name of the only begotten Son of [YHWH]. (John 3:18 NKJV)

The inheritance to which we are born is one that nothing can destroy or spoil or wither. It is kept for you in heaven, and you, because you put your faith in [YHWH], are under the protection of his power until salvation comes—the salvation which is even now in readiness and will be revealed at the end of time. (1st Peter 1:4-5 NEB)

152. When The Going Gets Tough

First read: Psalms 130:5

As you continue to journey you may seek relief from your pestilent inner conflict. You walk off the road foolishly, though you want to stay on. You fall down, though the predictable and equally undesirable throbbing of your scraped knees confirms that you would rather remain standing. It may help you to deal with your conflict by realizing that you're walking on temporal ground that you'll be walking on only temporarily. Relief is only a few miles away; just keep walking.

Then one of the elders answered, saying to me, "Who are these arrayed in white robes, and where did they come from?" And I said to him, "Sir, you know." So he said to me, "These are the ones who come out of the great tribulation, and washed their robes and made them white in the blood of the Lamb. Therefore they are before the throne of [YHWH], and serve him day and night in his temple. And he who sits on the throne will dwell among them. They shall neither hunger anymore nor thirst anymore; the sun shall not strike them, nor any heat; for the Lamb who is in the midst of the throne will shepherd them and lead them to living fountains of waters. And [YHWH] will wipe away every tear from their eyes." (Revelation 7:13-17 NEB)

What are we to do when the going gets tough? Recognize that it is a part of the Father's plan, and that if Messiah was able to endure while walking in the flesh, then we, who have been gifted with the Holy Spirit and grace, also have the ability to persevere. For Heaven's sake we must. There will exist thousands of external stimuli that will attempt to steer the believer in the wrong direction. But as long as our senses remain sharpened from praying persistently and daily devoting ourselves to Scripture, then the stimuli cannot make us stumble. Much stumbling stems from not allowing the Holy Spirit to have complete control over the will. Referring to the seed of sin, the eager believer says, "Yes, part permanently." Messiah, in his wisdom says, "No, part continuously." There is nothing wrong with the prayer, except that members of the Body fail to understand its implications. The Son wants nothing more than for his creation to ask the Father for a heart replacement. Such a request shows an acknowledgment that when born, our heart was already torn. And thus in its fractured condition, we were all dead upon delivery. But thanks to the Father for sending us his best so that immediately upon request we are revived to be restored.

Blessed be [YHWH], the Father of [Yeshua], who according to his abundant mercy has begotten us again to a living hope through the resurrection of [Yeshua] from the dead. (1st Peter 1:3a NEB)

How awesome that even though dead upon delivery, we should be delivered from death. There is indeed a reason to shout. Believers should bask in this joy during the moments when they become frustrated with their flesh. The request for a willing spirit is really a request for the Holy Spirit to take charge of your will, so that when the flesh becomes pesky, the former can put it to rest. This is the victory promised to us by Messiah. There is soon coming a day when all believers will indeed part with sin permanently, but until that day arrives we must continue to die. Delivered from death in order to die daily?

This perishable being must be clothed with the imperishable, and what is mortal must be clothed with immortality. And when our mortality has been clothed with immortality, then the saying of the Scriptures will come true: "Death is swallowed up; victory is won!'" O Death, where is your victory? O Death, where is your sting?" The sting of death is sin, and sin gains its power from the law; but, [YHWH] be praised, he gives us the victory through our Lord [Yeshua]. Therefore, my beloved brothers, stand firm and immovable, and work for [Yeshua] always, work without limit, since you know that in [Yeshua] your labor cannot be lost. (1st Corinthians 15:53-58 NEB)

While fighting with our flesh will, at times, seem more irksome than at others, it is essential that believers recognize that the fight is fleeting. It is also bearable. It is bearable because Messiah says that it is and because he has not left his sheep bereft. Two gifts that remain largely untouched by members who need them so much: The Holy Spirit and the Church. When the going gets tough then believers have some place to go; and a Helper who will not only lead them there, but if they are hungry and humble enough, they have a Helper who will also meet them there.

If you love me, keep my commandments. And I will pray to the Father, and he will give you another Helper, that he may abide with you forever—the Spirit of truth, whom the world cannot receive, because it neither sees nor knows the Spirit; but you know the Spirit, for the Spirit dwells with you and will be in you. I will not leave you orphans; I will come to you. (John 14:15-18 NKJV)

153. Living Out Loud: The Spirit Filled Church IV

First read: 1st Corinthians 12:4-11

In the meantime, enjoy the gifts of spring with the showers it brings. After a tough winter you should be reinvigorated for repairing, as signs of renewal up high remind you of what you are reaching for down below. It won't be long now. Summer is around the corner with some encouraging gifts from the sun. If winter, in its chill, kept you alert and on track, then summer will propel with its blaze on your back.

Once awakened, it is impossible to go about the business of rebuilding the Church without the use of effective tools. Consider this: most well-meaning bodies remain at the foundational level for any number of reasons. There are some churches who insist on trying to establish a new foundation, rather than building on the one that has already firmly been set into place; first by Yeshua Messiah, and then by his apostles. They are wasting valuable time attempting to reinvent a wheel that isn't taking them anyplace at all. Only they can't see it. If, in wisdom, someone attempts to relay some truth, their efforts are rebuffed with accusations of "adhering too much to tradition" or "being stuck in the past." The truth is that these traditions, as established by the early church leaders, need revisiting. Their traditions proved quite effective in healing the sick, saving the lost, sighting the blind, encouraging the faint, strengthening the weak, and raising the dead. Some shepherds, in discarding the old as obsolete, are rendering their flock useless, and instead are ensuring that they all remain stuck in the mud.

Take heed unto yourselves, and to all the flock, in which the Holy Spirit hath made you bishops, to feed the church of the [Yeshua] which he purchased with his own blood. I know that after my departing grievous wolves shall enter in among you, not sparing the flock;and from among your own selves shall men arise, speaking perverse things, to draw away the disciples after them. Wherefore watch ye, remembering that by the space of three years I ceased not to admonish every one night and day with tears. (Acts 20:28-31 ASV)

Stand firm, then, brothers, and hold fast to the traditions which you have learned from us by word or by letter. And may [Yeshua] himself and [YHWH] the Father, who has shown us such love, and in his grace has given us such unfailing encouragement and such bright hopes, still encourage and fortify you in every good deed and word. (2nd Thessalonians 2:15-17 NEB)

Another reason a body may remain at the foundational level is that while they have an understanding and have accepted the principles that have long been set, they are clueless as to how to proceed to the next level. The Holy Spirit provides insight into building the walls, as well as the doorways and the windows. In addition, the Spirit equips every member of the Church with the specific skills each will need while rebuilding. However, if the body who's been sealed, but who has not yet been filled with the Spirit, has not received baptism, the process becomes stagnant. What you could have is a multitude of eager workers with no blueprint. The Spirit-filled body understands that the Holy Spirit is the foreman who is the giver of all tools. The Holy Spirit knows precisely how the Son created each member of the crew and for what purpose. In knowing the mind of Yeshua, the Holy Spirit accurately distributes each tool in the right season, for the right reason. Without the Holy Spirit's filling, and hence, active participation, it is impossible to effectively rebuild the Church. And while Messiah takes delight in the worker with eager hands, he shakes his head in sorrow at those who attempt to build without tools. Bare hands work, but significantly retard the process and only result in unnecessary and unintended bruising.

> There are varieties of gifts, but the same Spirit of [YHWH]. There are varieties of service, but the same [Yeshua]. There are many forms of tasks, but all of them, in all men, are the work of the same [YHWH]. In each of us the Spirit is manifested in one particular way, for some useful purpose. One man, through the Spirit, has the gift of wise speech, while another, by the power of the same Spirit, can put the deepest knowledge into words. Another, by the same Spirit, is granted faith; another, by the one Spirit, gifts of healing, and another miraculous powers; another has the gift of prophecy, and another ability to distinguish true spirits from false; yet another has the gift of ecstatic utterance of different kinds, and another the ability to interpret it. But all these gifts are the work of one and the same Spirit, distributing them separately to each individual at will. (1st Corinthians 12:4-11 NEB)

Perhaps the most damaging reason a body will remain at the foundational level is because they insist on building with man-made tools, rather than with the tools that only the Holy Spirit can provide. To build a spiritual Body with man-made tools is foolish indeed. Messiah is holy and righteous and he expects his Body to reflect. Man, absent of the Holy Spirit's power, is deficient and thus so becomes everything he attempts to use in building. These bodies can't understand why their walls keep crumbling, why their windows continue cracking, and why their framing keeps failing. Messiah will either tear them down himself or allow the enemy to tear; continuing to take them back to the foundation; bringing them back to their knees—on the ground until they get it. Human efforts will always result in human failures. Except that with the Church, there are always spiritual consequences as well. The Holy Spirit is urging all members of the Body (those members whom have already been sealed) to receive the gift of baptism, so that all might become spiritually empowered and equipped to rebuild the Church. The Spirit-filled body is a purposeful body, and with its imparted power it is able to move prayerfully, to act passionately, and to build powerfully. Paul, in speaking to a group of Spirit-sealed converts in the churches of Ephesus, says:

> Do not give way to drunkenness and the dissipation that goes with it, but let the Holy Spirit fill you: speak to one another in psalms, hymns, and songs; sing and make music in your hearts to [Yeshua]; and in the name of [Yeshua] give thanks every day for everything to [YHWH] our Father. (Ephesians 5:18-20 NEB)

154. House of Healing

First read: Matthew 7:24-27 / 1st Corinthians 3:1-15

There's a humble house that stands atop a humble hill
Built to house the humble, the sick, and the lost
The Carpenter who crafted perfected his skill
By dying atop a wooden cross

Each jagged nail they pounded through his skin
Built one more layer where dried dirt had been
Brick by brick with blood that spilled to seal
Was how the house was built to save and heal

The Architect who drew the unique design
Knew that some would soon think it less than ideal
But the ones who were truly desperate to feel
It was these he had in mind

But what's happened to that humble house intended to protect?
Why is there broken glass atop the wooden floors?
Where is the multitude the Carpenter envisioned to perfect?
And why are there now a plethora of doors?

Who is responsible for letting evil dwell?
Who is to blame for the decomposing smell?
When did the house become a half-way house of buy?
When did the house become a sore spot to the eye?

How come more floors exist, each with their own name?
When did the house become a home to those who lie?
How come the Carpenter's house no longer looks the same?
While an "eastern wind" is brewing with foul aim?

The humble house atop the hill is now full of wears and tears
The Carpenter is pleading for immediate repairs
Before this storm tears down his house—
frame by frame

There is no time for second guessing
No time for window dressing
No time for pointing fingers with judgment at the end
No time for wondering if your works will offend

The house must rid itself of squatters who protest
The rules for repairing must never bend again
No allowing for complacency every now and then
Ignore those who will watch and laugh at you in jest

The rebuilding guide for the humble house remains, for most, unused
This, despite the fact that most can read
The work, though vast, can hasten, if the tenants invite the bruised
And if the tenants will mature and take the lead

(continued)

If the foremen will commit to utter truth
If the foremen will commit to raise the youth
If the foremen will refrain from pedantic orations
If the foremen will refrain from commanding undue adulation

If the tenants learn to use the tools the Carpenter did leave
If the foremen will recapture those bereft in isolation
And assuage the doubts of all those tenets filled with consternation
If the tenants learn to love all guests the house receives

Then the house that sits atop the hill will weather any storm
The builders' work will stand through holy fire
The Carpenter doesn't care if his house depicts the norm
All builders would be wise to avoid his ire

Let all the sick come in
Regardless of where they may have been
But keep out those who refuse a cure
Before all those well become impure

Tear down walls that foster separate lives
Keep the house hospitable for those who come to tour
If the guests decide to stay then ensure that they mature
Be ready to take their baggage, the moment each arrive

The humble house atop the hill must be a house of hope for all
It must be a house of unity and not a house for brawl
This house of hope must arm itself from those who prowl at night
It must be filled with tenants who have learned to stand and fight

The Carpenter will soon return to test what has been laid
He doesn't wish to come enraged and with charges to indict
But to all whose work either helps or harms
he is certain to repay

155. **Bon Appétit**

First read: Hebrews 5:12 - 6:3

Can you handle the heat? This is the question you should be asking yourself as spring parts company. If the answer is no, then you're in luck. Does summer ever have the gift for you. While walking, you will need to learn how to withstand heat. There will be some days where the sun's rays will seem merciless. And unfortunately, summer doesn't guarantee the luxury of allowing for the daily relief found in earth's tears.

"Yeshua loves me this I know, for the Bible tells me so. Little ones to him belong, they are weak, but he is strong. Yes, Yeshua loves me. Yes, Yeshua loves me. Yes, Yeshua loves me. For the Bible tells me so."

Incidentally, the Bible also tells us more. Such truth is awesome indeed. And as Christians, it benefits us to remain cognizant of the potency of Yeshua's love for us. If you are witnessing to an unbeliever who's worried that his or her past life-style is too much for Messiah to bear, inform them that at one point he bore an even heavier burden. They need to know that the price he paid covered a multitude of sins and that theirs is none too great for Yeshua to forgive. If, as a believer, you find yourself in the midst of doubt, as it's doubtless that such times will arise, then a gentle reminder is in order. God Almighty is always in control and remains loving for eternity.

Consider and hear me, [YHWH]; enlighten my eyes, lest I sleep the sleep of death, lest my enemy say, "I have prevailed against him," lest those who trouble me rejoice when I am moved. But I have trusted in your mercy; my heart shall rejoice in your salvation. I will sing to [YHWH], because he has dealt bountifully with me. (Psalms 13:3-6 NKJV)

However, if you're a seasoned Christian, and yet are still solely relying on the opening lyrics to sustain your relationship with the Father, then you're on your way to being spit out; in losing your flavor—you need more salt. Actually, before you get more salt you need to ask yourself, "What do I have to put it on?" If the answer is nothing but a glass of milk, then you have an even bigger problem. It is doubtful anyone would enjoy drinking a glass of milk in which even a teaspoon of salt has been added. Peter does remind us in his first letter to the Jewish converts that we must thirst for milk for our soul's nourishment. Peter is also speaking to an audience of recent converts. In the book of Hebrews, however, the author believes that grown men, that is, members of the Body who have matured in their relationship with Yeshua, should have the ability to digest solid food, because they are old enough to understand the difference between right and wrong, good and evil. Those who have matured in their faith should already have a grasp on the foundations of faith; the significance of repentance; the power of prayer; the deliverance of the dead through bodily resurrection; and eternal judgment.

The truth is that there are indeed members of the Body who have been walking for a while and haven't been introduced to any of the aforementioned principles that the author of Hebrews calls the rudiments of Christianity. These members have only been drinking milk. No wonder you're sluggish; you're spiritually emaciated. No need to turn on the television to see what starvation looks like; many of us need only to look in the mirror. The truth is that there are multitudes in Africa with more meat on their bones.

> [Yeshua] answered, "I tell you this: the truth is, not that Moses gave you the bread from heaven, but that my Father gives you the real bread from heaven. The bread that [YHWH] gives comes down from heaven and brings life to the world." (John 6:32-33 NEB)

After knowing that Yeshua loves us, it's time to get to know him. How many within the Body daily ask our Father in heaven to give to them this day their daily Bread? The only way to get to know him is by walking with him daily and becoming intimate with him. The more intimate we become with the Word, the more intimate we become with the Father. Not long after meeting Yeshua, we should begin eating meat. At first it may seem tough to chew all that Yeshua has to offer, but keep chewing and soon you shall swallow. However, after eating the same piece of meat for a while, it too can become bland. Make sure you add some salt. Careful though, not to allow your salt to lose its flavor, because when seasoned Christians have lost their flavor, it's time to spit them out.

> Salt is a good thing; but if salt itself becomes tasteless, what will you use to season it? It is useless either on the land or on the dung-heap: it can only be thrown away. If you have ears to hear, then hear. (Luke 14:34-35 NEB)

156. No Awe - No Law

First read: Joel 1-3

After the winter, if you can't handle the heat then you won't be inclined to drag your feet. Make no mistake, you will want to drag your feet. The pep in your step picked up after winter will drop once more, as you feel life draining with each mile you walk. Careful. You will be tempted to walk off the road to sit in the shade for just a second or two. The trees you sit under were, last winter, a bit smaller, but, oh, look how since winter they grew.

If you say "our Father" to the One who judges every man impartially on the record of his deeds, you must stand in awe of him while you live out your time on earth. (1st Peter 1:17 NEB)

What should motivate us to carry out the commands of Messiah? Fear of the disciplining rod? Some would shake in denial, rather than nod their heads in affirmation. But, in truth, there is nothing wrong or unscriptural about fearing the rod. The Body of Messiah wouldn't exist in its present crippled condition if more fear permeated throughout his Church. "But, I just believe that love is the answer," some would say, "because the Bible says that perfect love casts out all fear." Indeed the Bible does say as much, but the reality is that few walking on the road to Glory are actively perfecting through a consecrating relationship with Messiah. Truthfully, the fear of Yeshua is an invaluable gift that no Christian should walk without. Fear, if delivered by the Holy Spirit, can serve as an intrinsic check against moral relativism.

Behold, the eye of the [YHWH] is on those who fear him, on those who hope in his steadfast love... (Psalms 33:18a ESV)

[YHWH] will give ear and humble them. He who is enthroned from of old, ... because they do not change and do not fear [Yeshua]. My companion stretched out his hand against his friends; he violated his covenant. His speech was smooth as butter, yet war was in his heart; his words were softer than oil, yet they were drawn swords. (Psalms 55:19-21 ESV)

It worked for Joseph in the Tanakh who, despite repeated advances from Potiphar's wife, refused to engage in an extra-marital affair.

And after a time his master's wife cast her eyes on Joseph and said, "Sleep with me." But he refused and said to his master's wife, "Behold, because of me my master has no concern about anything in the house, and he has put everything that he has in my charge. He is not greater in this house than I am, nor has he kept back anything from me except you, because you are his wife. How then can I do this great wickedness and sin against [YHWH]?" And as she spoke to Joseph day after day, he would not listen to her, to lie beside her or to be with her. (Genesis 39:7-10 ESV)

The moment our fear sets in, temptation will begin. Remember that while temptation is never from the Father, he will allow for it as an exercise of strength and a test of faith.

It is crucial for members of the Body to realize that Satan does not want believers fearing YHWH. It is to his advantage that believers continue to see them as "the big guys in the sky" or as our little genie in the bottle. No awe? Then there's no need to obey any of their laws; neither is there any inspiration. As seasons change and you continue growing in your faith, know that Satan will also continue growing in his fixation to prevent you from perfecting. Every former temptation will intensify as both Satan's and sin's appeal to your lower flesh increases with vigor. Hunger pains. Agonizing? Occasionally. But, the Holy Spirit through the grace of the Father will enable you to endure.

Remembering that [Messiah] endured bodily suffering, you must arm yourselves with a temper of mind like his. When a man has thus endured bodily suffering he has finished with sin, and for the rest of his days on earth he may live, not for the things that man desire, but for what [YHWH] wills. (1st Peter 4:1-2 NEB)

Consider that each attempt is another opportunity to display your devotion to Messiah. You are not earning salvation by resisting the devil's wiles, but are reflecting your sanctification. It is ignorance that leads to insolence.

157. Wealthy With Wisdom VII

First read: Proverbs 9:10-18

While journeying, certain trees will look inviting; reject their invitation and keep walking. You had plenty of shade during the spring and more than enough during the winter—lest you forgot already. The shade under these trees is shady; especially with the scintillating fruit dripping with moisture. Just one bite? Alright. Eat it and it will be the last bite you ever take. For these scintillating pieces of fruit were in season, last season. They are rotten now; only you can't tell as easily because the sun's rays are not shining in their direction and so they are hidden in the dimness of shade. Keep moving.

Sin is tempting, though the temptation is not the sin itself. [Messiah] was tempted and yet did not sin. Eve was tempted in the Garden of Eden by the serpent that showed her the fruit and she sinned. Indeed death entered the human race the moment Eve ate, but dimness set in when she decided to touch. Where the simpleton walks, sin follows lock and step. YHWH took the man and put him in the garden of Eden to work it and keep it. And Yeshua commanded the man, saying, "You may surely eat of every tree of the garden, but of the tree of the knowledge of good and evil you shall not eat, for in the day that you eat of it you shall surely die" (Genesis 2:15-17 ESV).

Now the serpent was more crafty than any other beast of the field that [Yeshua] had made. He said to the woman, "Did [Yeshua] actually say, 'You shall not eat of any tree in the garden?'" And the woman said to the serpent, "We may eat of the fruit of the trees in the garden, and [Yeshua] said, 'You shall not eat of the fruit of the tree that is in the midst of the garden, neither shall you touch it, lest you die.'" (Genesis 3:1-3 ESV)

When Messiah forbids it's because we're his and he wants to protect. Satan protests everything Messiah tries to protect by professing to have our best interest at heart. It was Lucifer's protesting and professing that led to his fall in the beginning; protesting YHWH's authority and professing their equality. The prophet Isaiah paints a putrid picture:

How you are fallen from heaven, morning start, son of the dawn. How you are cut down to the ground, you who weakened the nations. For you have said in your heart: "I will ascend into heaven, I will exalt my throne above the stars of [YHWH]; I will also sit on the mount of the congregation. On the farthest sides of the north; I will ascend above the heights of the clouds, I will be like [YHWH]." Yet you shall be brought down to Sheol, to the lowest depths of the Pit. (Isaiah 14:12-15 ESV)

Along with a third of the former heavenly host, Satan has been using the same strategies to trip up YHWH's children, and he started with Adam and Eve—protesting and professing. He wants all to believe that the Bread of Life is actually stale.

It was not sinful for Eve to look longingly the fruit, for sin had not yet permeated the human body. No, it wasn't sinful—it was stupid. Where the simpleton walks, sin follows lock and step. Adam was none the wiser for allowing the fruit to pass into his own hands. Unfortunately, rather than protesting, he ingested; choosing instead to follow his wayward wife. Members of the Body must develop a passion for protecting their own bodies, and each others, by exercising holy wisdom. When Satan begins professing lies, respond by professing Messiah. Satan professes lies because he knows the truth. Your success in resisting his wiles is contingent upon your own knowledge, and your demise upon your stupidity. How well do you know the Truth?

> You know about [Yeshua] of Nazareth, how [YHWH] anointed him with the Holy Spirit and with power. He went about doing good and healing all who were oppressed by the devil, for [YHWH] was with him. (Acts 10:38 NEB)

158. The Hour of Power

First read: 2nd Samuel 22:1-51

If you can't handle the heat, then summer will teach you, more than any other season, the significance of perseverance. On the days where you just know the next step will be your last, you must take another and fast. The longer you hesitate the more likely you'll remain in that state.

[YHWH], save me by your name, and vindicate me by your might. [YHWH], hear my prayer; give ear to the words of my mouth. (Psalms 54:1-2 ESV)

Who among the Body would dare allege to never having felt like they wanted to throw in the towel? Though the temptation is there when there's heat in the air, members must hang on. You're going to need your towel to keep the sweat out of your eyes so that you can still see where you're going. The other temptation, when in the midst of misery, is to freeze. It's a common defense mechanism and a natural reaction to stop dead in your tracks when the sun's on your back. But the believer must keep walking, knowing that it is the Son's position that you persist and persevere. There is danger in standing still for too long; mirages will begin to appear on the side of the road. Remember, that which will materialize will provide exactly what you're looking for—momentary relief. Except that in accepting what's offered, relief will quickly pass, and in its place will regret stand, ready to rebuke. We find in reading the accounts of David that there were times of terror; days and nights in which his enemies were in such pursuit that his faith could have easily failed:

Save me, O [YHWH]. For the waters have come up to my neck. I sink in deep mire, where there is no foothold; I have come into deep waters, and the flood sweeps over me. I am weary with my crying out; my throat is parched. My eyes grow dim with waiting for [Yeshua]. (Psalms 69:1-3 ESV)

While metaphorical in delivery, none should mistake the depths of David's despair. Christians are never to assume that while on earth, YHWH will shield them from some depths of despair. The Bible never makes any such promises. There is a depth so deep where Messiah never wants his sheep to be. The pit of despair is the devil's lair, and Messiah will not deliver his sheep into the hands of the enemy without just cause. In the fifth chapter of 1st Corinthians the apostle Paul speaks of such an occasion, concerning a member of the Body who is engaging in an illicit sexual act with the wife of his father.

Nonetheless, the depths of despair are there and from time to time members will find themselves struggling to stay afloat. From David we can learn why closeness with our King is crucial. Rather than questioning the Father's existence—common during times of calamity—David immediately asked for YHWH's assistance. Unfortunately, most in the Body have not yet matured to the point of assurance. They have yet to faithfully understand that the Father knows the precise hour in which to display his perfect power. As such, some seek solace from a fist, a kiss, or momentary bliss, the list is endless. Others will seek God Almighty but are uninterested in waiting for his response; so they dismiss, and often at the dawn of deliverance. Our depths of despair may seem daunting on occasions, but what Messiah wants his sheep to believe is that there is no end to the depth of his love for us; neither is there of the Father's. Our perception of the Messiah's protection isn't always in perspective. The truth is that God Almighty will hold out his hands when he knows that we can no longer stand. In the meantime, Messiah expects all to persevere, and all to keep walking.

Give ear to my words, [YHWH]; consider my groaning. Give attention to the sound of my cry, my King and [Yeshua], for to you do I pray. [YHWH], in the morning you hear my voice; in the morning I prepare a sacrifice for you and watch. (Psalms 5:1-3 ESV)

159. Helping in the Highs

First read: 2nd Samuel 10:6-19

Remember that you will have other people walking with you. If you are hot, most likely you are not the only one. Share your feelings of discomfort with those walking beside you. After a minute or two you'll be surprised by how much cooler you feel and how your pace has picked up from the reel. No, the sun hasn't stopped beaming, but now you have looked outside yourself and at somebody else. Somehow sharing with another seems to soften the weather. Don't be like the traveler behind you who was walking beside you, but started reeling. When asked if they were hot too, they looked back at you with sweat glistening—no, cascading—down their face and said, "Of course not, mind your own business." So you did, and began to carry on a conversation with the traveler on the other side. While the one behind you braked with bowed head and began bathing, and then baking in the puddle forming beneath. Sadly, it won't be long before they make their way to the shade. There they will sit and there they will fade; drowning in their pool of denial.

When the going gets rough it's great to know that we have people to help us keep going. At least that's what Messiah desires that we remember while walking on the road to Glory. Just because we walk a narrow road, it doesn't mean that we have to walk it alone. The narrowness of the road is just another indication that next to intimacy with him, YHWH values interpersonal relationships and expects that among his people, a reasonable level of intimacy will exist as well. Reasonable is the operative word. All members must remember that no earthly relationship should ever attempt to replace what the Father has willed for himself and man. Many times we seek to fill a void that Yeshua intentionally placed inside of man for the sole purpose of uniting with his soul. What results are "break-up to make-up" relationships, forever accursed by co-dependency. It is with a sigh of relief that members of the Body can attest to rarely facing such entanglements. However, there is always an opposite end to a continuum. There is a cost in refusing to interact beyond the casual greeting or the common griping. When the going gets really tough, can you get beyond the fluff?

A man of many companions may come to ruin, but there is a friend who sticks closer than a brother. (Proverbs 18:24 ESV)

Sadly, for most the answer is no. Members of the Body must learn to say, "Yes." It is senseless to suffer in silence when the road is swarming with those who still suffer. Yes, there are plenty of the suffering sitting on the side of the road; and if those members more mature don't begin talking, then those younger will soon begin walking—off to the side and under the shade. In the same light, members must also learn how to receive. Pride will lead those to the side, but it is obstinacy that will keep them there. There is no shame in admitting that at times "it's too hot." And there are some in the Body whom Yeshua has assigned the task of cooling off, even while still in the sun. So why run? While on occasions we'd rather the sun sit out and chill, Paul reminds us of Messiah's purpose in refusing to relent:

"My grace is all you need;" power comes to its full strength in weakness. I shall therefore prefer to find my joy and pride in the very things that are my weakness; and then the power of [Messiah] will come and rest upon me. Hence I am well content, for [Messiah's] sake, with weakness, contempt, persecution, hardship, and frustration; for when I am weak, then I am strong. (2nd Corinthians 12:9-10 NEB)

Messiah's power is revealed in more ways than one, as is his grace. Though presently, there is perhaps no greater amount of grace or power to be found of Messiah, than in looking to his Body. His arms, legs, eyes, nose; his hands, feet, ears, and toes. When parts of a body are weakened, can each count on the rest of the Body to strengthen?

160. Full-time Forgiveness

First read: 1st Samuel 24:4-22

If there is another lesson to be gleaned from summer, it is that the heat can bring out the worst in people. Water that escapes from your pores won't leave without taking the salt with it. And when the surface it hits, out come the fits. It is one thing to share with another your feelings of discomfort. It's another to displace the bitterness of your salt onto those traveling with you. Stay leery of these travelers before they add to your weariness. Remember? These will be the ones who would rather drink the salty water cascading down their face, than to drink from the cup of fresh water you offer them; they want the gallon. The recurring hot air blowing around should condition you for what will blow from them. Yes, offer them assistance, but don't exert the extra energy you are going to need for the remainder of the summer by staying and accepting their abuse. You will find yourself emotionally drained. Instead, pour them another cup, set it down at their feet and continue to walk. There is no need to add salt to their wounds by replying with wounding words. Perhaps it will rain after another mile or two and their salt will wash away. Perhaps it won't rain at all that day.

It's no wonder that YHWH referred to David as a man after his own heart. Outside of Yeshua Messiah of Nazareth and perhaps Joseph from Genesis, the Bible makes mention of no other man more deserving of personal vengeance than the youngest son of Jesse. Here was a lad who, from his youth, devoted his life to the service of other people. In fact, this was the same youth who, though berated by his brothers, boldly stepped out in faith and defeated the nine-foot Philistine known as Goliath from Gath. David was called into the service of Saul. While technically still the king of Israel, Saul had been spiritually dethroned by YHWH for flagrant disobedience and was now the recipient of Yeshua's disciplining hand.

Now the Spirit of [YHWH] departed from Saul, and a harmful spirit from [Yeshua] tormented him. (1st Samuel 16:14 ESV)

David's job was to alleviate Saul's seasonal afflictions through song. What started off as gratitude, quickly turned into unwarranted gales of jealous rage; threatening the friendship and lives of both David and Saul's son, Jonathan.

Do not repay wrong with wrong, or abuse with abuse; on the contrary, retaliate with blessings, for a blessing is the inheritance to which you yourselves have been called. (1st Peter 3:9 NEB)

At what point as Christians do we tell ourselves, "Enough is enough"? Members might be tempted to tell themselves and others, "I'm no doormat." Such is a vain attempt at self-preservation when Messiah commands us to continuously deny self. It is not the case that YHWH desires for his children to accept verbal and physical abuse at the cost of life and limb. Messiah, thankfully, already endured on our behalf. Except for those who have been molded for martyrdom, all members are encouraged to walk while empowered.

However, despite the commandment of Messiah, there are those in the Body who are more concerned with saving face than they are with turning the other cheek. Moreover, there are those who have come to establish with others conditions for their clemency. As long as the offense doesn't fall outside selfishly drawn parameters, then a pardon is permissible. So long as the member is not a repeat offender, then our grace is guaranteed. What a remarkable concept—conditional clemency. Funny how in relating to a seeking neighbor, Messiah never mentioned it.

Then Peter came up and said to him, "Lord, how often will my brother sin against me, and I forgive him? As many as seven times?" [Yeshua] said to him, "I do not say to you seven times, but seventy times seven. (Matthew 18:21-22 ESV)

For those non-mathematicians out there, seventy times seven is equal to four hundred and ninety. If engaging in such a full-time job, then there is no time to remain offended. While seven is an odd number, seventy times seven should serve as a reminder to all that in time and if needed, it is Messiah who will get even. But, believers must also remember that Messiah would rather that no one suffer. And so, if turning the other cheek helps in saving a lost sheep, then being a mat isn't so bad after all. You're welcome.

161. Begrudging

First read: Ephesians 4:25-27

I shall hold my tongue until the sun has gone down
from the words that did bruise like a knife
It is worth the drain and strain on my life
and I shall take this grudge to the ground

My shoulder, so cold, is worth the heartache
My silence speaks much louder than words
Though I confess it seems rather absurd
with the smile that I wear, 'cause it's fake

Forgiveness, no doubt, is out of the question
Like a child twice denied I shall pout
I am certain by now he's ashamed, no doubt
and that surely he has learned his lesson

But, what lesson is this you might ask me?
That one should never think to offend
or our friendship will come to an end
Or lest they hear my wrathful decree

Because I am perfect in every way
and so have never made one mistake
Because I'm a joy, whether sleep or awake
I hope you rot till you drop from decay

162. Submitting To The Son

First read: 2nd Chronicles 13:1-22

On a scorcher when the sun is burning your face, you would do well to walk with the torch. In other words: don't try walking backwards, facing away from the sun. With your foolish strategizing, a hole sits patiently waiting for company. With your trickery, a dead limb lies eagerly awaiting your trip. You will feel the heat on your face during the summertime and occasionally it might get a little toasty; don't avoid a little color. However, in the long run you are better off walking while facing ahead and enduring a little heat. Because as long as you are facing forward, you can ensure that you will keep moving. Moving is an essential element of your journey. Eventually the sun will go down. If you fall into a hole or trip over a branch while walking backwards, you will be on the ground for a while, and the brilliance will continue beaming in your face. If you want to avoid unnecessary suffering, don't try to outmaneuver the sun; you may find yourself lying in a pile of manure.

While he was still speaking, a bright cloud suddenly overshadowed them, and a voice called from the cloud: "This is my Son, my Beloved, on whom my favor rests, listen to him." (Matthew 17:5a NEB)

The first chapter of Romans makes it clear that prior to the believer's relationship with the Father through justification by faith through the Son, all were enemies of YHWH. Let no member of the Body stand content while believing that such behavior is only suggestive of those outside. Paul made his business in writing to several of the early churches, including the ones in Colossae, Corinth, and Galatia, to remind those who had joined the fold that they were indeed new creatures; that their old selves had been crucified with Messiah. It was the painful truth that those in the Body still sinning were behaving as if they'd never left the enemy ranks. Sadly, not much has changed today. There are still those who proudly parade down the aisles between the pews, convinced that their eternal security lies within the walls of the Church. Unfortunately, their actions on the rest of the week demonstrate that their connection to the Head of the Church is anything but secure. While many in the Church are admiring the parade, Messiah is frowning at the charade.

But to the wicked [YHWH] says: "What right have you to recite my statutes or take my covenant on your lips? For you hate discipline, and you cast my words behind you. If you see a thief, you are pleased with him, and you keep company with adulterers. You give your mouth free rein for evil, and your tongue frames deceit. You sit and speak against your brother; you slander your own mother's son. These things you have done, and I have been silent. You thought that I was one like yourself; but now I rebuke you and lay the charge before you." Mark this, then, you who forget [YHWH], lest I tear you apart, and there be none to deliver. (Psalms 50:16-22 ESV)

The reality is that these members fail to realize that Messiah is only going to keep tugging on their hearts for a little while longer before he grows tired of fighting. The kingdom of Heaven is still available, though its gates are drawing to a close. Over the past 2000 years its doors have been closing. It is neither the will of the Father or the Son that any person gets shut out. And yet there are "believers" who are currently standing with only one foot in the door. Unacceptable. Messiah wants the feet, the heart, the soul, and the mind. There are times when the rod is more effective than the hand in capturing the attention of a wayward wanderer. Though an unpleasant experience (for both parties involved), such subjection should lead to soulful submission. God Almighty's intention from the start was to capture the heart.

To king Jeroboam and the wayward Israelites did Abijah, king of Judah, have to remind that fighting YHWH is a futile venture, and that submission is always a better option than attempted subversion. Both the envoy and the enemy claim to have a stake in the kingdom of Heaven. Yet, one daily submits while the other seeks to subvert. The King allows his subjects to choose their own role, but the road to Glory allows for only one.

I believed, even when I spoke: "I am afflicted;" I said in my alarm, "All mankind are liars." What shall I render to [YHWH] for all his benefits to me? I will lift up the cup of salvation and call on the name of [YHWH], I will pay my vows to [YHWH] in the presence of all his people. Precious in the sight of [Yeshua] is the death of his saints. O [YHWH], I am your servant; I am your servant, the son of your maidservant. You have loosed my bonds. I will offer to you the sacrifice of thanksgiving and call on the name of [Yeshua]. I will pay my vows to [YHWH] in the presence of all his people, in the courts of the house of [Yeshua], in your midst, O Jerusalem. Praise [YHWH]. (Psalms 116:10-19 ESV)

First read: 2nd Chronicles 30:1-22

If walking through fire is a breeze for you, congratulations. You will find that you are in the minority; be thankful for your gift. Others will have their own gifts that were given specifically to them for their journey. Rather than bemoaning a gift you don't have, take the ones you do and use them to ensure that those walking with you have a more bearable walk. Summer provides the best opportunity for looking outside your "self" to find ways to alleviate the suffering of those around. There will be plenty of opportunity to help the waving wake sitting on the side of the road, as well as the foolish who senselessly fall while on the road. Those in either category will be easy to spot as you travel. And in spotting them you will often forget the suffering of those who are still standing and still walking, while still on the road. However, during the summer, their needs will become obvious, as their faces, pinched and wet, will tell all. Listen and answer. Don't, because of your ease, lengthen your stride to avoid looking at their agony. In your haste to get away you will soon waste away, as the sun will eventually catch up with even you. The summer you don't want to hasten, nor should you stall. Simply walk with normal pace and soon you'll feel the fans of fall.

For you are my lamp, [YHWH] lightens my darkness. (2nd Samuel 22:29 ESV)

The pollutants that have been allowed to remain in the Body for too long have taken a toll on its various parts and it is time that they are removed. Yet, there exists those members who, by the grace of YHWH-Rophe (YHWH-Who-Heals), have been granted the gift of an early recovery. With their recovery has come the responsibility of helping others to restore. This is a responsibility that none should take lightly. It is tempting to consider our work done once we have found the light. In our pride we fail to consider that it was Messiah who gave us sight and that it was the Holy Spirit that led us to that light. The road set before the believer was designed so that yes, he could lead the blind to have sight. But, it was also intended for the believer whose vision is still blurred. These members have "found" the road to Glory, but look pitiful with their blackened eyes and battered limbs. It seems as if they never walk for long without finding themselves stuck in another mud-pile or at the bottom of another hole. With such an excess amount of pollution distorting their judgment and clouding their vision, in watching, it's as if their sole purpose for traveling was to torture their souls. "Man," we say, "will they ever get it right?" Not too bright. That goes for the believer who believes that these fellow travelers are just too much of a pain to petition on their behalf. Petition to whom? To the One who placed both of you on the road to Glory.

Remember, Christians can't sanctify—only Messiah can. Those struggling to stay out of the pits while on the road are not struggling with salvation like those snoozing on the side, but rather with sanctification. And if the actions of a blurred believer keep his vision blurry, then he who sees clearly ought to cry out for mercy. It is the disciple who recognizes that as long as there is even a single member limping around on crutches, then there is still work to be done within the Body.

The precepts of [YHWH] are right, rejoicing the heart; the commandment of [Yeshua] is pure; enlightening the eyes. . . (Psalms 19:8 ESV)

Hezekiah saw that while a number in the Hebrew assembly had hallowed themselves in preparation for their feast of Unleavened Bread, the celebration could not commence until every member had been hallowed. Rather than shaking his fist in condemnation at those daft, he instead fell to his knees and petitioned on their behalf. YHWH heard and healed. Members should remember that the re-sanctification of the sanctuary requires the help of he who sanctifies. Consider what engendered your success and then pray for the success of others.

I am [YHWH]. I have called you in righteousness. I will take you by the hand and keep you. I will give you as a covenant for the people, a light for the nations to open the eyes that are blind; to bring out the prisoners from the dungeon; from the prison those who sit in darkness. (Isaiah 42:6-7 ESV)

164. New Colors True Colors

First read: Ezra 3-4:5

Just when you thought you would collapse from a heat stroke, you receive a stroke of luck. Actually, it isn't luck at all that you're receiving. Seasons do change for sure; for what is sure, will occur, when it's time. And for sure you will never be so happy to see fall. By now you will be worn, wearied from the walk amidst the heat and revolving hot air. You will feel depleted from the absorbent amount of water lost, and maybe a little salty as a result. Tis the season for letting go. It may or may not be noticeable to all as the leaves begin to fall. In truth, some will be so focused on their own journey that they will fail to enjoy the changes around them. Don't allow this to discourage you from letting go. Sooner or later they will fall and when they're down they will have no choice but to look on the ground. And there they will see: yellow, brown, orange, and red—dead; changed, but charming. It will inspire all to lose their deadness. In the fall, nothing is as queer as seeing only a few colorful leaves sporadically scattered here and there. On the contrary, the real beauty is experienced in watching the changing leaves of all, both short and tall.

The Father will give his children enough space and time to mature on their own; to grow older and wiser in putting childish things away. However, the Father will lend a helping hand to help his people stand when, through words and deeds, most have shown that change is nowhere in their plans. Change is forever in the mind of Messiah because he knows the will of his Father; and so Yeshua tells Philip and Andrew:

> The hour has come for the Son of Man to be glorified. In truth, in very truth I tell you, a grain of wheat remains a solitary grain unless it falls into the ground and dies; but if it dies, it bears a rich harvest. The man who loves himself is lost, but he who hates himself in this world will be kept safe for eternal life. If anyone serves me, he must follow me; where I am, my servant will be. Whoever serves me will be honored by my Father. (John 12:23-26 NEB)

Yeshua was alluding to his death on the cross; necessary so that he could rise from the dead. Through his inference, Messiah was also imparting a significant truth. For his disciples, death was too a necessity. Death is a prerequisite for all who want to live. However, one has to develop such a loathing for sin and the status quo until everything around looks dingy. There are plenty on the road to Glory who accepted another's invitation to join, and have been walking ever since. There's just one problem: their fall was fruitless because it was rootless. Maybe this is why the enemy is able to entice so much with his greenery on the other side. When the believer has crucified self, that is, their lower nature, and has walked for several miles in the Spirit, eventually even the dreariest of days will beam with brilliance when compared to the luster of Satan's garden.

After years in Babylonian captivity, Cyrus, the king of the Babylonian empire, was moved by YHWH to allow the Jews to rebuild Solomon's temple. Unfortunately, the eagerness shared in the beginning of the rebuilding soon began to erode. There were people living within the land whose aim was to thwart the purposes of the Father. So they began to discourage those who sought to restore. Their goal was to defeat the Jews and prevent them from enjoying the land given to them by YHWH.

Likewise, as God Almighty begins to revive and restore, after first allowing many to break some and others to break more, there will exist those heckling spectators who will insist that you are making a spectacle of yourself. Some will come from the sidelines and from the enemy, sent intentionally to enervate, in hopes that you stay down. Others will be fellow travelers walking on the same road, still in love with their self and the dinginess around. Ignore those wearing tiny spectacles and know that what will be, will be spectacular. Falling is dying, though essential if change is to come. But, the colors that emerge are second to none.

So you, my friends, have died to the law by becoming identified with the body of [Messiah], and accordingly you have found another husband in him who rose from the dead, so that we may bear fruit for [YHWH]. While we lived on the level of our lower nature, the sinful passions evoked by the law worked in our bodies, to bear fruit for death. But now, having died to that which held us bound, we are discharged from the law, to serve [YHWH] in a new way, the way of the Spirit, in contrast to the old way, the way of a written code. (Romans 7:4-6 NEB)

165. The Holy Spirit: Dead or Alive II

First read: Acts 2:1-21

Besides respite from the heat and hot air from the Winds; fall will offer the unique gift of showing you the beauty in releasing the old. Take the gift without hesitation. The changing of the leaves as they're blowing in the breeze of wind's wisdom will reveal to you the liberation in letting go. But, only when it's time will you know. In the fall, there is nothing that looks as queer as seeing green leaves on the ground. However, when it is time, no need to avoid losing a part of you; it will be necessary in restoring all of you. Notice how light you feel in doing so; as light as the leaves drifting from trees. Most assuredly, it will be an equally pleasant experience for those around as they witness the results.

In [Yeshua] you also trusted, after you heard the word of truth, the gospel of your salvation; in whom also, having believed, you were sealed with the Holy Spirit of promise, who is the guarantee of our inheritance until the redemption of the purchased possession, to the praise of [Yeshua]. (Ephesians 1:13-14 NEB)

It is a shame that many in the Body believe that the activities of the Holy Spirit are really a sham; the Spirit who desires to empower all who have been imparted. Admittedly, it doesn't help to know that there have been those claiming membership to the Body who have also misrepresented the goodness of Yeshua. Misrepresenting the Holy Spirit is a sure way of falling out of grace with the Father, and unless grace is extended to the repentant sinner, eternity, for them, looks bleak indeed. Yeshua is patient and knows the limitations of his creation. Messiah is equally aware of the evil that has been operating in the spiritual realm, serving as stumbling blocks for his lost and wayward sheep: a righteous judgment upon the rebellious children of YHWH. Shortly, however, such excuses will no longer be excusable.

As for times of ignorance, [YHWH] has overlooked them; but now he commands mankind, all men everywhere, to repent, because he has fixed the day on which he will have the world judged, and justly judged, by a man of his choosing; of this he has given assurance to all by raising him from the dead. (Acts 17:30-31 NEB)

Not because all Satanic activity will cease to exist. On the contrary, Revelation states that the final end for Satan and his angels won't transpire until they are tossed into the lake of fire. However, the Holy Spirit was given as a gift to equip Messiah's sheep in helping to detect and defend themselves against the wolves in sheep clothing. While it is true that until now, many imparted have been duped and deprived of the Holy Spirit's baptism, there are currently faithful bodies of believers who are prayerfully seeking revival; not just for their own bodies, but for the entire Body. Thankfully, our Father is about to respond. This is no time for fear, but for rejoicing and then quickly preparing for properly rebuilding. The only thing that will deprive one from benefiting is persistent disobedience to the Scriptures. Peter speaks of this to the Sanhedrin after being set free by a messenger of the Lord:

> Peter replied for himself and the apostles: "We must obey [YHWH] rather than men. [YHWH] raised up [Yeshua] whom you had done to death by hanging him on a gibbet. He it is whom [YHWH] has exalted with his own right hand as leader and savior, to grant Israel repentance and forgiveness of sins. And we are witnesses to all this, and so is the Holy Spirit given by [YHWH] to those who are obedient to him." (Acts 5:29-32 NEB)

Salvation was YHWH's gift offered to unbelievers while we were still yet sinners, as was his seal via the Holy Spirit. However, the Holy Spirit's filling is a separate gift offered by the Father, but only upon daily request. Like the Spirit's initial sealing, it is expected that repentance will have transpired before our request to be filled is made. We request to be filled daily in order to daily disrupt the flow of sin. It is the Father's grace alone that is capable of disrupting the flow of sin (and the Holy Spirit is indeed a gracious gift from YHWH), not our best efforts or better intentions; not a careful recitation of the Lord's Prayer or the Apostles Creed; not getting dressed in our Sabbath best to make a fashionable appearance at Messiah's Supper, that is, Communion; and not humming the words to our favorite hymns and praise music.

Refusing to repent is flagrant disobedience to God Almighty. Those who insist on living in disobedience will continue to live in doubt. Ironically, it is doubt that keeps most people resistant to the Holy Spirit. For some it is fear of the unknown. For others it is worry of losing face. In being daily filled with the Holy Spirit, members of the Body will have a new outlook on their spiritual journey. With renewed vitality it will occur to all how dreary life was prior to their empowerment.

166. A Reflective Moment

The Power of Prayer

First read: Ephesians 6:18

When I shut up the heavens so that there is no rain, or command the locust to devour the land, or send pestilence among my people, if my people who are called by my name humble themselves, and pray and seek my face and turn from their wicked ways, then I will hear from heaven and will forgive their sin and heal their land. Now my eyes will be open and my ears attentive to the prayer that is made in this place. (2nd Chronicles 7:13-15 ESV)

When is the ideal time to pray? What if I were to tell you that YHWH's will is for believers to be in constant prayer, whether morning, noon, or night—would you consider? If the answer is no, then consider this—we are commanded do so. Of late I have made it a habit to inquire about the prayer life of fellow believers. Most often this conversation takes place when a problem has arisen and my brother or sister is seeking sound advice. After listening to the circumstance, I've followed with the question, "Have you talked to the Father about it?" I think the question startles most people because, as believers, we have grown accustomed to turning to our Father as a last resort, rather than as the primary source. I have been getting the impression that many Christians still have a difficult time relating to Yeshua because many don't really believe that he is real. I know it may sound rudimentary, but it is vital that believers remember that Messiah really does hear all and see all. For these characteristics to mean anything, we must cease viewing Christianity as some ideal philosophy and begin deepening our understanding of Messiah's identity. He is real. The Father is interested in what happens to his children. The Son is interested in serving as the gateway to knowing who the Father is and in serving as the Shepherd for his sheep. The Holy Spirit wants to give members the wisdom and empowerment needed to strengthen their relationship with the Father and other members of his household. And, lastly, the Father is interested in gracing us to walk the road to Glory.

> Our theme is the word of life. This life was made visible; we have seen it and bear our testimony; we here declare to you the eternal life which dwelt with the Father and was made visible to us. What we have seen and heard we declare to you, so that you and we together may share in a common life, that life which we share with the Father and his Son [Yeshua]. And we write this in order that the joy of us all may be complete. (1st John 1:2-4 NEB)

While YHWH is indeed slow to anger, he has grown tired of being an afterthought. For a parent, what joy is there found in knowing that your children only pay you any attention when they want something? On earth, it is natural for children to wean themselves away from the protective wings of their parents. From the time of their youth we begin instilling values of independence as a way of survival in the "real world." Unfortunately, the Church has erred in not correcting members who attempt to model the same relationship pattern with our Heavenly Father. On the contrary, a sign of spiritual growth and maturity comes in acknowledging and acting upon the truth that our survival depends upon our daily dependence on God Almighty. In the same vein, our growth is dependent upon our remaining attached to the Vine.

If you dwell in me, and my words dwell in you, ask what you will, and you shall have it. (John 15:7 NEB)

When we are able to recognize our need for YHWH then our prayer life should change significantly. Petitioning YHWH for the material should not serve as our sole purpose in praying. When was the last time you spent your prayer time thanking YHWH for his goodness? What about asking him what his thoughts are on a decision you need to make, rather than asking him to bale you out of a mess you helped to create. Need to vent? Cry? Are you happy, worried, upset? Tell our Father about it. He is listening.

In the laundry list that we often find ourselves giving to YHWH, where on the list does the Holy Spirit fit in? The purpose of prayer should center on our spiritual growth and development. When it does, then Yeshua promises that the Father will take care of everything else. However, it is impossible to center on the spiritual without the intervention of the Holy Spirit. Why, then, is the Third Person often treated as a fifth wheel?

167. What Will Be

First read: 1st Chronicles 28:1-21

Looking up at the trees during the fall can lead to an intimidating encounter. As the shades cast menacing shadows, silhouettes of melting splendor, you may feel tempted to bemoan the past. In thinking of what once was, you'll fail to consider what will be. You must know that what will be, will be beautiful. Remember that objects cast in shadows are deceptive distortions of reality. Change is uncomfortable, but don't allow it to be gripping.

Nothing quite says I love you like the encouraging words of a loving Father to his Son, whose life is about to take a new direction, and one that will at times prove difficult. We read in the Gospels the heartening message of the Father to Messiah upon his juncture in the Jordan:

> After baptism [Yeshua] came up out of the water at once, and at that moment heaven opened; he saw the Spirit of [YHWH] descending like a dove to alight upon him; and a voice from heaven was heard saying, "This is my Son, my Beloved, on whom my favor rests." (Matthew 3:16-17 NEB)

This was said prior to Yeshua's walk in the wilderness, preceding his ministry. We find a similar praise in the seventeenth chapter of Matthew when Yeshua is transfigured while atop the mountain. It's said prior to Yeshua's journey to Jerusalem, preceding his crucifixion. Though physically discomforted while walking in the wilderness for forty days without food or water, Yeshua was concerned with, but not consumed with what was at the moment. During his interlude with the enemy, Yeshua was focused on, but not fixed on what was in the present. While walking to Jerusalem, where he knew what awaited him, Yeshua dealt with, but did not dwell on what was in his midst.

> Now my soul is in turmoil, and what am I to say? Father, save me from this hour. No, it was for this that I came to this hour. Father, glorify thy name. A voice sounded from heaven: "I have both glorified it and I will glorify it again." (John 12:27-28 NKJV)

It may seem that while kneeling in Gethsemane, Yeshua was more immersed in, than involved in his immediate circumstances. He was. He was immersed in intimacy with his Father because he knew that their separation was imminent. In a minute he would be nailed to a cross, saving the lost. However, while in Gethsemane he rose from the ground and walked to his cross, because he could see: Not where he was now, but where he would be; at the right hand of his Father. He is. It didn't make the separation any less painful, but it did make it bearable.

Then what can separate us from the love of Christ? Can affliction or hardship? Can persecution, hunger, nakedness, peril, or the sword? "We are being done to death for thy sake all day long." as Scripture says; "We have been treated like sheep for slaughter."—and yet, in spite of all, overwhelming victory is ours through him who loved us. For I am convinced that there is nothing in death or life, neither angels or demons, in the world as it is or the world as it shall be, in the forces of the universe, in heights or depths—nothing in all creation that can separate us from the love of [YHWH] in [Yeshua]. (Romans 8:35-39 NEB)

And David said to his son Solomon, "Be strong and of good courage, and do it; do not fear nor be dismayed, for [Yeshua]—my God—will be with you. He will not leave you nor forsake you, until you have finished all the work for the service of the house of [YHWH]. Here are the divisions of the priests and the Levites for all the service of the house of [YHWH]; and every willing craftsman will be with you for all manner of workmanship, for every kind of service; also the leaders and all the people will be completely at your command." (1st Chronicles 28:20-21 ESV)

David said this to his son Solomon, prior to his building YHWH's temple. Though not provided with great details, readers can only imagine the seasonal anguish that must have accompanied Solomon during his seven years of painstaking precision while constructing. Indeed, a perpetual vision of the masterpiece must have remained etched in his head so he could see—not what was then, but what would be. The believer, then, has at least two from which to pattern their temple rebuilding years after. One deficient, though successful in his task, and the other, Yeshua himself. Scripture is not without sound advice and encouragement from the Holy Spirit, given to those who have accepted Messiah's invitation to engage in restoring the Father's temple. Through Paul the Apostle we are told:

Brethren, join in following my example, and note those who so walk, as you have us for a pattern. For many walk, of whom I have told you often, and now tell you even weeping, that they are the enemies of the cross of [Messiah]: whose end is destruction, whose god is their belly, and whose glory is in their shame—who set their mind on earthly things. For our citizenship is in heaven, from which we also eagerly wait for the Savior, [Yeshua], who will transform our lowly body that it may be conformed to his glorious body, according to the working by which he is able even to subdue all things to himself. (Philippians 3:17-21 NKJV)

168. Pray For Peace

First read: 1st Chronicles 23-24

It is difficult for you to see what lies ahead, especially in the fall. The menacing shadows, mixing with the blowing winds and falling leaves may undoubtedly leave you confused while you travel. Don't follow for long or you will find yourself blown off track. You may be tempted to hasten your pace to hammer through the whirlwind. Careful, or you soon may find yourself nailed to the ground. Enjoy the change that will be confusing at times. However, the confusion should only be brief as you are adjusting to your changing state, and finally, familiarizing yourself with what follows. During the moments when you feel the most confused or unsure, turn to those around you and share. They too will be asking questions relating to how, what, why, and where.

Then the high priest rose up, and all those who were with him (which is the sect of the Sadducees), and they were filled with indignation, and laid their hands on the apostles and put them in the common prison. But at night a messenger of [Yeshua] opened the prison doors and brought them out, and said, "Go, stand in the temple and speak to the people all the words of this life. And when they heard that, they entered the temple early in the morning and taught. But the high priest and those with him came and called the council together, with all the elders of the children of Israel, and sent to the prison to have them brought. (Acts 5:17-21 NEB)

When El Elyon (God Most High) is ready to act, there is absolutely nothing in creation that can impede. When he has made a decision to move, it usually means that some will move along, others ahead, and still others will get moved out of the way. What is there left to say? Nothing. It is best that believers succumb to his will and hang on for the ride that will follow shortly. Perhaps what is most frustrating to members of the Body is knowing that YHWH rarely acts in ways that are breathtaking, because he wants us to continue breathing. Yet, still we often find ourselves begging for him to intervene in our lives. When he finally does, we are beside ourselves with worry. However, while YHWH is working through his winds and storms, those faithful should pray for peace.

Pray for the peace of Jerusalem. May they be secure who love you. Peace be within your walls and security within your towers. For my brothers and companions' sake I will say, "Peace be within you." For the sake of the house of [YHWH], I will seek your good. (Psalms 122:6-9 ESV)

To all his children, YHWH will provide his peace. King Solomon's name means "Man of Peace." YHWH promised David that he would grant Israel peace during the reign of his son. His peace would be essential if Solomon was to undergo the task of building YHWH's house. It was important that YHWH removed all outside barriers before Solomon began the construction, and yet, still his peace was pertinent. Building the temple of YHWH? Not exactly stress free, but YHWH had decided that it was time to move. There are two temples that YHWH has since decided needs rebuilding so that he may dwell fully and actively. The first is the temple of his children, and the second is the temple of his Son, Yeshua Messiah, that is, the Body of Messiah, or the Church. Though in truth, the former needn't be fully rebuilt before the latter can begin to reshape. Both are broken and both need one another to repair. For almost two thousand years since Messiah ascended to his throne at the right hand of his Father, there has been repeated resistance from those without Messiah and repeated reluctance from those within the Body, to transform the Church into a place inhabitable by the Holy Spirit; not just a church here or there, but the whole Church. YHWH is ready to move. YHWH is about to move.

And so now: keep clear of these men, I tell you; leave them alone. For if this idea of theirs or its execution is of human origin, it will collapse; but if it is from [YHWH], you will never be able to put them down, and you risk finding yourselves at war with [YHWH]. (Acts 5:38-39 NEB)

Some will move along; others will move ahead; and still some will get moved out of the way. However, even before YHWH moves, the believer should begin to pray for peace. When there is uncertainty about how YHWH is acting, don't panic—pray for peace. When there is unfamiliarity with what YHWH is doing both to you and through you, and to those around you, don't panic—pray for peace. When there is a lack of understanding as to why YHWH is acting; where he is choosing to act; and through whom he is choosing to act, don't panic—pray for peace. And then pray that YHWH-Shalom (YHWH-is-Peace) will set your mind at ease.

Peace is my parting gift to you, my own peace, such as the world cannot give. Set your troubled hearts at rest, and banish your fears. (John 14:27 NEB)

During these moments of uncertainty, some of the faithful may choose to cower in fear; knowing that the enemy is near. Confusion only checks in when our faith begins to check out. Some confusion is normal, but it's best to keep it in check. Just remember that YHWH is in control and that when he makes the decision to move, it is always for the benefit of every believer.

Therefore [YHWH] said: "Inasmuch as these people draw near with their mouths and honor Me with their lips, but have removed their hearts far from Me, and their fear toward Me is taught by the commandment of men, therefore, behold, I will again do a marvelous work among this people, a marvelous work and a wonder; for the wisdom of their wise men shall perish, and the understanding of their prudent men shall be hidden." (Isaiah 29:13-14 NKJV)

169. Anchored

First read: Psalm 31:19-24

When circumstances rise
that threaten to unhinge
your faith in the Messiah,
the Prince of Peace

When your soul begins to cry
and your flesh begins to cringe;
it seems that rains continue
pouring without cease

breathe

When your body starts to ache
No comforting is near
And the doctors have revealed
some solemn news

When your heart won't let you fake
tiny smiles that once appeared;
bills won't stop coming
so debt has accrued

believe

When your job has let you down
You don't know where to turn;
Yet your family has needs
that must be met

When you've fallen on the ground
and your eyes have start to burn;
your vision is now blurred
from tears and sweat

cleave

When your love is not returned
by those who took your heart
The fire that once burned hot
has turned to ice

When the hurtful lessons learned
have left you cold, torn apart;
the thought of someone new
has you blinking twice

receive

There are no mountains too high
Neither valleys too low;
There are no rivers too deep
or nights too long

When the winds begin to sigh
The flowers no longer grow;
the birds in flight stop singing
their joyous song

retrieve

And draw back into your past
when your faith once sustained;
When you put your hope in Messiah,
gave him your fears

Although your faith didn't last,
you can cast aside your shame;
Now call on the Mighty One
and he'll draw near

receive

170. The Fight of the Fallen

First read: Ezekiel 28-32

Fall will also remind you that dropping dead weight is certain, whether you induced it or not. When the trees have withstood all they can, their limbs will start to fall. Make sure you are alert or you will find yourself sore; these aren't quite as light. Broken tree limbs are not nearly as aesthetically pleasing. However, all should keep looking and all should remain aware.

There are a multitude of certainties that the Christian has as a child of YHWH, and as a sibling of his Son. We are certain that there is life after death; that this world where we live isn't all that is left.

But the truth is, [Messiah] was raised to life—the first-fruits of the harvest of the dead. For since it was a man who brought death into the world, a man also brought resurrection of the dead. As in Adam all men die, so in [Messiah] all will be brought to life; but each in his own proper place:[Messiah] the fruit-fruits, and afterwards, at his coming, those who belong to [Messiah]. (1st Corinthians 15:20-23 NEB)

We are certain that there are those on earth who claim to have our best interest at heart, though theirs was blackened from our start. We are certain that as the curtains of this age draw to a close and members of the Body begin rousing from their slumber, the Holy Spirit will begin moving powerfully in eager anticipation and preparation. Until the rising of the Son, the Spirit's work will not be done:

And it shall come to pass afterward, that I will pour out my Spirit on all flesh; your sons and your daughters shall prophesy, your old men shall dream dreams, and your young men shall see visions. Even on the male and female servants in those days I will pour out my Spirit. And I will show wonders in the heavens and on the earth, blood and fire and columns of smoke. The sun shall be turned to darkness, and the moon to blood, before the great and awesome day of [YHWH] comes. And it shall come to pass that everyone who calls on the name of [Yeshua] shall be saved. For in Mount Zion and in Jerusalem there shall be those who escape, as [YHWH] has said, and among the survivors shall be those whom [Yeshua] calls. (Joel 2:28-32 ESV)

We are also certain that as the Holy Spirit begins to work overtime, so will the powers, authorities, potentates, and superhuman forces of hell. If any believers believe that Satan will sit idly by while millions of souls are saved from his eternal destination, they are mistaken. When the spiritual princes, so wicked and vile, realize that they are fighting a losing battle in the heavens, they will eventually tire and retreat. Satan will then refocus, as he redirects his forces in waging a full-fledge attack on YHWH's children. It is imperative that those whom YHWH has gifted with eyes and ears pray for increased acuity. Likewise, those arising from their slumber will need to become attuned in learning the art of war. And there's more. Satan is a terrorist. As such, his chief and most effective instrument in fighting is fear.

Christians have two weapons that work wonders both offensively and defensively. The first is faith and the second is truth. Satan instills fear by first planting seeds of doubt. However, doubting loses its potency the closer members are able to align their beliefs with the Truth. To know is to accept nothing less, while nonetheless, expecting anything.

Peter called to him: "[Yeshua], if it is you, tell me to come to you over the water." "Come," said [Yeshua]. Peter stepped down from the boat, and walked over the water toward [Yeshua]. But, when he saw the strength of the gale he was seized with fear; and beginning to sink, he cried, "Save me, [Yeshua]." [Yeshua] at once reached out and caught hold of him, and said, "Why did you hesitate? How little faith you have." They then climbed into the boat; and the wind dropped. And the men in the boat fell at his feet, exclaiming, "Truly you are the Son of [YHWH]." (Matthew 14:28-33 NEB)

Knowing the Truth will always engender peace even in the midst of panic. As darkness starts to rise know that it's because the sun is on the horizon. The fallen will fight harder as the night begins to fade; seething as they know their time is near. But believers must take courage as they focus on the prize; for very soon the Son shall reappear.

For behold, darkness shall cover the earth, and thick darkness the peoples; but [Yeshua] will arise upon you, and his glory will be seen upon you. And nations shall come to your light, and kings to the brightness of your rising. (Isaiah 60:2-3 ESV)

171. Oholah & Oholibah

First read: Ezekiel 23

Broken tree limbs can be hard lessons learned. If you aren't careful, you might find yourself tripping over quite a few branches. Though, here's a thought that may not have occurred to you before. While walking, when you happen to spot a few limbs on the ground, rather than stepping over them—gloating over your acuity—bend down to pick up the limb and throw it off to the side of the road for the sake of those traveling behind you who are still developing.

But [YHWH] forbid that I should boast of anything but the cross of Yeshua Messiah], through which the world is crucified to me and I to the world. (Galatians 6:14 NKJV)

A string of burglaries continue to take place in a neighborhood that has lavished itself in splendor. Eventually, someone wises up and suggests that all in the community install an alarm system. Your neighbors recently moved out because, while they had not yet been robbed, they were, nevertheless, frightened by the thought. Eventually, a new couple—the Novices—move in. Rather than rushing next door to ensure that your new neighbors are aware of the recent burglaries, and then volunteering to help them install an alarm, you greet them with a wince and tell them to keep their dog out of your yard. You don't want their mutt ruining your begonias and risk lowering your property value.

Well, whether you eat or drink, or whatever you are doing, do all for the honour of [YHWH]: give no offence to Jews, or Greeks, or to the church of [YHWH]. For my part I always try to meet everyone half-way, regarding not my own good but the good of the many, so that they might be saved. (1st Corinthians 10:31-33 NEB)

It may not have occurred to many members within the Body that part of being a family means doing our best to reduce the likelihood of failure on the part of our siblings. This becomes difficult for the members who live in a country where "I" is the most important letter in the word "united." In America many are bred from birth to believe that "I" should always be the first person and that independence is the name of the game. When it comes to making mistakes, it is less important that those around us learn not to imitate our failures, and more important that we come to secure our futures. As much as rugged individualism and personal responsibility screams of patriotism, there is little room for such sentiments in the Church. Indeed, believers must quickly understand that the most important letter in the word united isn't "I" neither is it "U.". It is actually a tie between "U" and "I" who, when tied together make "We."

Care as much about each other as about yourselves. Do not be haughty, but go about with humble folk. Do not keep thinking how wise you are. (Romans 12:16 NEB)

While Messiah does and will hold people personally responsible for failing to acknowledge him as Lord and Savior; where the Holy Spirit has inspired, he will also hold members of the Body individually responsible for failure to enlighten the spiritually ignorant. Paul explains to the Corinthians how Messiah will judge their efforts in building up his Body:

> Or again, you are [YHWH]'s building. I am like a skilled master-builder who by [YHWH]'s grace laid the foundation, and someone else is putting up the building. Let each take care how he builds. There can be no other foundation beyond that which is already laid; I mean [Yeshua] himself. If anyone builds on that foundation with gold, silver, and fine stone, or with wood, hay, and straw, the work that each man does will at last be brought to the light; the day of judgment will expose it. For that day dawns in fire, and the fire will test the worth of each man's work. If a man's building stands, he will be rewarded; if it burns, he will have to bear the loss; and yet he will escape with his life, as one might from a fire. (1st Corinthians 3:10-15 NEB)

> What for you is a good thing must not become an occasion for slanderous talk; for the kingdom of [YHWH] is not eating and drinking, but justice, peace, and joy, inspired by the Holy Spirit. (Romans 14:16-17 NEB)

Failing to guard our siblings against unnecessary or unseasonable suffering is essentially aiding in their wears and tears. Using the metaphorical sisters Oholah and Oholibah to describe the fate of Samaria and Jerusalem, YHWH once again paints plainly, a putrid picture of perversion. What is sad, however, is that while Oholibah was indeed responsible for her own actions, her older sister Oholah could have, in love, discouraged the younger from following in the same footsteps. Messiah is encouraging those members more mature who have stumbled, not to forget about their younger siblings. They are watching. Inevitably, they will make their own mistakes and the Father is not asking anyone to interfere in the Holy Spirit's convicting work. However, Messiah wants his disciples to remember that the letter "I" in Messiah stands for "Intercessor" and when dealing with the wayward, the Father would rather his experienced children wield their spiritual wisdom from hard lessons learned. Wisdom is always preferred over the rod, though, where the former lacks, the latter looms.

172. No Fear of The Fallen

First read: Zechariah 1-14

In truth, while walking you will not notice every fallen branch on the path you are walking. Nor should you fixate on the fallen branches; but, you must know that they are there. Messiah has ordained that the fallen branches stay in the midst of his more vibrant ones—at least for now, though not for too much longer. Remember that rebuilding the Body of Messiah is equally a strengthening exercise in as much as it is a sanctifying one. Some will stay and you will learn how to detect them from a mile away. And as you learn to identify, Messiah will expect you to help sharpen another's eye. It is vital that members understand that not all branches belong to the Vine, even though many will profess that, "Yeshua is mine." Let them profess, but the proof will be found in how they attest.

Here is the test by which we can make sure that we are in him: whoever claims to be dwelling in him, binds himself to live as [Yeshua] himself lived. (1st John 2:6 NEB)

A time is approaching when those fallen branches will be cast in such a light, to allow the whole world to see them in all their darkness. Then watch as they burn from afar. Until then, there will remain other fallen branches that you cannot see at all, but know that they are doing the work of their father. While you are rebuilding, they are rebelling. As the prophet Zechariah writes in describing a vision:

Then he showed me Joshua the high priest standing before the [Messenger] of [YHWH], and Satan standing at his right hand to oppose him. And [YHWH] said to Satan, "[Yeshua] rebuke you, Satan. [Yeshua] who has chosen Jerusalem rebuke you. Is this not a brand plucked from the fire?" (Zechariah 3:1-2 NKJV)

However, those with malicious intent rarely display their malevolence in such candid fashion. Clandestine is more of their style and they will often greet you with a smile, while remaining careful not to reveal the slit in between their tongue. No, you will not notice every fallen branch, but you must know that they're still there. Yet, neither should any believer work in fear, for Yeshua is always near his faithful and his eyes are watching. It may be unsettling to know that there is an enemy lurking about, actively seeking to sabotage the Savior's plan. Just remember that Satan can only do what the Savior says he can, and no more; believers simply need to know more.

Knowledge is indeed power. Intimately knowing the Father and his Word will keep you firmly in their grip. Zechariah had to remind the Israelites that their intimate connection rested in the rebuilding of a temple. Praise Messiah for shedding his blood so that a wall no longer separates us from the Father. Access rests on our affirmation of his Son as our Lord and Savior (and then faithfully acting upon that affirmation with the aid of the Holy Spirit) What a sad irony, then, that it is we who insist on erecting the walls. The Holy Spirit wants to remind all members of Messiah's flock that the Church has no walls, only limbs attached to a heart and Head. Moreover, it is not a building, but a Body made up of living vessels who need to be nurtured and fed. And so Messiah says: "Shepherds arise and take charge. I have sheep still asleep with the dead."

Woe to the idol shepherd that leaveth the flock! the sword shall be upon his arm, and upon his right eye: his arm shall be clean dried up, and his right eye shall be utterly darkened. (Zechariah 11:17 AKJV)

173. Abort: Apathy & Apostasy

First read: Malachi 1-3

There will be some branches that you will walk right over instinctively, as your past experiences will have sharpened your senses. However, there will still remain some that will afford a trip that you simply can't refuse.

But refuse it you must. Perhaps the prophet Malachi would not have given such a scathing message to the Israelites if they would have learned to refuse the rhetoric of their day. Take heed when the spiritual climate is at an all time low. Know that some will lurk in the shadows offering a message of change and hope, and who will extend their healing hands in helping all to cope. Know where their hands have been, because although outwardly smooth, theirs may have been soaking in sin. While the prophets Haggai and Zechariah were successful in encouraging the Israelites to finish their rebuilding of the temple, following its completion in 515 B. C, new problems began to surface. Beware. Apathy and Apostasy are fraternal twins. They don't look exactly identical, but both spring from the same womb, and with only a fragment of time separating their births. Malachi was sent at a time when Apathy had already arrived on the scene and Apostasy was beginning to rear its ugly head. When Apathy was born among the Israelites, Fear of YHWH, once highly favored, was suddenly discarded, while All Due Respect was simply disregarded. Through Malachi, YHWH reminded the Israelites that respecting him meant respecting his laws, which included sacrificing and offering up their best, rather than devouring their best and giving him the rest; prophetic teachings by the priests rather than perverted ones in which only they profited; marriages mirroring faithfulness, rather than ones marred by fornication; and advocating for honorable holiness, rather than endorsing relativistic righteousness. Not to mention abstaining from sorcery, witchcraft, and perjury; the mistreatment of hired help, the disregard for widows, the abuse of children, and the alienation of the aliens. Sound familiar? It is a gracious God indeed who, with perfect forbearance, tolerates such a tragic display of gratitude from a people whom he delivered from their graves. Apathy is a tragedy, but Apostasy is treacherous. Hence:

But there were also false prophets among the people, even as there will be false teachers among you, who will secretly bring in destructive heresies, even denying [Yeshua] who bought them, and bring on themselves swift destruction. And many will follow their destructive ways, because of whom the way of truth will be blasphemed. By covetousness they will exploit you with deceptive words...

Careful. Almost anything sounds appetizing to one who is apathetic.

...for a long time their judgment has not been idle, and their destruction does[a] not slumber For if [YHWH] did not spare the angels who sinned, but cast them down to hell and delivered them into chains of darkness, to be reserved for judgment; and did not spare the ancient world, but saved Noah, one of eight people, a preacher of righteousness, bringing in the flood on the world of the ungodly; and turning the cities of Sodom and Gomorrah into ashes, condemned them to destruction, making them an example to those who afterward would live ungodly; and delivered righteous Lot, who was oppressed by the filthy conduct of the wicked 8 (for that righteous man, dwelling among them, tormented his righteous soul from day to day by seeing and hearing their lawless deeds)—then [YHWH] knows how to deliver the godly out of temptations and to reserve the unjust under punishment for the day of judgment, and especially those who walk according to the flesh in the lust of uncleanness and despise authority. They are presumptuous, self-willed. They are not afraid to speak evil of dignitaries, whereas angels, who are greater in power and might, do not bring a reviling accusation against them before [Yeshua]. (2nd Peter 2:1-11 NKJV)

Those who choose to adopt Apostasy as their sibling will find their fate every bit as frightening as his. Remain leery of those who espouse a belief in a God who loves all, accepts all, and is in all, and who admonish you for thinking otherwise. It sounds wholesome and holy, but it's really full of holes. The truth? First, the Father loves all who are members of his household, including those still waiting to be adopted. He is not in love with sin. Second, the Father accepts all who accept his Son Yeshua Messiah as their Lord and Savior.

Thomas said, "[Yeshua] we do not know where you are going, so how can we know the way?" [Yeshua] replied, "I am the way; I am the truth and I am life; no one comes to the Father except by me." (John 14:5-6 NKJV)

There is no salvation in anyone else at all, for there is no other name under heaven granted to men, by which we may receive salvation. (Acts 4:12 NEB)

And finally, the God of the universe resides in all members of his household through the Holy Spirit. He is not some pantheistic deity living in all the flowers and trees; and so there should be no worshiping of these. While walking on the road to Glory, ask the Father to fill you continuously with the Holy Spirit to reside in the womb of your soul. Neither Apathy nor Apostasy must be allowed to steal even one breath of air (a dastardly pair). Instead, pray that your womb is fruitful in forever birthing Fortitude and Faith; a set of fraternal twins that, in the end, will ensure your safe arrival into the Father's arms.

Pure and undefiled religion before [YHWH] the Father is this: to visit orphans and widows in their trouble, and to keep oneself unspotted [untarnished] from the world. (James 1:27 NKJV)

174. Freedom from Falling

First read: Isaiah 32-35

When you fall, refuse to wallow in self-pity. Instead, look outside yourself and stand up, using your obstacle as an opportunity. Again, pick up the limb and toss it to the side of the road. When it is too heavy for you to carry by yourself, ask for a helping hand. Others around have either tripped over a similar branch recently, or a larger branch several miles back, and are stronger as a result of their fall. On occasion, it will be necessary to just continue walking, because trying to remove the obstacle at the present moment is not possible and your attempts to do so, with or without help, will only result in greater pain. Perhaps it is not yet time for that limb to be moved and perhaps you aren't the one to move it. Move on. If you can not move it, it is not a crime. What will happen, will occur, when it's time. Remember, in insisting on doing what you were not equipped to do, you add cracks to what you're trying to repair, and, in despair, you waste time.

It is our persistence in disobedience and refusal to repent that result in the limbs that are sent. Painful reminders in the middle of our journey that reflection is in order; the type of reflection which leads to repentance.

While Ezra prayed and made confession, weeping and casting himself down before the house of [YHWH], a very great assembly of men, women, and children, gathered to him out of Israel, for the people wept bitterly. (Ezra 10:1 ESV)

When believers, walking, begin to strut as if sin is in, then for the sake of their souls, Yeshua will help out. When the convert ceases to be convicted by the Holy Spirit, their lifestyle will once again emulate the convict's. As such, the chains once worn, which fell off when we were reborn, suddenly reappear. More than likely the convict did not keep his head saturated with holy wisdom, and so he bought into the lie from the devil that he was more free while still in prison.

You were bought at a price; do not become slaves of men. (1st Corinthians 7:23 NEB)

What should have been the liberation of a life-time was apparently short-lived. YHWH never leaves his children bereft in the midst of their struggles, but always provides for them a way out; gently reminding them of their costly freedom.

So he came to Nazareth, where he had been brought up, and went to synagogue on the Sabbath day as he regularly did. He stood up to read the lesson and was handed the scroll of the prophet Isaiah. He opened the scroll and found the passage which says, "The Spirit of [Yeshua] is upon me, because [YHWH] has anointed me to announce good news to the poor; [he has sent me to bind up the brokenhearted, to proclaim liberty to the captives (Isaiah 61:1 NRSV)], to proclaim release for prisoners and recovery of sight for the blind; to let the broken victims go free; to proclaim the year of [YHWH's] favor." (Luke 4:16-19 NEB)

After converting to Messiah, the Holy Spirit will continuously press the believer to express, at times his guilt, but always his gratitude. Justifiable guilt is for conversion, justified guilt is useful for convictions, but gratitude is necessary for our continual growth. However, when it becomes clear to Messiah that, within our walk, we have grown too tall then it is time to fall. The Father is not miserly with his mercy, but neither is he interested in dispensing freely at the expense of a disciple's freedom.

The time has come for judgment to begin; it is beginning with [YHWH]'s own household. And if it's starting with you, how will it end for those who refuse to obey the gospel of [Yeshua]? It is hard enough for the righteous to be saved; what then will become of the impious and sinful? So even those who suffer, if it be according to [YHWH]'s will, should commit their souls to him—by doing good; their Maker will not fail them. (1st Peter 4:17-19 NEB)

Self-examination is always the motivation behind an induced fall: Why didn't I abide even though "I" should have died to self? Why did I lust in my flesh and with mayhem did mesh with the world? But self-pity is never the key: "Oh, woe is me." Messiah does not discipline so that his disciples stay down in demise. Rather it is his wrath which should lead to their rise. Though, not to the same height as they were once before; but, to one where their wounds lead to wanting him more.

The reality is that God Almighty needs us at a place where we realize that our freedom is inextricably bound to our frequency of dependency. Our freedom is guaranteed as long as YHWH is our need. Messiah will always use his limbs as leverage. Limbs are a powerful deterrent for others who may seek to detour off the road to Glory. Having grown wiser from his woes, it is the concerned member who will endeavor to educate his brothers and sisters about the danger of the detour. No two jars of clay ever break exactly the same way and so it never hurts to share several stories of despair.

They travelled through the Phrygian and Galatian region, because they were prevented by the Holy Spirit from delivering the message in the province of Asia; and when they approached the Mysian border they tried to enter Bithynia; but the Spirit of [YHWH] would not allow them, so they skirted Mysia and reached the coast at Troas. (Acts 16:6-8 NEB)

Yet, be wise and know of the moments when the Father wills that your siblings need to suffer. Your obstruction will be met with objection. But, the Holy Spirit will help you discern if only you are willing to learn. Sometimes falling is the only movement forceful enough to break open binding chains and to awaken sleeping eyes. And though it pains the Father to hear his children wail, and it grieves the Son to see his sheep and shepherds writhe, he knows that when all is said in done—while losing much—Messiah will have saved their life for eternity.

A man gifted with the Spirit can judge the worth of everything, but is not himself subject to the judgment by his fellow-men. For who knows the mind of [Yeshua]? Who can advise him? We, however, posses the mind of [Yeshua]. (1st Corinthians 2:15-16 NEB)

175. The Day of the Lord

First read: Zephaniah 1-3

During the fall you may find yourself wondering what lies ahead. You've let go—now what?

By the time readers get to the book of Zephaniah, many will begin to wonder why Scripture often refers to the Day of the Lord and why its authors insist on painting such a tragic scene. It's because Messiah doesn't desire his flock to have to experience his wrath. While there are places in Scripture which employ metaphorical or other figurative language, none of Scripture is hyperbolic. There are shepherds who preach such lies to their sheep so as not to alarm them.

And it shall come to pass at that time that I will search Jerusalem with lamps, and punish the men who are settled in contentment, who say in their heart, "[YHWH] will not do good, nor will he punish." Therefore their goods shall become booty, and their houses a desolation; they shall build houses, but not inhabit them; they shall plant vineyards, but not drink their wine. The great day of [YHWH] is near; it is near and hastens quickly. The noise of the day of [YHWH] is bitter; there the mighty men shall cry out. That day is a day of wrath, a day of trouble and distress, a day of devastation and desolation, a day of darkness and gloominess, a day of clouds and thick darkness, a day of trumpet and alarm against the fortified cities and against the high towers. "I will bring distress upon men, and they shall walk like blind men, because they have sinned against [YHWH]; their blood shall be poured out like dust, and their flesh like refuse." Neither their silver nor their gold shall be able to deliver them in the day of [YHWH]'s wrath; but the whole land shall be devoured by the fire of his jealousy, for he will make speedy ends of all those who dwell in the land. (Zephaniah 1:12-18 ESV)

Verses like these are either ignored completely, interpreted so as to suggest that only the God of the Tanakh would perform such an act, but that the God of the B'rit Khadasha has promised that he would never do such a thing because he is a God of love, and so simply looks past our licentiousness. Or these types of verses are watered down to read: "YHWH will look at the sins of his children, shake his head in disappointment, send them to their room with no dinner, and when they go to bed with a little tummy ache, then they will know that he means business." No dinner? What an insult to suggest that God Almighty looks at sin so saccharinely. But, neither is it the case that the Father and the Son and the angels will be slapping each other high fives when the day of YHWH arrives. It will be a time of immense suffering, longing, and weeping, and many will hang their heads low. It will be a season of reaping their harvest of wine from the seeds that were sown long ago. But, they are reaping because they remained unrepentant. Our loving God keeps no records of the wrongs that were done by a people who fell prostrate and cried.

If you, O [YHWH], should mark iniquities, O [Yeshua], who could stand? But with you there is forgiveness, that you may be feared. (Psalms 130:3-4 ESV)

He does, however, remember the deeds that were done by those who fell, but then died. There death didn't result in repentance, but unauthorized respite.

Truth is lacking, and he who departs from evil makes himself a prey. [YHWH] saw it, and it displeased him that there was no justice. He saw that there was no man, and wondered that there was no one to intercede; then his own arm brought him salvation, and his righteousness upheld him. He put on righteousness as a breastplate, and a helmet of salvation on his head; he put on garments of vengeance for clothing, and wrapped himself in zeal as a cloak. According to their deeds, so will he repay, wrath to his adversaries, repayment to his enemies; to the coastlands he will render repayment. So they shall fear the name of [YHWH] from the west, and his glory from the rising of the sun; for he will come like a rushing stream, which the wind of [YHWH] drives. And a Redeemer will come to Jerusalem, to those in Jacob who turn from transgression, declares [YHWH]. (Isaiah 59:15-20 ESV)

Such imagery in the Tanakh is not merely used for effect, but as a tool to dissuade others from defecting. And it would be an effective tool if shepherds were candid, rather than cancerous, in their delivery. When the rod is sent it would be wise to consider the life of a disciplined disciple so that when the fall has past, your relationship will last. You will have let whatever is holding you go. Good. Now, stay focused on Yeshua and remember his rod. The Holy Spirit will aide if acknowledged. There is a Day of YHWH approaching that will prove life-changing for all who are interested in changing. Afterwards, for the rest of the insolent remaining, he says:

Then he will say to those at his left hand, Begone from me, you cursed, into the eternal fire prepared for the devil and his angels. For I was hungry and you gave me no food, I was thirsty and you gave me nothing to drink, I was a stranger and you did not welcome me and entertain me, I was naked and you did not clothe me, I was sick and in prison and you did not visit me with help and ministering care. Then they also [in their turn] will answer, Lord, when did we see you hungry or thirsty or a stranger or naked or sick or in prison, and did not minister to you? And he will reply to them, Solemnly I declare to you, in so far as you failed to do it for the least in the estimation of men of these, you failed to do it for me. Then they will go away into eternal punishment, but those who are just and upright and in right standing with [YHWH] into eternal life. (Matthew 25:41-46 AMP)

176. Refocus on Re-living

First read: Haggai 1-2

After the fall, when you have regain your footing, you need to continue walking because sooner or later you will find that there is still more to lose. But remember that in losing you are actually gaining so much more.

When Messiah sends a storm to blow your house down, he is sending a message. The message is that your foundation is cruddy and you need to consider returning to the One that was already laid before you; which you once accepted, but then decided that you wanted to try something different. You thought the new foundation was better than the older one because it appeared sturdier and it allowed you to place more bells and whistles on the outside, thereby attracting a larger crowd. The problem was that you spent so much time and effort improving the outside that you no longer had any resources to keep up the inside. Eventually the inside began to suffer; but alas there was nothing you could do. But, oh how the crowds did accrue. Messiah will send a storm to inform and to warn. He is informing his sheep that he is displeased with their performance and warning them to redirect their efforts on the task given to them prior to his ascension into Heaven. For those who may have forgotten, each has been called to assist in the building of the Church that has been so poorly tended to since the early disciples completed the initial stages, since the ascension of Messiah.

They used to meet by common consent in Solomon's Portico, no one from outside their number venturing to join them. But people in general spoke highly of them, and more than that, numbers of men and women were added to their ranks as believers in [Yeshua]. In the end the sick were actually carried out into the streets and laid there on beds and stretchers, so that even the shadow of Peter might fall on one or another as he passed by; and the people from the towns round Jerusalem flocked in, bringing those who were ill or harassed by demons, and all of them were cured. (Acts 5:13-16 NEB)

Though many will see his storms as indicative of his wrath, his warnings are actually illustrative of his grace. Messiah will knock down your house in hopes that you return to the foundation before he returns. His storms are an opportunity to repent and return before the obliteration of this earth and this heaven. .

For [YHWH] has not appointed us to [incur his] wrath [he did not select us to condemn us], but [that we might] obtain [his] salvation through [Yeshua] (the Messiah) Who died for us so that whether we are still alive or are dead [at (Messiah's) appearing], we might live together with him and share his life. Therefore encourage (admonish, exhort) one another and edify (strengthen and build up) one another, just as you are doing. (1st Thessalonians 5:9-11 AMP)

Therefore when the storm finally comes your way, it is not then time to say: "Whew, I'm glad I survived that one. Now I can take my insurance money and rebuild." How foolish. Yeshua wants his disciples to have a dwelling place in which to live, yes. However, he wants all to remember that he desires to have a dwelling place as well; preferably in our hearts and in the Church. When you have lost everything, only then will you begin to refocus on finding everything that matters. With your possessions gone now, will you now also lose yourself? Messiah says that it's a must if you want to follow him. The idea of having to start over from scratch can be draining, but consider what you're gaining in the process. Will you favor the Apostle Paul when you have lost it all?

> It is now my happiness to suffer for you. This is my way of helping to complete, in my poor human flesh, the full tale of [Yeshua]'s affliction still to be endured, for the sake of his body which is the church. (Colossians 1:24 NEB)

The prophet Haggai served as a source of encouragement to the Israelites who, after returning from exile in 538 B.C. had been instructed by YHWH to rebuild his temple. Apparently, after having lost it all they still had not yet lost themselves. More were focused on the rebuilding of their own homes than they were YHWH's temple. The Father had to remind them that their blessings would not be restored until they had first restored his house. When believers begin to grow in their knowledge of their blessing's source, only then will they be prepared to stay the course.

177. The Lady In Red

First read: Hosea 1-7

You may find that some around you will be stripped bare this fall. Undoubtedly, they will feel vulnerable and perhaps even shamed. Take the lessons you learned from the summer and begin encouraging those around you. You have been here before yourself, so you will know how to deal. Tell them to focus on the change inside, rather than on their chill. And then tell them to quickly look around so they can see that there are others just as bare, but as a result, have clothed their surroundings with splendor.

For at the very time when we were still powerless, then [Messiah] died for the wicked. (Romans 5:6 NEB)

In the ninth chapter of Romans we find the apostle Paul quoting from the Book of Hosea. At the least, it is a reminder that the Tanakh had a valuable role in instructing members of the early Church. Even a cursory glance at the epistles should provide evidence to readers that the concerns addressed by some of Messiah's earlier and most devout followers are, in fact, ecumenical in nature and transcendent in time. If any back then were living today, they would have the same concerns of past. Why? It's the same script, just a different cast. A Church with members even more gifted in the art of beguiling and even more committed to defiling their dress. It isn't that the dress was spotless—it never has been. The beauty is that Messiah chose us despite the deepness of our crimson. We were a whore to the core; the harlot in scarlet; the lady in red. In fact, when he found us we were still lying in bed—dead. In our shame, Messiah came and did what no one on earth would ever do. He took us for his wife and then did what no one on earth could ever do. He exchanged our red for his.

Then the soldiers took him inside the courtyard (the Governor's headquarters) and called together the whole company. They dressed him in purple, and plaiting a crown of thorns, placed it on his head. Then they began to salute him with, "Hail, King of the Jews." They beat him about the head with a cane and spat upon him, and then knelt and paid mock homage to him. When they had finished their mockery, they stripped him of the purple and dressed him in his own clothes. (Mark 15:16-20 NEB)

The soldiers accordingly came to the first of his fellow-victims and to the second, and broke their legs; but when they came to [Yeshua], they found that he was already dead, so they did not break his legs. But one of the soldiers stabbed his side with a lance, and at once there was a flow of blood and water. (John 19:32-34 NEB)

How gracious. But what is a Bridegroom to do when he discovers that his Bride chooses no longer to abide in him? When he learns that the stains of his blood no longer sustains her yearning; no longer captivates her heart? When he sees that she is more interested in her former attire, as an object of desire to all flesh that is foreign?

Let the Bride of Messiah cease to mirror the madam of the last hour:

> Then one of the seven messengers that held the seven bowls came and spoke to me and said, "Come, and I will show you the judgment on the great whore, enthroned above the ocean. The kings of the earth have committed fornication with her, and on the wine of her fornication men all over the world have made themselves drunk." In the Spirit he carried me away into the wilds, and there I saw a woman mounted on a scarlet beast which was covered with blasphemous names and had seven heads and ten horns. The woman was clothed in purple and scarlet and bedizened with gold and jewels and pearls. In her hand she held a gold cup, full of obscenities and the foulness of her fornication; and written on her forehead was a name with a secrete meaning: "Babylon the great, the mother of whores and of every obscenity on earth."
> (Revelation 17:1-5 NEB)

To avoid the uncanny appearance of the great adulterous, it is necessary for many members of Messiah's Body to begin stripping and soon. None should feel so shamed as to forget the condition Messiah first found them in—still dead in their sin. Remember how tattered and torn you were? And yet, indeed he did wed—in love—while exchanging his robe for your red.

> ...but [YHWH] shows his love for us in that while we were still sinners, [Messiah] died for us. Since, therefore, we have now been justified by his blood, much more shall we be saved by him from the wrath of [YHWH].
> (Romans 5:8-9 ESV)

178. Lively Leaves

First read: Daniel 9-12

The fall should be a time of rejoicing for the future, not for despairing over the present. The beauty of dying lies in relieving suffering and strife, so that in death you are receiving satisfaction with life.

[Yeshua] said, "I am the resurrection and I am life. If a man has faith in me, even though he die, he shall come to life; and no one who is alive and has faith shall ever die." (John 11:25-26 NEB)

Does the leaf feel fear when due to forces mightier than itself it is suddenly shaken from its familiar surroundings, tossed into the open air, blown from here to there, and finally abandoned upon the earth, left to examine its inherent worth? Once the green has finally faded, its cover is finally blown; and all that's left for the world to see is a soul, though once unknown. How bright. How liberating is its light. Able to liven the deadest still, to illumine the blackest night. The leaf only fears because it is unprepared for the winds to come. Yet, while thunderous and determined, not long after their arrival, the leaf shall sigh in relief. For only while falling in the midst of its descent, will the leaf discover a truth previously hidden by a shadow so dim. It was connected to a lifeless limb. What wickedness does darkness keep—to foul, to rot, to taint. Yes, to hide indeed a virulent point. In truth, the green was faint. Thank our God for his winds, his thunderous winds; whom he sends as an act of his grace. How better to be blown off of its lifeless branches, then to burn with the tree from its base.

The Book of Daniel speaks of some troubling times for his people. It is difficult for believers to understand why YHWH would allow for such atrocities to take place, and it leaves millions asking the question, "How can a loving God be so cruel?" In reality, God Almighty will act lovingly to protect his children from such cruelty. Messiah will act to protect his flock because so many shepherds have failed to adequately do so. It is against these men that Jude speaks of in his letter:

These men are a blot on your love-feasts, where they eat and drink without reverence. They are shepherds who take care only of themselves. They are clouds carried away by the wind without giving rain, trees that in season bear no fruit, dead twice over and pulled up by the roots. They are fierce waves upon the sea, foaming shameful deeds; they are stars that have wandered from their course, and the place for ever reserved for them is blackest darkness. (Jude 1:12-13 NEB)

These men draw a line between spiritual and unspiritual persons, although they are themselves wholly unspiritual. But you, my friends, must fortify yourselves in your most sacred faith. Continue to pray in the power of the Holy Spirit. Keep yourselves in the love of [YHWH], and look forward to the day when [Yeshua] in his mercy will give eternal life. There are some doubting souls who need your pity, snatch them from the flames and save them. There are others for whom your pity must be mixed with fear; hate the very clothing that is contaminated with sensuality. (Jude 1:19-22 NEB)

It is the purpose of the Body, the Church, to ensure that none of its members are attached to anything dead. But, oh how lustrous and luxurious do lifeless limbs look to the eyes mesmerized by the green. The filthy look flawless; what's poisonous looks polished; and though garbage, their bark sounds pristine.

When he had finished speaking, a Pharisee invited him to a meal. He came in and sat down. The Pharisee noticed with surprise that he had not begun by washing before the meal. But [Yeshua] said to him, "You Pharisees. You clean the outside of cup and plate; but inside you there is nothing but greed and wickedness. You fools. Did not he who made the outside make the inside too? But let what is in the cup be given in charity, and all is clean." (Luke 11:37-41 NEB)

Sometimes it takes a gust of wind to grab the attention of those who, while destined for heaven, are at the moment, are on their way to hell. Daniel was afforded the privilege of seeing YHWH's plans for his people. While Daniel's visions were filled with unpleasantries, at least one truth is worth gleaning: The Father's more painful plans are usually intended to compensate for those who would attempt to thwart their pleasurable purposes and promises. Messiah's purpose is for his disciples to share the Gospel and to share in the intimacy of his Body and his Father. His purpose is not to bring harm or judgment. His purpose never changes, but his plans may; depending upon the behavior and needs of his shepherds and sheep. YHWH's children will be replenished when they enter Heaven's gates; our tireless work will not have been in vain. However, it is the will of the Son that his hands and feet—the leaves from his tree—begin healing the nations even now.

179. Learning While Lamenting

First read: Lamentations 1-5

While traveling, you may come to discover that whatever the shapes of the clouds in reflecting the potential and perversions of the earth, you will always find among them, a silver lining. In so doing, you won't be inclined to focus on their monochromic mundanity. However, in order for such silver to be seen you must keep sharp your sight.

And here is one point, my friends, which you must not lose sight of: with [Yeshua] one day is like a thousand years and a thousand years like one day. It is not that [YHWH] is slow in fulfilling his promise, as some suppose, but that he is very patient with you, because it is not his will for any to be lost, but for all to come to repentance. (2nd Peter 3:8-9 NEB)

There is good news and bad news for the members in the Body of Messiah. For some, the good news is that Messiah is on his way back and in just a short time we will meet him in the air. For some it will be a day of rejoicing, because no longer will they have to endure the pains that come with pressing for perfection. No more frustration of the flesh. No more struggling with our sin. No more walking out our faith for days and then falling down again. While on the road to Glory we dare not lament because we recognize that falling doesn't always mean failure, especially if our sight has sharpened as the result of an unexpected jolt. The lament, then, is not intended for those who may stumble while sanctifying, and so may hobble for a few (as so many often do). Though a few bruises may ensue, these members are still walking on the road. No, the lament is not necessarily for those who limp as much as it is necessary for those who leave.

A servant who deals wisely has the king's favor, but his wrath falls on one who acts shamefully. (Proverbs 14:35 ESV)

For others, the day of Yeshua's surprised and brief return will be a day to mourn. Some statements of sobriety: there will be those in the Church who prefer those in society over their Savior. These will be the ones who weren't as serious about their faith when they found out how serious the Son was in expecting absolute devotion. As a consequence for their carefree inconsistency and wickedness, there shall be judgment.

As things were in Noah's days, so will they be when the Son of Man comes. In the days before the flood, they ate and drank and married, until the day that Noah went into the ark, and they knew nothing until the flood came and swept them all away. That is how it will be when the Son of Man comes. Then there will be two men in the field; one will be taken, the other left; two women grinding in the mill; one will be taken, the other left. (Matthew 24:37-41 NEB)

"But that's not fair," we say. "Why won't all get to meet in the air?" Because not all will be prepared to go. It's no different than two students who have the same opportunity to graduate on time with their classmates. One chooses to work now so that he may play later, while the other chooses to play now; he'll have to pay later. On graduation day there will be those who will delight in their diplomas, and then there will be those whose diplomas will be delayed. The Father wants all of his children to know that the graduation date is not far off and that based upon current observations, there are few ready. The Book of Lamentations gives an accurate depiction of a people who have been left to fend for themselves at the hands of an angry God. Lamentations reads as a requiem. But the dirge emerges only as a response to Israel's unrepentant dirt; painful illustrations of how some only learn through lamenting.

He has made my teeth grind on gravel, and made me cower in ashes; my soul is bereft of peace; I have forgotten what happiness is; so I say, "My endurance has perished; so has my hope from [YHWH]." Remember my affliction and my wanderings, the wormwood and the gall. My soul continually remembers it and is bowed down within me. But this I call to mind, and therefore I have hope: The steadfast love of [YHWH] never ceases; his mercies never come to an end; they are new every morning; great is your faithfulness. "[YHWH] is my portion," says my soul, "therefore I will hope in him." (Lamentations 3:16-24 ESV)

Such misery is never the will of our Maker. And yet while there will be those whose faithlessness or lack of fortitude will render them liars, and therefore liable, here, YHWH's final judgment is still not consummate. If they resist the wiles of the Anti-Messiah and return to the Bible that they spiritually rejected, then, even still, Messiah will be just to forgive and they'll live.

It will be a time of great distress; there has never been such a time from the beginning of the world until now, and will never be again. If that time of troubles were not cut short, no living thing could survive; but for the sake of [YHWH]'s chosen it will be cut short. (Matthew 24:21-22 NEB)

Then I saw thrones, and upon them sat those to whom judgment was committed. I could see the souls of those who had been beheaded for the sake of [YHWH]'s word and their testimony to [Yeshua], those who had not worshiped the beast and its images or received its mark on forehead or hand. These came to life again and reigned with [Messiah] for a thousand years, though the rest of the dead did not come to life until the thousand years were over. This is the first resurrection. Happy indeed, and one of [YHWH]'s own people, is the man who shares in this first resurrection. Upon such the second death has no claim; but they shall be priests of [YHWH] and of [Messiah], and shall reign with him for the thousand years. (Revelation 20:4-6 NEB)

180. A Reason for Every Season - IV

Training Season

First read: Numbers 1-10

Before moving ahead, here is a final precaution when looking up, down, or all around. During your journey, make sure that in avoiding a gaze in any particular direction, you don't become unaware of your own body. Looking outside your self does not necessitate ignoring yourself. Every single part of your body was created for a particular reason. While moving the body forward, make sure you are cognizant of how each part moves with it. In harmony should each step be. To help you remember, keep the images of a symphony playing in your head. First, however, you would do well in remembering that you are not the Composer. The piece before you, a masterpiece, was created by someone else, but with your particular journey in mind. As acting conductor count it a blessing to have the baton on loan. The tempo has already been set; it is your job to make sure that it is followed. You have the score, and you know how to read it, so read it. You have no one but yourself to blame if you find yourself lost. If you expect to hear euphonic music then expect to train your ear.

One, two, skip a few, thirty-five, thirty-six. Or at least that is what most would like to do when reading the book of Numbers. Is it really necessary for members of today's Body to know the number of registered males belonging to each Israelite tribe? How about the direction YHWH appointed each tribe to remain in when encamped; the names of each tribal chief, or the order they were to leave in when given the go ahead to move? Are Christians going to suffer from spiritual stagnation if they don't know the specific Tabernacle assignments given to the sons of Levi, Gershon, Kohath, and Merari, and members of their family? No. But it might stump the growth of one to believe that YHWH had these events recorded for the sake of taking up Biblical space, or for leaving behind a nice descriptive narrative of Hebrew history. There are numerous truths found in reading these accounts; one of which points to the fact that Yeshua is indeed involved with the details of his creation.

Praise [YHWH]. For it is good to sing praises to our God; for it is pleasant, and a song of praise is fitting. [YHWH] builds up Jerusalem; he gathers the outcasts of Israel. He heals the brokenhearted and binds up their wounds. He determines the number of the stars; he gives to all of them their names. Great is [YHWH], and abundant in power; his understanding is beyond measure. (Psalms 147:1-5 ESV)

Before journeying, the Israelites needed to know precisely what the Father expected of them, relative to their given assignments. Even in commissioning and encouraging his disciples to go out, Messiah does concern himself with how his own Body is functioning within. Before members of the Body can effectively share the Gospel, each must go through a season of training. Training season is not a one time event, per say. Although Messiah has commissioned every member with a specific task as it relates to the Gospel, he doesn't provide them with every detail at once. He will provide the needed information when it is time, and it will be sufficient. However, before executing the task, the believer needs proper preparation. As members of Messiah's Body we may not always share the same opinion as to what is proper. But, if we will only remember that he is indeed the Head, and if we will only believe that our best interest is always in the mind and at the heart of Messiah, then we won't be offended or inclined to forget that our opinion, while welcomed, doesn't matter.

Seldom, if ever, will the season of preparation be free of battered winds or wearied limbs. But then God Almighty and Messiah want to ensure that when it is time for your light to shine, you will remain standing.

Blessed be [Yeshua], my rock, who trains my hands for war, and my fingers for battle; he is my steadfast love and my fortress, my stronghold and my deliverer, my shield and he in whom I take refuge, who subdues peoples under me. (Psalms 144:1-2 ESV)

181. Matters of the Heart

First read: Jeremiah 6-10

As the acting conductor you need to be keenly attuned to the workings of each instrument in your symphony. How does each instrument function and what role does each play in contributing to the overall sound produced? You need to be able to hear their distinctive sounds, so you need to know what each sounds like. How will you know when the instruments need tuning? Which instrument is it? Answering these questions will take time and intentional reflection as you are walking.

On another occasion he called the people and said to them, "Listen to me, all of you, and understand this: nothing that goes into a man from outside can defile him; no, it is the things that come out of him that defile a man." (Mark 7:14-15 NEB)

It will also take members who recognize that the vitality of the Body depends heavily on their veracity. As previously stated, in the Body of Messiah there is little room and time for personal business. While each should consistently examine their own relationship with the Father, equally should members monitor the performance of fellow travelers to ensure that those in danger of heart failure get the necessary treatment, before disaster strikes. It doesn't help when the shepherds or watchmen that Messiah has appointed refuse to point out those behaviors which have contributed to clogged arteries.

All you beasts of the field, come to devour, all you beasts in the forest. His watchmen are blind, they are all ignorant; they are all dumb dogs, they cannot bark; sleeping, lying down, loving to slumber. Yes, they are greedy dogs Which never have enough. And they are shepherds Who cannot understand; they all look to their own way; every one for his own gain, from his own territory. "Come," one says, "I will bring wine, and we will fill ourselves with intoxicating drink; tomorrow will be as today, and much more abundant." The righteous perishes, and no man takes it to heart; merciful men are taken away, while no one considers that the righteous is taken away from evil. He shall enter into peace; they shall rest in their beds, each one walking in his uprightness. (Isaiah 56:9-57:2 ESV)

Jeremiah was anointed by YHWH to deliver a painful, yet powerful message to the Israelites; one of judgment juxtaposed with hope. Israel was living under the authority of wicked kings who had contributed to the decline of her spiritual health. What should have provided her shepherds an opportunity to intervene in an exercise of faithful leadership, instead unveiled a blockage saturated with so much sin as to render the bodies incapable of surviving from within. The obstacle was obstinacy. It doesn't take long before blatant disrespect, continuously left unchecked, results in a hardened heart. Thus the admonition from the Apostle Paul to the church in Corinth:

Examine yourselves: are you living the life of faith? Put yourselves to the test. Surely you recognize that [Yeshua] is among you?—unless of course you prove unequal to the test. I hope you will come to see that we are not unequal to it. Our prayer to [YHWH] is that you may do no wrong; we are not concerned to be vindicated ourselves; we want you to do what is right, even if we should seem to be discredited. For we have no power to act against the truth, but only for it. We are well content to be weak at any time if only you are strong. Indeed, my whole prayer is that all may be put right with you. (2nd Corinthians 13:5-9 NEB)

It is with hope that members of today's Body begin sharing the same passion for one another's purity as the early disciples had for their congregations. When this passion surfaces, as can only come by way of the Holy Spirit, then it will be time for some pointing. Understand that pointing out oozing infection is a must. Those contaminated portions of the Body are infectious and they need cleansing.

'If your right eye leads you astray, tear it out and fling it away; it is better for you to lose one part of your body than for the whole of it to be thrown into hell. And if your right hand is your undoing, cut it off and fling it away; it is better for you to lose one part of your body than for the whole of it to go to hell. (Matthew 5:29-30 NEB)

Israel only exacerbated YHWH's outrage because shepherds simply placed dressing on her putrid pus. While walking in dimness, it's difficult to remember that Yeshua sees beyond the bandage and guise. He sees all the shepherds whose lips spew with lies; and he's displeased. Make no mistake: Messiah does delight in those who give generously and without a thought (and to all who can, the Spirit commands that we should).

Nevertheless, no payments will placate. Messiah is concerned with the heart. Neither tithes, offerings, nor any amount of sacrificial giving, is an acceptable exchange for sacrificial living. It is vital that theses shepherds return to their Rock, because Messiah takes exception with those misleading his flock.

Alas for you Pharisees. You pay tithes of mint and rue and every garden-herb, but have no care for justice and the love of [YHWH]. It is these you should have practiced, without neglecting the others. (Luke 11:42 NEB)

182. A Reflective Moment

Deeply Rooted

First read: Ephesians 3:18-19

He said: "A sower went out to sow. And as he sowed, some seed fell along the footpath; and the birds came and ate it up. Some seed fell on rocky ground, where it had little soil, and it sprouted quickly because it had no depth of earth; but when the sun rose the young corn was scorched, and as it had no root it withered away. Some seed fell among thistles; and the thistles shot up, and choked the corn. And some of the seed fell into good soil, where it bore fruit, yielding a hundredfold or, it might be, sixtyfold or thirtyfold. If you have ears, then hear." (Matthew 13:4-8 NEB)

One way to ensure that we remain grafted into the family of Messiah is to make certain that we're planted in fruitful soil. The Church is currently struggling with some members who have sown seeds on rocky ground and others who have sown among thistles. Members in both groups are in a precarious situation. Any one of three possibilities lay on the horizon, and unless these seeds are replanted, calamity shall soon hit.

This is what the parable means. The seed is the word of [YHWH]. Those along the footpath are the men who hear it, and then the devil comes and carries off the word from their hearts for fear they should believe and be saved. The seed sown on rock stands for those who receive the word with joy when they hear it, but have no root; they are believers for a while, but in the time of testing they desert. That which fell among thistles represents those who hear, but their further growth is choked by cares and wealth and the pleasures of life, and they bring nothing to maturity. But the seed in good soil represents those who bring a good and honest heart to the hearing of the word, hold it fast, and by their perseverance yield a harvest. (Luke 8:12-15 NEB)

Little children, let us not love in word or talk but in deed and in truth. By this we shall know that we are of the truth and reassure our heart before him; for whenever our heart condemns us,[YHWH] is greater than our heart, and he knows everything. (1st John 3:18-20 ESV)

As Yeshua explained to his disciples, the seeds planted on rocky ground are those believers whose faith is superficial at best and phony at worst. Unlike the seeds that fell along the footpath, they actually understood the message of the Gospel and accepted it—at least with their lips. However, the message went no further, it did not take root in the heart. These are the "believers" in the Church who, whether showing up regularly or seasonally, have nothing to account for their alleged faith. At one extreme are the superficial members who attend church because they believe it is the right thing to do. But, rather than viewing each message as an instrument for growth, they sit passively back in the pews. Their eyes are perhaps on the pastor, but their hearts and minds are a thousand miles away. The superficial members look the part, but are acting only partially, if at all. The joy that once abounded within them upon first hearing the word was, in fact, superficial as well. The emotion only lasted as long as the experience, and when it passed, so did their joy. These believers must understand that they can rekindle their fire, but only through active participation in the growth of the Body. Members more mature should seek to recapture these seeds and help them to find their place. Otherwise a seed unused may soon become bruised.

> Only you must continue in your faith, firm on your foundations, never to be dislodged from the hope offered in the gospel which you heard. This is the gospel which has been proclaimed in the whole creation under heaven; and I, Paul, have become its minister. (Colossians 1:23 NEB)

What about the phony believer; the one who eagerly accepted the message of the Gospel for its eternal rewards, but wants no part in the earthly responsibilities? These members fail to see the significance of going to church, and so most don't go.

> Let us hold fast the confession of our hope without wavering, for he who promised is faithful. And let us consider one another in order to stir up love and good works, not forsaking the assembling of ourselves together, as is the manner of some, but exhorting one another, and so much the more as you see the Day approaching. (Hebrews 10:23-25 NKJV)

Their feet may be on the road to Glory, but they aren't going anywhere, at least not anymore. Upon first believing they walk proudly and swiftly; that is, until they begin to see the road as it actually is—dusty, hilly, windy, narrow, and full of holes. Now suddenly they lose interest in walking.

> He continued his journey through towns and villages, teaching as he made his way towards Jerusalem. Someone asked him, "Sir, are only a few to be saved?" His answer was: "Struggle to get in through the narrow door; for I tell you that many will try to enter and not be able." (Luke 13:22-24 NEB)

These seeds find their security in simply being on the road, but at closer inspection you'll find that they aren't very secure after all. In fact, their plight lies in their insecurity as a believer. The phony believer struggles with trusting in Yeshua. They know that genuine service will require genuine suffering, but aren't convinced that Yeshua will deliver or that it's all worth it. Unlike the superficial member, these seeds aren't even interested in acting partially. They enjoy the Christian label, but are uninterested in Christian living.

> He answered, "Isaiah was right when he prophesied about you hypocrites in these words: "Inasmuch as these people draw near with their mouths and honor me with their lips, but have removed their hearts far from me, and their fear toward me is taught by the commandment of men." (Mark 7:6-8 NEB)

> While he was speaking thus, a woman in the crowd called out, "Happy the womb that carried you and the breasts that suckled you." He rejoined, "No, happy are those who hear the word of [YHWH] and keep it." (Luke 11:27-28 NEB)

For [YHWH] has no favorites: those who have sinned outside the pale of the Law of Moses will perish outside its pale, and all who have sinned under that law will be judged by the law. It is not by hearing the law, but by doing it, that men will be justified before [YHWH]. When Gentiles who do not possess the law carry out its precepts by the light of nature, then, although they have no law, they are their own law, for they display the effect of the law inscribed on their hearts. Their conscience is called as witness, and their own thoughts argue the case on either side, against them or even for them, on the day when [YHWH] judges the secrets of human hearts through [Yeshua]. So my gospel declares. (Romans 2:11-16 NEB)

These "believers" must realize that Messiah is unimpressed with lip service and remember that upon his return, he will expect to see some fruit. Members more mature should seek to recapture these seeds and remind them of their obligations, as well as act as agents of encouragement. Otherwise a seed with no fruit will become detached from its Root.

Already the axe is laid to the root of the trees; and every tree that fails to produce good fruit is cut down and thrown into the fire. (Matthew 3:10 NEB)

In all this, remember how critical the moment is. It is time for you to wake out of sleep, for deliverance is nearer to us now than it was when first we believed. It is far on in the night; day is near. Let us therefore throw off the deeds of darkness and put on our armor as soldiers of the light. Let us behave with decency as befits the day: no reveling or drunkenness, no debauchery or vice, no quarrels or jealousies. Let [Yeshua] himself be the armor that you wear; give no more thought to satisfying the bodily appetites. (Romans 13:11-14 NEB)

Thus defines the struggle of the believer whose seed has been sown among thistles. These members are probably in the most precarious situation of all struggling believers, because not long into their walk they decided to substitute divine visions for deadly mirages. As such, they are now walking zombies. At the moment, with little concept of time and an almost impenetrable shell, it will take committed warriors to arouse them from their wake. So then what are some of the characteristics of this dying breed? Well, those members more mature will have to exercise discernment in spotting them among the lost. They blend in so well with the way of the world, it's virtually impossible to distinguish them from the rest of those dying. Most believe that their saving grace lies in their willingness to acknowledge that Messiah exists. These believers have no problem in admitting that the road to Glory is real. Why would they? They once walked the road themselves. Unfortunately, as they were walking, enticing illusions began to crystallize on the side of the road. After first setting foot on the road to Glory, someone wise instructed them to, at all times, keep their mind filled with images of Heaven. The author of Hebrews, in lauding the likes of Abel, Sarah, and Noah, has a reminder for believers.

These all died in faith, not having received the promises, but having seen them afar off were assured of them, embraced them and confessed that they were strangers and pilgrims on the earth. For those who say such things declare plainly that they seek a homeland. And truly if they had called to mind that country from which they had come out, they would have had opportunity to return. But now they desire a better, that is, a heavenly country. Therefore [YHWH] is not ashamed to be called their God, for he has prepared a city for them. (Hebrews 11:13-16 NKJV)

For many once on the road, it was easy in the beginning to long for an eternity of living with YHWH, but it was short-lived. For that which they could not see was no longer as attractive as that which they could see, taste, and feel. Lust redirected the attention of these "believers" and now their seeds are among the weeds. Whether sex, status, money, or power, these "Christians" have become mesmerized by delusions of grandeur. What is most dangerous is that they've made repeated attempts to fuse their recklessness with their religion; giving the illusion that their lifestyle is acceptable. Sadly, many within the Body have decided to part from the truth, and instead follow in the wake. Attempting to compete with the world in trying to arouse those who slumber is tricky. Those members more mature must exercise caution in their quest. Conforming to the world, while rescuing those inside, is an all too common occurrence within the Church. Caution: the Bridegroom's ire is easily stoked and his judgments not unprovoked, when his Bride's maids attempt to unwisely conjoin what's been deemed an uneven yoke. Additionally, members must not rely on their own human strength to reclaim those among the thistles; for there in the thorns lies an enemy who won't release without a fight. Prepare yourself.

Finally then, find your strength in [Yeshua], in his mighty power. Put on all the armor which [YHWH] provides, so that you may be able to stand firm against the devices of the devil. For our fight is not against human foes, but against cosmic powers, against the authorities and potentates of this dark world, against the superhuman forces of evil in the heavens. Therefore, take up [YHWH]'s armor; then you will be able to stand your ground when things are at their worst, to complete every task and still to stand. (Ephesians 6:10-13 NEB)

183. YHWH's Gifts

First read: 1st Samuel 10:17-27

The sharpness of one's ear will depend less on the number of miles walked than it will on the degree of reflection they've engaged in with each step. As a matter of truth, some will have sharpened their ears long before others who are perhaps twenty or thirty miles ahead of them, due to induced reflection. Others will have been gifted by the Composer with heightened acuity from the time of their first step, but will still need refinement nonetheless. While refining, these travelers will still have an ability to hear. Focus less on the number of miles they have walked and more on the sound produced.

He was in the world, and the world was made through him, and the world did not know him. He came to his own, and his own did not receive him. (John 1:10-11 NKJV)

Why is it that believers have less of a problem asking YHWH for deliverance and more of one in accepting the instrument he chooses to use for delivering? It is easiest and most significant to recall how the Israelites jeered at Yeshua. Though under the watchful eye of the Romans, the Jews seemed less enthused by the proposition that Yeshua of Nazareth was to free them from their spiritual shackles. To the masses, it was his less than impressive disposition which detracted from his value. The Jews were looking for someone mammoth, majestic, and superior; Yeshua was mild, magnanimous, and submissive.

He was oppressed, and he was afflicted, yet he opened not his mouth; like a lamb that is led to the slaughter, and like a sheep that before its shearers is silent, so he opened not his mouth. By oppression and judgment he was taken away; and as for his generation, who considered that he was cut off out of the land of the living, stricken for the transgression of my people? And they made his grave with the wicked and with a rich man in his death, although he had done no violence, and there was no deceit in his mouth. (Isaiah 53:7-9 ESV)

Philip went to find Nathanael, and told him, "We have met the man spoken of by Moses in the Law, and by the prophets: it is [Yeshua] son of Joseph, from Nazareth." "Nazareth," Nathanael exclaimed, "can anything good come from Nazareth?" Philip said, "Come and see." (John 1:45-46 NEB)

To the religious leaders Messiah's pedagogy was unacceptable because his pedigree was undistinguished. In reality, they knew nothing of his family tree. YHWH has made the wisdom of this world look foolish.

As [YHWH] in his wisdom ordained, the world failed to find him by its wisdom, and he chose to save those who have faith by the folly of the Gospel. (1st Corinthians 1:21 NEB)

Before sending his only Son, the Father sent other gifts at the request of his children. There was Moses and Aaron, Saul, and David, to name a few. Like Yeshua, each of these gifts was also rejected because of his wrapping.

Simeon blessed them and said to Mary his mother, "This child is destined to be a stone which men reject; and you too shall be pierced to the heart. Many in Israel will stand or fall because of him, and thus the secret thoughts of many will be laid bare." (Luke 2:34-35 NEB)

Unlike Yeshua, none of these men were perfect, and yet, somehow YHWH saw first that they were fit for service. Even the prophet Samuel had to learn a valuable lesson in grasping YHWH's perception of value:

When they came, he looked on Eliab and thought, "Surely [YHWH]'s anointed is before him." But [YHWH] said to Samuel, "Do not look on his appearance or on the height of his stature, because I have rejected him. For [YHWH] sees not as man sees: man looks on the outward appearance, but [YHWH] looks on the heart." Then Jesse called Abinadab and made him pass before Samuel. And he said, "Neither has [YHWH] chosen this one." Then Jesse made Shammah pass by. And he said, "Neither has [YHWH] chosen this one." And Jesse made seven of his sons pass before Samuel. And Samuel said to Jesse, "[YHWH] has not chosen these." Then Samuel said to Jesse, "Are all your sons here?" And he said, "There remains yet the youngest, but behold, he is keeping the sheep." And Samuel said to Jesse, "Send and get him, for we will not sit down till he comes here." And he sent and brought him in. Now he was ruddy and had beautiful eyes and was handsome. And [YHWH] said, "Arise, anoint him, for this is he." (1st Samuel 16:6-12 ESV)

YHWH does not see as man sees. What man sees in determining the worth of an individual often follows suit with what the world sees as worthy. Believers of the Body must learn that the worth of the world is worthless compared to what Messiah has to offer for the deliverance of his sheep. Though, the difficulty in accepting his instruments lies in the inability to hear their sound. There are multitudes of sounds that members have become accustomed to hearing, coming from a host of instruments in which they have echoed. Polished, practiced, and prominent; these describe the preference of man. Broken, bruised, and branded; these describe the gifts of YHWH. What YHWH has to give, man doesn't want. And what YHWH wants, man won't give up. To reject his gifts is to reject him who gives.

Thus says [Yeshua], the Holy One of Israel, and the one who formed him: "Ask me of things to come; will you command me concerning my children and the work of my hands? I made the earth and created man on it; it was my hands that stretched out the heavens, and I commanded all their host. I have stirred him up in righteousness, and I will make all his ways level; he shall build my city and set my exiles free, not for price or reward," says [Yeshua]. (Isaiah 45:11-13 ESV)

Who among the Body will reject his Head?

184. Faith In The Fire

First read: Daniel 3

In order for euphony to sound, you must simultaneously read your score while leading your symphony. You can't read your score if it's packed away in one of your bags, adding to your weight. You should have your music in your hands at all times. It should be in your hands as you walk and it should be in your hands when you fall. Holding the music in your hands is not always going to keep you from tripping, but you will find inspiration while reading on the ground. It will remind you that the show must go on. The symphony can't play if the acting conductor isn't leading, and so you will need to get back up. Even the most seasoned conductor still needs to look at his music.

In this you greatly rejoice, though now for a little while, if need be, you have been grieved by various trials, that the genuineness of your faith, being much more precious than gold that perishes, though it is tested by fire, may be found to praise, honor, and glory at the revelation of [Yeshua], whom having not seen you love. Though now you do not see him, yet believing, you rejoice with joy inexpressible and full of glory, receiving the end of your faith—the salvation of your souls. (1st Peter 1:6-9 NKJV)

Fire is one of those constants that all believers on the road to Glory will have an encounter with at least once; at the most—undisclosed. There are the fires from Heaven and then flaming are the fires from Hell; but only those walking in the Spirit can tell the difference. To suggest that only flames from Hell are painful is to show signs of spiritual immaturity, which can lead a believer down a dark and deceptive path. On the contrary, the flames of Hell are usually gratifying in the short-run. Its flames start off at a temperature just warm enough to keep one enraptured in their lustful behavior. And then you begin to burn. In the long-run, if you haven't found faith while in the midst of the flames, then you shall soon come to learn the stench of the rotting soul.

As for those who had been scattered, they went through the country preaching the word. (Acts 8:4 NEB)

Conversely, the heavenly flames of the Holy Spirit will rarely feel agreeable in the beginning. During a fiery baptism the Holy Spirit will grant believers a sneak preview of what awaits them upon entering Yeshua's presence in Paradise. However, almost immediately after, the novice may begin associating the convicting acts of the Holy Spirit with bouts of betrayal. "Hey," we say. "Where's all the pleasure I was promised?" Whoever promises earthly pleasure to a convict in promoting a conversion is not carrying out Messiah's commission.

Loving pleasure leads to poverty. Wine and luxury will never make you wealthy. (Proverbs 21:17 ESV)

And this is my prayer, that your love may grow ever richer and richer in knowledge and insight of every kind, and may thus bring you the gift of true discrimination. Then on the Day of [Yeshua] you will be flawless and without blame, reaping the full harvest of righteousness that comes through [Yeshua], to the glory and praise of [YHWH]. (Philippians 1:9-11 NEB)

Indeed the promise of Messiah to a convert is that the Holy Spirit will continue to convict so that we may appear blameless on the day of his return. Though, conviction is not condemnation. The former leads to purity while the latter paralyzes. In the long-run, the soreness that often accompanies sanctification will yield an eternity of satisfaction.

Of one thing I am certain: the One who started the good work in you will bring it to completion by the Day of [Yeshua]. (Philippians 1:6 NEB)

In the end, the only assurance we have in surviving the flames is by keeping faith in the Word. Our faith won't keep us away from the flicker, but what the Spirit doesn't singe will only grow thicker. Indeed, as the flames of Heaven draw a believer closer to his Savior, and likewise, the Father, the flames of Hell will flicker with fury. Perhaps no other figures in the Bible knew better of this predicament than Shadrach, Meshach, and Abednego; Daniel's faithful friends who defied in failing to comply with King Nebuchadnezzar's commands. Remember how just one phrase placed them in front of the blaze?

Shadrach, Meshach, and Abednego answered the king, "Nebuchadnezzar, we don't need to explain these things to you. If you throw us into the hot furnace, the God we serve can save us. And if he wants to, he can save us from your power. But even if [YHWH] does not save us, we want you to know, King, that we refuse to serve your gods. We will not worship the gold idol you have set up." (Daniel 3:16-18 ESV)

It was their boldness that brought them before the flames, and their belief that brought them out. Messiah delivered the same promise to his disciples, whom he told would also feel the fire's ire.

And be on your guard, for men will hand you over to their courts, they will flog you in the synagogues, and you will be brought before governors and kings, for my sake, to testify before them and the heathen. But when you are arrested, do not worry about what you are to say; when the time comes, the words you need will be given you; for it is not you who will be speaking: it will be the Spirit of your Father speaking in you. (Matthew 10:17-20 NEB)

Yeshua never told his disciples that they wouldn't take any heat from following him or for remaining loyal. He, in fact, warned them of it and prepared them for it. All of the disciples would eventually be doused in the flames for their faith, and thus Yeshua faltered not in his. Though the flames of fire burn bright, the light of the Lamb's burns brighter.

Then one of the seven messengers that held the seven bowls full of the seven last plagues came and spoke to me and said, "Come, and I will show you the bride, the wife of the Lamb. " So in the Spirit he carried me away to a great high mountain, and showed me the holy city of Jerusalem coming down out of heaven from [YHWH]. It shone with the glory of [YHWH]; it had the radiance of some priceless jewel, like jasper, clear as crystal. It had a great high wall, with twelve gates, at which were twelve angels; and on the gates were inscribed the names of the twelve tribes of Israel. There were three gates to the east, three to the north, three to the south, and three to the west. The city wall had twelve foundation-stones, and on them were the names of the twelve apostles of the Lamb. (Revelation 21:9-14 NEB)

It is the solidity of our faith that Messiah died to see. He faithfully shed his blood, now where are we?

185. A Reason for Every Season - V

A Season for Silence

First read: Joshua 6:6-10

No piece worth listening to is one-dimensional; beauty is found in balance. The Composer did not create a one-dimensional masterpiece, so questions you may have concerning the dynamics will be found in the score. The score will tell you of the moments when you need to be quiet. There is no joy to be found in a piece that is consistently shrill—it's deafening. What's more, every accidental sharp or flat sound produced will be accentuated. After a while, no one will want to hear and soon no one will be able to hear—not even you. Playing at such a volume persistently may energize, but such practice is folly when it wears everyone else down in the process. This means you won't hear anyone trying to help you fine-tune.

> Having then gifts differing according to the grace that is given to us, let us use them: if prophecy, let us prophesy in proportion to our faith; or ministry, let us use it in our ministering; he who teaches, in teaching; he who exhorts, in exhortation; he who gives, with liberality; he who leads, with diligence; he who shows mercy, with cheerfulness. (Romans 12:6-8 NKJV)

There is something to be said for the voice which has the unique ability to inspire, to motivate, to awaken one from the dead. These members are vital to the Body of Messiah and typically are the ones that Yeshua has endowed with strong evangelistic skills. It is their passion that penetrates; permeating the most hardened of hearts, down to the fibers of the sulking soul. While Messiah has commissioned all to spread the Good News, the evangelist has been placed at the front of this platoon. This spirit of boldness which hallmarks the Spirit-filled Body is an asset too, for the wayward believer who is threatening to defect from the ranks of the righteous. While situations arise in which YHWH speaks directly to us through the actions or words of another, there are moments when the mouth of a member, while intending to help, can itself hinder YHWH's deliverance. There are members who need reminding that the Father is capable of working even during seasons of silence. Joshua, the man whom YHWH appointed to replace Moses to lead the Israelites across the Jordan, had to instruct the eager believers to spend their first six days circling the perimeter of Jericho in silence. They were ready to experience the victory that YHWH had promised them, instantly. But the wisdom of YHWH moved Joshua to give his willing army an unexpected plan. It must have seemed odd to the Israelites, this plan of circling in silence. But, in his actions, the Father, on occasion, prefers the odd over the ordinary. Oddity often inspires a spirit of dependence. And dependence on God Almighty alone is a prerequisite if we expect his deliverance. YHWH's reason for his seasons of silence is always for the benefit of the believer. There are some who need a gentle reminder that for those whose hearts have been broken, the truth can be spoken with softness. Messiah was always cognizant of his crowd. Not just because he was the Son of YHWH, but, before he spoke, he saw. In foretelling of the future Messiah, the prophet Isaiah spoke of Yeshua and said:

> He will not cry aloud or lift up his voice, or make it heard in the street; a bruised reed he will not break, and a faintly burning wick he will not quench; he will faithfully bring forth justice. He will not grow faint or be discouraged till he has established justice in the earth; and the coastlands wait for his law. (Isaiah 42:2-4 ESV)

Believers, then, are encouraged to remain mindful of the needs of the masses. Not everyone around needs to hear at the same volume, though everyone around needs to hear. The message must match the words of Yeshua, but the way it's conveyed may be veered. While a narrow-mind will assist the believer in staying on the narrow road, some bending is required when reaching out to those on the side. Seasons of silence are also necessary in reminding the believer that a humble heart beats the loudest. Our journey on the road to Glory should be filled with daily instruction from the Holy Spirit, and at times from members of the Body whom have been inspired. Yet, no sound will be heard of its beat, from the heart which is hard from conceit. And without a beating heart, what use is this member to the rest of the Body? To keep it softened and us useful, YHWH will call for silence so that we may hear and learn. In wisdom and with gratefulness the believer will rejoice during these seasons; for there is hardly time for resting while on the road.

> He leads the humble in what is right, and teaches the humble his way. All the paths of [YHWH] are steadfast love and faithfulness, for those who keep his covenant and his testimonies. (Psalms 25:9-10 ESV)

186. Muzzling the Mouth

First read: Psalms 141:3

Remember, you are refining while on the road to Glory. You can't fine-tune if either you or everyone else has tuned out. Caution. Some people on your journey will be for whatever reason, tone-deaf; they can't distinguish music from mayhem. Some can, but will insist that the two are the same. "Any sound produced is music," they will say. Don't listen; you need to tune them out. Learn to discern. Make sure that those who are helping you fine-tune can hear the same sounds you do and are looking on the same sheet of music. Every day is not the day for forte. Know which instruments to soften and know when to soften them.

And the tongue is in effect a fire. It represents among our members the world with all its wickedness; it pollutes our whole being; it keeps the wheel of our existence red-hot, and its flames are fed by hell. Beasts and birds of every kind, creatures that crawl on the ground or swim in the sea, can be subdued and have been subdued by mankind; but no man can subdue the tongue. It is an intractable evil, charged with deadly venom. (James 3:6-8 NEB)

Nothing is quite as deafening to the ears of YHWH than the sound of division; it's isn't melodic, it is mayhem. There is a time to open one's mouth, and then there are moments when believers need to learn how to wear a muzzle. The Holy Spirit is in the business of teaching Messiah's flock, both found and lost, to discern the difference. When YHWH, through his grace, calls forth a lost sheep to join his Son's fold, it is vital that he or she responds with words: "I'm sorry and I'm dead. I have sinned because I am a sinner and I need Messiah in my life so that I may live."

Repent therefore and be converted, that your sins may be blotted out, so that times of refreshing may come from the presence of [YHWH], and that he may send [Yeshua] who was preached to you before, whom heaven must receive until the times of restoration of all things, which [YHWH] has spoken by the mouth of all his holy prophets since the world began. (Acts 3:19-21 NEB)

Such recovery is refused to those who, in their pride or obstinacy, choose to remain silent. And while the gift of salvation grants all authorization to live and to speak boldly about the goodness of the Father, it grants none a license for loose lips. Loose lips can rip a Body to shreds and can make the recovery process for individual members lonesome. It is foolery to foul up the entire Body with the lingering effects of diarrheic diction, and yet there are members whose gossiping will result in garnished wages unless repentance transpires. Perhaps there are those who believe that the Father is only concerned with more "serious" transgressions?

There are six things [Yeshua] hates. There are seven things he cannot stand [that are an abomination to his soul]: a proud look [haughty eyes], a lying tongue, hands that kill [spill the blood of] innocent people, a mind [heart] that thinks up evil plans, feet that are quick to do [run to] evil, a witness who lies, and someone who starts arguments [conflicts; fights] among families [brothers].(Proverbs 6:16-19 ESB)

I tell you this: there is not a thoughtless word that comes from men's lips but they will have to account for it on the day of judgment. For out of your own mouth you will be acquitted; out of your own mouth you will be condemned. (Matthew 12:36-37 NEB)

Let your bearing towards one another arise out of your life in [Yeshua]. (Philippians 2:5 NEB)

Rarely does gossip involve the whole truth; and yet even when it does, dissension is still the result. Division of the Body is an objective of the devil, therefore; it is wise for members to desist from being used as willing participants in his deadly game. How disdainful it is to Messiah for members of his flock to defend perverse contentions with "noble intentions." Igniting the flames of hell by sharing your "concerns" with members who have yet to find intimacy with Emmanuel is a sign of spiritual immaturity, and an indication of your own placement on the road to Glory. It is equally unwise to seek counsel concerning your journey from any spiritual Joe.

Do not give dogs what is holy; do not throw your pearls to the pigs: they will only trample on them, and turn and tear you to pieces. (Matthew 7:6 NEB)

Joe may not know Yeshua as well as he claims, and so shortly thereafter he will have defamed your name. When deciding who to tell when troubles turn up, believers need to learn to start with their Father; for there is no one who can counsel better. However, believers then need to ask him for discernment in deciding who next to share with. If you will comply then he will reply. Be patient and know that learning how to muzzle now will save the Body from misery later.

A worthless man plots evil, and his speech is like a scorching fire. A dishonest man spreads strife, and a whisperer separates close friends. A man of violence entices his neighbor and leads him in a way that is not good. (Proverbs 16:27-29 ESV)

187. Toxic Tongues

First read: Proverbs 18:21 / Ephesians 4:29

Abasing, ablazing, abjectly abrupt—
   Are the words that may eek from my lips

Begrudging, beguiling, benignly bankrupt—
   It is strife that I seek through my quips

Callous, careless, caustic, and cruel—
   If you should happen to cross me today

Deafening, decaying, and deafening drool—
   Are the words that I may choose to slay

Embarrass, embitter, embroil, exhaust—
   Oh, the power that lies in my tongue

Fermenting a fire or an icy frost—
   With the fragrance of flowers or wrong

Gossiping, gloating, griping, a gloss—
   And uttered without prayer or thought

Harmful, hateful, a hasty cost—
   Forgetting that our souls have been bought

Igniting, ignoble, immoral, implied—
   A venomous phrase or two

Jeering, judging, and self-justified—
   While praising our God from the pews

Knock, kindle, like a knife—
   that's stuck in the back

Loaded, licentious, the ruin of life—
   Ill-thought, ill-timed, no tact

Maim, maul, meddle, malign—
   While professing that Messiah is our Lord

Nonsense, noxious, numbly confined—
   To words that shall bring down his sword

Obloquies, obscenities, odious, and obstruct—
   With a few slight words to describe

Piercing, patronizing, and painful conduct—
   Though in jest, through the chest, with our gibes

Quakes, qualms, quarrels, a quiver—
   From the poisonous spout of our heads

Raunchy, reckless, a repelling river—
   Though to him, on the cross, we were wed

Salacious, sarcastic, sardonic, sour—
   The power to knock to the ground

Tarnishing, taunting, toxic abuse—
   The power to tear with a sound

Unashamed, unbridled, unaware, unwise—
   When passing judgment on those we see

Vexing, vengeful, our vain demise—
   By the One whose blood set us free

Weakening, whittling, wrenching, a weed—
   Whether whispered or uttered aloud

Exasperating and excessive, those wicked deeds—
   That Yeshua can hear in a crowd

Yes, YHWH yearns for his young to yoke—
   Their tongues to the word of his Son

Zealous, (and sometimes zany) words may—
   indeed provoke One's ire that can't be undone

188. A Reason for Every Season: VI

A Season for Sounding

First read: Joshua 6:13-20; 8-12

On that same note, pay attention to the score still. For you shall be alerted of the moments that you need to change the dynamics. There is no quicker way to induce lethargy than to have a piece where sound is barely heard, ever. It's worth noting that greater danger lies in playing with persistent pianissimo. First, remember that you are on the road to restoration and so you will have instruments that need tuning. However, if you are consistently playing at such a low volume then no one is going to pick up on your sour notes, and thus no one will know what needs tuning. You may find contentment in feigning perfection now, but there is someone waiting for you at the end of your journey who has perfect pitch. If you want to play in his symphony, then now is the time for fine-tuning. If not, no matter how melodic it may sound to you, all he will hear is noise; the response won't be music to your ears. Second, lethargy will eventually lull to sleep. If you or those around you are sleeping, it means that you are not alert. You need to stay alert. Everyone around you needs to remain alert. The temptation may exist to forever sound soothing. However, you may find yourself in trouble if no one else is moving.

In [Messiah] indeed we have been given our share in the heritage, as was decreed in his design whose purpose is everywhere at work. For it was his will that we, who were the first to set our hope on [Messiah], should cause his glory to be praised. (Ephesians 1:11-12 NEB)

And then they were given the go ahead. After circling in silence for six days, the Israelites were eager for day seven to arrive. Joshua gave the command, shouting commenced, and the walls came tumbling down. The city of Jericho was the first in a long series of campaigns in which YHWH delivered unto the Israelites, their enemies. Their shouting was heard from miles away, and neighboring nations, fearing for their own lives, sought victory by consolidating their forces. Such efforts by the enemy are in vain, however, when YHWH has already spoken. Likewise, there are moments in ministering when the Holy Spirit will direct believers to open up their mouth to speak. While hushed tones may prove effective in calling some from the side of the road, others will need a gong sounding in their ear in order to wake them from their daze. Many members in the Body are walking Jericho cities. There are elements within each that must still die before the Father can grant abundant life. But, at present, walls remain erect; preventing the painful penetration of truth from tearing down erosive lies. Unfortunately, restoration can only begin after repentance. Messiah is not impressed with those who insist on walking around masquerading silent perfection in hopes that no one will discover what lies beneath.

The Pharisees, who loved money, heard all this and scoffed at him. He said to them, "You are the people who impress your fellow-men with your righteousness; but [YHWH] sees through you; for what sets itself up to be admired by men is detestable in the sight of [YHWH]." (Luke 16:14-15 NEB)

The Body stands to heal when its members can be real. A reminder of what Paul wrote to the church in Ephesus:

Therefore, putting away lying, "Let each one of you speak truth with his neighbor," for we are members of one another. (Ephesians 4:25 NEB)

It is not always comforting to know that Messiah calls each of us to perpetually step outside of our boat. When the Father ushers in a season of sounding, at times he may call for the entire symphony to play or he may ask for only a section. Still yet, a solo performance might be in order. For many members of the Body, it is an alarming venture to speak the whole truth and nothing but. Yet, with God Almighty's help we can. With his help we must. While there are many hurting who need to hear of the Father's healing; many guilty who need hear of the Father's grace, there also exists the unjust who must know of Messiah's justice, and the swindler who should know of his sword. It is nice to hear that YHWH's angels are constantly protecting his children. They must also be told from whom they are protected, and the tricks of his trade. No, it isn't always pleasant to hear; but say it you must, and while having no fear.

Let the heavens rejoice, and let the earth be glad; let the sea roar, and all its fullness; let the field be joyful, and all that is in it. Then all the trees of the woods will rejoice before [Yeshua]. For he is coming, for he is coming to judge the earth. He shall judge the world with righteousness, and the peoples with his truth. (Psalms 96:11-13 NKJV)

189. A Reflective Moment

Slip of the Tongue

First read: Colossians 4:5-6

He who guards his mouth preserves his life, but he who opens wide his lips shall have destruction. (Proverbs 13:3 ESV)

Are you a cavalier Christian? Does the idea of having to monitor every syllable that comes out of your mouth annoy you? Being a Christian is no easy job, and yes, YHWH does have high expectations for each of his people. However, the bar he sets is neither too high, nor without reason. As ambassadors for Messiah, not only must we ensure that we aren't misrepresenting the interests of Heaven, we must keep, within our periphery, those who have made it their duty to discredit the Christian faith. Every opportunity they get to try and prove Messiah a liar, they take. And of late when Christians open their mouth, whether at the workplace, school, or any other mixed setting (which often even includes church), they are arming those seeking with ammunition to deny the existence of YHWH.

If anyone among you thinks he is religious, and does not bridle his tongue but deceives his own heart, this one's religion is useless. (James 1:26 NKJV)

Christians are today living in a time where cavalier living must desist. The number one assertion I heard at school by students who identified themselves as agnostics or atheists was that, to them, they saw no difference between one religion and another because those who are professing to believe aren't acting any differently from one another. Remember, as Christians we are beacons of light for those who are lost. However, at present it's proving difficult for the lost to see clearly because most of the lights are all pretty dim, one shining no brighter than any other. How then are Messiah's servants to carry out his instructions?

"You are a light for all the world. A town that stands on a hill cannot be hidden. When a lamp is lit, it is not put under the meal-tub, but on the lampstand, where it gives light to everyone in the house. And you, like the lamp, must shed light among your fellows, so that, when they see the good you do, they may give praise to your Father in heaven." (Matthew 5:14-16 NEB)

We are to carry out his instructions with due diligence. Every effort must be made to have tongues filled with compassion, humility, patience, kindness, and wisdom. Admittedly, it is not always easy.

Never pay back evil for evil. Let your aims be such as all men count honourable. If possible, so far as it lies with you, live at peace with all men. (Romans 12:17-18 NEB)

But, the non-believer must see that forbearance and forgiveness are distinguishing characteristics of Christianity. A believer's words should always be a beacon to win a lost soul, and always should his or hers serve as a compass.

Walk in wisdom toward those who are outside, redeeming the time. Let your speech always be with grace, seasoned with salt, that you may know how you ought to answer each one. (Colossians 4:5-6 NKJV)

Obviously there are times where our actions do speak louder than our words. And it's no less of a stumbling block for the Church to have believers whose actions routinely stand in stark contrast to what they profess. How quickly do the actions of a part adversely affect the perception of the whole. But at all times, our words must speak for themselves. There can be no slipping of the tongue, for such carelessness can prove costly. Each believer must only utter words shameful neither to Messiah nor the Body. Again, on a daily basis members should ask of the Father to be guided by the Holy Spirit in their conversations so that an opportunity never presents itself for an outsider to call into question the integrity of the Christian faith.

Hear this, all peoples. Give ear, all inhabitants of the world, both low and high, rich and poor together. My mouth shall speak wisdom; the meditation of my heart shall be understanding. (Psalms 49:1-3 ESV)

We use it to sing praises of [Yeshua] and the Father, and we use it to invoke curses upon our fellow-men who are made in [Yeshua]'s likeness. Out of the same mouth come praises and curses. My brothers, this should not be so. Does a fountain gush with both fresh and brackish water from the same opening? Can a fig-tree, my brothers, yield olives, or a vine figs? No more does salt water yield fresh. (James 3:9-12 NEB)

190. Delighting In Dichotomy

First read: Ecclesiastes 3:1-9

You will find while walking that balance is the key to play in. What is sensational is that the Composer created this piece just for you to play. What is magnificent about the music is that while everyone has the same score, not all of the dynamics are going to be uniformly positioned. Your symphony will sound slightly different, though being in perfect time, it should sound equally euphonic. As such, you should not expect to hear the exact same symphony from everyone. Don't assume that because one doesn't sound exactly like yours that it means their conductor or instruments are faulty; both are reflections of the Composer. Such assumptions will lead to your folly, as you will be so focused on the slight differences, that you will neither appreciate the beautiful sounds that are indeed produced, nor will you hear the sour notes that are suddenly coming from your own symphony.

It is tempting while walking to look around and begin making assumptions about our fellow travelers. It is easy to get frustrated with ourselves and with YHWH when we try to make sense of a world that doesn't fit into our individual schemas; when we don't understand the methods of our Maker. The Book of Ecclesiastes is a dichotomy, contrasting two ways of viewing the world. King Solomon minces no words in describing one as wise and the other as foolery. The believer's view of the world will depend upon his level of intimacy with the Father. Those whose intimacy with him is practically nil, will have a near nihilistic view of the world.

[YHWH] is righteous in all his ways and kind in all his works. [Yeshua] is near to all who call on him, to all who call on him in truth. He fulfills the desire of those who fear him; he also hears their cry and saves them. [YHWH] preserves all who love him, but all the wicked he will destroy. (Psalms 145:17-20 ESV)

They will also fall into the same thought patterns as some of the earlier Deists, in finding contentment in a distant deity. Some of the dangers are obvious while others perhaps are not so. Ironically, while espousing freedom, both nihilism and deism promote a rigid perception of God Almighty. It requires believers to see YHWH, shortly after creation, placing himself inside of a self-made box, with a self-made padlock on the outside—locking him in. Trying to figure out the plausibility of this feat would be as absurd as the belief is foolish. But, in practical and albeit, less extreme, circumstances such beliefs engender egocentric souls. Because these believers only view the Father from their perspective, any work of theirs outside of their schemata is speculative. Hence, Christianity is no longer just monotheistic; it is now also monolithic through the eyes of me. How bland. How perfect for the nihilist. On the other hand, with greater intimacy comes a heightened understanding of just how intimately YHWH is involved with his people. In a short time these believers become acutely aware of the purposefulness of each pulse. As such, they are able to recognize the purpose of Messiah in willing a Body that is diverse, while equally indivisible.

A body is not one single organ, but many. Suppose the foot should say, "Because I am not a hand, I do not belong to the body." it does belong to the body nonetheless. Suppose the ear were to say, "Because I am not an eye, I do not belong to the body." it does still belong to the body. If the body were all eye, how could it hear? If the body were all ear, how could it smell? But, in fact, [YHWH] appointed each limb and organ to its own place in the body, as he chose. If the whole were one single organ, there would not be a body at all; in fact, however, there are many different organs, but one body. The eye cannot say to the hand, "I do not need you;" nor the head to the feet, "I do not need you." Quite the contrary: those organs of the body which seem to be more frail than others are indispensable, and those parts of the body which we regard as less honorable are treated with special honor. To our unseemly parts is given a more than ordinary seemliness, whereas our seemly parts need no adorning. But [YHWH] has combined the various parts of the body, giving special honor to the humbler parts, so that there might be no sense of division in the body, but that all its organs might feel the same concern for one another. If one organ suffers, they all suffer together. If one flourishes, they all rejoice together. (1st Corinthians 12:14-26 NEB)

The Body of Messiah is to be made of diverse disciples in order to more effectively disseminate the Gospel to an equally diverse, but dying world; a world that is marching to the beat of a deadly drummer. The Body is to be united in the Truth and yet varied in her transmission. Our God is not a God of chance, but one of order and who is in charge. Thankfully, their purposes remain fixed despite the oft short-sighted perspective of their people.

For as the heavens are higher than the earth, so are my ways higher than your ways and my thoughts than your thoughts. For as the rain and the snow come down from heaven and do not return there but water the earth, making it bring forth and sprout, giving seed to the sower and bread to the eater, so shall my word be that goes out from my mouth; it shall not return to me empty, but it shall accomplish that which I purpose, and shall succeed in the thing for which I sent it. (Isaiah 55:9-11 ESV)

191. Meek Not Weak

First read: Micah 1-7

Your piece was especially crafted for you, and so you may have more measures that require the use of piano or pianissimo. Others may have pieces that, in fact, require more forte or fortissimo. Though, no masterpiece will be written absent of a mixture of all. If attuned to the score then your symphony should naturally produce a medley of mezzos.

Watch, stand fast in the faith, be brave, be strong. Let all that you do be done with love. (1st Corinthians 16:13-14 NKJV)

The meek shall inherit the earth. Yet, meekness is not weakness. Messiah does not call for his sheep to be weak. While we are called to humility, we must also take steps to ensure that those around us are being treated humanely.

For the love of money is a root of all kinds of evil, for which some have strayed from the faith in their greediness, and pierced themselves through with many sorrows. But you, O man of [YHWH], flee these things and pursue righteousness, godliness, faith, love, patience, gentleness. Fight the good fight of faith, lay hold on eternal life, to which you were also called and have confessed the good confession in the presence of many witnesses. I urge you in the sight of [YHWH] who gives life to all things, and before [Yeshua] who witnessed the good confession before Pontius Pilate, that you keep this commandment without spot, blameless until [Yeshua]'s appearing. (1st Timothy 6:10-14a NEB)

But that is not how you learned [Messiah]. For were you not told of him, were you not as Christians taught the truth as it is in Yeshua?—that, leaving your former way of life, you must lay aside that old human nature which, deluded by its lusts, is sinking towards death. (Ephesians 4:21-22 NEB)

Upon examining Scripture one should have no question as to the type of character that Christians are called to have. It is clear that all believers are called to renounce the ways of this world. But Messiah is reminding his sheep that denouncing comes with being a disciple as well. Frankly, there is too much injustice transpiring in the world for the Church to continue acting as a back seat spectator—interested but immobile. Thus, we are called to be both light and salt.

You are salt to the world. And if salt becomes tasteless, how is its saltiness to be restored? It is now good for nothing but to be thrown away and trodden underfoot. (Matthew 5:13 NEB)

Salt—oh, the healing it brings. But not before the sting. We are the salt of the world and Messiah is the Living water. Thus, those who live for the world, their sins are like festering wounds. Micah spoke against the Israelites, both Israel and Judah, because of the gross injustices their rulers were committing against the lowly. Messiah is not unaware of those shepherds and princes whose crimes are a must; who cheat in their lust; and whose wounds continue to pulsate with pus. As of now they haven't yet been found to have fault, because not enough members have been sharing their salt.

If your brother commits a sin, go and take the matter up with him, strictly between yourselves, and if he listens to you, you have won your brother over. If he will not listen, take one or two others with you, so that all facts may be duly established on the evidence of two or three witnesses. If he refuses to listen to them, report the matter to the congregation; and if he will not listen even to the congregation, you must then treat him as you would a pagan or a tax-gatherer. (Matthew 18:15-17 NEB)

Messiah has not called his sheep to salty behavior. Let no member be motivated to malign. We must still be kind and leave the vengeance to our Avenger who will one day repay those who wound his molded clay.

For [YHWH] has a day of vengeance, a year of recompense for the cause of Jerusalem. (Isaiah 34:8 ESV)

Strengthen the weak hands, and make firm the feeble knees. Say to those who have an anxious heart, "Be strong; fear not. Behold, [Yeshua] will come with vengeance, with the recompense of [YHWH]. He will come and save you." Then the eyes of the blind shall be opened, and the ears of the deaf unstopped. (Isaiah 35:3-5 ESV)

Nevertheless, it is right to speak out against those who attempt to darken the light. In accords with the teachings of Yeshua: where there is Justice there is light; where there is Empathy there is light; where there is Safety there is light; where there is Unity there is light; and where there is Sanctity there is light. While not every member of the Body is called to be the mouth, Messiah doesn't expect any to be mute. Yes, it is good to pray, but then know too when the Spirit has given you something to say, and then say it.

Who will dry the eyes of the sheep who weep;
who will take up their plight?
Who will stand up to the shepherds and princes
who plan their darkest at night?
Who will speak out against those who love evil,
against those who lust after sin?
Who will tell them that Yeshua is King
and he is soon coming back again?
And when Messiah comes back,
he'll be back with a sword
to slaughter the faithless and cruel.
He'll then sit on his throne—
while some will bemoan—
and with justice and truth, he will rule.

192. From The Heart: Set Apart

First read: Leviticus 18:1-5

Do not, in your attempt to satisfy those around, try to generate harmony by engendering sounds of mezzo-forte or mezzo-piano. If you look closely at your score, you will see a notation for neither. The Composer does not care for such blandness; it sounds like a cacophony. In merely blending in with everyone else—being kind to keep the peace—you are displeasing the Composer, who did not lend out the baton for you to blend in. You want to harmonize with those who are reading the same sheet of music, so that those who are reading a different score will clearly hear the difference. One can't clearly hear the distinction of everyone if the sound produced from every one is mezzo.

Even things without life, whether flute or harp, when they make a sound, unless they make a distinction in the sounds, how will it be known what is piped or played? For if the trumpet makes an uncertain sound, who will prepare for battle? (1st Corinthians 14:7-8 NKJV)

Another series of traditions recorded in the book of Leviticus that often reads like a to-do list are the laws of purification and atonement. YHWH was just as concerned with uncleanliness then as he is now. Unfortunately, it appears that the Israelites took Moses and Aaron more seriously then members of today's Body take Yeshua Messiah.

O [YHWH], are not your eyes on the truth? You have stricken them, but they have not grieved; you have consumed them, but they have refused to receive correction. They have made their faces harder than rock; they have refused to return. Therefore I said, "Surely these are poor. They are foolish; for they do not know the way of [YHWH], the judgment of their God." (Jeremiah 5:3-4 ESV)

The Father issued detailed instructions on how to handle those members of the Israelite community who, for one reason or another, found themselves ritually unclean. For some it was due to their eating specific forbidden foods. For others, either acquiring particular skin-infections or engaging in certain behaviors, was enough to send an Israelite into temporary exile, while undergoing intensive cleansing. The chief concern was that the infected, left in the community, would contaminate all those around still clean. A little leaven, remember:

"A little leaven leavens the whole lump." (Galatians 5:9 NKJV)

Leviticus is also depictive in describing the consequence for disregarding YHWH's commandments. Death. To some this might seem a rather harsh sentence, for say, disrespecting one's parents, engaging in homosexual acts, or committing adultery—all of which are deviant behaviors in American culture today. On the other hand, even this penalty shouldn't seem harsh to today's believers, for the wages of sin have never changed. Understandably for many Christians, condemnation of many sinful behaviors speaks of legalism, as is often the claim. News flash.

For the repentant Christian there is nothing legalistic about obeying YHWH's commandments. This claim is only acceptable by members of a Body who have yet to learn what the Father's intent is in setting his people apart.

And therefore, "come away and leave them, separate yourselves, says [YHWH]; touch nothing unclean. Then I will accept you," says [YHWH], the Ruler of all being; "I will be a father to you, and you shall be my sons and daughters. " Such are the promises that have been made to us, dear friends. Let us therefore cleanse ourselves from all that can defile flesh or spirit, and in the fear of [YHWH] complete our consecration. (2nd Corinthians 6:17-7:1 NEB)

Try to find out what would please [Yeshua]; take no part in the barren deeds of darkness, but show them for what they are. The things they do in secret it would be shameful even to mention. But everything, when once the light has shown it up, is illumined, and everything thus illumined is all light. (Ephesians 5:10-13 NEB)

The idea is to win lost souls. But, it should be much more than the idea, it should be the passion.

I have come to set fire to the earth, and how I wish it were already kindled. I have a baptism to undergo, and what constraints I am under until the ordeal is over. (Luke 12:49-50 NEB)

For it was the passion that led Yeshua Messiah to die on Calvary. An idea starts in the head, but passion comes from the heart. It is impossible to exude passion for saving the lost unless the heart of the believer has first been set completely apart from the rest of the world. The blind have no way of knowing they are blind unless someone who has sight informs them of their plight. Leviticus, then, is concerned with making sure that YHWH's people never forget that they were created to see. When the Israelites forgot, the Gentiles were offered sight.

So when they did not agree among themselves, they departed after Paul had said one word: "The Holy Spirit spoke rightly through Isaiah the prophet to our fathers, saying, 'And he said, "Go, and tell this people: 'Keep on hearing, but do not understand; keep on seeing, but do not perceive.' Make the heart of this people dull, and their ears heavy, and shut their eyes; lest they see with their eyes, and hear with their ears, and understand with their heart, and return and be healed.'" Therefore let it be known to you that the salvation of [YHWH] has been sent to the Gentiles, and they will hear it." (Acts 28:25-28 NKJV)

Members of the Body must insist that their hearts become, and remain, set apart from the rest of the world. All those around will continue to be dead if "winning the lost," remains in the head. Then obedience to the commandments is not solely an act of sacrifice or dedication to God Almighty, as it relates to self. It too strengthens the Christian's capacity to go forth in effectively executing the Great Commission.

Therefore say to the house of Israel, thus says [Yeshua]: "Repent and turn away from your idols, and turn away your faces from all your abominations. For any one of the house of Israel, or of the strangers who sojourn in Israel, who separates himself from me, taking his idols into his heart and putting the stumbling block of his iniquity before his face, and yet comes to a prophet to consult me through him, I [YHWH] will answer him myself. And I will set my face against that man; I will make him a sign and a byword and cut him off from the midst of my people, and you shall know that I am [YHWH]. And if the prophet is deceived and speaks a word, I, [YHWH], have deceived that prophet, and I will stretch out my hand against him and will destroy him from the midst of my people Israel. And they shall bear their punishment—the punishment of the prophet and the punishment of the inquirer shall be alike—that the house of Israel may no more go astray from me, nor defile themselves anymore with all their transgressions, but that they may be my people and I may be their God, declares [Yeshua]." (Ezekiel 14:6-11 ESV)

193. Meshing With Mayhem

First read: Isaiah 27-30

Perhaps you might think that an occasional mezzo note every once in a while is harmless. If so, you aren't thinking clearly. You are a creature of pleasure. In trying to please, you will try to appease. Many around you will be instantly turned off by your dynamics, both loud and soft. Both can be alarming and therefore, discomforting. Before too long, if those around are not at ease then watch as they float with the breeze, toward another symphony; one whose mezzo sounds mesh well with their mayhem. No one likes to be alone. In striving for company, you will wind up continuing to play to the tune of complaisance. You will do well to remember while looking ahead, you are performing for an audience of One. But, you can't see clearly if the mask you won't take off keeps obscuring your vision.

And the scribes and chief priests heard it and sought how they might destroy him; for they feared him, because all the people were astonished at his teaching. (Mark 11:18 NKJV)

Messiah couldn't have been clearer in delivering his instructions to the angel of the church at Laodicea:

These are the words of the Amen, the faithful and true witness, the prime source of all [YHWH]'s creation: "I know all your ways; you are neither hot nor cold. How I wish you were either hot or cold. But because you are lukewarm, neither hot nor cold, I will spit you out of my mouth. You say, 'How rich I am. And how well I have done. I have everything I want.' In fact, though you do not know it, you are the most pitiful wretch, poor, blind, and, naked. So I advise you to buy from me gold refined in the fire, to make you truly rich, and white clothes to put on to hide the shame of your nakedness, and ointment for your eyes so that you may see. All whom I love I reprove and discipline. Be on your mettle therefore and repent." (Revelation 3:14-22 NEB)

What is the particular disdain that Messiah has for sheep who claim citizenship in Israel, and yet live their lives as if they were still the iniquitous slaves of Egypt or Assyria? It has everything to do with diluting his power of deliverance for those who are looking to live in the light—no longer in the dark. It is not a coincidence that the Prophet Isaiah speaks of YHWH's judgment with both Israel and her enemies. They are receiving the same treatment because they are delivering the same testimony: "I live as though my soul is dead; my life is mine and mine alone. I'm content lying here in bed with my feet beneath the stone." For every wicked nation whom Israel emulates, her citizens shall receive the same fate. While on the island of Patmos, the Apostle John heard a warning from heaven concerning all those Israelites who insist on dwelling in Babylon.

Then I heard another voice from heaven that said: "Come out of her, my people, lest you take part in her sins and share in her plagues. For her sins are piled high as heaven, and [YHWH] has not forgotten her crimes. Pay her back in her own coin, repay her twice over for her deeds. Double for her the strength of the potion she mixed. Mete out grief and torment to match her voluptuous pomp. She says in her heart, 'I am a queen on my throne. No mourning for me, no widow's weeds.' Because of this her plagues shall strike her in a single day—pestilence, bereavement, famine, and burning—for mighty is [Yeshua] who has pronounced her doom." (Revelation 18:4-5 NEB)

There is too much at stake for Christians gaming with the Gospel, and Messiah has grown weary with those who won't quit. It is imperative that believers cease adulterating the Gospel in order to appease the masses. At this critical venture the Holy Spirit is urging members to place equal value in their walking as they do in their talking. As disciples, all should be leading the lost to the Son of YHWH—to the one who saves; yet, it is they who are being led back to the grave.

This is the path of those who have foolish confidence; yet after them people approve of their boasts. Like sheep they are appointed for Sheol; death shall be their shepherd, and the upright shall rule over them in the morning. Their form shall be consumed in Sheol, with no place to dwell. (Psalms 49:13-14 ESV)

Most assuredly, some will appear on the road and decide to leave after hearing and seeing the Truth. You would be wise not to follow suit. As the Apostle Paul declares to the young Timothy:

For the time will come when they will not endure sound doctrine, but according to their own desires, because they have itching ears, they will heap up for themselves teachers; and they will turn their ears away from the truth, and be turned aside to fables. But you be watchful in all things, endure afflictions, do the work of an evangelist, fulfill your ministry. (2nd Timothy 4:3-5 NKJV)

Members of the Body do unbelievers, new converts, and themselves a disservice in giving a false impression of the Gospel; proclaiming the Father's grace to those whose eyes have seen the Light, yet whose feet still tramp in the dark. But alas, those who lie through their lips and their lives; it is they who shall soon lie in stark.

[Yeshua] answered them: "The light is among you still, but not for long. Go on your way while you still have the light, so that darkness many not overtake you. He who journeys in the dark does not know where he is going. While you have the light, trust to the light, so that you may become men of light." After these words [Yeshua] went away from them into hiding. (John 12:35-36 NEB)

If we claim to be sharing in his life while we walk in the dark, our words and our lives are a lie; but if we walk in the light as he himself is in the light, then we share together a common life, and we are being cleansed from every sin by the blood of [Yeshua] his Son. (1st John 1:6-7 NEB)

194. A Faithful Proclamation

First read: 1st Thessalonians 4:13-5:11 / 2nd Thessalonians 2:1-17

We are sons of light and daughters of day
Awaiting the arrival of Messiah the King
Carefully molded jars of clay,
A life of love, our offering.
It matters not what critics say
Or what types of storms this life will bring
We march ahead with gracious strides
To pursue our Groom with faithful tunes
As a chaste and faithful Bride.

When the trumpet sounds and Messiah appears
When our bodies are stripped from its fleshly bin
We shall not faint from grief or tears
Or be held down by temporal sin.
Sounds of holy praise shall fill our ears
As our reign with YAH's own Son begins
And all the saints of YAH agree
It shall be a day full of grand arrays
A day of reigning free.

So let us not sleep as others do
Let us not wear the dark and worn clothes of night
Our deeds must not be misconstrued
For every step remains in sight.
We have bid our nights of shame adieu
And we walk awake in YAH's Son's light
Oh how delightful is YAH's grace
We ask; he gives; in turn, we live
And never shall we waste.

As we walk along we're equipped to face
Any bloodless battle, on or off the field
We shall not faint, but win this race
With belt for truth and faith for shield.
Soon my Savior's arms, we shall embrace
But for now, the sword of YAH we wield
The word of YAH shall thus resound
To all with ears who care to hear
It shall perplex, it shall astound

We wait and know it is not Messiah's desire
To return by stealth, and for those unprepared
To subject them all to his ire
A dreadful wrath still un-compared
An affliction by the convicting fire
Those who hid will now show; be made bare
So let us pray and press and press
For soon we'll hear that holy tune
And at last we'll enter rest

195. A Reflective Moment

And...action

First read: 1st Peter 2:12

Lights, camera, action. Like it or not, the camera is rolling on our lives twenty-four hours a day. Not an act goes unseen, and that works for both the spiritual and temporal worlds. As Christians we don't always realize the impact we are making on others, whether positive or negative. If we knew how often others judged our religion based on how they see us, would we act so carelessly? Maybe part of the problem is that many see Christianity as a religion to be acted out, rather than as a model to become. We shouldn't strive to act like a Christian, rather we should instead seek to be like Messiah.

Examine yourselves as to whether you are in the faith. Examine yourselves. Do you not know yourselves, that [Yeshua], through the Spirit, is in you?—unless indeed you are disqualified. But I trust that you will know that we are not disqualified. Now I pray to [YHWH] that you do no evil, not that we should appear approved, but that you should do what is honorable, though we may seem disqualified. For we can do nothing against the truth, but for the truth. (2nd Corinthians 13:5-8 NEB)

In the world of professional acting, actors usually fall into two broad categories. Technical actors are those who have refined their craft based upon years of studying and training. Every movement, whether on stage or in front of the camera, is contrived, based loosely on external stimuli. Technical actors have learned to react to situations based upon their surroundings, and the seasoned actor can easily give an impressive performance. Method actors are, on the other hand, in my opinion, superior in their abilities, and more believable, because their inspiration is almost always drawn from genuine emotions—from genuine experiences. When a method actor is crying, the character may be fictitious, but the tears are real. Emotions of past, which were internalized, are now brought to a head. Method actors aren't merely acting out their characters; they have fused who they are with who they are called to be and voila. What you have in front of you is not a character performing, but a person relating. As Christians, the analogy works well. Consider the following: Yeshua never fashioned his creation to engage in some technical, robotic relationship with him and the Father. Sadly, this is how many view Christianity, both believers and unbelievers alike. Every movement must be calculated. The more we invest in studying Christianity and all of its major characters then eventually we'll learn how to act like better Christians. Not only does this view fall short of the truth, it suggests that YHWH is more interested in and impressed with our knowledge of a religion, than he is in man developing and cultivating an intimate relationship with him. In following the fashion of technical acting, there is nothing wrong with wanting to study your craft. The history of Christianity is indeed a provocative one, filled with both comedic and tragic moments alike. Christians should desire to know more about the foundations of their beliefs by examining the role of the Church throughout the ages. However, the measure of our worth in the eyes of God Almighty must not be found through studying historical scripts we've come to term doctrine; but, by aligning who we are with an even more ancient script called Scripture. For it is in enveloping ourselves in the word of YHWH that we come to know, not the character known as Messiah, but the character of Messiah. And through the character of Messiah we come to know the Father.

My flesh is real food; my blood is real drink. Whoever eats my flesh and drinks my blood dwells continuously in me and I dwell in him. As the living Father sent me, so he who eats me shall live because of me. This is the bread which came down from heaven; and it is not like the bread which our fathers ate; they are dead, but whoever eats this bread shall live forever. (John 6:55-58 NEB)

What the Father desires from us is not a performance, but permanence. Performances eventually grow stale and people just stop watching. But, there is a raging fire that only the Holy Spirit can offer, and once ignited, it is the job of the Church to continue fanning its flames. Such permanence is achievable if members of the Body would craft their characters after the character of Messiah. Perhaps it's also helpful to remember that because we are on stage and always on display, critics will forever exist. But there's only One whose review actually matters. When the curtains go down, what will he say?

[YHWH] will judge the peoples. Establish justice for me, [Yeshua], according to my righteousness and according to my integrity. Please let the evil of the wicked be over, but set the righteous firmly in place because you, righteous [YHWH], are the one who examines hearts and minds. (Psalms 7:8-9 CEB)

But [YHWH] sits enthroned forever; he has established his throne for justice, and he judges the world with righteousness; he judges the peoples with uprightness. (Psalms 9:7-8 ESV)

196. It's A Mask Just Ask I

First read: 1st Kings 14:1-18

And now for some final words of wisdom while you are walking on the road to Glory. Remember that due to a variety of reasons and the vicissitudes of the seasons, your vision will become blurred at times. However, if you keep a clear head then you will never lose sight. What tools do you need to remain cognitive of possessing as you are looking ahead? The people ahead of you would be a good place to start. Though, it is going to be difficult to look at them or anything else through the narrow slits of your mask. You've been wearing it for some time now, so it has just about become a permanent fixture of your face. In wearing it, you have assumed it as an actual part of your identity, forgetting after each mile that it is fake. Oh, the mask is real—really aggrieving and deceiving—fatiguing each step. Secluding and diluting—concluding? No depth.

Face it, there aren't too many people around that we feel comfortable showing our real face to. As a matter of habit, a general trend within the Body is to mask our true selves so that nobody has the opportunity to reject who we are. It's a defense mechanism taught from childhood to shield matters of the heart so that no one else can see its tiny fractures. Parents warn their youth, "What goes on inside this house, stays in this house." The message is clear: keep all doors locked and windows shut so that no one can see what's inside. There's a problem in accepting this adage, however. Believers are on the road to Glory; we are to repair as we walk. The trend in the Body is for believers to become so accustomed to living in their brokenness, until they are no longer able to see that they're broken.

We grope for the wall like the blind, and we grope as if we had no eyes; we stumble at noonday as at twilight; we are as dead men in desolate places. (Isaiah 59:10 ESV)

Exactly how does this relate to the Christian walk? Well, Messiah expects each member to be transformed upon reaching the end of the road, and just prior to entering the gates of Glory. Transformation only seems desirable to those who are able to acknowledge that their existing state is unacceptable. Why would I acknowledge a need to change when I am content with who I am? The reality is that Messiah knows that none of his sheep enjoy carousing in the mud. The goal of each sheep, then, is to first admit that he or she is tired of being dirty. After confessing, they are led to the Shepherd for a shearing, so that all that is old can fall away; giving room and opportunity for a new and healthier coat to grow instead. Unfortunately, for many, doubt awaits them upon leaving the mud. They only make it to step one in the process of transformation, and then decide they would prefer to remain matted.

Whoever is wicked covets the spoil of evildoers, but the root of the righteous bears fruit. An evil man is ensnared by the transgression of his lips, but the righteous escapes from trouble. (Proverbs 12:12-13 ESV)

But now that you do acknowledge [YHWH]—or rather, now that he has acknowledged you—how can you turn back to the mean and beggarly spirits of the elements? Why do you propose to enter their service all over again? (Galatians 4:8-9 NEB)

Have you ever tried walking with mud matted to your body? It makes taking a step seem as if you have bricks inside your shoes. Sooner or later the sun comes out and the mud begins to mold and shape you into a creature that is filthier than the former. It won't be long now until the member is no longer able to move, and what remains has hardened on the outside, and has left the inside empty and useless. If this doesn't sound like a pleasant thought then consider this: believers need to begin shedding their muddy masks now before the Son comes back again. There is no disguise that will get past the eyes of the King of kings. It is commendable for believers to leave their pit, but that mustn't be it. Contempt will fall upon any sheep that are still unrecognizable to the Shepherd.

Yes, I am coming soon, and bringing my recompense with me, to requite everyone according to his deeds. I am the Alpha and the Omega, the first and the last, the beginning and the end. Happy are those who wash their robes clean. They will have the right to the tree of life and will enter by the gates of the city. Outside are dogs, sorcerers and fornicators, murderers and idolaters, and all who love and practice deceit. (Revelation 22:12-15 NEB)

197. Feigning Fixed

First read: Psalms 119:18

You will find that in keeping a mask on while walking, your steps are going to get heavier and you'll become weary. Even in moments or conditions in which there's no reason for you not to walk with ease, insisting on wearing the mask will still drain. Not just you, but those walking with you as well. In feigning fixed, others around will feel as if they can't relate to you in their brokenness.

For when I kept silent, my bones wasted away through my groaning all day long. For day and night your hand was heavy upon me; my strength was dried up as by the heat of summer. I acknowledged my sin to you, and I did not cover my iniquity; I said, "I will confess my transgressions to [YHWH]" and you forgave the iniquity of my sin. (Psalms 32:3-5 ESV)

The only reason that there are members in the Church who are feigning fixed is because these members don't yet realize that the Church is for the sick. The antidote for all who were dead in the grave was Messiah's blood on the cross. Yet, after one has been aroused from a deathly sleep, it takes a while for the blood to begin re-circulating in the body, so that the new believer has enough energy to walk without staggering with each new step. This is the role of the Church. The Church also has the responsibility of nursing the formerly dead back to health. The spiritually sleep will never enter the gates of Glory. And while the spiritually sick may enter, their journey, while in route, will be joyless and filled with unnecessary misery. It is not the will of the Father that any believer should hobble his way into heaven.

They arrived at Bethsaida. There the people brought a blind man to [Yeshua] and begged him to touch him. He took the blind man by the hand and led him away out of the village. Then he spat on his eyes, laid his hands upon him, and asked whether he could see anything. The man's sight began to come back, and he said, "I see men; they look like trees, but they are walking about." [Yeshua] laid his hands on his eyes again; he looked hard, and now he was cured so that he saw everything clearly. (Mark 8:22-25 NEB)

Indeed the man had been touched by Yeshua twice. After receiving the first touch it was clear that the Bethsaidan was no longer blind. But neither was his sight fully restored. Would his vision have been sharp enough so that he could've walk around town on his own without the help of "the people?" Perhaps. Perhaps he also would have needed a plethora of patches to cover up every scrape and bruise acquired from his reckless walking. Fortunately, when Yeshua asked the half-sighted man about his condition, the half-sighted was honest. His sincerity is what gave him his sight. Presently, there are millions of half-sighted people walking on the road to Glory; feigning as if they had twenty-twenty vision. It is sad to know that most of the millions are only feigning because of what they can actually see walking next to them; fellow travelers walking with an air of ease. Only a few are presently brave enough to reveal their handy patchwork. Shepherds must begin reminding their sheep that all who've confess are still needy and so no masks are needed. All sheep must remember that redemption only partially repairs the plight of the dead. As many shepherds have accurately attested—"If redemption was all, then immediately thereafter in heaven we'd all be, and having a ball." However, first there is the pain of redemption, and then there are the pains of restoration. Salvation to begin; sanctified at the end. With all of the hills, valleys, and enervating weather, walking on the road to Glory promises to be a weary experience in of itself. Not to mention the carrying of our weighty, but bearable, crosses. Therefore, it is foolery to feign when it does nothing but add to the drain. And yet still there is another incentive to removing the mask. Once the veil is gone then the time formerly spent on masquerading can now be spent on maturing; less time on hiding and more time on healing.

Is anyone among you in trouble? He should turn to prayer. Is anyone in good heart? He should sing praises. Is one of you ill? He should send for the elders of the congregation to pray over him and anoint him with oil in the name of [Yeshua]. The prayer offered in faith will save the sick man, [Yeshua] will raise him from his bed, and any sins he may have committed will be forgiven. Therefore confess your sins to one another, and pray for one another, and then you will be healed. A good man's prayer is powerful and effective. Elijah was a man with human frailties like our own; and when he prayed earnestly that there should be no rain, not a drop fell on the land for three years and a half; then he prayed again, and down came the rain and the land bore crops once more. (James 5:13-18 NEB)

198. Wealthy With Wisdom VIII

First read: Proverbs 28:13-14

The mask is really appealing. Though concealing, it reveals nothing too deep. Depraving because betraying; displaying no tears to weep. Perhaps you believe that you're serving as inspiration in keeping yourself together, being strong for the team. In reality, everyone else but you sees nothing but plastic. A mannequin may appear appealing at first glance—even after gazing for a short while. However, soon others will become disenchanted, as they begin to feel worthless in your presence. After saluting the occasional milestone, keep the mask on and the next several miles will be spent in seclusion. The mask is really misleading and impeding, appeasing for couth. Defiling and confining in disguising the truth.

We err if, as Christians, we believe that Messiah's purpose in coming the first time was to eradicate sin itself. It is agonizing to consider that the actions of one man and one woman should cause what often seems like an eternity of anguish. As believers, we should rejoice perpetually over what Messiah's birth did mean. It meant an opportunity for freedom. The Apostle Paul tried to articulate the torment of the soul while still a member of sin's chain gang.

For we know that the law is spiritual, but I am carnal, sold under sin. For what I am doing, I do not understand. For what I will to do, that I do not practice; but what I hate, that I do. If, then, I do what I will not to do, I agree with the law that it is good. But now, it is no longer I who do it, but sin that dwells in me. For I know that in me (that is, in my flesh) nothing good dwells; for to will is present with me, but how to perform what is good I do not find. For the good that I will to do, I do not do; but the evil I will not to do, that I practice. Now if I do what I will not to do, it is no longer I who do it, but sin that dwells in me. I find then a law, that evil is present with me, the one who wills to do good. (Romans 7:14-21 NKJV)

There are a multitude of members who have forgotten that Messiah's birth and death made room for a new guest to lodge. Messiah did not eradicate sin the first time, but he did eliminate our consignment to the enemy's ranks. Thus, the Apostle John's sobering pronouncement:

Here is the message we heard from him and pass on to you: that [YHWH] is light, and in him there is no darkness at all. If we claim to be sharing in his life while we walk in the dark, our words and our lives are a lie; but if we walk in the light as he himself is in the light, then we share together a common life, and we are being cleansed from every sin by the blood of [Yeshua] his Son. If we claim to be sinless, we are self-deceived and strangers to the truth. (1st John 1:5-8 NEB)

It is the Father's will that the recognition of the Holy Spirit living inside those who would call him Abba be manifested freely and faithfully through acts of love.

From where does an act of love come, if the heart is unable to choose? It is the believer's choice to either leave or live the life of a sinner; for because of Messiah, there is no longer any compulsion. However, sin itself retains it deadly potency until his second coming. It is vital that believers understand that Messiah made possible man's death to sin, not sin's death in man—not yet. What then makes it achievable for man to sin not, while he still has sin? It is an acknowledgment of the cleansing power of him who died, as well as his and the Father's grace. Though, it is not just a one time acknowledgment of, but rather a daily submission.

> If we confess our sins, he is just, and may be trusted to forgive our sins and cleanse us from every kind of wrong; but if we say we have committed no sin, we make him out to be a liar, and then his word has no place in us. My children, in writing thus to you my purpose is that you should not commit sin. But should anyone commit a sin, we have one to plead our cause with the Father, [Yeshua], and he is just. He himself the remedy for the defilement of our sins, not our sins only but the sins of all the world. (1st John 1:9-10 NEB)

Salvation is worthy of celebration. There is spectacular rejoicing with YHWH, as well as his heavenly host with each new addition to his family, However, the wool of Messiah's sheep is not white as snow the instant it is pulled from the mud; it's dingy, though still eligible for entry into the gates of Glory should their journey end tonight. The conversion experience is not one from "man" to "mannequin." Mannequins are lifeless and useless. Both the Body and the world need to see reality. From sinner to saint with sin; the change is from dead man, to man who is making it with Messiah. The Holy Spirit was given so that we could whiten while approaching the gates of Glory. But, make no mistake. Messiah sees clearly the sheep who stumble back into the mud because of wobbly legs, and those who jump back in after one or two kegs. To one he shall be just to forgive; to the other there shall be justice.

199. Wealthy With Wisdom IX

First read: Proverbs 23:17-18

What is appealing about your mask? Perhaps, the appeal lies in the fact that most around you will be wearing one as well. In attempting to fit in, for normalcy sake, you will want to keep it on. It is appealing because it keeps the discomfort level of those around you at an all-time low; especially if the mask you are wearing happens to be in season. In moments in which you need to express your sorrow, when you need to weep with the earth, your tears will fall; they will just be kept hidden. You may smile on the outside, while your soul is sulking on the inside, adding to the weight of the mask. How depraving it is to deny your soul the chance to share with others. You are not only betraying yourself, you are also betraying the souls of those walking with you who yearn for your help in repairing what lies beneath. In the beginning, it will seem appealing to take off the mask. However, after walking a number of miles, if you fail to reveal your soul to others, revealing just your face will lose its appeal. And, in continuing to cater to concealment, you will soon find yourself chained once more. The mask is really evading and enslaving; enraging all those who see. Depriving and dividing; relying only on me.

There are novice Christians, as well as ignorant veterans, who both still have yet to identify with the newness of Messiah. It is because they have never learned the purpose of Messiah, and so they have yet to understand how it applies to their life. The Apostle Paul, speaking to the church in Corinth explains the significance of transparency in carrying out Messiah's service of reconciliation:

With this fear of [Yeshua] before our eyes we address our appeal to men. To [YHWH] our lives lie open, as I hope they also lie open to you in your heart of hearts. (2nd Corinthians 5:11 NEB)

As believers, we are aware that Messiah died in order to reconcile all to the Father. It is both our knowledge of Messiah, as well as our knowing him, that makes the reconciliation real. His suffering and death was in plain sight so that all could see. In the eyes of the world the purpose was humiliation, but in the eyes of YHWH it was for humankind.

Pilate's soldiers then took [Yeshua] in the Governor's headquarters, where they collected the whole company round him. They stripped him and dressed him in a scarlet mantle; and plaiting a crown of thorns they placed it on his head, with a cane in his right hand. Falling on their knees before him they jeered at him: "Hail, King of the Jews." They spat on him, and used the cane to beat him about the head. When they had finished their mockery, they took off the mantle and dressed him in his own clothes. (Matthew 27:27-31 NEB)

And yet for many on the road to Glory, it is worry of humiliation that prevents them from fully revealing themselves in embracing the novelty of Messiah. This is proof of the ongoing struggle with "self" and its desire to identify with sin; but the proof defeats the purpose of Messiah.

For he was given up to death for our misdeeds, and raised to life to justify us. (Romans 4:25 NEB)

His purpose in dying for all was that men, while still in life, should cease to live for themselves, and should live for him who for their sake died and was raised to life. With us therefore worldly standards have ceased to count in our estimate of any man; even if once they counted in our understanding of [Messiah], they do so now no longer. When anyone is united with [Messiah], there is a new world; the old order has gone, and a new order has already begun. (2nd Corinthians 5:15-17 NEB)

Let this mind be in you which was also in [Yeshua], who, being in the form of God, did not consider it robbery to be equal with [YHWH], but made himself of no reputation, taking the form of a bondservant, and coming in the likeness of men. And being found in appearance as a man, he humbled himself and became obedient to the point of death, even the death of the cross. (Philippians 2:5-8 NKJV)

When first converted, there is a fire ignited that blazes with such brilliance; in eagerness to burn all that is false. Unfortunately, not long after their conversion experience, members began weighing the costs; an exercise that should have commenced prior to accepting Messiah.

Would any of you think of building a tower without first sitting down and calculating the cost, to see whether he could afford to finish it? Otherwise, if he has laid its foundation and then is not able to complete it, all the onlookers will laugh at him. "There is the man," they will say, "who started to build and could not finish." Or what king will march into battle against another king, without first sitting down to consider whether with ten thousand men he can face an enemy coming to meet him with twenty thousand? If he cannot, then, long before the enemy approaches, he sends envoys, and asks for terms. (Luke 14:28-32 NEB)

The cost of burning all that is false is a loss of "self" and pride. Where there is no pride, there is no humiliation. Moreover, there would be no worries of humiliation if men and women understood their universal condition. Even members of the Body who have accepted the antidote need to realize that the road to Glory really begins where their artifice ends. When believers spend ample time fighting to fit into an old world that they should've died to, then no time exists for living out the novelty of Messiah. It is impossible to be reconciled to both YHWH and world, and the King is uninterested in competing. It is of equal worth to consider the current plight of the Church. How can members of the Body effectively preach the ministry of reconciliation throughout when, presently, the Body is itself divided within? A plank needs removing so members can move.

Now I urge you, brethren, note those who cause divisions and offenses, contrary to the doctrine which you learned, and avoid them. For those who are such do not serve [Yeshua], but their own belly, and by smooth words and flattering speech deceive the hearts of the simple. (Romans 16:17-18 NKJV)

200. Helping the Hungry

First read: Amos 1-9

How long do you plan on wearing the mask? This is a question worth asking each step along the way. How long can you keep bearing the weight alone? The answer will differ for each person. You will find the reaction of others will differ as well, depending on where they are in their own walk. You don't really have the time to gamble with odds. Will the traveler walking next to you overlook your brokenness by refusing to look you in the eyes when talking? It's easy not to see what you aren't looking for. You can tell yourself that these travelers are not worth your time of day anyway, and so it doesn't really matter. You will be lying. The truth lies beneath your mask, for you know well that they do indeed matter.

One common mask worn by many members of the Body is the mask of indifference. Often it is our indulgences that lead to such appearances. Believers can become so wrapped up in their own affairs (or the more "spiritual" cares) that we become apathetic toward the struggling saints. While we will always have spiritual battles to fight and characters to refine, members mustn't forget to look at those—the poor, the sick, and the blind. Yes, the world contains the spiritually impoverished, and millions who have yet to see the light. And Messiah does expect the Body to carry out the Great Commission so that the Gospel may restore. However, Messiah expects so much more.

When he heard what had happened [Yeshua] withdrew privately by boat to a lonely place; but people heard of it, and came after him in crowds by land from the towns. When he came ashore, he saw a great crowd; his heart went out to them, and he cured those of them who were sick. When it grew late the disciples came up to him and said, "This is a lonely place, and the day has gone; send the people off to the villages to buy themselves food." He answered, "There is no need for them to go; give them something to eat yourselves." "All we have here," they said, "is five loaves and two fishes." "Let me have them." he replied. So he told the people to sit down on the grass; then, taking the five loaves and the two fishes, he looked up to heaven, said the blessing, broke the loaves, and gave them to the disciples; and the disciples gave them to the people. They all ate to their hearts content; and the scraps left over, which they picked up, were enough to fill twelve great baskets. Some five thousand men shared in this meal, to say nothing of the women and children. (Matthew 14:13-21 NEB)

It is the case that this passage is full of deep spiritual insights, which Messiah wants his disciples to grasp through the revelatory power of the Holy Spirit. Still, there is a simpler truth illustrated that shouldn't go unheeded. The people were hungry and Messiah commanded his disciples to feed them. Sure, they needed some spiritual food, and Messiah supplied before sending them away (so that he could be left alone to pray). But the people were also hungry.

The foolish person will no longer be called generous, nor the miser said to be bountiful; for the foolish person will speak foolishness, and his heart will work iniquity: to practice ungodliness, to utter error against [YHWH], to keep the hungry unsatisfied, and he will cause the drink of the thirsty to fail. Also the schemes of the schemer are evil; he devises wicked plans to destroy the poor with lying words, even when the needy speaks justice. But a generous man devises generous things, and by generosity he shall stand. (Isaiah 32:5-8 ESV)

The thief must give up stealing, and instead work hard and honestly with his own hands, so that he may have something to share with the needy. (Ephesians 4:28 NEB)

As brothers and sisters of Messiah the King, we are all of noble blood, and yet there are members in the Body whom the Father has blessed to be a blessing to others; but, whose current interest lies only in securing further blessings for themselves. In their hoarding and selfishness, they are, in fact, accumulating debt.

He who is faithful in what is least is faithful also in much; and he who is unjust in what is least is unjust also in much. Therefore if you have not been faithful in the unrighteous mammon, who will commit to your trust the true riches? And if you have not been faithful in what is another man's, who will give you what is your own? (Luke 16:10-12 NKJV)

A trumpet sounded in the prophet Amos's day and today it is being replayed. A trumpet call denouncing and warning those who have plenty, but give very little or none to those living in penury; to those who live in opulence, and yet, daily ignore the orphans; to those enjoying wealth, while the widows are wanting from war. And to those who show antipathy for the alien, Messiah says to forget not your former foreigner days. Yeshua has given us hands to pray with, but these same hands are also to be used for providing. The Father's people will not forever suffer at the hands of the self-centered. Save for repentance, ruin is impending and those riches won't last through the rains.

"And I will come near you for judgment; I will be a swift witness against sorcerers, against adulterers, against perjurers, against those who exploit wage earners and widows and orphans, and against those who turn away an alien— because they do not fear me," says [Yeshua]. (Malachi 3:5 ESV)

201. A House of Hate

First read: Obadiah 1:1-21

In failing to look other travelers in their eyes, you are enabling and exacerbating the problem for all. What results is resentment and frustration. You will resent them for not looking into your eyes, and they will, in turn, resent you for not looking into theirs; though neither will verbalize their frustration to each other. Mutual enragement is only the short-term result. In the long run, your mutual depriving will end in dividing. How can you repair others, and vice versa, when you aren't even walking together?

Let nothing be done through selfish ambition or conceit, but in lowliness of mind let each esteem others better than himself. Let each of you look out not only for his own interests, but also for the interests of others. (Philippians 2:3-4 NKJV)

The events foretold by the prophet Obadiah have some sad origins. The future of the Edomites, descendants of Esau, looked gloom because of their contemptible behavior toward their western neighbors, the Israelites, in the southern kingdom of Judah. Esau was the brother of Jacob.

For violence against your brother Jacob, shame shall cover you, and you shall be cut off forever. (Obadiah 1:10 ESV)

The verse is referring to a historical event which took place in 587 B.C. when Yeshua used the Babylonians as his disciplining rod against Judah. The Edomites took it upon themselves to rejoice over Judah's downfall and engaged in their own plundering of Jerusalem. What a pity for one nation to celebrate the destruction of another, especially when they have their roots in two brothers. But, the house of hate doesn't last at all. There is a long history of division which exists in the nation of Israel; beginning with Jacob and Esau, and continuing through the division of the Northern and Southern Kingdoms, Israel and Judah, respectively. The Edomites trace their heritage back to Esau, while the Israelites have as their patriarch, Jacob; both the twin sons of Isaac. While still in the womb, the division loomed. Unfortunately, resentment existed between the two of them before they were even born.

And Isaac prayed to [YHWH] for his wife, because she was barren. And [YHWH] granted his prayer, and Rebekah his wife conceived. The children struggled together within her, and she said, "If it is thus, why is this happening to me?" So she went to inquire of [YHWH]. And [Yeshua] said to her, "Two nations are in your womb, and two peoples from within you shall be divided; the one shall be stronger than the other, the older shall serve the younger." When her days to give birth were completed; behold there were twins in her womb. The first came out red, all his body like a hairy cloak, so they called his name Esau. Afterward his brother came out with his hand holding Esau's heel, so his name was called Jacob. Isaac was sixty years old when she bore them. (Genesis 25:21-26 ESV)

Believers are familiar with the rest of the account. Esau gave up his birthright for a bowl of soup. Jacob took Esau's blessing, throwing Isaac for a loop.

Now Esau hated Jacob because of the blessing with which his father had blessed him, and Esau said to himself, "The days of mourning for my father are approaching; then I will kill my brother Jacob." (Genesis 27:41 ESV)

If you are angry, do not let anger lead you into sin; do not let sunset find you still nursing it; leave no loop-hole for the devil. (Ephesians 4:26-27 NEB)

And Jacob lifted up his eyes and looked, and behold, Esau was coming, and four hundred men with him. So he divided the children among Leah and Rachel and the two female servants. And he put the servants with their children in front, then Leah with her children, and Rachel and Joseph last of all. He himself went on before them, bowing himself to the ground seven times, until he came near to his brother. But Esau ran to meet him and embraced him and fell on his neck and kissed him, and they wept. (Genesis 33:1-4 ESV)

Be generous toward one another, tender-hearted, forgiving one another as [YHWH] in [Messiah] forgave you. (Ephesians 4:32 NEB)

Regrettably, Esau's descendants failed to follow their patriarch's example in relating to their cousins the Israelites. As a result, Obadiah foretold of their fall. The Gentiles who were grafted into the Body of Messiah needn't follow in suit of their seniors. While division remains in the Church, each denomination leery of the others, believers mustn't forget that there is one Lord in Messiah, who has but one Body. Forgiveness is a must, followed by faithfulness then trust; and a desire to serve and grow-in-love by all. Bitterness and strife must cease amongst the Bride, or soon all within shall see the Body fall. In speaking to those who claimed his power was from the prince of darkness, Yeshua spoke these words:

Every kingdom divided against itself goes to ruin, and a divided household falls. (Luke 11:17 NEB)

202. Wealthy With Wisdom X

First read: Proverbs 16:1-33

The mask is really corroding and eroding—controlling your life; depressing in repressing your anguish and strife. You can only conceal your tears for so long before the water starts corroding the mask, and before too long, your soul. What may begin as appealing to all, will eventually wind up unveiling. The longer the mask is attached to your face, the harder it will be to take off in the event you decide to recognize the mask for what it is. Caution. A mask no longer looks appealing upon corroding. Your phantom, now replaced with foul, alienates those around who only enjoyed your company while you were acting. With the waxing of strife comes the waning of life. Before too long, you will find yourself standing on the side of the road, in the shade; waving with the wake of Those-Needy.

Pride goes before destruction, and a haughty spirit before a fall. Better to be of a humble spirit with the lowly, than to divide the spoil with the proud. (Proverbs 16:18-19 ESV)

Who in the Body would dare suggest to another member that wearing a mask is for their own protection? That it is okay to walk around with a smirk on your face, when your soul is calling for help? The wisdom ascribed to such actions promotes a spirit of perpetual suspicion. YHWH does not want his people to have a suspicious spirit. He does will that each have a discerning one.

When the festival was already half over, [Yeshua] went up to the temple and began to teach. The Jews were astonished: "How is it," they said, "that this untrained man has such learning?" [Yeshua] replied, "The teaching that I give is not my own; it is the teaching of him who sent me. Whoever has the will to do the will of [YHWH] shall know whether my teaching comes from him or is merely my own. Anyone whose teaching is merely his own, aims at honor for himself. But if a man aims at the honor of him who sent him he is sincere, there is nothing false in him." (John 7:14-18 NEB)

In walking around, forever suspicious of everyone, you're insisting on a solo sanctification. But sanctification is just as painful as the initial repentance required for salvation. They're both painful because both require a death to pride. It is pride that keeps many from the redemptive power of Messiah, and that same pride, if not killed daily, can keep one from asking for the help they need (the grace of the Father) in carrying their cross, or in wearing their heavy robe of righteousness. Some believers have yet to face this ordeal only because they know not the pangs of hunger.

In this present body we do indeed groan; we yearn to have our heavenly habitation put on over this one—the hope that, being thus clothed, we shall not find ourselves naked. We groan indeed, we who are enclosed within this earthly frame. (2nd Corinthians 5:2-3 NEB)

431

For to us, our hope of attaining that righteousness which we eagerly await is the work of the Spirit through faith. (Galatians 5:5 NEB)

Starving your flesh in the physical sense is no more excruciating then starving your spiritual flesh. And yet, we think that the hallmark of a saint is one who no longer starves. Not so. A saint walks perpetually starving while knowing their source of real sustenance. A saint doesn't deny their struggles, or pretend like they have been equipped to carry their own cross unto the gates of Glory.

"Come to me, all you who labor and are heavy laden, and I will give you rest. Take my yoke upon you and learn from me, for I am gentle and lowly in heart, and you will find rest for your souls. For my yoke is easy and my burden is light." (Matthew 11:28-30 NKJV)

Yeshua says to come to him so that our souls will find relief. But we will only find as much as we are willing to bear, and our load will only lighten as much as we willing to share—with his Body. With all members working in union, and with Messiah as the Head, there is no load too heavy for the Body to carry. There is nothing more dangerous to the Body of Messiah than a saint who has turned sour. It is possible. There are those shepherds who choose to ignore the character of Judas Iscariot. It is no accident that Judas was one of the twelve, and Scripture does not indicate nor imply that it was YHWH who aroused him to betray.

The Son of Man is going the way appointed for him in the scriptures; but alas for the man by whom the Son of Man is betrayed. It would be better for that man if he had never been born. (Mark 14:21 NEB)

Then Judas, his betrayer, seeing that he had been condemned, was remorseful and brought back the thirty pieces of silver to the chief priests and elders, saying, "I have sinned by betraying innocent blood." And they said, "What is that to us? You see to it." Then he threw down the pieces of silver in the temple and departed, and went and hanged himself. (Matthew 27:3-5 NKJV)

In fact, Messiah afforded him the same authority that was given initially to the other eleven:

Then he called his twelve disciples to him and gave them authority to cast out unclean spirits and to cure every kind of ailment and disease. (Matthew 10:1 NEB)

When day broke he called his disciples to him, and from among them he chose twelve and named them Apostles: Simon, to whom he gave the name of Peter, and Andrew his brother, James and John, Philip and Bartholomew, Matthew and Thomas, James son of Alphaeus, and Simon who was called the Zealot, Judas son of James, and Judas Iscariot who turned traitor. (Luke 6:12-16 NEB)

For he was one of our number and had his place in this ministry. (Acts 1:17 NEB)

Is self-righteousness a delusion to anyone other than self? Messiah does not will that any who follow him should feign perfection. The road to Glory is a refining one that allows the process of perfecting to begin once Yeshua has found you. Yet, beware of thinking, "I have arrived" the instant you have been revived. While indeed saved, you have only arrived at awareness. You were revived so that you one day could arrive at the gates of Glory—at the end of your journey. It is one thing to display confidence in Messiah. It is another to share the arrogance of Iscariot in his proximity to Messiah. Self-righteousness may appear to others as righteous at first and many will flock to attain. But, the self-righteous will point to self as the standard for holiness, while the righteous perpetually point to YHWH-Tsidkenu (YHWH-our-Righteousness) and Yeshua. Satan, always at the center of self, is willing to entice and is eager to water their seed. Eventually, what once was caught will begin to rot, unless the rotting can acknowledge their need. It is the unrighteous who need the blood of the Redeemer, but the righteous still need his Body for repairs. It does nothing but spoil the saint who, while toiling, begins walking and talking with airs.

203. By Grace

First read: Romans 6:1-23

By grace I was found still dead in my sin
while blinded by the darkness of night

By grace I was allowed to live yet again
and by grace I was given new sight

By grace I was uprooted from poisonous weeds,
whose seeds were planted to kill

By grace I was uprooted despite all my deeds
and by grace I have started to heal

By grace I was freed from a suffering cell
where peace could never be found

By grace I'm no longer eager to rebel
and by grace I am hearing new sounds

By grace I have been commanded to walk
on a road that at times will seem bleak

And while others around me are certain to balk,
by grace I've been commissioned to speak

By grace I've been girded with the belt of truth
and never shall it leave my waist

By grace I depart from the lies of my youth
and with it I will proceed with haste

By grace I've been given the breastplate of right
and to told to abstain from all that is wrong

By grace I am instructed to shine as a light,
and by grace I'm to help others along

By grace I've been given the shield of faith
to protect from the father of lies

By grace I can stare him face to face
and fight without batting one eye

By grace I've been issued the shoes of peace
to walk in as I boldly proclaim

By grace my proclaiming will never cease
and by grace I will strengthen the lame

By grace I was issued a helmet for heaven
and it will always remain on my head

By grace I will refrain from partaking of
leaven
that's ingested by those still dead

By grace have I been equipped with a sword
that can pierce both marrow and bone

By grace I will rip through all deadly cords
and by grace I will soon see my home

By grace I've been adopted into the family of
One,
yet, I still need to be covered in prayer;

By grace, with his blood I now serve the Son
and by grace he will lead me with care

By grace he will always extend his hands
when I reach up after a fall

By grace he will meet me wherever I land
and by grace he will help me stand tall

But my Redemer's grace, I know, will not
always excuse
though, he will never think twice to forgive

His grace is not for me to misuse or abuse
But, so that I may continue to live

By grace I've been given the Holy Spirit,
my Comforter, my Helper, my Friend

With wisdom imparted, I will learn to walk in it
And with grace I will walk 'til the end

434

204. **Only One**

First read: 1st Kings 18:1-40

Don't play with deception; for soon you will find yourself deceived. The control you have at first, won't last for long. Deception will allow you to think that you're in control in the beginning; it is part of the game. Unfortunately, unless you have learned the rules (most won't), you won't know how to win. Not long into the game the table will turn; if you aren't discerning you will be deceived. Deception is in control now, and while in control you will begin to erode. It is worth observing that even while corroding, you are still being deceived. Because erosion is a gradual process and many aren't attuned to their soul's sounds of anguish, it will happen unbeknown to you.

And, I will declare my judgments against them, for all their evil in forsaking me. They have made offerings to other gods and worshiped the works of their own hands. (Jeremiah 1:16 ESV)

If we, as believers, profess to believe in only one God, then why does YHWH see many of his children worshiping other gods? There are believers in the Body who think they are worshiping the God of Abraham, Isaac, and Jacob, but in reality their god is no where to be found in Scripture. Well, actually—

Sharing in [YHWH]'s work, we urge this appeal upon you: you have received the grace of [YHWH]; do not let it go for nothing. [YHWH]'s own words are: "In the hour of my favor I gave heed to you; on the day of deliverance I came to your aid." The hour of favor has now come; now, I say: has the day of deliverance dawned. (2nd Corinthians 6:1-2 NEB)

Elijah, the servant of YHWH, found himself proving to a backsliding Israel that their god, Baal, was false. In truth, Baal was never their god to begin with. The One and true God had never ceased being who he is; although for a while, the Israelites refused to acknowledge he who had graciously delivered their ancestors out of Egypt. Though Moses had earlier commanded the former captives not to entangle themselves in foreign cultures, the Israelites proved disobedient. The author of Kings records that Ahab, the seventh king of the divided kingdom of Israel was more wicked in the eyes of YHWH than all the kings before him. In reading of his ancestor's treachery, it's hard to fathom what could have been worse under Ahab's reign. How about marrying a woman who worships a false god? This unholy union led to the slaughtering of all but a hundred prophets who insisted on serving YHWH. The rest of Israel's population soon found themselves marching to the beat of a different drum—one that was dumb.

Has a nation changed its gods, even though they are no gods? But my people have changed their glory for that which does not profit. Be appalled, O heavens, at this; be shocked, be utterly desolate, declares [YHWH], for my people have committed two evils: they have forsaken me, the fountain of living waters, and hewed out cisterns for themselves, broken cisterns that can hold no water. (Jeremiah 2:11-13 ESV)

Do not unite yourselves with unbelievers; they are no fit mates for you. What has righteousness to do with wickedness? Can light consort with darkness? Can [Messiah] agree with Belial, or a believer join hands with an unbeliever? (2nd Corinthians 6:14-15 NEB)

How does it happen that members who once were so eager to serve the gracious Father are now mesmerized by gods who can neither speak nor hear? It didn't happen overnight to be sure. No, when the Church first began to divorce itself from the commandments of God Almighty in order to unite with the culture of the world, deception followed close behind. Actually, deception was holding culture's other hand. Because the Church failed to discern, she found herself entering into a polygamous marriage. Upon exchanging I do's, demons from hell emerged to begin their quest for subversion. To date, they've been deceptive, and millions of members within the Body have been deceived. Many find themselves praying to a god that doesn't exist. Others turn to the world to meet all of their needs, as they worship gods of sex, drunkenness, and greed. Eventually they start reaping what they've sown, and soon they return for help; praying to a god who doesn't exist. Like the prophets of Baal on Mount Carmel, "believers" will, in desperation, engage in the most erratic exercises, trying to get the attention of a god with no ears and no eyes.

Go, and proclaim these words toward the north, and say, "Return, faithless Israel, declares [YHWH]. I will not look on you in anger, for I am merciful, declares [Yeshua]; I will not be angry forever. Only acknowledge your guilt, that you rebelled against [YHWH] and [Yeshua] and scattered your favors among foreigners under every green tree, and that you have not obeyed my voice, declares [YHWH]. Return, faithless children, declares [YHWH]; for I am your master; I will take you, one from a city and two from a family, and I will bring you to Jerusalem. And I will give you shepherds after my own heart, who will feed you with knowledge and understanding. And, when you have multiplied and been fruitful in the land, in those days, declares [YHWH], they shall no more say, 'The ark of the covenant of [YHWH]. It shall not come to mind, or be remembered or missed; it shall not be made again." (Jeremiah 3:12-16 ESV)

For this reason [YHWH] has given them up to the vileness of their own desires, and the consequent degradation of their bodies, because they have bartered away the true [YHWH] for a false god, and have offered reverence and worship to created things instead of to the Creator, who is blessed for ever; amen. (Romans 1:24-25 NEB)

Fortunately, there are some faithful members within the Body who have been earnestly praying to YHWH. He has ears and has heard the cries of his faithful children. Praise YHWH for the fresh fire that will fall momentarily. The time is approaching when all false gods will be laid asunder, and all those who led astray will be forced to surrender.

He said, "Take care that you are not misled. For many will come claiming my name and saying, 'I am he', and, 'The Day is upon us.' Do not follow them." (Luke 21:8 NEB)

Nonetheless, from YHWH there is mercy for those members who, today, make the decision to leave behind all vain attempts to get ahead by worshiping multiple deities. For there's only One, and he can't be outdone.

205. Deep Deception

First read: Esther 7:1-10

It is a slippery slope in playing with deception; it won't stop playing until you are dead. As you'll recall, in standing on the side of the road while waving in your wake, others undiscerning or in their pride will interpret your wave for hi, and so, will continue walking "bye." Refuse to wear that which forsakes what is real. Truthfully, no one is really content in feigning what's fake; wearing so many faces in trying to appease; forgetting whom you are in trying to please. What may start off as your walking and wearing with ease, will soon add to your weight and leave you on your knees. That's pretty heavy, so why would you want to wear it?

There is no rest for the deceiver; that is, until they approach their death bed, which is forever looming in the distance. But what is it that begets deception? Desire, usually aimed at something perceivably out of reach for the perpetrator. Generally, an item that YHWH has decided is not in the best interest of the believer, and so "self" begins to whisper softly, "Oh, but you must have it." Since the Father chooses not to deliver then the "believer" decides to deceive. Once the member has detached himself from the Body of Messiah, the devil is free to engage in his own deception. What the detached member fails to understand is that he is playing with the master deceiver, whose purpose is to see you to your death. There is always the danger of stepping so far out of the Father's fence, that there will be difficulty in finding oneself back onto the road to Glory before the Master's return. The Holy Spirit advises all members to stay on the road to begin with, no matter how darkly it may appear in the distance. The deceiver must remember two truths. First, there is no place for him or her in the Body of Messiah.

Then away with all malice and deceit, away with all pretence and jealousy and recrimination of every kind. Like the new-born infants you are, you must crave for pure milk (spiritual milk, I mean), so that you may thrive upon it to your soul's health. Surely you have tasted that [Yeshua] is good. (1st Peter 2:1-2 NEB)

And second, to them who remain attached to the Vine, the deceivers will never prevail; their plans will fail. They will fail because a fight with a member of the family is a fight with both its King and Father:

And we know that the Son of [YHWH] has come and has given us an understanding, that we may know him who is true; and we are in him who is true, in His Son [Yeshua] is [YHWH] and eternal life. (1st John 5:20 NKJV)

Haman the Agagite, son of Hammedatha, and enemy to the Jews, had to learn these truths the hard way. Not content with the stately position given to him by King Ahasuerus, Haman felt insulted by Mordecai's refusal to pay him obeisance like the rest of Ahasuerus's attendants. "Death to Mordecai and the other Jews" was the reaction of Haman, resulting in continuous acts of intrigue and deception.

YHWH, however, in working behind the scenes through Esther, turned the plot upon its head. The mask of deception doesn't hold long past its conception.

A faithful witness does not lie, but a false witness breathes out lies. (Proverbs 14:5 ESV)

They bend their tongue like a bow; falsehood and not truth has grown strong in the land; for they proceed from evil to evil, and they do not know me, declares [YHWH]. Let everyone beware of his neighbor, and put no trust in any brother, for every brother is a deceiver, and every neighbor goes about as a slanderer. Everyone deceives his neighbor, and no one speaks the truth; they have taught their tongue to speak lies; they weary themselves committing iniquity. Heaping oppression and deceit on one another, they refuse to know me, declares [YHWH]. Therefore thus says [Yeshua]: "Behold, I will refine them and test them, for what else can I do, because of my people? Their tongue is a deadly arrow. It speaks deceitfully. With his mouth each speaks peace to his neighbor, but in his heart he plans an ambush for him. Shall I not punish them for these things? declares [YHWH], and shall I not avenge myself on a nation such as this? (Jeremiah 9:3-9 ESV)

For the believer, the mask doesn't really go with Messiah's robe of righteousness anyway, so all who are attempting to wear it need to let it go. It is Messiah within, who eliminates sin, but the road to Glory provides each member the opportunity to remove its residue. Though, it takes more energy to feign then it does to work on removing our stains.

206. Wealthy With Wisdom XI

First read: Proverbs 27:5-23

Perhaps, you didn't know it was going to be so heavy when you put it on? Okay, but what about after three or four miles? You had to have felt the weight, the baggage. No? Did you ever ask yourself why your feet seemed to drag like you were carrying bricks in two bags? No? Did you ever ask yourself why no one responded to your call or to the tears that they saw? No? Did you ever ask yourself why your head always seem to bow like your mood was afoul? No? Did you ever ask yourself why no one seemed to be around when you fell on the ground? Take off the mask now. Not only will you feel light on your feet, but everything around will be clearer, and you can begin to help others take off their masks. This is only part of the refining process, but a significant part, nonetheless. In learning who you really are, you begin to learn the true identity of others as well. How can you love who you don't even know? How can you learn of their seeds that were sown? How can they know that, in fact, you do care? How can anyone begin to repair?

But to all who did receive him, to those who have yielded him their allegiance, he gave the right to become children of [YHWH], not born of any human stock, or by the fleshly desire of a human father, but the offspring of [YHWH] himself. (John 1:12-13 NEB)

There is bitterness continuously permeating among various souls within the Body. It is resentment, self-inflicted, which results from a feeling of disconnection. Why should any of Messiah's flock feel like the red-headed step child of a biased Father? A disciple who feels disconnected is perhaps a disciple who is struggling to fully identify with the blood of Messiah. More than likely this disciple has little trouble acknowledging Messiah as his Savior and Lord. Yes, he understands that it was his Savior's blood that delivered him from sinful bondage. Yes, he grasps the concept that the shedding of Yeshua's blood makes him bound to service; and perhaps he does serve faithfully. However, he dares not identify with Messiah's blood that makes him his brother. How sad. How mistaken. What need is there to be real when you only resonate with Messiah as a transcendent figurehead of a remote religion? Where is the relationship?

Then His brothers and His mother came, and standing outside they sent to Him, calling Him. And a multitude was sitting around Him; and they said to Him, "Look, Your mother and Your brothers are outside seeking You." But He answered them, saying, "Who is My mother, or My brothers?" And He looked around in a circle at those who sat about Him, and said, "Here are My mother and My brothers! For whoever does the will of [YHWH] is My brother and My sister and mother." (Mark 3:31-35 NKJV)

For all who are led by the Spirit of [YHWH] are sons of [YHWH]. For you did not receive the spirit of slavery to fall back into fear, but you have received the Spirit of adoption as sons, by whom we cry, "Abba! Father!" The Spirit himself bears witness with our spirit that we are children of God. (Romans 8:14-16 ESV)

The redeemed can't begin to relate until they realize whose they really are. YHWH doesn't have any step-children, and Yeshua does not have any step-siblings. The blood of Messiah did establish his atonement and authority; but just as importantly, it established our adoption.

Peter began: "I now see how true it is that [YHWH] has no favorites, but that in every nation the man who is [YHWH]-fearing and does what is right is acceptable to him." (Acts 10:34-35 NEB)

For [YHWH] knew his own before ever they were, also ordained that they should be shaped to the likeness of his Son, that he might be the eldest among a large family of brothers; and it is these, so fore-ordained, whom he has called. And those whom he called he has justified, and to those whom he justified he has also given his splendor. (Romans 8:29-30 NEB)

While dying on the cross, Yeshua selflessly made it possible for his Father to become, "our Father which art in Heaven," but who also means to stay involved in our painful affairs on earth. Therefore, as family members who share the bond of Messiah's blood, there is no need to approach the Father with such trepid unfamiliarity. With veneration? Always. But, we must venerate while remembering that the veil has been torn.

[Yeshua] again gave a loud cry, and breathed his last. At that moment the curtain of the temple was torn in two from top to bottom. There was an earthquake, the rocks split and the graves opened, and many of [YHWH]'s saints were raised from sleep; and coming out of their graves after his resurrection they entered the Holy City, where many saw them. (Matthew 27:50-53 NEB)

When that day comes you will make your request in my name, and I do not say that I shall pray to the Father for you, for the Father loves you himself, because you have loved me and believed that I came from [YHWH]. (John 16:26-27 NEB)

When the disciple begins to understand his identity, only then will he be better equipped to identify with his siblings. Resentment abounds when the soul, longing to repair, feels cheated in isolation, because "self" is insisting on a solo sanctification. The only way to silence "self" is by growing in the Spirit. Though here is the conundrum: part of that growth is done in solitude, so that the believer learns how to discern the quiet voice of the Holy Spirit. Yet, the other part requires the member to rely on other members of the Body. Genuine growth is guaranteed when there are more members watering the seed.

First read: Acts 8:14-17

As you are walking ahead, always have your head filled with truth. Truth will set you free, in releasing your soul from captivity. Remember, other people will choose to perceive that truth is indeed relative. Truth will be the tool that enables you to remove your mask. Once removed, the truth will be easy to spot and to speak. It is difficult to speak truth when you are covered with lies. In attempting to help others remove their masks, you'll find that only a few will be receptive—most will be dismissive. Remember, other people will choose to perceive that truth is indeed relative. Perhaps you are not the person to successfully aid in removing their mask. Perhaps you are the person to simply loosen their mask, in informing or reminding them that what they are wearing is not real, while urging them to take it off sooner than later. Unfortunately, most will refuse to acknowledge their phantom; many will be unable to recognize. To them, their mask is real, and you won't be able to convince them otherwise. What they hear coming from you are lies. In wearing their several masks they will believe that you are trying to imprison them by accepting one truth. If your offer to help buff is continuously rebuffed, then you need to move on, because the clock is still ticking, and there are other people who can and will benefit from your assistance. If you insist on staying and trying to convince, battling for truth through duel, you will soon find yourself straddling the fence; and in folly, falling—a fool.

Nevertheless, when one turns to the Lord, the veil is taken away. Now [Yeshua] is the Spirit; and where the Spirit of [Yeshua] is, there is liberty. But we all, with unveiled face, beholding as in a mirror the glory of [Yeshua], are being transformed into the same image from glory to glory, just as by the Spirit of [YHWH]. (2nd Corinthians 3:16-18 NKJV)

And what is the danger? Because the majority of members within the Body refuse to acknowledge the convicting power of the Holy Spirit, and the same majority also denounce, as truth, the Spirit's empowerment of the Body through spiritual gifts, it will be an uphill battle in convincing them otherwise. Though, the danger might be lessened significantly if members would step out of their boat in a leap of faith and read Scripture. The truth is that Satan, the founder of death, enjoys the company he keeps among his sea of zombies. As such, he has been successful in convincing well-meaning shepherds to distort the personhood of the Holy Spirit.

Anyone who speaks a word against the Son of Man will receive forgiveness; but for him who slanders the Holy Spirit there will be no forgiveness. (Luke 12:10 NEB)

As previously mentioned, it is rare to hear outright heresy coming from the pulpit; Satan is much too crafty for such juvenile blasphemy. So, then, among mainstream Christian bodies, there will hardly be a word uttered that follows: "The Holy

Spirit doesn't exist." For the existence of the Holy Spirit has well since been established, and is supported by Scripture.

By this we know that we abide in him, and he in us, because he has given us of his Spirit. And we have seen and testify that the Father has sent the Son as Savior of the world. Whoever confesses that [Yeshua] is the Son of [YHWH], [YHWH] abides in him, and he in [YHWH]. And we have known and believed the love that [YHWH] has for us. [YHWH] is love, and he who abides in love abides in [YHWH], and [YHWH] in him. (1st John 4:13-16 NKJV)

Instead believers are told that the Holy Spirit has ceased to work through members today in the manner found in B'rit Khadasha Scripture. Upon careful examination, it is easy to see the fallaciousness of this assertion. If, by faith, we, as members of the Body, believe that upon accepting Messiah as our personal Lord and Savior, we have also received the promise of an eternal inheritance, and that our sins of old have been forgiven, then we are, in fact, supporting the assertion that we live under a New Covenant, and not the old. This is the same covenant, or testament, the believers of the early Church entered into, and there has not been a newer one since then. The same powerful Holy Spirit made available to them is still available to us now.

I wish you would bear with me in a little of my folly; please do bear with me. I am jealous for you, with a divine jealousy; for I betrothed you to [Messiah], thinking to present you as a chaste virgin to her true and only husband. But as the serpent in his cunning seduced Eve, I am afraid that your thoughts may be corrupted and you may lose your single-hearted devotion to [Messiah]. For if someone comes who proclaims another [Yeshua], not the [Yeshua] whom we proclaim, or if you then receive a spirit different from the Spirit already given to you, or a gospel different from the gospel you have already accepted, you manage to put up with that well enough. (2nd Corinthians 11:1-4 NEB)

And yet, there is still of course, an even subtler way in which to distort the personhood of the Holy Spirit. It is one thing to deny the timelessness and transcendence of the Third Person's power, it's another not to mention the Spirit at all. It's no wonder that some churches resemble a morgue, when the life-giving Spirit fails to ever be a topic mentioned, let alone taught. Messiah is not impressed with shepherds (who themselves are lacking the baptism of the Holy Spirit) who teach his flock to follow the commandments, but stop short of showing them how they might successfully do so.

Then [Yeshua] spoke to the multitudes and to his disciples, saying: "The scribes and the Pharisees sit in Moses' seat. Therefore whatever they tell you to observe, that observe and do, but do not do according to their works; for they say, and do not do. For they bind heavy burdens, hard to bear, and lay them on men's shoulders; but they themselves will not move them with one of their fingers. But all their works they do to be seen by men. They make their phylacteries broad and enlarge the borders of their garments. They love the best places at feasts, the best seats in the synagogues, greetings in the marketplaces, and to be called by men, 'Rabbi, Rabbi.'" (Matthew 23:1-7 NKJV)

When you seek to be justified by way of law, your relation with [Messiah] is completely severed: you have fallen out of the domain of [YHWH]'s grace. (Galatians 5:4 NEB)

Though not exactly the same, there is a similarity between this approach and the one employed by the Pharisees who also taught others to obey the law, but frowned upon the slightest infraction. It probably would have been rare to ever see a Pharisee smiling outside of their own circles. And when the Son of YHWH arrived on the scene to inform them that their efforts were both futile and antipodal (diametrically apposed) to what the Father required, the Pharisees' frown turned into a permanent scowl. Their efforts were futile because without YHWH's grace, via the indwelling Holy Spirit, such piety is impossible. They were antipodal to what the Father required because such efforts, as encouraged by the Pharisees, relied upon works for righteousness, rather than by salvation through faith in the Messiah. It was as if the Pharisees were promoting a sort of sanctification void of the Holy Spirit and void of justification by Messiah. Impossible.

Alas, alas, you are like unmarked graves over which men may walk without knowing it. In reply to this one of the lawyers said, "Master, when you say things like this you are insulting us too. " [Yeshua] rejoined: "Yes, you lawyers, it is no better with you. For you load men with intolerable burdens, and will not put a single finger to the load." (Luke 11:44-46 NEB)

[Yeshua] is the same yesterday, today, and for ever. So do not be swept off your course by all sorts of outlandish teachings; it is good that our souls should gain their strength from the grace of [YHWH], and not from scruples about what we eat, which have never done any good to those who were governed by them. (Hebrews 13:8-9 NEB)

Again, many shepherds of today are treading on dangerous ground. It is clear that most mainstream bodies understand that justification by Messiah is a prerequisite for entry into the kingdom. It is equally clear, however, that many mainstream bodies are unaware that Messiah also expects souls to be sanctified before approaching the heavenly gates. The Holy Spirit is urging the shepherds of these churches to get their act together. These are the bodies that have yet to experience painful repentance, and still prefer only casual glances into the mirror.

In truth, the only One to whom you have to convince of your repentance is Yeshua Messiah. However, everybody else should be able to clearly see. Those persons in the Body, Messiah will hold accountable for living an unholy life. However, for those whom YHWH has personally called to teach on such matters, they will have greater questions to answer.

And behold, a certain lawyer stood up and tested him, saying, "Teacher, what shall I do to inherit eternal life?" He said to him, "What is written in the law? What is your reading of it?" So he answered and said, "'You shall love

[YHWH] with all your heart and with all your soul and with all your might.' and 'you shall love your neighbor as yourself. '" And he said to him, "You have answered rightly; do this and you will live." (Luke 10:25-28 NKJV)

Perhaps the clearest observation, and the most troublesome, is that only a meager number of bodies understand what is essential to leading a life of holiness. And because of their failure to understand, shepherds all around are teaching their flock that it is impossible to do so, or they ignore the topic altogether. The bottom line? It is impossible to live a life of holiness without the Holy Spirit's baptism. A body is lifeless without its spirit. And yet the body is lifeless still if the Spirit has revived, but remains inactivated. The Body of Messiah was intended for holiness because its Head is Holy. But, without the active work of the Holy Spirit, many in the Body continue to bear an uncanny resemblance to those bodies still lying beneath the grass. Others, because of their failure to be daily filled by, and to daily yield to the Holy Spirit, will find themselves returning to their coffins and reverting to the dead. How unpleasant the day for those whom the Head finds dead upon his return.

What, then, is at present preventing some in the Body from receiving the Father's gracious gift of the Holy Spirit's baptism? Satan? Yes, but that's giving him too much credit. He can't keep the Holy Spirit from empowering, but he can entice shepherds and their flock to do so. How? Disobedience. Disobedience, which produces indifference.

208. The Prophecy of Prosperity

First read: Jeremiah 23-30

As you are walking, you will find that many, in wearing their masks, are riding the fence that separates the road from the garden of weeds. After attempting to aide, you need to leave before you are tempted to stay. They will offer you what is in their garden; you don't want any. While you are broken, they are fixed, and the two won't mix. If at first you don't succeed then don't be foolish—move on before they have a chance to fix you; for they will try.

It's not that Yeshua is against prosperity—he's not. He expects his Body to prosper and to aide generously those living in abject poverty. He is against those pastors and prophets who preach prosperity to souls who are still impoverished. The Son cares for the emaciated members of his body who are continuing to starve at the hands of irresponsible shepherds. That Satan has access to the Body of Messiah should come as no surprise. He, after all, had access to its Head while he walked in the wilderness. The Gospels are filled with admonitions from Messiah regarding the wolves who masquerade in sheep skin. At present there are swarms of venomous snakes who've invaded the ranks of the righteous. Their agenda is guised as the Gospel, but rather than focusing on repentance and renewal, they either speak of riches through repentance, or worse yet, riches rather than repentance. The danger is deceptively dim, and only through staying in Scripture and having a head saturated with the Holy Spirit's wisdom, can light expose him who is hungry.

Whoever denies the Son does not have the Father either; he who acknowledges the Son has the Father also. Therefore let that abide in you which you heard from the beginning. If what you heard from the beginning abides in you, you also will abide in the Son and in the Father. And this is the promise that he has promised us—eternal life. These things I have written to you concerning those who try to deceive you. But the anointing which you have received from him abides in you, and you do not need that anyone teach you; but as the same anointing teaches you concerning all things, and is true, and is not a lie, and just as it has taught you, you will abide in him. (1st John 2:23-27 NKJV)

In truth, the Tanakh books spoke of times when the Israelites lived lavishly, like the sons and daughters of a King. The prophetic books also speak of future times when God Almighty will restore Israel to her former glory, and her children will return to a land overflowing with milk and honey. Moreover, we have the following heavenly promises from Messiah himself:

Set your troubled hearts at rest. Trust in [YHWH] always; trust also in me. There are many dwelling-places in my Father's house; if it were not so I should have told you; for I am going there on purpose to prepare a place for you. (John 14:1-2 NEB)

The city was built as a square, and was as wide as it was long. It measured by his rod twelve thousand furlongs, its length and breadth and height being equal. Its wall was one hundred and forty-four cubits high, that is, by human measurements, which the messenger was using. The wall was built of jasper, while the city itself was of pure gold, bright as clear glass. The foundations of the city wall were adjourned with jewels of every kind, the first of the foundation-stones being jasper, the second lapis lazuli, the third chalcedony, the fourth emerald, the fifth sardonyx, the six cornelian, the seventh chrysolite, the eighth beryl, the ninth topaz, the tenth chrysoprase, the eleventh turquoise, and the twelfth amethyst. The twelve gates were twelve pearls, each gate being made from a single pearl. The streets of the city were of pure gold, like translucent glass. (Revelation 21:16-21 NEB)

These images are intended to encourage Messiah's disciples to continue in their devotion to him, through the Holy Spirit. However, it is not the prosperity of Paradise that these false prophets speak of when spewing their venom. No, their goal is to misrepresent the God of the Gospel so that "believers" are blinded to the Truth. Rather than placing trust in the Father to provide for their needs, they instead rely on their wealth, with its "neat-looking" seeds. It won't be long now before they're entangled in weeds. The Holy Spirit will convict man of his sin, while Satan and his prophets keep man focused within. When the true prophets and shepherds of Messiah begin preaching wrath as a "last call" pitch for repentance, most in their weeds still won't concede; maintaining their allegiance to the god of this world. Members who find themselves in these bodies would do well to pray for others in their flock, while holding fast to their Rock. However, if your prayers remain unheeded, leave and go to where you are needed. Messiah does not will that your soul stagnate by staying in the midst of such staleness. It is not you they will have rejected, but the Bread of Life. Those prophets and pastors who practice deceit, who prey upon those still searching, or are weak, will soon find themselves alone in the streets.

Many deceivers have gone out into the world, who do not acknowledge [Yeshua] as coming in the flesh. These are the persons described as the [Anti-Messiah], the arch-deceiver. Beware of them, so that you may not lose all that we worked for, but receive your reward in full. (2nd John 1:7-8 NEB)

209. Fatal Fruit - I

First read: 1st Kings 11:1-13

Inevitably, you will find yourself occasionally fencing for reasons not always apparent, so you need to know how to play. You need to know that the goal of your opponent is not simply to wound, but ultimately to defeat. It can happen in any number of ways. You could either be struck while on the fence; though your opponent will rarely display such open hostility, especially if you have only just begun walking. It will be more tempting to look at the masks of those on the fence. You will be magnetically drawn, like a moth to the flame. Careful. You will burn. Once you climb aboard, your opponent will entice with a piece of scintillating fruit. At this point you should immediately discern; for what fruit could possibly be edible coming from a garden of weeds?

Bear one another's burdens, and so fulfill the law of [Messiah]. For if anyone thinks himself to be something, when he is nothing, he deceives himself. But let each one examine his own work, and then he will have rejoicing in himself alone, and not in another. (Galatians 6:2-4 NKJV)

Oh, how the mighty have fallen. How does it happen that Satan is successful in using the same old recycled trash in luring YHWH's children off the road to Glory? Because he knows that even while walking in the Spirit, the lower nature of man stays famished. He also knows what man likes to eat when he's hungry. Again and again, the resounding message of our Maker is that man has the victory; if only they'd feast on the Word, rather than on their neighbor's flesh. The diet guided by the Holy Spirit must be ingested on a daily basis. It is tempting to think that after walking several miles on the road, the body no longer needs nutrients from its Root. But, in attempting to rely solely upon stored sustenance to sustain while walking, one welcomes an opportunity for the enemy to entice.

From the fruit of a man's mouth his stomach is satisfied; he is satisfied by the yield of his lips. (Proverbs 18:20 ESV)

King Solomon suffered from making a mistake that even well-seasoned members of the Body will often find themselves emulating. He came to a point where he believed he'd reached his pinnacle; a dangerous place to stand with so much air. Oh, how the mighty have fallen. There is no such thing as a pinnacle on the road to Glory because the road was designed so that the apex awaits the believer at the end of his journey. The only way to arrive is by continuously placing one foot in front of the other. The pinnacle is pointed and so there's only room for one person—self. That means there's no room for another traveler to assist by insisting that you daily eat of your spiritual Bread. Moreover, there is no one available to assist when an unexpected wind engenders your sway. Oh, how the mighty have fallen. And there you lay.

How blest are those who hunger and thirst for righteousness; they shall be filled. (Matthew 5:6 NEB)

For everyone has his own proper burden to bear. (Galatians 6:5 NEB)

And yet we must continuously crave to stay away from the grave. Satan won't have much success in alluring a believer who's always allured to the cross. For starters, members of the Body allured to the cross are always carrying their cross; it is jagged and heavy. The only way they have the strength to continue carrying it is by daily eating of their fruit. Next, in carrying their cross, members of the Body understand the cost, so they dare not put it down. They realize that their fate is in the hands of Messiah so, in being faithful, they're assured that their next bite won't be fatal. Finally, in understanding the cost, members are allured to the lost, rather than by them. The strategy and goal of every believer, then, is to get to the lost and show them the cross. Take what Satan intended to be fatal, and offer them a new faith, with a new fate. Take any piece of illicit fruit, graft it to a new root, and watch it grow. Oh how the weak will rise.

In the end he appeared even to me; though this birth of mine was monstrous, [ISV: as though I were born abnormally late]; for I had persecuted the church of [YHWH] and am therefore inferior to all other apostles—indeed not fit to be called an apostle. However, by [YHWH]'s grace I am what I am, nor has his grace been given to me in vain; on the contrary, in my labors I have outdone them all—not I, indeed, but the grace of [YHWH] working with me. (1st Corinthians 15:8-10 NEB)

And His mercy is on those who fear Him from generation to generation. He has shown strength with His arm; He has scattered the proud in the imagination of their hearts. He has put down the mighty from their thrones, and exalted the lowly. He has filled the hungry with good things, and the rich He has sent away empty. (Luke 1:50-53 NKJV)

210. A Reflective Moment

Fatal Fruit – II

First read: 2nd Kings 18-19

One day he got into a boat with his disciples and said to them, "Let us cross over to the other side of the lake." So they put out; and as they sailed along he went to sleep. Then a heavy squall struck the lake; they began to ship water and were in grave danger. They went to him, and roused him, crying, "Master, Master, we are sinking." He awoke, and rebuked the wind and the turbulent waters. The storm subsided and all was calm. "Where is your faith?" he asked. (Luke 8:22-24 NEB)

While journeying, storms will arise, and the believer will have to choose the person to whom they turn for help. It is our natural inclination when faced with threats from the world, to ask the world for help. Where is the logic in such actions? Can anyone imagine during wartime, members of one party turning to their enemy for assistance? It flies in the face of reason. The Assyrian king, Sennacherib, was determined to make the Israelites feel foolish for turning to God Almighty during their time of need. However, this is what David did while under constant attack from king Saul:

I sought [YHWH], and he answered me and delivered me from all my fears. Those who look to him are radiant, and their faces shall never be ashamed. This poor man cried, and [YHWH] heard him and saved him out of all his troubles. The messenger of [YHWH] encamp around those who fear him, and delivers them. (Psalms 34:4-7 ESV)

It bears repeating that the road to Glory is neither void of pitfalls, nor hecklers from the side of the road who have as their goal, to drive members off course. Believers would perhaps save themselves unnecessary anxiety if they discontinued their view of the road as "supposing to be trouble free." The Bible makes no mention of a God who shields his people from adversity. There is a God, however, who promises to protect his people while in the midst. The way to Heaven is high, and is filled with plenty of low valleys. The challenge for the believer is to stay on the road when the temptation arises to depart.

Keep back your servant also from presumptuous sins; let them not have dominion over me. Then I shall be blameless, and innocent of great transgression. (Psalms 19:13 ESV)

Like Job, believers must repent of moments when, in acting out of ignorance, they accuse YHWH of neglecting them, or of spitefully delivering them to the devil and his demons. Why would the Father act with such malice? On the other hand, members must not mistakenly expect him to immediately lift them out of a hole that they themselves have insisted on digging, even against their own better judgment. Not that the Good Shepherd is unconcerned about the suffering of his sheep; but sometimes suffering is the only way to make us see. Furthermore, after a moment of suffering and walking in a constant night, how appreciative we are for the gift of sight.

Thus says the king: "Do not let Hezekiah deceive you, for he will not be able to deliver you out of my hand. Do not let Hezekiah make you trust in [YHWH] by saying, '[YHWH] will surely deliver us, and this city will not be given into the hand of the king of Assyria.' Do not listen to Hezekiah, for thus says the king of Assyria: 'Make your peace with me and come out to me. Then each one of you will eat of his own vine, and each one of his own fig tree, and each one of you will drink the water of his own cistern, until I come and take you away to a land like your own land, a land of grain and wine, a land of bread and vineyards, a land of olive trees and honey, that you may live, and not die. And do not listen to Hezekiah when he misleads you by saying, '[YHWH] will deliver us.'" (2 Kings 18:29-32 ESV)

And this is the message of this kingdom with its present ruler. Yet, to all who are faithful to YHWH, he does indeed rescue; to all who are faithful. Though this world has much fruit to offer, believers must look up for their deliverance. Members of the Body must desist in placing their faith in the flesh. The curtains are closing on this present kingdom. While many are still in bondage, Messiah and his heavenly host are working to release. Hold fast and pray. Help is on the way to all who believe.

211. Garden Grass - I

First read: 1st Kings 21:1-29

With pinched face you begin to ponder. And while doing so, the opponent, in seeing your contemplation, points to the direction of the garden. How lush it looks. Yes, there are weeds, but it is hard to see them among the shade and all the greenery. The opponent asks how anything that comes from such plush could possibly be bad. Caution. In staring at the garden's greenery, you will be tempted to compare. Its luster will make the grass on your side of the fence seem dingy. Don't be fooled and don't despair. Everything will appear less polished on the road you are traveling when contrasted with what the opponent shows you. In rushing, you can't reason; you also can't remember. The grass on your side is greener after every storm.

He also allured you out of distress into a broad place where there was no cramping, and what was set on your table was full of fatness. But you are full of the judgment on the wicked; judgment and justice seize you. Beware lest wrath entice you into scoffing, and let not the greatness of the ransom turn you aside. Will your cry for help avail to keep you from distress, or all the force of your strength? Do not long for the night, when peoples vanish in their place. Take care; do not turn to iniquity, for this you have chosen rather than affliction. (Job 36:16-21 ESV)

It would seem that people are pre-wired to constantly compare themselves to one another. The world is full of people who stay miserable because their state of contentment is contingent upon whether or not they are able to keep up with the latest craze and fad. If someone else has and they are without, then it won't be long before you see them pout. This is an assured way of getting Satan's attention. Believers must remember that perpetual misery is the name of Satan's game. If he can keep the eyes of members turned away from the Father, and instead focused on their longing, then he is succeeding in thwarting the Father's purpose for their people. It is impossible to overstate the truth that what Yeshua ultimately desires to have is intimacy with those whom he created in his image. However, immediately with the eyes to the side and the lips poked out—out goes our faith, and in comes the doubt. The road to Glory becomes murky when believers choose to associate God Almighty's presence with his, or worldly, presents. How often have we asked our Father why it is we don't have such and such, or why we can't have so and so? How soon do we begin accusing Messiah of abandonment when what we desire or aspire won't come? It isn't he who has left, but rather the heart of the wavering worker has begun searching for greener pastures. Envy will, at times, lead the traveler to the side of the road where a fence sits separating truth from deception. The truth is that the road to Glory doesn't always appear glorious. It's not. In fact, for Messiah, the road to Glory was rather gory; as it also had been for just about all of his earlier disciples.

Then James and John, the sons of Zebedee, came to Him, saying, "Teacher, we want you to do for us whatever we ask." And he said to them, "What do you want me to do for you?" They said to him, "Grant us that we may sit, one on your right hand and the other on your left, in your glory." But [Yeshua] said to them, "You do not know what you ask. Are you able to drink the cup that I drink, and be baptized with the baptism that I am baptized with?" They said to him, "We are able." So [Yeshua] said to them, "You will indeed drink the cup that I drink, and with the baptism I am baptized with you will be baptized; but to sit on my right hand and on my left is not mine to give, but it is for those for whom it is prepared." (Mark 10:35-40 NKJV)

But, that isn't the whole story. There were magnificent moments for Messiah and his followers while journeying. Most often they occurred in times of intimacy; whether between Messiah and his Father, or Messiah and his disciples. Never did they happen during an exchange of presents, but always in the midst of the other's presence.

Six days later [Yeshua] took Peter, James, and John the brother of James, and led them up a high mountain where they were alone; and in their presence he was transfigured; his face shone like the sun, and his clothes became white as the light. And they saw Moses and Elijah appear, conversing with him. Then Peter spoke: "[Yeshua]," he said, "how good it is that we are here. If you wish it, I will make three shelters here, one for you, one for Moses, and one for Elijah." While he was still speaking, a bright cloud suddenly overshadowed them, and a voice called from the cloud: "This is my Son, my Beloved, on whom my favor rests; listen to him." (Matthew 17:1-5 NEB)

How glorious indeed. Immediately when Yeshua descended from the mountain, he continued his service. Messiah's first act upon returning to the road was to bring glory, not to himself, but to his Father, by curing and setting free a man who had, for years, been plagued with epilepsy. The truth? Caring for others leaves no time for comparing one another, which means there's no time to head to the fence.

212. A Reflective Moment

Greener Grass – II

First read: 1st Kings 21:1-29

It's deceiving to believe that what lies on the other side of the fence is some-how better for you than that which YHWH wills for you to have while walking on the road to Glory. What is the will of Yeshua for the believer as they journey? That each would find contentment in walking on the road, no matter how dusty or dingy the flowers, grass, and trees might seem. There is a difference, however, between finding contentment and feigning contentment. Yeshua does not will that his servants feign contentment because it only engenders masked resentment. It is with a sinful sense of entitlement that members begin to resent "not having." At some point in our walk, we are no longer grateful for the newly awakened state given to us by Messiah. It is as if the freely shed blood of Messiah for the redemption of man, once potent enough to liven the deadest of the dead, is now pointless instead. It is because members no longer remember the personal power of red, that green becomes eye-catching.

Not that I am alluding to want, for I have learned to find resources in my-self whatever my circumstances. I know what it is to be brought low, and I know what it is to have plenty. I have been very thoroughly initiated into the human lot with all its up and downs—fullness and hunger, plenty and want. I have strength for anything through him who gives me power. (Philippians 4:11-13 NEB)

Each step on the road to Glory is a gift by itself; we step only as the Father wills. How then can any resent what is sent by him and is meant for the good of the Body? Nothing on the other side of the fence can prepare the believer for the place Yeshua is preparing even now. Somehow through the fusing of Church and culture, members within the Body have been affected by the nuisance of now. This nuisance of now has engendered a generation infested with selfish hearts and impatient souls. Instant gratification always has inward intentions and with "me" as the perpetual subject. Instant gratification is in constant conflict with the cross. As believers, we are instructed to daily carry crosses that Messiah never promised would be feathery. His assurance of easy yokes and light burdens spoke of the believer's empowerment through the Holy Spirit. To handle the weight, he would make our burdens bear-able. However, those seeking instant gratification make no effort to carry their cross beyond their threshold for pain. "This is much too heavy," they say. At the instant their cross goes down, it is as if death had eluded them altogether. No death? No red.

What's deceiving about instant gratification is that it never satisfies the soul. YHWH created our souls to remain dissatisfied apart from intimate communion with him. What lies on the other side of the fence is foreign to the soul, though familiar to the flesh. It is the lower nature of man that finds contentment from feasting on the green that all believers have seen. We've seen it because we once lay beneath it. For under the blades of grass lay rows of graves, and from here is where members were rescued and washed. But, by fixing our attention on the scintillating fruit, Satan is able to prevent believers from remembering just how shady his trees really are.

> There is indeed no single gift you lack, while you wait expectantly for [Yeshua] to reveal himself. (1st Corinthians 1:7 NEB)

Again, believers mustn't believe that Messiah would have his servants walk without times of joy, or that they are the adopted children of a stingy Father who disregards their needs and wants. Yes, he rejoices with those who yearn for his presence. And to those who obey, he will provide presents, so that they may be shared with others. The Book of James offers some valuable insight for those whose feigned contentment has lead to contemptuous looks toward fellow travelers.

> Where do wars and fights come from among you? Do they not come from your desires for pleasure that war in your members? You lust and do not have. You murder and covet and cannot obtain. You fight and war. Yet you do not have because you do not ask. You ask and do not receive, because you ask amiss, that you may spend it on your pleasures. Adulterers and adulteresses. Do you not know that friendship with the world is enmity with [YHWH]? Whoever therefore wants to be a friend of the world makes himself an enemy of [YHWH]. Or do you think that the Scripture says in vain, "The spirit who dwells in us yearns jealously"? (James 4:1-5 NKJV)

To those who have been asking with purity and in faith, know that YHWH is going to respond.

213. Plowing For Plush

First read: Psalms 25:1-22

The opponent will most likely only beckon you over to the garden when it's scorching. This is why it is so important to look ahead. Don't be in a rush to get it now—your plush will come after your plow.

But this I say: he who sows sparingly will also reap sparingly, and he who sows bountifully will also reap bountifully. (2nd Corinthians 9:6 NKJV)

Being a laborer in Messiah's vineyard definitely has it draw backs, or at least it would seem that way when we insist on laboring in our flesh rather then in the Spirit. When laboring in the flesh, the focus is always on the drudgery. After all, there are days when the weather doesn't appear conducive for gardening. While we are busy planting seeds, the clouds suddenly let loose and the rain begins to pour. We want less while the Spirit says, "More." Without any rain, the seeds would remain beneath the ground, and all of our digging and tilling would have been in vain. In our flesh we focus only on self, so that long before the rain is done, we're calling on the sun. And then the sun comes out.

For we brought nothing into this world, and it is certain we can carry nothing out. And having food and clothing, with these we shall be content. But those who desire to be rich fall into temptation and a snare, and into many foolish and harmful lusts which drown men in destruction and perdition. For the love of money is a root of all kinds of evil, for which some have strayed from the faith in their greediness, and pierced themselves through with many sorrows. (1st Timothy 6:7-10 NKJV)

"Oh, it's too hot," you may say. In our flesh we forget that a little heat is also necessary for growth. Rather than ensuring that all of the buds get their day in the sun, we instead turn inward and wonder when we'll ever get done. That is when the Holy Spirit begins to remind us that when the Father feels that his children are ready to enter the garden; when the Son believes that a disciple of his is mature enough to work, then into the garden you'll go. After traveling a few miles and strengthening the muscles in your legs, it is time to begin working on the upper body. Messiah will place in your hands all the necessary tools and say, "Now, plow." If you thought that engaging in spiritual warfare was the only work expected of you, then you haven't been winning any battles lately. Satan should never be the focus of any believer traveling on the road to Glory; though he should always be kept in the periphery. It is the goal of every believer to ensure that nothing is obstructing him or her from the purpose of their King—to enlarge his kingdom. Spiritual warfare is only necessary because our vision would remain clouded if we didn't fight.

But as it is written: "Eye has not seen, nor ear heard, nor have entered into the heart of man the things which [YHWH] has prepared for those who love him." But [YHWH] has revealed them to us through the Spirit. For the Spirit searches all things, yes, the deep things of [YHWH]. (1st Corinthians 2:9-10 NKJV)

At times what lies ahead may indeed be a garden. It is imperative that believers ensure that the garden is located on this side of the fence and not on the other. A believer's private journey ought never to excuse him from public service. Think not so highly of yourself, that you have time for no one else. Remember that you cannot repair unless someone else is there, or several someones. Besides, there is no mention of a solo expedition in the Gospels, only the occasional solo excursion when God Almighty wills for such.

After this [Yeshua] appointed a further seventy-two and sent them on ahead in pairs to every town and place he was going to visit himself. He said to them: "The crop is heavy, but laborers are scarce; you must therefore beg the owner to send laborers to harvest his crop. Be on your way. And look, I am sending you like lambs among wolves. Carry no purse or pack, and travel barefoot." (Luke 10:1-4 NEB)

It is only the begrudging believer that has to worry about Satan enticing him or her away from the garden. The disciple who is focused on the drudgery of his plowing begins dreaming of greener pastures. Messiah is preparing a place for his faithful followers; for those whose present plowing will produce a plentiful harvest. And there is nothing wrong with eagerly anticipating the reward that awaits the righteous. Allow it to be but one motivator to continue in your plowing while the sun is beaming down. But stay leery of wondering and your feet won't start wandering. Don't wonder—work.

Do you not say, "Four months more and then comes harvest?" But look, I tell you, look round on the fields; they are already white, ripe for harvest. The reaper is drawing his pay and gathering a crop for eternal life, so that sower and reaper may rejoice together. That is how the saying comes true: "One sows, and another reaps." I sent you to reap a crop for which you have not toiled. Others toiled and you have come in for the harvest of their toil. (John 4:35-38 NEB)

214. Collaboration

First read: Esther 9:1-32

It won't appear enticing for another traveler to see the opponent defeat you right there on the fence. No, when the opponent sees that you are stepping away to get back to the road, the generosity will increase. You must understand that the easiest and most efficient way for the opponent to get as many travelers on the fence and into the garden is to have fellow travelers lending a hand. If you won't jump down to enter the garden on your own then the opponent will lend you a helping hand. You must ensure that you are fully armed in fencing with your opponents. Luckily, you will have all of your armor in your bag.

As previously mentioned, spiritual warfare is not the topic of the town within most churches today. Nevertheless, it is a topic that believers must learn to address with clarity and without fear. Though the focus of the believer should routinely center on the Father, it is wise that believers become and remain equally aware of this truth: As the curtain draws to a close and the King prepares to make his triumphant return, Satan will work to get believers to lose their focus. As long as the believer remains on the road, then no true harm will he incur, though at times Satan may feel closer than anyone would prefer. In the moments when truth seems a thousand miles away, it is best to remember the words of King David, who understood well the agony of an attack:

[YHWH], how many are my foes. Many are rising against me; many are saying of my soul, there is no salvation for him in [Yeshua]. But you, [YHWH], are a shield about me, my glory, and the lifter of my head. I cried aloud to [YHWH], and he answered me from his holy hill. I lay down and slept; I woke again, for [YHWH] sustained me. I will not be afraid of many thousands of people who have set themselves against me all around. (Psalms 3:1-6 ESV)

Most of our agony is manifested mentally and emotionally, which in turn may cause great physical discomfort. Messiah never promised that his disciples would be shielded from attacks; he only ensured our protection in the midst.

He delivers the afflicted by their affliction and opens their ear by adversity. (Job 36:15 ESV)

He also ensured that his disciples would have the ability to defend themselves. While the armor of YHWH is freely extended to every believer, after confessing sins and upon accepting Messiah, it is up to the believer to wear it daily. There is power in the belt; the coat of mail; the shoes; the shield; the helmet; the sword; and in prayer. There is power in the Son and there is potency in the number one.

Now this is the confidence that we have in him, that if we ask anything according to his will, he hears us. And if we know that he hears us, whatever we ask, we know that we have the petitions that we have asked of him. (1st John 5:14-15 NKJV)

Haman the Agagite, son of Hammedatha, posed a threat to Esther, Mordecai, and the other Jews, not because he was capable of killing them all by himself, but rather Haman's strength lay in his numbers. Were it not for YHWH's intervention, the Jews would have suffered a horrible death at the hands of Haman's army. Once again, believers would do well to remember that Satan is only as effective in debilitating as his numbers enable him. Satan is not omnipresent any more than he is omniscient or omnipotent. Satan is strategic, however. He is aware that as long as the Body of Messiah remains divided into many, she will remain forever diluted in defending, and practically ineffective in defeating. There is potency in the number one. Satan, his fallen angels and demons are united in their efforts to debilitate and destroy. YHWH and his angels are united in their intentions to defend and defeat. It is now time for the Body in the physical realm to collaborate, so that she no longer looks like bait.

And though a man might prevail against one who is alone, two will withstand him—a threefold cord is not quickly broken. (Ecclesiastes 4:12 ESV)

The Holy Spirit continues to urge members of the Body to put aside differences and instead turn to one another to create a viable defense. Where there is unity, the Father Son, and Holy Spirit are always found. But continue with division and watch what comes crashing to the ground.

For through faith you are all sons of [YHWH] in union with [Yeshua]. Baptized into union with him, you have all put on [Messiah] as a garment. There is no such thing as Jew and Greek, slave and freeman, male and female; for you are all one person in [Yeshua]. (Galatians 3:26-28 NEB)

215. A Reflective Moment

T. K. O.

First read: 1st Peter 5:8-10

Okay, it's time for some truth. Are you ready? The devil has already been defeated, but he isn't dead yet. On the contrary, Satan is alive and well, which is why Peter encouraged members of the Body to stay alert. The Holy Spirit is urging the Church now more than ever to wake up. Unbelievers aren't the devil's prey—they already belong to him. In fact, in their pride, they have unknowingly become a part of Satan's entourage. In this final stretch before the return of Messiah, Satan, his fallen angels, and demons are working overtime.

Be gracious to me, [YHWH], for man tramples on me; all day long an attacker oppresses me; my enemies trample on me all day long, for many attack me proudly. When I am afraid, I put my trust in you. In [YHWH], whose word I praise, in [Yeshua] I trust; I shall not be afraid. What can flesh do to me? All day long they injure my cause; all their thoughts are against me for evil. They stir up strife, they lurk; they watch my steps, as they have waited for my life. For their crime will they escape? In wrath cast down the peoples, [YHWH]. (Psalms 56:1-7 ESV)

It is important that believers are clear in understanding that Satan is not the opposite of YHWH—they are not evenly matched. YHWH is a heavy weight; omnipotent, omniscient, and omnipresent. Satan, while no feather weight, is none of the above. Satan is a created being; he had a beginning, and he has an end. Satan knows his final destination. In his hatred he wants as many of Yeshua's human creation to go with him. Those that he can't cause to retract their repentance, he will try to make their journey on the road to Glory a living hell. Satan has many tools, but two of his most powerful ones are deception and debilitation.

First, if he can't deceive you into believing that he doesn't really exist, then he can deceive you into believing that he is more powerful than he that lives in you. Second, if deception isn't working—if you have already put Satan in his place to where he can't defeat you spiritually (because you remind Satan that Messiah knocked him out with his blood on the cross, and the Father sealed all believers with his indwelling Holy Spirit) he will attack you mentally, emotionally, or physically.

Deliver me from my enemies, [YHWH]. Protect me from those who rise up against me; deliver me from those who work evil, and save me from bloodthirsty men. For behold, they lie in wait for me; fierce men stir up strife against me. For no transgression or sin of mine, [Yeshua], for no fault of mine, they run and make ready. Awake. Come to meet me and see. You, [YHWH], are [Yeshua]. Rouse yourself to punish all the nations; spare none of those who treacherously plot evil. Each evening they come back, howling like dogs and prowling about the city. There they are, bellowing with their mouths with swords in their lips—for "Who," they think, "will hear us?" But you, [Yeshua], laugh at them. You hold all the nations in derision. My Redeemer, I will watch for you. For you [Yeshua], are my fortress. [Yeshua] in his steadfast love will save me; [Yeshua] will let me look in triumph on my enemies. Kill them soon, lest the people forget. Make them totter by your power and bring them down, [Yeshua], our shield. For the sin of their mouths, the words of their lips, let them be trapped in their pride. For the cursing and lies that they utter, consume them in wrath; consume them till they are no more, that they may know that [YHWH] rule over Jacob to the ends of the earth. Each evening they come back, howling like dogs and prowling about the city. They wander about for food and growl if they do not get their fill. I will sing of your strength. I will sing aloud of your steadfast love in the morning. For you have been to me a fortress and a refuge in the day of my distress. My strength, I will sing praises to you. For you, [Yeshua], are my fortress, [YHWH] who shows me steadfast love. (Psalms 59:1-17 ESV)

Notice how Peter characterizes Satan as lion-looking. Again, while Satan is not omniscient, he is observant and so are his demons and fallen angels—his fellow traitors. Satan can't force you to sin because sin starts from within. He can, however, capitalize on it. Satan can't tempt you with what you haven't already shown him you struggle with. But, once the temptation surfaces, it is up to you to decide. "Am I going to give in to sin, or am I going to cling to the grace that the Father freely makes available to all who are actively running the race?" Except for the rare instances in which one is experiencing demon possession, the devil can't make you do it. Such utterance gives Satan more credit than he deserves, and denies the essence of the Father's gift of free will. Satan's easiest targets are passive Christians who spend more time focusing on their self-satisfying lusts.

Hear my voice, [YHWH], in my complaint. Preserve my mind from dread of the enemy. Hide me from the secret plots of the wicked, from the throng of evildoers, who whet their tongues like swords, who aim bitter words like arrows, shooting from ambush at the blameless, shooting at him suddenly and without fear. They hold to their evil purpose. They talk of laying snares secretly, thinking, "Who can see them?" They search out injustice, saying, "We have accomplished a diligent search." For the inward mind and heart of men are deep. But, [YHWH] shoots his arrow at them. They are wounded suddenly. (Psalms 64:1-7 ESV)

Okay, now that we have exposed the ugly truth, let's now focus on weapons. Active Christians who fill their time with Messiah pose a constant threat. There are both defensive and offensive weapons that Messiah has given us. One of the most powerful defensive weapons is prayer. Many believers underestimate the power of prayer; King David didn't; neither did the Son of YHWH.

But the talk about him spread all the more; great crowds gathered to hear him and to be cured of their ailments. And from time to time he would withdraw to lonely places for prayer. (Luke 5:16 NEB)

A life marked by constant prayer is a life assured that Messiah is there. When

Messiah is near, the devil and his demons flee in fear. It may sound a little hokey, but try it and see what happens. Our life style is yet another powerful defensive weapon. Once again, if everything we do is Messiah centered—the music we listen to, the movies we watch, and the company and conversation we entertain—if Messiah is in all, then there is no room for Satan.

Whoever commits sin also commits lawlessness, and sin is lawlessness. And you know that he was manifested to take away our sins, and in him there is no sin. Whoever abides in him does not sin. Whoever sins has neither seen him nor known him. Little children, let no one deceive you. He who practices righteousness is righteous, just as he is righteous. He who sins is of the devil, for the devil has sinned from the beginning. For this purpose the Son of [YHWH] was manifested, that he might destroy the works of the devil. (1st John 3:4-8 NKJV)

Finally, the Christian battle is a spiritual battle. When Satan fell, he took one-third of the angels with him. That still leaves two-thirds of the angels serving and fighting on YHWH's side.

Angels are not to be worshiped or served, rather they exist to serve and worship the Father and aid man (through messages and deeds—though, often unseen), and to help fight the forces of evil. [YHWH] has established his throne in the heavens, and his kingdom rules over all. Bless [YHWH], you his angels, you mighty ones who do his word, obeying the voice of his word. (Psalms 103:19-20 ESV)

But, [Yeshua] said to him, "Put your sword in its place, for all who take the sword will perish by the sword. Or do you think that I cannot now pray to my Father, and he will provide me with more than twelve legions of angels? (Matthew 26:52-53 NKJV)

The war has already been won and those who serve Messiah will know victory. However, the battles will continue until Messiah returns. Ask the Father to release his legions of angels to aid you in your spiritual battles. We have been given the gloves. The Holy Spirit is now imploring the Body to use them.

When a strong man fully armed is on guard over his castle his possessions are safe. But when someone stronger comes upon him and overpowers him, he carries off the arms and armor on which the man had relied and divides the plunder. (Luke 11:21-22 NEB)

216. Dueling With the Devil in Truth

First read: Ephesians 6:14-20

Stand firm, I say. Fasten on the belt of truth. (Ephesians 6:14a NEB)

I know the title of this section, in of itself, is enough to make any Christian cringe. If so, you're starting off on the wrong foot. The number one rule in engaging in spiritual warfare is that fear must never manifest while in the midst of battle.

[YHWH] is my light and my salvation; whom shall I fear? [Yeshua] is the stronghold of my life; of whom shall I be afraid? When evildoers assail me to eat up my flesh, my adversaries and foes, it is they who stumble and fall. Though an army encamp against me, my heart shall not fear; though war arise against me, yet I will be confident. (Psalms 27:1-3 ESV)

Though an unpopular topic in several churches and an unspoken one in most, Christians everywhere need to learn how to fight; their spiritual livelihood is on the line. Presently, the Body of Messiah is in a vulnerable position because the majority of its parts remain unprotected. Albeit still limited, Satan will continue in his successes until members show that they aren't afraid of scrapping. He won't desist until we begin resisting. Paul reminds the believers at Ephesus that the Christian struggle is not a human one. In an attempt to divert the attention away from himself, the crafty serpent has manipulated believers into constantly waging war against one another. The first piece of defensive armor mentioned in these Scripture verses is the belt of truth. It's no coincidence that Satan is referred to as the Father of Lies. Believers must remember that the devil has been around for some time, and so has had sufficient time to master his craft.

After meeting with the elders and conferring together, the chief priests offered the soldiers a substantial bribe and told them to say, "His disciples came by night and stole the body while we were asleep." They added, "If this should reach the Governor's ears, we will put matters right with him and see that you do not suffer." So they took the money and did as they were told. This story became widely known, and is current in Jewish circles to this day. (Matthew 28:12-15 NEB)

Although the eternal victory has already been guaranteed, Messiah died so that we might also have victory here on earth. However, if the Bride of Messiah is to prove triumphant, she must receive the truth and her maidens must accept it. The spiritual world, while unseen, is nevertheless real. It is not a figment of a zealous Christian imagination. Refusing to address the relationship between the spiritual world and the physical world doesn't thwart the activity apparent in both. It only allows the demonic forces and fallen angels to continue making a mockery of the people Messiah inherited from his Father. It is worth it for believers to revisit the accounts found in Scripture, where the spiritual world was spoken of as legitimate. The book of Daniel, whose author shares the same name is one of the most influential major prophets, along with Isaiah, Jeremiah, and Ezekiel, of the Tanakh, and records an account.

On the twenty-fourth day of the first month, as I was standing on the bank of the great river (that is, the Tigris) I lifted up my eyes and looked, and behold, a man clothed in linen, with a belt of fine gold from Uphaz around his waist. His body was like beryl, his face like the appearance of lightning, his eyes like flaming torches, his arms and legs like the gleam of burnished bronze, and the sound of his words like the sound of a multitude. And I, Daniel, alone saw the vision, for the men who were with me did not see the vision, but a great trembling fell upon them, and they fled to hide themselves. So I was left alone and saw this great vision, and no strength was left in me. My radiant appearance was changed, and I retained little strength. Then I heard the sound of his words, and as I heard the sound of his words, I fell on my face in deep sleep with my face to the ground. And behold, a hand touched me and set me trembling on my hands and knees. And he said to me, "O Daniel, man greatly loved, understand the words that I speak to you, and stand upright, for now I have been sent to you." And when he had spoken this word to me, I stood up trembling. Then he said to me, "Fear not, Daniel, for from the first day that you set your heart to understand and humbled yourself before [YHWH], your words have been heard, and I have come because of your words. The prince of the kingdom of Persia withstood me twenty-one days, but Michael, one of the chief princes, came to help me, for I was left there with the kings of Persia, and came to make you understand what is to happen to your people in the latter days. For the vision is for days yet to come." (Daniel 10:4-13 ESV)

Ready for some truth? Satan, as the spiritual ruler of this temporal world, has a hierarchical host of angels fighting on his side; and they each have their earthly mission. And what are these assignments? In returning to the tenth chapter of Daniel, we find a message being delivered to Daniel from a member of Yeshua's angelic host.

Again, one looking the form of a man touched me and strengthened me. And he said, " man greatly loved, fear not, peace be with you; be strong and of good courage." And as he spoke to me, I was strengthened and said, "Let my lord speak, for you have strengthened me." Then he said, "Do you know why I have come to you Daniel? But now I will return to fight against the prince of Persia; and when I go out, behold, the prince of Greece will come. But I will tell you what is inscribed in the book of truth: there is none who contends by my side against these except Michael, your prince." (Daniel 10:18-21 ESV)

The references to the prince of Persia and then the prince of Greece do not speak of human beings, but of fallen angels who have been given great authority and power over specific earthly kingdoms. In the passage above, these specific fallen angels were assigned to the kingdoms of Persia and Greece, respectively. These high-ranking fallen angels have tremendous influence over nations. It is important for Christians to remember that when Satan fell, in fact, one-third of the angelic force fell with him. It is also vital that Christians not live in fear of this truth, while remembering that two-thirds of YHWH's holy angels continue to fight on behalf of all spiritual Israel.

The necessity of these high-ranking fallen angels hinges on another significant truth: Satan is not omnipresent. This sacred attribute characterizes the Father, Son, and Holy Spirit only. Satan does not want members of the Body awakened from their slumber because an active Christian poses a constant threat to his kingdom. As long as members remain captivated by the allurements on the side of the road, Satan is indirectly adding to his army.

> So then let us not sleep, as others do, but let us keep awake and be sober. For those who sleep, sleep at night, and those who get drunk, are drunk at night. But since we belong to the day, let us be sober, having put on the breastplate of faith and love, and for a helmet the hope of salvation. (1st Thessalonians 5:6-8 ESV)

So, does this mean that a high-ranking fallen angel has been assigned to the United States? I believe so. Because in the same way that Daniel resided first in the Babylonian kingdom and then in the kingdom of Persia along with other exiled Jews, the United States too has within its borders exiled children of the Most High God, sheep of the Son of YHWH. As such, Satan has every reason to try and thwart YHWH's purpose. What is the job of this high-ranking fallen spirit who has been assigned to the "land of the free" and "home of the brave?" To keep YHWH's children enslaved in their sin, and to ensure that they continue to live in fear. It is with regret that I believe, that at present, Satan has been winning. What's worse is that currently his greatest stronghold is on the men of this nation (but not just them). And the medium most at his disposal is the media. However, this should come as no surprise. Television, radio, movies, or in laymen terms: Hollywood, MTV, BET, VHI, WB, UPN, FOX, etc. You name it and the devil has his hands in it. The truth? While slumbering, YHWH's people continue to trade their spirituality for sensuality, and Satan and his princes are succeeding in ensuring that Christians remain willing victims, rather than rising to the status of victor.

In the same vein that fallen angels exist in higher places, so too are those that have been given more intimate assignments. In other words, those that seek to influence the day to day activities of the believer. Here is yet another truth for members of the Body to consider: Satan is not omniscient. Once again, this attribute has been reserved for the Father alone. The Holy Spirit was omniscient before coming to the earth to minister to the Church. However, like Messiah who gave up his omnipresence when he came to the earth; so too the Holy Spirit has given up omniscience while on the earth. Instead, the Spirit carries out instructions from Messiah and knows only what is revealed through the Father. Do you ever wonder why at times it seems as if you continue to struggle with the same sin over and over again? Do you ever ask yourself why the log you keep tripping over seems invisible to the neighbor walking next to you? It's because Satan's imps know exactly how to make you stumble. How is this possible if Satan isn't omniscient? Because he is observant.

> But, some strolling Jewish exorcists tried their hand at using the name of [Messiah] on those tortured by demons; they would say, "I adjure you by [Yeshua] whom Paul proclaims." There were seven sons of Sceva, a Jewish chief

priest, who were using this method, when the demon answered back and said, "[Yeshua] I acknowledge, and I know about Paul, but who are you?" And the man with the demon flew at them, overpowered them all, and handled them with such violence that they ran out of the house stripped and battered. (Acts 19:13-16 NEB)

Once again, it's foolish for the believer to believe that Satan is unintelligent. Remember that although he is fallen, Satan is still an angelic being, and created with superior intelligence as it compares to human beings. Moreover, he knows the intricacies of human nature, which explains why he is able to manipulate so well. However, unless one has opened themselves up to demonic possession, Satan cannot make you do anything against your will. His spiritual access to the believer was severed when Yeshua died on the cross.

"Now is the hour of judgment for this world; now shall the Prince of this world be driven out. And I shall draw all men to myself, when I am lifted up from the earth." This he said to indicate the kind of death he was to die. (John 12:31-33 NEB)

But, whosoever is not living for Messiah, is living for self. And, whosoever is living for self is dying in sin. Satan tempted man. Man, giving into temptation, thus introduced sin into the world by disobeying YHWH. Ever since his fall, the demonic kingdom has been able to capitalize on man's sinful nature with relative ease. It is the power of suggestion, not possession, that Satan has artfully mastered over the past few millennium. Again, Satan, not possessing omniscience, did not know at that point that Eve was going to disobey YHWH, for there existed no previous behavior on which to base this knowledge. Nevertheless, Satan began his attack on humankind by suggesting to Eve that a) YHWH is a liar and b) that in giving his commandment, YHWH was attempting to keep her and Adam from experiencing some perceived greater good. Christians may take comfort in understanding the significant truth that the character of Satan never changes and neither do his strategies. In witnessing the susceptibility of man, the devil and his demons have become aware what continuously results in his fall.

Contend, [Yeshua], with those who contend with me. Fight against those who fight against me. Take hold of shield and buckler and rise for my help. Draw the spear and javelin against my pursuers. Say to my soul, "I am your salvation." Let them be put to shame and dishonor who seek after my life. Let them be turned back and disappointed who devise evil against me. Let them be like chaff before the wind, with the messenger of [YHWH] driving them away. Let their way be dark and slippery, with the messenger of [YHWH] pursuing them. For no cause they hid their net for me; with no cause they dug a pit for my life. Let destruction come upon him when he does not know it. And let the net that he hid ensnare him. Let him fall into it—to his destruction. Then my soul will rejoice in [YHWH], exulting in his salvation. (Psalms 35:1-9 ESV)

Believers continue to stumble either because they don't believe that consequences are impending, or they believe that their sinful activity is time better spent than is serving the Father. In either scenario, it is not without outside influence that such ideas become ideals. If Christians are to achieve victory while dueling with the devil, it is necessary that each learn the tricks of his trade. It is equally vital that each begin asking for help.

217. Dueling With the Devil in Righteousness

First read: Ephesians 6:14-20

For coat of mail put on integrity. (Ephesians 6:14b NEB)

The next piece of armor mentioned in Ephesians is the coat of mail; the battle piece traditionally used to cover the entire body. Paul declares that in dueling with the devil, the believer needs to ensure that his life is one marked by integrity, or righteousness. Translation? Right living. Living under the New Covenant, righteousness is sustained through YHWH's grace and the believer's decision to dwell in the power of the Holy Spirit. As a token of our gratitude and in compliance with his commandments, upon receiving the gift of righteousness, Messiah expects to see it consistently on display.

For [Messiah] ends the law and brings righteousness for everyone who has faith. (Romans 10:4 NEB)

Believers are made right when, by faith, they come to accept Yeshua Messiah as their Savior and Lord.. They do not have to earn their righteousness. This is why you are able to enter the gates of Glory should you die shortly after receiving your gift. Remember the thief on the cross? He did not live a righteous life. Indeed it was his flagrant unrighteous lifestyle which brought him to the cross. Under the Old Covenant, righteousness was attained by faithful works. Save for a slim few, virtually all fell short of the mark. Under the New Covenant, righteousness is attained by receiving YHWH's gift of salvation through his Son Yeshua Messiah. Messiah was ushering in the New Covenant even as his blood was pouring out of him. How gracious is Messiah to those who acknowledge their depravity and who recognize their deserved sentence as a result. How merciful is he to those who accept his identity and who choose to identify with his death in order to receive eternal life.

However, when a convict has received righteousness as a gift, he is now a convert—a free man. A parolee, while out of prison, is still serving his prison sentence. He is not truly free until his sentence has been completed. Messiah came to set us free. He has put provisions in place for the convert who is to enjoy his newly given freedom. Unfortunately, with a depraved nature, the devil will go to depths to venture into his quest to deceive YHWH's children. Presently, he has made significant gains with the surrounding culture in convincing all that YHWH painted in shades of gray when issuing his commandments. Moral relativity is the name of the game, and Christians everywhere need to bow out while understanding that in this game, everyone is a loser.

I have chosen the way of truth; your judgments I have laid before me. I cling to your testimonies; [YHWH], do not put me to shame. I will run the course of your commandments, for you shall enlarge my heart. (Psalms 119:30-32 NKJV)

There are those in the Church who have become convinced that YHWH is silent on certain questionable behaviors, which then gives believers the opportunity to decide for themselves what is morally acceptable. In essence, declaring themselves little gods. Once again, this was a strategy used by Satan in the Garden of Eden.

But, the serpent said to the woman, "You will not surely die. For [YHWH] knows that when you eat of it your eyes will be opened, and you will be like [YHWH], knowing good and evil." (Genesis 3:4-5 ESV)

Of course this was a lie. The reality is that as soon as Adam and Eve ate of the fruit, their vision became blurred, as did their offspring's. It took establishing the Law through Moses to clarify once again what YHWH meant by righteous living. The danger in flirting with sin is that believers begin laying groundwork for their own moral decay. There are several stages. When one first begins engaging, they are aware that the activity is wrong. Immediately after engaging there is a twinge of guilt; the Holy Spirit's reminder that repentance is in order. The next stage of moral deterioration is the indifference of the believer.

The devil had already put it into the mind of Judas son of Simon Iscariot to betray him. (John 13:2 NEB)

When repentance fails to transpire, Satan has been given permission to cloud the mind of the unfaithful. As his voice gets louder, the Holy Spirit's grows softer—not in defeat, but by default.

How stubborn you are, heathen still at heart and deaf to the truth. You always fight against the Holy Spirit. (Acts 7:51 NEB)

The believer must remember that the Holy Spirit is God, and in the same light, adheres to the credence:

No servant can be the slave of two masters; for either he will hate the first and love the second, or he will be devoted to the first and think nothing of the second. You cannot serve [YHWH] and money. (Matthew 6:24 NEB)

Neither can you serve YHWH while simultaneously serving any of the behaviors that belong to the lower nature:

I mean this: if you are guided by the Spirit you will not fulfill the desires of your lower nature. That nature sets its desires against the Spirit, while the Spirit fights against it. They are in conflict with one another so that what you will to do you cannot do. But if you are led by the Spirit, you are not under law. Anyone can see the kind of behavior that belongs to the lower nature: fornication, impurity, and indecency; idolatry and sorcery; quarrels, a contentious temper, envy, fits of rage, selfish ambition, dissensions, party intrigues, and jealousies; drinking bouts, orgies, and the like. I warn you, as I warned you before, that those who behave in such ways will never inherit the kingdom of [YHWH]. (Galatians 5:16-21 NEB)

Satan has been given dominion over the lower nature; it is his desire that all remain enslaved to it. By the believer's conscious decision to persist in sinful activity, they are choosing to allow their lower nature to rule. This is no place for the indwelling Holy Spirit.

Blessed is the man against whom [YHWH] counts no iniquity, and in whose spirit there is no deceit. (Psalms 32:2 ESV)

Perhaps the next stage of moral deterioration [and each believer should pray that they never enter this stage] is spiritual stagnation. Now that the devil has clouded the mind of the believer, and convinced him or her that their lower nature is, in fact, the nature to live by, there is little incentive for growth. It becomes difficult for fellow members to redirect this wayward Christian because they are convinced that their behavior is justifiable as a result of "original sin." This is yet another lie from the enemy. Their sinful lifestyle was justifiable prior to being justified by the grace of YHWH, through the death of Yeshua Messiah on the cross.

But Scripture has declared the whole world to be prisoners in subjection to sin, so that faith in [Yeshua] may be the ground on which the promised blessing is given, and given to those who have such faith. (Galatians 3:22 NEB)

And what was this promised blessing?

And so it is with us. During our minority we were slaves to the elemental spirits of the universe, but when the term was completed, [YHWH] sent his own Son, born of a woman, born under the law, to purchase freedom for the subjects of the law, in order that we might attain the status of sons. (Galatians 4:3-5 NEB)

In other words, our reason for sinning prior to knowing Messiah was that we were slaves to sin. However, for what purpose did Messiah die on the cross, if his death should result in the continuous rebellion of subjects? Christians have become convinced that while righteousness, marked by a life of holiness the goal, it is unattainable; it is, nonetheless, a relative and abstract ideal at best.

You have commanded your precepts to be kept diligently. That my ways may be steadfast in keeping your statutes. Then I shall not be put to shame, having my eyes fixed on all your commandments. I will praise you with an upright heart, when I learn your righteous rules. (Psalms 119:4-7 ESV)

The Holy Spirit is urging all members of the Body to tighten their belt of truth before the rest of their armor falls off. First, holiness should not be the goal, but rather the path taken leading to the goal, which is glorification. Second, there is only one path leading to glorification, not several. There are signs along the way, painted in black and white, clearly marking the correct route; designed to ensure that the believer stays on the road to Glory. However, most travelers struggle with staying on course because they choose not to read the given signs painted in black and white, preferring the flashier ones off to the side. Others choose to make their own signs.

How can a young man keep his way pure? By guarding it according to your word. With my whole heart I seek you; let me not wander from your commandments. I have stored up your word in my heart, that I might not sin against you. (Psalms 119:9-11 ESV)

Third, there is nothing abstract about righteousness or holiness. As it relates to the armor of YHWH, how can believers wear what they can not see? Once again, through his Word becoming flesh, the invisible YHWH provided a visible pattern in which the rest of us could model our lives after. Remember the words found in the book of Hebrews?

> The children of a family share the same flesh and blood; and so he too shared ours, so that through death he might break the power of him who had death at his command, that is, the devil; and might liberate those who, through fear of death, had all their lifetime been in servitude. (Hebrews 2:14-15 NEB)

> And therefore he had to be made like these brothers of his in every way, so that he might be merciful and faithful as their high priest before [YHWH], to expiate the sins of the people. For since he himself has passed through the test of suffering, he is able to help those who are meeting their test now. (Hebrews 2:17-18 NEB)

Thus, the believer has living proof that righteousness is real. The same coat of mail worn by Messiah, even unto the cross, has been made free and available to all members of his family. But there is a trade off. Repentance is the prerequisite for righteousness. If the believer is to receive the coat of arms, worn by Messiah himself, then he must in turn, give up his life of sin. It's interesting to note that, at present, the secular world seems to have a better grasp on the nature of true repentance than the Church herself.

In truth, the Church does appear to understand that expressing sorrow for one's sins befits the believer who wants to follow in the footsteps of Messiah. What's the purpose behind a grieving heart? A heart that grieves is a heart that believes past and current behaviors have been harmful, not only to self, but, more importantly, they have been hurtful to the Father, and the Church. A heart that grieves is a heart that conceives of the possibilities surrounding a changed lifestyle. It possesses the ability to envision what can be, rather than what was, while recognizing that what is, cannot remain. A grieving heart is a receiving heart, capable of accepting direction from the newly indwelling Holy Spirit, as well as the grace and correction of the Father. God Almighty can work with and through a grieving heart because spiritual walls have been torn down, which formally had, as its foundation, pride and fear. Sorrow isn't an emotion from which to always flee. On the contrary, the expression of sorrow not only hints at a believer's humanity, it can, at times, act as an agent of grace in reminding the soul that there is a time to let go.

Genuine repentance, however, has two faces; one no less difficult to look at than the other. If members of the Body are to snuggly wear Messiah's coat of mail in dueling with the devil, then each must learn self-discipline, as well as how to engage in disciplining one another.

> If one of your number has a dispute with another, has he face to take it to pagan law-courts instead of to the community of [YHWH]'s people? (1st Corinthians 6:1 NEB)

The devil has convinced both shepherds and sheep that YHWH's grace is sufficient to cover their persistent and reckless disregard for righteous living. Believers need to remember that YHWH's standards for Christians are much higher than they are for the lost. Does the Father frown upon the believer who, while growing, occasionally trips and tumbles to the ground? No. Messiah frowns upon the believer who wallows in the weeds of self-pity, while *staying* on the ground. He frowns upon those who stand around mocking the believer who has stumbled, rather than helping her up. And he scowls with fury at all who make it their business to trip up those who are still growing.

But, be careful that this liberty of yours does not become a pitfall for the weak. If a weak character sees you sitting down to a meal in a heathen temple—you, who "have knowledge"—will not his conscience be emboldened to eat food consecrated to the heathen deity? This "knowledge" of yours is utter disaster to the weak, the brother for whom [Messiah] died. In thus sinning against your brothers and wounding their conscience, you sin against [Messiah]. And therefore, if food be the downfall of my brother, I will never eat meat any more, for I will not be the cause of my brother's downfall. (1st Corinthians 8:9-13 NEB)

There is still a degree of personal responsibility that the Father expects each follower to exercise. In accepting from Messiah, the keys to life, expressing sorrow for one's sins shows that the believer has acknowledged Messiah's unlocking of his chains. However, abusing God Almighty's grace by refusing to drop the chains that has death as its master, is a sad sign that repentance is still an ideal, and not real.

So, sin must no longer reign in your mortal body, exacting obedience to the body's desires. You must no longer put its several parts at sin's disposal, as implements for doing wrong. No: put yourselves at the disposal of [YHWH], as dead men raised to life; yield your bodies to him as implements for doing right; for sin shall no longer be your master, because you are no longer under law, but under the grace of [YHWH]. What then? Are we to sin, because we are not under law but under grace? Of course not. You know well enough that if you put yourselves at the disposal of a master, to obey him, you are slaves of the master whom you obey; and this is true whether you serve sin, with death as its result; or obedience, with righteousness as its result. (Romans 6:12-16 NEB)

Why is there reluctance for some believers to drop their chains? It's ironic how the people who claim to fear the devil are the same ones who have little trouble serving him. Perhaps it is out of fear that they serve. If only members would realize that their fear is misplaced. There are shepherds who teach their sheep that YHWH is not to be feared. Woe unto those shepherds who insist on deceiving the flock. Woe unto those shepherds who are, at present, befriending jackals for selfish gain, while ignoring the sheep being ravished and slain by wolves.

Is it possible to serve a God who is both gracious and fearsome? Not only is it possible, if the members of the Body are to receive Messiah's coat of mail, then it is necessary that each understand this bi-conditional attribute of the Father. It's because of his grace and mercy that sinners become justified by faith, while they are still sinners. However, it is the believer's unwillingness to fear the Father that allows them to continue sinning even after having been justified. Genuine repentance requires the believer to not only express sorrow for their sinful life, each must also expect and work out their sanctification. While justification is an act of grace and mercy, undeserved and unearned, sanctification is an act of the will, through the grace of YHWH. It is the indwelling Holy Spirit who makes me holy, yet it is I who, because of, and through the grace of YHWH, strives for and am enabled to live a life of holiness.

Teach me, [YHWH], the way of your statutes, and I shall keep it to the end. Give me understanding, and I shall keep your law; Indeed, I shall observe it with my whole heart. Make me walk in the path of your commandments, For I delight in it. Incline my heart to your testimonies,and not to covetousness. Turn away my eyes from looking at worthless things,and revive me in your way. Establish your word to your servant,who is devoted to fearing you. Turn away my reproach which I dread, for your judgments are good. Behold, I long for your precepts; revive me in your righteousness.(Psalms 119:33-40 NKJV)

Members still walking in the flesh find it difficult to consistently wear Messiah's coat of mail. They need to realize that it will never fit snuggly because his coat was intended for the spirit. Until they began walking, that is. Until they decide to walk fully and consistently in the Spirit, it will always feel awkward. It looks pretty awkward too, just ask any unbeliever. Those members more mature would do well to point out this peculiarity and then help them to readjust properly. Make no mistake, Satan doesn't want you wearing Messiah's coat of mail; he doesn't want you living a life of righteousness. Actually, the gift of righteousness is what enables the believer to live a life of holiness. Satan wants believers to exchange their gift for an unholy lifestyle. He continuously whispers into the ears of the believer, telling them that it's impossible– "After all, you're only human." And believers continue to listen, entertain, and believe the father of lies, while sinning. Yeshua Messiah was not only human, but he was fully human; complete with the seed of sin and capable of disobeying his Father in experiencing the same temptations.

[Messiah] was innocent of sin, and yet for our sake [YHWH] made him one with the sinfulness of men, so that in him we might be made one with the goodness of [YHWH] himself. (2nd Corinthians 5:21 NEB)

Have this mind among yourselves, which is yours in [Yeshua],who, though he was in the form of God, did not count equality with [YHWH] a thing to be grasped, but emptied himself, by taking the form of a servant,being born in the likeness of men. And being found in human form, he humbled himself by becoming obedient to the point of death, even death on a cross. (Philippians 2:5-8 ESV)

But, Messiah never disobeyed, even when presented with the opportunity, because he was filled with the Father's grace, as well as filled with, and yielded to, the

Spirit. Yes, Yeshua was also fully Divine while walking the earth, but it wasn't his Divinity that prevented him from sinning, but rather his understanding of his identity as the Son of YHWH. Through his death on the cross, Messiah extended this opportunity to those whom the Father called before they were born. What, then, is gained by dropping our chains? Eternal life.

But [YHWH] be thanked that though you were slaves of sin, yet you obeyed from the heart that form of doctrine to which you were delivered. And having been set free from sin, you became slaves of righteousness. I speak in human terms because of the weakness of your flesh. For just as you presented your members as slaves of uncleanness, and of lawlessness leading to more lawlessness, so now present your members as slaves of righteousness for holiness. (Romans 6:17-19 NKJV)

218. Dueling With the Devil in Peace III

First read: Ephesians 6:14-20

Let the shoes on your feet be the gospel of peace, to give you firm footing.. (Ephesians 6:15 NEB)

It can't be overstated that the powers we wrestle against are not flesh and blood. Yet, often these are the people Satan will use to attack the believer—her own flesh and blood. Many families within the Body are currently under attack from the enemy; peace is absent from their household. The Gospel of peace is one manifestation of an even greater Gospel.

But, when the Pharisees heard that He had silenced the Sadducees, they gathered together. Then one of them, a lawyer, asked him a question, testing him, and saying, "Teacher, which is the great commandment in the law?" [Yeshua] said to him, "'You shall love [YHWH] with all your heart, with all your soul, and with all your mind.' This is the first and great commandment. And the second is like it: 'You shall love your neighbor as yourself.' On these two commandments hang all the Law and the Prophets." (Matthew 22:34-40 NEB)

If love is the standard by which all members of the Body are to operate in, then peace is a natural extension. "Agape" is the Greek translation of the word "love" as used in this context. Agape is the unexplainable and unconditional form of love that the Father has for the Body. The reason that believers are commanded to first love YHWH with all their heart, soul, and mind is that without complete union with the Father, it is impossible for man to extend the same type of love to his neighbor. In his usual perversion, Satan has convinced members to forgo their pursuit of Agape love, for the more worldly type, Eros. Unfortunately, where lust abounds, peace will never be found.

Paul spends time explaining to the less than peaceful church in Corinth why, above any gift the Holy Spirit can produce, love is the most desirable; lest any more confusion transpires. In explicating the subject Paul says,

Love is patient; love is kind and envies no one. Love is never boastful, nor conceited, nor rude; never selfish, not quick to take offense. Love keeps no score of wrongs; does not gloat over other men's sins, but delights in the truth. There is nothing love cannot face; there is no limit to its faith, its hope, and its endurance. (1st Corinthians 13:4-7 NEB)

Christians everywhere are familiar with the contents in this verse. However, the execution of its substance is thwarted by the devil. In reflecting over each component of these words, it becomes clear that members of the Body can wear the same shoes worn by earlier disciples, if each would seek to emulate their Head. It is when we allow our lower natures to get the best of us, that struggling ensues. Moreover, the Gospel of peace is selfless. Where there is disorder, it is because the believer has turned his eyes inward. What's manifested outside is always a reflection of who's controlling the inside. The gospel of peace requires the Holy Spirit to always have control. Members must discontinue allowing Satan to use them or their loved ones as puppets for executing his dirty work. Disunity among the Body remained a threat in most of the early churches. So much so that the Apostle Paul felt it necessary to reiterate the very words of Messiah to the church in Galatia,

> For you, brethren, have been called to liberty; only do not use liberty as an opportunity for the flesh, but through love serve one another. For all the law is fulfilled in one word, even in this: "You shall love your neighbor as yourself." But if you bite and devour one another, beware lest you be consumed by one another. (Galatians 5:13-15 NKJV)

Satan would like nothing more. It is no wonder, then, that in each of Paul's letter's, there contains a common salutation, "Grace and peace to you from YHWH our Father and the Lord Yeshua."

What's more, Paul gives reasons as to why each of the churches should take pleasure in their peace.

To the church in Rome:

> To all those in Rome who are loved by [YHWH] and called to be saints: Grace to you and peace from God our Father and the Lord [Yeshua Messiah]. (Romans 1:7 ESV)

Like those in the Roman church, believers today can find peace in knowing that YHWH, out of his unfathomable love, has extended a personal invitation for each member to live a life of holiness. By doing so, each can enjoy a life of intimacy that Satan himself once had, but lost. Because he lost it, the devil doesn't want anyone else to have the same opportunity. But, during times of temptation, the believer should remind himself that he belongs to Yeshua. Such turmoil is hardly pleasurable, yet it can still be peaceful.

> As for me, I will call upon [YHWH], and [Yeshua] shall save me. Evening and morning and at noon I will pray, and cry aloud, and he shall hear my voice. He has redeemed my soul in peace from the battle that was against me, for there were many against me. (Psalms 55:16-18 NKJV)

To the church in Corinth:

> Grace and peace to you from [YHWH] our Father and [Yeshua]. Praise be to [YHWH], the Father of [Yeshua], the all-merciful Father, the God whose consolation never fails us. He comforts us in all our troubles, so that we in turn may be able to comfort others in any trouble of theirs and to share with them the consolation we ourselves receive from [YHWH]. (2nd Corinthians 1:2-4 NEB)

Believers can have peace when in crisis because they are assured comforting while in the midst. This comforting is two-fold, both from the Father as well from fellow members of the Body. Remember that Satan's plan is to divide. Christians can outmaneuver the devil every time if they would use moments of temporal and temporary calamity as opportunities for spiritual collaboration. Disaster should not have to strike before believers decide to act as One.

Let me hear what [YHWH] will speak, for he will speak peace to his people, to his saints; but let them not turn back to folly. Surely his salvation is near to those who fear him, that glory may dwell in our land. Steadfast love and faithfulness meet; righteousness and peace kiss each other. Faithfulness springs up from the ground, and righteousness looks down from the sky. Yes, [YHWH] will give what is good, and our land will yield its increase. Righteousness will go before him and make his footsteps a way. (Psalms 85:8-13 ESV)

To the church in Galatia:

Grace and peace to you from [YHWH] the Father and [Yeshua], who sacrificed himself for our sins, to rescue us out this present age of wickedness, as [YHWH], the Father, willed; to whom be glory for ever and ever. Amen. (Galatians 1:3-5 NEB)

Everyday seems to provide ample evidence that Satan's kingdom is fighting tooth and nail in their final days. Each of us was nothing more than a ventriloquist's dummy before Messiah's death on the cross. But no more. His death meant our freedom. Believers can find peace in remembering that we no longer have to indulge the wiles of the devil. Furthermore, we know that Messiah is coming back to rescue again.

Seven times a day I praise you for your righteous rules. Great peace have those who love your law; nothing can make them stumble. I hope for your salvation, [YHWH], and I do your commandments. My soul keeps your testimonies; I love them exceedingly. I keep your precepts and testimonies, for all my ways are before you. (Psalms 119:164-168 ESV)

To the church in Ephesus:

Grace to you and peace from [YHWH] our Father and [Yeshua]. Praise be to [YHWH], the Father of [Yeshua], who has bestowed on us in [Messiah] every spiritual blessing in the heavenly realms. (Ephesians 1:2-3 NEB)

Finally, Christians can have peace with the assurance that until Messiah comes back, we have at our disposal every needed tool in combating the enemy; as well as to build up the Church. If only believers would ask and seek whole-heartedly. However, these spiritual blessings, as Paul refers to them, were not designed or intended for self-edification. In truth, the efficacy of the gospel of peace depends not only on it residing within each believer; it must resound among every believer. Such a commitment, however, requires a selfless heart. It also requires a faithful one.

Jerusalem, built as a city that is bound firmly together, to which the tribes go up, the tribes of [YHWH], as was decreed for Israel, to give thanks to the name of [Yeshua]. There thrones for judgment were set, the thrones of the house of David. Pray for the peace of Jerusalem. "May they be secure who love you. Peace be within your walls and security within your towers." For my brothers and companions' sake I will say, "Peace be within you." For the sake of the house of [YHWH], I will seek your good. (Psalms 122:3-9 ESV)

219. Dueling With the Devil in Faith

First read: Ephesians 6:14-20

And, with all these, take up the great shield of faith, with which you will be able to quench all the flaming arrows of the evil one. (Ephesians 6:16 NEB)

Ah, the great shield of faith. A significant piece of the armor indeed. And holding it is no easy task. It would be easy if all the believer had to do was stand in one spot. But we know that the life of the Christian is far from simple; in fact, it's a balancing act. The believer must hold the shield of faith while walking at the same time. As a matter of truth, the shield would be unnecessary if all the believer did was stand, because then there would be little, if any, interference from the enemy. What arrows need the devil throw at a member who is stagnant? Remember that the hallmark of the Christian faith is activity. So, it is the active Christian who must balance their walk while holding the shield in hand.

Love [YHWH], all you his saints. [Yeshua] preserves the faithful but abundantly repays the one who acts in pride. Be strong, and let your heart take courage, all you who wait for [YHWH]. (Psalms 31:23-24 ESV)

For most believers, it isn't that they've never held the shield. On the contrary, it was with shield in hand, graciously given, that each came to accept Messiah. However, not long after picking it up they began listening to foolish talk. Somehow the enemy convinced them that the shield would be too heavy for them to carry as they walked; so the believer had to make a hasty decision. Either he could continue walking without the shield and discover that he constantly finds himself venturing off to the side of the road, mesmerized by murderous mirages. Or, she could instead choose to hold her shield while standing in place; convinced that because she has already put on her helmet of salvation, there is nothing more to do. He will feign contentment in feeding his flesh, while his spirit goes hungry. She will feign satisfaction in standing in place, while her soul yearns to walk. Both of them should immediately hold the shield up to their ears when they first pick up, in recognizing that Satan's arrows come from a multitude of directions.

Therefore let everyone who is godly offer prayer to you at a time when you may be found; surely in the rush of great waters, they shall not reach him. You are a hiding place for me; you preserve me from trouble; you surround me with shouts of deliverance. (Psalm 32:6-7 ESV)

It is a lie that the shield of faith is too heavy for believers to hold while walking at the same time. And while the Holy Spirit apportions each shield according to the needs of each, every member has been provided with adequate defense. In fighting the enemy, the shield's potency rests not in its size. Rather, the strength of the shield rests in the power of the Holy Spirit, who provides the equipment in the first place. Believers must develop dexterity—that is, they must develop their ability to swiftly maneuver their shield, so that no matter the direction of Satan's arrows, they can successfully ward them off. However, this requires practice and it requires movement. Once again, our Heavenly Father and our Savior desire that we experience victory right here on earth. But, there is no other way to experience victory without first going through battle.

Make no mistake, the shield of faith will not deter Satan from attacking, and won't prevent the believer from staggering in the process, especially in the beginning. The good news is that persecution induces perseverance; perseverance engenders strength; and strength enhances dexterity.

Therefore, now that we have been justified through faith, let us continue at peace with [YHWH] through [Yeshua], through whom we have been allowed to enter the sphere of [YHWH]'s grace, where we now stand. Let us exult in the hope of the divine splendor that is to be ours. More than this; let us exult in our present sufferings, because we know that suffering trains us to endure, and endurance brings proof that we have stood the test, and this proof is the ground of hope. Such a hope is no mockery, because [YHWH]'s love has flooded our inmost heart through the Holy Spirit he has given us. (Romans 5:1-5 NEB)

After dueling with the devil for a while, the shield of faith will seem almost weightless. Believers will soon find that Satan's arrows will simply bounce off. Warning: watch where they land and resist the temptation to pick them up.

He who dwells in the shelter of [YHWH] will rest in the shadow of [Yeshua]. I will say of [YHWH], "He is my refuge and my fortress, my God, in whom I trust." Surely he will save you from the fowler's snare and from the deadly pestilence. He will cover you with his feathers, and under his wings you will find refuge; his faithfulness will be your shield and rampart. You will not fear the terror of night, nor the arrow that flies by day, nor the pestilence that stalks in the darkness, nor the plague that destroys at midday. A thousand may fall at your side, ten thousand at your right hand, but it will not come near you. You will only observe with your eyes and see the punishment of the wicked. If you make the Most High your dwelling—even [YHWH], who is my refuge—then no harm will befall you, no disaster will come near your tent. (Psalms 91:1-10 NIV)

You need to stick with the weapons that the Holy Spirit has provided for you in dueling with the devil.

For he will command his angels concerning you to guard you in all your ways. On their hands they will bear you up, lest you strike your foot against a stone. You will tread on the lion and the adder; the young lion and the serpent you will trample underfoot. (Psalms 91:11-13 ESV)

In developing dexterity, the believer will soon come to appreciate the ease in which they are able to maneuver their shield. What exactly are the devil's tactics? How does the believer know from where his fiery arrows will spring? It isn't difficult to figure out. Members of the Body would do well to remember: Attacking the senses is Satan's number one strategy. His second is to attack the intellect. And when he feels the necessity, he will aim to attack both simultaneously. He did it in the garden to the first son of YHWH; he did in the desert to the only begotten Son of YHWH; and he continues to do so today while roaming the earth. Remember, Satan is observant.

Now there was a day when the sons of [YHWH] came to present themselves before [Yeshua], and Satan also came among them. [YHWH] said to Satan, "From where have you come?" Satan answered [YHWH] and said, "From going to and fro on the earth, and from walking up and down on it." (Job 1:6-7 ESV)

Human beings tend to operate chiefly through either sensory or rational modes. For those believers whose religious experiences are aligned with their senses, Satan will do his best to manipulate so that these members are focused exclusively on gratifying their sensual desires. Satan's tactics will change depending upon each believer's level of spiritual maturity. The novice Christian whose primary mode of operating is through his senses can be easily punctured, as he is still growing into his coat of mail. Moreover, because their agility is still underdeveloped, they are not yet able to swiftly move their shield from one sensory area to the next. The eyes become the number one target.

Alas for you who are well-fed now; you shall go hungry. (Luke 6:25 NEB)

By crafty manipulation the serpent can convince this traveler that the fruit he sees on the side of the road to Glory looks too succulent to be poisonous. He also seduces him into believing that the fruit on the side of the road is of greater importance than is the fruit he should instead be producing while on the road. In practical terms, the wandering eye affects both men and women. As a matter of truth, there are many men and women in the Body who struggle with sexual immorality. Though, Satan has done wonders in convincing the Church that only men were plagued with this poison.

Marriage is honorable; let us all keep it so, and the marriage-bond inviolate; for [YHWH]'s judgment will fall on fornicators and adulterers. (Hebrews 13:4 NEB)

The shield of faith reminds believers everywhere to redirect their attention to that which is unseen. If the Church would only focus on the spiritual, then the material will cease being used as a weapon against her members. Consider the only gift Bartimaeus son of Timaeus, asked of the King of kings, when hearing of his arrival:

They came to Jericho; and as he was leaving the town, with his disciples and a large crowd, Bartimaeus son of Timaeus, a blind begger, was seated at the roadside. Hearing that it was [Yeshua] of Nazareth, he began to shout, "Son of David, [Yeshua], have pity on me." Many of the people told him to hold his tongue; but he shouted all the more, "Son of David, have pity on me." [Yeshua] stopped and said, "Call him;" so they called the blind man and said, "Take heart; stand up; he is calling you." At that he threw off his cloak, sprang up, and came to [Yeshua]. [Yeshua] said to him, "What do you want me to do for you?" "Master," the blind man answered, "I want my sight back." [Yeshua] said to him, "Go; your faith has cured you." And at once he recovered his and sight and followed him on the road. (Mark 10:46-52 The Storyteller's Companion to the Bible, Vol 9)

The eyes are a gift from Yeshua, made for taking in all the beauty that is his creation. Members should not, then, walk around with eyes closed in fear of failing in the flesh. In truth, all eyes must remain open. However, when images began to emerge that appear foreign to the Spirit (not to the flesh), Christians should shield their eyes with the shield of faith. Faithfully, the Spirit will say no to the flesh, and when your will responds in kind, the mirage will have just been replaced with a miracle.

My eyes are ever toward [YHWH], for he will pluck my feet out of the net. (Psalms 25:15 ESV)

The moment the eyes are shielded, Satan begins aiming for the ears. The sensuous Christian must remain cognizant of the fact that they are just as susceptible to stumbling through hearing, as they are through seeing. Perhaps the most obvious medium for Satan is music. And yet, carelessness, or the failure to exercise common sense, is often the largest stumbling block to believers. The relationship between music and mood is undeniable; having the ability to either alter or enhance. When believers choose instead to rely on their own faith, rather then using the shield provided by the Holy Spirit, disaster is impending. Faith in the flesh is what Satan would prefer members to exercise, because it is the flesh that will always prove faulty. Why listen to music which ignites a fire in the body, but leaves the Spirit feeling cold?

Do you not know that your body is a shrine for the indwelling Holy Spirit, and the Spirit is [YHWH]'s gift to you? You do not belong to yourselves; you were bought at a price. Then honor [YHWH] in your body. (1st Corinthians 6:19-20 NEB)

Protecting our ears with the shield of faith ensures that nothing entering will offend the Holy Spirit, who inhabits every believer.

An intelligent heart acquires knowledge, and the ear of the wise seeks knowledge. (Proverbs 18:15 ESV)

However, music is not the only medium used by Satan to arouse sin. Speech is just as alluring. Particularly for the novice Christian whose passion to know and to grow hasn't yet been quenched by members less enthused. It is vital that they begin asking the Father for wisdom, discernment, and understanding via the Holy Spirit. If not, the devil is enthused to entice.

But you, my children, are of [YHWH]'s family, and you have the mastery over these false prophets, because he who inspires you is greater than he that inspires the godless world. They are of that world, and so therefore is their teaching; that is why the world listens to them. But we belong to [YHWH], and a man who knows [YHWH] listens to us, while he who does not belong to [YHWH] refuses us a hearing. That is how we distinguish the spirit of truth from the spirit of error. (1st John 4:4-6 NEB)

Does Satan have agents doing his dirty work? Yes. They're called wolves in sheep clothing. And they will tell you anything that your flesh wants to hear. But, here is what the Apostle Paul has to say about them:

Such men are sham-apostles, crooked in all their practices, masquerading as apostles of [Messiah]. There is nothing surprising about that; Satan himself masquerades as a messenger of light. It is therefore a simple thing for his agents to masquerade as agents of good. But they will meet the end their deeds deserve. (2nd Corinthians 11:13-15 NEB)

Hence, the advice given by James to believers in seeking out those in the Body who claim to have wisdom.

Who among you is wise or clever? Let his right conduct give practical proof of it, with the modesty that comes from wisdom. (James 3:13 NEB)

There are also well-meaning believers in the Church who offer advice which sounds insightful and harmless. However, unless they themselves have sought wisdom via the Holy Spirit, folly is not outside the realm of possibility. Even still are the shepherds whose speech, while stirring, contains no substance. Those believers who allow emotion exclusively to guide them on their journey may soon find themselves lost. Though soothing to the ear, words devoid of holy wisdom may destroy the soul. The shield of faith will remind believers to cross-check all that they hear and ensure that the words of men are attuned to the word of [YHWH].

Wisdom rests in the heart of a man of understanding, but it makes itself known even in the midst of fools. (Proverbs 14:33 ESV)

For the believer whose religious faith is primarily grounded in their intellect, rather than through their senses, danger still lurks. It is true that [YHWH] endowed his people with the gift of reason. It is equally true that there are those in the Body who could stand to remember that emotional experiences can only carry one so far in their walk with Yeshua. Sooner or later everyone comes down from the mountain to spend some time in the valley. Without a clear head while descending, members may find themselves lying on the ground, edging closer to the pit of despair. Remember the pit of despair? The devil's lair.

You must be made new in mind and spirit, and put on the new nature of [YHWH]'s creating, which shows itself in the just and devout life called for by the truth. (Ephesians 4:23-24 NEB)

On the other hand, while reason is instrumental in helping one to grasp truth, Satan can use the intellect for the purpose of reducing truth to myth. For many in the Body, Christianity isn't really an experience at all. It is nothing more than an idea, though an ideal one. Faith and reason do not stand in contrast to one another, contrary to popular sentiments. The two are complimentary, enjoying a symbiotic relationship. For faith without reason is blind. Messiah does not encourage blind faith, in knowing that without sight, without a constant vision of his image, his people perish. We are able to exercise faith in Messiah because we possess the mind of Messiah. After directing Timothy on proper relationships in the Church, Paul writes:

> This is what you are to teach and preach. If anyone is teaching otherwise, and will not give his mind to wholesome precepts—I mean those of [Yeshua]—and to good religious teaching, I call him a pompous ignoramus. He is morbidly keen on mere verbal questions and quibbles, which give rise to jealousy, quarreling, slander, base suspicions, and endless wrangles: all typical of men who have let their reasoning powers become atrophied and have lost their grip of the truth. (1st Timothy 6:3-5 NEB)

Reason without faith, that is, without the Holy Spirit's shield of faith, is faulty and self-corruptive, or soul-destructive. Believers must constantly guard their minds against secularized theology. There is nothing esoteric about the word of YHWH, except for what the Father chooses to keep hidden until such appointed times. Those whom Messiah has appointed as shepherds must take great care not to intellectualize the personhood of Messiah so much, that their flock forgets that they serve a living Shepherd. Satan is interested in convincing believers that the varied doctrines and denominations of Christianity are of greater significance than Messiah himself. Sound doctrine is vital, but then, so is sound discipleship. If a believer's walk is hindered by pedantic pulpit talk (though cloaked in self-righteous sophistry), then the shepherd needs to question his own placement on the road to Glory. In as much as Paul cautioned Timothy in the early Church, the same admonition holds true today for those whose minds remain unshielded.

> The Spirit says expressly that in after times some will desert from the faith and give their minds to subversive doctrines inspired by demons, through the specious falsehoods of men whose own conscience is branded with the devil's sign. (1st Timothy 4:1-2 NEB)

In dueling with the devil, the Holy Spirit doesn't just equip members of the Body with armor. There are also a multitude of gifts with which the Holy Spirit eagerly awaits to distribute. Unfortunately, at present, few believers are benefiting; because of shepherds who teach that such gifts are now extinct. Spiritual discernment and wisdom are a must, if members of the Body are to effectively shield their minds from Satan's arrows. Woe to those shepherds who insist on rendering their flock powerless. The Head of the Body has always been Satan's number one target. Praise be to YHWH that it was Messiah who instead crushed Satan's head. And yet, until the return of Messiah, each believer must fight faithfully to ensure that their own heads remain protected.

> The salvation of the righteous is from [YHWH]; he is their stronghold in the time of trouble. [YHWH] helps them and delivers them; he delivers them from the wicked and saves them, because they take refuge in him. (Psalms 37:39-40 ESV)

220. A Reflective Moment

Thief in the Night

First read: 1st Thessalonians 5:1-11

Does the thought of Yeshua coming like a thief in the night terrify you? This phrase has often been used in describing the return of Messiah. There's a problem, however. Messiah's thief-like return was never intended for the working Christian. In other words, for those in the Body who are working diligently, for those who are persevering even in the midst of persecution, Messiah's return will be a pleasant and welcomed event. There should exist not the slightest bit of fear for the servant who is serving when the Master returns—only eager anticipation. Nevertheless, the "thief in the night" description is valid and necessary.

Keep awake, then; for you do not know on what day [Yeshua] is to come. Remember, if the householder had known at what time of night the burglar was coming, he would have kept awake and not have let his house be broken into. Hold yourselves ready, therefore, because the Son of Man will come at a time you least expect him. (Matthew 24:42-44 NEB)

As Christians, we do one another, and especially non-believers, a disservice when choosing to present Yeshua as a one-dimensional docile figure—the ever sacrificial lamb. The truth of the matter is that Yeshua, as the Son of YHWH, is a bi-conditional being; and his bi-conditional nature can be examined in more than one way. For example, we know that Yeshua, while walking the earth, was identified as both the Son of YHWH and the Son of Man. These two titles reveal the duality of Yeshua Messiah as being both fully Divine and fully human—the sovereign servant. Additionally, in describing the Son's purpose, we understand it best when referring to him as both Lamb and Lion.

A king's wrath is like the growling of a lion, but his favor is like dew on the grass. (Proverbs 19:12 ESV)

Then I saw standing in the very middle of the throne, inside the circle of living creatures and the circle of elders, a Lamb with the marks of slaughter upon him. He had seven horns and seven eyes, the eyes which are the seven spirits of [YHWH] sent out over all the world. And the Lamb went up and took the scroll from the right hand of the One who sat on the throne. (Revelation 5:6-7 NEB)

The Lamb, in illustrating his sacrificial commitment to saving mankind, is perhaps the most comfortable characterization of Yeshua; perhaps because it is the least intimidating of the two, and equally serves as the most intimate depiction. It isn't that this is an inaccurate characterization. Yeshua' principal function was to die on the cross—to offer himself as a sacrifice for the sins of the multitude.

The next day he saw [Yeshua] coming towards him. "Look," he said, "there is the Lamb of [YHWH]; it is he who takes away the sin of the world." (John 1:29 NEB)

His perpetual innocence is significant, as it is one attribute distinguishing him from YHWH's people and it made his sacrifice acceptable. Nevertheless, however comfortable it may be for Christians to view Messiah in this light, it is an incomplete characterization. Messiah completed his primary function when he came to earth the first time. His secondary function, though not diminutive in comparing to the first, will be to act as avenger. And it is with a lion's ferocity that Messiah will return. The symbolism of the lion is also that of a ruler, a kingship. And indeed Messiah will reign on earth, just as he currently reigns in Heaven now.

It shall come to pass in that day that [YHWH] will punish on high the host of exalted ones, and on the earth the kings of the earth. They will be gathered together, as prisoners are gathered in the pit, and will be shut up in the prison; after many days they will be punished. Then the moon will be disgraced and the sun ashamed; for [Yeshua] will reign on Mount Zion and in Jerusalem. (Isaiah 24:21-23 ESV)

Moreover, Messiah's bi-conditional nature is manifested through his dual loving and just nature. When the Son of YHWH came the first time it was an act of love. Members of the Body would do well to remember and act upon this momentous truth. Round two will display the justness of Messiah. Make no mistake; it is not the will of YHWH that his Son should return as a thief in the night to an unsuspecting and inactive flock. It his Son's will that members of the Body continuously prepare with faithful service. The Holy Spirit is beckoning members of the Body to arise from their slumber, and to throw away those seeds of complaisance. But, in truth, what motivation exists to engage in meaningful service when the servants don't really believe that the Master is on his way back?

Who then is a faithful and wise servant, whom his master made ruler over his household, to give them food in due season? Blessed is that servant whom his master, when he comes, will find so doing. Assuredly, I say to you that he will make him ruler over all his goods. But if that evil servant says in his heart, "My master is delaying his coming," and begins to beat his fellow servants, and to eat and drink with the drunkards, the master of that servant will come on a day when he is not looking for him and at an hour that he is not aware of, and will cut him in two and appoint him his portion with the hypocrites. There shall be weeping and gnashing of teeth. (Matthew 24:45-51 NKJV)

221. Dueling with the Devil in the Word

First read: Ephesians 6:14-20

The strategy is simple, but you must pay attention. First, there is no use bemoaning your current situation. For whatever reason, you are there and you must stand your ground on the fence; until you can safely get back to your side. The opponent won't make it easy.

For sword, take that which the Spirit gives you the words that come from [YHWH]. (Ephesians 6:17b NEB)

In using the sword, there are both direct and indirect tactics that will prove effective. Once again, we may turn to the Master in learning how to duel with the devil through the word. For those members of the Body who mistakenly believe that an attack from Satan is a sign that they're being punished by the Son, a return to the Gospels is necessary. The synoptic Gospels of Matthew, Mark, and Luke make mention of the Father's own Son being led into the wilderness (and by the Holy Spirit) so that he could be tested and tempted. Once again, the purpose of Yeshua's coming to earth was not only to die on the cross. He also came so the rest of his household might learn from him. The Father sent the Eldest to earth to show his younger siblings how complete faithfulness and obedience to the Father, through the power of the Holy Spirit and the gifts of grace and righteousness, yields a life of holiness.

In very truth, anyone who gives heed to what I say and puts his trust in him who sent me has hold of eternal life, and does not come up for judgment, but has already passed from death to life. (John 5:24 NEB)

And therefore he had to be made like these brothers of his in every way, so that he might be merciful and faithful as their high priest before [YHWH], to expiate the sins of the people. For since he himself passed through the test of suffering, he is able to help those who are meeting their test now. (Hebrews 2:17-18 NEB)

Remember that Satan's arrows will generally come in various forms. However, in the same way as Yeshua was tempted, Satan will usually stick to three modes: flesh—usually taking the form of lust; opulence—primarily through materialism; and fear—either of failure, rejection, bodily harm, or even death. While YHWH never tempts, rest assured that, much like the account of Job, YHWH does indeed test. And like Job, oft times a test from YHWH may manifest as temptation or a trial from Satan.

Simon, Simon, take heed: Satan has been given leave to sift all of you like wheat; but for you I have prayed that your faith may not fail; and when you have come to yourself, you must lend strength to your brothers. (Luke 22:31-32 NEB)

In Satan's role as the Accuser, he tries, in vain, to convince YHWH that his people don't really love him; that his unconditional love will never be reciprocated.

Satan even tried this with YHWH's only Son. But being the faithful Son that Yeshua is, while in the wilderness, Satan was shown to be the eternal liar that he is.

So, a temptation of the flesh may equally be a test of forfeiture:

Then he called the people to him, as well as his disciples, and said to them. "Anyone who wishes to be a follower of mine must leave self behind; he must take up his cross, and come with me." (Mark 8:34 NEB)

Forfeiture involves giving up something in order to gain something else. Giving up self involves giving up our lower nature (despite our temporal conditional sinful nature) and all of its lustful desires. In the wilderness, Satan used food. There are those in the Body who struggle with gluttony. Nevertheless, through the prevalence of pornography, as well as homosexual, adulterous, and promiscuous premarital activity, sexual lust is Satan's number one choice of fleshly temptation. Are members in the Body willing to give up their convict clothes in order to wear the clothes of a free man?

A temptation of opulence may equally be a test of obedience:

A man in the crowd said to him, "Master, tell my brother to divide the family property with me." He replied, "My good man, who set me over you to judge or arbitrate?" Then he said to the people, "Beware. Be on your guard against greed of every kind, for even when a man has more than enough, his wealth does not give him life." (Luke 12:13-15 NEB)

Yeshua makes it clear that his followers cannot serve both him and money. In serving money, one is serving Satan. In their obsession with gaining glitter—gold and silver—members are losing their soul. And though they have won the world, the "believer" will lose out on eternal life.

Finally, a temptation of fear may equally be a test of faith:

Whoever cares for his own safety is lost; but if a man will let himself be lost for my sake and for the Gospel, that man is safe. (Mark 8:35 NEB)

Indeed, negative feelings are never pleasant. Though he took pleasure in obeying his Father, Yeshua by no means looked forward to the pain he was to experience while on the cross—both physical and emotional. He only knew it would be worth it. If Yeshua had allowed fear to overtake him in Gethsemane, the rest of us would still be lost and still in bondage. Yeshua, then, walked to Calvary in faith, not in fear. So too, members must also walk faithfully and not allow Satan to scare them into inactivity.

Now for a moment of truth: In dueling with the devil using the words of YHWH, it is imperative that believers know the word. It is equally imperative that believers learn to speak; for there is power in the spoken word.

When you are fencing, you will find yourself on the defense and offense, so with your words as sword, do not mince.

Full of the Holy Spirit, [Yeshua] returned from the Jordan, and for forty days was led by the Spirit up and down the wilderness and tempted by the devil. All that time he had nothing to eat or drink, and at the end of it he was famished. The devil said to him... (Luke 4:1-3a NEB)

It is important for believers to remember, once again, that Satan's typical approach in tempting is not through possession, but suggestion. As a spirit, it is uncommon for Satan to speak directly and audibly to human beings. Satan spoke to Yeshua the same way he speaks to the rest of us who are human, through mental suggestions. In their wisdom, parents and teachers often advise children on how to respond to the common bully. "If you will simply ignore them, eventually they will just go away." Not only is this advice foolish, but it is untrue. The bully may grow weary of his present approach if he finds that he isn't getting a response, and so may grant his victim a temporary reprieve.

But, a bully who is intent on wreaking havoc, or inflicting harm on their prey, will simply conjure up a device more devious than the previous, and often times a more harmful one.

So they brought the boy to him; and as soon as the demon saw him it threw the boy into convulsions, and he fell to the ground and rolled about foaming at the mouth. [Yeshua] asked his father, "How long has he been like this?" "From childhood," he replied; "often it has tried to make an end of him by throwing him into the fire or into water." (Mark 9:20-22a NEB)

While speaking to a crowd during the course of his ministry, Yeshua offered this insight in dealing with spiritual warfare:

When an unclean spirit [or demon] comes out of a man it wanders over the deserts seeking a resting-place; and if it finds none, it says, "I will go back to the home I left." So it returns and finds the house swept clean [or unoccupied], and tidy. Off it goes and collects seven other demons more wicked than itself, and they all come in and settle down; and in the end the man's plight is worse than before. (Luke 11:24-26 NEB)

Whether via possession or suggestion, the devil responds well to passivity, though not favorably for his target. Satan and his demons are bullies and relentless ones.

I am weary with my moaning; every night I flood my bed with tears; I drench my couch with my weeping. My eye wastes away because of grief; it grows weak because of all my foes. Depart from me, all you workers of evil, for [YHWH] has heard the sound of my weeping. [YHWH] has heard my plea; [YHWH] accepts my prayer. All my enemies shall be ashamed and greatly troubled; they shall turn back and be put to shame in a moment. (Psalms 6:6-10 ESV)

In no way does it benefit the believer to simply act as if the devil isn't there. It, in fact, adversely affects him or her. The believer must resist the devil and only then will he flee. Resistance implies activity not passivity. In traditional warfare an act of resistance may, on occasion, involve the use of defensive tactics. Typically, however, in the midst of a resistance, victory is a viable option only if soldiers are willing to engage using offensive strategies; i.e. picking up their own swords, as well as their shields. This is what Messiah employed when he was tempted by Satan. The devil's suggestion to Yeshua was that he give in to his fleshy desires; that he compromise his identity and test his Father. These suggestions were intended to be the means to Yeshua's end. With the same craftiness that he employed in the Garden of Eden, Satan was again attempting to cast doubt into the mind of this man, in hopes that he might disobey his Father and receive the same sentence as the previous one. Little did Satan know, however, that the Word became flesh to rectify, redeem, and restore what Adam and Eve had ruined. Or perhaps Satan did know and was attempting to thwart YHWH's plan. In either scenario, praise be to YHWH. Yeshua succeeded where Adam failed.

> ... "The first man, Adam, became an animate being, whereas the last Adam has become a life-giving spirit. Observe, the spiritual does not come first; the animal body comes first, and then the spiritual. The first man was made of the dust of the earth; the second man is from heaven. The man made of dust is the pattern of all men of dust, and the heavenly man is the pattern of all the heavenly. As we have worn the likeness of the man made of dust, so we shall wear the likeness of the heavenly man." (1st Corinthians 15:45-49 NEB)

Tell your opponent or opponents (whichever the case) that you know the truth. You know that they are wearing masks; you know that their fruit is rotten; you know that their weeds are crippling; you know that their greenery is deceiving; and you know what they are trying to do. Tell them that you know that your journey is not an easy one, but that you know what awaits you at the end. They will respond quickly, "Aren't your feet sore? Wouldn't you like to rest for a while?" Quickly reply in truth by admitting that your feet are sore, but that you've packed plenty of shoes and know when to change into a new pair. Tell them that it won't delete the sores on your feet, but always wearing a fresh pair will deplete the soreness. They will quickly respond. "But aren't you hot in wearing all those clothes? Wouldn't you rather come and lie in the shady garden, rather than suffer under the rays of the sun?"

We often think of Satan's defeat beginning as Messiah was led up to The Skull. In truth, though, the devil's demise began in the desert, the moment Yeshua opened his mouth.

Let us look at the way Yeshua did not respond to Satan. First, notice that Yeshua, the Son of YHWH, did not attempt to insult Satan's intelligence or his powers of observation by denying that he was famished; by denying that he was human. Neither did Yeshua deny the attractiveness in Satan's offer of giving him all the worldly kingdoms. Both sin's power and poison lay in its appeal.

> She is loud and wayward; her feet do not stay at home; now in the street, now in the market, and at every corner she lies in wait. She seizes him and kisses him, and with bold face she says to him, "I had to offer sacrifices, and today I have paid my vows; so now I have come out to meet you, to seek you eagerly,

and I have found you. I have spread my couch with coverings, colored linens from Egyptian linen; I have perfumed my bed with myrrh, aloes, and cinnamon. Come, let us take our fill of love till morning; let us delight ourselves with love. For my husband is not at home; he has gone on a long journey..." (Proverbs 7:11-19 ESV)

They then called them in and ordered them to refrain from all public speaking and teaching in the name of [Yeshua]. But Peter and John said to them in reply: "Is it right in [YHWH]'s eyes for us to obey you rather than [YHWH]? Judge for yourselves. We cannot possibly give up speaking of things we have seen and heard." (Acts 4:18-20 NEB)

Accordingly, choosing whether or not to sin is a question of allegiance, not of appearance.

He who is not with me is against me, and he who does not gather with me scatters. (Luke 11:23 NEB)

As if through hypnosis, Satan will encourage believers to gaze long enough at his mirages until the truth becomes irrelevant. So then, the believer must exercise the same wisdom in first acknowledging their humanness and the weaknesses that accompany. Second, the believer must determine and then vocally assert to whom their allegiance is due. This is a reminder to both you and Satan. Third, if Messiah is the answer, then the believer must respond in faith.

"...But if it is at all possible for you, take pity upon us and help us." "If it is possible?" asked Yeshua. "Everything is possible to one who has faith." (Mark 9:22b-23 NEB)

In faith, the servant is assured that through the indwelling Holy Spirit, YHWH's grace is sufficient enough to keep them from sinning. When Satan tempted Yeshua through his flesh...

[Yeshua] answered, "Scripture says, 'Man cannot live on bread alone; he lives on every word that [YHWH] utters.'" (Matthew 4:4 NEB)

And through materialism:

[Yeshua] answered, "Scripture says, 'You shall do homage to [YHWH] and worship them alone.'" (Luke 4:8 NEB)

Yeshua knew that in feeding the flesh, you're forfeiting the spirit; and that likewise, in satisfying the spirit, you are starving self. In order to follow Messiah, it is self that must starve. He was also aware of man's appetite for wealth, if left unchecked. A wealthy appetite makes for an unhealthy heart, leaving no room for YHWH. Scripture suggests no hesitancy in Yeshua's response. He was so sure of whom he was and whose he was, that his answers seemed almost automated. It cut like a double-edge sword because, in responding, he was simultaneously confirming both his and Satan's identity.

Need it be reiterated that Satan is no idiot? He knows Scripture. He also knows that most "believers" do not. This means that there are multitudes within the Body walking around with practically no offensive weapon. Those who proudly purport, "I'm no Biblical scholar," are like soldiers walking around shamelessly parading their dull blades. They are no more effective in resisting the devil than is the soldier without a sword. In fact, the former look foolish as Satan effortlessly knocks their swords to the ground with his flaming arrows. No Word, no sword. Messiah doesn't need eminent scholars in his fold; he does need effective soldiers.

Quickly reply in truth by acknowledging that it is indeed hot and that yes, your clothes can seem unbearable at times, but that seasons change and so the sun's rays are not always beaming down. Furthermore, concede in truth that while it isn't always easy, you don't mind going bare when respite is in need; and that you would rather feel the warmth or blaze of the sun any day, than lie in the shady garden, wasting your time away.

It should, then, come as no surprise that Satan will aim his most fiery arrows at the believer's sword. What good is the rest of the armor, if members of the Body are ignorant to the manner in which to wear it? Even still, the defensive nature of the armor becomes useless if members don't know how to use it. There exists only one instruction manual capable of providing the necessary information and, sadly, it remains unused.

I will meditate on your precepts and fix my eyes on your ways. I will delight in your statutes; I will not forget your word. Deal bountifully with your servant, that I may live and keep your word. (Psalms 119:15-17 NKJV)

Christians need to realize that they are rendering themselves powerless when choosing to ignore the word of YHWH. Even the well-meaning believer must understand that his poor intentions are again likened to the young soldier rushing out to do battle with his armor practically falling off. And, though given a sword by his father, in his wisdom he thinks it best to leave his sword at home, worried that it will get too bloody during the midst of war. Hopefully, a more experienced warrior will spot this youth in error and usher him back home to retrieve his weapon. It is with greater hope that the more experienced warrior (by guiding him through the manual) will also teach the youth how to use his weapon. Satan has done a fine job in creating distractions. The believer doesn't need to search for an excuse to stay away from the Bible; excuses are continuously handed to him on a platter. There was a time in history when immorality was clearly defined, but as Satan's kingdom is now working overtime in their final days, even these have become blurred.

Fornication and indecency of any kind, or ruthless greed, must not be so much as mentioned among you, as befits the people of [YHWH]. No coarse, stupid, or flippant talk; these things are out of place; you should rather be thanking [YHWH]. For be very sure of this: no one given to fornication or indecency, or the greed which makes an idol of gain, has any share in the kingdom of [Messiah] and of [YHWH]. Let no one deceive you with shallow arguments; it is for all these things that [YHWH]'s dreadful judgment is coming upon his rebel subjects. Have no part or lot with them. For though you were once all in darkness, now as Christians you are light. (Ephesians 5:3-8 NEB)

It is an alarming scene to see and hear Christians debating over what YHWH deems as acceptable or unacceptable behavior. The typical stage reveals a large cast with passionate impromptu dialogue. However, no one has bothered to look at the script. It is a lie that YHWH is unclear about certain behaviors. What is truthful is there are those in the Body who become frustrated when trying to reconcile what "self" wants, to what YHWH has said they must deny. A little leaven starts spreading and poisonous seeds begin to take root. The Holy Spirit is urging members to return to the Word, while leaving behind the world.

I hold back my feet from every evil way, in order to keep your word. I do not turn aside from your rules, for you have taught me. How sweet are your words to my taste, sweeter than honey to my mouth. Through your precepts I get understanding; therefore I hate every false way. Your word is a lamp to my feet and a light to my path. I have sworn an oath and confirmed it, to keep your righteous rules. (Psalms 119:101-106 ESV)

There are also those behaviors that some would count as amoral, simply because they don't appear blatantly evil. Sin rarely does. For an example, working hard to provide comfortable accommodations for one's family seems like an admirable goal, right? Why would YHWH condemn such? Well, for starters, the goal is focused on the material when Messiah is insistent that the spiritual take priority. "Can't I do both simultaneously?" Many try. None succeed. In our quest for comfort, we compromise. Time spent with YHWH is replaced by more time spent at work, and the family also suffers. It's simple really. Any activity that takes precedence over YHWH becomes idolatry. Idolatry is a sin, and sin is immoral, not amoral.

A final question to consider. Is it possible to have the wrong sword? Yes. Satan has done a fine job in even penetrating the word of YHWH. He first did it while the Living Word hung on the cross. When that attempt failed he turned to the written word. Using the erudition of men who are content and impressed with their own wisdom, Satan has successfully created versions of Scripture that through the years have come to dilute, and in essence, refute, the Truth.

But you must not be called "rabbi"; for you have one Rabbi, and you are all brothers. Do not call any man on earth "father"; for you have one Father, and he is in heaven. Nor must you be called "teacher"; you have one Teacher, the [Messiah]. The greatest among you must be your servant. For whoever exalts himself will be humbled; and whoever humbles himself will be exalted. (Matthew 23:8-12 NEB)

A common claim among devout members of the Christian faith is their belief in the inerrancy of Scripture. In other words, the infallibility of YHWH's word. What a ludicrous claim to make in a world that mass produces a plethora of various translations of the same word. All versions are backed by Biblical scholars and theologians who claim that their translation is the most accurate and theirs is the one that believers need to ensure they have. Most will also denounce all others as faulty. News flash. They're all faulty, because all have had man's sinful touch added here and there; men and women who came to the table with their preconceived notions about the Father, Son, and Holy Spirit rooted primarily in the traditions of older and equally sinful church and Biblical scholars, at worst, or, at best, rooted in the beliefs of other scholars who, while having been Spirit sealed, remained Spiritually unfilled. Hence, members of the Body of Messiah should have no problem ascribing to the errant nature of Scripture, as they equally espouse a belief in a sovereign God. There is a difference between what the original authors of Scripture wrote, under the Divine inspiration of the Holy Spirit, and what has been filtered in and out throughout the last 2000 years. Of course, Scripture has always been and continues to remain "living and powerful" (Hebrews 4:11 NKJV) because of the sovereignty and providence of YHWH. None of man's attempts to adulterate it have diminished the life-changing power of the Word.

Nothing happens without his knowledge or allowance, even if it doesn't always have his blessing. The doctrine of YHWH's permissive will is established throughout Scripture and it began in the Garden of Eden. It was YHWH's will that Adam and Eve refrain from eating the fruit of the tree, but YHWH's permissive will allowed them to disobey. Indeed the whole Bible, from cover to cover, is an ode to YHWH's permissive will. It is an illustration of what happens when YHWH allows the effects of man's free will to take its course (while decisively intervening at will to ensure the fulfillment of his eternal plan), even when man's sinful nature causes a costly chain of events that has eternal consequences—again, the original fall.

The truth about YHWH is that he can take man's foolery and use it as a tool to teach his children valuable lessons (no matter how painful), and then finally use their resulting degraded status to usher in and demonstrate his grace—again, man's original fall. Nowhere does Scripture ever state or imply that it was YHWH's will from the foundation of the earth for man to disobey him. However, once we did, while the natural consequences immediately began to take their course YHWH's grace immediately began to take form. It would take several thousand years before man would see the complete fruition of YHWH's grace, through the shedding of his Son's blood. Even still, with Messiah's death on the cross, man wrestles with sin. We will continue to wrestle until Messiah returns to put an end to the seed of sin. The same seed that Adam and Eve ingested when they disobeyed YHWH is the same one that all future generations inherited. Yet, YHWH still intends for us to benefit from his grace even now. He gives us grace to resist the temptations of the fleshly seed so that we do not have to give in to sin.

The autographs, or, original Scriptures, were inerrant. And the Hebrew Scriptures we have today are close to the original because they have been carefully guarded and preserved by the Jewish scribes over the centuries. However, as previously mentioned, through some translations and false doctrinal teachings, sinful man has stripped YHWH's word of its undefiled and Divine dignity, and in more than one period in history. As such, I believe that the Church today does not have the same form that Messiah intended for his Body to have all along. Consequences have resulted, including the massive division that presently exists among the Body. Some words have been altered and others have been deleted, as have some books. However, we serve a God that regularly moves through man's mess, so that his message still gets delivered. The Holy Spirit has not allowed the message of the Gospel to be altered in any way. The heart of the word has remained intact, though the flesh around it has had a number of facelifts. And while many have praised the results and gawked at its beauty, I do not think that YHWH is impressed with the mess.

Finally, I offer this word of caution. The wisdom of this world suggests that it is a noble venture to mass produce versions of Scripture that is reader friendly and easy to digest. But, Satan is the sage of this age, and believers must know that what many of them have been ingesting into their body is poisoned. Just because a translation is easier to read, doesn't necessarily mean believers should be reading it. Nonetheless, believers must also know that while our present form of Scripture is in error, it is not irrelevant. This book you are reading now is intended to encourage all of YHWH's children to return to the word, but carefully, and with wisdom, discernment, and understanding from the Holy Spirit. Truthfully, the Holy Spirit is the only effective voice, an invaluable weapon that Christians must have activated in dueling with the devil.

222. **How to Honor**

First read: 2nd Kings 17:1-41

You should've never taken the hat off when it was first given to you; for it is designed to be form-fitting and irremovable, no matter the conditions. And once it is placed on your head, it is indeed snug and irremovable unless you take it off, which you did. Because in comparing yourself to everybody else, you found that the hat wasn't in season and that those sporting the same gear were in the minority. Hence, you decided that you wanted to be normal, like everybody else, and so you too removed yours and placed it snuggly in your bag, beside your sheet music, which you found, while comparing, to be equally non-trendy. Now here you stand on the fence facing your opponent, as memories of senseless falling race through your head. You also remembered why you took off the hat. It wouldn't fit snuggly on your head, no thanks to your impeding mask.

It is impossible to honor the Son without giving honor to the Father. And no man may honor the Father and not give the Son the same. The Father and Son are inseparable. But, though intimate they are, Messiah made it clear that his desire was that we too might share in his fellowship. Yeshua came to earth to clean, so the Father might be seen.

When it was Simon Peter's turn, Peter said to him, "You, Lord, washing my feet?" [Yeshua] replied, "You do not understand now what I am doing, but one day you will." Peter replied, "I will never let you wash my feet." "If I do not wash you," [Yeshua] replied, "you are not in fellowship with me." "Then, Lord," said Simon Peter, "not my feet only; wash my hands and head as well." (John 13:6-9 NEB)

So then whoever eats the bread or drinks the cup of [Yeshua] in a way that is unworthy [of him] will be guilty of [profaning and sinning against] the body and blood of [Yeshua]. Let a man [thoroughly] examine himself, and [only when he has done] so should he eat of the bread and drink of the cup. For anyone who eats and drinks without discriminating and recognizing with due appreciation that [it is Messiah's] body, eats and drinks a sentence (a verdict of judgment) upon himself. That [careless and unworthy participation] is the reason many of you are weak and sickly, and quite enough of you have fallen into the sleep of death. For if we searchingly examined ourselves [detecting our shortcomings and recognizing our own condition], we should not be judged and penalty decreed [by the divine judgment]. (1st Corinthians 11:27-31 AMP)

How can we refuse to honor the One who daily washes our dirt? You say you do, in fact, honor Yeshua? Messiah is honored by his followers who accept his gift of salvation. Once accepted, Messiah is honored by those who display their gratitude by keeping his gift; even when everyone around questions its value. Is Messiah's gift so valuable to you that it remains hidden and tucked away for "safe" keeping? Or is its value clear because everyone who's near you desires to have the same gift that you do? Messiah is honored when his gift is displayed openly and without shame, so that those who are lame might see the soles of your feet, and know that the Father wills for them too to walk with Messiah. Are you still walking with the gift that Messiah once gave, or have you tired of the gift you received when you bathed?

> For whoever is ashamed of me and mine, the Son of Man will be ashamed of him, when he comes in his glory and the glory of the Father and the holy angels. (Luke 9:26 NEB)

It's common to hear the believer proclaim his or her allegiance to Yeshua. Make no mistake; Yeshua hears them all loud and clear. He hears those who honor him with their lips in speech and song. It's no different today then it was with the people from Babylon, Cuthah, Avva, Hamath, and Sepharvaim, whom the Assyrian king brought to settle in Samaria. Even after being taught how to honor the living God, these foreigners endeavored to do the impossible. Each attempted to serve multiple masters. Perhaps they believed their mistake had been in worshiping their own gods, while ignoring YHWH. If so, they were mistaken. Honoring Messiah doesn't mean that, out of guilt, we begin to include him in our vast repertoire of music. Two-faced behavior is the result of worshiping two Masters. However, members of the Body have only One heart, and are lead by only One Head. Therefore, with one face, one mouth, and in the direction of one prize, should believers continue to walk; this is what honors Messiah.

> For [Messiah] is like a single body with its many limbs and organs, which, many as they are, together make up one body. For indeed we were all brought into one body by baptism, in the one Spirit, whether we are Jews or Greeks, whether slaves or free men, and that one Holy Spirit was poured out for all of us to drink. (1st Corinthians 12:12-13 NEB)

> Sinners, make your hands clean; you who are wavery, see that your motives are pure. Be humble, mourn and weep. Turn your laughter into humility and your gaiety into meekness. Humble yourselves before [YHWH] and he will lift you high. (James 4:8-10 NEB)

223. The Fate of the Faithless I

First read: 2nd Kings 6:8-20

They will quickly respond, "But, how can you be certain that you will even make it to the end of your destination in the amount of time given? What if the wind blows you off track? How do you even know where you are going or that someone is going to be there to meet you when you arrive? Wouldn't you rather stay here, where you can clearly see all that is available to you?" Quickly reply in truth by granting the partial validity of their claims. Tell them that you are not always certain that there is someone at the end of the road, that there are times of doubt when you find yourself asking some of the same questions. However, tell them that there are a few intangibles that you insist on accepting as actual while journeying because you can feel their presence. "Like what?" they will respond. Tell them like the wind. Whether blowing hot or cold, faint or fierce, you can neither see nor touch, but its existence is obvious. And during periodic moments of stillness, you still believe in the wind's being, because of its plethora moments of movement. When it moves, you move, so that when it's still and you can't feel, you can still keep moving.

Meanwhile our eyes are fixed, not on the things that are seen, but on the things that are unseen: for what is seen passes away; what is unseen is eternal. (2nd Corinthians 4:18 NEB)

How often are you required to defend your faith? If the answer is never, then perhaps you aren't really doing any work. It is inevitable that while in the field, the follower of Messiah will be forced to defend his faith. The call of the Great Commission will, on occasion, require answering the questions of those who will question; it is to the benefit of the believer and the Body to have an answer prepared.

But for your part, stand by the truths you have learned and are assured of. Remember from whom you learned them; remember that from early childhood you have been familiar with the sacred writings which have the power to make you wise and lead you to salvation through faith in [Yeshua]. Every inspired scripture has its use for teaching the truth and refuting error, or for reformation of manners and discipline in right living, so that the man who belongs to [YHWH] may be efficient and equipped for good work of every kind. (2nd Timothy 3:14-17 NEB)

In a culture that is blinded by materialism and sensuality, it isn't difficult to understand why many insist on believing in only what they can see. They call those who walk by faith foolish, and yet they are the ones who keep stumbling and tripping over their own logical presuppositions. However, one truth is for certain. They will never accept as truth what the believer pitches with uncertainty. There is nothing wrong with acknowledging that comprehending Christianity completely is far from easy. In fact, "the call" could prove perilous by responding to the unbeliever that you have all of the answers, because it would be untrue. Furthermore, the believer's responsibility is not to serve as a permanent mouth piece for the Master. Rather, it is to lead the cracked to the Potter so that he is able to complete his work. Nevertheless, members of the Body have been equipped to answer the most common of questions, and should not shirk their duty to answer with confidence.

For all that may be known of [YHWH] by men lies plain before their eyes; indeed [YHWH] himself has disclosed it to them. His invisible attributes, that is to say his everlasting power and deity, have been visible, ever since the world began, to the eye of reason, in the things he has made. There is therefore little defense for their conduct; knowing [YHWH], they have refused to honor him as God, or to render him thanks. Hence all their thinking has ended in futility, and their misguided minds are plunged in darkness. (Romans 1:19-21 NEB)

Those who insist on believing in only what they see, need only to open their eyes. Nature is YHWH's natural way of revealing himself. But, YHWH's spiritual self is reserved for and revealed only to those who have first agreed to reveal their broken spirits to him, through Messiah. Concealing our brokenness to the Potter is a sign that we don't believe he is capable of restoring.

So now, my friends, the blood of [Yeshua] makes us free to enter boldly into the sanctuary by the new, living way which he has opened for us through the curtain, the way of his flesh. We have, moreover, a great priest set over the household of [YHWH]; so let us make our approach in sincerity of heart and full assurance of faith, our guilty hearts sprinkled clean, our bodies washed with pure water. (Hebrews 10:19-22 NEB)

What ground then does the faithless follower have to stand on when the wondering wanderer starts to ask? When your ground begins to crumble, you'll have no room to grumble.

224. The Fate of the Faithless II

First read: 2nd Kings 12:1-21

Don't just stop there; give them another intangible. Tell them time is something that exists, but that you cannot see. Whether in sync with your own steps, nipping at your heels, or flying past you and urging you to catch up, you can neither see nor touch, but its existence is obvious. The rising and setting of the sun, and the changing of seasons for life-giving reasons, are both observable. The flowers that wither and bloom and the caterpillars, who from ground to sky grow wings to fly, are both substantial. Tell them that you can neither see nor touch wind or time. And while hard to define, you believe that there is One behind it all. You can't see what awaits you at the end of your journey. But, you believe that One is waiting for you and so you will keep walking.

The word I spoke, the gospel I proclaimed, did not sway you with subtle arguments; it carried conviction by spiritual power, so that your faith might be built not upon human wisdom but upon the power of [YHWH]. (1st Corinthians 2:4-5 NEB)

Defending our faith through words is one thing, actions is another. Messiah appreciates those servants who, through speaking, obey the call of the Great Commission. It is the Christian whose faith is shown through action—that is, active obedience—who shall hear the words, "Well done my good and faithful servant." As Paul describes in the book of Romans, all of nature surrounding man echoes the sound of obedience and radiate proof that each have a Maker. Not a river runs dry nor does a flower die without the approval of YHWH, and yet both are still given free reign to run their course. What, then, is man to take from his observations of nature? That YHWH has also given all believers free reign to run their course is an acceptable truth, yes. That each faithfully completes its journey without an indication of its end, but with reliance upon Yeshua, who authored their beginning. Absolutely.

In past ages he allowed all nations to go their own way; and yet he has not left you without some clue to his nature, in the kindness he shows: he sends rain from heaven and crops in their seasons, and gives you food and good cheer in plenty. (Acts 14:16-17 NEB)

And, so the marker of the faithful is one whose obedience indicates acknowledgment that his soul is reliant upon his Maker. These members of the Body are effective workers because they have enough faith to continue running, even when they can't see the finish line. Unfortunately, there exists the ineffective worker whose make-up is marked by inactivity. They see the rising and the setting of the sun and still no work is done. They see the changing of the seasons, and yet still come up with a million reasons as to why work needing completion today can be put off for tomorrow. These workers take pleasure in stopping to smell the roses, but then they just stop. Perhaps a mature member of the Body needs to gently remind them that the clock is ticking, and those same roses could be dead tomorrow. In gasping over Yeshua's creation, believers need to equally grasp his concept of serving; time is of the essence. What of the faithless?

> I passed by the field of a sluggard, by the vineyard of a man lacking sense, and behold, it was all overgrown with thorns; the ground was covered with nettles, and its stone wall was broken down. Then I saw and considered it; I looked and received instruction. A little sleep, a little slumber, a little folding of the hands to rest, and poverty will come upon you like a robber, and want like an armed man. (Proverbs 24:30-34 ESV)

> The Father loves the Son and has entrusted him with all authority. He who puts his faith in the Son has hold of eternal life, but he who disobeys the Son shall not see that life; [YHWH]'s wrath rests upon him. (John 3:35-36 NEB)

Telling others that we believe in what we don't see because of what can already be seen is admirable. However, our "belief" isn't believable to YHWH when he can't see actions that prove we do.

> But someone may object: "Here is one who claims to have faith and another who points to his deeds." To which I reply: "Prove to me that this faith you speak of is real though not accompanied by deeds, and by my deeds I will prove to you my faith." (James 2:18 NEB)

225. Dueling With the Devil in Salvation

First read: Ephesians 6:14-20

Their responses aren't as quick anymore. They drop their swords momentarily and in attempting to deliver the final blow they say, "Yeah, but you are going to fall from this fence one way or another. Either you can choose to topple and land safely in this garden where you can lie peacefully for eternity, or you can plunge head first on the hard and dirty ground, where you will lie bemoaning, bruised, bashed, and broken." Until this moment you had almost forgotten about your head. However delivered, be thankful for the reminder. For in your bag, along with your sheet music, is a hat that you should've been wearing in the first place. A hat that was given to you by a fellow traveler, a stranger you met toward the start of your journey. This is a special hat, made for wear in all seasons— during any weather. It has extra padding on the inside that won't break your fall, but will keep your skull from breaking when you land. It also has a visor; not intended for keeping you from the sun's rays, but for preventing blindness when it's shining in your face. You may be able to do so at the end of your journey, but for now, such familiarity with the sun should be avoided; equally rejoice in and have respect for its proximity.

Take salvation for helmet. (Ephesians 6:17a NEB)

The head is perhaps the most vulnerable part of the body. Obtaining salvation is perhaps the most essential purpose of the believer—for now the journey truly begins. However, in the same way that all other pieces of armor are offered freely, the helmet's efficacy and security lies not in the agreement of the believer to receive and wear such a gift, but in his faithful decision to keep it on. There are a number of spiritual truths that jump out from this passage, but the one that speaks to the issue at hand is this: In the same way that one can put on armor; one can also remove their armor. This is not a far-fetch extrapolation of the text. While the passage is largely metaphorical, take any piece mentioned in the text and the reader will arrive at the same conclusion. For example, the sword, which is the word that comes from YHWH, is not with you automatically. You have to learn the verses so that the Holy Spirit can recall them to you when the time is appropriate. This, like every other piece of armor, truth, integrity, peace, and faith, is a lifestyle choice and commitment. Salvation is no different; it is also a lifestyle. A believer's choice to live a life marked by holiness, truth, integrity, peace, faith, and prayer is living one that demonstrates their decision and commitment to keeping their gift of salvation on their head, at all times. Conversely, a believer who decides, for whatever reason, that they are no longer interested in holiness and instead are committed to reverting to their previous lifestyle of falsity, deception, rancor, and faithlessness, have made the decision to remove their helmet of salvation. There is no reason why the only piece of armor incapable of being removed by the wearer is the helmet.

Away then with all that is sordid, and the malice that hurries to excess, and quietly accept the message planted in your hearts, which can bring you salvation. Only be sure that you act on the message and do not merely listen; for that would be to mislead yourselves. A man who listens to the message but never acts upon it is like one who looks in a mirror at the face nature gave him. He glances at himself and goes away, and at once forgets what he looked like. But the man who looks closely into the perfect law, the law that makes us free, and who lives in its company, does not forget what he hears, but acts upon it; and that is the man who by acting will find happiness. A man may think he is religious, but if he has no control over his tongue, he is deceiving himself; that man's religion is futile. (James 1:21-26 NEB)

To better understand how the helmet of salvation works, let's use the analogy of a prison story, using the name "Daniel." Before Messiah's death on the cross, all of creation was imprisoned. Daniel attributed his confinement to the crime committed by Adam and Eve. When Moses brought forth the Law as granted by YHWH, this resulted in a parole. However, from the beginning, the Law could never grant freedom; for parole is only a temporary condition, pending the good behavior of all convicts. Daniel's nature was so deprived, however, that upon release, he not only carried with him the badge of "convict," but his actions continued to emulate the character of a criminal—a repeat offender. In truth, Daniel wanted to do right. But try as he did, he always missed the mark; and so, always found himself breaking the law. Whether in prison or paroled, he remained captive; his death inevitable.

It follows, then, that as the issue of one misdeed was condemnation for all men, so the issue of one just act is acquittal and life for all men. For as through the disobedience of the one man the many were made sinners, so through the obedience of the one man the many will be made righteous. Law intruded into this process to multiply law-breaking. But where sin was thus multiplied, grace immeasurably exceeded it, in order that, as sin established its reign by way of death, so [YHWH]'s grace might establish its reign in righteousness, and issue in eternal life through [Yeshua] our Lord. (Romans 5:18-21 NEB)

YHWH saw and grieved over the condition of Daniel, who remained incarcerated. And, while still in prison, YHWH saw fit to provide an opportunity to release him from his prison permanently. It is unfathomable to consider why YHWH would decide to set free an idolater, adulterer, murderer, liar, fornicator, and thief. But he did. What's unbelievable still is that YHWH's decision was made, not while Daniel was on parole engaging in good behavior. Instead, it was made during a time when he had since been taken back to the cell for repeatedly violating the conditions of his parole; his execution date had already been set. In an act of unmerited grace, YHWH sent his own Son to die in Daniel's place. The death of Messiah was so that the rest of humanity might live, and live in freedom. The moment Yeshua gave up his spirit the warden himself came and unlocked the prison cell. Daniel asked if he had come to take him to the execution chambers. The warden shook his head.

Standing in the open door with a look of disbelief, Daniel asked if he was being let out on good behavior. The warden smiled, while again shaking his head no. Daniel continued standing in place; frozen from lack of understanding. The warden told him,

"I have some good news, someone came and died in your place; you are a free man."

"Free? Daniel asked. "You mean I'm out on parole again?"

"No," said the warden, "You are free."

"Sir, what does that mean?"

The warden paused for a moment and looked at the man patiently.

"It means that you will no longer have to look at these walls again. It also means that you no longer have to engage in the behavior that kept you behind these bars. It means that you are free to live as a productive member of society."

As the warden spoke, excitement began to swell within Daniel, as he began to understand what his newly given freedom meant. As Daniel was about to exit his cell, the warden held up his hand,

"Wait, I have something to give you." The warden reached into a bag he'd been holding to pull out a set of new clothes. "Here, you and someone close to me wear roughly the same size. I figured you'd want to change into something new."

"Thanks warden," Daniel answered, "but I really don't mind wearing what I have on. I'm just so thankful to know that from now on I'll be an ex-con instead of a convict. "

"But, that's just it Daniel," said the warden, "you are not an ex-con."

"Pardon me?" asked Daniel.

"Exactly," said the warden, "I just did. And because you have been pardoned, you can't wear the clothes of a convict; they will only remind you of your former days, and you will be tempted to revert. No, I give to you these new clothes, because you are a new person now." The warden continued, "But don't try to put these new ones over the ones you're wearing now because I'm telling you that they won't fit. You must take off the old ones first. Moreover, the material is also different, so it will take some getting use to. The fit is pretty snug, so you'll need to lose a few pounds. It shouldn't be too difficult to do though, once you quit eating this prison food and start on a healthier diet."

Looking flustered Daniel responded, "But, I don't understand. Now that I'm free and can't go back to my old life, what am I suppose to do?"

The warden smiled. "I'm glad you asked. While you are growing into your new clothes, you are to go and visit other prisons and prisoners and share your story. You are to tell them that the same freedom which was given to you is available to them as well. If you happen to run into any convicts on parole, remind them that they aren't really free yet, and then tell them the good news also. Think of it as community service; as your way of giving back to society. "

"That's asking a lot," said Daniel.

The warden laughed and replied, "I said you were free, I never said you wouldn't be working." He continued, "But don't sweat it; the more there are set free, the more you will have helping you."

Now it was Daniel's turn to smile. "I guess you're right. I never saw it that way."

The warden continued, "I'm also not saying it's going to be easy. In fact, I am telling you that it won't be. There will be those who will try to prevent you from going into the prisons because they won't want to release their prisoners. It will be a struggle, but you will have the tools to go in anyway."

"Where are they?" asked Daniel.

"Right here in this same bag that your new clothes are in," said the warden.

They went through the whole island as far as Paphos, and there they came upon a sorcerer, a Jew who posed as a prophet, Bar-Jesus by name. He was in the retinue of the Governor, Sergius Paulus, an intelligent man, who had sent for Barnabas and Saul and wanted to hear the word of [YHWH]. This Elymas the sorcerer (so his name may be translated) opposed them, trying to turn the Governor away from the Faith. But Saul, also known as Paul, filled with the Holy Spirit, fixed his eyes on him and said, "You utter impostor and charlaton [swindler, you rascal]! You son of the devil and enemy of all goodness, will you never stop falsifying the straight ways of [Yeshua]? Look now, the hand of [Yeshua] strikes: you shall be blind, and for a time you shall not see the sunlight." Instantly mist and darkness came over him and he groped about for someone to lead him by the hand. When the Governor saw what had happened he became a believer, deeply impressed by what he learned about [Yeshua]. (Acts 13:6-12 NEB)

The warden continued, "There will also be those convicts who aren't interested in obtaining freedom because they are either uninterested in working, or are too afraid of the struggles which will ensue. There will be those leery of you and your story. They've come across self-proclaimed converts in the past, but their lifestyles, either through words or deeds, or both, weren't convincing in trying to convert. These convicts have seen plenty of artifices, but they have yet to see any authenticity; you will be their first. Share with them anyway. It will be their choice to remain where they are, just as I am giving you a choice."

If people hear my words and don't keep them, I don't judge them. I didn't come to judge the world but to save it. Whoever rejects me and doesn't receive my words will be judged at the last day by the word I have spoken. I don't speak on my own, but the Father who sent me commanded me regarding what I should speak and say. I know that his commandment is eternal life. Therefore, whatever I say is just as the Father has said to me." (John 12:47-50 CEB)

"And now, Daniel," continued the warden "I must speak seriously to you. I want you to understand that the pardon offered now won't be offered forever. In truth, the days for issuing pardons are near the end. You must act quickly, as must others who are to be set free. Those who refuse the pardon, or the conditions that come with it, will be executed. It is my desire that everyone accept the pardon that I am freely offering; for the one who died this morning died for all prisoners. However, not all will accept. It will be a sad day for them. Nevertheless, you must share with all anyway; their fate is in my hands, not yours."

All that the Father gives me will come to me, and the man who comes to me I will never turn away. I have come down from heaven, not to do my own will, but the will of him who sent me. It is his will that I should not lose even one of all that he has given me, but raise them all up on the last day. For it is my Father's will that everyone who looks upon the Son and puts his faith in him shall possess eternal life; and I will raise him up on the last day. (John 6:37-40 NEB)

Daniel nodded in understanding. "I get everything you just said, but I just have two more questions before I leave."

"Yes, Daniel?"

"The convicts, how will you know of the ones who have been set free?"

The warden responded, "Oh, I'll be able to tell easily. Whether in prison, or out on parole, those who are not set free will still be wearing their convict clothes. Where there is no authenticity, all will look the same to me."

When the king came in to see the company at table, he observed one man who was not dressed for a wedding, "My friend," said the king, "how do you come to be here without your wedding clothes?" He had nothing to say. The king then said to his attendants, "Bind him hand and foot; turn him out into the dark, the place of wailing and grinding of teeth." For though many are invited, few are chosen. (Matthew 22:11-14 NEB)

The warden continued, "Those who have been set free, on the other hand," he reached down to grab the same bag containing the clothes for Daniel, "will be wearing the same clothes fashioned after someone close to me. They are not all the same color, but are roughly the same size. All will have to grow into their own; and, they look nothing like the convict's clothes. In the same way that I now admonish you Daniel, be sure to share with everyone else that under no circumstances are they to take off their new clothes once they decide to change. For whosoever is caught without their clothes on the day of execution—which has already been set—they too shall share the same fate as the common criminal."

This then is my word to you, and I urge it upon you in [YHWH]'s name. Give up living like pagans with their good-for-nothing notions [their deeds that are committed in the flesh]. Their wits [minds] are beclouded, they are strangers to the life that is in [YHWH], because ignorance prevails within them and their minds have grown hard as stone. Dead to all feeling, they have abandoned themselves to vice, and stop at nothing to satisfy their foul desires. But that is not how you learned [Messiah]. For were you not told of him, were you not as Christians taught the truth as it is in [Yeshua]?—that, leaving your former way of life, you must lay aside that old human nature which, deluded by its lusts, is sinking toward death. You must be made new in mind and spirit, and put on the new nature of [YHWH]'s creating, which shows itself in the just and devout life called for by the truth. Then throw off falsehood; speak the truth to each other, for all of us are the parts of one body. (Ephesians 4:17-25 NEB)

As Daniel stood looking gravely into the eyes of the warden, he found himself shaking in alarm. The warden, in seeing Daniel's condition, changed his tone to lessen Daniel's fear. He didn't want Daniel to leave with the wrong impression.

"I tell you these things out of love Daniel. If you obey my instructions, you will not have to worry about judgment. Though the day of execution will be a terrible day for those who refuse my pardon, for everyone else, it will be a day of celebration." The warden hugged Daniel and then told him to go in peace.

After first changing his clothes, Daniel suddenly remembered he had one more question.

"Warden, I wanted to ask one more question. Who was it that died this morning—in my place?"

Turning around full circle the warden looked directly at Daniel and answered, "My Son."

As Daniel gazed into the eyes of the warden, he realized that they held not sorrow, but joy. The warden wanted to show Daniel that his eyes were full of empathy and not anger.

"Go in peace, Daniel," he said, and then he left.

Daniel looked on until the warden was out of sight. Tears begin rolling down his face, as he considered all that had just occurred. With the prison cell open, and the change of clothes, Daniel wondered if he was ready to accept the challenge.

Just as formerly you were disobedient to [YHWH], but now have received mercy in the time of their disobedience, so now, when you receive mercy, they have proved disobedient, but only in order that they too may receive mercy. For in making all mankind prisoners to disobedience, [YHWH]'s purpose was to show mercy to all mankind. (Romans 11:30-32 NEB)

Oh, it sat on your head okay, but it was always loose, threatening to topple off at any moment. "How aggravating," you thought. And when you complained, a wise traveler walked by and told you that you could not wear both the mask and the hat; that you needed to choose one or the other. You didn't notice that the traveler was one of the few who wore a hat but no mask. You did notice that some of the people walking were imitating you. Most feigned contentment, choosing instead to hide their pain. You wanted to feel like part of the normal crowd. United you stood and united you continued to fall. How fortunate for you to have survived all those falls free from head injury. What about now—now that you've removed your mask? Don't be foolish. Put on the hat that never should you have removed. Reply to your opponents in truth by asserting your assurance. Tell them that you fear no brokenness because you've already been broken. Tell them that you fear no bruises because you've already been bruised. Tell them that you have no reason to bemoan because, in spite of your brokenness and bruises, here you are still standing today. Finally, tell them that you will not now, nor will you ever, lie in their shady garden. Don't waste additional time adding a few more cents. Turn facing the dirt road and jump off the fence.

What then is Satan's goal when aiming for the believer's head, while in the midst of his attacks? Because he can't remove the helmet, no matter the number of flaming arrows, he wants to convince members of the Body to leave it off. The helmet of salvation must be worn daily to thwart Satan's attacks. Satan knows that his arrows are impenetrable when members are wearing their armor. However, he also knows how hot they are. Members must not allow the heat of Satan's arrows, nor their intensity, to dissuade them from keeping on their helmet or any other part of their armor. In truth, the armor is no light piece of equipment and at times it may seem unbearable, but bear it we must. While on earth, it is in our armor that our protection lies. And on those occasions when it seems the defensive gear isn't enough, it's time to open our mouths, raising our swords.

226. Living Out Loud: The Spirit Filled Church V

First read: Acts 2:42-47

One final word of wisdom while walking toward your destination. In sticking with self-actualization as your marker for success, you will soon experience self-annihilation. You will realize that you are closer toward restoration the moment you recognize that in reaching your goal, it really isn't about you at all. In meeting the needs of others, their basic needs, you find your needs being met; physiological, safety, belonging, and esteem. Here is a final puzzle to ponder; for it is a question of accountability. As you are looking ahead, ask yourself, "Who am I accountable to?" With your mask off you should have no problem seeing.

Meanwhile those who had been scattered after the persecution that arose over Stephen made their way to Phoenicia, Cyprus, and Antioch, bringing the message to Jews only and to no others. But there were some natives of Cyprus and Cyrene among them, and these, when they arrived at Antioch, began to speak to pagans [Gentiles] as well, telling them the good news of [Yeshua]. The power of [Yeshua] was with them, and a great many became believers, and turned to [Yeshua]. (Acts 11:19-21 NEB)

The question bears repeating: Who am I accountable to? You are closer to the answer, but not there yet. The question of accountability is a tricky one. Look carefully. In answering, follow a few easy math steps.

First: Divide everyone like you are normally inclined to do into two different groups: "Me' and "Them."

Second: Set up the equation.

(I) am accountable 2 + (They) are accountable 2 = We are accountable 4 (each other)

But, he wanted to vindicate himself, so he said to [Yeshua], "And who is my neighbor?" [Yeshua] replied, "A man was on his way from Jerusalem down to Jericho when he fell in with robbers, who stripped him, beat him, and went off leaving him half dead. It so happened that a priest was going down by the same road; but when he saw him, he went past on the other side. So too a Levite came to the place, and when he saw him he went past on the other side. But a Samaritan who was making the journey came upon him, and when he saw him was moved to pity. He went up and bandaged his wounds, bathing them with oil and wine. Then he lifted him on to his own beast, brought him to an inn, and looked after him there. Next day he produced two silver pieces and gave them to the innkeeper, and said, "Look after him; and if you spend any more, I will repay you on my way back." Which of these three do you think was neighbor to the man who fell into the hands of the robbers?" He answered, "The one who showed him kindness." [Yeshua] said, "Go and do as he did." (Luke 10:29-37 NEB)

The equation is simple really. In declaring "for," take "to" plus "to," add the two numbers to tally your score. The number resulting? Not "to", but "for." If you find yourself perplexed or ill-equipped to solve the problem, then look to the rising of the sun and remember that four is two to the second power. You can't do it alone, so don't try. You should feel almost weightless after arriving at the answer. Not only are you mask free, but you also realize that in looking outside your self, you are less likely to compare yourself to someone else when you are caring for someone else. How liberating. Ponder over the equation a little longer. Notice anything outstanding? Did you notice how simple it was to solve? Why do you and others around insist on complicating the equation by adding extra variables?

For my part, my brothers, I could not speak to you as I should speak to people who have the Spirit. I had to deal with you on the merely natural plane, as infants in [Messiah]. And so I gave you milk to drink, instead of solid food, for which you were not yet ready. Indeed, you are still not ready for it, for you are still on the merely natural plane. Can you not see that while there is jealousy and strife among you, you are living on the purely human level of your lower nature? When one man says, "I am Paul's man." and another, "I am for Apollos." are you not all too human? (1st Corinthians 3:1-4 NEB)

There is nothing more lovely to Yeshua than to see his Bride's maidens operating as one Body. There is no sign of division in a truly and completely Spirit-filled church because there is recognition that the needs of another should have precedence over the needs of self. A Spirit-filled Body is a unified Body. It is in unison that the Body speaks in boldness. It is with agreement that the Spirit-filled Body expels those members who have for their agendas, subversion. With one accord, the Spirit-filled Body goes about their business of rebuilding the Church, while remaining aware of structures that may topple the moment their eyes turn away from the task. A Spirit-filled body understands that because Satan's kingdom is united in its efforts to debilitate or destroy, the Church must avoid dissension.

I entreat you, then—I, a prisoner for the [Yeshua]'s sake: as [YHWH] has called you, live up to your calling. Be humble always and gentle, and patient too. Be forbearing with one another and charitable. Spare no effort to make fast bonds of peace the unity which the Spirit gives. There is one body and one Spirit, as there is also one hope held out in [YHWH]'s call to you; one [Yeshua], one faith, one baptism; one God and Father of all, who is over all and through all and in all. (Ephesians 4:1-6 NEB)

So shall we all at last attain to the unity inherent in our faith and our knowledge of the Son of [YHWH]—to mature manhood, measured by nothing less than the full stature of [Messiah]. We are no longer to be children, tossed by waves and whirled about by every fresh gust of teaching, dupes of crafty rogues and their deceitful schemes. No, let us speak the truth in love; so shall we fully grow up into [Messiah]. He is the head, and on him the whole body depends. Bonded and knit together by every constituent joint, the whole frame grows through the due activity of each part, and builds itself up in love. (Ephesians 4:13-16 NEB)

Let your magnanimity be manifest to all. (Philippians 4:5 NEB)

227. My Brother's Keeper

First read: Galatians 6:1-5 / James 5:19-20

Listen,
do I speak lies?
How can I now describe
my passion for my brother's soul?
I'll try

Like this,
In Messiah alone-
the only man I know
with perfect love both day and night;
disowned

Still yet,
He rose again;
Deliverer of sin
And life for those who trust in him;
all men

Since now,
I have his heart
I can perfect his art
To love unconditionally
I'll start

Today,
to bear his pain
walk with him through his rain
until the sun comes out once more;
I'll gain

Today,
I'll share his cross
I'll help him pay the cost
To walk behind Yeshua with faith-
no loss

Today,
he won't be caught
by sin he won't be bought
nor will he find himself ensnared
to rot

I'm his
with hearts aligned;
to him I've been assigned
I am my brother's keeper and
he's mine

228. Intimate While Eminent

First read: 1st Chronicles 21 – 22:1

While journeying, think of everyone around as an employee within your company, and you are the interim COE. The Chief of Everything. You have more responsibilities and greater power than a CEO, because on this journey you are ultimately accountable for everyone in your company, but you are not accountable to anyone. Your performance is being evaluated. How well are you caring for your employees? Are you providing opportunities for growth? Are you valuing their time? Are you listening to their concerns? Are you responding to their concerns? Are you being fair and just to everyone in your company, maintaining an open door policy for all; or does your door just revolve around a select few? Are you helping to repair broken relationships among co-workers; or do you believe that you have more important things to do, and that this is the responsibility of someone lesser than you?

The words were still on his lips, as they entered the cloud which cast a shadow over them; they were afraid as they entered the cloud, and from it came a voice: "This is my Son, my Chosen; listen to him." When the voice had spoken, [Yeshua] was seen to be alone. The disciples kept silence and at that time told nobody anything of what they had seen. Next day when they came down from the hills he was met by a large crowd. All at once there was a shout from a man in the crowd: "Master, look at my son, I implore you, my only child. From time to time a demon seizes him, gives a sudden scream, and throws him into convulsions with foaming at the mouth, and it keeps on mauling him and will hardly let him go. I asked your disciples to cast it out, but they could not." [Yeshua] answered, "What an unbelieving and perverse generation. How long shall I be with you and endure you all? Bring your son here." But before the boy could reach him the demon dashed him to the ground and threw him into convulsions. [Yeshua] rebuked the demon, cured the boy, and gave him back to his father. And they were all struck with awe at the majesty of [YHWH]. (Luke 9:34-43 NEB)

So the Word became flesh; he came to dwell among us, and we saw his glory, such glory as befits the Father's only Son, full of grace and truth. (John 1:14 NEB)

How often Christians have been told that they have been set aside for a higher calling. Paul reminds Gentile believers in the book of Romans that once they have accepted Messiah as their personal Lord and Savior, then they become grafted into the family of YHWH, and are now too a member of Israel.

Then he left that place and went away into the territory of Tyre. He found a house to stay in, and he would have liked to remain unrecognized, but this was impossible. Almost at once a woman whose young daughter was possessed by a demon heard of him, came in, and fell at his feet. (She was a Gentile, a

Phoenician of Syria by nationality.) She begged him to drive the demon out of her daughter. He said to her, "Let the children be satisfied first; it is not fair to take the children's bread and throw it to the dogs." "Sir," she answered, "even the dogs under the table eat the children's scraps." He said to her, "For saying that, you may go home content; the demon has gone out of your daughter." And when she returned home, she found the child lying in bed; the demon had left her. (Mark 7:24-30 NEB)

Moses spoke these words to the Israelites as he delivered to them the commandments of YHWH:

For you are a holy people to [YHWH], and [YHWH] has chosen you to be a people for himself, a special treasure above all the peoples who are on the face of the earth. (Deuteronomy 14:2 ESV)

Paul sheds further light on who the real Israelites are:

It is impossible that the word of [YHWH] should have proved false. For not all descendents of Israel are truly Israel, nor, because they are Abraham's offspring, are they all his true children; but, in the words of Scripture, "Through the line of Isaac your descendants shall be traced." That is to say, it is not those born in the course of nature who are children of [YHWH]; it is the children born through [YHWH]'s promise who are reckoned as Abraham's descendants. (Romans 9:6-8 NEB)

If a genuine believer then we can claim to share Messiah's royalty right? After all, our heavenly Father has given the Kingship over to Yeshua Christ; and the author of Hebrews reminds believers that Messiah is among other things, our Elder brother. Where does that leave the rest of us? It leaves us as members of a royal family who have been given specific responsibilities. Every member is responsible for one another, but members are also responsible to Messiah and his Father. Let not any believer fall into the same trap as David who, at one moment in his kingship, became arrogant. In his eminence he forgot his responsibility to be intimate with his subjects and so he sinned. Counting the Israelites served to remind David of how powerful he was. Perhaps he thought that his prominence gave him permission to sin; it wasn't the first time.

And who made of us a royal house, to serve as the priests of [YHWH], his Father—to him be glory and dominion for ever and ever. Amen. (Revelation 1:6 NEB)

Yes, but Messiah does not expect members of his royal family to waste their days reveling in their royalty. Instead, members are to ensure that their lives revolve around building and restoring relationships.

[Yeshua] called them to him and said, "You know that in the world the recognized rulers lord it over their subjects, and their great men make them feel the weight of authority. That is not the way with you; among you, whoever wants to be great must be your servant, and whoever wants to be first must be the willing slave of all. For even the Son of Man did not come to be served but to serve, and to give up his life as a ransom for many." (Mark 10:42-45 NEB)

Then the man who had been given one bag came and said, "Master, I knew you to be a hard man: you reap where you have not sown, you gather where you have not scattered; so I was afraid, and I went and hid your gold in the ground. Here it is—you have what belongs to you." "You lazy rascal," said the master. "You knew that I reap where I have not sown, and gather where I have not scattered? Then you ought to have put my money on deposit, and on my return I should have got it back with interest. Take the bag of gold from him, and give it to the one with ten bags. For the man who has will always be given more, till he has enough and to spare; and the man who has not will forfeit even what he has. Fling the useless servant out into the dark, the place of wailing and grinding of teeth." (Matthew 25:24-30 NEB)

229. Rules for the Road

First read: Isaiah 61-66

Make no mistake by accepting three truths. One, you are not accountable to anyone but the One who placed you on this journey. No one is going to determine if you get a raise, or are promoted or demoted when you reached your destination. Two, you are performing for an audience of One. At the end of this journey, your performance will be considered in order to know what will happen to you inside the gates of Glory. As COE, even you have an opportunity for growth and expansion. Whether you move up or down, the direction you choose now will determine your direction later. Look behind you; look beside you; look around you—who are you accountable for? As many as you can count. Lastly, look ahead and see that as it may appear that you started walking only yesterday, your journey could end as soon as tomorrow while journeying. Keep these truths in your head, and on the days in which your vision is blurred from surrounding conditions, you won't lose sight. Whether hazed by heat or dimmed by night, remember these truths and you'll always have light. Keep moving. Tick. Tick. Tick

Then the messenger of the [Yeshua] said to Philip, "Start out and go south to the road that leads down from Jerusalem to Gaza." (This is the desert road.) So he set out and was on his way when he caught sight of an Ethiopian. This man was a eunuch, a high official of the Kandake, or Queen, of Ethiopia, in charge of all her treasure. He had been to Jerusalem on a pilgrimage and was now on his way home, sitting in his carriage and reading aloud the prophet Isaiah. The Spirit said to Philip, "Go and join the carriage." (Acts 8:26-29 NEB)

For the believer, there are a few simple rules that, if followed, will not make their journey pain free, but will keep them in good standing with the One who sits upon the throne. First, Yeshua's anger is stoked when his disciples base their decision of whether or not to obey on what others will have to say. From the gate, too many members of the Body are concerned with getting approval from their peers, when not one will decide their eternal fate.

I do not look to men for honor. But with you it is different, as I know well, for you have no love for [YHWH] in you. (John 5:41-42 NEB)

We therefore make it our ambition, wherever we are, here or there, to be acceptable to him. For we must all have our lives laid open before the tribunal of [Messiah], where each must receive what is due to him for his conduct in the body, good or bad. (2nd Corinthians 5:9-10 NEB)

Second, if you are a disciple of Messiah's then it means that he expects your light to shine for all to see. It is foolish to speculate over whose life you are to illumine. There are too many in the Body whose loathing of some colors keeps their light fairly faint; and yet they want to be called saints of their Father. To them, your Savior wishes that you'd comply with this "favor."

[Yeshua] said to him, "'You shall love [YHWH] and [Yeshua] with all your heart, with all your soul, and with all your mind. ' This is the first and great commandment. And the second is like it: 'You shall love your neighbor as yourself. '" (Matthew 22:37-39 NEB)

A man may say, "I am in the light;" but if he hates his brother, he is still in the dark. Only the man who loves his brother dwells in the light; there is nothing to make him stumble. But one who hates his brother is in darkness; he walks in the dark and has no idea where he is going, because the darkness has made him blind." (1st John 2:9-11 NEB)

Members who are pleased with their poisonous actions and words must know that hearts with such hatred have no place in Heaven, because none have a place with the Head; with no love for another because of their color, in truth, to Messiah you're still dead. The hands of Messiah should extend to all who are in sight; and those same hands should also embrace; no matter their race.

We love because he first loved us. But, if a man says, "I love [YHWH]." while hating his brother, he is a liar. If he does not love his brother whom he has seen, it cannot be that he loves [YHWH] whom he has not seen. And indeed this command comes to us from [Messiah] himself: that he who loves [YHWH] must also love his brother. (1st John 4:19-21 NEB)

Third, while we are to be a light to a dark and dying world, we must equally protect against the squelching of our fire, which only ignites the ire of Emmanuel. Resist intimacy with those who imitate him whose fate is doused in flames. Your walk is not a game but, if you insist on perceiving yours as such, know that your opponent never plays by the rules and you are bound for ruin.

Make no mistake: Bad company is the ruin of a good character. (1st Corinthians 15:33 NEB)

My dear friend, do not imitate bad examples, but good ones. The well-doer is a child of [YHWH]; the evil-doer has never seen [YHWH]. (3rd John 1:11 NEB)

Finally, while on the road to Glory, the number of miles for each believer's walk has already been determined. No day is guaranteed to anyone, save for the extended grace of YHWH. The expectation is that our time granted on earth be spent preparing for our family reunion, not in ruining our family. As a Body, we rejoice over members when they're delivered from the clutches of death. Now, let us continue to pray for the hastening of that day when our Redeemer will return. The journey won't be trouble-free; but, then, neither was the road to Calvary. Messiah walked to release us from confinement, in hopes that all would seek and find him; and through him, the Father. All praise is due to Messiah the King for the freedom that his death did bring. There is little we can give in return to compare with the magnitude of his gift; so the least we could give is our all. With every stride and with faith in him, we must fight and always strive to win: while remembering that we *died* to sin. Amen.

Appendix A: SALVATION

Understanding Salvation

Thus far Satan has been successful in giving members of the Body a false sense of security. There are multitudes in the Church who have come to ignore the teachings of Messiah, and now mistakenly believe that words are enough to keep them from pronounced judgment, that the confessions on their tongues sufficiently cover all future disobedience to the Word of YHWH. This didn't work under the Old Covenant; neither does it under the new.

It is the soul that sins, and no other, that shall die; a son shall not share a father's guilt, nor a father his son's. The righteous man shall reap the fruit of his own righteousness, and the wicked man the fruit of his own wickedness. It may be that a wicked man gives up his sinful ways and keeps all my laws, doing what is just and right. That man shall live; he shall not die. None of the offenses he has committed shall be remembered against him; he shall live because of his righteous deeds. Have I any desire, says [Yeshua], for the death of a wicked man? Would I not rather that he should mend his ways and live? It may be that a righteous man turns back from his righteous ways and commits every kind of abomination that the wicked practice; shall he do this and live? No, none of his former righteousness will be remembered in his favor; he has broken his faith, he has sinned, and he shall die. You say that [YHWH] acts without principle? Listen, you Israelites, it is you who act without principle, not I. If a righteous man turns from his righteousness, takes to evil ways and dies, it is because of these evil ways that he dies. Again, if a wicked man turns from his wicked ways and does what is just and right, he will save his life. If he sees his offenses as they are and turns his back on them all, then he shall live; he shall not die. "[YHWH] acts without principle," says the Israelites. No, Israelites, it is you who act without principle, not I. Therefore, Israelites, says [Yeshua], I will judge every man of you on his deeds. Turn, turn from your offenses, or your iniquity will be your downfall. Throw off the load of your past misdeeds; get yourselves a new heart and a new spirit. Why should you die, you men of Israel? I have no desire for any man's death. This is the very word of [Yeshua]. (Ezekiel 18:20-32 ESV)

Later on [Yeshua] went up to Jerusalem for one of the Jewish festivals. Now at the Sheep-Pool in Jerusalem there is a place with five colonnades. Its name in the language of the Jews is Bethesda. In these colonnades there lay a crowd of sick people, blind, lame, and paralyzed. Among them was a man who had been crippled for thirty-eight years. When [Yeshua] saw him lying there and was aware that he had been ill a long time, he asked him, "Do you want to recover?" "Sir," he replied, "I have no one to put me in the pool when the water is disturbed, but while I am moving, someone else is in the pool before me." Yeshua answered, "Rise to your feet, take up your bed and walk." The man recovered instantly, took up his stretcher, and began to walk. That day was a Sabbath. So the Jews said to the man who had been cured. "It is the Sabbath. You are not allowed to carry your bed on the Sabbath." He answered, "The man who cured me said, 'Take up your bed and walk.'" They asked him, "Who is the man who told you to take up your bed and walk?" But the cripple who had been cured did not know; for the place was crowded and [Yeshua] had slipped away. A little later [Yeshua] found him in the temple and said to him, "Now that you are well again, leave your sinful ways, or you may suffer something worse." The man went away and told the Jews that it was [Yeshua] who had cured him. (John 5:1-15 NEB)

If Christians are to effectively duel with the devil in salvation, its truth must be understood. In truth, salvation is a gift from YHWH. Shepherds in the Church do well in informing those lost that they can perform no work good enough to merit what YHWH offers freely. Under the Old Covenant, the Israelites were given the Law as a means of making apparent what had previously been indistinguishable to them. That is, good from evil. The various sacrifices described in the book of Leviticus give Christians a visual of what YHWH then required for the expiation of sin. As Moses delivered YHWH's instructions to the Israelites, he made clear both the rewards available for those who obeyed, and likewise, the consequences for the disobedient. In the book of Ezekiel we see a reminder given to the Israelites who have mistakenly come to believe that any prior acts of righteousness will cover their multitude of sins, whether present or future. However, Yeshua is unequivocal in speaking through Ezekiel. A believer's faith in YHWH is characterized by a life of active obedience, which is the marker of righteousness. So too, then, a life characterized by disobedience, which was disobedience to the Law, was a sign of unfaithfulness to YHWH, and therefore also, a symbol of wickedness. Again and again, the Israelites found themselves reaping the judgment of YHWH; a result of turning away from YHWH after learning the truth. YHWH, in his sovereignty, and in order to complete his Divine plan, made a provision by sending his Son to earth. Messiah's sinless life made him the perfect sacrifice—his death, the perfect atonement. No more must Christians be subjected to rituals of old in an attempt to make themselves right with YHWH. Salvation through Messiah is the sole catalyst leading to justification. When, by faith, a believer accepts that Messiah died for his sins, by this faithful action he has also been justified. It is the next point, however, that Satan has managed to make blurry for the Body.

Salvation and the gift of Righteousness

For if by the wrongdoing of that one man death established its reign, through a single sinner, much more shall those who receive in far greater measure [YHWH]'s grace, and his gift of righteousness, live and reign through the one man, [Yeshua]. (Romans 5:17 NEB)

How is the believer able to live and reign with Yeshua? Yes, by receiving YH-WH's grace—that is, the grace he extended to us while we were still sinners—but, also by receiving his gift of righteousness. At present there are those in the Church who are enthralled with a game invented by Satan, which YHWH takes no pleasure in playing, "Let's Make a Deal."

> The kind of religion which is without stain or fault in the sight of [YHWH] our Father is this: to go to the help of orphans and widows in their distress and keep oneself untarnished by the world. (James 1:27 NEB)

These are the members who indirectly tell YHWH that they will gladly accept his gift of grace as long as he keeps his gift of righteousness. What responsibility does the believer have in living righteously if they've never received the gift of righteousness? The helmet of salvation does not come by itself, lest the believer forgets already, the coat of mail. When Messiah returns he expects to see every member of his body still wearing their full armor; for this is how he will identify his own.

> Those who live on the level of our lower nature have their outlook formed by it, and that spells death; but those who live on the level of the spirit have the spiritual outlook, and that spells life and peace. For the outlook of the lower nature is enmity with [YHWH]; it is not subject to the law of [YHWH]; indeed it cannot be: those who live on such a level cannot possibly please [YHWH]. But that is not how you live. You are on the spiritual level, if only [YHWH]'s Spirit dwells within you; and if a man does not possess the Spirit of [Messiah], he is no Christian. (Romans 8:5-9 NEB)

The Helmet comes with responsibilities

Many within the Body are inclined to believe that the helmet, freely given by YHWH, brings with it no responsibilities; almost as if the helmet in of itself guarantees one's admission into heaven. Is it, then, possible for a man to wear the helmet of salvation which comes from the Father, and at the same time continue to live a life of sin, which comes not from the Spirit? Absolutely not, though Satan has convinced many that it is. No wonder the Body is filled with "members" content with acknowledging that they are still sinners. If Messiah died once so that we could die daily, an act that was never committed under the Old Covenant, and a function that could never have been carried out by the Law, then how is it that "Believers" still find themselves willfully persisting in sin? Both the author of Romans and Hebrews attribute such behavior to a lack of faith. Most shepherds excuse such persistence as a byproduct of our sinful make-up. In truth, however, there is a contrast between the conditional and the descriptive sinner. The former is a biblical portrayal of man's universal depraved nature, due to his initial descent in the garden.

> But death held sway from Adam to Moses, even over those who had not sinned as Adam did, by disobeying a direct command—and Adam foreshadows the Man who was to come. (Romans 5:14 NEB)

Even after being justified and redeemed by the blood of Yeshua Messiah, and receiving our daily allotment of the Father's and Son's grace (but only upon request), man retains his sinful condition until Messiah's second coming; the seed of sin will remain lodged within. On the other hand, the descriptive sinner is a consistent and conscientious sinner. This is also a universal description of all men, but it should no longer hold true for all who have accepted, and currently wear upon their heads, the gracious helmet of salvation.

But [YHWH]'s act of grace is out of all proportion to Adam's wrongdoing. For if the wrongdoing of that one man brought death upon so many, its effect is vastly exceeded by the grace of [YHWH] and the gift that came to so many by the grace of the one man. (Romans 5:15 NEB)

At stated previously, it was not possible to live such a life of sinlessness prior to the death of Yeshua on the cross—unless YHWH himself apportioned such grace as he saw fit to carry out his Divine plan. The helmet of salvation, then, brings with it not only a hope of what is still unseen; a hope that was unavailable under the Old Covenant. No, the helmet of salvation also brings freedom, through YHWH's grace. This freedom is that which Satan actively strives to withhold from YHWH's people.

The children of a family share the same flesh and blood; and so he too shared ours, so that through death he might break the power of him who had death at his command, that is, the devil; and might liberate those who, through fear of death, had all their lifetime been in servitude. (Hebrews 2:14-15 NEB)

The man by the pool

We are then able to conclude that the blood shed on Calvary was powerful enough to set us free. It is worth noting that at the pool in Bethesda, Yeshua did not immediately cure the cripple, but first asked him if he wanted to recover. It is a sad but truthful commentary that, at present, there are many in the Church content with their spiritual sickness, and so in their own eyes, recovery is still an option not worth considering. For others, recovery would be worth considering if ever they were told the truth, that Salvation was never a means to partial recovery, with one foot outside of the prison and the other still lingering inside. If half of the body is still lying on the sick-bed, while the other half is on the ground, how then can the believer "get up and walk?"

Here are some additional potent truths to be gleaned from the passage of Scripture found in John 5:1-15 and its message of salvation: First, it is significant that this pool lay among five colonnades. Why? Historically, in Roman society, most colonnades were built in pairs. In other words, you typically would have seen one with an even number of columns. This one had five and John purposefully makes mention of it. Numbers are significant in Scripture. The number five is often linked with YHWH's divine grace. Therefore, how significant that Messiah would meet this sickly man here. For Messiah indeed was sent by the grace of YHWH to heal all of us who were sickly with sin.

Now, this man's sickness, as is often the case in the book of Luke, is both literal and allegorical. I believe that all of Messiah's healings in Scripture are both literal and allegorical. And as this Scripture passage points out allegorically, all forms of sinful living are indeed crippling and we all are crippled in sin long before meeting Messiah. Like the man in this passage, there are a plethora of hindrances we encounter when trying to make ourselves well, prior to a genuine encounter with Yeshua. And yet, all human attempts are futile. It is indeed an act of YHWH's grace that we are called to be healed of, and released from, our sinful bondage. Yet, we are not compelled to comply with Messiah's inquiry when he meets us. He wants us to know that his gracious gift is available because he indeed predestined us to receive it. However, the choice is still ours to make.

And once justified, our ability to walk with Messiah and to work out our sanctification toward glorification is instantaneous. It is because we do receive Messiah's indwelling Holy Spirit—YHWH's seal. We are not to allow the word of man to detract us from doing what the Word of YHWH says we have the power to do, and what he says we ought to be doing.

Once we come to know Messiah, the expectation is that we leave our sinful lifestyle permanently; for this is the definition of true repentance. It does not suggest perfection, but it does suggest a life of perfecting through the power of the indwelling Holy Spirit and by YHWH's grace. No, we will not depart from our sinful seeds (hence the constant struggle with sin and our need to remain attached to the Vine) until Messiah's return. But, we are to depart permanently from our sinful deeds and to stay away from all sinful weeds which produce those deeds.

Remember, there is no doubt that this man was healed. He had a genuine encounter with Messiah, as evidence by his new found ability to walk. And yet when Messiah saw him again, he told him if he didn't leave his sinful life, something worse would happen to him.

What is there left to conclude, but that Messiah was referring to a spiritual and eternal something, rather than an earthly or temporal one? There are consequences from turning away or falling away from the faith. If it were not possible, what reason would exist for Messiah to make such a statement? And if Messiah was only referring to someone who wasn't really healed to begin with (to address those who claim that all members of the faith who fall away do so because they were never genuine believers to begin with) then the verses preceding his warning would have been intentionally phrased differently.

Can we lose our salvation?

Language is vital and part of the problem the Church has faced over the years in understanding the gift of salvation. For an example, the words and phrases that many well-meaning shepherds choose to use when delivering messages, such as, "losing your salvation." When the issue is phrased in this manner, I would agree that it is indeed impossible. For how can one lose what has been given to him as a gift? Of course, I am not talking about misplacing something; anyone can misplace an object that has been given to him as a gift and hence, lose it. I am instead talking about having something taken away from you. Generally speaking, you can only lose something that you have earned or worked for. Let's say a job, perhaps. You apply for and receive a job. Many would say that you have somehow earned this job, right? It is equally possible to lose that job, whether it be with cause (you were fired) or without cause (you were laid off), the job is still lost. Or, what about a child who, by doing chores or receiving good grades in school, has earned some privileges as a result? Those same privileges can be taken away or lost if the child suddenly becomes derelict. The common denominator in the two examples is that the reward was earned. The provider of the reward takes whatever it is back if certain conditions are no longer met.

However, if someone gives you a gift, then the only way you can lose it, using the same language as above, is if the giver reneges on his gift and demands it back. Making the suggestion that YHWH would commit such an offense by providing his gift of salvation and then taking it back, is unbiblical and blasphemous. There is no indication in any of the Gospels or Epistles that the Christian faith is based upon such conditions. The helmet of salvation is a gift given, not a reward earned. The debate surrounding the idea of "losing your salvation" is, therefore, counterproductive and unnecessarily divisive. On the other hand, there is something worth questioning. Can a believer who once received the helmet of salvation as a gift, somehow no longer be in possession of it, and therefore suffer the same eternal consequences as someone who had never received the gift in the first place? I believe the answer is yes. Yet, the words of YHWH remain true.

> "You are my witnesses," declares [YHWH], "and my servant whom I have chosen, that you may know and believe me and understand that I am he. Before me no god was formed, nor shall there be any after me. I, I am [Yeshua], and besides me there is no Savior. I declared and saved and proclaimed, when there was no strange god among you; and you are my witnesses," declares [YHWH], "and I am [Yeshua]. Also henceforth I am he; there is none who can deliver from my hand; I work, and who can turn it back?" (Isaiah 43:10-13 ESV)

No one, human or spiritual foe, can steal your gift, the helmet of salvation, away. Believers should never fear that Satan or any of his minions will somehow successfully remove what Messiah has given to them as their security. However, a gift, though once received, can at any time be rejected by its recipient. No, the former believer did not "lose his salvation," and no, she did not have it snatched away. But they may have given it up, willingly, through their actions and deeds.

No one who has not yet accepted Messiah into their heart is going to call him Lord. A non-believer would have no motivation to do so—why would he? Why would someone who hadn't accepted Messiah into their life prophesy in a name they never really believed in? How would they have the power to cast out demons or perform miracles if they were never empowered by the Holy Spirit? It didn't fly with Simon the former sorcerer in the book of Acts; a newly but still spiritually immature convert to the faith. [Acts 8:9-24] Messiah's warning to the healed man at the pool of Bethesda is symbolic to member's of today's Body. "Leave your sinful ways, or you may suffer something worse."

What then? Are we to sin, because we are not under law but under grace? Of course not. You know well enough that if you put yourself at the disposal of a master, to obey him, you are slaves of the master whom you obey; and this is true whether you serve sin, with death as its result; or obedience, with righteousness as its result. (Romans 6:15-16 NEB)

Paul makes it clear in this verse that even though a believer has the Holy Spirit, he still has the choice to place himself at the disposal of either, the Holy Spirit, and thus Messiah, or his seed of sin. The Holy Spirit is not in the business of forcing anyone to obey. The Holy Spirit's goal is to inspire within each believer adoration for the Father, which results in faithful loving and living. Contrary to what many well-meaning shepherds mistakenly teach Messiah's flock, the New Covenant did not change the consequences of sinful living. It has always been death. What the New Covenant did do was usher in the reign of YHWH's grace for everyone who receives YHWH's gift of salvation, through his Son. First, the grace to free one from their prison of sin. Now, the grace to remain free from our prison of sin with his grace and with the help of the Holy Spirit. Soon, the grace will come from Messiah's destruction of our prison of sin when he comes to reclaim his Bride.

It is surely just that [YHWH] should balance the account by sending trouble to those who trouble you, and relief to you who are troubled, and to us as well, when [Yeshua] is revealed from heaven with his mighty angels in blazing fire. Then he will do justice upon those who refuse to acknowledge [YHWH] and upon those who will not obey the gospel of our Lord [Yeshua]. They will suffer the punishment of eternal ruin, cut off from the presence of [Yeshua] and the splendor of his might. (2nd Thessalonians 1:6-9 NEB)

Notice the two groups that Paul describes in this passage to the Thessalonians: Those who refuse to acknowledge YHWH and those who will not obey the gospel of Yeshua. Ironically, both groups can be identified as non-committers. The first group never committed to Messiah because they never acknowledged him or the Father to begin with. The second group did acknowledge Messiah and the Father, but were not committed to the Gospel, hence their disobedience to the Gospel. In the end, if left unrepentant, members of both groups will incur Messiah's wrath. Acknowledging Messiah assumes that we have accepted him into our lives and, as such, have accepted his gift, or helmet of salvation. It will be that helmet still worn which will get us through the gates of Glory.

Disowning

To disown assumes that there was once ownership, but there is no longer. It is synonymous with the words "repudiate" or "renounce." If a member of a royal household decides to renounce his title, it means he has decided to "give up" the title and all claims that come with it. The word renounce in no way suggests that the member of the royal household was never really a member to begin with. You can't renounce a title that you never really held. Even more so, renounce does not mean that you lost it. It is a voluntary action. A person who renounces their title has not had it taken from him. That believers are members of a royal priesthood should come as no surprise. And some, through their faithless deeds and disobedience, have renounced their title and disowned their King. Peter speaks of these wicked men in his second book.

> Israel had false prophets as well as true; and you likewise will have false teachers among you. They will import disastrous heresies, disowning the very Master [Yeshua] who bought them, and bringing swift disaster on their own heads. They will gain many adherents to their dissolute practices, through whom the true way will be brought into disrepute. 3 In their greed for money they will trade on your credulity with sheer fabrications. But the judgement long decreed for them has not been idle; perdition waits for them with un-sleeping eyes. 4 [YHWH] did not spare the angels who sinned, but consigned them to the dark pits of hell, where they are reserved for judgement. ... Thus [YHWH] is well able to rescue the godly out of trials, and to reserve the wicked under punishment until the day of judgement.   (2nd Peter 2:1-4,9 NEB)

There is no other place for them to go after Messiah has disowned them, except for their final resting place, which, according to the book of Revelation, won't be so restful. Who is this "them" that Peter is referring to? These are not a predetermined select group of people that Messiah has predestined to hell, so that they were bound to disown him anyway. "Them" refers to anyone, or in the words of Messiah, "whosoever." Whosoever decides to disown Messiah through their faithless actions and disobedience. Peter is but citing one example of these groups of defectors. And, like the angels who defected from the holy ranks, these men know exactly what they are doing in trying to seduce members who are still genuine into departing from the road to Glory. What is particularly dangerous about these men, however, is that they still claim membership in the Church. That is why Peter refers to them as false teachers. They are not false because they weren't ever true (though this was admittedly the case with Israel's false prophets). They are false because they are no longer following the Truth, though to undiscerning eyes they appear to be. Remember that appearances can be deceptive. This is why the Holy Spirit's filling is vital. Readers should also note how Peter makes it clear that these disowners were indeed once on the road to Glory, but they decided to leave. No one snatched them off and no one pushed them off. To claim that in this passage Peter is speaking of people who were never genuine believers to begin with, is to claim that they were never placed on the road to Glory. These passages do not support that attractive assertion.

He was still speaking to the crowd when his mother and brothers appeared; they stood outside, wanting to speak to him. Someone said, "Your mother and your brothers are here outside; they want to speak to you." [Yeshua] turned to the man who brought the message, and said, "Who is my mother? Who are my brothers?" and pointing to the disciples, he said, "Here are my mother and my brothers. Whoever does the will of my heavenly Father is my brother, my sister, my mother." (Matthew 12:46-50 NEB)

Here Messiah is making clear what the qualifications are for being identified as a member of his Father's household—the same household that the Father has placed the Son in charge of. It is whoever does the will of the Father. What is the will of the Father? That all would renounce their allegiance to Satan's kingdom and give their allegiance to his Son, Yeshua Messiah, by accepting his helmet of salvation, and that their allegiance be consistently demonstrated through a lifestyle of faithful obedience.

There is nothing in creation that can hide from him; everything lies naked and exposed to the eyes of the One with whom we have to reckon. (Hebrews 4:13 NEB)

Messiah is not simply going to frown at his "naughty" sheep, while sighing, "tsk tsk." He's not going to tap them on the head with his staff and send them to the back of the line, but allow them to still enter his kingdom. No, Messiah is clear. These goats will not be allowed in. Period. They will be sent to the same place as the goats who never accepted him in the first place. It will be as if they had never received a talent to begin with, never received the helmet of salvation—though they had. It will be rather sad.

Now that by obedience to the truth you have purified your souls until you feel sincere affection toward your brother Christians, love one another whole-heartedly with all of your strength. You have been born anew, not of mortal parentage but of immortal, through the living and enduring word of [YHWH]. (1st Peter 1:22-24 NEB)

This is the only way of being identified as an adopted son of the Father. Hence, it follows logically that all who do not do the will of the Father are not siblings of Messiah, and therefore will have no part in the eternal kingdom. But the Father also wills so much more.

For the grace of [YHWH] that brings salvation has appeared to all men, teaching us that, denying ungodliness and worldly lusts, we should live soberly, righteously, and godly in the present age, looking for the blessed hope and glorious appearing of our great God Savior [Yeshua], who gave himself for us, that he might redeem us from every lawless deed and purify for himself his own special people, zealous for good works. (Titus 2:11-14 NEB)

Holiness

The One who called you is holy; like him, be holy in all your behavior, because Scripture says, "You shall be holy, for I am holy." (1st Peter 1:15 NEB)

You yourselves like living stones are being built up as a spiritual house, to be a holy priesthood, to offer spiritual sacrifices acceptable to [YHWH] through [Yeshua]. (1st Peter 2:5 ESV)

Your holiness is the hallmark of your helmet. The word holy means "designated for and dedicated to the service of YHWH." He who is holy is descriptively sinless. Though, holy is not synonymous for perfect. Take it from the lips of the Apostle Paul.

It is not to be thought that I have already achieved this. I have not yet reached perfection, but I press on, hoping to take hold of that for which [Messiah] once took hold of me. My friends, I do not reckon myself to have got hold of it yet. All I can say is this: forgetting what is behind me, and reaching out for that which lies ahead, I press towards the goal to win the prize which is [YHWH]'s call to the life above, in [Yeshua]. (Philippians 3:12-14 NEB)

In the eyes of YHWH, upon receiving the gracious helmet of salvation, believers are perfectly suitable for a life of holiness, but it does not mean that they are perfect. For he who is perfect is conditionally sinless. That describes not a single person still walking this earth. While living a holy life, believers shall be perfecting through the consecrating power of Messiah within, via the Holy Spirit.

If we claim to be sinless, we are self-deceived and strangers to the truth. If we confess our sins, he is just, and may be trusted to forgive our sins and cleanse us from every kind of wrong; but if we say we have committed no sin, we make him out be a liar, and then his word has no place in us. (1st John 1:8-10 NEB)

That means that while on the road to Glory, believers will make some mistakes and stumble. Will the stumbling be sinful? Maybe. But, that is why there is grace and forgiveness at the Father's throne. Stumbling does not mean that your helmet has fallen off. After stumbling, with your helmet still on and intact, get back up and keep walking on the road to Glory. However, the antonym of holiness is heathenness. You cannot, therefore, live the life of a heathen and claim to also still have on your head the helmet of salvation. Scripture is clear in stating that these "members" are no members of YHWH's household; they are no siblings of Messiah's.

Here is the message we heard from him and pass on to you: that [YHWH] is light, and in him there is no darkness at all. If we claim to be sharing in his life while we walk in the dark, our words and our lives are a lie; but if we walk in the light as he himself is in the light, then we share together a common life, and we are being cleansed from every sin by the blood of [Yeshua] his Son. (1st John 1:5-7 NEB)

What gives? At some point while walking on the road to Glory, there were members who were coaxed into giving up their helmet. They left the road a long time ago, though well-meaning shepherds have convinced them that they are, in fact, still on. But, to those who still insist that a profession of faith can stand without faithful deeds; who believe that Messiah is impressed and contented with the spouting of man-made creeds, I point to 1st John.

Here is the test by which we can make sure that we know him: do we keep his commands? The man who says, "I know him," while he disobeys his commands, is a liar and a stranger to the truth; but in the man who is obedient to his word, the divine love has indeed come to its perfection. (1st John 2:3-5 NEB)

And what does Messiah command?

[Yeshua] said to him, "'You shall love [YHWH] with all your heart, with all your soul, and with all your mind.' This is the first and great commandment. And the second is like it: 'You shall love your neighbor as yourself.' On these two commandments hang all the Law and the Prophets." (Matthew 22:37-40 NKJV)

So how does Messiah's commandments apply to the helmet of salvation and the road to Glory? The hallmark of the helmet is holiness, and holiness is characterized by a lifestyle of faithful obedience to Yeshua's two commandments. So, those who had at one time in their life obeyed Yeshua, but who no longer do so, as evidenced by their disobedient lifestyle, are no longer wearing their helmet of salvation. Shepherds must desist in giving wayward sheep false comfort. Messiah is not content with those who had at one time made a genuine profession and so walked in the light, but are now carousing in the dark. They are not still safe. What's more? Shepherds must begin acknowledging that many in their congregations are still in the dark.

He who has [YHWH] for his father listens to the words of [YHWH]. You are not [YHWH]'s children; that is why you do not listen. (John 8:47 NEB)

In very truth I tell you, if anyone obeys my teaching he shall never know what it is to die. (John 8:51 NEB)

If there are sheep who no longer live as Messiah lived, they are no longer truly living. For Messiah emulated holiness while he walked the earth because Messiah is holy. Indeed, Messiah is our helmet of salvation. No Christ-emulated lifestyle? No helmet of salvation.

Let us behave with decency as befits the day: no reveling or drunkenness, no debauchery or vice, no quarrels or jealousies. Let [Yeshua] himself be the armor that you wear; give no more thought to satisfying the bodily appetites. (Romans 13:13-14 NEB)

By whose standard do we determine whether or not a believer's head is covered? Messiah's. If a man is defiled, then he is no longer holy. Remember that holiness is the hallmark of the helmet. Thus, no one can claim that their outside behavior in no way indicates what's truly on the inside. "But Messiah knows my heart," many claim. Indeed he does. If you claim to dwell in him and hence claim membership into his household, then you have no business ever engaging in any of the offenses mentioned above. Both the Apostle Paul and Messiah make it clear that no one who remains unrepentant for conducting themselves as such will step one foot inside the gates of Glory. For he who has received the gift of salvation has renounced the life of a descriptive sinner.

Branches cut off

> You will say, "Branches were lopped off so that I might be grafted in." Very well: they were lopped off for lack of faith, and by faith you hold your place. Put away your pride, and be on your guard; for if [YHWH] did not spare the native branches, no more will he spare you. Observe the kindness and severity of [YHWH]—severity to those who fell away, divine kindness to you, if only you remain within its scope; otherwise you too will be cut off. (Romans 11:19-22 NEB)

There is nothing esoteric about this passage of Scripture, and yet many shepherds enjoy pontificating over its points. Such pedantic talking won't help those who need to return to the road and once again begin walking. These branches that Paul speaks of are the Israelites. They were lopped off for their lack of faith, ie., lack of faithful living. It is the purpose of us B'rit Khadasha believers having the Tanakh within our reach—to teach:

> You should understand, my brothers, that our ancestors were all under the pillar of cloud, and all of them passed through the Red Sea; and so they all received baptism into the fellowship of Moses in cloud and sea. They all ate the same supernatural food, and all drank the same supernatural drink; I mean, they all drank from the supernatural rock that accompanied their travels—and that rock was [Messiah]. And yet, most of them were not accepted by [YHWH], for the desert was strewn with their corpses. (1st Corinthians 10:1-5 NEB)

Again, this is not a passage of Scripture endorsing selective salvation—per say. The passage demonstrates that all Israelites were saved from drowning in the Red Sea. Those who were rejected were Pharaoh's army; all others were, in essence, graciously given a helmet of salvation and allowed to pass safely through. All readers should keep in mind that it was YHWH's choice to redeem the Israelites out of Egypt and out of Pharaoh's clutches. They were special by YHWH's decree, not by human deeds—lest any man should boast. All were baptized and all were allowed to partake in what Messiah—their rock—had to offer. So what happened to them? Why were they lopped off?

> These events happened as symbols to warn us not to set our desires on evil things, as they did. Do not be idolaters, like some of them; as Scripture has it,

"The people sat down to feast and stood up to play." Let us not commit fornication, as some of them did—and twenty-three thousand died in one day. Let us not put the power of [Messiah] to the test, as some of them did—and were destroyed by serpents. Do not grumble against [YHWH], as some of them did—and were destroyed by the Destroyer. (1st Corinthians 10:6-10 NEB)

You already know it all, but let me remind you how [Yeshua], having once delivered the people of Israel out of Egypt, next time destroyed those who were guilty of unbelief. (Jude 1:5 NEB)

They were lopped off for their faithless actions. Shepherds must desist telling their flock that such punishments are only indicative of an Tanakh wrathful Rock. What happened to the Israelites was not merely an Old Covenant consequence.

All these things that happened to them were symbolic, and were recorded for our benefit as a warning. For upon us the fulfillment of the ages has come. If you feel sure that you are standing firm, beware. You may fall. (1st Corinthians 10:11-12 NEB)

Who is Paul speaking to? Believers. We must remember that when writing the epistles, including Corinthians and Romans, Paul was writing to a Believing audience—not a pagan one. It is time for the Church to arise from her slumber. There are those lying on the side of the road to Glory, strung out with pieces of rotting fruit. Many have been told that they were never really on the road to begin with. That is a lie. The account Paul gives in this chapter is applicable to today's Believers. It is possible for someone to have graciously accepted the helmet of salvation, become baptized into the Body of Messiah, received the bountiful blessings which accompany the life of a believer, and then still decide, for various reasons, to start living a sinful lifestyle. Their rescue from Satan's kingdom (that is, Egypt), from the clutches of Satan (that is, Pharaoh), their initial salvation (that is, their safe passage through the Red Sea), their water baptism, partaking of the Lord's supper, and other righteous acts—does not give them license for licentious living. Should they decide to partake, they should not expect to escape Messiah's wrath. Branches are barren because they've born no fruit. You can't bear fruit if, after professing Messiah as your Lord and Savior, you decide to return to your sinful lifestyle.

With all this in view, you should try your hardest to supplement your faith with virtue, virtue with knowledge, knowledge with self-control, self-control with fortitude, fortitude with piety, piety with brotherly kindness, and brotherly kindness with love. These are gifts which, if you possess and foster them, will keep you from being either useless or barren in the knowledge of [Yeshua]. The man who lacks them is short-sighted and blind; he has forgotten how he was cleansed from his former sins. (2nd Peter 1:5-9 NEB)

There will be consequences for those whose branches remain barren when Messiah returns. Notice Messiah uses the words "of mine." Who belong to him, but those who had one time been grafted in? Again, here Messiah is speaking words of wisdom and caution to those who make the decision to follow him. This entire speech (John 14-17) and the prayer that follows, takes place before he is arrested. In no way is Messiah speaking here of people who would never profess him.

> Therefore, brothers, be all the more diligent to confirm your calling and election, for if you practice these qualities you will never fall. For in this way there will be richly provided for you an entrance into the eternal kingdom of our Lord and Savior [Yeshua Messiah]. (2nd Peter 1:10-11 ESV)

Barren Branches

Allow me to momentarily offer a side-note here. A branch can remain barren not only because of a return to a sinful lifestyle. As previously mentioned, it can also remain bare because no fruit was ever there, due to faithless inactivity.

> But can you not see, you quibbler, that faith divorced from deeds is barren? Was it not by his action, in offering his son Isaac upon the altar, that our father Abraham was justified? Surely you can see that faith was at work in his actions, and that by these actions the integrity of his faith was fully proved. Here was fulfillment of the words of Scripture: "Abraham put his faith in [YHWH], and that faith was counted to his as righteousness;" and elsewhere he is called "[YHWH]'s friend." You see then that a man is justified by deeds and not by faith in itself. The same is true of the prostitute Rahab also. Was not she justified by her action in welcoming the messengers into her house and sending them away by a different route? As the body is dead when there is no breath left in it, so faith divorced from deeds is lifeless as a corpse. (James 2:20-26 NEB)

Now wait a minute, justified by deeds? Isn't that Old Covenant talk? Yes. But, it is also New Covenant talk, too. When anyone invites Yeshua Messiah into their heart, they are performing a deed. This act is what justifies an unbeliever and extends to them the gift and helmet of salvation. Nevertheless, Messiah expects this act to become accentuated by other faithful actions; as an expression of their justification. Where there is no expression of one's justification, there is equally no proof. Proof is not found in the confession. Rather the proof of your confession is found in your expression. Where there is no proof, there will be a penalty. The book of Isaiah also references this.

> Fear not; you shall not be put to shame, you shall suffer no insult, have no cause to blush. It is time to forget the shame of your younger days and remember no more the reproach of your widowhood; for your husband is your maker, whose name is [Yeshua]; your redeemer is the Holy One of Israel who is called God of all the earth. [Yeshua] has acknowledged you a wife again, once deserted and heart-broken, [Yeshua] has called you a bride still young though once rejected. (Isaiah 54:4-6 A Theological Commentary to the Midrash: Pesiqta deRab Kahana By Jacob Neusner, University Press of America, Jan 1, 2001, p. 203)

Israel not forgotten

Though I digress just a little, this passage of Scripture is, nonetheless, important. It is a reminder to all Gentile converts that Yeshua has not forgotten about the Jews. As Paul makes mention in Romans, they were "lopped of for their lack of faith" they were divorced from their Maker. However, we know they will be redeemed again in the near future.

> Put away your pride and be on your guard; for if [YHWH] did not spare the native branches, no more will he spare you. Observe the kindness and the severity of [YHWH]—severity to those who fell away, divine kindness to you, if only you remain within its scope; otherwise you too will be cut off, whereas they, if they do not continue faithless, will be grafted in; for it is in [YHWH]'s power to graft them in again. For if you were cut from your native wild olive and against all nature grafted into the cultivated olive, how much more readily will they, the natural olive branches, be grafted into their native stock. For there is a deep truth here, my brothers, of which I want you to take account, so that you may not be complacent about your own discernment: this partial blindness has come upon Israel only until the Gentiles have been admitted in full strength; when that has happened, the whole of Israel will be saved, in agreement with the text of Scripture: "From Zion shall come the Deliverer; he shall remove wickedness from Jacob. And this is the covenant I will grant them, when I take away their sins." In the spreading of the Gospel they are treated as [YHWH]'s enemies for your sake; but [YHWH]'s choice stands, and they are his friends for the sake of the patriarchs. For the gracious gifts of [YHWH] and his calling are irrevocable. Just as formerly you were disobedient to [YHWH], but now have received mercy in the time of their disobedience, so too, when you receive mercy, they have proved disobedient, but only in order that they too may receive mercy. For in making all mankind prisoners to disobedience, [YHWH]'s purpose was to show mercy to all mankind. (Romans 11:20b-32 NEB)

Who is the Bride?

There is no need for disagreement to arise concerning who the Bride of Messiah is. There presently exists Gentile converts who insist that they are the Bride, and Jewish converts who claim the same thing with equal zeal. Both are correct, but neither in isolation—only in union. There are places in the Bible where the marriage motif is applied exclusively to either the former or latter converts, so both have a stake in their claim. The Gentile converts often use Paul's letter to the Church in Ephesus.

However, in the passage above from the book of Isaiah, the reference to the wife and bride is specifically speaking of the Jewish people. It is a prophesy that has yet to be fulfilled; when the Jews (the orthodox who do not currently refer to themselves as Messianic Jews) will acknowledge that Yeshua Messiah is the promised Messiah, and through their faithful acknowledgment they shall be re-grafted onto the Vine. It will be a renewing of their marriage vows, per say. It is at this point that the Bride of Messiah, in all her unified splendor, will be adorned and ready to partake in the marriage supper with her Bridegroom. The book of Proverbs also contains passages of Scripture which allude to the relationship between a husband and a wife. Again, these are literal passages, but they are not devoid of spiritual truths as well. Here is one passage that stands out:

> He who commits adultery lacks sense; he who does it destroys himself. He will get wounds and dishonor, and his disgrace will not be wiped away. For jealousy makes a man furious, and he will not spare when he takes revenge. He will accept no compensation; he will refuse though you multiply gifts. (Proverbs 6:32-35 ESV)

What does Messiah desire from his wife? Fidelity. Messiah is a jealous husband; YHWH is a jealous God. On the day of vengeance, there will be wrath for him who woos his wife away, and wrath for her who chose to stray. Using the second definition, readers can conclude that Messiah is asking his disciples to continue in their descriptively sinless lifestyle, as they are now able to do so with Messiah's permanent dwelling, via the Holy Spirit, as well as the grace he and his Father afford to those who ask. Readers are informed that only those fruitful branches will be rewarded eternally. The only way to ensure that believers are eternally rewarded is to ensure that they remain attached to the Vine, which is Yeshua Messiah.

Then What's the Difference?

Those who renounce their title, who take off their helmet, who adulterate their marriage, who detach themselves from the Vine, and so become withered; who commit such actions and remain unrepentant—their eternal destiny will be torturous. As Paul promises in Romans, these branches will be lopped for their faithless deeds. Some might ask, "Well then, what is the difference between the Old and New Covenant? Why did Messiah come if Believers were going to be treated just like the Israelites in the Tanakh?" Messiah came so that Gentiles who confessed his name would indeed be treated like the Israelites of the Tanakh, by being adopted into YHWH's household. That is, they would receive the same love and affection as children of the God of Abraham, Isaac, and Jacob and the promise of his protection and blessings. However, believers can't profess to want to be treated as equals to their elder siblings, in the eyes of YHWH, and then not want their heavenly Father to treat them equally. Believers cannot, on one hand, expect to receive YHWH's devotion, while at the same time, rejecting his other beloved children or rejecting his discipline when deserved.

Division

Since Messiah's ascension into heaven, Satan has been working overtime in coming against the Body of Messiah. Nothing but discord and division can arise from faulty doctrine. Within the Body, the denominational split over the doctrine of salvation is but one example of what can happen when a little leaven begins spreading. Make no mistake, there is truth and there are lies. There are a multitude of believers in the Church who have mistakenly placed their faith in the hands of man when it is Messiah who will determine their fate. Messiah wasn't impressed with the religious elite of his day. Most of his scathing remarks were directed at them, not the sinners. The men who prided themselves on their knowledge and on keeping the Law had the admiration of man, while receiving stern admonition from the Son of Man. Neither a Masters of Divinity nor a Doctorate in Theology, in of themselves, makes anyone qualified to preach the Gospel. The majority of seminaries in the United States provide their students with only semi-truth. The history of the Church, the richness of Hebrew history, archaeological findings of Biblical significance, Biblical language acquisition; these are worthy of learning and of sharing with Messiah's flock. However, sound Biblical doctrine need not be learned behind the walls of academia. Remember that while perhaps the preeminent theologian of his day, not an ounce of Paul's learning prior to his conversion drew him closer to Messiah. Indeed, all of his knowledge brought more harm to the Body of Messiah then it helped. What's more? While his actions were harmful, his intentions were sincere. Prior to his conversion, Paul actually thought he was doing YHWH a favor.

> I myself once thought it my duty to work actively against the name of [Yeshua] of Nazareth; and I did so in Jerusalem. It was I who imprisoned many of [YHWH]'s people by authority obtained from the chief priests; and when they were condemned to death, my vote was cast against them. In all the synagogues I tried by repeated punishment to make them renounce their faith; indeed my fury rose to such a pitch that I extended my persecution to foreign cities. (Acts 26:9-11 NEB)

And yet he was humble enough to acknowledge that he had been in error.

> And certain men came down from Judea and taught the brethren, "Unless you are circumcised according to the custom of Moses, you cannot be saved." (Acts 15:1 NEB)

Undoubtedly, these were newly converted Jewish-Christians who were still trying to hold on to their old traditions and who believed that any Gentile who wanted to be truly converted to Messiah needed to first pass through one of their Jewish rituals. Their intentions may have been benign, but what they were teaching was poisonous. Circumcision for salvation? Not what Messiah preached at all. In fact, in the words of Paul:

> Circumcision has value, provided you keep the law; but if you break the law, then your circumcision is as if it had never been. Equally, if an uncircumcised

man keeps the precepts of the law, will he not count as circumcised? He may be uncircumcised in his natural state, but by fulfilling the law he will pass judgment on you who break it, for all your written code and your circumcision. The true Jew is not he who is such in externals, neither is the true circumcision the external mark of the flesh. The true Jew is he who is such inwardly, and the true circumcision is of the heart, directed not by written precepts but by the Spirit; such a man receives his commendation not from men but from [YHWH]. (Romans 2:25-29 NEB)

In short, what these Jewish Believers, the Judaizers, were insisting on was nonsense. That controversy arose when the Church was barely established, while unfortunate, didn't necessarily pronounce irredeemable disaster. This deceptive doctrine was defeated. How?

That brought them into fierce dissension and controversy with Paul and Barnabas. And so it was arranged that these two and some others from Antioch should go up to Jerusalem to see the apostles and elders about this question. (Acts 15:2 NEB)

Rather than accept the doctrine as dogma, members from the Antiochian church were sent to the recognized architects of the faith for answers. What is significant to remember is that the apostles and elders in Jerusalem were respected, not because of their earthly erudition, but because they were men both sealed and filled with the Holy Spirit. All but one apostle were chosen by Messiah, and the elders were selected by a body of Spirit-filled believers with specific credentials.

Therefore, friends, look out seven men of good reputation from your number, men full of the Spirit and of wisdom, and we will appoint them to deal with these matters, while we devote ourselves to prayer and to the ministry of the word. This proposal proved acceptable to the whole body. They elected Stephen, a man full of faith and of the Holy Spirit, Philip, Prochorus, Nicanor, Timon, Parmenas, and Nicolas of Antioch, a former convert to Judaism. These they presented to the apostles, who prayed and laid their hands on them. (Acts 6:3-6 NEB)

Peter spoke directly to members of the Pharisaic party who had confessed and converted, but who, in dimness, were still distorting.

Then why do you now provoke [YHWH] by laying on the shoulders of these converts a yoke which neither we nor our fathers were able to bear? No, we believe that it is by grace of [Yeshua] that we are saved, and so are they. (Acts 15:10-11 NEB)

And yet, should any who profess to believe choose to disbelieve you—let go and let YHWH. After responding, the apostles and elders sent their visitors back to Antioch with a letter to deliver to those questioning. Notice the ending words.

It is the decision of the Holy Spirit, and our decision, to lay no further burden upon you beyond these essentials: you are to abstain from meat that has been offered to idols, from blood, from anything that has been strangled, and from fornication. If you keep yourselves free from these things you will be doing right. Farewell. (Acts 15:28-29 NEB)

The dispute was settled; though, not by relying upon their own thoughts, traditions, feelings, opinions, or ideas. Because the apostles and elders were filled with the Holy Spirit, they were led by the Holy Spirit. God had made the decision. A Spirit-filled man can discern the voice of YHWH and will respond in obedience. Perhaps the most significant observation to be made here is that unlike the ecumenical councils which would eventually follow, notice how the Council in Jerusalem ended with unanimity. Notice too in the following passage that the unanimous decision of the Spirit-filled council resulted in an increase in the number of converts; and how the leaders worked in spite of the spiritual obstacles presented to them by the Holy Spirit.

As they went on their way through the cities, they delivered to them for observance the decisions that had been reached by the apostles and elders who were in Jerusalem. So the churches were strengthened in the faith, and they increased in numbers daily. And they went through the region of Phrygia and Galatia, having been forbidden by the Holy Spirit to speak the word in Asia. And when they had come up to Mysia, they attempted to go into Bithynia, but the Spirit of [YHWH] did not allow them. So, passing by Mysia, they went down to Troas. (Acts 16:4-8 NEB)

False Teachings

Factions can't form when everyone is united by their faith. When the focus is within, then and only then will dissension begin. What Messiah calls dissension within his Body has euphemistically come to be referred to as denominations. I believe that Messiah is most unimpressed. In fact, it is distressing. There should not exist various versions of the doctrine of salvation. While it is true that, thankfully, none within the Body are presently proclaiming a salvation by works earned, it is no less dangerous that many are preaching a salvation with little to no expectations; that our freely given righteousness comes not with responsibilities. It is no less problematic that many are teaching that a prince who turns prodigal still has permanence without repentance. Let no shepherd place themselves in a position to be rebuked on the day they stand before the judgment throne of Messiah. Messiah is concerned with his sheep knowing the truth and nothing but the truth. He has no tolerance for any shepherd whose pride allows them to continue perpetrating the poison already circulating among his Body. Those who are in love with their degrees and the titles they bring; those in love with their doctrines and creeds while their sheep can barely breathe; those who insist on adhering to lies, though impressed with their tithes—they all will have to give an account to the Shepherd for every sheep who remains lost as a result of their obstinacy.

But I have this against you, you have lost your early love. Think from what a height you have fallen; repent, and do as you once did. Otherwise, if you do not repent, I shall come and remove your lamp from its place. (Revelation 2:4-5 NEB)

I know how hard pressed you are, and poor—and yet you are rich; I know how you are slandered by those who claim to be Jews but are not—they are Satan's synagogue. Do not be afraid of the suffering to come. The devil will throw some of you in prison, to put you to the test; and for ten days you will suffer cruelly. Only be faithful till death, and I will give you the crown of life. (Revelation 2:9-10 NEB)

But, I have a few matters to bring against you: you have in Pergamum some that hold to the teaching of Balaam, who taught Balak to put temptation in the way of the Israelites. He encouraged them to eat food sacrificed to idols and to commit fornication, and in the same way you have some who hold to the doctrine of the Nicolaitians. So repent. If you do not, I shall come to you soon and make war upon them. (Revelation 2:14-16 NEB)

Nevertheless, I have a few things against you, because you allow that woman Jezebel, who calls herself a prophetess, to teach and seduce my servants to commit sexual immorality and eat things sacrificed to idols. And I gave her time to repent of her sexual immorality, and she did not repent. Indeed I will cast her into a sickbed, and those who commit adultery with her into great tribulation, unless they repent of their deeds. I will kill her children with death, and all the churches shall know that I am he who searches the minds and hearts. And I will give to each one of you according to your works. Now to you I say, and to the rest in Thyatira, as many as do not have this doctrine, who have not known the depths of Satan, as they say, I will put on you no other burden. But hold fast what you have till I come. And he who overcomes, and keeps My works until the end, to him I will give power over the nations. (Revelation 2:20-26 NKJV)

Be watchful, and strengthen the things which remain, that are ready to die, for I have not found your works perfect before [YHWH]. Remember therefore how you have received and heard; hold fast and repent. Therefore if you will not watch, I will come upon you as a thief, and you will not know what hour I will come upon you. You have a few names even in Sardis who have not defiled their garments; and they shall walk with me in white, for they are worthy. He who overcomes shall be clothed in white garments, and I will not blot out his name from the Book of Life; but I will confess his name before my Father and before his angels. (Revelation 3:2-5 NKJV)

Because you have kept my command and stood fast, I will also keep you from the ordeal that is to fall upon the whole world and test its inhabitants. I am coming soon; hold fast to what you have, and let no one rob you of your crown. (Revelation 3:10-11 NEB)

I know your ways: you are neither hot nor cold. How I wish you were either hot or cold. But because you are lukewarm, neither hot nor cold, I will spit you out of my mouth. You say, "How rich I am. And how well I have done. I have everything I want in the world. In fact, though you do not know it, you are the most pitiful wretch, poor, blind, and naked. So I advise you to buy from me gold refined in the fire, to make you truly rich, and white clothes to put on to hide the shame of your nakedness, and ointment for your eyes so that you may see. All whom I love I reprove and discipline. Be on your mettle therefore and repent. (Revelation 3:15-19 NEB)

Today's Body of Messiah

While the seven lamps in the 1st chapter of Revelation are real historic churches on what was then Asia Minor, the messages from Messiah, delivered by messengers, apply just as fervently to the ecumenical Church of today. If Messiah were sending a message to today's Church (and indeed he is), the one given to the Church in Sardis is the one I believe applies to today's Church. In other words, we are living in the Sardis Church age today. Like those of the past, Messiah is aware that in today's Body, there are those who have been faithful and diligent in deeds and service. There are believers who, with discernment, have refused to entertain spiritual charlatans, as well as those who shamelessly carouse in darkness. There are those who have persevered amidst the harshest of conditions (even those who have been physically tortured for their testimony). Thus, the same promise of Paradise remains for those who remain righteous. However, Messiah is equally conscience of all the poison that continues to abound within. He knows of those who once confessed but who no longer profess; of those who serve out of selfishness rather than for the Shepherd and his flock; of those who teach false doctrine and those who blindly adhere, of those who proclaim a Gospel of comfort, rather than one of sacrifice; of those interested in blending with the darkness of the world, rather than in being light to attract those in darkness. Messiah is aware of the stench and it has been heart-wrenching. Enough. The same consequences will commence should repentance fail to transpire. Genuine repentance. There are far too many shepherds preaching that the rapture is new age nonsense. They must desist. Messiah is coming soon to redeem his Bride and those who are ready will not be left behind. Those who are will be given over to the Anti-Messiah, as a judgment.

Do you not remember that when I was still with you I told you these things? And now you know what is restraining, that he may be revealed in his own time. For the mystery of lawlessness is already at work; only He who now restrains will do so until He is taken out of the way. And then the lawless one will be revealed, whom [Yeshua] will consume with the breath of His mouth and destroy with the brightness of His coming. The coming of the lawless one is according to the working of Satan, with all power, signs, and lying wonders, and with all unrighteous deception among those who perish, because they did not receive the love of the truth, that they might be saved. And for this reason [YHWH] will send them strong delusion, that they should believe the lie, that they all may be condemned who did not believe the truth but had pleasure in unrighteousness. (2nd Thessalonians 2:5-12 NKJV)

Hell

The Bible is clear on YHWH's wrath. Shepherds must desist from teaching their sheep that his wrath is metaphorical or hyperbolic. They need to hear the truth. Hell is not the final resting place for all who are unfaithful, who renounce their righteousness. Hell is where they go when they die, yes, but, not for eternity. Remember the rich man who was miserly to Lazarus and to all who were beggars and poor? Daily they came in hopes of respite and relief, but the rich man chose to ignore them.

One day the poor man died and was carried away by the angels to be with Abraham. The rich man also died and was buried, and in Hades, where he was in torment, he looked up; and there, far away, was Abraham with Lazarus close beside him. "Abraham, my father," he called out, "take pity on me. Send Lazarus to dip the tip of his finger in water, to cool my tongue, for I am in agony in this fire." (Luke 16:23-24 NEB)

And yet, here is their eternal fate:

Then I saw a great throne and him who sat on it, from whose face the earth and the heaven fled away. And, there was found no place for them. And I saw the dead, small and great, standing before [YHWH], and books were opened. And another book was opened, which is the Book of Life. And the dead were judged according to their works, by the things which were written in the books. The sea gave up the dead who were in it, and death and Hades delivered up the dead who were in them. And they were judged, each one according to his works. Then death and Hades were cast into the lake of fire. This is the second death. And anyone not found written in the Book of Life was cast into the lake of fire. (Revelation 20:11-15 NEB)

Work

Now that we've examined this message, let us focus on another question. Are there those in our culture who have left the Church, but were never really a member to begin with? Yes, I believe there are. Messiah speaks distinctly of this group in the Book of John. In the sixth chapter Yeshua had just finished feeding "the five thousand." That same night his disciples set sail for Capernaum and Yeshua later joins them in the middle of a storm, walking on water. The next morning crowds from the feeding began to search for Yeshua.

Not finding him where they last saw him, they decided to set sail, also to Capernaum, in search of Messiah.

They found him on the other side. "Rabbi," they said "when did you come here?" [Yeshua] replied, "In very truth I know that you have come looking for me because your hunger was satisfied with the loaves you ate, not because you saw signs. You must work, not for this perishable food, but for the food that lasts, the food of eternal life." (John 6:25-27 NEB)

It is a fact that the people were in search of something authentic. It is apparent that these were needy people, and that Yeshua was aware of their needs and empathetic to them. He had fed them the night before. Readers need to pay careful attention, though, to what the people wanted and what Yeshua knew they needed; for this is where I believe the disconnect still lies today. They knew that Yeshua was capable of providing for their material needs, he had demonstrated that the night before with the miraculous feeding. The problem was that the physical was what they chose to focus on. Messiah didn't ignore it, but he knew that their spiritual hunger would never be satiated unless they began to refocus. Seeds of discontent began to sink in the moment Yeshua mentioned the word work. The words "eternal life" were perhaps a bit disconcerting as well. Why? Well, work implies that in seeking to reach the goal, one has to give up something or things to receive it. It implies sacrifice. Most notably, sacrificing time and "self." In using the word work here, Messiah was not suggesting that the helmet of salvation wasn't a gift. He was reminding, however, that once the helmet has been given, now there is work to be done. Our faithful lifestyle in loving YHWH with all of our heart, soul, and mind, and loving our neighbor as ourselves; and in carrying out the Great Commission—these are how we are adding to our plates, which we will receive when dining during our heavenly banquet. But more importantly, our future heavenly dishes are inconsequential without taking that first bite of the Bread of Life. Our faithful lifestyle is demonstrative of our daily diet of that same Bread, which never grows stale. The phrase "eternal life" implies that our goal should be centered on something other than on those temporal things of this world. Those searching for Yeshua were hoping that he would continue to meet their material needs, and that if he wasn't, at least he could show them how they could meet their own. How patient our Messiah is. Though he kept attempting to deliver spiritual truths, those searching couldn't get beyond the temporal desires.

Why did they not believe, though they had seen Yeshua work a miracle? Perhaps, it was because they already had in their minds what they wanted; a physical savior. Someone who would come and save them from their worldly turmoil under the existing political climate. They had already seen a glimpse of Messiah's physical power the night before and so had every reason to believe that this was just a preview of what was to come later. They insisted on comparing him to Moses. This only frustrated them more. Moses, after all, had shown signs, to the Israelites and Egyptians both, before physically delivering them out of Pharaoh's clutches. They didn't understand the spiritual significance of what Moses did for them. They didn't grasp that what Moses did was only a precursor to what Messiah would later come to do. The Israelites would eventually reject Messiah for the same reasons many of his followers would begin to leave him momentarily.

Shortsightedness fueled by a desire for instant gratification is what led to their departure. The problem is that instant gratification is only gratifying for an instant, though at times it seems like an eternity to our flesh—and so we indulge. Messiah, our Creator, came to satisfy our spirit, not to gratify our lower nature. Satisfying our spirit, however, is on the one hand, instantaneous at the moment of salvation. But, on the other hand, we have to keep it continuously satisfied. This is the process of sanctification through the inner-workings of the Holy Spirit, resulting in the outer-workings of the faithful believer. Everyone is intrigued with the wonders of religion; few are interested in the work which must accompany Christianity and with having a relationship with Messiah. Those who want no part in the work depart from the start. Instead, they leave in search of something more wonderful. No wonder they remain aimless. And the more truth they hear, the more they flinch and jeer.

This led to a fierce dispute among the Jews. "How can this man give us his flesh to eat?" they said. [Yeshua] replied. "In truth, in very truth I tell you, unless you eat the flesh of the Son of Man and drink his blood you can have no life in you. Whoever eats my flesh and drinks my blood possesses eternal life, and I will raise him up on the last day. My flesh is real food; my blood is real drink. Whoever eats my flesh and drinks my blood dwells continuously in me and I dwell in him. As the living Father sent me, and I live because of the Father, so he who eats me shall live because of me. This the bread which came down from heaven; and it is not like the bread which our fathers ate: they are dead, but whoever eats this bread shall live forever. This was spoken in synagogue when [Yeshua] was teaching in Capernaum. Many of his disciples on hearing it exclaimed, "This is more than we can stomach. Why listen to such talk?" (John 6:52-60 NEB)

Yeshua was relaying to his disciples that he was the incarnate Word of YHWH. He wanted them to know that the words from his mouth provided nourishment for their spirits. But, do you see how absurd it is to try and accept spiritual truths while insisting on looking through temporal lenses? That is why Yeshua told his disciples that we must worship YHWH in spirit and in truth. So those who depart from the start were never really interested in the truth to begin with, only in its temporal semblances.

[Yeshua] was aware that his disciples were murmuring about it and asked them, "Does this shock you? What if you see the Son of Man ascending to the place where he has been before? The spirit alone gives life; the flesh is of no avail; the words which I have spoken to you are both spirit and life. And yet there are some of you who have no faith." For [Yeshua] knew all along who were without faith and who was to betray him. So he said, "This is why I told you that no one can come to me unless it has been granted to him by my Father." From that time on, many of his disciples withdrew and no longer went about with him. (John 6:61-65 NEB)

There are those who are drawn to Messiah by faith, but then their faith begins to falter. Then there are those who are drawn to the belief system, but who want nothing to do with Messiah. They were never truly disciples. Their fidelity remains attached to the precepts of a religion and the self-satisfaction it brings, but it was never drawn to a relationship with the Prince. There was never any intimacy with Emmanuel, only an empty homage to a religion promoting honorable living. This is again likened much to the Apostle Paul's experiences during his missionary journeys. He would come across the curious, that is, until he began to speak to the truth about Messiah. Upon hearing about Messiah, the curious were no longer so curious. There is one account when Paul was speaking before the Court of Areopagus. Located in Athens, this court met regularly to discuss ethical, cultural, and religious matters. It was made up of members who identified themselves as Epicureans and Stoics. As such, they were deeply impressed with learning newfound philosophies—earthly erudition. The former believed that pleasure was the end of all things and that wisdom was the way to achieve it. The latter basically advocated ethical and moral living, but as a philosophy of perfection, not as a religious duty based upon a relationship with a deity—namely, YHWH. Neither believed that anything was left after death. Thus, they were interested in hearing Paul's theology, but only as a possible addition to their collection of pagan philosophies. Almost comically, when Paul began speaking of Yeshua and the resurrection, they were intrigued by the idea of these two "gods." The court and those around remained intrigued throughout Paul's theological discourse until the truth became evident. Yeshua Messiah and Resurrection were not the latest gods, the new flavors of the month. When Paul made it clear that Yeshua Messiah was the man chosen by YHWH, as the Son of YHWH, to one day judge all mankind, and that he was himself resurrected (a verb, not a proper noun) from the dead, most lost their intrigue.

When they heard about the raising of the dead, some scoffed; and others said, "We will hear you on this subject some other time." And so Paul left the assembly. (Acts 17:32-33 NEB)

But, Paul's discourse did not fall upon all deafened ears.

However, some men joined him and became believers, including Dionysius, a member of the Court of Areopagus; also a woman named Damaris, and others besides. (Acts 17:34 NEB)

Though it is not the will of Messiah or the Father, sinful human nature, coupled with the gift of freedom of choice, dictates that some will be drawn by the Truth that they hear. Most will be repelled by it and veer.

But, you simply cannot have one part:

Turning to the Jews who had believed him, [Yeshua] said, "If you dwell within the revelation I have brought, you are indeed my disciples; you shall know the truth, and the truth will set you free. (John 8:31-32 NEB)

And not the other One:

Even if your daily activities [including going to Church on Sundays or synagogue on Saturdays] are good, YHWH's grace won't be extended until your activities have ended and you have embraced his Son's helmet of salvation.

True Believers

We now turn to another important matter that needs clearing up. There are well-meaning shepherds who use Scripture to teach what I call the doctrine of "superficial salvation." This doctrine suggests that if a believer falls away from the faith, it means that they were never really saved to begin with. As just examined, there are a group of people who do indeed fall into this category. However, the majority of the faithless who fell were not fakers from the first. Let's look at a couple of verses often used and then clarify.

> My children, this is the last hour. You were told that [Anti-Messiah] was to come, and now many antichrists have appeared; which proves to us that this is indeed the last hour. They went out from our company, but never really belonged to us; if they had, they would have stayed with us. They went out, so that it might be clear that not all our company truly belong to it. You, no less than they, are among the initiated; this is the gift of the Holy One, and by it you all have knowledge. It is not because you are ignorant of the truth that I have written to you, but because you know it, and because lies, one and all, are alien to the truth. (1st John 2:18-21 NEB)

Juxtapose this text with one found in Acts, in speaking of Judas Iscariot—

> For he was one of our number and had his place in this ministry. (Acts 1:17 NEB)

How do you reconcile the two verses? First, I reiterate the truth that it is indeed possible for there to be those among the Body of Messiah who do not truly belong to the Body. As they relate to the Church, there are the temporally benign (though their spiritual plight is still severe). Then there are the temporally malignant who often appear benign, and only those with spiritual discernment from the Holy Spirit may sniff them out. These antichrists that John speaks of could refer to the malignant wolves in sheep clothing that Messiah mentions several times in the Gospels. They could also refer to members of the Body who at one time offered a genuine confession (Judas Iscariot and types like him fall into this category), and later decided to forfeit their gift. Upon their forfeiture they can either benignly continue with their disbelief (again, benign as it relates to the Body of Christ) or, like Judas Iscariot, their arrogance could induce temporal malevolence. So then how does one explain the phrase "but never really belonged to us?" Like this:

Let's say that you are on a sports team (let's call them the Sheep). One day one of the members of your team decides that he no longer wants to be on yours, but instead wants to join a rival one (we'll call them the Wolves). He leaves and so now the sheep disappointedly make the claim,

"Whatever. Who needs him anyway; he was never a real Sheep to begin with."

"Yeah," quips another, "if he had been, he wouldn't have left us."

Now, in fact, the betrayer was obviously a member of the Sheep's team at one time. If his name can be found on the roster, it would be absurd for anyone to dispute this claim, no matter how disappointed they are. Neither claim, the first nor second, contradicts John's claim, "They went out, so that it might be clear that not all our company truly belong to it." In present times it could equally be said that not all people who claim to be Christians are, in fact, genuine Christians. Whether they are among a body of believers as undercover agents of Satan's, (no matter how unconventional it sounds—these are the wolves in sheep clothing), or are interested in blending in with the world as a cultural Christian, there will come a time in the near future when the one Truth will sound loud and clear and the dark clouds are removed. (Currently it is easy for the wolf and the worldly to blend in, with so many denominations having bits of the Truth among them here and there.) Then the genuine, committed believer will follow in rank and file. The posers will detest the Truth they hear, shirk the light that can be seen, and flee into darkness where they are more comfortable. One was never a believer to begin with; the other was only half-spirited. Neither truly belonged to the company. Think about the student at the high school football game who remains seated; calmly clapping, while everyone else stands up shouting uproariously at the game-winning touchdown. Is that student really a true blue fan? Chances are they won't be going to many more football games, if any more.

Shepherds need to ensure that when delivering the hopeful message of eternal security, they are taking care to deliver it in its strictest sense, what some might coin the "conservative view." (I use liberal and conservative only as already established terms. I don't really like either word; as I believe they create division.) What I mean is that Paul, in the Epistles, was appropriately relieving any anxiety that a believer might have in questioning his sure footing in his faith. A stumble here or there, due to growing pangs associated with working out our sanctification, in no way implies that a believer is in danger of forfeiting his gift. The broadest view, or the more "liberal" interpretation, should be avoided at all cost: the idea that someone who chooses to leave the road altogether, either hasn't really left or that he was somehow never on the road to begin with. While such efforts genuinely try to reconcile a conundrum, it is unnecessary, and may lead to unintentional snobbery on the part of those still on the road. At worse, if left unqualified, it might result in a dangerous blurring, so that the believer no longer is able to clearly distinguish between the narrow road to Glory and the broader dead-end road leading to the grave, and the expectations that Messiah has for those who choose to remain on the former.

A different Gospel

One final example of how a believer can begin wearing their helmet of salvation, but then at some point in their journey no longer have it on, is as follows: They can renounce their title by accepting what Paul calls, "a different gospel." These are people who come to know the Truth, accept the Truth, and even live the Truth. That is, until someone comes along with their own version of the truth. Paul cautioned many early, sincere converts, who were in danger of renouncing their title, though they didn't know it. In particular, there were Gentile converts in the Galatian churches who were becoming befuddled in their beliefs because of Judaizers, the Jewish converts who were preaching that salvation was only really possible if the Gentiles came to obey the Torah, which included getting circumcised. They were preaching a genuine conversion by way of keeping the commandments; directly antipodal to the Gospel of Messiah. Here is what Paul had to say to those who were beginning to believe:

> Mark my words: I, Paul, say to you that if you receive circumcision [Messiah] will do you no good at all. Once again, you can take it from me that every man who receives circumcision is under obligation to keep the entire law. When you seek to be justified by way of law, your relation with [Messiah] is completely severed: you have fallen out of the domain of [YHWH]'s grace. For to us, our hope of attaining that righteousness which we eagerly await is the work of the Spirit through faith. If we are in union with [Yeshua] circumcision makes no difference at all, nor does the want of it; the only thing that counts is faith active in love. (Galatians 5:2-6 NEB)

Paul couldn't have used clearer language. There is no reason why any shepherd should be teaching "once saved always saved," when the words "your relation with Messiah is completely severed: you have fallen out of the domain of YHWH's grace," are plain. In other words, for those who came to genuinely accept Messiah at one point in their life, but then decided to accept another gospel which contradicts what the true Gospel says, the consequences are clear: you have renounced your title, and by default, removed your helmet of salvation. This is why it is dangerous for a sincere convert, although perhaps unbeknown to themselves, to begin listening and accepting additional doctrine that falls outside the message of Messiah's Gospel. Thankfully, because of YHWH's sovereignty and his grace, the message of the Gospel has remained intact, despite the rest of his word becoming tainted by the hands of unscrupulous men, armed with their own selfish agenda.

Encouragement

You were running well; who was it that hindered you from following the truth? Whatever persuasion he used, it did not come from [YHWH] who is calling you; "a little leaven," remember, "leavens all the dough. " United with you in [Yeshua], I am confident that you will not take the wrong view; but the man who is unsettling your minds, whoever he may be, must bear [YHWH]'s judgment. (Galatians 5:7-10 NEB)

Paul is using the words of Messiah who gave this same warning to his disciples after feeding the multitude. Then he was speaking of Pharisees and Sadducees; here Paul is speaking of any self-appointed "message giver" who happens to identify himself with the faith. Remember that Paul is speaking specifically of the Judaizers. The Judaizers claim membership into the Body of Messiah—the Pharisees and Sadducees don't. Almost like two book-ends, believers are warned from accepting any foul religious doctrines, no matter whom they come from, whether from outside or within the faith. It is a high call to consistent spiritual discernment, through the indwelling Holy Spirit. It is important to note that Paul's union with Yeshua and his confidence, in no way permanently seals the deal for the converts in question. It is similar to his message to the Philippians.

Of one thing I am certain: the One who started the good work in you will bring it to completion by the Day of [Yeshua]. (Philippians 1:6 NEB)

Paul is certain that the God who graciously showed them the road to Glory, and graciously extended the invitation to step onto (and provided the means to do so), will continue with his graciousness until Messiah returns; as long as the believer remains on the road.

May [YHWH] himself, the God of peace, make you holy in every part, and keep you sound in spirit, soul, and body, without fault when [Yeshua] comes. He who calls you is to be trusted; he will do it. (1st Thessalonians 5:23-24 NEB)

In both passages Paul is using encouraging words. And in his letter to the Thessalonians he even offers up a prayer, of which YHWH certainly heard and honored (yet, YHWH isn't going to keep anyone who isn't interested in being kept, and who demonstrates such disinterest by their consistent disobedience to his Son; YHWH's grace does not override man's freewill; it does powerfully remind man of his new nature in Messiah.) But, Paul can't know with certainty, the course of action that the Galatian converts will choose to take in the future, regarding this leaven. I would submit that if he wasn't concerned about the converts possibly accepting the leaven, leading to inadvertent apostasy, then he never would have written the letter to begin with. It is because of the unassuming and indirect nature of the possible apostasy that Paul is writing with such fervency. These converts are not consciously choosing to reject the gospel of Messiah and thus making the deliberate choice to fall from the faith. Nevertheless, by deliberately accepting a false gospel—like an unwelcomed appendage that places additional truths onto the Truth—they have fallen away from the true faith by default. Paul concludes, and Messiah confirms, that their acting without spiritual discernment makes it their fault. Thus, there are consequences for them, as well as for those who are spreading and legitimizing the leaven. It is not a harsh or unfair judgment for those who might be unaware. Rather it is a letter encouraging all converts to take their faith seriously; to desist with cavalier Christian living; and to instead, strive towards spiritual maturity; for it is indeed a matter of life or death.

Reverts

> My brothers, if one of your number should stray from the truth and another succeed in bringing him back, be sure of this: any man who brings a sinner back from his crooked ways will be rescuing his soul from death and cancelling innumerable sins. (James 5:19-20 NEB)

To whom is James writing? Converts. Like Paul and Peter, James is not writing to an unbelieving audience. In this verse James calls his audience, his brothers. He is acknowledging their familial status as children of YHWH, and as brothers of Messiah. First, his final words establish the fact that it is possible for any genuine convert to revert back to a convict. He doesn't say, "if one of your number, who wasn't really one of your number to begin with..." Second, James acknowledges that while other believers have the responsibility of redirecting the "revert" back to repentance, they may not be successful—"should [they] stray from the truth and another succeed in bringing him back..." In other words, there is a 50/50 chance. Messiah only expects effort on the part of the seasoned convert. The responsibility of repenting and returning is on the one who reverts. If he who reverts fails to re-convert before his earthly death, or before Messiah returns, then he shall receive the same sentence as any other descriptive sinner. As mentioned in the book of Ezekiel, his former righteousness will not save him from eternal retribution. There's another book that contains strong admonition to believers to avoid falling from the faith and to continue in their saintly perseverance, the book of Hebrews.

> See to it, brothers, that no one among you has the wicked, faithless heart of a deserter from the living [YHWH]; but day by day, while the word "Today" still sounds in your ears, encourage one another, so that no one of you is made stubborn by the wiles of sin. For we have become [Messiah's] partners if only we keep our original confidence firm to the end. (Hebrews 3:12-14 NEB)

The words could not be any plainer. The author of Hebrews is addressing an audience of converts, and he is encouraging them to watch out for the spiritual welfare of their fellow converts, as members of the same family that we are. The warning would not sound if it wasn't warranted. There is no reason to believe that any author of the Scriptures would waste time delving into hypothetical scenarios. There is a sense of urgency that rings in all the B'rit Khadasha books. And unlike many present-day shepherds, these architects did not teach their flock that the God of the B'rit Khadasha deals with his children in a different fashion then the God of the Tanakh.

> When Scriptures says, "Today if you hear his voice, do not grow stubborn as in those days of rebellion." who, I ask, were those who heard and rebelled? All those, surely, whom Moses had led out of Egypt. And with whom was

[YHWH] indignant for forty years? With those, surely who had sinned, whose bodies lay where they fell in the desert. And to whom did he vow that they should not enter his rest, if not those who had refused to believe? We perceive that it was unbelief which prevented their entering. (Hebrews 3:15-19 NEB)

I must keep reiterating that the author of Hebrews is speaking to a group of converts. Readers, especially shepherds, fail to acknowledge this point, and thus, Scripture gets distorted. He is recalling an event in the Tanakh when the Hebrews, whom Moses delivered from Egypt, begin to persist in sin. The consequence for their persistence was death. Let us compare. Messiah delivered us from spiritual Egypt, that is, our former life of bondage and sin. In looking at verse 14 again we see these words: "For we have become Messiah's partners if only we keep our original confidence firm to the end."

This is a conditional statement. "If. . . then." Not just that, but it contains the word "only." The strength of the passage implies that the single verse could easily read, "if and only if." Such an assertion carries a necessary condition, rather than a sufficient one. In other words, if we are to maintain our partnership with Messiah, then we must keep our original confidence (the same confidence that we held when we first accepted Messiah's gift of salvation—there is no other way). Because it is a necessary condition, rather than a sufficient one, if the claim is not true, then the condition is unmet. If we do not have the original confidence we had, we no longer maintain a partnership with Messiah. It has become severed. Those guilty are no longer safe from judgment. The confidence the Hebrews had in YHWH upon their initial deliverance from Egypt was not maintained. Thus, among some persistent complaints, accusations, and sinful behavior, discipline was carried out. YHWH vowed that those who had refused to believe would not enter his rest; they would not enter the promise land. Many shepherds, mistakenly, solely teach of a restrictive disbelief. By restrictive, I mean they only admonish those who currently are outside of Messiah's fold. To them, disbelief is limited to those who are atheist or agnostic. Truthfully, those who have never accepted Messiah are unbelievers. Messiah and the other architects of the Christian faith, on the other hand, espoused a definition that was more inclusive. Unbelievers are also those who have come to accept Messiah and yet also choose to walk in disobedience. They show their disbelief in Messiah by disobeying his Gospel and his commandments. The author of Hebrews is attempting to illustrate the correlation between the Tanakh and B'rit Khadasha with the behaviors of those who lived under the former and those who currently live under the latter. We live under the latter. All of Messiah's shepherds must accept the fact that under the New Covenant, just because the conditions for attaining righteousness was altered, and just because the invitation to obtaining was broadened, it doesn't mean that the requirements for sustaining it were changed. They weren't. Neither were the consequences for failing to live it. It's easy to see why many theologians contend that the Apostle Paul was the author of Hebrews. The same recalling of the Tanakh to B'rit Khadasha converts is made by him when writing to the Church in Corinth, with the same warning.

You should understand, my brothers, that our ancestors were all under the pillar of cloud, and all of them passed through the Red Sea; and so they all received baptism into the fellowship of Moses in cloud and sea. They all ate the same supernatural food, and all drank the same supernatural drink; I mean, they all drank from the supernatural rock that accompanied their travels—and that rock was [Messiah]. And yet, most of them were not accepted by [YHWH], for the desert was strewn with the corpses. These events happened as symbols to warn us not to set our desires on evil things, as they did. Do not be idolaters, like some of them; as Scripture has it, "The people sat down to feast and rose up to revel. Let us not commit fornication, as some of them did—and twenty-three thousand died in one day. Let us not put the power of [Messiah] to the test, as some of them did—and were destroyed by serpents. Do not grumble against [YHWH], as some of them did—and were destroyed by the Destroyer. All these things that happened to them were symbolic, and were recorded for our benefit as a warning. For upon us the fulfillment of the ages has come. If you feel sure that you are standing firm, beware. You may fall." (1st Corinthians 10:1-12 NEB)

Evidence for the inclusive definition of disbelief can be found as we continue to chapter four of Hebrews.

Therefore we must have before us the fear that while the promise of entering his rest remains open, one or another among you should be found to have missed his chance. (Hebrews 4:1 NEB)

Here is a plea for converts to resist cavalier Christianity. There is similarity between the messages in verse 12 of 1st Corinthians, chapter 10 and verse 1 of Hebrews chapter 4. No genuine convert is above apostasy. Those who believe they are need to make sure that such confidence is rooted in their consistent commitment to Messiah, as Messiah is committed to them.

Insincere belief

For indeed we have heard the good news, as they did. But in them the message they heard did no good, because they brought no added mixture of faith to the hearing of it. (Hebrews 4:2 NEB)

Notice where the blame lies. The Israelites heard the good news—Moses told them. They accepted it—they left Egypt, but it did them little good. Why? Because they brought "no added mixture of faith to the hearing of it." They had faith enough to believe Moses. However, they did not continue in their faith; the faith necessary to sustain them in the desert. The author of Hebrews makes the comparison to his converted audience. They also heard the Good News and had faith enough to accept it. The same grace afforded to the Israelites in Egypt who fled, was strengthened when given to the ex-convicts who converted. We are graciously given the faith by YHWH to accept the Gospel. Of course, we still have to choose to accept it and then to act upon it. For he who call us, also enables us to respond, but he doesn't force us to. Again when we were created, we were equally enabled to resist. The expectation was for us not to do so. Now the author is imploring the converts to distinguish themselves from the Israelites by bringing with them, the faith to follow through. This is what the Israelites failed to do. It is not YHWH's responsibility, but the Christian's. YHWH will provide the faith needed to remain faithful. It is the believer who must inquire to acquire. And still yet, it is the believer who must yield—daily. Christianity is a relationship and Christians must stop arrogantly expecting YHWH to do all the work. Messiah did his job on the cross and graces us with the gift to live. He also promises to give all who are weary, rest. Yet, I grant that few Christians these days are deserving of any rest, because few have actually been doing any work. Those strewn in the desert never entered YHWH's rest because of their lifestyle of unbelief, though they had one time believed. We who are Christians eagerly await the chance to enter YHWH's rest. Messiah will return one day soon and those who have earned it will enter. Earned? Yes. We receive YHWH's gift of salvation, undeserved and unearned.

Work out your own salvation

However, Paul and Peter both reminded the early converts that it was their job to work out their salvation.

So you too, my friends, must be obedient, as always; even more, now that I am away, than when I was with you. You must work out your own salvation in fear and trembling; for it is [YHWH] who works in you, inspiring both the will and the deed, for his own chosen purpose. (Philippians 2:12-13 NEB)

The work that we shall rest from is the natural weariness which abounds from following Messiah. To the grateful, his work is not drudgery, but it can be both spiritually and physically draining. There is no shame or condemnation in admitting such. What work do we speak of? Spreading the Gospel, enlarging the Kingdom, feeding the poor, caring for the abused, orphaned and widowed, visiting the invalid and incarcerated, speaking out against injustice, consistently resisting fleshly temptation, engaging in spiritual warfare, persevering amidst persecution...to name a few. And yet, if as a believer, your weariness abounds not from working for YHWH's household, but solely for your own, then a personal spiritual inventory is in order. Paul reminds us that YHWH works in us. He inspires, and yet the perspiring must come from us.

Let us then make every effort to enter that rest, so that no one may fall by following this evil example of unbelief. (Hebrews 4:11 NEB)

After reminding the converts of what happened to their elders, the author of Hebrews warns them not to follow in step. He has vividly described but a single shade of unbelief and then warns the converts not to paint in the same shade if they are interested in seeing Heaven and all its glorious splendor.

Since therefore we have a great high priest who has passed through the heavens, [Yeshua] the Son of [YHWH], let us hold fast to the religion we profess. For ours is not a high priest unable to sympathize with our weakness, but one who, because of his likeness to us, has been tested every way, only without sin. Let us therefore boldly approach the throne of our gracious [YHWH], where we may receive mercy and in his grace find timely help. (Hebrews 4:14-16 NEB)

And here is the marker of a great architect, and a model that every shepherd should emulate when pasturing their flock. The author of Hebrews ends the chapter by once again encouraging the converts to remain converted, but he doesn't just end there. He acknowledges that it will not be an easy feat; indeed, it is going to be work.

Messiah's humanity

The writer of Hebrews also reminds converts of Messiah's humanity; an important fact that many shepherds neglect to effectively articulate. For the Believer, Messiah's humanity is every bit as significant as is his Deity. Shepherds do not do their sheep, nor Messiah, any favors by focusing exclusively on the Divinity of our Savior. Yes, his Divinity prior to his birth is relevant; none should cease from sounding this truth. However, Believers would relish a relationship with Messiah more if they could relate to him more. Messiah wants them to. Not only that, but Believers must always remember that Yeshua Messiah, though he sinned not, had the seed of sin within him. Messiah had the ability to sin, and wrestled with the seed just like the rest of us. Messiah was descriptively sinless from birth until death, but he shared our sinful condition. To proclaim this truth is not to degrade Messiah's Divinity. His sinful condition detracts not an iota from his title as the Son of YHWH. Denying it, however, does cheapen his connection as the Son of Man. To suggest that he was only like us because he wore skin is silly. How could Messiah have been tested if he didn't have the ability to fail? What kind of test is that? Yeshua was the perfect sacrifice on the cross, not because of his Deity, but because of his consistent decision, despite being tested, of never becoming a descriptive sinner. The Father knows what we personally go through everyday, because the Son knows. He has been there. Because he has walked the same road, he knows the help that we are going to need in order to hold fast to our religion. We need his and the Father's grace. We also need the Father's gracious gift in the Holy Spirit actively working through us. The Holy Spirit wasn't just sent to seal and to remain dormant; though that is what the majority of converts have come to believe. That is what they have been taught.

In the days of his earthly life he offered up prayers and petitions, with loud cries and tears, to [YHWH] who was able to deliver him from the grave. Because of his humble submission his prayer was heard: son though he was, he learned obedience in the school of suffering, and, once perfected, became the source of eternal salvation for all who obey him, named by [YHWH] high priest in the succession of Melchizedek. (Hebrews 5:7-10 NEB)

What was this school of suffering the author of Hebrews is referring to? It did include the hours he spent in agony on the cross. However, while horrific in every detail, his school of suffering extended well beyond his trial and death. Any man could have been betrayed by loyal followers, given over to the local authorities while offering no resistance, accepted a death sentence, and died a humiliating death, though he committed no crime. Though admirable, it wouldn't have been unique. Messiah simply would have been a martyr for a worthy cause, as his disciples would indeed follow. What made Messiah worthy of his high priesthood was the years he spent in the school of suffering.

For years Messiah suffered with the same seed of sin that the rest of humanity has suffered with ever since the original fall. Every single time Yeshua was presented with the opportunity to sin and he chose not to, he was perfecting his obedience to the Father. Where there is no struggle, there is no suffering. If Yeshua simply dismissed every sinful advance because there was no seed attracted to it, if there was never a struggle between his flesh and his Spirit, what suffering ensued? Messiah did not have some supernatural magnetic force around him while he walked to deflect sinful advances. He did perpetually carry his shield of faith. Moreover, what was Satan appealing to in the desert when he tried to get Messiah to disobey his Father, if not the same fleshy seed that he and his kingdom regularly appeals to when tempting the rest of us? His obedience was perfected in his final seconds as a student enrolled in the school of suffering. Again, to suggest that Messiah only enrolled in this school for a few hours, though excruciating, and that they were enough to promote him to high priesthood, fails to make Messiah indistinguishable from many of his devout followers, who were also dealt a deathly blow. Messiah's lifetime commitment to remain descriptively sinless puts him in a class all by himself. After dying on the cross, he graduated with honors. He is currently using the education to strengthen his disciples during their time on earth.

Die to the seed of sin

We know that [Messiah], once raised from the dead, is never to die again: he is no longer under the dominion of death. For in dying as he did, he died to sin, once for all, and in living as he lives, he lives to [YHWH]. In the same way you must regard yourselves as dead to sin and alive to [YHWH], in union with [Yeshua]. (Romans 6:9-11 NEB)

The sin that Paul is referring to here is the seed of sin. Messiah died to the seed of sin when he died on the cross. The seed of sin only reigns in the body as long as death itself does. Messiah, though the Son of YHWH he was, made himself answerable to death while in the form of man. So when Messiah died on the cross, by default, he also died to sin. This is the connection Paul is trying to make with believers. Though the seed of sin still remains within (hence we are all still subject to physical death, as a consequence), in accepting YHWH's gift of salvation, we claim to have died with him; that is, we shared in his death spiritually. Now with our new lives, the seed of sin should no longer reign in us either. The seed itself will still remain until our salvation is completed when Messiah returns, but it should no longer reign. Where the seed of sin once reigned, should now be the Holy Spirit's domain.

But [YHWH] be thanked, you, who once were slaves of sin, have yielded whole-hearted obedience to the pattern of teaching to which you were made subject, and, emancipated from sin, have become slaves of righteousness (to use words that suit your human weakness)—I mean, as you once yielded your bodies to the service of impurity and lawlessness, making for moral anarchy, so now you must yield them to the service of righteousness, making for a holy life. (Romans 6:17-19 NEB)

Here's yet another one:

What the law could never do, because our lower nature robbed it of all potency. [YHWH] has done: by sending his own Son in a form like that of our own sinful nature, and as a sacrifice for sin, he has passed judgment against sin within that very nature, so that the commandment of the law may find fulfillment in us, whose conduct, no longer under the control of our lower nature, is directed by the Spirit. (Romans 8:3-4 NEB)

The Law, itself holy, was designed to lead the Israelites to a life of holiness. But, it was impossible because of the strength of our lower nature, imprisoned by the seed of sin. Messiah was sent to share our sinful condition, so that he could offer himself as the ultimate sacrifice. Yet, he was only acceptable because of his descriptively sinless lifestyle—from birth to death. Only now is the Law able to do what it was originally designed to do: Leading believers to a life of holiness through obedience to its precepts, the same precepts that Messiah commanded.

Do not suppose that I have come to abolish the Law and the prophets; I did not come to abolish, but to complete. (Matthew 5:17 NEB)

...that by two immutable things, in which it is impossible for [YHWH] to lie, we might have strong consolation, who have fled for refuge to lay hold of the hope set before us. This hope we have as an anchor of the soul, both sure and steadfast, and which enters the Presence behind the veil... (Hebrews 6:18-19 NEB)

True enough. Those who have chosen to grasp that hope through Messiah will continuously receive encouragement from YHWH, through the Holy Spirit, to continue grasping it. As long as we continue with our grasp we are "safe and sure." Conversely, at the moment any choose to release their hold, they are no longer "safe and sure." Only their repentance will return them to their grasp. Shepherds must desist with teaching that although one may release, they are still safe; they are not.

But the priesthood which [Yeshua] holds is perpetual, because he remains for ever. That is why he is also able to save absolutely those who approach

[YHWH] through him; he is always living to plead on their behalf. Such a high priest does indeed fit our condition—devout, guileless, undefiled, separated from sinners, raised high above the heavens. He has no need to offer sacrifices daily, as the high priests do, first for his own sins and then for those of the people; for this he did once and for all when he offered up himself. (Hebrews 7:24-27 NEB)

The author of Hebrews recognizes that Yeshua is able to save absolutely, "those who approach YHWH through him." This sounds like an open invitation. The text does not read, "only those who YHWH previously selected to approach him, through him." Messiah is characterized as flawless—he is. Some might be tempted to suggest that the word "undefiled" must mean that Messiah, in fact, did not possess the seed of sin. That's not what the word "defiled" is referring to here. Defiled is referring to the rest of us who engaged in sinful behavior prior to accepting Christ; behavior that Messiah never engaged in, so he remained undefiled from birth to death. Under the Old Covenant, high priests had to offer sacrifices for themselves and the people, not because of their condition, but because of their behavior. The Law brought attention to the egregious acts of YHWH's children:

Law intruded into this process to multiply law-breaking. But where sin was thus multiplied, grace immeasurably exceeded it. (Romans 5:20 NEB)

Paul is essentially spelling out the conditions which led to the Israelites developing a lifestyle of sinful behavior. YHWH knew that the Israelites were not going to be able to keep the Law, which is why he provided for the expiation of their sins through the high priests. It is the seed of sin which is attracted to the perversion or absence of all that YHWH says is good. The seed of sin sets itself against holiness; the standard established in the Law. Prior to the Law, the seed of sin sat sulking and bored. But when Moses introduced the Law to the Israelites, for the seed of sin, it was like a devious child being let loose at a candy store. The Law is not to blame for the Israelites disobedience. Rather, the blame lies within. Just because the Law provided the opportunity for the seed of sin to act, it was still the Israelites' choice to act upon their seed's urging. Thus the high priest worked on behalf of the Israelites sins, not the seed producing them. Messiah had the same urging, but Messiah never responded favorably to the seed. That's what makes him fit to intercede on behalf of all humanity.

And therefore he is the mediator of a New Covenant, or testament, under which, now that there has been a death to bring deliverance from sins committed under the former covenant, those whom [YHWH] has called may receive the promise of the eternal inheritance. (Hebrews 9:15 NEB)

We have already established the fact that "those whom YHWH has called" is everyone. The word "only" (the adverb of exclusivity) is not used in the passage.

For if we persist in sin after receiving the knowledge of the truth, no sacrifice for sins remains: only a terrifying expectation of judgment and a fierce fire which will consume [YHWH]'s enemies. If a man disregards the Law of Moses, he is put to death without pity on the evidence of two or three witnesses. Think how much more sever a penalty the man will deserve who has trampled under foot the Son of [YHWH], profaned the blood of the covenant by which he was consecrated, and affronted [YHWH]'s gracious Spirit. For we know who it is that has said, "Justice is mine: I will repay. " and again, "[Yeshua] will judge his people." It is a terrible thing to fall into the hands of the living [YHWH]. (Hebrews 10:26-31 NEB)

There is no reason for the author of Hebrews to issue a warning against engaging in a particular behavior if it weren't possible to do so. An unrepentant revert profanes the blood of the covenant, shed by Messiah, by returning to the lifestyle of bondage that Messiah freed him from, and that Messiah intended him to remain free from. The fact that he has the ability to remain free from his former fetters because of the newly indwelling Holy Spirit, as well as the Father's grace, are three distinct feature of the New Covenant. Features that were, on the whole, absent from the old one. To deny that the Holy Spirit is powerful enough to keep a yielding convert perpetually free until Messiah's return, is blasphemous. This is one of the reasons the Spirit was sent in the first place. I believe that YHWH takes issue with anyone calling him a liar through his selfish disregard for his expectations and through ignoring the Father's gracious gift. The revert also sets a bad precedence for any future convert who doesn't yet understand what freedom means, but who is consistently eyeing all those who profess to be free, and in whose name.

Remain Faithful

But recall the former days in which, after you were illuminated, you endured a great struggle with sufferings: partly while you were made a spectacle both by reproaches and tribulations, and partly while you became companions of those who were so treated; for you had compassion on me in my chains, and joyfully accepted the plundering of your goods, knowing that you have a better and an enduring possession for yourselves in heaven. Therefore do not cast away your confidence, which has great reward. For you have need of endurance, so that after you have done the will of [YHWH], you may receive the promise: "For yet a little while, and he who is coming will come and will not tarry. Now the just shall live by faith; but if anyone draws back, my soul has no pleasure in him." But we are not of those who draw back to perdition, but of those who believe to the saving of the soul. (Hebrews 10:32-39 NKJV)

Remaining consistent with the same encouraging theme, the author of Hebrews concludes this chapter by urging the converts to continue with the enthusiasm they had when they first converted; a message that still needs sounding among the Body of Messiah. Unlike the majority of members in America's Church today, these followers of Messiah knew what it was like to suffer for their faith and yet they had remained faithful to this point. This is why the author is confident that the converts would remain converted. There is nothing that compares to having your faith tested than passing through fire. If you can remain sincere after having been singed then you're in good standing. Nonetheless, being singed doesn't guarantee your security. Successfully singed believers still have to make the choice to remain faithful. In remaining faithful until Messiah's return, the convert will receive his eternal reward. Even after remaining faithful through fire, if after passing through, the convert decides to revert without repenting then he, too, will receive no reward. The last line is a reassuring one, based perhaps on his knowledge of their past persecution, and their persistence in the midst. It is not, however, an unalterable fact. It can't be because the author knows nothing of their future circumstances, nor of the future choices they will make in response to those circumstances. I conclude again by asserting that we will be judged by the faith we demonstrate daily. Our faith of yesterday stands on its own merit, as does our faith exercised today, and the faith we had better exercise tomorrow.

Discipling

There can be no other foundation beyond that which is already laid; I mean [Yeshua] himself. If anyone builds on that foundation with gold, silver, and fine stone, or with wood, hay, and straw, the work that each man does will at last be brought to light; the day of judgment will expose it. For that day dawns in fire, and the fire will test the worth of each man's work. If a man's building stands, he will be rewarded; if it burns, he will have to bear the loss; and yet he will escape with his life, as one might from a fire. (1st Corinthians 3:11-15 NKJV)

Part of the foundation laid by Messiah was proper discipleship. Messiah led by example and prepared his disciples for what was to come. Believers everywhere have been commissioned by Messiah to make disciples unto all nations. Each convict that comes our way is a like a pile of rubble ready to be built. When the convict is saved by the Messiah, he is ready for building; his foundation has already been laid and sealed. Discipling is the art of building and the Bible is our manual. Messiah expects his experienced carpenters and other tradesmen to help erect that building. If the building suddenly comes crumbling to the ground due to adverse circumstances through indifferent workers, if that building remains on the ground before Messiah returns, more than one worker will answer to the Architect. Thus, while the doctrine coined, "perseverance of the saints" mustn't persevere among the saints any longer, all saints everywhere must persist in working out their salvation until they reach the gates of Glory.

We turn now to other dastardly doctrines rampant among some denominations, while thankfully absent among others. Though, as long as any member within the Body of Messiah either teaches or accepts such foolery, the Bride is still unready for her Groom's return. "Unconditional election" and "irresistible grace," as they are popularly referred, ring of reverence, but they still reek. When taking the piece-meal approach to Scripture, it is understandable how many will find evidence to support these religious ideologies.

Nonetheless, Messiah never intended for his words to be taken in pieces, as if his disciples were partaking in a buffet. The slices used to support, when placed in context of the whole Bible and the message of the Gospel, continue to look thin. Those who choose to digest will remain hungry for the truth. If shepherds would spend less time defending man-made doctrine, they would have the additional time needed to properly disciple Messiah's sheep. Like the "perseverance of the saints," the unconditional election and irresistible grace doctrines both threaten the stability of the helmet of salvation. But even among those member's whose own helmet remain securely fastened, in spite of their adherence to these doctrines, failure to disregard them will leave believers with a distorted view of the Gospel and of their God.

Appendix B: Unconditional Election

All Men are Depraved

It is true indeed that YHWH's decision to save has nothing to do with man's condition prior to his conversion. For we all accept that all men are depraved and spiritually dead before accepting Messiah as Lord and King.

What then? Are we Jews any better off? No, not at all. For we have already [drawn up the accusation] that Jews and Greeks alike are all under the power of sin. This has scriptural warrant: "There is no just man, not one; no one understands, no one who seeks [YHWH]. All have swerved aside, all alike have become debased; there is no one to show kindness; no, not one, no one who understands, no one who seeks [YHWH]. Their throat is an open grave, they use their tongues for treachery, adder's venom on their lips, and their mouths is full of bitter curses. Their feet hasten to shed blood, ruin and misery lie along their paths, they are strangers to the high-road of peace, and reverence for [YHWH] does not enter their thoughts. (Romans 3:9-18 NEB)

But now, quite independently of law, [YHWH]'s justice has been brought to light. The Law and the prophets both bear witness to it: it is [YHWH]'s way of righting wrong, effective through faith in [Messiah] for all who have such faith—all, without distinction. For all alike have sinned, and are deprived of the divine splendor, and all are justified by [YHWH]'s free grace alone, through his act of liberation in the person of [Yeshua]. (Romans 3:21-24 NEB)

Even for a just man one of us would hardly die, though perhaps for a good man one might actually brave death; but [Messiah] died for us while we were yet sinners, and that is [YHWH]'s own proof of his love towards us. (Romans 5:7-8 NEB)

Mark what follows. It was through one man that sin entered the world, and through sin death, and thus death pervaded the whole human race, inasmuch as all men have sinned. (Romans 5:12 NEB)

Time was when you were dead in your sins and wickedness, when you followed the evil ways of this present age, when you obeyed the commander of the spiritual powers of the air, the spirit now at work among [YHWH]'s rebel subjects. We too were of their number: we all lived our lives in sensuality, and obeyed the promptings of our own instincts and notions. In our natural condition we, like the rest, lay under the dreadful judgment of [YHWH]. But [YHWH], rich in mercy, for the great love he bore us, brought us to life with [Messiah] even when we were dead in our sins; it is by his grace you are saved. (Ephesians 2:1-5 NEB)

Formerly you were yourselves estranged from [YHWH], you were his enemies in heart and mind, and your deeds were evil. (Colossians 1:21 NEB)

No Room for Boasting

As Paul continues to declare in the epistles, no one has any room for boasting. While the world will continuously make distinctions in man, placing some on pedestals, while viewing others as pedestrian, YHWH has never and will never. Still, I believe there are conditions to being elected. The only distinction that YHWH routinely makes among men are those who have been adopted into his household by professing his Son, Yeshua Messiah, as their Lord and Savior, and those who are still lost. But whether lost or found, all began beneath the ground.

There are two popular B'rit Khadasha passages often used by shepherds to defend the doctrine of unconditional election:

Tell me now, you who are so anxious to be under the law, will you not listen to what [Yeshua] says? It is written there that Abraham had two sons, one by his slave and the other by his free-born wife. The slave-woman's son was born in the course of nature, the free woman's through [YHWH]'s promise. This is an allegory. The two women stand for two covenants. The one bearing children into slavery is the covenant that comes from Mount Sinai: that is Hagar. Sinai is the mountain in Arabia and it represents the Jerusalem of today, for she and her children are in slavery. But the heavenly Jerusalem is the free woman: she is our mother. For Scripture says, "Rejoice, barren woman who never bore child, break into a shout of joy, you who never knew a mother's pangs; for the deserted wife shall have more children than she who lives with the husband." And you, my brothers, like Isaac, are children of [YHWH]'s promise. But just as in those days the natural-born son persecuted the spiritual son, so it is today. But what does Scripture say? "Drive out the slave-woman and her son, for the son of the slave shall not share the inheritance with the free woman's son." You see, then, my brothers, we are no slave-woman's children. Our mother is the free woman. [Messiah] set us free, to be free men. Stand firm, then, and refuse to be tied to the yoke of slavery again. (Galatians 4:21-5:1 NEB)

It is impossible that the word of [YHWH] should have proved false. For not all descendants of Israel are truly Israel, nor, because they are Abraham's offspring, are they all his true children; but, in the words of Scripture, "Through the line of Isaac your descendants shall be traced." That is to say, it is not those born in the course of nature who are children of [YHWH]; it is the children born through [YHWH]'s promise who are reckoned as Abraham's descendants. For the promise runs: "At the time fixed I will come, and Sarah shall have a son." But that is not all, for Rebekah's children had one and the same father, our ancestor Isaac; and yet, in order that [YHWH's] selective purpose might stand, based not upon men's deeds but upon the call of [YHWH], she was told, even before they were born, when they had as yet done nothing, good or ill, "The elder shall be servant to the younger." and that accords with the text of Scripture, "Jacob I loved and Esau I rejected." (Romans 9:6-13 NEB)

Abel, but not Cain. Shem, but not Ham or Japheth. Abraham, but not Nahor or Haran. Sarah and not Hagar, Isaac and not Ishmael, Jacob and not Esau. This selected sibling motif (Sarah and Hagar were not siblings) is a recurring one throughout the Tanakh. It is but one example of how and why the Tanakh is a significant part of the Believing experience. And why more shepherds should spend time teaching from it. For some time now the selected sibling motif has been used by many to prove that YHWH, in fact, chooses some and not others. These passages in Galatians and Romans speak to the same truth: YHWH decided from the beginning, that only certain ones would become beneficiaries of a New Covenant and others would not. In Galatians Paul states that only Sarah's offspring and not Hagar's would become the beneficiary. Likewise, in Romans we find that only Jacob's offspring would benefit and not Esau's, for YHWH rejected Esau. So it proves that some are elected and others are not, right? Or so the story goes. Wrong. But then again, right.

Remember that Paul says in Galatians that the Sarah/Hagar comparison, while a true story, is also an allegory. He uses these two women specifically because he's trying to remind the Gentile converts that adherence to the Old Covenant (represented by the slave-girl Hagar), by following the Torah as a means of obtaining righteousness, means bondage. Conversely, Sarah, the mother of Isaac, who would become the father of Jacob, who would become Israel and found a new nation, represents freedom. It is through the lineage of Isaac, through Jacob, that Yeshua Messiah would be born from the tribe of Judah, a son of Jacob. Paul reminds the converts that animosity did exist between the siblings, struggles did ensue. However, just as Hagar and her son were driven out after the birth of Isaac, so must today's believers drive out the slave-girl and her son.

Ask, Seek, and Knock

And so I say to you, ask, and you will receive; seek; and you will find; knock, and the door will be opened. For everyone who asks receives, he who seeks finds, and to him who knocks, the door will be opened. Is there a father among you who will offer his son a snake when he asks for fish, or a scorpion when he asks for an egg? If you, then, bad as you are, know how to give your children what is good for them, how much more will the heavenly Father give the Holy Spirit to those who ask him. (Luke 11:9-13 NEB)

To prove that you are sons, [YHWH] has sent into our hearts the Spirit of his Son, crying "Abba." "Father." You are therefore no longer a slave but a son, and if a son, then also by [YHWH]'s own act an heir. (Galatians 4:6-7 NEB)

The Greek word Abba can be translated literally as Father, but it is suppose to have a warm, affectionate, familial sound to it. In our current society, the word "Daddy" gives the more formal "Father" that affectionate quality. No, it is not a perquisite to go before the Father; nor will he love you any more or less if you don't call him Daddy. I can tell you, however, that I believe he does delight in it. Every believer, since they have been sealed with the Holy Spirit, is capable of walking righteously. But again, all need to ask the Holy Spirit to assist them via the Father. Paul says that this is the only way to ensure that believers will not be guided by their lower natures. Let none be arrogant as to believe that once they have accepted Messiah into their hearts, they need no further help.

Holy Spirit, Our Helper

If the Holy Spirit is daily activated, by request of the Father, there is no way that a repented believer should ever revert back to the days of old. There is no reason to backslide to a life that was "lived" while you were still on your backside—still dead. Paul says that the Holy Spirit, your Helper, won't let you. That doesn't mean that you no longer have free will, as if you have been possessed. It means that the Holy Spirit is actively fighting against what your lower nature is now urging you to do. Before, your lower nature—your only nature—didn't need to urge. It only had to whisper, and you complied. Now you have a choice and the Holy Spirit will enable you to make the right decision every time, if you choose to yield.

Yielding to the Holy Spirit because you are now filled with the Holy Spirit doesn't mean that you won't stumble on the road anymore. Daily yielding to the Holy Spirit does mean that you won't ever leave the road again. Mistakes are bound to happen as you continue to grow in Yeshua. But, that is why Messiah's death on the cross is so significant. What you consider a mistake, is most likely still sinful in the eyes of our holy God. Forgiveness is only a request away. And no, you haven't removed your helmet of salvation—unless you have left the road.

Jacob and Esau and Pharaoh

"Jacob I loved, Esau I rejected" is another comparison similar to the one in Galatians with Sarah and Hagar. Jacob represents those would come to be spiritually reborn, as was he. Remember, Jacob was chosen before he was even born. It didn't matter that he was a sinful wretch. YHWH loved him anyway and through repentance, Jacob was renamed Israel. Believers of today share an identical story. Esau represents the natural child who remains in his natural state.

For Scripture says to Pharaoh, "I have raised you up for this very purpose, to exhibit my power in my dealings with you, and to spread my fame all over the world." Thus he not only shows mercy as he chooses, but also makes men stubborn as he chooses. You will say, "Then why does [YHWH] blame a man? For who can resist his will?" Who are you, sir, to answer [YHWH] back? Can the pot speak to the potter and say, "Why did you make me like this?" Surely the potter can do what he likes with the clay. Is he not free to make out of the same lump two vessels, one to be treasured, the other for common use? But what if [YHWH], desiring to exhibit his retribution at work and to make his power known, tolerated very patiently those vessels which were objects of retribution due for destruction, and did so in order to make known the full wealth of his splendor upon vessels which were objects of mercy, and which from the first had been prepared for splendor? (Romans 9:19-23 NEB)

Paul makes it clear in his opening lines that the rest of this passage is focused on Pharaoh and the Egyptians who lived with him, and YHWH's specific purpose in creating them. Yes, after giving them a number of opportunities to repent on their own, Yeshua eventually did harden Pharaoh's heart and YHWH did use them for his purposes. Egypt and Pharaoh are also the prototypes for the spiritual battle that has been waging sense the fall of Satan. Egypt represents a life of sin, Satan's kingdom. Pharaoh - Satan. Moses is a sort of Christ-like figure, in a strict sense. YHWH sent Moses to redeem the Israelites from Egypt. YHWH sent his Son to earth, Satan's temporary domain, to redeem his children.

Appendix C: Limited Atonement

Not far from Each One of Us

He created every race of men of one stock, to inhabit the whole earth's surface. He fixed the epochs of their history and the limits of their territory. They were to seek [YHWH], and, it might be, touch and find him; though indeed he is not far from each one of us, for in him we live and move, in him we exist; as some of your own poets have said, "We are also his offspring." (Acts 17:26-28 NEB)

Suffering

Paul knows what suffering is; and Paul has endured. In fact, in writing this last letter, his execution is imminent. Paul writes to his spiritual protégée to show that he not only talks the talk, but he has walked the walked—willingly. As such, he is encouraging Timothy to do the same.

As for me, already my life is being poured out on the altar, and the hour for my departure is upon me. I have run the great race, I have finished the course, I have kept faith. And now the prize awaits me, the garland of righteousness which [Yeshua], the all-just Judge, will award me on that great Day, and it is not for me alone, but for all who have set their hearts on his coming appearance. (2nd Timothy 4:6-8 NEB)

Finally, it is important for readers to remember that suffering for Messiah is not attractive to an unbeliever, so there is no reason to believe that Paul's endurance would persuade an unbeliever to convert. Therefore, it would make little sense to believe that the glorious and eternal salvation that Paul speaks of is referring to the initial gift of salvation.

If the world hates you, it hated me first, as you know well. If you belonged to the world, the world would love its own, but because you do not belong to the world, because I have chosen you out of the world, for that reason the world hates you. Remember what I said: A servant is not greater than his master. As they persecuted me, they will persecute you; they will follow your teaching as little as they have followed mine. It is on my account that they will treat you thus, because they do not know the One who sent me. (John 15:18-21 NEB)

But, notice the conditions that come with the promise of protection (that is spiritual protection, not necessarily always physical).

We know that no child of [YHWH] is a sinner; it is the Son of [YHWH] who keeps him safe, and the evil one cannot touch him. (1st John 5:18 NEB)

Security of the Believer

Because you put your faith in Yeshua, the security of a believer's inheritance and of Yeshua's continual protection is not unconditional. Limited atonement? Sure. You are atoned for your sins by Yeshua Messiah, as long as you faithfully continue to walk on the road to Glory. If you walk off, but repent and return, YHWH is still just to forgive. Messiah will receive you once again as one of his sheep, and you will once again benefit from his atonement. However, Messiah's atonement does not stretch beyond the road, and so neither does his protection or the Father's provisions. If you choose to leave, as evidenced by your faithless lifestyle, you have now forsaken your inheritance. Remember the prodigal son?

> From Simeon Peter, servant and apostle of [Yeshua], to those who through the justice of [YHWH] and Savior [Yeshua], share our faith and enjoy equal privilege with ourselves." (2nd Peter 1:1 NEB)

I love how non self-centered Peter's opening lines are here. This disciple was routinely in Messiah's inner-circle of three (along with James and John). This is the guy whom Yeshua proclaimed the rock. Peter, out of all the disciples, had cause to gloat and to self-promote. While believers should be able to recount Peter's numerous errors, both during Yeshua' ministry and his own (remember Paul's open rebuke to him in the letter to the Galatians?), in reading his letters, believers should equally be aware of his later spiritual maturity. In one sentence Peter illustrates his righteousness. The designated rock begins by acknowledging his servant-hood status, relative to the Rock. As is the case with all of Scripture, Peter's letter was written to both a present audience, as well as a future one. That future audience is, "those who share our faith." The best part about this verse is that despite Peter's special designation by Yeshua, he places himself on equal footing with the rest of his brothers and sisters, "to those who through...enjoy equal privileges with ourselves..."

Appendix D: IRRESISTIBLE GRACE

YHWH's grace is not irresistible. Yeshua's creation was given free will as a gift. YHWH's grace is only necessary because the first man and women disobeyed him and his Son. When Messiah walked the earth, he called many to him. Many chose not to come and follow. Others followed him, but then chose to leave. Irresistible grace is not loving. YHWH desires for his children to love him, but he would never force them to. There is nothing adoring about a Bride-in-waiting who is forced to love her Groom-to-be. The Holy Spirit does pull on the hearts of the lost, reminding them that their emptiness will never be fulfilled by drinking from a cup of emptiness. However, the Holy Spirit also does not selectively search. YHWH is sovereign. There is a divine purpose and plan for the entire world. As such, there are Biblically recorded moments (and there will continue to be until the end of this present world) when YHWH, in his sovereignty, does call on specific people, at specific times, to fulfill a specific purpose. The Apostle Paul is an example of this Divine act. While on his way to continue in his maliciousness, he was met by his Maker. This was not a chance encounter.

> Meanwhile Saul was still breathing murderous threats against the disciples of [Yeshua]. He went to the High Priest and applied letters to the synagogues at Damascus authorizing him to arrest anyone he found, men or women, who followed the new way, and bring them to Jerusalem. While he was still on the road and nearing Damascus, suddenly a light flashed from the sky all around him. He fell to the ground and heard a voice saying, "Saul, Saul, why do you persecute me?" "Tell me Lord," he said, "who you are." The voice answered, "I am [Yeshua], whom you are persecuting. But get up and go into the city, and you will be told what you have to do." Meanwhile the men who were traveling with him stood speechless; they heard the voice but could see no one. Saul got up from the ground, but when he opened his eyes he could not see, so they led him by the hand and brought him into Damascus. He was blind for three days, and took no food or drink. (Acts 9:1-9 NEB)

Yet, as direct as Messiah's encounter was with Paul, it did not itself preclude Paul from telling Messiah no. Remember Jonah? Fortunately for Paul, he did comply. Jonah did not...at least not in the beginning. What happened? YHWH created an unpleasant situation for Jonah, which eventually resulted in a change of mind and heart. The fact that YHWH, in his love, patiently and graciously persisted with Jonah, and that Jonah finally responded, in no way suggests that his persistence was irresistible. Jonah resisted, but then after careful reflection, he wised up. Sometimes pain is the only way to induce the reflection which leads to wiser actions. It is indeed wise to accept YHWH's gracious gift of salvation through his Son, Yeshua Messiah.

> Or do you think lightly of his wealth of kindness, of tolerance, and of patience, without recognizing that [YHWH]'s kindness is meant to lead you to a change of heart? In the rigid obstinacy of your heart you are laying up for yourself a store of retribution, for the day of retribution, when [YHWH]'s just

judgment will be revealed, and he will pay every man for what he has done. (Romans 2:4-6 NEB)

What is the prophetic relevance for today? The same message that YHWH had Jonah deliver to a nation of sinners, is still unfinished. It is the same message that Messiah wants his disciples delivering to the world. It is Messiah's will that those whom he calls become his disciples. As such, as Messiah wills, and through the Holy Spirit, some hearts will be tugged more directly then others, for the expressed purpose of fulfilling the Father's plan. So what of this passage of Scripture?

On the following Sabbath almost the whole city gathered to hear the word of [Yeshua]. When the Jews saw the crowds, they were filled with jealously, and contradicted what Paul said with violent abuse. But Paul and Barnabas were bold in their reply. "It was necessary," they said, "that the word of [Yeshua] should be declared to you first. But because you reject it and thus condemn yourselves as unworthy of eternal life, we will now turn to the nations." For these are our instructions from [Yeshua]: "I have appointed you to be a light for the nations, and a means of salvation to earth's farthest bounds." When the Gentiles heard this, they were overjoyed and thankfully acclaimed the word of [Yeshua], and those who were marked out for eternal life became believers. (Acts 13:44-48 NEB)

As previously indicated, YHWH has a time table that is often inconceivable to the rest of us who are not YHWH. It is the case that not everyone is going to become a believer at the same time. When Paul continued his missionary journey with Timothy and Silas, they were directed by the Holy Spirit to go to some places and not others.

They traveled through the Phrygian and Galatian region, because they were prevented by the Holy Spirit from delivering the message in the province of Asia; and when they approached the Mysian border they tried to enter Bithynia; but the Spirit of [Yeshua] would not allow them, so they skirted Mysia and reached the coast at Troas. During the night a vision came to Paul: a Macedonian stood there appealing to him and saying, "Come across to Macedonia and help us." After he had seen this vision we at once set about getting a passage to Macedonia, concluding that [YHWH] had called us to bring them the good news. (Acts 16:6-10 NEB)

It is equally the case that if YHWH has already preordained such an opportunity (to accomplish his sovereign will) for a group of individuals, at a set time, then grace is going to be extended to them. But two facts also need to be remembered: One, the extension of his grace does not mean that those to whom it has been extended, will receive it. Again, YHWH's grace can be resisted. Two, the extension of YHWH's grace to a specific person or group of persons, at an appointed period, does not preclude his extension of grace to others around at another period. The word of YHWH would eventually reach the province of Asia, in YHWH's own time, and there would be converts.

Greetings from the congregations in Asia. Many is greetings in [Yeshua] from Aquila and Prisca and the congregations at their house. (1st Corinthians 16:19 NEB)

The only fact we know for certain from this passage is that a group of members, upon hearing the word of YHWH, were graciously offered faith by YHWH to receive the truth, and they chose to accept it. In doing so, they became believers. This pattern of behavior accords well and is consistent with Scripture.

For the Scripture says, "Whoever believes on him will not be put to shame." For there is no distinction between Jew and Greek, for the same Lord over all is rich to all who call upon him. For "Whoever calls on the name of [Yeshua] shall be saved." How then shall they call on him in whom they have not believed? And how shall they believe in him of whom they have not heard? And how shall they hear without a preacher? And how shall they preach unless they are sent? As it is written: "How beautiful are the feet of those who preach the gospel of peace, Who bring glad tidings of good things." But they have not all obeyed the gospel. For Isaiah says, "[YHWH], who has believed our report?" So then faith comes by hearing, and hearing by the word of [YHWH]. (Romans 10:11-17 NEB)

There is no mention or inference by Paul in this verse that those who have not responded to the good news, have not responded because they did not receive an inner call from the Holy Spirit.

Appendix E: HAMMERING ON THE HELMET

Deception is nothing new

After examining and pondering over these sentiments the question now becomes, "Which view is antipodal to the Gospel and therefore a dangerous doctrine to adhere to and to teach?" It is this author's contention that the more liberal interpretation and espousal of the eternal security, or the "perseverance of the saints" doctrine is such; as is the doctrine of irresistible grace. I will offer up proof, then an analysis, and finally I will conclude with some brief remarks.

I am astonished to find you turning so quickly away from him who called you by grace, and following a different gospel. Not that it is in fact another gospel; only there are persons who unsettle your minds by trying to distort the gospel of [Messiah]. (Galatians 1:6-7 NEB)

Be on your guard; see that your minds don't get captured by hollow and delusive speculations, based on traditions of man-made teaching and centered on the elemental spirits of the world and not on [Messiah]. (Colossians 2:8 NEB)

Why let people dictate to you: "Do not handle this, do not taste that, do not touch the other."—all of them that must perish as soon as they are used? That is to follow merely human injunctions and teaching. True, it has an air of wisdom, with its forced piety, its self-mortification, and its severity to the body; but it is of no use at all in combating sensuality. (Colossians 2:21-23 NEB)

The Spirit says expressly that in after some times some will desert from the faith and give their minds to subversive doctrines inspired by demons, through the specious falsehoods of men whose own conscience is branded with the devil's sign. They forbid marriage and inculcate abstinence from certain foods, though [YHWH] created them to be enjoyed with thanksgiving by believers who have inward knowledge of the truth. (1st Timothy 4:1-3 NEB)

As stated earlier, while these false doctrines (though perhaps benignly inspired) indeed plague the Church today, we are not witnessing anything new. The Apostle Paul confronted this same issue head on when he wrote his letter to the Churches in Galatia, Philippi, and Colossae. In his letter to the Galatians, Paul openly rebukes those Gentile converts living in what is today modern day Turkey, because of their quick departure from the true gospel of Yeshua Messiah. Paul and Barnabas visited this area on their first missionary journey, as outlined in the book of Acts. It is safe to conclude that the journey, while met with some complications, was nevertheless, successful.

As you know, it was bodily illness that originally led to my brining you the Gospel, and you resisted any temptation to show scorn or disgust at the state of my poor body; you welcomed me as if I were a messenger of [YHWH], as you might have welcomed [Yeshua] himself. (Galatians 4:14 NEB)

However, eventually Paul received word that problems were arising. Gentile converts were now floundering in their faith because they were listening to Judaizers; Jewish converts to the new faith of Christianity who were teaching the Gentile converts that they had to subscribe to the Torah, namely through circumcision, in order to be truly saved. In short, they were teaching an earned justification and righteousness by works and deeds, rather than by unearned and undeserved grace, via faith in Messiah Yeshua. Unlike the situation which arose prior to the Counsel in Jerusalem, Paul is clear as to the malignant motivation of these Judaizers:

> Yet even my companion Titus, Greek though he is, was not compelled to be circumcised. That course was urged only as a concession to certain sham-Christians, interlopers who had stolen in to spy upon the liberty we enjoy in the fellowship of [Yeshua]. These men wanted to bring us into bondage, but not for one moment did I yield to their dictation; I was determined that the full truth of the Gospel should be maintained for you. (Galatians 2:3-5 NEB)

> The persons I have referred to are envious of you, but not with an honest envy: what they really want is to bar the door to you so that you may come to envy them. (Galatians 4:17 NEB)

> It is all those who want to make a fair outward and bodily show who are trying to force circumcision upon you; their sole object is to escape persecution for the cross of [Messiah]. For even those who do receive circumcision are not thoroughgoing observers of the law; they only want you to be circumcised in order to boast of your having submitted to that outward rite. (Galatians 6:12-13 NEB)

They were envious of the freedom that the Gospel of Messiah afforded its adherents; freedom from rabbinical teaching that fell outside Torah. Envy can often inspire erroneous teachings. It is unfortunate that the Judaizers failed to understand that this same freedom applied to them. There was nothing to be envious about because the Gospel of Messiah placed them all, Jewish and Gentile converts alike, on the same footing. Perhaps many of them were envious that their God could now be shared with a group of people that had not been a part of the original promise. Perhaps they were jealous that Messiah's Gospel was an inclusive Gospel. This sometimes happens in a family when one of the parents decides to get remarried after a painful divorce. When a blended family arises, often the natural child of one parent is resentful that he or she has to share their parent with their step-sibling, and vice a versa. That is sadly the way it is on earth. The Jewish converts should have understood, and believers of today must understand, that in YHWH's house there are no step-siblings. Whether you are of Jewish or Gentile descent, black or white, male or female, American or non—Messiah is the common denominator.

> For through faith you are all sons of [YHWH] in union with [Messiah Yeshua]. Baptized into union with him, you have all put on [Messiah] as a garment. There is no such thing as Jew and Greek, slave and freeman, male and female; for you are all one person in [Messiah Yeshua]. But if you thus belong

to [Messiah], you are the "issue" of Abraham, and so heirs by promise. (Galatians 3:26-29 NEB)

Three categories of deceivers

We know the motivation of the Judaizers. What of those shepherds today who distort the Gospel of Messiah? What is their motivation? I think it first necessary to divide the shepherds into three different categories. Though all are wrong, it's important to distinguish between the three so that readers understand the present position of Messiah concerning their current leaders.

And now I appeal to the elders of your community, as a fellow-elder and a witness of [Messiah's] sufferings, and also a partaker in the splendor that is to be revealed. Tend that flock of [YHWH] whose shepherds you are, and do it, not under compulsion, but of your own free will, as [YHWH] would have it; not for gain but out of sheer devotion. (1st Peter 5:1-2 NEB)

The first category is the deceived, who are themselves inspired by the Deceiver and are thus deceiving others. Their intentions are good, but their rhetoric is still poisonous. These are the leaders of cults with semblances of the Truth, such as the Mormons and Jehovah Witnesses. This category too includes those leaders of the Universalist and Unitarian churches.

Who is the liar? Who but he that denies that [Yeshua] is the Christ? He is [Anti-Messiah], for he denies both the Father and the Son: to deny the Son is to be without the Father; to acknowledge the Son is to have the Father too. (1st John 2:22-23 NEB)

But do not trust any and every spirit, my friends; test the spirits, to see whether they are from [YHWH], for among those who have gone out into the world there are many prophets falsely inspired. This is how we may recognize the Spirit of [YHWH]: every spirit which acknowledges that [Yeshua] has come in the flesh is from [YHWH]. That is what is meant by "antichrist; " you have been told that he was to come, and here he is, in the world already. (1st John 4:1-3 NEB)

The second category is the deceived, who are inspired by the Deceiver via their own perverse ambitions, and are thus deceiving others. These are the shepherds of mainstream Christian churches with social agendas. They preach gospels designed to enrich their churches, while their sheep remain spiritually (and in some cases, temporally) impoverished. Others who fit into this category are those shepherds who promote gospels resulting in continual racial division within the Body of Messiah. They place one race on a pedestal and leave the other ones out to pasture, allowing the world to capture their hearts and minds. Still, there are those shepherds within this category who have their own political agenda, and so their messages include the promotion of homosexuality and radical feminism. However, their messages are nowhere to be found in the Gospel of Messiah.

Bear in mind that [Yeshua]'s patience with us is our salvation, as Paul, our friend and brother, said when he wrote to you with his inspired wisdom. And so he does in all his other letters, wherever he speaks of this subject, though they contain some obscure passages, which the ignorant and unstable misinterpret to their own ruin, as they do the other scriptures. But you, my friends, are forewarned. Take care, then, not to let these unprincipled men seduce you with their errors; do not lose you own safe foothold. But grow in the grace and in the knowledge of our Lord and Savior [Yeshua Messiah]. To him be glory now and for all eternity. (2nd Peter 3:15-18 NEB)

Finally, there is the third category. These are the shepherds who, like the second category, are also found amongst mainstream Christian bodies. They are also deceived and have been inspired by the Deceiver via the impression and intellectual dogma of man, but, like those in the first category, are still deceiving others. These include sects of Protestant denominations whose shepherds are more interested in teaching man-made doctrine than they are in teaching the doctrines of Scripture. These also include portions of the Catholic faith that teach erroneous doctrine. Such denominations and sects would rather promote their founder's teachings than Messiah's alone. Scripture should be taught, exclusively, to Messiah's sheep.

It is these shepherds who, having loved the traditions of man and man's erudition, have allowed Satan to have his greatest impact to date. Those in this third category are, in fact, the most dangerous (though danger still lurks in the other two) because while they see the wrongs in the first two, they are themselves pleased with their own poison (though in their own eyes they see no such poison). These are the shepherds who are more concerned with preserving their specific Protestant denomination than they are with seeing a united Body of Messiah. Many of those who promote "Calvinist" or "Wesleyan" doctrine and who defend them vehemently, fall into this category. Within the Body of Messiah only one doctrine should sound and that is Messiah's. Presently, many of those in this third category may wear the helmet of salvation, but, I believe, their Savior is displeased. Many of their sheep are without their helmet, and others, while having theirs on, are stumbling unnecessarily, and are currently hobbling their way to the gates of Glory.

The Gospel of Messiah

Some of those in the first two categories, I'm convinced (although YHWH only is the judge), currently do not wear the helmet of salvation and so are not on the road to Glory. Sadly, many are still lost and are presently, surely, on the road to perdition. I conclude in reminding all shepherds that the Gospel of Messiah is clear and simple. Messiah died on the cross so that those who choose to have faith in him should not perish but have everlasting life. He was sent by the Father to reconcile depraved humanity to the Father. While the Father wants all who were made in his Son's image to have eternal life while on earth, and to enjoy life in the hereafter, only those who accept Messiah's gift of salvation will be allowed to enter the gates of Glory. Messiah's gift is a choice, and though extended to persons at various time intervals, any can refuse. Messiah expects those who do accept his gifts of salvation, righteousness, and the Father's gift of the Holy Spirit to alter and conduct their faithful lifestyle in such a holy manner that proof of their conversion experience is clear to all; but, most importantly, that it is clear to him and the Father. Believers have the individual, as well as the corporate responsibility of ensuring that once they are placed on the road to Glory, they, and those saints walking next to them, persevere and stay on the road. It isn't the only sealing of, but also the daily filling of and yielding to the Holy Spirit, as well as the daily asking for the Father's grace, that will ensure that believers do stay on the road, though some stumbling will still occur. As we have pointed out previously in many Scriptures, those travelers who leave the road are no longer righteous nor saved from judgment and hell. If they remain unrepentant, at the return of Messiah or at their death, they too will be denied entrance into the gates of Glory. Other souls, though saved themselves, won't get to enjoy hearing the appreciative, affirming feedback from Messiah, "Well done, good and faithful servant .... Enter into the joy of your lord" (Matthew 25:21). They will enter into the afterlife with little rewards.

EPILOGUE: A Prophecy

In November of 2010 I had an alarming dream. In the dream I was in the heavens and I saw the sun, which I knew to be representative of Yeshua, the Son of YHWH. Next, I saw a white horse flying from the east, passing across the sun, and finally heading in my direction.

At first I gazed at the beauty of the white horse, even as it steadily approached me. But, then as it approached my face, the horse turned from white to red, and its nostrils flared. I closed my eyes, but I could still feel it breathing on me. Then I woke up.

The Holy Spirit revealed to me the interpretation of the dream. The white horse symbolized judgment, like the one spoken of in Revelation. It was a symbol of false peace. The red horse also symbolized judgment, again, like the one in Revelation. It was a symbol of war. The white horse flying from the east to the west symbolized the geographic region from which the horse came. I knew that it stood for Islam. The west stood for the United States.

The message was as follows: Messiah says that judgment is impending for the United States. If it transpires, it will come from Islam; specifically, it will come from Iran, whose radical Muslims hate the United States. This is not a judgment for the future, but for the present. If it happens, it will be before the rapture of the Church; an unintended part of the great tribulation. Moreover, if it happens, it will be while President Barack Obama is still in office.

My Thoughts On This Prophecy

First Judgment - Potentially

President Obama is not the Anti-Messiah. I believe that Messiah takes issue with those in his flock who refer to him as such. It is disrespectful and unbecoming behavior of a Believer. The Bible commands us to pray for our leaders, not to ridicule them. Some believers have questioned President Obama's faith. Such questions are warranted, but President Obama is not, to my knowledge, a Muslim. However, currently his faith in Messiah is questionable. For those who are concerned about his spiritual condition, they should pray and leave it in the hands of our heavenly Father. That does not mean you have to support his policies if they fall outside Biblical principles. If they do, then you shouldn't.

There are some within the Body of Messiah who reject President Obama because of his skin color. We know that Messiah is not pleased over this. For those to whom it applies, repentance is in order before disciplining occurs.

In order for the judgment of this prophecy not to occur on America, the Church in America needs to repent of its multitude of sins. The judgment will be harsh and painful. The military might of America will not help, the political make-up of America will not help. This will not be the fault of Republicans or Democrats, but the Church. It happened during Jeremiah's day, and it will happen again if the United States does not take this warning seriously.

Second Judgment – Actually

Yet, regardless of whether or not the Church in America repents, the whole world is still entering into a time of judgment. I sense that Messiah has declared that the weather will continue to get more severe until the rapture of the Church. It will look different to different people, depending on the specific area of the world. For the United States and the rest of the western hemisphere, it will mean more tornadoes and hurricanes, stronger winds and heavier rain. The temperatures in the summers and winters will also become more extreme. There have already been some of these trends to date. However, this prophetic word speaks to even more severe weather patterns that have never been seen before in earth's history.

There will be some loss of lives, and even more loss of homes. People will walk in despair, as they witness their earthly treasures disappear. This will be a season intended for reflection and repentance. It will provide an opportunity to share the Gospel to persons who otherwise would not pay attention. Everyone will be affected, including members of the Church. This period will be known as the great tribulation, as interpreted by some in Scripture. Other parts of the world will see an increase in flash floods and earthquakes. Some have already begun to see examples of these; the recent flood in the Philippines is but one example.

Again, there will be loss of lives and homes; even among those in the Church. This will be the time for American Believers to change their focus from within, and start, in mass, reaching out to those without. This will require many in the United States to leave and to relocate to other countries; many will have to leave their families behind. It would be inappropriate for Believers to react in fear; rather, all should respond in faith. Shepherds should begin preparing their flocks now. This is an alarm; a trumpet. It would be wise for all to keep their ears open, and their hearts soft, so that the enemy doesn't use you for his purposes. Denominations are going to be detrimental during this time period; the Church must be united. There will be many who, after reading this book, will decide to leave the Church, should shepherds begin teaching its truths. While this is not the will of YHWH, he respects every man's, woman's and youth's free will.

Into the Light

From centuries of darkness plagued with sin
By hearts content with "self" and with hate
From eras filled with tongues and berates,
That filled the soul, but kept it hollow within
It helped to shape a nation's fate
The wars,the blood, the lives that were shattered
The tears,which fell from eyes,they were loud
Like the rain that falls from heavy clouds
Though stretching for years, as if time didn't matter
The sun sat behind,until the proud
Decided they were through with all their vile
Were done with the crimes of guilty hands
Of guilty speech, and guilty feet that walked the land
Then from behind the clouds, the sun beamed for miles
Onto the face and hearts of man

Throughout the book, I made references to my mother. The comments were primarily negative, as those were the experiences that I had with her growing up before I went into foster care. However, my relationship with my mother today is positive. Through the grace of YHWH there has been healing and forgiveness on both sides. My life is evidence of the power of YHWH's grace and healing.

FROM GRACE TO GLORY

is available at:

olivepresspublisher.com

amazon.com

barnesandnoble.com

christianbook.com

deepershopping.com

parable.com

and other online stores

Store managers:

Order wholesale through
Ingram Book Company or
Spring Arbor
or by emailing:

olivepressbooks@gmail.com